Microsoft Press

Desktop Applications with
Microsoft
Visual C++ 6.0
MCSD
Training Kit

**For Exam
70-016**

PUBLISHED BY
Microsoft Press
A Division of Microsoft Corporation
One Microsoft Way
Redmond, Washington 98052-6399

Library of Congress Cataloging-in-Publication Data
Desktop Applications with Microsoft Visual C++ 6.0 : MCSD Training Kit
  / Microsoft Corporation.
      p. cm.
   Includes index.
   ISBN 0-7356-0795-8
    1. Electronic data processing personnel--Certification.
   2. Microsoft software--Examinations Study guides.   3. C++ (Computer
program language)   4. Microsoft Visual C++. I. Microsoft
Corporation.
   QA76.3.D47   1999
   005.26'8--dc21   99-33877

Printed and bound in the United States of America.

1 2 3 4 5 6 7 8 9 QMQM   4 3 2 1 0 9

Distributed in Canada by Penguin Books Canada Limited.

A CIP catalogue record for this book is available from the British Library.

Microsoft Press books are available through booksellers and distributors worldwide. For further information about international editions, contact your local Microsoft Corporation office or contact Microsoft Press International directly at fax (425) 936-7329. Visit our Web site at mspress.microsoft.com.

Acquisitions Editor: Eric Stroo
Project Editor: Victoria Thulman

Contents

About This Book

Welcome to *Desktop Applications with Microsoft Visual C++ 6.0 MCSD Training Kit*. By completing the chapters and associated Lab exercises in this course, you will acquire the knowledge and skills necessary to develop solutions using Visual C++ 6.0.

This book addresses the objectives of the Microsoft Certified Solution Developer (MCSD) Exam 70-016, *"Designing and Implementing Desktop Applications with Microsoft Visual C++ 6.0."* This book provides content that supports the skills measured by the 70-016 exam. Review questions at the end of each chapter test your knowledge of the chapter material, and help you prepare for the exam.

Note For more information on becoming a Microsoft Certified Solution Developer, see "Microsoft Certified Professional Program" later in this section.

Intended Audience

This course is designed for individuals interested in developing their skills in Microsoft Visual C++ 6.0 while developing desktop applications. Topics include using the Microsoft Solutions Framework (MSF); building applications with the Microsoft Foundation Classes (MFC); creating user interfaces; implementing application behaviors; and working with persistent data. Also included are adding database support to applications; creating Component Object Model (COM) components and ActiveX controls; using MFC and the Active Template Library (ATL); Internet programming; error handling, debugging, and testing; and application deployment.

Prerequisites

This book assumes that you have a good working knowledge of C++ application development and are acquainted with but not knowledgeable about Microsoft Visual C++ 6.0 and the Microsoft Windows Application Programming Interface (API). Before beginning this self-paced course, you should have:

- A thorough working knowledge of the C++ language as described by the ANSI standard, including language features such as templates and exception handling.
- A good understanding of the principles of object-oriented software development.
- A good basic understanding of the operation of a Windows application, and the features of the Windows user interface.

Course Overview

This course combines text, graphics, and review questions to teach you about designing and implementing desktop applications with Visual C++ 6.0. The course assumes that you will work through the book from beginning to end. However, you can choose a customized track and complete only the sections that interest you. If you choose to customize your course, see the "Before You Begin" section in each chapter for important information regarding prerequisites.

The book is divided into the following chapters:

- **Chapter 1,** *Preparing for Application Development* In this chapter, you will learn about the elements of designing a Visual C++ application using MSF design concepts. You will study the issues that you should consider in planning your design. You will also be given an overview of the Visual C++ development tools through a description of the installation options.

- **Chapter 2,** *Visual C++ Development Environment* This chapter discusses the development environment and the tools that enable you to create applications using Visual C++. You will use the MFC AppWizard to generate a development project, which contains source code and resource files that you can compile into a working executable program. You will explore features of the Visual C++ development environment and learn how to configure options for your project. You will also learn how to use Microsoft Visual SourceSafe to manage source code control for a software development team.

- **Chapter 3,** *Building Applications with the Microsoft Foundation Classes* In this chapter, you will learn about specific MFC classes and their role in Windows application development. You will learn how the MFC framework implements the basic components of a Windows application, and how it provides an architecture that enables the processing, display, and storage of the application's data.

- **Chapter 4,** *Creating the User Interface* This chapter explores some of the elements of a typical Windows application user interface. You will edit application menus and toolbars, and add code to handle user selections. You will update the interface to communicate information to the user. You will also learn how dialog boxes are used in an application, and you will use the dialog editor to create a dialog box template.

- **Chapter 5,** *Implementing Application Behaviors*   This chapter discusses some of the MFC programming techniques that you can use to implement the operational behavior of an application. You will learn how to make use of dialog box classes, and also how to take advantage of the multithreading capabilities of the Win32 platform. You will learn more about the techniques used to display application data to an on-screen window or a printer. You will also implement Help for an MFC application.

- **Chapter 6,** *Persistent Data*   In this chapter, you will learn ways to make your application data and settings persistent. You will use the MFC **CFile** class for general file input/output (I/O) operations. You will also use the serialization facilities of the MFC framework to save and restore structured application data. Finally, you will save individual data items, such as application settings, in the system registry.

- **Chapter 7,** *Adding Database Support*   In this chapter, you will learn about a variety of data access interfaces available to Visual C++ application developers. These interfaces include features of MFC that provide support for data access and ActiveX Data Objects (ADO), Microsoft's standard interface to essentially all forms of external data.

- **Chapter 8,** *Introducing the Component Object Model*   This chapter provides a conceptual introduction to COM. COM is a binary standard that defines a way for software objects, developed in different languages or operating on different platforms, to communicate with each other and with other applications. Also included in this introduction are ActiveX controls. ActiveX controls are COM components designed for placement in an ActiveX control container, such as an application dialog box or a Web page, to perform a self-contained function.

- **Chapter 9,** *Creating COM Components*   In this chapter, you will create a simple COM component using the ActiveX Template Library (ATL). You will review aspects of the source code generated for your COM object by the ATL wizards, and learn about other approaches to generating COM components.

- **Chapter 10,** *COM Clients*   This chapter explains how applications and components can act as clients of COM server components by making use of the services that the component provides. You will learn how the Visual C++ compiler simplifies the creation of COM client code. You will also learn techniques for creating COM objects that contain instances of other COM objects.

- **Chapter 11,** *Creating ActiveX Controls*   In this chapter, you will create a simple ActiveX control using MFC, and analyze the MFC-generated code. You will then develop the same control using the ActiveX Template Library (ATL). You will thus be able to compare the two development methods and assess which method might be most appropriate in a particular development scenario.

- **Chapter 12, *Internet Programming*** This chapter introduces some of the features of Visual C++ 6.0 that allow you to create Internet-based applications. You will learn how you can use Dynamic HTML to create application user interfaces, and how you can add Web-browsing capabilities to your applications and components. You will study how to develop an application that creates ActiveX documents—documents that can be hosted by Microsoft Internet Explorer for viewing and editing over the Web. You will also learn how to create Internet Server API (ISAPI) DLLs that enhance the services provided by Microsoft Web servers.

- **Chapter 13, *Error Handling, Debugging, and Testing*** In this chapter, you will learn about the three steps that make up the second half of the software development process: error handling, debugging, and testing. These final steps are an essential part of the development process, and merit at least as much attention as that given to the designing and coding phases.

- **Chapter 14, *Deploying Desktop Applications*** In this chapter, you will learn some of the ways a Windows application created with Visual C++ can be efficiently deployed. After presenting an overview of deployment methods, the chapter shows how to use InstallShield, a tool that helps automate the creation of installation programs for Visual C++ projects. You will also learn how installation programs install ActiveX controls and other COM components, and how the Microsoft Zero Administration for Windows (ZAW) initiative will affect program installation in the future.

Features of This Book

The following features are designed to enhance the usefulness of this course:

- Each chapter opens with a "Before You Begin" section, which provides information about chapter prerequisites.

- Each chapter is divided into lessons. Most lessons contain procedures that give you an opportunity to use the concepts presented, or explore the part of the application described in the lesson. All procedures are preceded by an arrow symbol.

- Each lesson ends with a short Lesson Summary of the material presented.

- The Review section at the end of the chapter lets you test what you have learned in the lesson.

- The Appendix, "Review Questions and Answers," contains all of the book's review questions and corresponding answers.

- The Glossary contains key terms and definitions used in the course.

Conventions Used in This Book

Before you start reading any of the chapters, it is important that you understand the terms and notational conventions used in this book.

Notational Conventions

- *Italic* is used for emphasis when defining new terms or indicating place-holders. *Italic* is also used for references to book, chapter, and section titles.

- **Bold** is used to emphasize selections you make during labs and procedures and to highlight elements such as functions, methods, and classes.

- Names of files and folders might appear in Title Caps. Unless otherwise indicated, you can use all lowercase letters when you type a file or folder name in a dialog box or at a command prompt.

- File name extensions appear in all lowercase.

- Acronyms appear in all uppercase.

- Monospace type represents code samples, examples of screen text, or entries that you might type at a command prompt or in initialization files.

- Square brackets [ ] are used in syntax statements to enclose optional items. For example, [*filename*] in command syntax indicates that you can choose to type a file name with the command. Type only the information within the brackets, not the brackets themselves.

Keyboard Conventions

- A plus sign (+) between two key names means that you must press those keys at the same time. For example, "Press ALT+TAB" means that you hold down ALT while you press TAB.

- A comma (,) between two or more key names means that you must press each of the keys consecutively, not together. For example, "Press ALT, F, X" means that you press and release each key in sequence. As another example, "Press ALT+W, L" means that you first press ALT and W together, and then release them and press L.

- You can choose menu commands with the keyboard. Press the ALT key to activate the menu bar, and then sequentially press the keys that correspond to the highlighted or underlined letter of the menu name and the command name. For some commands, you can also press a key combination listed in the menu.

- You can select or clear check boxes or option buttons in dialog boxes with the keyboard. Press the ALT key, and then press the key that corresponds to the underlined letter of the option name. Alternately, you can press TAB until the option is highlighted, and then press the spacebar to select or clear the check box or option button.

- You can cancel the display of a dialog box by pressing the ESC key.

About the Companion CD

The companion CD contains sample exam questions and the files used in the hands-on labs and procedures in the text.

Using the Lab Files

The companion CD contains files required to perform the hands-on lab exercises. To copy the lab files to your hard drive, run the Setup.exe program in the root directory of the CD and follow the instructions that appear on your screen.

By default, the lab files are copied to the \DAVC folder. Each chapter in the book has its own subfolder. (For example, material relating to Chapter 1 can be found in \DAVC\Chapter1.) Each of these folders might contain the following subfolders:

- The \Code folder contains source files and code snippets that you can use as you complete the labs or exercises in the lessons. These files are referenced at the top of the code listing. The icon shown in the left margin identifies the sections of code contained on the CD. You can cut and paste these files to save yourself some typing. (Be sure to exclude the labels.)

- The \Data folder contains other data files that you will use in the course of developing and testing the lab exercises.

- The \Exercises folder contains files related to the exercises in the lessons.

- The \Lab folder contains project files for the labs that appear at the end of each chapter. Most \Lab folders will have the following subfolders:

    - The \Partial folder contains the application as it looks at the beginning of each lab.

    - The \Solution folder contains a completed version of the lab solution. This project has had each step applied and can be used to review the completed lab.

The recommended procedure is to follow the labs in numerical order. Save your work and use it in the next lab to continue developing the example application. If you do not complete a lab, you can start the next lab using the project in the \DAVC\Chapter *n*\Lab\Partial folder, which will allow you to proceed from the appropriate starting point.

You should check your work against the project in the \DAVC\Chapter *n*\Lab\ Solution folder after you complete each lab.

Beneath the \DAVC folder is the \Database folder, which contains files that you use to set up the database used by the labs.

Self Test Software Visual C++ 6.0 Sample Exam

To practice taking a certification exam, you can install the sample exam from Self Test Software (STS) contained on the companion CD. Designed in accordance with the actual Microsoft certification exam, this sample includes questions to help you assess your understanding of the materials presented in this book. Each question includes feedback with an associated course reference so that you can review the material presented. Visit the STS Web site at *www.selftestsoftware.com* for a complete list of available practice exams.

The Self Test Software demonstration for Exam 70-016 is located in the \Exam folder. To install the sample exam on your hard drive, run the Mp016.exe program in this folder and follow the instructions that appear on your screen.

Microsoft Visual C++ 6.0 Starts Here

This companion CD also contains the *Microsoft Visual C++ 6.0 Starts Here* product to help you become more familiar with Visual C++ 6.0. It is located in the \MVC6SH folder (on the companion CD). For installation instructions, refer to the Readme.txt file.

SQL Server 7.0 Trial Edition

On a separate CD, you will find a 120-day limited trial edition of Microsoft SQL Server 7.0 that you can install to enable you to complete the labs. Please refer to the "Getting Started" section for information on how to install SQL Server and how to set up the databases that are used by the labs in this courseware.

Getting Started

To complete the exercises in this book, your computer must meet the following hardware and software requirements.

Hardware Requirements

All hardware should be on the Microsoft Windows Hardware Compatibility List located at *www.microsoft.com/hcl*.

Computer/Processor	Personal computer with a Pentium-class processor; 166-megahertz (MHz) or higher processor recommended
Memory	24 megabytes (MB) of RAM for Microsoft Windows 95 or later (32 MB recommended); 32 MB for Microsoft Windows NT 4.0 (64 MB recommended)
Hard Disk Space	Visual C++: 300 MB typical; 360 MB maximum
Microsoft Developer Network (MSDN)	57 MB typical; 493 MB maximum
Internet Explorer (IE)	43 MB typical; 59 MB maximum

Windows NT 4.0 Option Pack	40 MB for Windows 95 or later; 200 MB for Windows NT 4.0
SQL Server 7.0	170 MB typical; 266 MB maximum
Drive	CD-ROM drive
Display	VGA or higher-resolution monitor; Super VGA recommended
Operating System	Windows 95; Microsoft Windows 98; Windows NT Workstation 4.0 with Service Pack 4 or later; Windows NT Server 4.0 with Service Pack 4 or later
Peripheral/Miscellaneous	Microsoft Mouse or compatible pointing device

Software Requirements

The following software is required to complete the exercises in this course:

- Visual C++ 6.0, Professional or Enterprise Edition
- Visual SourceSafe
- Windows NT 4.0 Option Pack including Microsoft Internet Information Server or Microsoft Personal Web Server
- SQL Server 7.0 (trial version included with this courseware)
- Internet Explorer 4.01 with Service Pack 2 or higher

Installation Instructions

These instructions describe how to install the software you need to complete the exercises and labs in this book, including the following:

- Windows NT 4.0 Option Pack
- Internet Information Server 4.0 (if you are running Windows NT Server 4.0)
  - or -
  Personal Web Server (if you are running Windows NT Workstation 4.0, Windows 95, or Windows 98)

  Both products can be downloaded free of charge from Microsoft's Web site at *www.microsoft.com*.
- SQL Server 7.0 Standard Edition (if you are running Windows NT Server 4.0)
  - or -
  SQL Server 7.0 Desktop Edition (if you are running Windows NT Workstation 4.0, Windows 95, or Windows 98)

  A limited 120-day trial edition is included with this courseware.
- SQL databases that have been created for use with the labs in this book.

  These are installed from the companion CD to the \Database folder on your hard drive.

Installing the Windows NT 4.0 Option Pack

The Windows NT 4.0 Option Pack contains Internet Information Server (IIS), which can be installed on Windows NT Server 4.0; and Personal Web Server (PWS), which can be installed on Windows NT Workstation 4.0, Windows 95, or Windows 98. You can obtain the Windows NT 4.0 Option Pack from the Web at *www.microsoft.com/ntserver/nts/downloads/recommended/nt4optpk/default.asp*

Note To install all the components of the Windows NT 4.0 Option Pack, networking and the TCP/IP protocol must be installed.

▶ **To install and configure the Windows NT 4.0 Option Pack including IIS on Windows NT Server 4.0**

1. Download and run the Setup.exe file. Because you have Service Pack 4 or greater installed, the following message appears: "Setup detected that Windows NT 4.0 SP4 or greater is installed on your machine. We haven't tested this product on SP4. Do you wish to proceed?" Click **Yes**. If the message appears again, click **Yes** again.

2. When the Windows NT 4.0 Option Pack Setup window appears, click **Next**.

3. Click **Accept** to agree with the terms of the license agreement.

4. Choose a **Typical** installation. Choose the directories in which to install the files or accept the defaults, and then click **Next**.

5. For SMTP and NNTP Service Setup, choose the directories you want or accept the defaults, and click **Next**.

6. Click **Finish** when installation is complete.

7. Click **Yes** to restart the computer, and accept the systems settings change.

Installing Personal Web Server

Personal Web Server (PWS) comes as a version of the Windows NT 4.0 Option Pack that is configured for installation on Windows NT Workstation 4.0, Windows 95, or Windows 98. You can download PWS from the Web at *www.microsoft.com/windows/ie/pws/default.htm*.

Note To install all the components of the Personal Web Server, networking and the TCP/IP protocol must be installed.

▶ **To install and configure Personal Web Server on Windows NT Workstation 4.0**

1. Download and run the Setup.exe file. Because you have Service Pack 4 or greater installed, the following message appears: "Setup detected that Windows NT 4.0 SP4 or greater is installed on your machine. We haven't tested this product on SP4. Do you wish to proceed?" Click **Yes**. If the message appears again, click **Yes** again.

2. When the Windows NT 4.0 Option Pack Setup window appears, click **Next**.

3. Click **Accept** to agree to the terms of the license agreement.

4. Choose a **Typical** installation. Choose a directory in which to install the Default Web home directory or accept the default, and then click **Next**.

5. Click **Finish** when installation is complete.

6. Click **Yes** to restart the computer, and accept the systems settings change.

▶ **To install and configure Personal Web Server on Windows 95 or Windows 98**

1. Download and run the Setup.exe file. If you are installing on Windows 95, the following message might be displayed: "Setup has installed Winsock2 on your machine and needs to reboot to complete the installation." When prompted to restart your system, click **Yes**. After your computer restarts, the Personal Web Server Setup window appears.

2. In the Personal Web Server Setup window, click **Next**.

3. Click **Accept** to agree with the terms of the license agreement.

4. Choose a **Typical** installation. Choose a directory in which to install the Default Web home directory or accept the default, and then click **Next**.

5. Click **Finish** when installation is complete.

6. Click **Yes** to restart the computer, and accept the systems settings change.

Installing SQL Server 7.0 Standard Edition

▶ **To install and configure SQL Server 7.0 Standard Edition on Windows NT Server 4.0**

1. Insert the SQL Server 7.0 CD-ROM. Autorun starts.

2. Choose **Install SQL Server Components**.

3. Choose **Database Server – Standard Edition**.

4. In the Select Install Method window, choose the **Local** installation and click **Next**.

5. In the Welcome window, click **Next**.

6. Click **Yes** to agree with the terms of the license agreement.

7. Complete the User Information with your name (required) and company information (optional).

8. Choose **Typical** as the Setup Type, set the Destination Folder for Program Files and Data Files to **c:\mssql7**, accept the defaults, and click **Next**.

9. In the Services Accounts window, choose **Use the same account** for each service. Choose **Use the Local System account** for Service Settings. Click **Next**.

10. Click **Next t**o start copying files.

11. Choose **Per Seat** as the licensing mode and click **Continue**.

12. When the per-seat licensing agreement is displayed, select the **I agree that** check box and click **OK**.

13. After the necessary files are copied to your hard drive, click **Finish** in the **Setup Complete** dialog box.

14. Exit the SQL Server setup program.

15. Restart your computer to configure the Data Access Component. (If you skip this step, you will not be able to import data from a text file later in these instructions.)

Installing SQL Server 7.0 Desktop Edition

► **To install and configure SQL Server 7.0 Desktop Edition on Windows NT Workstation 4.0**

1. Insert the SQL Server 7.0 CD-ROM. Autorun starts.

2. Choose **Install SQL Server Components**.

3. Choose **Database Server – Desktop Edition**.

4. In the Select Install Method window, choose the **Local** installation and click **Next**.

5. In the Welcome window, click **Next**.

6. Click **Yes** to agree with the terms of the license agreement.

7. Complete the User Information with your name (required) and company information (optional).

8. Choose **Typical** as the Setup Type, set the Destination Folder for Program Files and Data Files to **c:\mssql7**, accept the defaults, and click **Next**.

9. In the Services Accounts window, choose **Use the same account** for each service. Choose **Use the Local System account** for Service Settings and click **Next**.

10. To start copying files, click **Next**.

11. After the necessary files are copied to your hard drive, click **Finish** in the **Setup Complete** dialog box.

12. Exit the SQL Server setup program.

13. Restart your computer to configure the Data Access Component. (If you skip this step, you will not be able to import data from a text file later in these instructions.)

▶ **To install and configure SQL Server 7.0 Desktop Edition on Windows 95 or Windows 98**

1. Insert the SQL Server 7.0 CD-ROM. Autorun starts.

2. Choose **Install SQL Server Components**.

3. Choose **Database Server – Desktop Edition**.

4. In the Welcome window, click **Next**.

5. Click **Yes** to agree with the terms of the license agreement.

6. Complete the User Information with your name (required) and company information (optional).

7. Choose **Typical** as the Setup Type.

8. Set the Destination Folder for Program Files and Data Files to **c:\mssql7**, accept the defaults, and click **Next**.

9. To start copying files, click **Next**.

10. When setup is complete, click **Yes** to restart your computer, and then click **Finish**.

SQL Server 7.0 Database Configuration for All Operating Systems

▶ **To create the Stocks SQL Server database**

1. On the **Start** menu, choose **Programs/SQL Server 7/Enterprise Manager**.

2. Expand SQL Server(s) up to and including the local computer name.

3. Right-click the **Databases** object. Select **New Database** and type **Stocks** in the **Name** text box. Accept all defaults and click **OK**.

4. Verify that the Stocks database was created, by opening the **Databases** object and viewing the Stocks database.

▶ **To create the Pricehistory table in the Stocks database**

1. On the **Tools** menu of the SQL Enterprise Manager, choose **SQL Server Query Analyzer**.

2. Open the CreatePHTable.sql script from the \Database folder that was installed from the companion CD. Using the **DB:** drop-down list box, change the database window to the Stocks database. Press F5 to execute the script, or click the **Execute Query** button (with a green right arrow icon) on the toolbar of the SQL Server Query Analyzer. The following message appears: "The command(s) completed successfully."

3. Minimize the SQL Server Query Analyzer.

▶ **To import data into the Pricehistory table in the Stocks database**

1. Using the Enterprise Manager, expand SQL Server(s) up to and including the local computer name.

2. Expand the **Databases** object and click the **Stocks** database. On the right side of the screen, choose **Import Data**.

3. When the DTS Import Wizard opens, click **Next**.

4. From the **Sources** drop-down list, choose **Text file**. In the **File name** box, type the path for the PHImportData.txt file that was installed from the companion CD to the \Database folder, and click **Next**.

5. In the Select file format window, check that **Delimited** is chosen, accept all defaults, and click **Next**.

6. Verify that **Comma** is chosen as the **Column Delimiter** and click **Next**.

7. In the **Destination** drop-down box, verify that **Microsoft OLE DB Provider for SQL Server** is selected. In the **Server** box, check that your local server name is displayed. Choose **Use SQL Server authentication**, type **sa** as the username, and leave the password blank. Choose **Stocks** as the **Database** and click **Next**.

8. In the **Select Source Tables** dialog box, change **Destination table** to **[stocks].[dbo].[pricehistory]**, and click **Next**.

9. Ensure that the **Run immediately** check box is selected and click **Next**.

10. In the **Completing the DTS Wizard** dialog box, click **Finish**.

11. The following message appears: "Successfully transferred 1 table(s) from flat file to Microsoft SQL Server." Click **OK**.

12. When the **Transferring Data** dialog box appears, click **Done**.

13. Open the SQL Server Query Analyzer and click the **New Query** button on the toolbar. Type the following command: **select * from pricehistory**.

14. Press F5 to execute the script, or click the **Execute Query** button on the toolbar of the SQL Server Query Analyzer. The data from the table appears in the results window.

Using This Book to Prepare for Certification

Where to Find Specific Skills in This Book

The following tables provide lists of the skills measured on the Microsoft Certified Solution Developer (MCSD) Exam 70-016 and where in this book you will find information relating to each skill.

Note Exam skills are subject to change without notice and at the sole discretion of Microsoft.

Deriving the Physical Design

Skills measured	Location in book
Explain the elements of an application that is based on the MFC framework.	
Identify differences between developing an MFC application for Windows NT, Windows 95, and Windows 98.	Chapter 3, Lesson 1
Explain when to use the Platform Software Development Kit (SDK) for an MFC application and when to use the functionality provided by the MFC framework.	Chapter 3, Lesson 1
Choose whether to use an MFC regular DLL or an MFC extension DLL.	Chapter 3, Lesson 1
Explain how command messages are routed between a user interface object and a handler function.	Chapter 3, Lesson 3
Describe the Document/View architecture.	Chapter 3, Lesson 4
Explain the MFC drawing, printing, and print preview architecture.	Chapter 3, Lesson 4
Explain how the MFC architecture supports multi-threading.	Chapter 5, Lesson 3
Evaluate whether access to a database should be encapsulated in an object.	
Evaluate whether a database should be incorporated in the application.	Chapter 7
Identify which type of library to use. Valid libraries include MFC, ATL, and the SDK.	Chapter 7
Identify which type of object to use. Valid object types include ADO, ODBC, and RDO.	Chapter 7, Lesson 1
Design the properties, methods, and events of components.	Chapter 9, Lesson 1

Establishing the Development Environment

Skills measured	Location in book
Establish the environment for source-code control by using Visual SourceSafe. Issues include multiple user/multiple location development and versioning of the source code.	Chapter 2, Lesson 3
Install the Visual C++ development tools that are necessary for developing a desktop application on various platforms. Platforms include Windows NT Workstation, Windows NT Server, Windows 95, and Windows 98.	Chapter 1, Lesson 2

Creating the User Interface

Skills measured	Location in book
Implement the navigation for the user interface.	
Create and integrate toolbars in an MFC application.	Chapter 4, Lesson 1
Implement ToolTips for toolbar buttons.	Chapter 4, Lesson 1
Implement and write to the status bar in an MFC application.	Chapter 4, Lesson 1
Given a scenario, select the appropriate options to create a new application by using the MFC AppWizard.	Chapter 2, Lesson 1
Create and edit user interface objects by using the resource editors.	Chapter 4
Create a new class by using ClassWizard.	Chapter 4, Lesson 1, Lab 4
Add member variables by using ClassWizard.	Chapter 5, Lesson 1
Add a message handler for an event by using ClassWizard.	Chapter 5, Lesson 1
Create data input forms and dialog boxes.	
Create a static menu by using the menu editor.	Chapter 4, Lesson 1
Create a dialog box by using the dialog editor.	Chapter 4, Lesson 2
Create property sheets by using ClassWizard.	Chapter 5, Lesson 1
Create dialog box classes and members by using ClassWizard.	Chapter 4, Lesson 2 Chapter 5, Lesson 1
Use the **CFormView** class to create a view that contains controls.	Chapter 7, Lesson 2
Validate user input.	
Validate user input by using DDV.	Chapter 5, Lesson 1
Validate user input by using ClassWizard.	Chapter 5, Lesson 1

Skills measured	Location in book
Process user input from a form or a dialog box by using DDX.	Chapter 5, Lesson 1
Use an ActiveX user interface control.	
Insert a control into a project by using the Components and Controls Gallery.	Chapter 7, Lesson 3
Handle an event from an ActiveX user interface control.	Chapter 10, Lab 10
Dynamically create an ActiveX user interface control.	Chapter 11, Lab 11
Use the MFC AppWizard to create an ISAPI DLL that can dynamically change Web content.	Chapter 12, Lesson 2
Incorporate Dynamic HTML scriptlets into a Visual C++ desktop application.	Chapter 12, Lesson 1
Create or modify an MFC application to store and retrieve personalized user settings from the registry.	Chapter 6, Lesson 3
Display data from a data source.	
Implement standard serialization by using **Serialize**.	Chapter 6, Lesson 2
Implement persistence by using **CFile**.	Chapter 6, Lesson 1
Display data by using **CArchive**.	Chapter 6, Lesson 2
Connect a recordset to dialog box controls.	Chapter 7, Lesson 2
Instantiate and invoke a COM component.	Chapter 10
Add asynchronous processing.	
Create secondary threads.	Chapter 5, Lesson 3
Download ActiveX user interface controls.	Chapter 14, Lesson 4
Implement online user assistance in an application.	
Implement status bars.	Chapter 4, Lesson 1
Implement ToolTips.	Chapter 4, Lesson 1
Implement context-sensitive Help.	Chapter 5, Lesson 4
Create Help for an application that provides links to a Web page containing Help files.	Chapter 5, Lesson 4
Implement error handling.	
Implement exception handling.	Chapter 13, Lesson 1
Given an error, determine how to handle the error.	Chapter 13, Lesson 1
Use an active document.	Chapter 12, Lesson 2

Creating and Managing COM Components

Skills measured	Location in book
Create a COM component that implements business rules or logic.	
Create a COM component by using ATL.	Chapter 9, Lesson 1
Create a COM component by using the SDK.	Chapter 9, Lesson 2
Create a COM component by using MFC.	Chapter 9, Lesson 2
Create an ATL COM in-process COM component and an ATL COM client to access it.	Chapter 9, Lesson 1 Chapter 10, Lesson 1
Create an ATL COM out-of-process COM component and an ATL COM client to access it.	Chapter 9, Lesson 1 Chapter 10, Lesson 1
Create ActiveX user interface controls.	
Create an ActiveX user interface control by using ATL.	Chapter 11, Lesson 2
Create an ActiveX user interface control by using the SDK.	Chapter 8, Lesson 5
Create an ActiveX user interface control by using MFC.	Chapter 11, Lesson 1
Create a COM component that reuses existing components.	
Explain the difference between aggregation and containment.	Chapter 10, Lesson 2
Add error handling to a COM component.	Chapter 13, Lesson 2
Log errors into an error log.	Chapter 13, Lesson 1
Create and use an active document.	Chapter 12, Lesson 2
Debug a COM component.	Chapter 13, Lesson 4
Create a COM component that supports apartment-model threading. Models include single-threaded apartment, multithreaded apartment, or both.	Chapter 8, Lesson 4

Creating Data Services

Skills measured	Location in book
Access and manipulate data by using ad hoc queries. Methods include ODBC, ADO, DAO, RDO, and data source control.	Chapter 7, Lessons 2, 3
Handle database errors.	Chapter 7, Lesson 2

Testing and Debugging the Solution

Skills measured	Location in book
Determine appropriate debugging techniques.	
Use library debugging support.	Chapter 13, Lesson 4
Use the IDE.	Chapter 13, Lesson 4
Use Depends.	Chapter 13, Lesson 5
Use Spy++.	Chapter 13, Lesson 6
Given a scenario, describe the type of debugging support that Visual C++ provides for resolving programming errors.	Chapter 13
Step through code by using the integrated debugger.	Chapter 13, Lesson 4
List and describe the MFC macros that are used to debug applications.	Chapter 13, Lesson 3
Identify and describe the elements of a test plan. Elements include beta testing, regression testing, unit testing, integration testing, and stress testing.	
Evaluate the need for beta testing.	Chapter 13, Lesson 7
Incorporate stress tests.	Chapter 13, Lesson 7

Deploying an Application

Skills measured	Location in book
Create a Setup program that installs an application and registers the COM components.	Chapter 14, Lessons 1, 2
Use .cab files to package and distribute an application.	Chapter 14, Lesson 1
Plan disk-based deployment or CD-based deployment for an application.	Chapter 14, Lesson 4
Plan Web-based deployment for an application.	Chapter 14, Lesson 4
Plan network-based deployment for an application.	Chapter 14, Lesson 4
Given a scenario, evaluate the use of Microsoft Systems Management Server as an aid to deploying a solution.	Chapter 14, Lesson 5
Create a setup program that installs an application and allows for the application to be uninstalled.	Chapter 14, Lesson 2
Evaluate Zero Administration for Windows (ZAW) as an aid to deploying a solution.	Chapter 14, Lesson 5

Maintaining and Supporting an Application

Skills measured	Location in book
Fix errors, and take measures to prevent future errors.	Chapter 13
Deploy application updates.	Chapter 14, Lesson 4

Microsoft Certified Professional Program

The Microsoft Certified Professional (MCP) program provides the best method of proving your command of current Microsoft products and technologies. Microsoft, an industry leader in certification, is on the forefront of testing methodology. Its exams and corresponding certifications are developed to validate your mastery of critical competencies as you design and develop, or implement and support, solutions with Microsoft products and technologies. Computer professionals who become Microsoft certified are recognized as experts and are sought after industry-wide.

The MCP program offers five certifications, based on specific areas of technical expertise:

- **Microsoft Certified Professional** Demonstrates in-depth knowledge of at least one Microsoft operating system. Candidates can pass additional Microsoft certification exams to further define their skills with the Microsoft BackOffice integrated family of server software products, development tools, or desktop programs.

- **Microsoft Certified Professional—Specialist: Internet** Designates MCPs with a specialty in the Internet, who are qualified to plan security, install, and configure server products, manage server resources, extend servers to run CGI scripts or ISAPI scripts, monitor and analyze performance, and troubleshoot problems.

- **Microsoft Certified Systems Engineer (MCSE)** Demonstrates the ability to effectively plan, implement, maintain, and support information systems in a wide range of computing environments with Windows 98, Windows NT, and BackOffice.

- **Microsoft Certified Solution Developer (MCSD)** Demonstrates the ability to design and develop custom business solutions with Microsoft development tools, technologies, and platforms, including Microsoft Office and BackOffice.

- **Microsoft Certified Trainer (MCT)** Demonstrates the instructional and technical ability to deliver Microsoft Official Curriculum through a Microsoft Certified Technical Education Center (Microsoft CTEC).

Microsoft Certification Benefits

Microsoft certification, one of the most comprehensive certification programs available for assessing and maintaining software-related skills, is a valuable measure of an individual's knowledge and expertise. Microsoft certification is awarded to individuals who have successfully demonstrated their ability to perform specific tasks and implement solutions with Microsoft products. As with any skills assessment and benchmarking measure, certification brings a variety of benefits to the individual, and to employers and organizations. Not only does certification provide guidance for what an individual should know to be proficient, but it also provides an objective measure for employers to consider when hiring IT professionals.

Technical Support

Every effort has been made to ensure the accuracy of this book and the contents of the companion CD. Microsoft Press provides corrections for books through the World Wide Web at:

http://mspress.microsoft.com/support/

If you have comments, questions, or ideas regarding this book or the companion CD, please send them to Microsoft Press via e-mail to:

tkinput@microsoft.com

or via postal mail to:

Microsoft Press
Attn: Desktop Applications with Microsoft Visual C++ 6.0
   MCSD Training Kit Editor
One Microsoft Way
Redmond, WA 98052-6399

Please note that product support is not offered through the above addresses.

About the Authors

This course was developed for Microsoft Press by ARIS Corporation. ARIS is an innovative, professional services and software company that works with clients globally to maximize the usefulness of existing information technologies and the integration of new technologies. ARIS enables companies and government agencies to find and implement client/server and Internet solutions to improve their business operations. The company's consulting and training services utilize leading-edge technologies, primarily from Microsoft, Oracle, PeopleSoft, Sun Microsystems and Lotus. ARIS is a Microsoft Solutions Provider Partner.

ARIS has offices across the United States and in the United Kingdom and Germany, with over 900 employees worldwide. For more information about the products or services offered by ARIS, visit the Web site at *www.aris.com.*

ARIS produced this course with the assistance of Software Architects Inc., Witzend Software, and other contributing authors. Software Architects, Inc. (*www.swarchitects.com*) specializes in custom software in all environments from Windows to Unix on a wide variety of application domains. Additionally, Software Architects, Inc. offers a series of practical, custom-developed, intensive courses at all levels of Windows programming. Witzend Software (*www.witzendsoft.com*) is a Seattle-based company that provides custom programming services, specializing in Visual C++ and COM. Individuals who participated in the production of this course include:

Lead author, project lead, and courseware designer:	Julian Lindars, MCSD
Contributing authors:	Dr. Bruce Krell (Software Architects, Inc., *swarch.krell@prodigy.net*)
	Beck Zaratian (Witzend Software)
	Bob McCoy, MCT
	Scott F. Wilson (KiZAN Corporation)
Additional material:	Ruth Hogan, MSCE

CHAPTER 1

Preparing for Application Development

About This Chapter

In this chapter, you will learn about the elements of designing a Microsoft Visual C++ application using Microsoft design concepts. You will study the issues that you should consider in planning your design. You will also be given an overview of the Visual C++ development tools through a description of the installation options.

Before You Begin

To complete Lab 1 at the end of this chapter, you should have set up the Microsoft SQL Server 7.0 database and run the scripts to create the STUpload database, as described in the preceding section, *About This Book*.

Lesson 1: Defining the Solution with the Microsoft Solutions Framework

Developing large, complex software projects is risky. Statistics on large information technology (IT) projects show that a significant number of software projects fail. Some of the reasons for project failure include the following:

- Constantly changing requirements
- Volatile or incomplete specifications
- Poor quality coding
- A scope that is too large
- Inadequate staffing
- Poor process
- Unclear goals

To address the problems of software development, Microsoft Consulting Services developed the Microsoft Solutions Framework (MSF). MSF is based on best practices from within Microsoft product groups, technology partners, and corporate customers. Consider using the framework to benefit your own development efforts and applying the MSF concepts as you plan a multi-developer project.

This lesson explains the features of MSF and how they relate to implementing Visual C++ applications.

After this lesson, you will be able to:
- Describe the elements of MSF.
- Explain the role of MSF in the design and development process.

Estimated lesson time: 30 minutes

Overview of MSF

MSF is a collection of models, principles, and practices that helps organizations become more effective in their creation and use of technology to solve their business problems. MSF helps by providing measurable progress and adaptable guidance that is flexible enough to meet the changing needs of a modern business. The core building blocks for this MSF-based solutions guidance are the six major models:

- MSF Enterprise Architecture Model
- MSF Risk Management Model

- MSF Team Model for Application Development
- MSF Process Model for Application Development
- MSF Application Model
- MSF Design Process Model

We describe each model briefly and elaborate on the specific uses of each later in this lesson.

MSF Enterprise Architecture Model

The MSF Enterprise Architecture Model provides a consistent set of guidelines for rapidly building enterprise architecture through versioned releases. This model aligns information technology with business requirements through four perspectives: Business, Application, Information, and Technology. Using this model helps shorten the enterprise architecture planning cycle.

MSF Risk Management Model

The MSF Risk Management Model provides a structured and proactive way to manage project risks. This model sets forth a discipline and environment of proactive decisions and actions to continuously assess potential problems, determine what risks are important to confront, and then implement strategies to deal with those risks. Using this model and its underlying principles and practices helps teams focus on what is most important, make the right decisions, and be more prepared for the future.

MSF Team Model for Application Development

The MSF Team Model for Application Development (MSF Development Team Model) provides a flexible structure for organizing project teams. This model clearly emphasizes roles, responsibilities, and goals for team success, and increases team member accountability through its team-of-peers approach. This model's flexibility allows for adaptation depending on project scope, team size, and team members' skills. Using this model and its underlying principles and practices helps produce more engaged, effective, resilient, and successful teams.

MSF Process Model for Application Development

The MSF Process Model for Application Development (MSF Development Process Model) provides structure and guidance through a project's life cycle that is milestone-based, iterative, and flexible. This model describes an application development project's phases, milestones, activities and deliverables; and these elements' relationship to the MSF Development Team Model roles. Using this model helps improve project control, minimize risk, improve quality, and shorten delivery time.

MSF Application Model

The MSF Application Model provides a logical, multi-layer, services-based approach to designing and developing software applications. The implementation of user services, business services, and data services allows for parallel development, improved use of technology, easier maintenance and support, and optimal flexibility in distribution, because the services that make up the application can reside anywhere, from a single desktop to servers and clients around the world.

MSF Design Process Model

The MSF Design Process Model provides a three-phase, user-centric continuum that allows for a parallel and iterative approach to design for the greatest efficiency and flexibility. The three design phases—Conceptual, Logical, and Physical—provide three different perspectives for three different audiences—the users, the project team, and the developers. Moving through each of these design phases shows the translation of user-based scenarios to services-based components so that application features can be traced back to user requirements. Using this model helps ensure that applications are created not just for the sake of technology, but to meet business and user requirements.

Presentation of MSF in This Book

Throughout this lesson, we use some of the basic concepts of MSF to provide a foundation for our discussions of application design and implementation. We concentrate on the aspects of MSF that are directly related to the process of application development—specifically the Team model, the Process model, the Application model, and the Design Process model. For a broader and more detailed treatment of MSF, read *Analyzing Requirements and Defining Solution Architectures: MCSD Training Kit for Exam 70-100* (Microsoft Press, 1999).

Using the MSF Development Team Model

Rather than being a methodology, MSF is a framework that can be adapted to suit the particular needs of any organization. The MSF Development Team Model is one aspect of this framework. The model describes how teams should structure themselves and what principles they should follow to be successful at developing software.

The MSF Development Team Model is specific in nature, but as part of the framework, it should be viewed as a starting point. Different project teams can implement aspects of the framework differently, depending on project scope, team size, and team members' skills.

Specific responsibilities must be carried out and specific goals must be met for any project to be successful. These responsibilities and goals serve to provide continual direction for all the team members. Key project responsibilities and goals include the following:

- **Customer satisfaction** Projects must meet the needs of their customers and users to be successful. It is possible for a team to meet budget and time goals but still be unsuccessful in meeting its goals, because customer needs have not been met.

- **Delivery within project constraints** Most projects measure success using "on time, on budget" metrics.

- **Delivery to specifications based on user requirements** The Functional Specification describes in detail the deliverable to be provided by the team to the customer. This specification represents an agreement between the team and the customer as to what will be built, and constitutes the basis for "Doing what we say we will do."

- **Release after identifying and addressing all issues** All software is delivered with defects. The team's goal is to ensure that those defects are identified and addressed before the product is released. Addressing defects can involve everything from fixing the defect in question to documenting work-around solutions. Delivering a known defect that has been addressed along with a work-around solution is preferable to delivering a product containing unidentified defects that might "surprise" the team and the customer later.

- **Enhanced user performance** For a product to be successful, it must enhance the way that users work. Delivering a product that is rich in features and content but can't be used is considered a failure.

- **Smooth deployment and ongoing management** The effectiveness of deployment directly affects the perceived quality of a product. For example, a faulty installation program might imply to users that the installed application is similarly faulty. The team must do more than simply deploy the product; it must deploy the product smoothly, and then support and manage the product.

The MSF Development Team Model addresses the need to meet these key goals by assigning tasks to six team roles: Product Management, Program Management, Development, Testing, User Education, and Logistics Management. Each goal requires a different discipline, so each team role embodies a different discipline. The people who carry out the team roles must have the unique perspective and set of skills necessary to meet each goal.

Table 1.1 on the next page shows the correspondence between the six roles of the MSF Development Team Model, and the six key goals of an effective project team. Because each goal is critical to the success of a project, the roles that correspond to these goals are seen as peers with equal say in decisions. There is no project master, but simply a team that knows what to do and is properly equipped to do it.

Table 1.1   Goals and corresponding team roles

Goal	Team role
Customer satisfaction	Product Management
Delivery within project constraints	Program Management
Delivery to product specifications	Development
Release after identifying and addressing all issues	Testing
Enhanced user performance	User Education
Smooth deployment and ongoing management	Logistics Management

Using the MSF Development Process Model

The MSF Development Process Model fulfills a key function of project development by specifying which activities should be performed and when. The model has two other important aspects: its close relationship with the MSF Development Team Model and the benefits to the organization of using them together; and the MSF Development Process Model's underlying practices and principles. The latter include:

- Using versioned releases.
- Creating living documents.
- Scheduling for an uncertain future.
- Managing tradeoffs.
- Managing risks.
- Maintaining a fixed ship date mindset.
- Breaking large projects into manageable parts.
- Performing daily builds.
- Using bottom-up estimating.

Traditional approaches to software development, such as the Waterfall and Spiral Models, often cannot meet the needs of current enterprise application development environments.

With the Waterfall Model, a project progresses through sequential steps, from the initial concept through system testing. This model identifies milestones along the course of the project and uses them as transition and assessment points. This approach works well for a project in which requirements can easily be specified at the beginning, but might not work well for a complex project where requirements can change during the project's life cycle. Additionally, practitioners of this model rely heavily on volumes of documentation and a single review process for each stage. These two Waterfall practices usually lead to overextended "analysis paralysis" and adversarial relationships between developers, customers, and users.

Using the Spiral Model, the application evolves over a number of iterations. Early passes through the Spiral life cycle provide increasingly tight definitions of the product, with middle and later iterations adding features and functionality to the application. The Spiral Model seeks to confront project risks early in a software project and address them in early product releases.

Due to its iterative nature, the Spiral Model supports creative adjustments along the way, thus evolving and hopefully improving the quality of product. The highly iterative Spiral process requires significant amounts of process and documentation automation to become efficient. In practice, customers and users might develop a general sense of instability because the product can change too rapidly for them to grasp. Finally, many Spiral projects lack a known ending point, so they continue to iterate indefinitely with no financial or business end within site.

As shown in Figure 1.1, the MSF Development Process Model combines the strengths of these two models, providing the benefits of milestone-based planning from the Waterfall Model and the benefits of the iterative creative process from the Spiral Model.

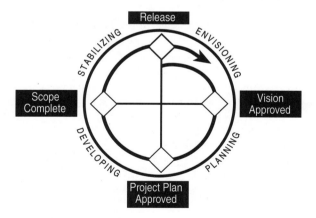

Figure 1.1   The MSF Development Process Model.

The MSF Development Process Model has three primary traits:

- A phased process (the four wedges of the diagram in Figure 1.1)
- A milestone-driven process (the diamonds separating the phases)
- An iterative process (the process arrow aiming back into the first phase)

Although Figure 1.1 shows the four phases as quarters, the phases do not necessarily require equal amounts of time to complete. Different business and technological environments will require different time and resource ratios for the various phases.

Phased Process

The MSF Development Process Model consists of four interrelated phases. Each of these phases represents deliverables for which a baseline should be established before the development process can move to the next phase of the project. The four phases and their primary tasks are:

- Envisioning, which must produce a shared vision.
- Planning, which must produce a detailed project plan and application architecture.
- Developing, which must produce a well-built, complete product.
- Stabilizing, which must produce a stable, deployable product.

Milestone-Driven Process

The MSF Development Process Model is based on milestones that are points for review and synchronization, rather than points for freezing the application or its specifications. They enable the team to assess the project's progress and make midcourse corrections, such as adjusting the scope of the project to reflect changing customer requirements, or reacting to risks that might materialize during the course of the project.

The MSF Development Process Model uses two types of milestones: *major milestones* and *interim milestones*. Each milestone, whether major or interim, is marked by one or more *deliverables*. Deliverables are physical evidence that the team has reached a milestone.

Major Milestones

Each phase of the development process culminates in an externally visible major milestone. *Externally visible* means that the milestone and its deliverables are visible to entities outside the project team, such as the customer or operations personnel.

A major milestone is a point in time when all team members synchronize their deliverables. Additionally, those external to the project team such as the customer and users; operations, support, and help desk personnel; the distribution channel (commercial software); and other key project stakeholders, should be updated on the project status.

A significant role of major milestones is to allow for a stage-by-stage assessment of the project's viability. The project team and the customer, having reviewed the deliverables for the current phase, jointly make the decision whether or not to move into the next phase. Thus, major milestones serve to move the project from one phase to another.

Interim Milestones

Within each phase of the MSF Development Process Model are various interim milestones which, like major milestones, are review and synchronization points rather than freeze points. Unlike major milestones, however, interim milestones are *internally visible*—that is, visible only to project team members.

Interim milestones indicate early progress and break large work assignments into smaller pieces that are easier to address.

Versioned Process

The MSF Development Process Model is a versioned process in the sense that it is designed to be repeated during the life cycle of a given product. Each succeeding completion of the MSF Development Process Model allows for the addition of features and functionality to satisfy changing business requirements.

Using the MSF Application Model

An application model is a conceptual view of an application that establishes the definitions, rules, and relationships that will structure the application. Additionally, an application model serves as a basis for exchanging ideas during the logical design (rather than the physical design) of an application. The application model shows how the application is structured, not how it will be implemented.

The MSF Application Model provides a multi-layer services-based approach to designing and developing software applications. MSF views an application at a logical level as a network of cooperative, distributed, and reusable services that supports a business solution. Application services are units of application logic that include methods for implementing an operation, function, or transformation. These services should be accessed through a published interface that is driven by the interface specification, and focus value toward the customer rather than the provider. Services should map directly to user operations.

The MSF Application Model is Microsoft's recommended approach to designing distributed, multi-tier client-server applications. This model aims to:

- Promote a consistent approach to design and development of client-server applications.
- Provide a standard set of definitions for the application logic in a multi-layer application.
- Make it easier to use component technology to implement distributed, multi-tier applications that have the flexibility, scalability, and maintainability needed to address the needs of mission-critical, enterprise-wide applications.
- Shift from the traditional view of monolithic applications supporting specific business processes to the concept of systems of interoperable applications built upon a common set of components.
- Describe a way of consistently applying the skills and resources of an application development organization across multiple projects.
- Define a framework for organizing teams, introducing parallelism into the development process and identifying the required skills.

The MSF Application Model describes applications as using three services: user, business, and data. A service is a unit of application logic that implements operations, functions, or transformations applied to objects. Services can enforce business rules; perform calculations or manipulations on data; and expose features for entering, retrieving, viewing or modifying information. These services allow for parallel development, improved use of technology, easier maintenance and support, and flexibility in distributing the application's services. In addition, these services can reside anywhere in the environment, from a single desktop to servers and clients around the world.

Application Architectures

An application architecture is a conceptual view of the structure of an application. As shown in Figure 1.2, each application has three distinct layers: the user layer, the business layer, and the data layer. Each application also contains the following types of code: presentation, business-rule processing, data processing, and data storage. Application architectures differ in how this code is packaged to form a particular application product.

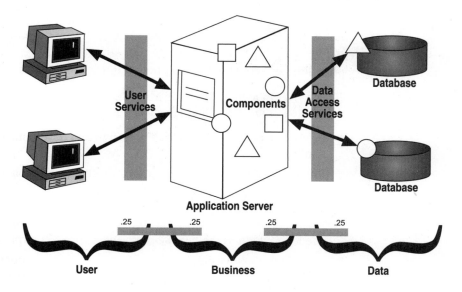

Figure 1.2   The Application Model and its application layers

Many current applications have a *two-tier architecture,* also known as *client/ server architecture.* In a two-tier architecture, a client process handles the data processing and presentation parts of the application. Data is stored on centrally administered server computers. Clients connect directly to the servers they need, often for the lifetime of the application's use.

Client/server applications work well in controlled environments in which the number of users can be estimated and managed, and resources can be allocated accordingly. However, when the number of users is unknown or very large, the client/server architecture breaks down. Because each client connects to data servers directly, the number of available data connections limits scalability. Opportunities for reuse are limited because the clients are bound to the data-base formats. Each client application contains data processing logic, making the applications relatively large. (This type of client is sometimes called a *fat client.*) If the data processing logic ever needs to change, new applications must be distributed to every client computer.

A slight improvement comes from moving parts of the data processing, or business logic, to the data servers—for example, by using SQL Server stored procedures. This architecture is sometimes called "two-and-a-half tier." Applications built on this model are somewhat more scalable, but not scalable enough to meet the needs of highly distributed applications. In addition, opportunities for reuse are limited.

Scalability and reuse can be improved significantly by introducing a third tier to the application architecture. With *multi-layer architecture*, also known as *N-tier architecture*, the user, business, and data tiers are logically separated, as illustrated in Figure 1.3.

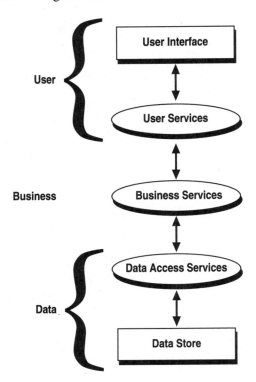

Figure 1.3   Multi-layer application architecture

The three tiers perform the following functions:

- **User layer** The user layer presents data to the user and, optionally, lets the user edit data. The two main types of user interfaces (UIs) for personal computer-based applications are native and Web-based. Native UIs use the service of the underlying operating system. On the Microsoft Windows platform, for example, native UIs use the Microsoft Win32 API and Windows controls. Web-based UIs are based on HTML and Extensible Markup Language (XML), which can be rendered by a Web browser on any platform.

- **Business layer** The business layer is used to enforce business and data rules. The presentation tier uses the services of the business tier. However, the business tier is not tied to any specific client; its services are available to all applications. Business rules can be business algorithms, business policies, legal policies, and so on—for example, "Users get a 10 percent discount for ads placed before Tuesday night" or "Six percent sales tax must be collected for all orders delivered to the Commonwealth of Kentucky." Data rules help to ensure the validity and occasionally the integrity of the stored data—for example, "An order header must have at least one detail record" or "Money must not be lost or generated during transfers between bank accounts." Business rules are typically implemented in isolated code modules, which are usually stored in a centralized location so that multiple applications can use them.

- **Data layer** The business tier has no knowledge of how or where the data it works on is stored. Instead, it relies on the data access services, which perform the actual work of storing and retrieving the data. The data access services are also implemented in isolated code modules, encapsulating knowledge of the underlying data store. If the data store moves or changes format, only the data access services need to be updated. Each data access module typically is responsible for the integrity of a set of data—for example, data placed in relational tables or the Microsoft ActiveX Data Objects (ADO) and OLE DB technology. For the purpose of N-tier design, the data store is simply the DBMS—the systems required to serve data from tables, as well as optimize information retrieval, such as database indexes. Examples of data stores are SQL Server, Microsoft Exchange Server, Microsoft Database Engine (MSDE), Microsoft FoxPro, Microsoft Access, and Microsoft Jet.

It might be slightly confusing to talk about logical architecture as part of the Physical Model. It is important to understand that logical architecture encompasses a wide range of physical architectures and implementations that specify where services are deployed. In other words, applications are constructed as logical networks of consumers and suppliers of services. Services are merely units of application logic that provide well-defined functionality.

The terms *multi-layer* and *N-tier* don't imply separate computers. The N-tier application architecture promotes scalable applications. To create highly scalable applications, resources such as database connections must be shared. Instead of each client application consuming resources to access data servers directly, client applications communicate with business services. One instance of a business service can support many clients, reducing resource consumption and improving scalability, as shown on the next page in Figure 1.4 and Figure 1.5. Because business services do not manage data directly, it's easy to replicate these services to support even more clients. Services can often be designed and implemented independently of any particular client applications, providing flexibility and the potential for reuse in many applications. By encapsulating application logic behind well-defined public interfaces, developers create a body of reusable services that can easily be combined in new ways to create new applications. In addition, common functionality can easily be updated in response to changing business requirements, without impacting the client applications that rely on the functionality. This aspect reduces the management and deployment costs of changing requirements.

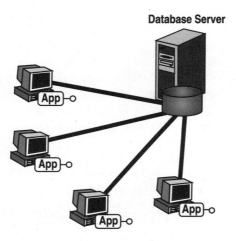

Figure 1.4   Client/server systems

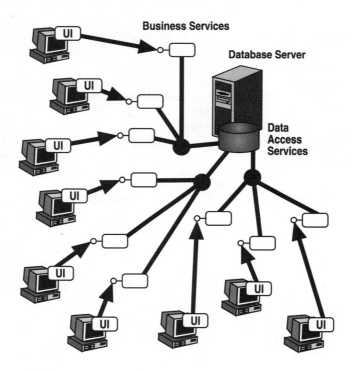

Figure 1.5   N-tier systems

The multi-layer application architecture can also help developers deal with existing, or legacy systems. Developers can "wrap" access to existing systems within business logic, data access, or data store services. Client applications need to worry only about how to access the business logic, not about how to access all the different legacy systems on which they might rely. If the legacy system is modified or replaced, only the wrapper needs to be updated.

Using the MSF Design Process Model

The MSF Design Process consists of three distinct types of design work: conceptual, logical, and physical. Each of these generates a model of the same name: the Conceptual Design Model, the Logical Design Model, and the Physical Design Model.

Each part of the process approaches the design task from a different perspective and defines the solution differently, as shown in Table 1.2.

Table 1.2   Design task approaches to the three parts of the MSF Design Process

Type of design work	Perspective	Action
Conceptual	Views the problem from the perspective of the user and business	Defines the problem and solution in terms of scenarios
Logical	Views the solution from the perspective of the project team	Defines the solution as a set of cooperating services
Physical	Views the solution from the perspective of the developers	Defines the solution's services and technologies

The output of each part is used as the input for the succeeding part, as Figure 1.6 illustrates.

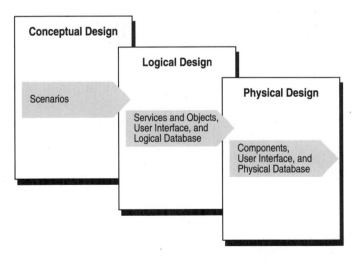

Figure 1.6   The output of the three interdependent design process models

The goals of the three parts are:

- **Conceptual Design** Identify business needs and understand what users do and what they require. Conceptual Design generates scenarios that reflect complete and accurate requirements by involving the customer, users, and other stakeholders.

- **Logical Design** Organize the solution and the communication among its elements. Logical Design takes the business problem identified in Conceptual Design scenarios and formulates an abstract model of the solution. Following the workflow in Figure 1.6, Logical Design takes the scenarios from Conceptual Design and produces objects and services, UI prototypes, and a logical database design.

- **Physical Design** Apply real-world technology constraints, including those dealing with implementation and performance, to the output of Logical Design by specifying the details of the solution. The output of Logical Design is used to produce components, UI specifications, and physical database design.

The MSF Design Process moves from tangible requirements (use cases) to an abstract application design (Conceptual Design), then to a rationalized application design (Logical Design), then to a concrete application design (Physical Design), and finally, to the tangible product. Conceptual Design is the initial translation of the use cases (the language of the users) to the application design (the language of the application developers). Logical Design is the developers' perspective and serves as a translator between the high-level application concepts—the business and user requirements—and the detailed application design.

Conceptual Design does not take into account the approach or the technologies needed to build the solution. Rather, Conceptual Design corresponds to rough sketches and scenarios for building a house. These elements are easily understood models jointly created by the customer, user, and architect. Conceptual Design is the translation of business and user requirements from the language of the users to the language of the developers.

Logical Design starts to get into the details of the application that the team will build to fulfill business needs and user requirements. Logical Design thus corresponds to the floor plan and elevation of a house, where elements such as spatial relationships are organized. In this part of the process, the architect's team lays out the design's relationships and communication paths.

Physical Design addresses the technology that will be used. This design adds detail to the architecture and reflects real-world implementation constraints.

Essentially, the different parts of the MSF Design Process address the needs of different "readers" while still serving as parts of a functional whole. Instead of forcing readers to digest what might be a very large and detailed document, this model allows readers to focus only on the information—the part of the whole— that is pertinent to them. The model also allows the use of formal or informal techniques as appropriate.

The design evolves as each step in the process contributes more detail to the Functional Specification. And as the design evolves, every aspect is traceable from any point back to the original business problem, for verification and testing purposes.

Although the MSF Design Process resides primarily within the Planning Phase of the MSF Development Process Model, the work of design often begins before the Planning Phase is officially started, and it continues to some extent up to the point when the code is frozen (near the end of the Developing Phase). The baselines for each of the three parts of the process are established during the Planning Phase. As shown in Figure 1.7, the three design activities occur in a staggered, parallel manner, with the early output of one activity signaling that the next activity should begin.

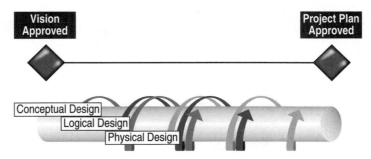

Figure 1.7   The overlapping, iterative, and spiral qualities of the MSF Design Process

The Conceptual Design activity begins when the team agrees upon a vision statement, which can occur before the team reaches the formal Vision Approved Milestone. The Logical Design and Physical Design activities parallel those of Conceptual Design, and all three sit squarely in, but are not limited to, the Planning Phase of the MSF Development Process Model.

It is the parallel execution of all three design activities that allows the product's conceptual, logical, and physical design to have the following three qualities:

- **Overlapping** The activities are parallel, with Conceptual Design typically starting first, followed by Logical Design and then Physical Design. They are not sequential, so one doesn't have to finish before the next can begin. In fact, Logical Design and Physical Design can begin even before the baseline for Conceptual Design is established.
- **Iterative** The activities have their own cycles of validation, design testing (as opposed to code testing), and redesign.
- **Spiral** Each iteration of all three activities represents progress toward the Project Plan Approved Milestone of the Planning Phase.

Obviously, a minimum degree of sequencing must occur as a practical matter. Conceptual Design must start before Logical Design, which must start before Physical Design. Similarly, the baseline for Conceptual Design must be established before the baseline for Logical Design, which must be established before the baseline for Physical Design.

Design Considerations

The promotion of understanding among members of the project team is a primary consideration when determining how to manage the inherent *complexity* of large-scale business applications and when trying to assess the level of detail that should be included in the design. If too little detail is included, the team runs the risk of missing relevant interactions. If too much detail is included, the design might become overly complicated.

The experience and skill of C++ developers are especially valuable to the logical design process, as the principles of object-oriented software development are very similar to the methods used to establish a logical design. This section outlines some of the key concepts used in the logical design process—concepts that will be familiar to anyone with experience in developing object-oriented software solutions.

Modularity

The team starts the Logical Design process by defining the major services of the system. A service represents some collection of processes that work together to accomplish a task. The principle behind modular design is that the final product will be constituted by the combination of the major services. Each service is deliberately designed to perform a particular function as a stand-alone unit that must work with other parts of the system.

Abstraction

Abstraction is the process of examining and distilling the properties and features of a distinct item, and the classification of groups of items through the recognition of essential common characteristics. Abstraction enables us to classify and organize our day-to-day world by concentrating on the defining characteristics and behavior of an object while ignoring its non-essential details. This process enables us to deal with what would otherwise be overwhelmingly complex situations.

Typically, C++ developers are accustomed to abstracting real-world objects, and more abstract entities, into *classes* that specify the characteristics of the software objects in the application. For example, designers of a postal delivery system might design classes to represent letters, packets, van routes, and airline schedules; as well as entities internal to the software environment such as caches, event schedulers, and barcode input handlers.

Encapsulation

Encapsulation is a fundamental principle of structured design, object-oriented design, and object-based component design. In structured design, encapsulation provides the notion of a "black box"—a compiled, unit-tested module that can be assumed to perform a limited, well-defined function correctly. In object-oriented design, it provides the basis for abstraction. Abstraction focuses upon the essential characteristics of some object, relative to the perspective of the viewer. Software components encapsulate behaviors, which they expose as services to client programs.

Encapsulation is the technique for packaging information (data and process) in such a way as to hide what should be hidden, and make visible what is intended to be visible. A component should describe the services that it can provide and specify the data types of the input and output parameters. It should not expose the means by which it provides its advertised services—in particular, it should ensure that its inner state is not exposed in such a way that it can be corrupted by external factors.

When developers decide to expose some aspect of a component, they use an interface. An *interface* describes the services that a component can provide to a client. To ensure that a component is easy to use, and difficult to abuse, it should hide as much as possible about its inner workings from the outside world.

Encapsulation allows a system to be assembled out of parts. The idea of encapsulation is applicable at all levels of design—from the largest subsystem to the smallest code routines and functions.

Cohesion and Coupling

Cohesion refers to how closely the operations within a service are related. The goal of any design is to maximize the beneficial cohesion among its constituent parts. High cohesion allows a module's purpose or function to be more easily abstracted so that its behavior can be more easily and accurately specified.

Coupling refers to the relationships between services. The less information that links services to each other, the freer the designer is to compose a solution without causing perturbations within the individual services themselves, or the existing assembly of those services. One service should depend as little as possible on other services. However, where a dependency exists, the connection between those services should be as clear and straightforward as possible. This leads to easier definition and greater simplicity in determining interfaces.

The constituent units of a well-defined service have loose inter-unit coupling and high internal cohesion. As an example, consider a hi-fi music system built of three separate services—an amplifier, a CD player, and a tape deck. The internal components of the amplifier, such as the transistors and the resistors, don't do much on their own. They rely upon a relationship of high internal cohesion with the other parts of the amplifier module to perform their task. On the other hand, the modular units of the hi-fi system exhibit a loosely coupled relationship—they are usually connected together by a few cables, and can easily be interchanged.

Separation of Interface and Implementation

Services exhibit external characteristics that make them available as building blocks. Each service has an interface that allows it to be used, but the interface hides internal implementations so those implementations can be replaced without affecting the rest of the system. For this approach to work effectively, developers must recognize that each service contains some capability that needs to be represented to the outside world. A description of this capability can be used as a contract with other modules. Any other service that complies with this contract can access the capability.

A contract sets up the rules for interaction between the supplier and the consumer. For example, we know that when we use a public telephone, we have to insert some coins and dial a number. We trust that if we do this correctly, the call will be connected or, if the call is unsuccessful, the money will be returned. Likewise, users of a software component know that as long as the conditions of the interface "contract" are met, any consumer can call upon it as a supplier and receive the specified service. This is known as an open-ended contract. It is important that interfaces be designed as open-ended as possible to facilitate modularity and reuse.

The interface is defined logically, independent of its implementation, providing common access to any potential user. The contractual nature of the interface places the responsibility for fulfilling the request on the supplier of that capability. If we type the number correctly, it is the phone company's responsibility to handle the necessary details to connect us to the intended party. Interface implementations are replaceable as long as the replacement can service the same public interface. This allows services to evolve as conditions and requirements change, or as improvements are made. For example, the phone company can often upgrade the handset in a telephone booth. As long as it maintains the familiar dial pad and coin slot interface, we can continue to use the handset without difficulty.

Clearly specifying interfaces is necessary for services to be designed and coded independently. With well-defined interfaces, these independently coded services can be reliably integrated into a fully functional application. The inter-service independence afforded by clearly specified interfaces allows for easier maintenance and greater flexibility with regard to future upgrades.

Developing Desktop Applications

In this course, we will be applying the Application Model in the creation of desktop applications. By "desktop applications," we do not just mean applications like Microsoft Word that run self-contained on a single computer. We define desktop applications to include client/server applications—particularly those based on the so-called "fat client model," where the business services and the presentation services are implemented together as a locally deployed application retrieving data from a remote data source. This model tends to assume business rules of limited complexity and of limited deployment scope.

Where appropriate, a desktop application should make use of the component-based design described by the Application Model to take advantage of the flexibility, scalability, and reliability offered by a component-based architecture.

Lesson Summary

MSF is a suite of models, principles, and guides for building and deploying software. MSF is a collection of best practices used by the Microsoft product groups and Microsoft Consulting Services.

MSF implements the following models and perspectives, which contribute to the development cycle:

- **MSF Development Team Model** Defines a team of peers working in interdependent and cooperating roles.
- **MSF Development Process Model** Helps the team establish guidelines for planning and controlling results-oriented projects based on project scope, the resources available, and the schedule.

- **MSF Application Model** Helps the team design distributed applications that take optimum advantage of component reuse. It establishes standards and guidelines for designing distributed client/server and multi-tier applications that can be implemented using Microsoft's component-based tools and technologies.

- **MSF Design Process Model** Shows how applications must be designed from both a user and business perspective. It specifies three iterative design phases, tying together the Team Model, Process Model, and Application Model in a solution-oriented context.

- **Conceptual design perspective** Focuses on the needs and technological capabilities of the business and of the users. The output of conceptual design is typically documented as scenarios.

- **Logical design perspective** Focuses on project team understanding. The solution is described in terms of the constituent parts of the system and how they interact. The output of logical design consists of high-level functional specification documents.

- **Physical design perspective** Focuses on providing information necessary to allow developers to implement the solution. Physical design focuses on the organization, structure and technology of the solution. The output of physical design consists of lower-level specification documents such as flowcharts, object models, and pseudocode.

Sometimes developers participate only in the physical design of a solution. However, logical design should not be neglected, as it plays an important role in software development. The purpose of the logical design process is to promote a greater understanding of the system by the entire project team, helping team members to determine how to manage the inherent complexity of large-scale business applications. Management of this complexity is achieved through the application of design concepts similar to those employed by object-oriented software developers.

Lesson 2: Installing the Visual C++ Development Tools

In this lesson, you will learn about the options offered by Microsoft Visual Studio 6.0 when installing the Enterprise Edition of Visual C++ 6.0 using a custom installation. The installation setup program is a good place to gain an overview of the features offered by the Visual C++ development environment, as it groups together all the installable options that are available to you in one logically organized, browsable location. If you already have Visual C++ installed, you can still follow through this lesson to further your understanding of the installation options.

After this lesson, you will be able to:

- Understand the choices presented to users when installing Visual C++ 6.0.

Estimated lesson time: 30 minutes

Microsoft Visual C++ Installation

Visual C++ comes as part of the Visual Studio development suite or as a stand-alone product. In either case, you start the installation process by running the Setup.exe file from the root directory of the CD.

Note If you are using Windows NT 4.0, you will need to install the Windows NT Service Pack 3 before you can install Visual C++.

First you will be presented with a dialog box providing you with the opportunity to browse the Readme file. This file contains important information that will likely impact your development effort, so you should at least scan its contents.

Next, you will be presented with the user license agreement. Once you have read and accepted the user license agreement and entered your product number and user ID, you will be taken to a dialog box that presents you with setup options. At this point, choose a **Custom** setup and click **Next**.

On the screen that appears, accept the default installation location by clicking **Next**. The setup process will begin. Read the information screens and click **Next** until you arrive at the Custom Setup screen, shown in Figure 1.8 on the next page. (This figure displays the Visual Studio version of this screen, which shows options to install the other products in the Visual Studio suite.)

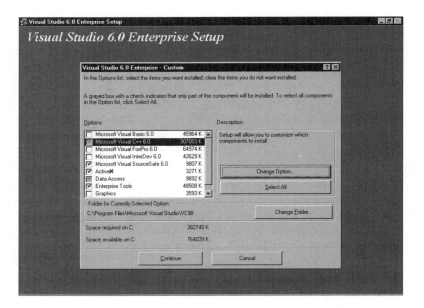

Figure 1.8   **The** Visual Studio Custom Setup screen

If you already have Visual C++ installed, you'll want to get to the maintenance dialog box that allows you to add or remove components for your current installation. You access this dialog box by selecting the **Workstation** option. This maintenance dialog box is identical to the setup screen, so you can use it to explore the installation options.

The custom setup screen appears with a default set of installation options selected, which you can change as required. A check mark next to an installation option means that the option will be installed. Many of the options are arranged in a hierarchical order. If one of the items in the **Options** list is selected and the **Change Option** button is made available, you can click it to reveal further suboptions beneath the currently selected option. **OK** and **Cancel** can be used to move up the option hierarchy, saving or discarding the changes you have made to the option selection on each screen.

If an option check box is selected but shaded, only some of its suboptions are selected, meaning that only some of its options will be installed.

The following exercise shows you how to use the Custom Setup or Maintenance screen to configure your installation options.

▶ **To configure installation options**

1. In the **Options** list of the Custom Setup or Maintenance screen, select the **Microsoft Visual C++ 6.0** option as shown in Figure 1.8.

2. Click the **Change Option** button.

3. In the **Options** list, select the **VC++ Runtime Libraries** option. Click the **Change Option** button.

   Note that the **CRT Source code** option is not selected. Note, too, that the option requires 5805 KB of disk space. Having the C run-time source code available means that you can use the debugger to step through the C source code of the standard C libraries. If the CRT source code is unavailable, you will only see assembly language instructions when you use the debugger to step into a C library function. Having this source code available can also be instructional in that it demonstrates how professional C programmers handle a particular programming situation.

4. If you would like to have the CRT library source code available, and you can spare the half-megabyte of disk space that this option requires, select the check box next to that option.

5. If you have changed any of the options that are currently displayed in the **Options** list and you want to save the changes, click **OK** to revert to the previous screen in the hierarchy. Otherwise, click **Cancel** to leave the options as they were.

Tip If you make changes at one level and click **OK**, and then click **Cancel** at a higher level, the lower level changes are still reflected in your setup. If you want to cancel the lower level changes, you must go to the dialog box on which they were made and reverse them, and then click **OK** in that dialog box.

---

6. When you have finished configuring the options, return to the main Custom Setup or Maintenance screen, and proceed with the installation by clicking the **Continue** button. To abandon the installation, click **Cancel**.

Installation Options

The rest of this lesson consists of a brief explanation of most of the Visual C++ installation options. Using the Custom Setup or the Maintenance screen, locate each of the options listed in the following sections and determine whether or not you require them to be installed on your computer.

Visual Studio

You have an all or nothing choice of options with Visual Studio, and you should hence select the default choice of **All**. The default choice installs the development environment, wizards, and debugger.

The Visual C++ UI consists of an integrated set of windows, tools, menus, toolbars, directories, and other elements that allow you to create, test, and refine your application in one place. You can also work on other types of documents within Visual C++, such as Microsoft Excel or Microsoft Word documents.

Run-Time Libraries

The **VC++ Runtime Libraries** selection, which you read about in the previous exercise, offers four choices:

- **Static CRT Libraries** Multithread-capable libraries. These libraries are linked to your application at link time, increasing the size of the executable file. An advantage to static linking is that the executable (.exe) file contains the entire application. A disadvantage is that a change in the program or a library requires a rebuild of the entire application.

- **Shared CRT Libraries** Dynamically linked to your application at run time. Accordingly, the application's .exe file is smaller than the same application when statically linked to the libraries. Advantages to dynamic linking include builds that take less time to create, and the ability to redistribute a smaller executable program if you make changes in the application. A disadvantage to dynamic linking is that you have to ensure that users of your program have the link libraries installed on their computers.

- **CRT Source Code** Installs the source code for the C++ run-time debug libraries. Having the source code readily available makes programming and debugging easier. You can refer to the code to see how other programmers handle a particular programming situation.

- **Single Threaded CRT Libraries** Used when you choose static linking and single threading as build options.

Each of the libraries has an optimized release version without debug symbols and a debug version with no optimizations, but with debug symbols. When you choose to include the source code, you can step into library functions during debugging sessions.

Developers of desktop applications on the Win32 platform (that is, Windows 95, Windows 98, and Windows NT) will often want to take advantage of multithreading capabilities offered by these platforms. If you are developing programs that need to run on older 16-bit platforms, you will need to link to the single-threaded CRT libraries.

MFC Library

The MFC Library is a collection of C++ classes that provide a framework for programming on the Windows platform. Building on the work of expert Windows developers, you can quickly and easily generate applications, libraries, and software components. MFC makes rapid development available for all aspects of Windows programming, including the development of UIs, Internet development, component technology, and database access—all without sacrificing programming freedom and flexibility. MFC provides the *AppWizard*, a step-by-step visual tool that allows the developer to quickly and easily generate frameworks to set up a basic application structure; and to generate code to implement fundamental application behaviors.

The **VC++ MFC and Template Libraries** option includes the following MFC libraries:

- **Static Libraries** Installs the headers, libraries, and debug symbols for static linkage to MFC.

- **Shared Libraries** Installs the headers, libraries, and debug symbols for dynamic linkage to shared MFC DLLs.

- **Static Libraries for Unicode** Same as static libraries, except that the linkage is to the *Unicode* version of MFC. Unicode is a 16-bit character set supported by Windows NT that makes character sets of more than 65,000 characters available. You would use Unicode to develop international versions of your application that are required to support languages with large character sets such as Chinese. Note, too, that all internal strings used by Windows NT, such as user account names and device names, are Unicode strings, so you will need to install the Unicode libraries if you are planning to write programs that retrieve and manipulate these strings directly.

- **Shared Libraries for Unicode** The dynamic linking, shared version of the MFC Unicode library.

- **Browser Database** Installs the browser database for the debug versions of the MFC libraries. The browser allows you to view a graphical representation of the inheritance hierarchy of your classes and of the relationships between them. Makes jumping to MFC source code from within your code quick and easy. However, including browser information in your project does increase the compilation time and the executable program size.

- **Source Code** One of the best ways to learn how to program with MFC is to look at the code and step through it using the debugger.

ActiveX Template Library

This option is in the same dialog box as the **MS Foundation Class Libraries** option. Choose **MS ActiveX Template Library** (ATL) to install the headers, libraries, and source files for ATL.

ATL is a set of template-based C++ classes with which you can easily create Component Object Model (COM) objects. ATL simplifies the often-complicated process of COM development, but with less overhead than MFC. ATL's ability to generate small, fast components is especially useful if you are developing for an Internet environment. ATL has special support for fundamental COM features including stock implementations of key COM interfaces, and helper classes that simplify working with COM objects and data types. COM and ATL are covered in depth later in this book.

Build Tools

The **Build Tools** option installs the compiler, linker, NMAKE, and other tools used to build applications and components.

Data Access

The **Data Access** option is in the main selection dialog box, at the same level as the C++ options. These options include:

- **ADO, RDS, and OLE DB Providers** OLE DB is a new low-level interface that introduces a universal data access paradigm. That is, OLE DB is not restricted to the Indexed Sequential Access Method (ISAM), the Microsoft Jet database, or even relational data sources, but is capable of dealing with any type of data regardless of its format or storage method. For practical purposes, this means that you can access data that resides in an Excel spreadsheet, in text files, or even on a mail server such as Exchange.

  OLE DB is a set of interfaces that exposes data from a variety of sources using COM. OLE DB interfaces provide applications with uniform access to data stored in diverse information sources. These interfaces support the amount of DBMS functionality appropriate to the data source, enabling it to share its data.

  ADO enables you to write a client application to access and manipulate data in a data source through a provider. ADO is designed as an easy-to-use application level interface to OLE DB providers. ADO's primary benefits are ease of use, high speed, low memory overhead, and a small disk footprint.

  RDS client-side and server-side components work together to bring data over the Internet or over an Intranet to a Web page. These RDS components also allow updated information to be sent back across the network and merged into a database.

- **Microsoft ODBC Drivers** Open Database Connectivity (ODBC) provides an API that different database vendors implement via ODBC drivers specific to a particular DBMS. Your program uses this API to call the ODBC Driver Manager, which passes the calls to the appropriate driver. The driver, in turn, interacts with the DBMS using Structured Query Language (SQL).

- **Jet Installable ISAM Drivers** The Microsoft Jet database engine is a database management system that retrieves data from and stores data in user and system databases. The Microsoft Jet database engine can be thought of as a data manager component with which other data access systems, such as Microsoft Access and Microsoft Visual Basic, are built. The installable ISAM drivers allow you to access various ISAM data sources, such as the DBase III file format, using the Jet engine.

- **Remote Data Objects and Controls** Remote Data Objects (RDO) is a thin object layer interface to the ODBC API. It is specifically designed to access remote ODBC relational data sources.

- **Data Environment** The data environment selection adds a grid control, and supporting functionality, to permit design-time data manipulation.

We suggest that you install the default Data Access options, but consider whether you would ever need to write applications that connect to an ISAM data source using the Jet engine, and look through the **Microsoft ODBC Drivers** options to see whether the preselected set is likely to meet your needs.

Enterprise Tools

The tools included with the Enterprise Edition of Visual Studio are as follows:

- **Application Performance Explorer (APE)** Models your application design and tests the expected performance and interactions of a distributed architecture. You can save favorite design architectures and use them as the basis for new configurations and performance tests.

- **Repository** Provides a common place to keep information about objects and relationships between objects. In doing so, it provides a standard way to describe object-oriented information used by software tools: Software tools use information composed of various classes of objects; objects expose interfaces; properties, methods, and collections compose interfaces; collections contain relationships to other interfaces; and therefore, collections relate objects to other objects. A software tool is modeled in the Repository through an information model. Each information model is stored in the Repository database as a Repository type library.

- **Visual Component Manager** A tool with which to organize, find, and insert components into a Visual Studio project, addressing three requirements for storing and organizing components: publishing, finding, and reusing them. Using the Visual Component Manager, you can identify existing objects available for reuse.

- **Visual C++ Enterprise Tools** Adds enhanced data tools support and support for SQL debugging.

- **Visual Modeler** A tool for designing three-tier distributed applications using class and component diagrams. With Visual Modeler, you can visually design models of the classes and components your application needs, and then convert these models to Visual C++ code.

- **Visual Studio Analyzer** A tool for evaluating, analyzing, and debugging the structure, performance, and interactions of a distributed application from an application perspective, rather than a component or code perspective. Visual Studio Analyzer uses an event-oriented model to record component interactions for analysis.

General Tools

General tools are included with all versions of Visual C++. We suggest that you install all of the following:

- **MFC Trace Utility** Helps you debug windows programs. You can trace displays to a debugging output window or console, to messages about the internal operation of the MFC library, as well as to warnings and errors if something goes wrong in your application. Trace only works in debug versions of applications. Trace sets the trace flags in Afx.ini. These trace flags determine what message categories the application sends to the debugging window or console.

- **Spy++** A Win32-based utility that gives you a graphical view of the system's processes, threads, windows, and window messages.

- **Win32 SDK Tools** Adds a handful of tools that are useful while developing and debugging applications. For instance, DDESpy allows you to monitor dynamic data exchange (DDE) activity in the operating system. PView (process viewer), another SDK tool, lets you examine and modify many characteristics of the processes and threads running on your system.

- **OLE/COM Object Viewer** Displays all registered controls. The object viewer reads a control's type library and displays the control's interfaces, as well as registry and other pertinent information.

- **ActiveX Control Test Container** Helps the control developer test and debug ActiveX controls. Test Container allows you to test the control's functionality by changing its properties, invoking its methods, and firing its events.

- **VC Error Lookup** A simple dialog box application that looks up system and module error codes and displays the text of the error code.

Visual SourceSafe 6.0

On the main installation screen, you will find an option to install Visual SourceSafe 6.0 (VSS). VSS helps you manage your projects, regardless of the file type (text files, graphics files, binary files, sound files, or video files), by saving them to a database. If you need to share files between two or more projects, you can share them quickly and efficiently. When you add a file to VSS, the file is backed up on the database, made available to other people, and changes that have been made to the file are saved so you can recover an old version at any time. Members of your team can see the latest version of any file, make changes, and save a new version in the database.

Lesson 3 in Chapter 2 teaches you how to implement a source-code control system using VSS, so you should ensure that it is installed. During installation, you might be asked to choose between support for the old or new VSS database formats. Generally you should select the newer format—you can upgrade existing VSS databases using the VSS utility DDCONV.EXE

Completing the Installation

After you have configured your installation by selecting the appropriate options from the main and sub installation screens, you click the button labeled **Continue** to start installing the software. You will be prompted to reboot your computer to complete the installation. After the reboot, you will be prompted to install the version of the Microsoft Developers' Network (MSDN) library that comes with your copy of Visual C++. You should do this, as the MSDN library is the means by which online Help and documentation are provided for Visual C++.

Lesson Summary

Visual C++ provides a rich environment for the developer. This environment contains an essential set of tools and utilities to allow you to produce efficient, bug-free code. The libraries and frameworks offered in the environment allow you to create code and application structures for common programming situations, allowing you to concentrate your time and skills on the creation of unique solutions.

The overview of the major installation options provided in this lesson serves as an introduction to many aspects of the Visual C++ development suite that we will cover in more depth throughout this training kit. These include:

- Visual Studio and debugging tools
- Microsoft Foundation Classes (MFC)
- ATL
- Data Access Technologies
- Visual SourceSafe (VSS)

Lab 1: Introducing the STUpload Application

The purpose of this lab is to introduce the application that you will develop throughout the labs in this course. You will be presented with the customer requirements and are encouraged to think about the solution in terms of the MSF models.

Customer Requirements

Your customer, StockWatch Data Services, Inc. (SDS), is an information services company that specializes in providing stock market information to brokers and fund managers. SDS receives a large volume of data every week in the form of ASCII text files automatically downloaded from mainframe computers around the world. Their request is for an application, which will allow operators in the company data center to load the data contained in these text files, perform visual verification that the data is correct, and upload verified data to a central database server. The application must meet the following requirements:

- The application will be deployed on a Microsoft Windows NT 4.0 network accessible by up to 50 users, all of whom will be working from desktop computers in the data center.

- Data downloaded from mainframe computers around the world will arrive on the operators' computers in the form of text files attached to electronic mail messages. The text files have the file extension *.dat*.

- Each file will contain data from one particular market, for example NASDAQ or the London Stock Exchange, although each file might contain data for a number of funds.

- The text files will be in standard 8-bit ASCII format and will consist of one header row detailing the source market and the file date, and any number of data rows in which the fields are delimited by fixed column widths, as illustrated in Figure 1.9.

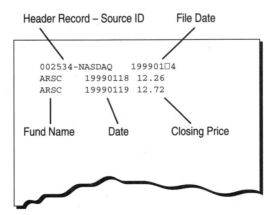

Figure 1.9   The format of the ASCII download file

- The text files often contain duplicate lines, lines with zero price values, or lines containing corrupted data, and the application needs to ensure that such lines are filtered out, and only valid data lines are loaded into the application.

- The application should allow users to load the text file, and then display all of the fund names contained in that file in a list.

- When the user chooses one of the fund names, the price data for that fund will be displayed in a line graph for visual verification that the data appears correct.

- Once the operator is satisfied that the data contained in the file is accurate, he or she can upload it to the central database server.

- This server runs SQL Server 7.0, located within the data center domain.

- This server will be handling updates from all of the installations of our application, as well as requests for data from other applications.

- To each row appended to the database table, two additional fields will need to be added to enable an audit trail of the uploaded data: one to record the upload date, and another to contain the name of the user who uploaded the record.

- Duplicate records should not be allowed on the table.

- Once the data from a text file has been loaded into the application, it can be saved in the application's own document format.

- The application documents will be retained as an archive.

- The operator will be able to load any number of .dat files into the application so that several text files can be merged into one upload transaction and one archive file.

- The customer has specified that this is to be the first of several applications that will append records to a database.

- The customer has requested that the application modules that update the database be designed for maximum reusability within a Windows NT environment.

- The application will allow the user to query the central database, specifying a fund name, a start date, and an end date for the query.

- The user will be able to browse through a read-only result set—for example, to ensure that the data he or she is about to upload does not already exist on the server.

- The existence of a live connection to the database will be indicated on the UI.

- If the database is offline, the user will still be able to load and view text files and save them as application documents, which can be reopened and uploaded when the database connection becomes available.

Steps Toward a Solution Design

Consider how the concepts you learned in Lesson 1 might help you think about the design of your solution from both the logical and the physical design perspectives.

Logical Design

Think about who is going to use the application, and where. The client has initially specified that about 50 users, all in the same Windows NT domain, will be uploading data to a central server. This scenario suggests that you should be thinking in terms of a fairly small-scale client/server application. However, you might consider asking the client about their expansion plans. Is this application likely to grow so that it is distributed across more than one department, or across more than one site? Is the usage of the application likely to grow to the point where insufficient resources (such as concurrent database connections) start to affect the performance of the application?

You might also ask the client if they foresee a need to extend the application to include a Web-based interface. If the company is already running an intranet, you might ask whether it might not be better to host the application inside a browser to allow staff to access the application from any computer anywhere. This option could also simplify deployment and upgrade issues.

You should also consider the business rules that the application is to implement. Consider whether the business rules need to be implemented in their own middle-layer component tier, or whether they can be integrated into the presentation tier or the data tier. The business rules in our scenario are few. The business rule specifying that duplicate rows are not allowed on the database can be taken care of by a primary key constraint—a rule specified for a table that won't allow the addition of duplicate rows to the table. The requirements that relate to the "cleaning up" of garbage data and duplicate lines from the text files can easily be implemented in the client application.

SDS decides that, given their budget and their business projections, an application based on a client/server model will be most suitable for their present requirements. They agree that a two-tier architecture is an appropriate model. However, they reiterate their requirement that the database update modules should be designed for maximum reusability, with the possibility of future expansion in mind.

To meet this requirement, you design the database update module as a set of co-operating components with clearly defined interfaces describing services that can be used by other client applications. You do not need to implement these components as a separate tier—they can be installed as part of the desktop application and distributed as application DLLs. In the future, however, they can be reused as part of the middle tier of a distributed application.

Physical Design

The physical design of your solution is what comprises the labs in this book. Your client might be surprised that you are using Visual C++ to implement the solution. They might feel that you could develop a solution that is just as adequate, and that you could do so more quickly by using Visual Basic.

Visual C++ does have many features that, in the hands of an experienced C++ developer, allow rapid application development. For example, the MFC AppWizard will be used to generate the basic structure of the client-side application, onto which you will be able build your application-specific functionality. The visual design features of Visual C++ will enable you to quickly develop the UI and link user-interface elements to code. MFC provides efficient, easy-to-use data structures, such as variable-length strings and object collections. The ADO data control can be used to visually design a database query screen in minutes. ATL can be used to implement the reusable component-based database update module that the client requires.

The overall result is that Visual C++ enables you to rapidly develop applications and components that are smaller and faster than those built with any other Windows development tool. Components built using ATL are quite efficient—ATL was created to meet the need for extremely lightweight components in the Internet environment. This means that your clients can be sure that the database access components you will build for them using ATL will be suitable for deployment in future Web-based applications. Also, the use of COM means that the services that the components provide will be available to a wide range of clients on a variety of platforms.

STUpload Application

In this first lab, you will simply get acquainted with the STUpload application. Each lab throughout the course will build upon the previous lab so that when you are finished with the course, you will have a complete working application that meets the specification of your imaginary customer, SDS. Your Chapter1\ Lab folder contains the finished version of the STUpload.exe file and the Chapter1\Data folder contains a sample data file Ch1Test.dat, which contains data for you to load into the application and to upload to the database server.

The recommended procedure is to build the STUpload application in the order presented by each lab. Follow the labs in numerical order. Save your work and use it in the next lab to continue developing the STUpload application. If you do not complete a lab, you can start the next lab with the project in the \Labs\Lab*n*\Partial folder, which will allow you to proceed from the appropriate starting point.

You should check your work against the \Labs\Lab*n*\Solution folder project after you complete each lab.

▶   To run the STUpload application

1. Double-click the **STUpload.exe** application icon in the Labs\Lab1\Solutions folder. The STUpload application opens.

2. Explore the application menus. Hover the pointer over any unfamiliar toolbar buttons to learn their function.

3. On the **Data** menu, click **Import**.

4. Use the **File** dialog box to locate the Ch1Test.dat file in the Chapter1\Data folder. Click the file and click **Open** to import the text file in the STUpload application.

5. Read the message box that reports the status of the import, and then click **OK** to complete loading the file.

6. The Select Fund window appears. Click the ARSC item to view the price history for the ARSC fund, as shown in Figure 1.10.

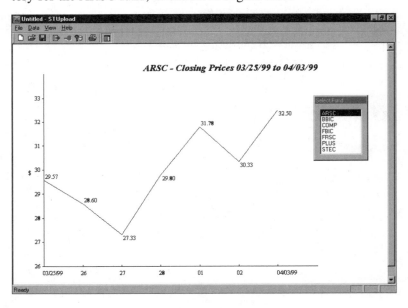

Figure 1.10 The STUpload application

7. On the **File** menu, click **Save**. Save the file as **Lab1.stu** in the Chapter1\Data folder.

8. On the **Data** menu you will notice two additional items, **QueryDatabase** and **Upload**. These options will not work on your machine until you have configured the application's connection to the database and registered the data Upload COM component on your machine. You will perform both of these tasks in the course of these labs.

9. Close the STUpload application.

Review

The following questions are intended to reinforce key information presented in this chapter. If you are unable to answer a question, review the appropriate lesson and try the question again. Answers to the questions can be found in the Appendix.

1. What is MSF?

2. Which models are most directly related to the development of business-oriented software solutions?

3. What is the main focus of the logical design perspective?

4. How might a client/server application implement the three tiers of an application?

5. What are some of the benefits that MFC offers to developers?

6. You are writing an MFC application that will allow your network administrator to manage user accounts on an NT network. Which libraries should you install?

7. What kind of data can you access through an OLE DB provider?

CHAPTER 2

Visual C++ Development Environment

About This Chapter

In this chapter, you will learn about the development environment and the tools that enable you to create applications using Microsoft Visual C++. You will learn how to use the MFC AppWizard to generate a development project, which contains source code and resource files that you can compile into a working executable program. You will explore features of the Visual C++ development environment, and learn how to configure options for your project. You will also learn how to use Microsoft Visual SourceSafe to manage source code control for a software development team.

Before You Begin

To complete the lessons in this chapter you must have installed the Visual C++ development tools as described in Lesson 2 of Chapter 1.

Lesson 1: Creating an MFC Project

This lesson introduces you to Visual C++ development projects and shows you how to use the AppWizard to create projects based on the Microsoft Foundation Classes (MFC). You will use the AppWizard to generate a framework of code and resources that can be compiled into a working executable program. This program can be used as a basis for the development of an application to suit your specific requirements.

After this lesson, you will be able to:

- Describe how projects and workspaces are organized in Visual C++.
- Describe the types of projects you can create with the AppWizard.
- Understand the steps involved in using the AppWizard to create an MFC executable application.

Estimated lesson time: 30 minutes

Projects, Configurations, and Workspaces

In Visual Studio, application source code files and the files that specify application resources, such as menus, toolbars and dialog boxes, are grouped together into *projects*. A project allows you to edit your files and manage the relationships—such as build dependencies—between them.

In a Visual C++ project, settings for the build tools such as the compiler, resource compiler, and linker are centrally controlled through the **Project Settings** dialog box. You can specify any number of independent *configurations* of settings for your project. When you use the AppWizard to create a project, both Debug and Release configurations are created for you automatically.

Projects are always contained within a *workspace*. By default, a single project will be created inside a workspace, and both configurations will have the same name. To organize your development more effectively, you can group related projects together into a single workspace. You can also set dependency relationships between them to ensure build consistency between projects that share files.

Although your workspace might contain more than one project, you work on only one project at a time, known as the *active project*. Figure 2.1 on the facing page is an illustration of a workspace that includes three projects. Note that the active project is displayed in bold type.

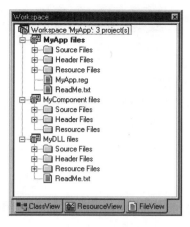

Figure 2.1   Workspace window (FileView)

Creating a New Project

The starting point for any development in Visual C++ is the Visual C++ **New Project** dialog box (shown in Figure 2.2), which lists project types.

▶   **To show the New dialog box**

Start Visual C++ by clicking **Start**, pointing to **Programs**, pointing to **Microsoft Visual C++ 6.0**, and then clicking **Visual C++**. On the **File** menu, click **New**.

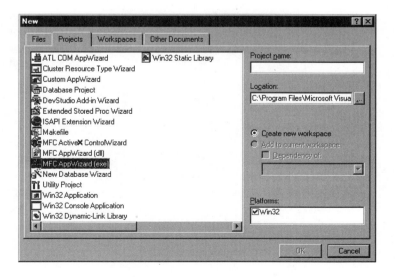

Figure 2.2   Visual C++ **New** dialog box (Enterprise Edition)

You use the **New** command to create new workspaces, projects, source files, or resource files. You can also create blank documents for other Microsoft applications such as Microsoft Word or Microsoft Excel.

Visual C++ Project Types

The Visual C++ **New Project** dialog box gives you the option of creating a project for the development of applications, components, or libraries using the following methods:

- **MFC development** The MFC development option generates a framework based on MFC, which you can use to develop applications, DLLs, or ActiveX controls. Other project types, such as those generated by the Internet Server API (ISAPI) Extension Wizard, are also based on an MFC framework.

  Although MFC saves you time and effort in the creation of Windows programs, simple programs might not justify the code size and performance overhead of MFC. To use MFC in an application, you need to link the MFC static libraries to your code or ensure that the MFC DLLs are installed on each computer that will run your application. Consider whether your application needs the types of application framework created by the MFC project options.

- **Win32 development** The Win32 options allow you to create simple Windows-based programs without the overhead of MFC. You can choose to create an empty project configured with the appropriate settings for generating Windows programs, which allows you to start developing a Windows application from scratch. Alternatively, you may choose to have the wizard implement the basic architecture of a Windows application. The wizard will handle basic tasks such as registering your window classes, setting up a message loop to process user input to the program, and implementing a basic window procedure to perform actions based on messages generated by the user input. You also have an option to create a Windows DLL. Here, too, you may create a completely empty project or create a project with sample code that shows you how to export classes, functions, and variables from a DLL. You can also choose to create a simple console application that will run without a graphical user interface from the command prompt, or choose an option to create a static library for linking to an executable program at build time. These options allow you to include support for MFC, which you might do if you want to take advantage of the MFC string or collection classes.

- **ATL development** The ActiveX Template Library (ATL) is a set of template-based C++ classes that helps you create small, fast COM objects. We will be covering ATL in depth in Chapters 9 through 11. The ATL COM AppWizard allows you to create a COM server, a DLL, or an .exe file that can host COM components. Once you have used the wizard to create your ATL project, you can add a number of different types of ATL-based COM objects. These can include simple COM objects, objects that can be used with Microsoft Transaction Services or in Active Server Pages, Microsoft Management Console SnapIns, ActiveX user-interface controls, and OLE DB data providers and consumers. Other project types, such as those generated by the DevStudio Add-in Wizard, are also based on ATL templates.

- **Miscellaneous projects** A number of C++ development options do not fall into the above categories. These include options that allow you to create DLL resources to run on Microsoft Internet Information Server (IIS) or on Microsoft Cluster Server. You can also write your own Visual Studio add-ins, create general-purpose utility projects, and develop your own custom AppWizards.

Note The Enterprise edition of Visual C++ contains some project options not found in the Standard or Professional editions. These allow you to work with DEFINTION (ODBC) databases directly from Visual Studio and to create SQL Server extended stored procedures.

Using the AppWizard

In this exercise, you will use the AppWizard to create an MFC executable project.

▶ **To launch the AppWizard**

1. Select the **MFC AppWizard (exe)** option (shown in Figure 2.2 on page 41).
2. Type **MyApp** in the **Project name** box and click OK.

Note AppWizard will create your project in the default location in the directory: C:\Program Files\Microsoft Visual Studio\MyProjects. If you want, you can enter a different location in the **Location** edit box.

The first dialog box of the MFC AppWizard, shown in Figure 2.3, appears.

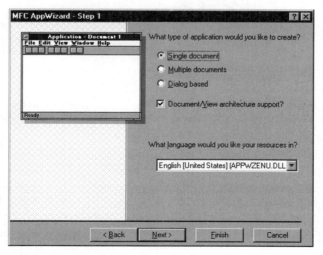

Figure 2.3   MFC AppWizard—Step 1

Step 1 of the MFC AppWizard gives you the option to choose whether your project is to produce a single-document interface (SDI) application (the **Single document** option); a multiple-document interface (MDI) application (the **Multiple documents** option); or an application that is based around a dialog box (**Dialog based** option). SDI applications permit only one document, displayed within the application's main window, to be open at a time. MDI applications allow multiple documents, displayed in multiple child windows, to be opened within a single instance of an application. Dialog-based applications use a dialog box as their main application window rather than the style of window that displays a client area inside a frame. Lesson 4 in Chapter 3 discusses these application types in more detail.

You can get help on any of the options in the AppWizard by selecting the appropriate option and pressing F1.

The following steps show you how to make MyApp.exe an SDI application.

▶   **To create a project using AppWizard**

1. Change the application type option from **Multiple documents** to **Single document**. Click **Next** to proceed to the next dialog box (shown in Figure 2.4).

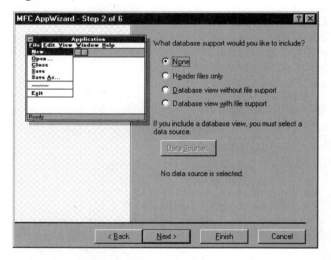

Figure 2.4   MFC AppWizard—Step 2

2. A discussion of MFC database support can be found in Chapter 7, *Adding Database Support*. Leave **None** selected and click **Next** to proceed to the next dialog box (shown in Figure 2.5).

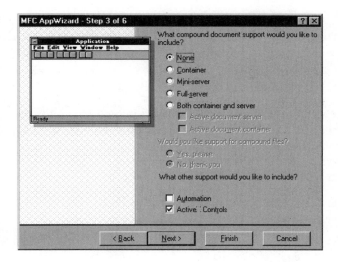

Figure 2.5   MFC AppWizard—Step 3

3. This dialog box presents you with options associated with ActiveX technologies. ActiveX technologies use COM to enable software components to interact with one another, regardless of the language in which they were created. OLE is another COM-based technology used for creating and working with compound documents—documents that can contain data of different formats, created by different applications. We cover COM and the ActiveX technologies in depth in Chapters 8 through 12. Leave the default options selected, and click **Next** to move to Step 4 (shown in Figure 2.6).

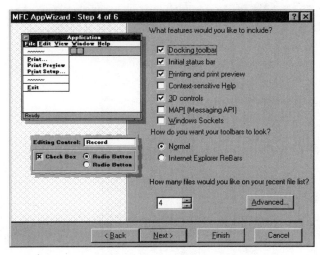

Figure 2.6   MFC AppWizard—Step 4

4. The AppWizard options presented allow you to specify the features your application will support. Leave the default options selected and click **Advanced**.

5. The **Advanced Options** dialog box has two tabs. The **Document Template Strings** tab (shown in Figure 2.7) allows you to set options for the document type associated with your application. This is useful so that Windows can associate a document type with an application. A user can then double-click a filename and have Windows automatically start the application appropriate for using that file. The **Window Styles** tab (shown in Figure 2.8) provides settings that allow you to specify display characteristics of the application window.

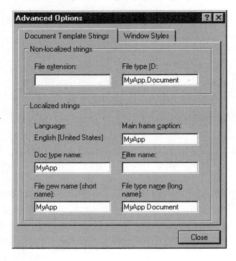

Figure 2.7   The **Document Template Strings** tab of the **Advanced Options** dialog box

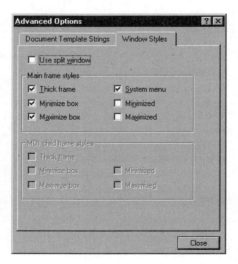

Figure 2.8   The **Window Styles** tab of the **Advanced Options** dialog box

6. On the **Document Template Strings** tab, type **mya** in the **File extension** box and click **Close**. Click **Next** to move to the next dialog box (shown in Figure 2.9).

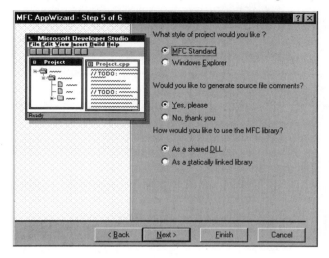

Figure 2.9 MFC AppWizard—Step 5

7. The first option on this dialog box allows you to create an application with an interface similar to that provided by Windows Explorer—essentially a tree control view and a list control view side by side in a split window. Leave **MFC Standard** selected. Leave the second option set to the default. The last option deals with how the MFC Libraries are to be distributed with your application. Leave the **As a shared DLL** option selected, and click **Next** to continue to proceed to the final AppWizard dialog box, shown in Figure 2.10.

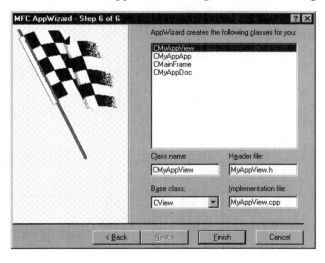

Figure 2.10 MFC AppWizard—Step 6

8. The final AppWizard dialog box (shown in Figure 2.10) provides information about the classes and files that will be created for you. You can change the automatically generated names if you are not happy with the defaults. Notably, it allows you to change the base class from which your view class is derived. The view class is used in an MFC application to display the application data. Click the **Base class** drop-down list to see the options available.

Powerful features are available from this drop-down list. Many of the base classes listed incorporate functionality based on Windows common controls, which you can use to help you organize the display of your application data. If you select **CRichEditView**, you can construct an application based on a full-featured text editor. With **CHtmlView**, your application would be based on an HTML browser. The default **CView** provides your application with a blank window where you can display your application data in any form you choose. **CScrollView** is similar to **CView**, but it creates a scrollable view that enables you to display more data than can be shown in a single screen window.

9. In the **Base Class**, click **CScrollView**. Click **Finish** to proceed to the **New Project Information** dialog box. The AppWizard presents a summary of the project so that you can double-check the selections you've specified. The AppWizard cannot be rerun (against the same project) once the project has been generated. For this lesson, simply read the summary and click **OK**. The project is created and opened for you in a new workspace.

10. The **MyApp Classes** icon will appear in the Workspace window. Click the icon's plus sign to view the classes that the AppWizard has created. In the next lesson, you will compile these classes into a working application. Double-click the **CMyAppApp Class** icon to view the source code for the class declaration.

Lesson Summary

The source code and resource files that make up an application or component are grouped together in *projects*. Projects enable you to easily manage your files and build settings. You can specify any number of independent *configurations* of settings for your project. Related projects may be grouped together into a single *workspace*.

Visual C++ provides a number of project wizards that provide frameworks from which you can develop different types of applications and components, using a variety of technologies.

The MFC AppWizard allows you to quickly and easily create a set of classes and resources that can be compiled to produce a complete MFC executable application. By using the AppWizard you can:

- Create SDI, MDI, or dialog-based applications.
- Add database, ActiveX, or OLE support to your application.
- Specify application features such as toolbars or context-sensitive help.
- Choose from a number of specialized base classes for your application view.

Lesson 2: Exploring the Development Environment

Microsoft Visual Studio 6.0 provides developers a rich, visual environment, known as the *integrated development environment* (IDE). A common IDE is shared by Visual C++, Microsoft Visual J++, and Microsoft Visual InterDev, and it can host projects created with these tools as well as other types of files.

In this lesson, you will examine some of the features of the Visual C++ development environment typically used in the course of developing applications.

After this lesson, you will be able to:

- Understand the elements of the Visual C++ user interface, including its windows, menus, and toolbars, and how they can be configured and customized.
- Get help from within the development environment.
- Change the project configuration settings.
- Build the MyApp project.

Estimated lesson time: 30 minutes

Visual C++ User Interface

Figure 2.11 shows the MyApp project workspace as it was at the end of Lesson 1. It is divided into two main areas: the workspace window and the edit window.

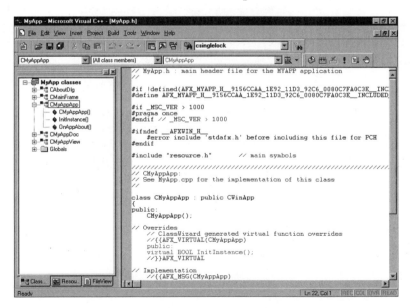

Figure 2.11   Features of the Visual C++ user interface

The *workspace* window uses hierarchical tree controls to display a graphical view of the objects in your workspace. As you saw in Lesson 1, the projects in the workspace form the root items of this hierarchy. The workspace window offers three different views of the contents of your project, which are accessed by the three tabs along the bottom of the window:

- **ClassView** Presents an object-oriented view in terms of the C++ classes, their data members, and their member functions. Double-clicking any of these objects will take you directly to their definition or implementation in the source code.

- **ResourceView** Displays resource objects grouped by category. Double-clicking any object will load the appropriate editor.

- **FileView** Shows all the editable files in your project.

Right-clicking an object in any of the views will bring up a shortcut menu with a set of object-related options.

The *edit* window is the area in which you work on open files, either with the program editor or one of the resource editors. If you would like more space while editing, click the **Full Screen** command on the **View** menu.

Menus and Toolbars

The Visual C++ development environment provides you with a complete set of menus that enable you to manage files and project workspaces, configure the environment, and access the help system, source control, and other external tools. Most of the menus have corresponding toolbars that allow you to select options with a single button click. Toolbars in Visual C++ are fully configurable. You can specify which toolbars are displayed and which buttons are included on a toolbar. This means that you can configure your environment so that your most commonly used options are easily accessible.

A new installation of Visual C++ shows the three most commonly used toolbars. The **Standard** toolbar, which contains the most frequently used commands for working with files; the **Build** MiniBar, which contains the most frequently used commands for building and running applications; and the **WizardBar**, which provides commands for working with classes.

Right-clicking an empty area of any of the toolbars or the main window frame will show you a list of available toolbars and will allow you to toggle their display status on or off.

The following exercises will demonstrate how you can customize your user interface and will provide you with a means to turn a full-screen edit window on or off with a single mouse click or keystroke.

► **To add a toolbar button to a toolbar**

1. From the **Tools** menu, choose **Customize**. The **Customize** dialog box appears.

2. Click the **Commands** tab.

3. In the **Category** list, click **View**.

4. Click the **Full Screen** icon (the third from the left in the top row of icons), and note that a description of the command appears below the **Category** drop-down list. The dialog box should now look like the one shown in Figure 2.12.

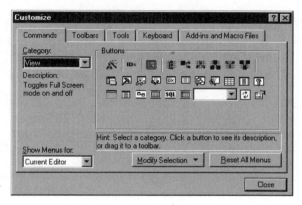

Figure 2.12   The **Commands** tag of the **Customize** dialog box

5. Drag the **Full Screen** icon onto your Standard toolbar.

6. Close the **Customize** dialog box.

7. Open a program source file by double-clicking a file in FileView.

8. Test your new button by clicking it to show the source file in full-screen mode. When you want to switch back from full-screen, click the button again.

Note While the **Customize** dialog box is open, you can delete buttons from toolbars by right-clicking them and choosing **Delete** from the shortcut menu. You can also delete buttons by simply dragging them off the toolbar you want to remove them from and dropping them anywhere but on another toolbar.

► **To assign a shortcut key**

1. On the **Tools** menu, click **Customize**. The **Customize** dialog box appears.

2. Click the **Keyboard** tab.

3. In the **Category** list, click **View**.

4. In the **Commands** box, click **ToggleFullScreen**. Note that a description of the command appears below the **Category** drop-down list.

5. Click in the **Press new shortcut key** edit control, and then press PAUSE on your keyboard.

6. Click **Assign**. The dialog box should now appear as it is shown in Figure 2.13.

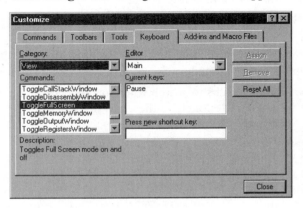

Figure 2.13   Assigning a shortcut key

7. Close the **Customize** dialog box.

8. Test the effect of pressing PAUSE. Your edit window should switch back and forth between window mode and full-screen mode.

Setting Environment Options

Display the **Options** dialog box (Figure 2.14) by clicking **Options** on the **Tools** menu. This tabbed page allows you to configure the design environment options for your installation of Visual C++. These options affect the appearance and behavior of the integrated tools that make up the development environment and apply to all projects and configurations of project settings.

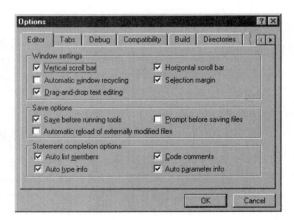

Figure 2.14   The **Options** dialog box

The **Options** dialog box can be used to configure:

- Aspects of the code editor, from basics such as window settings and save options, to advanced features such as automatic code completion and colored syntax highlighting. The editor can even be configured to emulate other popular editors such as BRIEF.
- The information displayed by the debugger.
- Options for integrated source control.
- The directory paths to search when loading executable files and when looking for source files, include files, and library files.

Getting Help

Visual Studio 6.0 ships with its own release of the Microsoft Developer Network (MSDN) library. This is an essential reference for developers, containing more than a gigabyte of technical programming information, including documentation, technical articles, sample code, the Microsoft Knowledge Base, and anything else you might need to develop solutions using Microsoft technology.

The MSDN library runs in its own HTML-based environment, complete with a fast, intelligent search engine. It is integrated with the Visual C++ development environment so that context-sensitive help is always available from within the Text editor (and from the output windows) simply by pressing F1.

Microsoft has provided further assistance in the form of context-sensitive Automatic Statement Completion. This feature, also known as IntelliSense, puts the MFC, Win32, and ATL libraries at your fingertips by displaying class members, function prototypes, identifier declarations, and code comments at the insertion point while you're editing your code. IntelliSense instantly shows all the available options. IntelliSense also optionally completes recognized words for you, saving you from continually having to type lengthy class or member names.

Project Configuration Settings

Display the **Project Settings** dialog box, shown in Figure 2.15 on the next page, by clicking **Settings** on the **Project** menu. This dialog box is used to configure a wide range of options for the project, including options for compilers and the linker used by Visual C++.

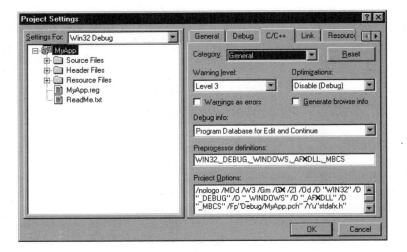

Figure 2.15 The **Project Settings** dialog box

Changes made to any settings on any of the tabbed pages apply only to the currently selected project and the build version specified in the **Settings For** list. Each build type of each project has its own combination of settings. To maintain the same settings for all build versions of a project, select **All Configurations** in the **Settings For** list. When changing project settings, be careful to check the build version you are modifying. It is easy to apply settings to the wrong build version if you aren't careful.

▶ **To alter project settings**

1. On the **Project** menu, click **Settings**. The **Project Settings** dialog box appears.

2. Click the **C/C++** tab.

3. In the **Category** list, click **C++ Language**.

4. In the **Settings For** box, click **All Configurations**. Note that now only the settings common to all configurations are displayed in the **Common Options** box on the property sheet.

5. Select **Enable Run-Time Type Information (RTTI)** to make RTTI available for all configurations of the MyApp project. Note how the /GR compiler switch is added to the **Common Options** box.

6. Click **OK** to close the **Project Settings** dialog box and save your changes.

When editing settings at the project level, the current project should be selected in the tree view in the left pane. You can move through the project's category folders and the individual files in the category folders. The settings available to you on the property sheets in the dialog box will correspond to the object that you selected in the tree. A common setting that occurs at file or folder level is the exclusion of a particular file, or set of files, from a build.

The **Debug**, **C/C++**, and **Link** tabs actually contain several pages of settings within a single page. To switch between these different groups of settings, select one of the options from the **Category** list on each page.

Some of the options you can set using the **Project Settings** dialog box are:

- **General Settings** Here you can specify whether to link your executable program with the static MFC libraries (in case you change your mind after specifying this in Step 5 of the AppWizard). You can also specify directories for your output files.

- **Debug Settings** Here you can pass command-line arguments to your program when it is started in the debugger. You can also use I/O redirection as you would from the command prompt.

- **C/C++ Settings** Here you can set general compiler settings, language features, calling conventions, processor-dependent settings, optimizations, preprocessor definitions, and so on.

- **Linker Settings** Here you can specify additional libraries to link to your executable program.

Building a Project

Now that you have a better understanding of the working environment, you are going to build the MyApp application from the project you created in Lesson 1.

▶   **To build MyApp.exe**

1. On the **Build** menu, click **Set Active Configuration**. Ensure that **MyApp— Win32 Debug** is selected and click **OK**.

Tip When you are working with multiple projects and configurations, consider using the full **Build** toolbar rather than the **Build** MiniBar. The **Build** toolbar contains drop-down list box controls that allow you to switch between projects or configurations quickly and easily. These controls also remind you which project or configuration you are currently working on.

---

2. On the **Build** menu, click **Build MyApp.exe**

   or

   On the **Build** MiniBar (shown in Figure 2.16), click **Build**

   or

   Press F7.

Figure 2.16   The **Build** button on the **Build** Minibar

The program will compile and link, and the MyApp.exe file will be generated in the Debug directory.

▶   **To test your program**

1. On the **Build** menu, click **Execute MyApp.exe**

   or

   On the **Build** MiniBar, click the **Execute Program** button (the red exclamation mark that is two buttons to the right of the **Build** button)

   or

   Press CTRL+F5.

   Notice that the *output window* appears at the bottom of the screen. The output window contains a number of views that are accessible by clicking the tabs at the bottom. The appropriate view is generally displayed automatically according to what kind of output is being generated by the environment. As the build process runs, the **Build** tab displays messages from the compiler and linker.

2. Once the build process has completed, test the functionality that has been provided for free by the AppWizard. On the **File** menu, click **Open** to see how a standard file dialog box is opened for you. You will need to implement File Open and Save routines yourself.

3. On the **File** menu, click **Print Preview** and see how the Print Preview architecture is already in place. Code that you add to display output in your application main window will also display in this Print Preview window, formatted as it would appear on printed pages.

4. Click **Close** to close the Print Preview window, and choose **Exit** from the **File** menu to close the MyApp application.

Lesson Summary

Visual Studio 6.0 provides a rich, visual environment for developers, known as the integrated development environment, or IDE.

A new installation of Visual C++ will arrange a project for you. Along with the menus and toolbars, the user interface is organized into three main areas: the workspace window, the edit window, and the output window. The workspace window offers three different views of the contents of your project. ClassView presents an object-oriented view in terms of the C++ classes, their data members, and their member functions. ResourceView displays resource objects grouped by category. FileView presents a view of all the editable files in your project.

Visual C++ provides a wide range of toolbars that you can hide, show, and configure according to your needs. You can configure toolbars using the **Customize** command on the **Tools** menu.

Visual C++ provides a fully configurable environment. You can configure the environmental options for your installation of Visual C++ using the **Options** command on the **Tools** menu.

Visual Studio 6.0 ships with its own release of the MSDN library, an essential reference for developers.

Visual C++ provides a central location for configuring project settings. You can use the **Project Settings** dialog box to configure the options for the compilers and the linker used by Visual C++. You can specify any number of different configurations of project settings.

Lesson 3: Source Code Control

Source code control provides the ability to track changes made to source code files and is an important part of team software development. Visual C++ provides facilities for integrating a source code control system into the development environment.

In this lesson, you will learn how to set up a source code control system using Microsoft Visual SourceSafe (VSS) 6.0, which comes as a part of Visual Studio 6.0, and you will use the features of Visual SourceSafe from within the Visual C++ development environment.

After this lesson, you will be able to:

- Understand how Visual SourceSafe is used to implement a source code control system.
- Describe how to use the Visual SourceSafe Administrator to set up a new database, add a user, and maintain passwords.
- Describe how to place a Visual C++ development project under source code control.
- Describe how the integrated source code control features of Visual C++ simplify the tasks of maintaining source code control for the developer.

Estimated lesson time: 30 minutes

Setting Up Source Code Control Using Visual SourceSafe

To maintain the security and consistency required of a source code control system, VSS stores a central copy of your source code files in a database. Files of any type, including text files, graphic files, binary files, sound files, and video files, can be stored under source control. When you add a file to VSS, the file is stored in the database and made available to other people. Members of your team can see the latest version of any file, make changes, and save a new version in the database. Changes that have been made to the file are saved so that you can recover an old version at any time.

As a developer of a source code control system, you will keep a *read-only* copy of the source files in a working folder on your local hard drive. When you want to modify a file, you *check out* the file from the VSS database. This places an editable copy of the file in your working folder and prevents other users from overwriting the current versions. When you have finished making changes, you *check in* the file to make your newly edited version the latest version that is available to the other developers. If you want to abandon the changes that you have made, you can undo the check out, thereby replacing your local edited version with the previous copy of the file held in the database.

To make sure that you have the latest version of all the files in the project, you use the **Get Latest Version** command to copy the current versions of the project source files to your working folder.

By default, a user cannot check out a file that is already checked out to another. This ensures that only one person at a time is modifying a file. Suppose that developer A and developer B are allowed to work on the same file at the same time. If A saves his changes, and subsequently B saves hers, all the changes made by A will be lost. The VSS administrator can change the default setting to allow multiple simultaneous checkouts of a single file and prevent overwrites of other changes. This will require some extra work on the part of the administrator, who must use the VSS **Merge** facility to ensure that the simultaneous changes do not conflict.

When you check out a source code file for editing, you must always be sure that you have the latest version of all the other files in the project. Otherwise, you might make changes that render your code incompatible with other recently-edited modules. VSS supplies the **Get Latest Version** command to copy read-only copies of source files to your working folder.

Files are organized within a VSS database in projects. A project typically contains all the files required to develop a software component, although projects can be defined in any way that is meaningful to the user. Projects tend to be organized in the same way as file directories.

It is usual to appoint an administrator to be responsible for the VSS database. The administrator uses the Visual SourceSafe Administrator program to control the location of the database, maintain the user list and access rights of each user, and back up the database.

The Visual SourceSafe Explorer is a utility that provides users with an interface to VSS projects. However, many of the common tasks—checking files in and out, getting latest versions, and so forth—are directly available to developers from within the Visual C++ development environment. The integration of VSS with Visual C++ actually simplifies the process of source code control for the developer.

Note The source code control features of Visual C++ are designed to work with other products in addition to Visual SourceSafe. Any source code control system that conforms to the Microsoft standard source code control interface will allow you to access source code control functionality directly from the Visual C++ menus.

Setting up a VSS Database

In the following exercise, you will be using the VSS Administrator program to set up a VSS database for the MyApp code that you created in Lesson 1. If you have not yet installed the VSS Workstation components, you should do this now.

▶ **To install the VSS Workstation components**

1. Run Setup.exe from the root directory of the Visual Studio CD 1.
2. Select **Workstation Tools And Components**. Click **Next**.
3. On the Visual Studio setup screen, click **Add/Remove**.
4. On the Visual Studio maintenance screen, select **Microsoft Visual SourceSafe 6.0**. Click **Continue** to install VSS.
5. When the installation is complete, close the Visual Studio setup program.

A VSS Workstation installation sets up a private VSS database on your computer and the VSS client software. In a live team development situation, you would install the VSS Server components and create a shared VSS database on a secure, regularly backed-up server.

▶ **To create the MyVSS database**

1. On the **Start** menu, point to **Programs**, point to **Microsoft Visual Studio 6.0**, point to **Microsoft Visual SourceSafe**, and click **Visual SourceSafe 6.0 Admin**.
2. Log on to VSS as **Admin** with no password. If the program warns you that the Admin account has no password, just click **OK**.
3. On the **Tools** menu, click **Create Database**. The **Create New VSS Database** dialog box appears.
4. In the text box, type **C:\Source Control\MyVSS**. Leave the check box selected. Click **OK** to create a new VSS database named MyVSS at the specified location and to create any necessary directories.

▶ **To open the MyVSS database**

1. On the **Users** menu, click **Open SourceSafe Database**.
2. In the **Open SourceSafe Database** dialog box, click **Browse**. Use the **File** dialog box to locate and open the srcsafe.ini file in the C:\Source Control\MyVSS folder.
3. Click **OK**. The MyVSS database should now appear in the **Open SourceSafe Database** dialog box. Make sure that it is selected and click **Open**.
4. Click **OK**.
5. Note that the name of the current database appears in the window's title bar.

▶ **To set the Admin password**

1. Make sure the **Admin** user is selected.

2. On the **Users** menu, click **Change Password**.

3. In the **Change Password** dialog box, leave the **Old Password** box blank. Type and confirm a new password.

▶ **To set yourself up as a user**

1. On the **Users** menu, click **Add User**.

2. Using the **Add User** dialog box, type your user name and a password. Note that you can use a check box to specify that a user has read-only access. Leave this unselected.

3. Click **OK**.

Placing the MyApp Project Under Source Code Control

You are now going to add the project you created in Lesson 1 to the **MyVSS** database. This is most easily accomplished from within the Visual C++ development environment.

▶ **To add the MyApp project to the MyVSS database**

1. Start Visual C++. Open the MyApp workspace.

2. Right-click an empty area of the main window frame. On the toolbars menu, click **Source Control**.

3. The **Source Control** toolbar, shown in Figure 2.17, appears. Commands in the following exercises refer to buttons on this toolbar. Alternatively, you can use the equivalent commands from the **Source Control** submenu of the **Project** menu.

Figure 2.17   Source Control toolbar

4. Click **Add To Source Control** (as shown in Figure 2.17).

5. The **Visual SourceSafe Login** box appears. Make sure that **MyVSS** is displayed in the **Database** box. Enter the user name and password that you created for yourself on the **MyVSS** database.

6. When you click **OK**, the **Add To SourceSafe Project** dialog box appears, displaying the **MyApp** project name. Click **OK** (and **Yes** to create the new project) to add your MyApp project to source control.

Note The **$/** symbol signifies the *root project* of the database. All projects in a VSS database are subprojects of the root project.

---

7. The **Add To Source Control** dialog box appears with all the files in your project selected. Click **OK** to add the selected files to source control.

Using the VSS Explorer

In the next exercise, you will view your new VSS project using VSS Explorer.

▶   **To view the MyApp VSS project**

1. Start VSS Explorer (shown in Figure 2.18) by clicking the **Source Control** button on the rightmost side of the **Source Control** toolbar.

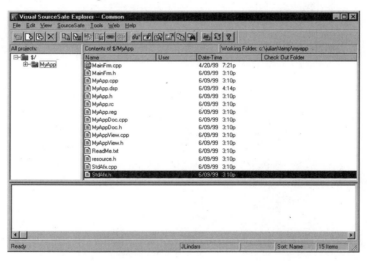

Figure 2.18   Visual SourceSafe Explorer

2. Experiment with the interface by expanding the folders in the left pane and looking at which files have been placed in the project. Explore the menus and use the ToolTip feature to identify the buttons on the toolbar.

▶   **To check out a file**

1. Click the MyApp folder in the left pane.
2. Click the ReadMe.txt file in the right pane.

3. On the **SourceSafe** menu, click **Check Out** (or use the corresponding toolbar button).

4. Click **OK** to check out the ReadMe.txt file. Notice how Visual SourceSafe Explorer displays the checked-out status.

5. Switch back to Visual C++. Look at the project files in the FileView window. Notice that the file icons are now gray to indicate that they are under source control. Notice that the ReadMe.txt file has a check mark to indicate that it is checked out.

6. Switch back to VSS Explorer.

▶   **To check in a file**

1. In VSS Explorer, click the **ReadMe.txt** file in the right pane.

2. As an alternative to using the menu and toolbar, check in the ReadMe.txt file by right-clicking the file and clicking **Check In** on the shortcut menu.

3. Click **OK** to check in the ReadMe.txt file.

Close VSS Explorer and return to Visual C++. You might now want to try repeating the above actions from within the Visual C++ development environment. You will find that the procedure is virtually identical. You can use commands on the **Source Control** submenu of the **Project** menu, the **Source Control** toolbar buttons, or you can right-click the icon in the FileView window.

Source Code Control Configuration

The integrated source code control features of Visual C++ are configured from the **Source Control** tab of the **Options** property sheet (shown in Figure 2.19), which is available from the **Tools** Menu. Note that you may have to use the arrow keys to bring the **Source Control** tab into view.

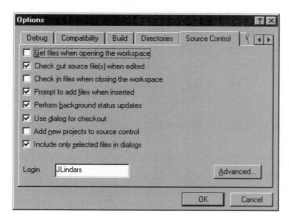

Figure 2.19   Source Control tab options

Figure 2.19 shows the default settings for source control options. These settings will affect the way you work with Visual C++ in the following ways:

- **Check out source files when edited** When you attempt to edit a file that is not already checked out to you, a **Check Out** dialog box will appear to allow you to check out the file. (Note that you are prohibited from editing files that are not checked out to you.)

- **Prompt to add files when inserted** When you add files to a project, you will be prompted to add them to source control.

- **Perform background status updates** The status of the files under source code control is updated as a background task rather than immediately.

- **Use dialog for checkout** When you check out files directly from ClassView, ResourceView, or FileView, a dialog box appears prompting you to confirm the action. If this option is not selected, the selected files are checked out immediately.

- **Include only selected files in dialogs** When you elect to perform an action (such as **Add to Source Control** or **Check In**) on selected files in ClassView, ResourceView, or FileView, only those selected files will appear in the dialog box. Otherwise, all of the files to which the action could be applied are listed in the dialog box.

You can also set the following options:

- **Get files when opening the workspace** When this option is set, VSS asks you if you want to get the latest versions of all files not checked out to you when the workspace is opened. This might not always be what you want, especially if your development is in an interim stage.

- **Check in files when closing the workspace** When this option is set, VSS prompts you to check in any files that are checked out to you when you close your Visual C++ workspace. Again, this might not be a good idea if your development is still in progress. Other users might get incomplete versions of your files.

- **Add new projects to source control** When this option is set and you create a new project, you will be prompted to add the new project to source control.

Clicking **Advanced** on this property sheet exposes a relevant subset of the source code control program's configuration settings.

Reusing Visual SourceSafe Files

You can reuse files within the same VSS project or between VSS projects. Some of the commands for reusing files are **Share**, **Branch**, and **Merge**.

Sharing

In VSS, one file can be shared among multiple projects. Changes to the file from one project are automatically seen by other projects sharing the same file. For example, suppose you want to share all the header files in your MyApp project with another project. To share a file, you create a share link between two (or more) projects. The same file then appears in those projects at the same time. When you check in the file to any one of the projects, your changes are automatically updated in all of the linked files.

▶ **To share all the MyApp header files with another project**

1. Open Visual SourceSafe Explorer.
2. To create another project with which to share files, right-click the **MyApp** project icon and click the **Create Project** button.
3. In the **Create Project** dialog box, type **NewProject** as the project name and click **OK**.
4. Click the newly created **NewProject** icon.
5. On the **SourceSafe** menu, click **Share**.
6. In the **Share with** dialog box, click the **MyApp** project in the projects pane.
7. In the **File to share** text box, type ***.h** and press ENTER to display only the MyApp header files.
8. Select *all* the files in the list of header files displayed. (Click the first item in the list, and then press and hold SHIFT while clicking the last item in the list.) Click **Share**.
9. Click **Close**. Note that the shared files have been added to the NewProject project and that they have special icons to indicate their shared status.

▶ **To display all the projects that share a specific file**

1. Right-click one of the files with a shared file icon. From the shortcut menu, select **Properties**.
2. Click the **Links** tab on the property sheet. The projects that share this file will appear in the list box.

Branching

Normally when you share files, only one version of the file exists. However, you might want to create a custom copy of the file for a particular project. For example, suppose you want to create a custom version of the MyAppDoc.h file in the NewProject project. To achieve this, you can use the VSS *branching* feature. Branching duplicates files from one project and uses the duplicates to create a new version of the project. These duplicate files can be altered without affecting the original version of the files. At a later stage, you can use the *Merge* facility to merge the changes in both these versions to recreate a single version of the file.

▶ **To create a custom version of the MyAppDoc.h file in the NewProject project**

1. In Visual SourceSafe Explorer, click the **NewProject** project. In the right pane, click the **MyAppDoc.h** file.
2. On the **SourceSafe** menu, click **Branch**.
3. Click **OK**. Note how the file icon reverts to a non-shared type.

Merging

As mentioned above, files that have been branched into parallel versions can be merged back into one file. For example, suppose now that your team has made changes to the original version of MyAppDoc.h in the MyApp project, and you want to merge these changes into the custom version that is contained in the NewProject project. Merging compares the differences between files and creates a single file containing all the changes.

▶ **To merge different versions of the MyAppDoc.h file**

1. In the Visual SourceSafe Explorer, click the **NewProject** project. In the right pane, click the **MyAppDoc.h** file.
2. On the **SourceSafe** menu, click **Merge Branches**.
3. In the **Merge to $/ NewProject /MyAppDoc.h** dialog box, select the **MyApp** project. Note how the versions that are to be merged are displayed in the **Versions** column. Click **Merge**, and then click **OK** in the message box that follows.

Merging might commonly take place when the administrator enables multiple checkouts of the same file to allow parallel development to take place on a single source file. Users can also merge the differences between an existing local copy of a file and the most up-to-date version saved in the VSS database by using the **Get Latest Version** command.

Viewing Version History

VSS contains several features you can use to keep track of version history. The **Show History** feature is commonly used to view a summary of a file's version history.

► **To show the version history of the MyAppDoc.h file**

1. In the Visual SourceSafe Explorer, click the **NewProject** project. In the right pane, click the **MyAppDoc.h** file.
2. On the shortcut menu, click **Show History**.
3. Click **OK** to accept the default options. The file's version history is displayed.
4. Close the History window.

Archiving a VSS Project

The Visual SourceSafe Administrator program makes it easy for you to archive your SourceSafe project. By clicking **Archive Projects** on the **Archive** menu, you can back up your project files to a compressed file as a secure backup. You can also use **Archive Projects** along with the **Restore Projects** command to move projects between VSS databases.

► **To archive the MyApp project**

1. Open the VSS Administrator program. You should be taken directly to the **MyVSS** database you created earlier.
2. On the **Archive** menu, click **Archive Projects**.
3. In the **Choose Project to Archive** dialog box, select the **MyApp** project and click **OK**.
4. With the MyApp project displayed in the Archive Wizard **Projects to archive** box, click **Next**.
5. In Step 2 of the Archive Wizard, select the **Save data to file** option and specify **C:\SourceControl\backup.ssa** as an archive file name. Click **Next**.
6. In Step 3 of the Archive Wizard, select **Archive all of the data** and click **Finish**.
7. When the archive process is complete, close the VSS Administrator program.

To restore from an archive, simply open the database you want to restore to from within the VSS Administrator program. Choose **Restore Projects** from the **Archive** menu, and use the Restore Wizard to locate and load the .ssa file that contains the archive.

Lesson Summary

Source code control provides the ability to track changes made to source code files and is an important part of team software development. Visual SourceSafe (VSS) 6.0, which comes as a part of Visual Studio 6.0, is a source code control system that is fully integrated with the Visual C++ development environment.

VSS stores a central copy of your source code files in a database. Members of your team can see the latest version of any file, make changes, and save a new version in the database. Changes that have been made to the file are saved so that you can recover an old version at any time.

Users of a source code control system keep a *read-only* copy of the source files in a working folder on their local hard drive. When you want to modify files, you can use the Visual SourceSafe Explorer program to check out the file from the VSS database. This places an editable copy of the file in your working folder. When you have finished making changes, you check in the file to make your newly edited version the latest version that is available to the other developers. To make sure that you have the latest version of all the files in the project, you use the **Get Latest Version** command to copy the current versions of the project source files to your working folder.

The VSS Administrator Program allows you to set up and administer a VSS project for your development team. You can use this program to control access to the VSS database and to archive and restore projects.

Visual SourceSafe is fully integrated with the Visual C++ development environment. Visual C++ can be configured to perform many of the source code control tasks automatically—for example, you can configure the environment so that when you add files to a Visual C++ project, you will be prompted to add them to source control.

The Visual SourceSafe **Share** command allows you to share a single copy of a file between multiple projects. The VSS **Branch** command allows parallel development on different versions of the same file, and the **Merge** command allows you to merge the changes made to two different versions of a file into a single file.

The **Show History** command is one of the many features you can use to keep track of a file's version history.

Lab 2: Creating the STUpload Development Project

In this lab, you will use the MFC AppWizard to create a project for the STUpload.exe application introduced Lab 1. You will be able to use this project as a basis for development labs in subsequent chapters.

▶   **To create the STUpload project**

1. Open Visual C++.

2. On the **File** menu, click **New**.

3. Select the **MFC AppWizard (exe)** option.

4. Type **STUpload** as the project name.

5. Click **OK**.

6. STUpload will allow the user to work on only one document within a single instance of the application. Change the application type setting from **Multiple Documents** to **Single Document**. Click **Next** to proceed to Step 2, the database support screen.

7. STUpload will provide the facility to query a database, but it will use ActiveX Data Objects to achieve this. Therefore, you do not need to implement MFC database support. Leave **None** selected and click **Next** to proceed to Step 3, the compound document options screen.

8. You will not be implementing compound document support for STUpload, so leave **None** selected and click **Next** to proceed to Step 4, the application features screen.

9. Accept the default options in this dialog box, and then click **Advanced** to open the **Advanced Options** dialog box.

10. In the **File Extension** text box of the **Document Template Strings** page, type **stu** as the file extension. Click **Close** to close the **Advanced Options** dialog box.

11. In the **Filter Name** box, the **File New Name** box and the **File Type Name** box, change the word **STUplo** to read **STUpload**.

12. Click **Close** to close the **Advanced Options** dialog box, and click **Next** to proceed to Step 5 of the AppWizard.

13. Leave the default options set and click **Next** to proceed to Step 6 of the AppWizard.

14. You are going to implement a scrollable view for the STUpload application to allow you to view windows that are larger than the screen area. To enable this feature, you will derive your view class from the MFC **CScrollView** class, which implements scroll bars and scrolling behavior. Make sure that the **CSTUploadView** class is selected in the upper pane, and click **CScrollView** in the **Base Class** drop-down list.

15. Click **Finish**, check through the **New Project Information** screen, and click **OK** to create the project.

16. When the project is created, expand the **STUpload Classes** icon in the ClassView window to view the classes that AppWizard has created for you. Press F7 to build the project.

17. Press CTRL+F5 to run the STUpload application. On the **File** menu, click **Open**. Note how the standard file dialog box is expecting you to open STUpload files with the .stu extension that you specified in Step 4 of the AppWizard. Select **Cancel** to close the **Open File** dialog box.

18. Using the mouse, drag the bottom-right corner of the STUpload application window, and shrink the window until it is only a couple of inches square. Note how scrollbars appear automatically along the edges of the window client area.

19. On the **File** menu, click **Exit** to close the STUpload application.

Review

1. What project configurations are created for you automatically by the MFC AppWizard?

2. Where, in the AppWizard, can you configure features of the application windows?

3. What kinds of help are available from the Visual C++ IDE?

4. What can you set on the **C/C++** tab of the **Project Settings** dialog box?

5. Why might you need to use the **Get Latest Version** command of Visual SourceSafe?

6. Under what circumstances might you use the Visual SourceSafe **Merge** facility?

C H A P T E R   3

Building Applications with the Microsoft Foundation Classes

About This Chapter

In Chapter 2, you saw how to use the Microsoft Foundation Classes (MFC) AppWizard to create projects based on Microsoft Foundation Classes. In this chapter, you will learn about specific MFC classes and their role in Windows application development. You will learn how the MFC framework implements the basic components of a Windows application and how it provides an architecture that enables the processing, display, and storage of the application's data.

Before You Begin

Before you start this chapter, you should have read and completed the lessons in Chapter 2, *Visual C++ Development Environment*.

Lesson 1: Overview of MFC

The MFC Library is a collection of C++ classes and global functions designed for the rapid development of Microsoft Windows–based applications. MFC offers many advantages to C++ developers at all levels, from beginners to seasoned professionals. It simplifies Windows programming, shortens development time, and makes code more portable without reducing programming freedom and flexibility. MFC provides easy access to hard-to-program technologies like ActiveX and Internet programming. MFC makes it easy to program user interface features such as property sheets, print preview, shortcut menus, and customizable floating toolbars complete with ToolTips.

In this lesson, you will learn how the MFC Library is organized, and how it is designed to encapsulate the Microsoft Win32 API—the low-level application that programmers interface to the Windows operating system services. You will also learn about some of the more important platform issues that need to be considered when using the MFC Library.

After this lesson, you will be able to:
- Describe the general structure of the MFC Library and how it relates to the Win32 API.
- Describe some of the issues that should be considered when developing for the different Win32 Platforms: Microsoft Windows NT, Microsoft Windows 95, and Microsoft Windows 98.
- Describe the general categories of the MFC classes and their hierarchical organization.
- Describe when to use an MFC extension DLL.

Estimated lesson time: 40 minutes

MFC and the Win32 API

The term *Win32* is used to describe an Application Programming Interface (API) that is common to all of the Microsoft 32-bit Windows platforms. These platforms currently include Windows 95, Windows 98, Windows NT, and Microsoft Windows CE. (Note: This book will not cover information specific to Windows CE.) The Win32 API is a set of functions, structures, messages, macros, and interfaces that provides a consistent interface to enable you to develop applications for any of the Win32 platforms. Table 3.1 lists some of the services provided by the Win32 API.

Table 3.1   Win32 API Services

Win32 API service	Description
Window Management	Provides the means to create and manage a user interface.
Window Controls	Provides a set of common user interface controls. Using the common controls helps keep an application's user interface consistent with that of the shell and other applications. It also saves a significant amount of development time.
Shell Features	Provides access to system objects and resources such as files, storage devices, printers, and network resources.
Graphics Device Interface	Provides functions and related structures used to generate graphical output for displays, printers, and other graphical devices.
System Services	Provides access to the resources of the computer via features of the underlying operating system.

Because the Win32 API is distributed as a set of C functions, users of Visual C++ can simply include the appropriate header files and then call the Win32 API functions from their code. Before MFC was available, Windows applications were developed using only the Win32 API—a time-consuming process. Experienced Win32 programmers would invariably reuse code and develop libraries to speed up the development of basic, often-repeated Windows programming tasks. MFC is a formalization of this process that makes this reusable code available to all C++ developers.

MFC was developed to simplify and speed up the development of Windows applications by providing a set of C++ classes that encapsulate key features of the Win32 API. As a C++ programmer, you will be familiar with the way in which a good class design can be used to encapsulate complex features of a software object behind a clear and concise interface.

For example, the Win32 concept of a window is encapsulated by the MFC class **CWnd**. That is, a C++ class called **CWnd** encapsulates the HWND handle (HWND is a Win32-defined data type that represents a Win32 window). Encapsulation means that the **CWnd** class contains a member variable of type HWND, and the class's member functions encapsulate calls to Win32 functions that take an HWND as a parameter. An example of this is the Win32 function:

```
BOOL ShowWindow(HWND hWnd, int nCmdShow);
```

that is encapsulated by the MFC function:

```
BOOL CWnd::ShowWindow(int nCmdShow);
```

MFC class member functions typically have the same name as the Win32 function they encapsulate.

MFC hides some lower-level aspects of Windows programming through encapsulation, although low-level access is always available if needed. Encapsulation also helps to protect against the possibility that pointer values such as window handles or file handles might become corrupted, or that operations might be performed on an invalid pointer.

When to Use MFC and When to Use the Win32 API

You should use the MFC Library whenever you need to develop anything but the simplest of applications. The advantages of the simplified development model and the benefits of reusing MFC code far outweigh any gains in speed and size made by choosing not to link the MFC Library to your application. Applications that have a command-line user interface, or no user interface, might be as easy to implement as non-MFC applications. Even for these applications you might find MFC helpful because of the application support it provides through utility classes like its string classes and generic collection classes.

MFC encapsulates most, but not all, of theWin32 API. Although you can perform most of the common Windows programming tasks through the use of the MFC classes, you will sometimes need to make direct calls to the Win32 API functions. This usually becomes necessary when you need to access system functionality at a fairly low level. For example, if you were developing a utility to modify user accounts on a network, you would be required to use the Win32 networking functions because there are no MFC classes that provide access to Windows NT network management functions.

Win32 Platform Considerations

As mentioned earlier, Windows 95, Windows 98, and Windows NT are all 32-bit operating systems that use the same Win32 API. Each operating system is intended to serve a different purpose and therefore has unique characteristics in addition to the common features shared with the other Win32 operating systems. These differences necessitate functions in the Win32 API that are operating system–specific.

To learn more about which functions are specific to which operating systems, search in the Visual C++ Help file for "Differences in Win32 API Implementations." This search will result in a useful article that details the differences to be considered when using the Win32 API for the Windows NT, Windows 95, and Windows 98 platforms.

If you need to find out which operating system is currently running your application, perhaps to conditionally branch out part of your code that is specific to one platform, you can use the API function **GetVersionEx()**, as illustrated by the code sample that follows.

```
OSVERSIONINFO vinfo;
vinfo.dwOSVersionInfoSize = sizeof(OSVERSIONINFO);

::GetVersionEx(&vinfo);

switch(vinfo.dwPlatformId)
{
case VER_PLATFORM_WIN32_WINDOWS :
    // Windows 95 / 98 specific code

case VER_PLATFORM_WIN32_NT :
    // Windows NT specific code
}
```

The higher level of abstraction that MFC provides removes you from many platform-specific considerations. Most of the MFC code you write will run across the Windows 32-bit platforms without difficulty, but to ensure that your applications will run without problems, you should be aware of a few platform-specific issues.

Unicode Issues

The ANSI character set used on 16-bit platforms such as MS-DOS and Microsoft Windows 3.1 uses a single byte to represent a character. Since one byte can represent only 256 unique characters, the ANSI character set is insufficient to represent a language with a large number of characters, such as Chinese. Unicode addresses this problem by using two bytes to represent each character. The 16-bit Unicode character set has the capacity to encode 65,536 characters, and so has become a worldwide character-encoding standard.

Windows NT supports both Unicode and ANSI strings. All Windows NT internal character strings, including Windows NTFS File System (NTFS) names, are Unicode strings. The Win32 API provides conditionally defined data types and generic versions of functions that are implemented differently according to whether the _UNICODE symbol is defined for a build of your program. For example, when the _UNICODE symbol is defined, the TCHAR data type is defined as *wchar_t*, a 16-bit character encoding type; otherwise, it is defined as *char*, the normal 8-bit character encoding type.

Windows 95 and Windows 98 support only ANSI strings—not Unicode strings. To ensure that your application string data is portable across all Win32 platforms, you should always use the generic data types and functions.

The MFC string class **CString** is based on the TCHAR data type. Its constructors, assignment operators, and comparison operators are all Unicode-aware. This means that you can use the **CString** class transparently, safe in the knowledge that it will implement Unicode or ANSI strings as appropriate to the build environment. However, you must be careful to extend the platform independence embodied in the **CString** class into your own code. To make your application more Unicode-aware, you must also consider the following:

- Use the _T macro to conditionally code literal strings to be portable to Unicode. For example, use _T("MyString") where you might otherwise use "MyString."
- When you pass strings to functions, pay attention to whether function arguments require a length in characters or a length in bytes. The difference is important if you're using Unicode strings.
- Use portable versions of the C run-time string-handling functions. For example, use "_tcslen" rather than "strlen" and _"tcscat" rather than "strcat."
- Use the following data types for characters and character pointers:
    - TCHAR where you would use char.
    - LPTSTR where you would use char*.
    - LPCTSTR where you would use const char*. **CString** provides the operator LPCTSTR to convert between **CString** and LPCTSTR.

File System Considerations

NTFS is a high-performance file system that can be installed on Windows NT systems as an alternative to the older File Allocation Table (FAT) file system used by Windows 95 and Windows 98. In addition to providing Unicode support, NTFS is more robust than FAT and provides direct support for file- and folder-level security.

When programming with MFC, you have fewer worries about the underlying file system. If you use the MFC class **CFile** to handle access to disk files, filenames will be converted to the correct TCHAR data type. **CFile** also provides error handling for "access denied" situations. It is important to be aware that file security on a corporate network will be more rigorously enforced than the test directories on your development computer, so your applications should never assume that a file will be accessible. Where you can, use system environment variables in pathnames (*SystemRoot*, for example, which points to the directory in which the operating system is installed) to avoid dependency on hard-coded paths. System environment variables can be retrieved by the **_tgetenv()** API function.

Screen Coordinates

Under Windows 95 and Windows 98, all screen coordinates are limited to 16 bits. If you develop on a Windows NT computer, be aware that routines that draw to the screen using coordinate values that lie outside the range −32768 to 32767 will not work properly on Windows 95 and Windows 98 platforms.

MFC Class Hierarchy

The MFC Library is implemented as a set of C++ classes. One of the main methods of code reuse in C++ is the *inheritance* mechanism. A C++ class can be derived from, and inherit the characteristics of, a parent class. The MFC Library, in common with many other C++ class libraries, organizes its contents into an inheritance hierarchy. This hierarchy contains a large number of classes of specific functions that are derived from a small number of base classes that implement the general functionality common to all their descendants.

As an example, Figure 3.1 shows the inheritance structure of the **CDialog** class. This MFC class represents a Windows dialog box.

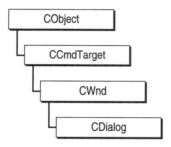

Figure 3.1   Inheritance structure of the **CDialog** class

At the top of the hierarchy is the **CObject** class. **CObject** is the base class for a large number of the MFC classes. **CObject** provides basic services, including serialization (loading and saving data objects to a file); run-time class information; diagnostic and debugging support (validations and dumps); and compatibility with collection classes.

The **CCmdTarget** class is the base class for all objects that are capable of handling Windows messages. You will learn more about this in Lesson 3, *MFC Application Framework*, later in this chapter.

The **CWnd** class mentioned at the beginning of this chapter represents a window. The fact that the **CDialog** class is derived from the **CWnd** class illustrates the idea that a dialog box is a specialized type of window.

Viewing the MFC Object Hierarchy

In this practice exercise, you will learn how to use the Visual C++ Help system to view the MFC Hierarchy Chart, which displays the entire set of MFC classes and their inheritance relationships.

▶ **To view the MFC Hierarchy Chart**

1. Start Visual C++. On the **Help** menu, click **Index**. The Visual Studio version of the MSDN Library will open, with the insertion point positioned in the **Type in the keyword to find** text box.

2. In the **Type in the keyword to find** text box, type **hierarchy chart**.

3. In the **keyword** list, double-click **hierarchy chart**. The MFC Hierarchy Chart will appear in the right pane. Resize this pane so that you can see as much of the chart as possible.

4. Explore the Hierarchy Chart. Note how the classes are organized into groups denoted by bold labels. Note which classes are derived from **CObject**, which are derived from **CCmdTarget**, and which are derived from **CWnd**. You might want to keep this chart open for reference while you proceed with this lesson.

MFC Class Categories

When learning about the MFC classes, you might find it helpful to organize them into categories, as described in Table 3.2.

Table 3.2   MFC Class Categories

MFC class category	Description
Application architecture	The application architecture classes represent the basic architectural elements of an application and include **CWinApp**, which represents the application itself.
User interface	The user interface classes typically encompass the elements of a Windows-based application that are visible to the user. These include windows, dialog boxes, menus, and controls. The user interface classes also encapsulate the Windows device context and graphics device interface (GDI) drawing objects.
Collections	MFC provides a number of easy-to-use collection classes including **Arrays**, **Lists**, and **Maps**. These come in both template and non-template versions.
General purpose	MFC includes a number of general-purpose classes that do not encapsulate functions in the Win32 API. These classes represent simple data types such as points and rectangles, and more complex data types such as strings.
ActiveX	MFC provides classes that simplify the process of adding ActiveX capabilities to your applications and significantly reduce development time. The ActiveX classes work with the other application framework classes to provide easy access to the ActiveX API.
Database	Accessing data by connecting to databases is one of the most common Windows environment programming tasks. MFC provides classes that enable operations on databases through Open Database Connectivity (ODBC) and the Data Access Object (DAO).
Internet	Creating applications that interact with the Internet, across intranets, or both, is becoming a major focus of developers. MFC includes the WinInet APIs and the Internet Server API (ISAPI), which provide classes for client-side and server-side applications, respectively.
Global functions	MFC provides some functions that are not members of classes. These global functions generally have the prefix Afx and provide the programmer with general-purpose utilities. A commonly used example is **AfxMessageBox()**.

MFC DLLs

The AppWizard gives you the choice to use the MFC Library either as a shared DLL or as a static library linked to your application's executable file. If you choose the shared DLL option, you have to be sure that the MFC Library MFC*xx*.DLL (*xx* stands for the version number you are using), and the Visual C++ standard library MSVCRT.DLL are both available on the user's computer. To ensure that this is the case, the DLLs are usually packaged and shipped with the application.

Note Unicode applications must link to the MFC*xx*U.DLL version of the library.

By choosing to link to a shared DLL, you can greatly reduce the size of your executable program. It makes sense to adopt this strategy if you are going to install a large number of MFC-based applications on one computer. This way, all the applications can share one set of DLLs rather than unnecessarily consuming disk space with multiple copies of the same DLLs.

MFC Extension DLLs

In the course of C++ software development, you will frequently develop custom classes that you later reuse in other applications. Like the MFC Library, these custom classes are often packaged as DLLs. Classes that are made available to other applications via a DLL are said to be *exported*—that is, their public member functions and data members are made visible to the client applications. For example, the MFC DLLs export the **CString** class. This means that applications that link to the MFC DLLs can create and use **CString** objects in their code.

You can click **MFC AppWizard (dll)** in the **New Projects** dialog box to create DLLs to export your own classes. The AppWizard refers to DLLs of this type as *regular DLLs*.

Regular DLLs can use MFC classes in their implementation. However, consider what happens if you want to export a class that is *derived* from an MFC class. Suppose you implement a class for a custom dialog box **CMyDialog** that derives its functionality from the MFC **CDialog** class and provides a set of public member functions that a client application can call to set and retrieve values from the controls. How do you ensure that the base class (**CDialog**) is properly exported and that its public member functions and data members are available to client applications?

To enable MFC applications to use **CMyDialog** as an MFC class, to call the **CDialog** base class member functions, and to reference **CMyDialog** with **CDialog** pointers, you need to package the class in a special type of DLL known as an *MFC extension DLL*. An MFC extension DLL implements reusable classes derived from existing MFC classes. MFC extension DLLs allow you to provide an "extended" version of MFC.

Extension DLLs are built using the shared DLL version of MFC. Only MFC executables (or DLLs) that are built with the shared version of MFC can use an extension DLL. Both the client application and the extension DLL must use the same version of the MFC DLLs.

To build an MFC extension DLL, click **MFC AppWizard (dll)** in the **New Projects** dialog box, and select **MFC Extension DLL** on the first page of the MFC DLL AppWizard (shown in Figure 3.2).

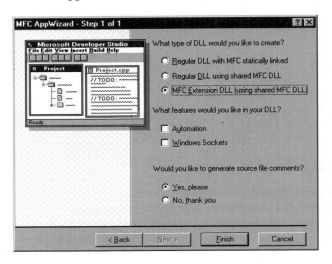

Figure 3.2   Creating an MFC extension DLL

Lesson Summary

The Microsoft Foundation Class Library is implemented as a collection of C++ classes designed primarily for creating Microsoft Windows–based applications.

MFC is designed to encapsulate the most commonly used functions of the Win32 API. The Win32 API is a set of functions, structures, messages, macros, and interfaces exposed by the operating system, which you can use to develop applications on any of Microsoft's 32-bit platforms. MFC simplifies Windows development by hiding some of the more complex features of the Win32 API. MFC should be used wherever possible to save development time and effort. Even though you use MFC, you can still use the Win32 API when you need to perform certain low-level tasks not supported by MFC.

Although the Win32 API is designed as an interface to all Windows 32-bit operating systems, there are a few differences among the platforms. For example, Windows NT uses Unicode strings internally and supports NTFS but Windows 95 and Windows 98 do not. Although the use of MFC insulates developers from most of the platform differences, you must still be aware of platform issues.

MFC is implemented as a hierarchical set of C++ classes that use the C++ inheritance mechanism to provide a reusable and extensible code base for Win32 developers. MFC class categories include:

- Application architecture classes.
- User interface classes.
- Collection classes.
- General purpose classes.
- ActiveX classes.
- Database classes.
- Internet classes.
- Global functions.

An application that uses the MFC classes in its implementation can either statically link the MFC Library to the application's executable file or share the MFC DLLs with other MFC applications. Using the shared DLLs saves disk space on the user's computer, but you must make sure that the appropriate MFC DLL and MSVCRT.DLL are both available to the installed version of the application.

You can create your own regular DLLs or MFC extension DLLs. An MFC extension DLL implements reusable classes derived from existing MFC classes. Extension DLLs are built using the shared DLL version of MFC.

Lesson 2: Win32 Application Architecture

To understand how MFC implements a Windows application, you need to understand the architecture of the Win32 platform and the applications that run on it. In this lesson, you will learn about the basic structure and operation of a Win32 application.

After this lesson, you will be able to:

- Describe the relationship between processes, threads, and applications.
- Describe the role of messages within the Windows operating system.
- Describe the essential steps required to create a basic Win32 application.

Estimated lesson time: 30 minutes

Windows Application Fundamentals

A proper understanding of the target platform is essential to developing effective applications. This section explains the architectural elements of the Win32 operating systems that will enable you to write well-behaved applications and take full advantage of the operating system services.

Processes and Threads

An application written for Windows consists of one or more processes. A *process*, in the simplest terms, is an instance of an executing program. A process has an address space and resources assigned to it, and one or more threads run in the context of the process.

A *thread* is the basic unit to which the operating system allocates processor time and is the smallest piece of code that can be scheduled for execution. A thread runs in the address space of the process and uses resources allocated to the process.

A process always has at least one thread of execution, known as the *primary thread*. You can create additional *secondary threads* to carry out background tasks, to take advantage of the multitasking capabilities of Windows 32-bit operating systems. Using more than one thread in an application is known as *multithreading*.

Application Startup

When an application is started, the operating system creates a process and begins executing the primary thread of that process. When this thread terminates, so does the process. This primary thread is supplied to the operating system by the startup code in the form of a function address. All Windows applications define an entry-point function named **WinMain()**. The address of the **WinMain()** function is supplied as the primary thread.

The application then proceeds to create windows, which will constitute the user interface. Before windows can be displayed on the screen, the different types of *window classes* need to be registered with the operating system. Window classes are templates that supply the details of how windows are to be created. In the window class registration process, windows are associated with a *window procedure* through which you can specify what the window displays and how the window is to respond to user input by determining how the window will respond to system messages.

Windows Messages

Whereas a window is the primary form of communication between the user and the application, internal communications between the operating system, applications, and application components are conducted through various types of *system messages*. For example, when creating an instance of an application, the operating system sends a series of messages to the application, which responds by initializing itself. Keyboard and mouse activity cause the operating system to generate messages and send them to the proper application. The primary task of a Windows-based application can be seen as the processing of the messages that it receives. This processing involves the routing of messages to their intended target windows and the execution of expected responses to those messages according to the messages' types and parameters. It is the task of the application developer to map these messages to the functions that will handle them and to provide an appropriate response to the message.

How an Application Processes Messages

Each thread of execution that creates a window is associated with a *message queue*. A message queue is a data structure in which the operating system will store messages for a window. All Windows applications have a main application window and all main application windows have a *message loop*. A message loop is program code that retrieves messages from the message queue and dispatches the messages to the appropriate window procedure. The window procedure might provide application-specific handling for the message or pass the message on to the *default window procedure*—a system-defined function that provides default processing for messages. For example, a message sent to notify the application that the user minimized the application's main window will be handled in the same way by virtually all applications. In such a case, the default window procedure handling is appropriate.

Figure 3.3 on the following page shows how messages are queued in the system and processed by the application. Notice how messages might be generated by the **PostMessage()** and **SendMessage()** functions as well as by hardware events. You might use these Win32 API functions or, more likely, their MFC counterparts

CWnd::PostMessage() and **CWnd::SendMessage()** to send Windows messages to or from your application. The **PostMessage()** function places a message in the message queue associated with a window, and returns without waiting for the window to process the message. **SendMessage()** sends a message to a window and does not return until the window procedure has processed the message.

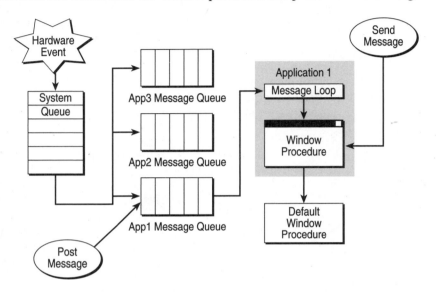

Figure 3.3   Windows NT message processing

Essential Elements of a Windows Application

Our discussion of Windows application architecture can be summarized by the following essential tasks that you must perform when creating a Win32 application:

- Implement a **WinMain()** function to serve as the entry-point to the program.
- Register each window class and declare an associated window procedure.
- Create an instance of the application's main window.
- Implement a message loop to relay messages to the appropriate window procedure.
- Implement the window procedure to handle the messages.

Creating a Win32 Application

This practice exercise will show you how to use Visual C++ to create a simple, non-MFC Windows application that illustrates how to implement the preceding five tasks.

► **To create a Win32 application**

1. Start Visual C++.

2. On the **File** menu, click **New**.

3. Select the **Win32 Application** option.

4. Type **MyWin32App** as the project name.

5. Click **OK**. The Win32 AppWizard appears. Select **A typical "Hello World" application**, and then click **Finish**.

6. In the **New Project Information** dialog box, click **OK** to create the project.

7. When the project has been created, click the **FileView** tab of the **Workspace** pane. Click the plus sign to expand MyWin32App files. In a similar fashion, expand the Source Files folder.

8. Double-click the **MyWin32App.cpp** file icon in order to view the generated source code.

9. Look through this code and find the following items:

   ■ A **WinMain()** function that calls the initialization functions and implements the main message loop.

   ■ A function named **MyRegisterClass()** that registers the window class of the application's main window.

   ■ A window procedure function **WndProc()** that is associated with the main window in the **MyRegisterClass()** function. This window procedure handles the WM_COMMAND message (messages from menu items, controls, or accelerator keys); the WM_PAINT message (sent when the system makes a request to paint a portion of an application's window); and the WM_DESTROY message (sent when a window is being destroyed). All other messages are passed to the default window procedure.

   ■ A function named **InitInstance()** that creates and displays an instance of the main application window.

Lesson Summary

In this lesson, you learned about the basic architecture of an application running on the Win32 platform and the basic steps required to implement a simple Windows application using the Win32 API.

A process can be defined as an instance of an executing program. Each process has at least one thread of execution known as the primary thread. When an application is run, a new process is created, and the address of the application's **WinMain()** function is passed to the operating system. The **WinMain()** code is run on the primary thread of the process.

A Windows application waits for messages generated by hardware events, system events, or other applications and components. Messages are processed by procedures associated with the application window objects. The developer provides these procedures in order to supply an application with its desired behavior.

Lesson 3: MFC Application Framework

Now that you have an understanding of the Windows application architecture, you are ready to learn how MFC implements a basic Windows application.

In addition to the encapsulation of the Win32 API, MFC defines a small group of classes to represent common application objects, and establishes relationships within this group to implement fundamental Windows application behaviors. These application architecture classes, along with a number of global functions, comprise an *application framework* that you can use as a basis for constructing applications. You can use the MFC AppWizard to generate a set of classes that is derived from the framework classes. You can build upon these classes to construct an application to suit your individual requirements.

After this lesson, you will be able to:
- Describe how the MFC application framework implements a Windows application.
- Describe the role of the application class and the main window class in the application framework.
- Describe how the AppWizard can be used to generate a basic framework application.
- Describe how Windows messages are handled by the application framework.

Estimated lesson time: 40 minutes

MFC Application Architecture

The MFC application framework implements a basic Windows application architecture by providing:

- A class to represent the application.
- An implementation of the **WinMain**() function.
- A class to represent the main application window.

Application Class

The MFC class **CWinApp** represents the application as a whole. **CWinApp** is derived from **CWinThread**, the class that represents a thread in an MFC application. **CWinApp** represents the primary thread of an application's process, and encapsulates the initialization, running, and termination of a Windows-based application. These behaviors are implemented by the member functions described in Table 3.3.

Table 3.3   CWin App Member Functions

CWinApp member function	Purpose
InitInstance()	Initializes each new instance of your application running under Windows. Displays the application's main window.
Run()	Provides the implementation of the message loop.
OnIdle()	Called by the framework when no Windows messages are being processed. You can override this function to perform background tasks.
ExitInstance()	Called each time a copy of your application terminates.

An application built on the MFC framework must implement exactly one class derived from **CWinApp**. You must also provide your own overridden version of the **InitInstance()** member function. The **InitInstance()** function is called directly by the **WinMain()** function, and is the proper location for initialization specific to your application.

WinMain() Function

The framework provides a standard **WinMain()** function for your application. **WinMain()** calls a number of global functions to perform standard initialization services such as registering window classes. It then calls the **InitInstance()** member function of the application object to initialize the application. Next **WinMain()** calls the **Run()** member function of the application object to run the application message loop. The message loop will continue to acquire and dispatch messages until a WM_QUIT message is received, at which point it calls the application object's **ExitInstance()** function and returns. **WinMain()** will then call cleanup routines and terminate the application.

Main Window

An essential component of a Windows application is the *main window,* which represents the principal interface to your application. This might be a simple dialog box; or it might be a *frame window*, which is a resizable window that houses the application menu, the toolbars, and the window client area. In either case, a framework application should provide a class—derived from the **CDialog** class or from the **CFrameWnd** class—that the application can use to create the main window object. The main window is initially displayed by the application object's **InitInstance()** function.

As an exercise, return to the MyApp project you created in Chapter 2 to view the framework classes that have been created for you.

▶ **To view the MyApp framework classes**

1. Open the MyApp workspace by clicking **Open Workspace** on the **File** menu. If you saved your work in the default directory, the workspace name will appear in the list. If not, navigate to where you saved the workspace. Double-click **CMyApp.dsw** to open the workspace.

2. In ClassView, expand the first item in the list, **MyApp classes** (if it is not already expanded), to view the classes created for this project by the AppWizard.

3. Expand the **CMyAppApp** class to view the overloaded methods created by the AppWizard for this class. Your Workspace pane should now look like Figure 3.4.

Figure 3.4   The MyApp project ClassView

4. Double-click **CMyAppApp** to view the class declaration. Note how this class is derived from the MFC class **CWinApp**.

5. Double-click **InitInstance**() to view its source code. Look through the code and the comments to gain an idea of the sort of initializations that are performed by this function. The implementation of **InitInstance**() that the AppWizard generates will perform initializations in accordance with the options you chose while stepping through the AppWizard.

Application Framework Message Handling

In Lesson 2, you learned that one of the key tasks of Windows application development is the mapping of system messages to routines that will handle them. In Win32 applications constructed without MFC, you supply a window procedure for each type of window class that is registered. These window procedures are often implemented as switch statements based on the value of the message ID. In an application based on the MFC framework, messages are handled by member functions of the application's classes. These can be classes that you create yourself or classes generated by the AppWizard for your application. The mapping of messages to their appropriate handler function is achieved by the use of *message maps*.

Message Maps

A message map is a table, declared within a class definition, that maps system messages to the member functions of the class. The message map contains entries that link the message IDs to the handler functions. The message map recognizes four types of messages, as described in Table 3.4.

Table 3.4   MFC Message Types

Message type	Description
Windows	Windows messages are generated by the operating system. They inform the application about window creation, impending window destruction, mouse and keyboard events, changes to the system colors, and anything else that can affect the operation of the application. The identifiers for these messages generally begin with the WM_ prefix. Windows messages are usually handled by the window to which Windows sends the message, such as an application's main frame window, or by a dialog box.
Command	Command messages are generated from user interaction with the user interface—for example when the user selects a menu item, clicks a toolbar button, or presses a shortcut key. When one of these events occurs, a WM_COMMAND message with command-specific parameters is sent to the application. Command messages are routed by the framework to the application objects. This *command routing* is a feature that allows the application to handle the message in the class most closely associated with the message.
User interface update command	User interface update command messages are generated from within an application by the application framework—that is, they are MFC-specific. They signal the application to update the status of user interface elements such as menu items or toolbar buttons. For example, before a menu is displayed, the application framework will send the application an appropriate update command message that gives the application the opportunity to modify the menu command state—whether it should be available, unavailable, or displayed with a check mark.
Control notification	Control notification messages are sent from controls and other child windows to their parent windows. These are generally sent as WM_COMMAND messages with control notification parameters. For example, an edit control sends its parent a WM_COMMAND message containing the EN_CHANGE control notification code when the user has taken an action that might have altered text in the edit control.

Creating Message Maps

MFC makes it easy to implement message maps. Any class that is derived from the **CCmdTarget** class is capable of supporting a message map. All the framework classes generated with the AppWizard will be created with a basic message map structure. You can use the ClassWizard tool to create new classes that implement message maps and to maintain the message maps of existing classes by adding and removing message map entries. Use ClassWizard to maintain your classes' message maps wherever possible to save time and to ensure that the message maps are correctly implemented.

Adding Handler Functions Using ClassWizard

In this section, you will learn how to use ClassWizard to add handlers for a Windows message and for a command message. In subsequent chapters, you will learn how to implement user interface update command messages and control notification messages. By looking at the code that is generated, you will learn how message maps are implemented in an MFC application.

In the following exercise, you will add a handler to display a message box when the user clicks in the client area of your MyApp application window. The *client area* is the area enclosed by the frame window, where application data is usually displayed.

▶   **To add a handler for a Windows message**

1. Return to the MyApp project.

2. Press CTRL+W to open ClassWizard. Click the **Message Maps** tab.

3. In the **Class Name** list, click **CMyAppView**. This indicates that you want to handle a message sent to the application's *view* class. The view class encapsulates the main window's client area.

4. In the **Object IDs** list, click **CMyAppView**.

5. In the **Messages** list, click **WM_LBUTTONDOWN**. This message is sent to the application when a user clicks the left mouse button in the window client area.

6. Click **Add Function**. ClassWizard creates a stub function to which you can add your own code. All Windows messages are handled by overloaded virtual functions on the **CWnd** base class. The name of the overloaded virtual function will start with "On" and is followed by the name of the message, with the initial "WM_" removed, and only the first letter of each word capitalized. In this case, the stub function created is named **OnLButtonDown()**.

7. Click **Edit Code**. The MyAppView.cpp file is opened and the insertion point is positioned at the top of the **OnLButtonDown()** function implementation.

8. Replace the // TODO comment line with the following code:

```
AfxMessageBox("You clicked?");
```

so that your code reads as follows:

```
void CMyAppView::OnLButtonDown(UINT nFlags, CPoint point)
{
    AfxMessageBox("You clicked?");
    CView::OnLButtonDown(nFlags, point);
}
```

9. Press F7 to build the MyApp project, and then press CTRL+F5 to run the application. Click with the left mouse button in the application client area to test that the WM_LBUTTONDOWN message is handled as expected. Close the MyApp application.

In the following exercise, you will add a handler for a command message that is generated when the user clicks **Paste** on the **Edit** menu in the MyApp application.

► **To add a handler for a command message**

1. From within the MyApp project, press CTRL+W to open ClassWizard. Click the **Message Maps** tab.

2. In the **Class Name** list, click **CMyAppApp**. Remember that command messages can be handled by any of the application classes. Because our handler function does very little, we will make it a member of the application class. The class most closely associated with the command should handle command messages. For example, the CMainFrame class would best handle a command that simply modifies attributes of the main frame window, such as hiding or showing a toolbar.

3. In the **Object IDs** list, click **ID_EDIT_PASTE**. This is the command ID that is passed as a parameter of the WM_COMMAND message generated when **Paste** is clicked on the **Edit** menu.

4. In the **Messages** list, click **COMMAND**. This indicates that we are to handle a command message and not a user interface update command message.

5. Click **Add Function**. A dialog box appears, suggesting the name **OnEditPaste()** for your handler function. This is because you are defining a new function to handle the message rather than overloading an existing virtual function of the parent class. Click **OK** to accept the name.

6. Click **Edit Code**. The MyAppView.cpp file is opened and the insertion point is positioned at the top of the function implementation.

7. Replace the // TODO comment line with the following code:

```
AfxMessageBox("MYAPP does not support the Paste command");
```

so that your code reads as follows:

```
void CMyAppApp::OnEditPaste()
{
    AfxMessageBox("MYAPP does not support the Paste command");
}
```

8. Build and run the CMyApp application. Click **Paste** on the **Edit** menu to test that your handler function behaves as expected. Note that the framework disables menu items for commands for which you haven't provided handlers.

Understanding the Message Map Code

When you use ClassWizard to add handler functions, it automatically performs the following tasks for you:

- It declares the handler function in the class header file.
- It creates a handler function stub in the class implementation file.
- It adds an entry for the handler to the message map.

▶   **To see the declaration for the CMyAppApp::OnEditPaste() function**

1. In ClassView, double-click **CMyAppApp** to view the class definition in the file MyAppApp.h.

2. Locate the code toward the bottom of the class definition that reads:

```
//{{AFX_MSG(CMyAppApp)
afx_msg void OnAppAbout();
afx_msg void OnEditPaste();
//}}AFX_MSG
DECLARE_MESSAGE_MAP()
```

Note the **DECLARE_MESSAGE_MAP** macro. This is an essential part of the message map implementation and is added to the class by the AppWizard or ClassWizard. You will learn how to create classes using ClassWizard in subsequent chapters.

You have already seen, and added code to, the function stub that ClassWizard provides.

▶ **To view the message map entry for the CMyAppApp::OnEditPaste()
    function**

1. Return to the CMyApp.cpp file. If it has been closed, you can open it by
   double-clicking the **OnEditPaste()** function icon in ClassView (beneath the
   CMyAppApp class icon).

2. Near the top of the CMyApp.cpp file is the message map that looks like this:

```
BEGIN_MESSAGE_MAP(CMyAppApp, CWinApp)
    //{{AFX_MSG_MAP(CMyAppApp)
    ON_COMMAND(ID_APP_ABOUT, OnAppAbout)
    ON_COMMAND(ID_EDIT_PASTE, OnEditPaste)
    //}}AFX_MSG_MAP
    // Standard file based document commands
    ON_COMMAND(ID_FILE_NEW, CWinApp::OnFileNew)
    ON_COMMAND(ID_FILE_OPEN, CWinApp::OnFileOpen)
    // Standard print setup command
    ON_COMMAND(ID_FILE_PRINT_SETUP, CWinApp::OnFilePrintSetup)
END_MESSAGE_MAP()
```

You can see that ClassWizard has added an **ON_COMMAND** entry macro to
the message map. The structure of this macro is quite straightforward. The first
parameter is the ID of the command. (You will learn more about assigning command IDs in the next chapter.) The second parameter is the name of the handler
function.

The **OnLButtonDown ()** function handles the WM_LBUTTONDOWN message
and is declared in MyAppView.h as:

```
afx_msg void OnLButtonDown(UINT nFlags, CPoint point);
```

The corresponding message map entry in MyAppView.cpp is:

```
ON_WM_LBUTTONDOWN()
```

Because Windows messages are handled by overloaded virtual functions on
the **CWnd** base class, there is no need to supply the handler function name as
a parameter. The MFC framework automatically maps the message to the appropriate virtual function. Windows messages often have additional information
attached to them in the form of parameters. The framework will take care of
extracting the information from these parameters and passing it to the handler
functions. If you look at the **CMyApp::OnLButtonDown** function declaration,
you will see that it takes the following: two parameters, derived from the
WM_LBUTTONDOWN message parameters, which indicate the current screen
position of the mouse pointer; and a flag value to indicate whether any of the
"virtual keys" (for example, CTRL or SHIFT) are also being depressed.

Message Map Entry Macros

MFC defines four message map entry macros, listed in Table 3.5, to correspond to the four types of messages that can be handled by the message map.

Table 3.5   Message Map Entry Macros

Message type	Macro form	Parameters
Standard Windows message	ON_WM_*XXX* (where *XXX* is the name of the message)	None
Command message	ON_COMMAND	Command ID, Handler Name
Update command	ON_UPDATE_COMMAND_UI	Command ID, Handler Name
Control notification	ON_*XXX* (where *XXX* is the name of the parameter indicating the control notification)	Control ID, Handler Name

You may have noticed that all ClassWizard-generated code is placed within comment blocks beginning with {{AFX_MSG and ending with }}AFX_MSG. These tags denote areas that are modified by ClassWizard. You are allowed to add message map entries or handler function declarations manually, but you should add them *outside* of these sections. Failure to do so might result in improper functioning of ClassWizard. The AFX_MSG modifier that precedes the handler declaration is also used by ClassWizard. As far as the compiler is concerned, it has no value.

Deleting Message Map Entries

If you use ClassWizard to delete message map entries, it will also delete the function declaration in the class header file. It will not delete the function implementation, which might contain code that you have written.

▶   **To remove the CCMyAppApp::OnEditPaste() function**

1. From within the CMyApp project, press CTRL+W to open ClassWizard. Click the **Message Maps** tab.

2. In the **Class Name** list, click **CCMyAppApp**.

3. In the **Member functions** list, click **OnEditPaste**.

4. Click **Delete Function**. A message box appears, warning you that you must delete the function implementation yourself. Click **Yes**.

5. Click **OK** to close ClassWizard.

6. Locate the function implementation in MyApp.cpp and delete it.

7. Build and execute the application to ensure you removed the function properly and to see the effect on the **Edit** menu.

Command Routing

You will recall that command messages are routed by the framework to the application objects. This *command routing* feature allows the application to handle the message in the class most closely associated with the message. The MFC application framework routes commands through a standard sequence of command-target objects (defined by the classes in your application that are derived from **CCmdTarget** and implement message maps) to see if any of them provide a handler for the command. Each command-target object checks its message map to see if it can handle the incoming message.

This command routing sequence can sometimes be used to your advantage. For example, you can set up an application shortcut key to send a command message with **ID_SAVE_WINDOW_STATE**. This shortcut key indicates that the user wants to save the current window's settings. Some window objects in the system might provide their own implementations of the associated handler function **OnSaveWindowState()**. Other windows, such as temporary dialog boxes and help screens, might not. The command routing sequence will check the message map of the currently active window to see if it implements the function **OnSaveWindowState()**. If it does not, the message map of the parent window will be checked. If that does not provide a handler, the message map of the application object can be checked.

The command routing sequence varies according to context. To find out more about command routing, search for "command routing" in the Visual C++ Help file.

Lesson Summary

The MFC application framework is a small group of interrelated classes that, together with a number of global functions, implement a basic Windows application. Using the AppWizard, you can easily generate a set of classes, derived from the framework classes, on which they can build an application to suit their own particular requirements.

The framework classes include the **CWinApp** class, which encapsulates the application as a whole. It exposes several functions that are called by the framework's implementation of the **WinMain()** function to handle the initialization, running, and termination of a Windows-based application. The **CFrameWnd** class encapsulates a frame window, which is a main application window that is capable of hosting application menus, toolbars, and a window client area.

In an application based on the MFC framework, messages are handled by member functions of the application's classes. The mapping of messages to their appropriate handler function is achieved by the use of message maps, a feature supported by classes derived from the MFC class **CCmdTarget**. Message maps are tables that are declared within a class definition to link message IDs to member functions of the class. You should use the ClassWizard tool to add and remove message map entries.

In this lesson, you learned how to use ClassWizard to add handlers for Windows messages. Windows messages are generated by the operating system to inform the application of changes in the Windows environment. These changes include mouse and keyboard events and command messages. Command messages are generated by user interaction with user interface elements such as menus and toolbars.

Command messages are routed by the framework to the application's command target objects in a specific sequence until an object is found that provides the appropriate handler. This command routing is a feature that allows the application to handle the message in the class most closely associated with the message.

Lesson 4: Document/View Architecture

The purpose of an application is to perform operations on a set of data. When you are working on the logical design of your application, you will need to specify how the application data is going to be structured, and how it is to be presented to users so that they can interact with it.

The MFC document/view architecture provides a single, consistent way of co-ordinating application data as well as views of that data. The document/view architecture is implemented by the classes created when you generate an application using the AppWizard. This lesson will describe the features of the document/view architecture and explain how the application framework implements it.

After this lesson, you will be able to:

- Describe the features of the document/view architecture and the benefits they offer to the application developer.
- Describe how the application framework objects act together to implement the document/view architecture.
- Describe how the document/view architecture can be used to display a visual representation of the application data on an output device such as a screen or a printer.

Estimated lesson time: 40 minutes

Documents and Views

In the MFC framework, a document is simply an object that acts as a container for the application data. A view is a window object, usually associated with the client area of an onscreen window, through which the user interacts with the data contained in the document.

This logical separation of application data and its visual representation means that a document can be associated with a number of different views. For example, when editing a Microsoft Word document, you can switch between Normal View, Page Layout View, and Outline View. All of these views draw upon the same data—they simply display it differently. Any changes made in one view are reflected in the other views.

Benefits of the Document/View Architecture

The document/view architecture assists you by simplifying the process of rendering application data on the screen in a way that enables users to interact with the data. This functionality can be designed completely from scratch through the overloading of the view's drawing function, the handling of mouse and keyboard interaction with the view, and the handling of menu commands. Alternatively, you can elect to use a predefined view that is based on a control. These capabilities let you develop an application similar to Windows Explorer by using a Tree View and a List View side by side in a split window. An Edit View, based on a rich-text edit control, can be used as the basis of a text-editor.

The document/view architecture also simplifies printing and print previewing by using the same drawing logic (contained in the view's drawing function) to render the application's data on the view, on a print preview window, or on a printer.

The document/view architecture provides much of the logic for saving documents to disk and loading them back into memory. This process of saving and loading documents, known as *serialization*, allows you to save and retrieve data in the custom object format used by your application, as well as in any of the object formats derived from the MFC **CObject** class. Serialization of application data is covered in Chapter 6, *Saving User Settings and Implementing Serialization*.

Document/view architecture is important because applications that use documents and views derive the greatest benefit from the application framework. Although most of the discussion about Visual C++ and MFC functionality assumes the use of the document/view architecture, you can use MFC without implementing a document/view architecture. The benefits associated with document/view architecture also carry with them a potentially significant performance and size cost.

In some cases, document/view might not be the right choice for your application. For example, an application that compresses text files might require only a dialog box that requests file names and displays a progress bar. A main frame window and a view are not needed, so the document/view architecture would provide little, if any, benefit in this instance. In this case, you could use the dialog-based application framework that the AppWizard provides.

SDI and MDI Applications

As you learned in Chapter 2, in addition to generating a dialog-based application, the MFC AppWizard can generate frameworks for two types of document/view-based applications: single document interface (SDI) and multiple-document interface (MDI). SDI applications permit only one document frame window at a time. The Paint and WordPad applications that come with Windows are examples of SDI applications. MDI applications allow multiple document windows to be open within the same instance of an application. In an MDI application, the user can open multiple MDI child windows in the main window.

These child windows are themselves frame windows, each containing a separate document. Microsoft Word and Microsoft Excel are examples of MDI applications. The SDI and MDI application types are shown in Figures 3.5 and 3.6.

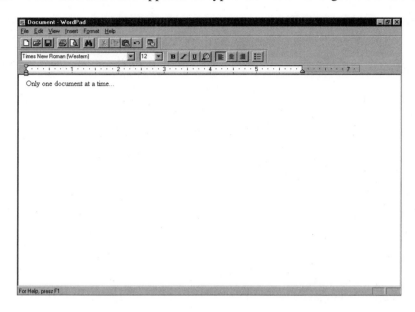

Figure 3.5   An SDI application

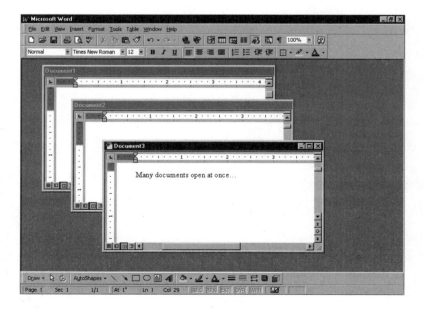

Figure 3.6   An MDI application

Objects in the Document/View Architecture

The AppWizard generates the basic framework of an MFC document/view application for you. As always, you can modify and extend the generated code to obtain the degree of customization and control that you require.

This framework for documents and views implemented in classes is derived from the MFC base classes **CDocument** and **CView**. The **CWinApp**, **CFrameWnd**, and **CDocTemplate** classes work in conjunction with **CDocument** and **CView** to ensure that all the pieces of the application fit together.

Table 3.6 lists the application objects and related MFC base classes in a document/view-based application and describes the major tasks each object performs.

Table 3.6   Document/View-Based Application Objects and Related MFC Base Classes

Object	Derivation and task
Document	Derived from **CDocument**. Specifies your application's data.
View	Derived from **CView**. As the user's window to the data, the view class specifies how the user sees your document's data and interacts with it.
Frame window	Derived from **CFrameWnd**. Views are displayed inside document frame windows. In an SDI application, the document frame window is also the main frame window for the application.
Document template	Derived from **CDocTemplate**. A document template orchestrates the creation of documents, views, and frame windows. A particular document-template class creates and manages all open documents of one type.
Application	Derived from **CWinApp**. Controls all of the objects in this table and specifies the application's behavior, such as initialization and cleanup.

Document/view application objects cooperatively respond to user actions, bound together by commands and other messages.

Document Template Objects

Document templates are created and maintained by the application object. One of the key tasks performed during your application's **InitInstance()** function is to construct one or more document templates of the appropriate kind. The following code shows how this is achieved in an SDI application:

```
// From CMyAppApp::InitInstance()
CSingleDocTemplate* pDocTemplate;
pDocTemplate = new CSingleDocTemplate(
    IDR_MAINFRAME,
    RUNTIME_CLASS(CMyAppDoc),
    RUNTIME_CLASS(CMainFrame),          // main SDI frame window
    RUNTIME_CLASS(CMyAppView));
AddDocTemplate(pDocTemplate);
```

When a document template object is created, it associates a document class with a group of resources (such as menus and icons), a frame window, and a view. The template is added to the application by using the **CWinApp::AddDocTemplate()** function.

In an SDI application, the user views and manipulates a document through a view contained inside the main frame window, derived from **CFrameWnd**. Figure 3.7 shows the relationship between the document/view objects in a running SDI application.

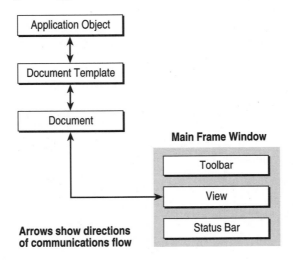

Figure 3.7   Objects in an SDI application

MDI applications use a **CMultiDocTemplate** object, which keeps a list of many open documents of one type. MDI applications use a class derived from **CMDIFrameWnd** to implement the application main window. Views are contained within MDI child windows, implemented by the **CMDIChildWnd** class. An MDI child window looks much like a typical frame window, except that it appears inside an MDI frame window rather than on the desktop. An MDI child window does not have a menu bar of its own, but instead shares the menu of the MDI frame window. The framework automatically changes the MDI frame menu to represent the currently active MDI child window.

The construction of an application's **CMultiDocTemplate** object is illustrated in the following code snippet.

```
// From CMyMDIAppApp::InitInstance()
   CMultiDocTemplate* pDocTemplate;
   pDocTemplate = new CMultiDocTemplate(
       IDR_MYMDIATYPE,
       RUNTIME_CLASS(CMyMDIAppDoc),
       RUNTIME_CLASS(CChildFrame), // custom MDI child frame
       RUNTIME_CLASS(CMyMDIAppView));
   AddDocTemplate(pDocTemplate);
```

Document Objects

The document object in an MFC document/view application is implemented in a class derived from **CDocument**. This class loads, stores, and manages the application's data. It will also contain the functions that are used to access and work with that data. To support the close connection between documents and views, each document object maintains a list of all the associated views, accessed through the **CDocument::GetFirstViewPosition()** and **CDocument::GetNextView()** functions.

The **CDocument** class also provides the **UpdateAllViews()** member function, which iterates through all the views associated with a document and notifies each one that it should redraw itself (by calling the **CView::OnUpdate()** member function).

Your application's views should be updated whenever changes are made to the application data that affect how that data will appear on the screen.

View Objects

The view object physically represents the client area of an application. Logically it represents a view of the information contained in the document class and allows the user input through the mouse and keyboard. Whereas a document object can have any number of views associated with it, a view always belongs to just one document. Views in your application will be derived from the **CView** class unless you specify that the AppWizard should use one of its specialized subclasses. These include **CScrollView**, which will provide your view with scrolling functions; and **CListView** and **CTreeView**, which allow you to base the representation of your data on the list and tree common controls.

The **CView** class provides a **GetDocument()** member function, which supplies a pointer to the associated document object.

Drawing, Printing, and Print Preview Architecture

The final section of this lesson takes a closer look at the **CView** class and how it is used to display a visual representation of the application data on an output device, such as a screen or a printer.

Device Contexts and the GDI

Windows provides a layer of abstraction between applications and output devices, known as the Graphics Device Interface (GDI). The GDI presents a standard programming interface to applications, allowing you to write code that is guaranteed to produce consistent output on all GDI-compatible devices.

The GDI manages a data structure called a *device context*, which maintains information about the current drawing attributes of a device. This might include information such as the color palette, the text font, the width of the pen used to draw lines, and the brush style used to fill areas. The Windows API provides a number of GDI functions for drawing lines and shapes, filling areas, and printing text. These functions render their output to a device context—they take a handle to a device context as a parameter.

In MFC, the device context, as well as many general GDI operations, is encapsulated by the CDC class, which provides creation and initialization functions for a device context and drawing functions that you can use to render your application's output. A number of classes that provide for a variety of specific needs are derived from CDC, including those listed in Table 3.7.

Table 3.7   CDC Derived Classes

CDC Derived Class	Description
CPaintDC	Encapsulates a device context that is prepared for painting an invalid region of a client window, in response to a WM_PAINT message. The constructor calls **CWnd::BeginPaint()**, which creates the device context and prepares the client area for graphic output. The destructor calls **CWnd::EndPaint()** to perform clean up operations.
CClientDC	Encapsulates a device context that represents only the client area of a window.
CWindowDC	Encapsulates a device context that represents the whole window, including its frame.
CMetafileDC	Encapsulates drawing into a Windows metafile—a collection of structures that stores a picture in a device-independent format.

Drawing in a View

The graphical output of your application's data is handled by the view object's **OnDraw()** member function. The **CView**-derived class that AppWizard generates for you provides a stub **OnDraw()** function, to which you must add code to display a representation of your application data. The stub **OnDraw()** function looks like this:

```
void CMyAppView::OnDraw(CDC* pDC)
{
    CMyAppDoc* pDoc = GetDocument();
    ASSERT_VALID(pDoc);
    // TODO: add draw code for native data here
}
```

Note that a pointer to a CDC object is passed to the **OnDraw()** function. This pointer is used to call the device context drawing functions to render your application's output. Note, also, that the stub implementation sets up a pointer to your application's document object. You use this pointer to retrieve the application data.

The following exercise demonstrates a very simple implementation of the **OnDraw()** function.

▶   **To implement the OnDraw() function**

1. Return to the MyApp project you created in the previous lesson.

2. In ClassView, right-click the **CMyAppDoc** class icon.

3. On the shortcut menu that appears, click **Add Member Variable**.

4. In the **Add Member Variable** dialog box, type **CString** in the **Variable Type** box and **m_string** in the **Variable Name** box.

5. Leave the **Access** type set as **Public** and click **OK** to create the variable.

6. Expand the **CMyAppDoc** class icon and confirm that the m_string member variable has been added.

7. Locate the **CMyAppDoc** constructor icon, the member function displayed beneath the **CMyAppDoc** class icon with the name **CMyAppDoc**. Note the key icon, which indicates a protected class member. Double-click the **CMyAppDoc** constructor icon to edit the constructor code.

8. Add the following line of code to the body of the constructor:

```
m_string = "Hello World!";
```

9. Expand the **CMyAppView** class icon. Double-click the **OnDraw()** function icon to edit the function code.

10. Add the following code to the **OnDraw()** function in place of the //TODO comment:

```
CSize TextSize = pDC->GetTextExtent(pDoc->m_string);
CRect rect(10, 10, 10+TextSize.cx, 10+TextSize.cy);
rect.InflateRect(4, 4);

pDC->Rectangle(&rect);
pDC->TextOut(10, 10, pDoc->m_string);
```

11. Build and run the program. Check that "Hello World!" is displayed inside a rectangle in the upper left corner of your application's view.

You will learn more about displaying application output in Chapter 5, *Implementing Application Behaviors*. For now, note the following points:

- The device context pointer is used to call the GDI member's functions of the MFC CDC class to display the application output.

- The document pointer is used to retrieve application data.

- The drawing code is designed so that when the application data changes, it will always be displayed in a consistent fashion—the rectangle will always neatly frame the text. Try assigning a longer string to the **CMyAppDoc:: m_string** member in the **CMyAppDoc** constructor. Recompile and rerun the program to verify that it displays correctly.

How OnDraw() is Called by the Framework

When a document's data changes in a way that will affect the visual representation of the data, the view must be redrawn to reflect the changes. Typically, this happens when the user makes a change through a view on the document. Any code that updates the document data should call the document's member **UpdateAllViews()** function to notify all views on the same document to update themselves.

UpdateAllViews() calls each view's **OnUpdate()** member function. The default implementation of **OnUpdate()** invalidates the view's entire client area. You can override **OnUpdate()** to invalidate only those regions of the client area that map to the modified portions of the document.

When a view becomes invalid, Windows sends it a WM_PAINT message. The view's default **OnPaint()** handler function responds to the message by creating a device context object of class **CPaintDC** and passing it to the view's **OnDraw()** member function. You have already seen how the **OnDraw()** function uses this device context object to draw a representation of your data.

Printing and Print Preview

In Windows programming, sending output to the printer is very similar to sending output to the screen. This is because the GDI is hardware-independent. You can use the same GDI functions for screen display or for printing simply by using the appropriate device context. If the CDC object that **OnDraw()** receives represents the printer, the output from **OnDraw()** goes to the printer.

This explains how MFC applications can perform simple printing without requiring extra effort on your part. The framework takes care of displaying the **Print** dialog box and creating a device context for the printer. When the user chooses the **Print** command from the **File** menu, the view passes this device context to **OnDraw()**, which draws the document to the printer.

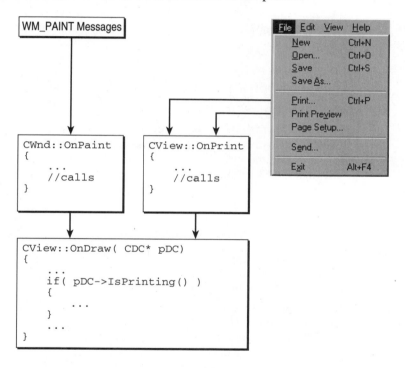

Figure 3.8   How **OnDraw()** is called by the framework

There are, however, some significant differences between printing and screen display. When you print, you have to divide the document into distinct pages and display them one at a time, rather than display whatever portion is visible in a window. As a corollary, you have to be aware of the size of the paper (whether it's letter size, legal size, or an envelope). You might want to print in different orientations, such as landscape or portrait. The **CView** class provides a set of print-related functions to enable you to implement the logic for the printing routines.

Lesson Summary

The MFC document/view architecture is implemented by the application framework to provide a single, consistent way of coordinating application data and views of that data. A document is an object that acts as a container for the application's data. A view is a window object, usually associated with the client area of an onscreen window, through which the user interacts with the data contained in the document.

The document/view architecture provides many benefits to the application developer. The document/view architecture simplifies the display of the application data on the screen so that users can interact with the data. Printing and print previewing are also simplified because the same drawing logic is used to render the application's data on the view window, on a print preview window, or on a printer. The document/view architecture provides much of the logic for *serialization*—the saving of documents to disk and loading them back into memory.

The framework classes generated by the MFC AppWizard work together to implement the document/view architecture. The application object contains at least one document template object that associates a document class (derived from the MFC class **CDocument**) with a group of resources, with a frame window class, and with a view class (derived from the **CView** class).

Document/view applications can expose a single document interface (SDI) or a multiple document interface (MDI). SDI applications permit only one document, displayed within the application's main frame window, to be open at a time. MDI applications allow multiple documents, displayed in multiple MDI child windows, to be opened in a single instance of an application.

Drawing on an output device such as a screen or a printer is handled by the Graphical Device Interface (GDI). The GDI presents a standard programming interface that allows you to write device-independent graphical output code. The GDI manages a data structure called a device context, which maintains information about the current drawing attributes of a device. GDI drawing functions render their output to a device context. MFC encapsulates device contexts, and the associated GDI drawing functions, in the **CDC** class.

The application's drawing logic is implemented by the view's **OnDraw()** function. The **OnDraw()** function is called by the framework, and is passed a pointer to a **CDC** object that represents the current device context. You add code to the **OnDraw()** function to display a visual representation of your application data, which is contained within the application's document object. The same drawing code is used to render output to your application's view, to a print preview window, and to the printer.

Lab 3: Displaying Application Data

In this lab, you will learn how to use the classes generated by the MFC AppWizard to implement the basic document/view architecture. Using the STUpload project that you created for Lab 2, you will learn how to:

- Use the document class to store the application data.
- Use the **OnDraw()** function of your view class to display the application data on screen.

You will recall from the discussion of the STUpload application in Lab 1 that your client, StockWatch Data Services, requires that the data be loaded into the application from an ASCII data file. Each of the data rows in the text file will contain three values: a fund name, a date, and a closing price. Your first task should be to establish an appropriate structure for the data that you are trying to model. You can then implement this structure as part of the application's document class.

A data file can be thought of as a collection of data rows. Therefore, an appropriate way to proceed would be to:

1. Create a class that represents a data row.
2. Create a collection of these data row classes.

To save you time and effort, we have implemented the data row class and a class that encapsulates a collection of these data row classes. The data row class, **CStockData**, is implemented with the following data members:

```
double m_dblPrice;
COleDateTime m_date;
CString m_strFund;
```

The **COleDateTime** class is an MFC class that encapsulates date and time values. The **CString** class is MFC's variable length string class. Information on both of these classes is available in the Visual C++ Help file.

We have supplied the definition and implementation of the **CStockData** class in the StockData.h and StockData.cpp files in the \Chapter 3\Code directory on the companion CD. The files also define constructors, accessor functions, and comparison operators for the class, as well as the **GetAsString()** function to display the object's data as a string.

We have supplied the **CStockDataList** class, declared in \Chapter 3\ Code\StockDataList.h as follows:

```
class CStockDataList : public CList<CStockData, CStockData &>
```

The **CStockDataList** class is derived from the MFC template-based collection class **CList**. The template takes two parameters: the first specifies the type of object to be contained in the list and the second specifies the type used to reference objects stored in the list.

MFC provides a number of template-based classes to implement data collections, such as **CArray** and **CMap**. We have chosen to use the **CList** class because it provides the facility to insert items at any location in the list. You can find out more about MFC collection classes by searching for "MFC collection classes" in the Visual C++ Help file.

You are going to import the source files into your project so that you can use the **CStockData** and the **CStockDataList** classes.

▶ **To import the source files into your project**

1. Using Windows Explorer, copy the files StockData.h, StockData.cpp, StockDataList.h, and StockDataList.cpp from the \Chapter 3\ Code directory to your STUpload working directory.

2. Open the STUpload project that you created in Lab 2.

3. In the Workspace window, switch to FileView.

4. Right-click the **STUpload Files** icon. On the shortcut menu, click **Add Files to Project**.

5. Browse to the **STUpload** directory (you are probably already there). Select the StockData.h, StockData.cpp, StockDataList.h, and StockDataList.cpp files and click **OK**. The files will be inserted into the project.

6. In the Workspace window, switch to Class View. The STUpload classes tree now contains the **StockData** and **StockDataList** classes. Expand the class icons and look at the member data and functions that are provided.

Now you have a class that can be used to represent the application data. The **CStockDataList** class represents all the records loaded from one of the ASCII data files used by StockWatch Data Services. The next task is to create an instance of your application data class inside your document class, so that your document class contains your application data. You can achieve this by creating a variable of the **CStockDataList** type as a member of the **CSTUploadDoc** class.

▶ **To add the m_DocList data member to the CSTUploadDoc class**

1. In ClassView, right-click the **CSTUploadDoc** class icon.

2. On the shortcut menu, click **Add Member Variable**.

3. In the **Add Member Variable** dialog box, type **CStockDataList** in the **Variable Type** box.

4. Type **m_DocList** into the **Variable Name** box.

5. Set the access specifier to **Protected**. Press **OK** to add the variable.

6. Double-click the **CSTUploadDoc** class icon in ClassView to open the CSTUploadDoc.h file and jump to the top of the class declaration.

7. Check that ClassView has added the line

```
#include "StockDataList.h"
```

to the top of the CSTUploadDoc.h file.

Because you have added m_DocList as a protected member variable, you will need to add a function that will provide read-only access to the list.

▶ **To add an accessor function for the protected m_DocList member**

Add the following line to the **public** section of the **CSTUploadDoc** class declaration:

```
const CStockDataList & GetDocList() { return m_DocList; }
```

You are not going to add functions to load records from a text file in this lab. However, you are going to add a few **CStockData** items to the **CSTUploadDoc::m_DocList** member so that you can learn how to display the document data in the application's view. As a temporary measure, you will add a few fake **CStockData** records in the **CSTUploadDoc** constructor. We have provided an implementation of the constructor in the file \Chapter 3\Code\Ch3_01.cpp on the companion CD.

▶ **To add the fake CStockData records**

1. Using Windows Explorer, locate the \Chapter 3\Code directory on the companion CD.

2. Double-click the Ch3_01.cpp file to open it in Visual C++. The new **CSTUploadDoc** constructor function displays as shown on the next page.

```
CSTUploadDoc::CSTUploadDoc()
{
    m_DocList.AddTail(CStockData(_T("ARSC"),
        COleDateTime(1999, 4, 1, 0, 0, 0),
        22.33));
    m_DocList.AddTail(CStockData(_T("ARSC"),
        COleDateTime(1999, 4, 2, 0, 0, 0),
        23.44));
    m_DocList.AddTail(CStockData(_T("ARSC"),
        COleDateTime(1999, 4, 3, 0, 0, 0),
        24.55));
    m_DocList.AddTail(CStockData(_T("ARSC"),
        COleDateTime(1999, 4, 4, 0, 0, 0),
        25.66));
    m_DocList.AddTail(CStockData(_T("ARSC"),
        COleDateTime(1999, 4, 5, 0, 0, 0),
        26.77));
}
```

The code adds five **CStockData** objects to the **CSTUploadDoc::m_DocList** member. Select the entire function and press CTRL+C to copy the code to the clipboard.

3. Close the Ch3_01.cpp file.

4. In ClassView, double-click the **CSTUploadDoc** constructor icon to jump to the constructor implementation. The default blank constructor should display as follows:

```
CSTUploadDoc::CSTUploadDoc()
{
    // TODO: add one-time construction code here
}
```

5. Select and delete the entire blank constructor. Press CTRL+V to paste in the replacement constructor.

For the purposes of illustration, you will provide a simple implementation of the **CSTUploadView::OnDraw()** function. You will implement a much more sophisticated drawing function in Chapter 5, *Implementing Application Behaviors*.

► **To implement the CSTUploadView::OnDraw() function**

1. Using Windows Explorer, locate the \Chapter 3\Code directory on the companion CD.

2. Double-click the Ch3_02.cpp file to edit it in Visual C++. The new **OnDraw()** function displays as follows:

```
void CSTUploadView::OnDraw(CDC* pDC)
{
    CSTUploadDoc* pDoc = GetDocument();
    ASSERT_VALID(pDoc);

    // Save the current state of the device context
    int nDC = pDC->SaveDC();

    // Create font for axis labels
    CFont aFont;

    if(aFont.CreateFont(16, 0, 0, 0, 0, 0, 0, 0, 0, 0, 0, 0,
        FF_MODERN, 0))
        pDC->SelectObject(&aFont);

    else
    {
        AfxMessageBox("Unable to create font");
        return;
    }

    const CStockDataList & pData = pDoc->GetDocList();

    int yPos = 10;
    int nTextHeight = pDC->GetTextExtent("A").cy;

    POSITION pos = pData.GetHeadPosition();

    while(pos)
    {
        CStockData sd = pData.GetNext(pos);

        pDC->TextOut(10, yPos, sd.GetAsString());
        yPos += nTextHeight;
    }

    // Restore the original device context
    pDC->RestoreDC(nDC);
}
```

The code uses functions of the **CList** class to iterate across the **CSTUploadDoc:: m_DocList** member, and uses the **CStockData::GetAsString**() function to provide a string version of the data that can be displayed using the **CDC::TextOut**() function. Note how the CDC functions **SaveDC**() and **RestoreDC**() are used to save and restore the state of the device context at the beginning and end of the function. This is recommended practice whenever you make calls to functions that modify the device context. This function modifies the device context by selecting a new font with the **CDC::SelectObject**() function.

3. Select the entire function and press CTRL+C to copy the code to the clipboard.

4. Close the Ch3_02.cpp file.

5. In ClassView, double-click the **CSTUploadView::OnDraw**() icon to jump to the function implementation. The default function should display as follows:

```
void CSTUploadView::OnDraw(CDC* pDC)
{
    CSTUploadDoc* pDoc = GetDocument();
    ASSERT_VALID(pDoc);
    // TODO: add draw code for native data here
}
```

6. Select and delete the entire **OnDraw**() function. Press CTRL+V to paste in the new version.

You can now build and run your STUpload application. The five stock records should display as shown in Figure 3.9.

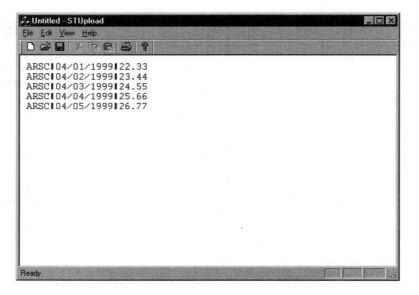

Figure 3.9   STUpload at the end of Lab 3

Review

1. When developing an MFC application, under what circumstances might you need to call the Win32 API directly?

2. What services are provided by the **CObject** class?

3. Why would you use an MFC extension DLL?

4. Which member function of which MFC class implements the application message loop?

5. What type of classes can implement message maps?

6. Name four categories of Windows messages that can be handled by message maps.

7. What is the function of a document template object?

8. Which MFC class encapsulates GDI drawing functions?

9. How do you ensure that the client area of your application's main window always displays an up-to-date picture of the application data?

C H A P T E R   4

Creating the User Interface

About This Chapter

This chapter explores some of the elements of a typical Microsoft Windows application user interface. You will learn how to edit application menus and toolbars, and how to add code to handle user selections. You will learn how to update the interface to communicate information to the user. You will also learn how dialog boxes are used in an application, and how to use the dialog editor to create a dialog box template.

Before You Begin

Before you start this chapter, you should have read Chapters 2 and 3, and completed the exercises in the text.

Lesson 1: Windows Application User Interfaces

In this lesson, you will explore elements of the user interface that are created for you when you generate a document/view-based application using the MFC AppWizard. You will learn how to use the Microsoft Visual C++ resource editors to edit standard interface features to suit your own requirements, how to handle user menu or toolbar selections, and how to update the interface to communicate information to the user.

After this lesson, you will be able to:

- Describe the icons that you are required to supply for a program that meets the Microsoft Windows 98 or Microsoft Windows NT logo requirements, and how to use the graphics editor to design icons.
- Describe how to edit menus and toolbars.
- Describe how to implement accelerator keys for menu and toolbar commands.
- Describe how to add code to handle menu or toolbar selections.
- Describe how to dynamically update the appearance of menu and toolbar commands.
- Describe how to write to the status bar.

Estimated lesson time: 50 minutes

Application and Document Icons

An application that meets the Windows 98 or Windows NT logo requirements must define standard (32x32 pixels) and small (16x16 pixels) icons for both the application and the document type. Icons are application resources that are associated with Windows icon (.ico) files. The MFC application framework automatically defines default icon resources and creates icon files for you.

All application resources such as icons, menu commands, dialog boxes, controls, and so on have a unique numeric identifier known as a *resource ID*. The resource.h file defines memorable names to correspond to these IDs.

Figure 4.1 illustrates the icons, resource IDs, and icon files that are created for the MyApp sample application.

Icon	Resource ID	File
	IDR_MAINFRAME	MyApp\res\MyApp.ico
	IDR_MYAPPTYPE	MyApp\res\MyAppDoc.ico

Figure 4.1   MFC default icons

Your program's application object calls **CWinApp::RegisterShellFileTypes()** to register the icons with the Windows file manager when the program starts.

The Graphics Editor

The graphics editor supplied with Visual C++ has an extensive set of tools for drawing images. In addition to creating and editing images in bitmap (.bmp) format, you can edit .gif or .jpg images, and convert .gif or .jpg images to bitmaps.

To access the graphics editor, open a graphical resource by double-clicking an object in ResourceView. This allows you to access the special features that support icon files and toolbar bitmaps. Figure 4.2 shows the graphics editor opened to edit the standard-sized default document icon.

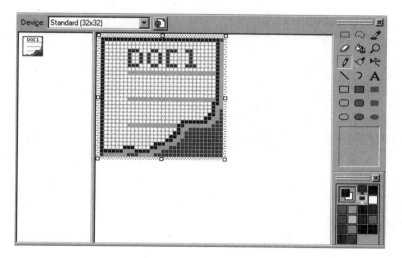

Figure. 4.2   The graphics editor

► **To edit the default icons**

1. Return to the MyApp project you modified in Chapter 3.

2. In **ResourceView**, expand MyApp Resources.

3. Expand the Icon folder.

4. Double-click the **IDR_MAINFRAME** object to open the icon in the graphics editor.

Experiment with the drawing features of the graphics editor. Note that you can switch between the Standard (32x32) icon format and the Small (16x16) icon format using the **Device** list in the upper left corner of the editor pane.

You can use **New Device Image** to create icons in other device formats. The graphics editor provides different pencil and brush styles, area fill, and text tools; it also allows you to select an area of your icon to move, resize, or copy to the clipboard.

If you are feeling creative, you might like to design your own icons for the MyApp application. The easiest way to do this is to edit the existing icons, leaving their resource IDs as they are. When you build the application, your changes to the .ico files will be saved.

Editing Application Menus

Menus offer a convenient and consistent way for you to group commands, and an easy way for users to access them. An application generated by the MFC AppWizard will generally include a main menu resource appropriate to the options selected by the developer. Figure 4.3 depicts a typical menu generated for an SDI application and illustrates the elements of a menu interface.

Figure 4.3   SDI application menu

The menu as a whole is created with a resource ID of **IDR_MAINFRAME**. You will recognize that this is the same ID as the application icon that you read about in Chapter 3. When a document template object is created, it is associated with a resource ID that specifies a group of resources to be used by the document type. These might include menu, toolbar, icon, accelerator table, and string resources.

Using the menu editor supplied with Visual C++ (shown in Figure 4.4), you can visually construct a menu and edit the properties of the menu commands.

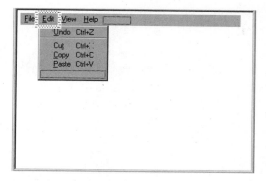

Figure 4.4   The menu editor

In the following exercises, you will learn how to add and remove menus, and you will add menu commands to the MyApp application menus. You'll start by removing the standard **Edit** menu that is depicted in Figure 4.4. You would want to do this if your application was not going to support the selection of objects in the view, or the **Cut**, **Copy**, and **Paste** commands that work on selected objects. In its place, you will add a new menu—the **Data** menu. The **Data** menu will contain commands that will allow the user to connect to a remote database, and to upload application data. You will add two commands to the menu: the **Connect** command and the **Upload** command.

▶   **To remove the Edit menu**

1. In the MyApp project, click the **ResourceView** tab and expand the MyApp Resources folder.

2. Expand the Menu folder.

3. Double-click the **IDR_MAINFRAME** menu resource to open the menu editor.

4. Click **Edit** on the menu bar and then press DELETE. Click **OK** to confirm the deletion of the **Edit** menu.

▶   **To add the Data menu**

1. Click the blank menu command to the immediate right of the **Help** menu.

2. Drag the blank command to place it between the **File** and **View** menus.

3. Double-click the blank menu command to display its properties. Type **&Data** as the **Caption** property. The ampersand (**&**) has the effect of designating the character following it as an access key. An access key is used to select the menu using the keyboard. By preceding the "D" in Data with an ampersand, users can select the **Data** menu by pressing ALT+D.

Note If you want to include the ampersand character in a menu name, use two ampersands as in: "Mutt && Jeff". This would result in the menu name "Mutt & Jeff".

▶ **To add the Connect command to the Data menu**

1. If the **Data** menu is not already selected, click **Data**.

2. Click the blank command under the **Data** menu title.

3. Type the string **&Connect...\tCTRL+C**.

    ■ **\t** is the tab character.

    ■ **CTRL+C** denotes the shortcut key you will assign to this menu command in a following exercise.

4. As you start typing, the **Menu Item Properties** dialog box will appear. In the **Prompt** box, type **Connect to database**. This is the text to display on the status bar when the command is selected.

5. Click the thumbtack icon in the upper-left corner of the **Menu Item Properties** dialog box. This will keep the dialog box open while you move between different menu commands.

6. Click another command, and then click **Connect** again. The dialog box for the **Import** command should now look as it does in Figure 4.5.

Figure 4.5   The **Menu Item Properties** dialog box

7. Notice that the editor has constructed the **ID_DATA_CONNECT** command ID by appending the command name to the menu name. You can change this ID if you want, but generally you just accept the default.

Each selectable menu command (everything but menu titles or separator bars) is associated with an ID that allows it to be mapped to a handler function. Remember that when a menu command is selected, the framework generates a WM_COMMAND message, which is handled by one of the application objects. This message takes the menu command's command ID as a parameter. You will learn how to associate the command ID with a handler function later in this chapter in the section *Handling Menu and Toolbar Selections*.

► **To add the Upload command to the Data menu**

Following the steps just described, add another command to **Data** menu. This command caption should be **&Upload...\tCTRL+U**, and the prompt string should be **Upload data to the database**. Allow the menu editor to generate the command ID **ID_DATA_UPLOAD**.

Adding Shortcut Keys

You will remember that the captions for commands in the **Data** menu referred to keys that could be used as shortcut keys—namely, CTRL+C for the **Connect** command and CTRL+U for the **Upload** command. Shortcut keys are used as keyboard shortcuts for program commands that are also available on a menu or toolbar, though you can also define key combinations for commands that don't have a user-interface object associated with them.

Shortcut keys, or *accelerator keys* as they were once known, are defined in an *accelerator table*, a Windows resource that contains a list of the defined keys and the command identifiers that are associated with them. The accelerator table can be edited by using the accelerator editor (shown in Figure 4.6).

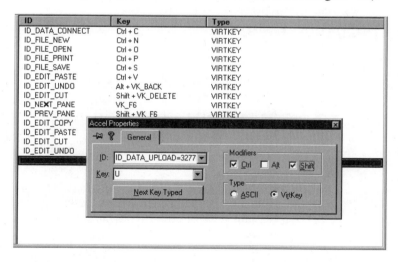

Figure 4.6 The accelerator editor

In this exercise, you will add the CTRL+C and CTRL+U key combinations to the application's accelerator table using the accelerator editor.

► **To define a shortcut key**

1. In ResourceView, expand the Accelerator folder.

2. Double-click the **IDR_MAINFRAME** accelerator resource to open the accelerator editor.

   Notice that the CTRL+C shortcut key is already defined for the **ID_EDIT_ COPY** command ID. To change the association, double-click the **CTRL+C** entry at the top of the table.

3. In the **Accel Properties** dialog box, select **ID_DATA_CONNECT** from the **ID** list. Close the **Accel Properties** dialog box to update the ID.

4. To add a new shortcut key, double-click the blank entry at the bottom of the table. In the **ID** list, click **ID_DATA_UPLOAD**.

5. Type **u** in the **Key** box.

6. Select the **Ctrl** check box and clear the **Shift** check box. The accelerator editor pane should look similar to the one in Figure 4.6 on the previous page.

7. Close the **Accel Properties** dialog box. The shortcut key is added to the table.

Editing Application Toolbars

When AppWizard generates an application, it will create a standard toolbar resource that includes buttons that are associated with commonly used commands from the **File** and **Edit** menus. The toolbar is one of the groups of resources that is associated with the application's document template, and thus has the same **IDR_MAINFRAME ID** as the application icon, accelerator, and menu resources.

A toolbar resource is associated with a bitmap file, which contains the button images. The file associated with the **IDR_MAINFRAME** toolbar is named toolbar.bmp. The framework places a copy of this file in the \Res folder beneath the project folder. If you create additional toolbars from within ResourceView, additional bitmaps with names that reflect the toolbar resource IDs will be created in this folder.

All the button images in the toolbar must be the same size, and are by default 16 pixels wide and 15 pixels high. The bitmap file contains all of the images side by side in the order they appear in the corresponding resource definition. For this reason, it is recommended that you edit this file using the special features of the graphics editor, which are accessible only by double-clicking a toolbar object in the ResourceView window. These features allow you to manipulate the bitmap in manageable, button-sized chunks, and to maintain the relationship between buttons and command IDs.

Figure 4.7 shows the graphics editor being used to edit a toolbar.

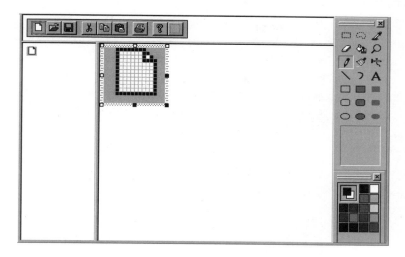

Figure 4.7   Editing toolbars with the graphics editor

In this exercise, you will delete the **Cut**, **Copy**, and **Paste** toolbar buttons.

► **To delete toolbar buttons**

1. In ResourceView, expand the MyApp resources.

2. Expand the Toolbar folder and double-click the **IDR_MAINFRAME** toolbar resource to open the toolbar editor.

3. Drag the **Cut** button off the toolbar.

4. Repeat the process for the **Copy** and **Paste** buttons.

In this exercise, you will add buttons to correspond to the **Connect** and **Upload** commands that you added earlier.

► **To add toolbar buttons**

1. Click the blank button to the right of the toolbar.

2. Drag the button to the desired location on the toolbar. For this exercise, drag it to the left of the **Print** button.

3. Use the graphics editor facilities to design the simple icon shown in Figure 4.8, which represents a connection to a database.

Figure 4.8   The **Connect Toolbar** button

4. Press ENTER. The **Toolbar Button Properties** dialog box will appear.

5. In the **ID** list box, click **ID_DATA_CONNECT**. Click another toolbar button to assign the new ID.

6. Click the **Connect** toolbar button to redisplay the properties. Note how the prompt string associated with the **ID_DATA_CONNECT** command ID is now displayed. Add the string **\nConnect** to the end of the prompt string. This is to specify the ToolTip text for the button.

7. Repeat the previous steps to add another toolbar button for the **Upload** command shown in Figure 4.9. Associate this button with the command ID ID_DATA_UPLOAD, and add the string **\nUpload** to specify the ToolTip text.

Figure 4.9   The **Upload** Toolbar button

8. Build and run the MyApp application. Test the changes you have made to the menu and toolbar. Notice that the commands that you have added appear dimmed. This is because these commands do not yet have handlers associated with them. However, you are still able to check that the prompt strings and the ToolTips display properly.

Handling Menu and Toolbar Selections

In Lesson 3 of Chapter 3, you learned how to use ClassWizard to handle the command messages that are generated when a user selects a menu or toolbar command. In the following exercises, you will add handlers for the **Connect** and **Upload** commands.

The command routing feature of the MFC application framework allows you to define class handlers inside the class most closely associated with the handler function. You might decide that a connection to a remote database is best conceived as a feature of the application as a whole, in which case you would consider handling the **Connect** command in your **CMyAppApp** application class.

In this case, the **Connect** command handler function would contain code to locate and connect to a remote database. You would probably want to record the current state of the database connection in a Boolean variable so that the application would always be able to tell whether there was a live connection to the database. This variable would be set to TRUE after a successful connection to the database and set to FALSE after disconnection or if the connection failed. For the purposes of our example, you will not need to implement the database connection code. Instead, you will simulate connection and disconnection by creating the Boolean variable m_isDatabaseConnected as a member of the **CMyAppApp** class. The **Connect command** function will then switch the variable between TRUE and FALSE.

▶ **To add the m_isDatabaseConnected member to the CMyAppApp class**

1. On the **ClassView** tab, right-click the **CMyAppApp** class icon.

2. On the shortcut menu, click **Add Member Variable**.

3. In the **Add Member Variable** dialog box, type **BOOL** in the **Variable Type** box.

4. Type **m_isDatabaseConnected** into the **Variable Name** text box.

5. Ensure that the **Public Access** option is set. Click **OK** to add the variable. You can see the new variable by expanding the **CMyAppApp** class.

Note When developing MFC code, we will use the MFC-defined BOOL type (an integer type) rather than the C++ built-in bool type. This is to maintain compatibility with the MFC functions, which predate the adoption of the bool type as an ANSI standard and use the BOOL type for Boolean parameters and return values.

---

6. Double-click the **CMyAppApp** class constructor icon to edit the constructor code.

7. Add the following line of code to the body of the constructor (inside the opening and closing braces) to initialize the m_isDatabaseConnected variable:

```
m_isDatabaseConnected = FALSE;
```

In this exercise, you will add a function to handle the **Connect** command.

▶ **To add the OnDataConnect() handler function to the CMyAppApp class**

1. From within the MyApp project, press CTRL+W to open ClassWizard. Click the **Message Maps** tab and do the following:

   ■ In the **Class Name** list, click **CMyAppApp**.

   ■ In the **Object IDs** list, click **ID_DATA_CONNECT**.

   ■ In the **Messages** list, click **COMMAND**.

2. Click **Add Function**. A dialog box appears and suggests the name **OnDataConnect()** for your handler function. Click **OK** to accept the name.

3. Click **Edit Code**. The MyApp.cpp file is opened and the insertion point is positioned at the top of the function implementation.

4. Replace the // TODO comment line with the following line of code:

```
m_isDatabaseConnected = m_isDatabaseConnected ? FALSE : TRUE;
```

Your next task is to add a handler for the **Upload** command. The purpose of this function is to upload the application data to the database. As application data is contained within an application's document class, the **CMyAppDoc** class seems to be the appropriate place for the **OnDataUpload()** function. For the purposes of this example, all your function will do is display a message box.

▶ **To add the OnDataUpload() handler function to the CMyAppDoc class**

1. Repeat the previous steps, but this time add the **OnDataUpload()** function to the **CMyAppDoc** class to handle the **ID_DATA_UPLOAD** command.

2. When editing the **OnDataUpload** function, replace the // TODO comment line with the following code:

```
AfxMessageBox("Upload successfully completed");
```

3. Build and run the MyApp application.

4. Now that you have added handlers, the new menu and toolbar commands are available. The **Connect** command will have no effect yet, but the **Upload** command displays a message box.

Dynamically Updating Menu and Toolbar Commands

Even if we had provided full implementations of the **OnDataConnect()** and the **OnDataUpload()** functions, in terms of logical design, the user interface as it stands would still need adjustments. Consider the following points:

- We have no indication of the current state of the data connection—whether the database is connected or disconnected. Thus we do not know what the effect of our selecting the **Connect** command will be.

- The **Upload** command, the purpose of which is to upload application data to a remote database, depends on the existence of a current live connection to the database. As the program stands, a user can select the **Upload** command when there is no connection, a situation in which the upload is bound to fail.

- Menu and toolbar commands often need to be updated to convey the state of the application to the user. If a menu command or a toolbar button switches between on and off states, the command should be "checked" to indicate the on state. You can arrange menu commands and toolbar buttons into what are known as *radio groups*. In a radio group, only one of the group buttons can be selected at a time. The act of selecting a radio button automatically de-selects any other selected buttons in the group.

- Menu commands and toolbar buttons that cannot perform any useful function within the current state of the application should be made unavailable. For example, an option that allows you to upload data to a remote database should be unavailable when the remote database is offline.

- It is possible to change the text of a menu command according to the application context. You should use this option carefully, as it is generally confusing for the user to have menu command captions changing in the middle of a program.

The MFC application framework provides us with an easy way to update the appearance and status of menu commands and toolbar buttons by allowing us to provide handler functions for user-interface update command messages.

User Interface Update Command Handlers

You will recall from the discussion of MFC message handling in Chapter 3 that the application framework generates user-interface update command messages, which signal the application to update the status of user-interface elements. When this occurs, the message maps of command target objects in the command routing are searched for ON_UPDATE_COMMAND_UI entries, which associate command IDs with update handler functions. This process occurs for shortcut menus as they are opened, and for toolbar buttons during application idle time.

You can create user interface update handler functions to modify the appearance of menu commands and toolbar buttons. The framework passes the functions a single parameter—a pointer to a **CCmdUI** object. The **CCmdUI** class gives access to the user-interface element associated with the handler and allows you to update a menu command or toolbar button using one of the member functions described in Table 4.1.

Table 4.1   CCmd UT Member Functions

Function	Purpose
Enable	When set to TRUE, makes a menu command or toolbar button available. When set to FALSE, makes a menu command unavailable. Unavailable commands are dimmed.
SetCheck	When set to TRUE, places a check mark next to a menu command and makes toolbar buttons available. When set to FALSE, removes the check mark from a menu command and makes toolbar buttons unavailable.
SetRadio	Works like **SetCheck**, except that it operates on user-interface commands acting as part of a radio group. Clearing the other commands in the group is not automatic unless the commands themselves maintain the radio-group behavior.
SetText	Sets the text of the user-interface command. Has no effect on toolbar buttons.

In the following exercises, you will add user-interface update command handlers to the **CMyAppApp** class to modify the status of the **Connect** and **Upload** commands and the corresponding toolbar buttons.

▶ **To add the OnUpdateDataConnect() handler function to the CMyAppApp class**

1. From within the MyApp project, press CTRL+W to open ClassWizard. Click the **Message Maps** tab and do the following:

   - In the **Class Name** list, click **CMyAppApp**.
   - In the **Object IDs** list, click **ID_DATA_CONNECT**.
   - In the **Messages** list, click **UPDATE_COMMAND_UI**.

2. Click **Add Function**. A dialog box appears and suggests the name **OnUpdateDataConnect()** for your handler function. Click **OK** to accept the name.

3. Click **Edit Code**. The MyApp.cpp file is opened and the insertion point is positioned at the top of the function implementation.

4. Replace the // TODO comment line with the following code:

```
pCmdUI->SetCheck(m_isDatabaseConnected);
```

A Boolean parameter is passed to the **SetCheck()** function. TRUE selects the command and FALSE clears it. The effect of the code just added will be to provide a visual indication as to the state of the m_isDatabaseConnected variable used to signify a successful live connection to the database.

In the next exercise, you will add the user-interface update command handler for the **Update** command.

▶ **To add the OnUpdateDataUpload() handler function to the CMyAppApp class**

1. Repeat the steps above, but this time add the **OnUpdateDataUpload()** function to the **CMyAppApp** class to handle the UPDATE_COMMAND_UI message for the **ID_DATA_UPLOAD** command.

2. When editing the **OnUpdateDataUpload()** function, replace the // TODO comment line with the following code:

```
pCmdUI->Enable(m_isDatabaseConnected);
```

The **Enable()** function also takes a single Boolean parameter. TRUE makes the command available and FALSE makes it unavailable. The effect of the code will be to make the **Upload** command available only when there is a live connection to the database. A live connection will be signified by CMyAppApp::m_ isDatabaseConnected being set TRUE.

3. Build and run the MyApp program. Notice how the **Connect** menu command and the corresponding toolbar button are affected by being selected. Note, too, how the selection of the **Connect** command makes the **Upload** command available.

Writing to the Status Bar

In some cases, simply updating menu and toolbar commands is not an adequate method of conveying information about the status of your application. For example, consider the MyApp example application above. As it stands, the **Connect** command simply allows you to connect to and disconnect from a single data source. What if there were a number of alternative data sources available and the application was often required to switch between them?

In this case, you might use the **OnDataConnect**() function to display a list of data sources from which the user can select. The connection status would need to be displayed on the user interface either as the name of the currently selected data source or as a string indicating that no data source is currently selected.

The appropriate place to display this type of information is on the application's *status bar*. You have already seen how an MFC application uses the status bar to display text that you supply as a menu command prompt. If you run your MyApp application, you will see that it also displays the status of the CAPS LOCK, NUM LOCK and SCROLL LOCK keys in separate indicator panes (indicators) on the status bar.

MFC support for status bars is encapsulated in the **CStatusBar** class. **CStatusBar** allows you complete control over the number and style of status bar indicators and the text they display.

The framework stores indicator information in an array with the leftmost indicator at position 0. By default, the first indicator is "elastic"—it takes up the status-bar length not used by the other indicators, so the other panes are right-aligned. It is in this indicator that the MFC framework displays menu and toolbar prompt strings.

When you create a status bar, you use an array of string IDs (which identify entries in a string table resource) that the framework associates with the corresponding indicators. You can then use either a string ID or an index to access an indicator.

The recommended way to update text on a status bar indicator is to use an ON_UPDATE_COMMAND_UI entry in a message map to associate a user-interface update handler function with an indicator's string ID. You can then use the **SetText**() function of the handler's *CCmdUI* parameter to display text in the indicator. Note that ClassWizard does not automate the association of indicator IDs with handler functions, so you are obliged to add these message map entries manually.

It is possible to update the indicator text by using the **CStatusBar::SetPaneText()** function. Even so, you will need to create an update handler. Without an update handler for the indicator, MFC automatically disables the indicator, erasing its content.

In the exercises that follow, you will replace the MyApp default status bar indicators for the CAPS LOCK, NUM LOCK, and SCROLL LOCK keys, with a single database connection indicator. This indicator will display the name of the current data source, which will be stored as a variable in the application class. If the application is disconnected from a data source, the string "Database not connected" will appear. For the purposes of this exercise, you will not implement a data source selection routine, but simply hard-code a single name to appear.

In the following exercise, you will add a data member to the **CMyAppApp** class to hold the name of the current data source.

▶ **To add the m_strDSN member to the CMyAppApp class**

1. On the **ClassView** tab, right-click the **CMyAppApp** class icon.
2. On the shortcut menu, click **Add Member Variable**.
3. In the **Add Member Variable** dialog box, type **CString** in the **Variable Type** box.
4. Type **m_strDSN** in the **Variable Name** box.
5. Ensure that the **Public Access** option is set. Click **OK** to add the variable. You should see it appear under the **CMyAppApp** class on the MyApp classes tree.
6. Double-click the **CMyAppApp** class constructor icon to edit the constructor code.
7. Add the following line of code to the body of the constructor to initialize the m_strDSN variable with the name of a data source:

```
m_strDSN = "MyDatabase";
```

In the following exercise, you will create a string ID for the new indicator.

▶ **To create the ID_INDICATOR_DB indicator ID**

1. In the MyApp workspace window, click the **ResourceView** tab.
2. Expand the String Table folder.
3. Double-click the **String Table** resource to open the string table editor.

4. Locate the string IDs that represent the indicators. Each of these IDs begins with **ID_INDICATOR_**.

5. Right-click the last of these entries: **ID_INDICATOR_REC**.

6. On the shortcut menu, click **New String**.

7. In the **ID** box, type **ID_INDICATOR_DB**.

8. In the **Caption** box, type **Database not connected**. This is a default string that must always be supplied for a string table entry. Use the space bar to type 15 blank spaces after the string. The framework will use the length of the string, including spaces, to size the indicators. The blank spaces ensure that the indicator pane is large enough to take the longest string that it is required to display. Your screen should now look something like Figure 4.10.

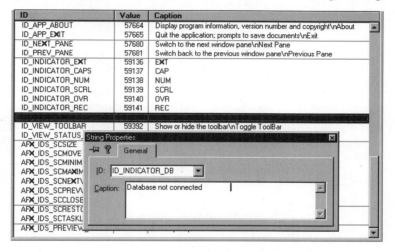

Figure 4.10 Adding a string to the string table

9. Press ENTER to add the new string. Close the string table editor.

Now you will modify the application's status bar creation code so that it creates the ID_INDICATOR_DB pane instead of the three standard key lock indicators.

▶ **To set up the MyApp status bar indicators**

1. In the MyApp workspace window, click the **FileView** tab.

2. Expand the Source Files folder.

3. Double-click the **MainFrm.cpp** file icon to edit the file.

4. Locate the code that declares the status bar indicator array. You'll find it just below the message map. The code reads as follows:

```
static UINT indicators[] =
{
    ID_SEPARATOR,           // status line indicator
    ID_INDICATOR_CAPS,
    ID_INDICATOR_NUM,
    ID_INDICATOR_SCRL,
};
```

5. Delete the last three elements of the array so that only **ID_SEPARATOR** remains. Add the **ID_INDICATOR_DB** identifier as the second element. The code should now read as follows:

```
static UINT indicators[] =
{
    ID_SEPARATOR,           // status line indicator
    ID_INDICATOR_DB,
};
```

If you look through the **CMainFrm::OnCreate()** function further down the file, you will see that this array gets passed to the **CStatusBar::SetIndicators()** function that is called for the **CMainFrame::m_wndStatusBar** object.

Now you must manually implement the message map entry and handler function to enable the framework to update the indicators.

► **To add the message map entry**

1. Locate the message map. It should be just above the array that you edited in the previous exercise.

2. Add the following entry macro to the message map:

```
ON_UPDATE_COMMAND_UI(ID_INDICATOR_DB, OnUpdateDB)
```

Note that all message map entries that are not created by ClassWizard should be placed outside the {{AFX_MSG_MAP comment block. The entire message map should read:

```
BEGIN_MESSAGE_MAP(CMainFrame, CFrameWnd)
    //{{AFX_MSG_MAP(CMainFrame)
    // NOTE - ClassWizard will add and remove mapping macros here.
    // DO NOT EDIT what you see in these blocks of generated code!
    ON_WM_CREATE()
    //}}AFX_MSG_MAP
    ON_UPDATE_COMMAND_UI(ID_INDICATOR_DB, OnUpdateDB)
END_MESSAGE_MAP()
```

▶   **To add the handler function**

1. In the MyApp workspace window, click the **FileView** tab.
2. Expand the Header Files folder.
3. Double-click the **MainFrm.h** file icon to edit the file.
4. At the bottom of the **CMainFrame** class declaration, just above the
   DECLARE_MESSAGE_MAP macro, add the following function definition:

```
afx_msg void OnUpdateDB(CCmdUI *pCmdUI);
```

   Note that this entry is also outside the {{AFX_MSG comment block.

5. Switch back to the MainFrm.cpp file. At the bottom of the file, add the following code to implement the **OnUpdateDB()** function:

```
void CMainFrame::OnUpdateDB(CCmdUI *pCmdUI)
{
    CMyAppApp * pApp = dynamic_cast<CMyAppApp *>(AfxGetApp());
    ASSERT_VALID(pApp);

    if(pApp->m_isDatabaseConnected)
        pCmdUI->SetText("Connected to: "+ pApp->m_strDSN);
    else
        pCmdUI->SetText("Database not connected");
}
```

This function is straightforward. The code checks for a live database connection by checking the CMyAppApp::m_isDatabaseConnected variable. If
m_isDatabaseConnected contains TRUE, then the function retrieves the name
of the current data source from CMyAppApp::m_strDSN and displays it on
the status bar pane. Otherwise it displays the string "Database not connected."

Note the use of the MFC global function **AfxGetApp()**, which returns a
pointer to the main application object. This function must be cast to the
CMyAppApp * type so that you can reference the CMyAppApp member
variables. To cast down the inheritance hierarchy, you should use the
dynamic_cast<>() operator.

Note Before you can use the **dynamic_cast<>()** operator, you must make sure
that you have selected the **Enable Run-Time Type Information (RTTI)**
check box on the language settings of the **C/C++** page in the project settings.
(See Lesson 2 of Chapter 2 for details on how to do this.)

Note the use of the **ASSERT_VALID** debug macro to check the validity of
the pointer.

6. Build and run the MyApp program. Test the **Connect** command to see how the text on the status bar is updated to indicate the database connection status. In subsequent exercises, you will change the **Connect** command so that instead of it simply switching on and off, it will open a dialog box where you can select a data source. In this scenario, you will rely entirely on the status-bar indicator to inform the user of which data source (if any) the application is connected to.

Lesson Summary

A document/view–based application generated by the MFC AppWizard provides a fully featured user interface that you can adapt to suit your own requirements. Along with the application classes and code, the AppWizard creates a group of resources that can contain application icons, menus and toolbars, and a string table.

These resources can be edited using tools that come as part of the Visual C++ development environment. The graphics editor can be used to edit icons and toolbar buttons. The menu editor allows you to edit menus visually. There are also editors for string table entries and shortcut key associations.

While using these editors, you can also edit the property pages of the objects that you are editing. These property pages allow you to set the text for menu options, status bar prompt strings and ToolTips, and set command IDs for menu and toolbar options.

Command IDs are used to map menu or toolbar selections to handler functions. Using ClassWizard, you can easily add message map entries and create handler functions for any of the classes derived from **CCmdTarget**. Similarly, you can use ClassWizard to add user-interface update command handlers. These are functions that are called by the framework to allow you to update the status or appearance of user interface elements. The framework passes these functions a pointer to a **CCmdUI** object as a parameter. The **CCmdUI** class gives access to the user-interface element associated with the handler, and provides member functions that allow you to alter the appearance or status of menu or toolbar commands.

You can also convey information on the status bar about the status of your application. The MFC class **CStatusBar** allows you complete control over the number and style of status bar indicators and the text they display. You can set up an array of status bar indicators that are associated with string IDs in the application's string table. You can use these IDs or the array index to access and update individual status bar panes. The recommended way to update text in a status bar pane is to use an ON_UPDATE_COMMAND_UI entry in a message map to associate a user-interface update handler function with an indicator's string ID. You can then use the **SetText()** function of the handler's *CCmdUI* parameter to display text in the pane. ClassWizard cannot be used to add handler functions for indicator IDs, so you are obliged to add these message map entries manually.

Lesson 2: Creating Dialog Boxes

In this lesson, you will learn about the different types of dialog boxes used within a Windows application. You will learn how you can visually design and edit a dialog box using the Visual C++ dialog editor, and how to create an instance of a dialog box within your application.

After this lesson, you will be able to:

- Describe the types of dialog boxes used in a Windows application.
- Describe how to use the Visual C++ dialog editor to create a dialog box template.
- Describe how to edit the properties and controls of a dialog box.
- Describe how to use ClassWizard to create a dialog box class from a template.
- Describe how to use the dialog box class to create an instance of a dialog box within your code.

Estimated lesson time: 30 minutes

Dialog Boxes

Anyone who has ever used a Windows application should be familiar with the concept of a dialog box. A dialog box is a child window of the main application window that is used to display application status information or to get input from the user. A dialog box contains *controls*, which are small standardized window objects that can be manipulated by the user to perform an action, or used by the application to display information to the user. For example, a user can enter text into an *edit* control, or set a simple on/off option through a *check box* control. The user can select from a predefined list of options in a *list box* control. The application can relay information to a user through a static *text* control or with a dynamic *progress bar* control. *Button* controls are generally used to start an application procedure or close the currently open dialog box.

Types of Dialog Boxes

There are two types of dialog boxes that accept user input. *Modal* dialog boxes take control of an application interface and require the user to supply information or cancel the dialog box before continuing with the application. Each AppWizard-generated application provides an **About** dialog box, which is a good example of a simple modal dialog box. Select the **About** command from the **Help** menu in your MyApp application to see how a modal dialog box operates.

Modal dialog boxes are used everywhere; *modeless* dialog boxes are less common. Modeless dialog boxes do not take control of an application interface, but allow you to work on other areas of the application without closing the dialog box. You can switch between application windows and a modeless dialog box as required.

A good example of a modeless dialog box is the **Menu Item Properties** dialog box that you used in the previous lesson to set the command ID and command text of the application menu commands. Try opening the menu editor and editing the properties of one of the menu commands. If you keep the **Menu Item Properties** dialog box open by clicking on the thumbtack icon in the upper-left corner, the dialog box will remain open as you move between menu commands in the editor. You can even add and delete menu commands while the **Menu Item Properties** dialog box is open.

The **Menu Item Properties** dialog box is actually a special type of dialog box known as a *property sheet*. A property sheet presents the user with a tabbed, index card–like selection of property pages, each of which features standard dialog box–style controls. Property sheets are usually used to configure options or settings for objects or applications. They can be modal or modeless in operation.

Creating a Dialog Box Template

The first stage in creating a dialog box is to use the Visual C++ dialog editor to create a *dialog box template*. A dialog box template is a reusable application resource that is a binary description of a dialog box and the controls it contains. The dialog editor (shown in Figure 4.11) is a visual tool that allows you to lay out the template of a dialog box and its controls on screen, edit their properties, and test their operations.

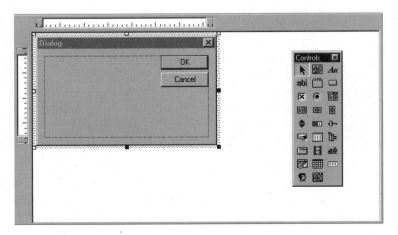

Figure 4.11   The Visual C++ dialog editor

Note the **Controls** toolbar, which might be docked. You place a control on the dialog box template by selecting the appropriate tool on the **Controls** toolbar. This action turns your pointer into a control placement tool (usually a crosshair pointer) of the appropriate type.

In the following exercises, you will use the dialog editor to create a template for a dialog box belonging to the MyApp application, which will allow the user to connect to a data source. The user will use a list box control to select a data source name. A read-only edit control will convey information about each data source as its corresponding list item is selected. The dialog box will contain edit controls to allow the user to enter logon information consisting of a user ID, a password, and a numeric privilege level. A check box option will allow users to indicate whether subsequent sessions of the application should attempt to connect to the current data source. The dialog box will contain two buttons, **Connect** and **Cancel**. **Connect** will allow the user to try and connect to the currently selected data source, and **Cancel** will cancel the operation.

The **Connect to Data Source** dialog box is shown in Figure 4.12. You can use this illustration as a guide when working through the following exercise.

Figure 4.12   The **Connect to Data Source** dialog box

▶ **To create the Connect to Data Source dialog box template**

1. In the MyApp workspace pane, click **ResourceView** and expand the MyApp resources folder.

2. Right-click the Dialog folder. Click **Insert Dialog**. A new blank dialog box appears with default **OK** and **Cancel** command buttons.

3. Click the title bar of the dialog box to select it. Don't click one of the command buttons, because doing so would select the button rather than the entire dialog box.

4. Use the resize handle on the bottom-right corner of the dialog box to stretch it to 230 pixels wide by 200 pixels tall. The size of the dialog box in pixels is displayed on the status bar when the dialog editor is open.

▶ **To edit the dialog box properties**

1. With the dialog box selected, press ENTER.

2. On the **General** tab, change the dialog resource ID by typing **IDD_ CONNECTDIALOG** in the **ID** box. IDD_ is the standard prefix used for dialog resource IDs.

3. In the **Caption** box, type **Connect to Data Source**.

4. Close the **Dialog Properties** dialog box.

▶ **To add a caption for the list box control**

1. On the **Controls** toolbar, click the **Static Text** tool.

2. With the crosshair pointer, draw a static text box against the top left corner of the drawing guide.

3. With the static text box selected, start typing the text **&Data Source:** The **Text Properties** sheet will appear automatically, and your typing will be entered into the **Caption** box.

▶ **To add a list box control to the dialog box**

1. On the **Controls** toolbar, click the **List Box** button.

2. Use the crosshair pointer to draw a list box beneath the list box caption that you just created. (Refer to Figure 4.12 for a guide to the correct size and position.)

3. Select the list box and press ENTER to edit the properties.

4. On the **General** tab, type **IDC_DSNLIST** in the **ID** box.

5. Explore the other pages on the property sheet. (Press F1 for context-sensitive help.) When you are done, close the list box property sheet.

▶ **To add a read-only edit control to the dialog box**

1. On the **Controls** toolbar, click the **Edit Box** tool.

2. With the crosshair pointer, draw an edit control box beneath the list box. Position it as shown in Figure 4.12.

3. Click the edit control to select it, and press ENTER.

4. On the **General** tab, change the control ID by typing **IDC_DESCRIPTION** in the **ID** box.

5. On the **Styles** tab, select the **Multiline** and **Read Only** check boxes.

6. Close the **Edit Properties** dialog box.

▶ **To add the logon information edit controls to the dialog box**

1. Using the **Static Text** tool, create captions for the logon information edit controls shown in Figure 4.12. Type the captions **User &ID:**, **&Password:**, and **&Access Level:**.

2. Using the **Edit Box** tool, create an input box for the User ID command (shown in Figure 4.12). Set the control ID to **IDC_USERID**.

3. Create an input box for the Password. Set the Control ID to **IDC_PASSWORD**. On the **Styles** tab of the property sheet, select the **Password** check box. This style displays the characters typed by the user as asterisks to preserve the privacy of the user password.

4. Create an input box for the **Access Level** command. As shown in Figure 4.10, this should be smaller than the other two input boxes. Set the control ID to **IDC_ACCESS**. On the **Styles** tab of the property sheet, select the **Number** check box so that the edit control will accept only numeric input.

▶ **To add a check box control to the dialog box**

1. On the **Controls** toolbar, select the **Check Box** tool.

2. With the crosshair pointer, draw a check box control beneath the read-only edit control, as shown in Figure 4.12. Extend the control far enough to the right to accommodate the text shown in the illustration.

3. Click the check box control to select it.

4. Press ENTER to edit the properties.

5. On the **General** tab, change the control ID by typing **IDC_CHECKCONTROL** in the **ID** box.

6. In the **Caption** box, type **Attempt to connect at application & startup**.

7. Close the **Edit Properties** dialog box. If the entire caption text is not showing, use the resize handle to extend the control to the right.

▶ **To reorganize the button layout**

1. Click **OK**. Type **Connec&t**. The **Push Button Properties** sheet will appear automatically and your typing will be entered in the **Caption** box. Do not change the control ID.

2. Close the **Push Button Properties** sheet. Reorganize the **Connect** button and the **Cancel** button as shown in Figure 4.12.

Often, users need to be able to select values from some controls in a dialog box and alter values in others. For example, they might need to make a selection from a list box or enter text in a text box. They usually need to make a selection between two command buttons. To facilitate this movement, the controls need to be selectable. When a particular control is selected, it is said to have the *focus*.

When a control has the focus, the user is able to interact with that control. The control with the focus is readily apparent. It looks different from the other controls because it appears with an outline or contains the insertion point or is distinguished in some other way. This provides a clear signal about which control will be affected by the user's actions.

A user can navigate through the controls displayed on a dialog box by using the TAB key. When the user presses the TAB key, the focus changes from one control to the next. Not all of the controls on a dialog box can necessarily receive the focus. For example, a static text control cannot. But each control capable of receiving the focus gets a turn. The order in which their turns come is known as the *tab order*.

The tab order of the controls in a dialog box is set by the developer. The tab order provides a means for navigating among the controls using only the keyboard. This order can be an important aspect of a heavily used application, where the thousands of times a month a user might need to move a hand from the keyboard to manipulate the mouse can add up to lost productivity and increased fatigue.

Pressing the TAB key moves forward through the tab order. Pressing SHIFT+TAB moves backward through the tab order. When a dialog box is initially displayed, the first selectable control receives the focus.

On a dialog box with numerous controls, the user may need to press the TAB key many times to reach the control of interest. Access keys are handy in these cases. To provide an access key for a selectable control, place a static text control in the tab order immediately prior to the control to which it is to be assigned and include an ampersand in the displayed text for the static text control.

When the user presses the access key for the static text control, focus goes to the first selectable control in the tab order after the static text control to which that access key was assigned.

▶   **To set the tab order**

1. On the **Layout** menu of the Visual Studio main window, click **Tab Order**. Numbers representing the current tab order will appear in the upper left corner of each control in the dialog box.

2. Click the **Data Source** caption, then the list box control, then each of the input box captions, and then each of the associated input boxes. Next, select the **Attempt to connect at application startup** check box, then click **Connect**, and finally click **Cancel**. The order in which you click determines the tab order.

3. Click outside the dialog box to finish setting the tab order.

▶ **To test the dialog box**

1. Click the **Test** button or press CTRL+T. An instance of your dialog box appears.

2. Try testing the tab order. Test the access keys to ensure the tab order was set correctly to permit moving among controls using the access keys. Try selecting the different sample commands in the list box, and then try closing the dialog box with the **Continue** or **Cancel** button.

Creating and Using a Dialog Box Class

Once you have created a dialog box template, you need to create a class to represent the dialog box in your code. The dialog box class should be derived from the MFC class **CDialog**. This class might contain member variables to represent controls and data items in the dialog box, and methods to handle events arising from user interaction with the controls. The task of creating a dialog box class, and the binding of controls to class data members, is greatly simplified by automatic features of ClassWizard.

In this lesson, you will use ClassWizard to create a class for your **Connect to Data Source** dialog box and you will learn how to display the dialog box in your application. You will learn how to work with dialog data and with dialog box controls in Chapter 5.

▶ **To create the CConflictDialog class**

1. With the **IDD_CONNECTDIALOG** dialog box open in the dialog editor, press CTRL+W to open ClassWizard. You will see the **Adding a Class** dialog box shown in Figure 4.13.

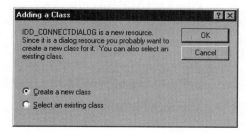

Figure 4.13   Adding a new dialog class

2. With the **Create a new class** option selected, click **OK**. The **New Class** dialog box appears.

3. In the **Name** text box, type **CConnectDialog**. Note the file name that is created by default.

4. Click **OK**. The **CConnectDialog** dialog class is created and selected in the **Class Name** box of ClassWizard.

5. Click **OK** to close ClassWizard.

Displaying the Dialog Box

Once you have created a dialog class, displaying a modal dialog box is simply a matter of creating an instance of the dialog class in your code and calling the base class method **CDialog::DoModal()**. The base class functions **CDialog::OnOK()** and **CDialog::OnCancel()** provide default handling of the IDOK and IDCANCEL messages generated (by default) by the **OK** and **Cancel** buttons. Both of these functions call the **CDialog::EndDialog()** method to close the dialog box. The **DoModal()** function returns the ID of the button used to close the dialog box.

An application generated by the MFC AppWizard provides a dialog template and a dialog class for the **About** dialog box. The code to display the **About** dialog box is located within the **OnAppAbout()** member function of the application object, which is the handler function for the **ID_APP_ABOUT** command ID. The following code snippet illustrates how the **OnAppAbout()** function in your MyApp application displays the **About** dialog box:

```
void CMyAppApp::OnAppAbout()
{
    CAboutDlg aboutDlg;
    aboutDlg.DoModal();
}
```

Modeless dialog boxes are handled differently. Rather than calling **DoModal()** to activate a modeless dialog box, you call the **CDialog::Create()** function and pass the resource ID of the dialog box template as a parameter. If the dialog resource has the property **WS_VISIBLE**, the dialog box appears immediately. If it does not, you must call the base class member function **CWnd::ShowWindow()** to display the dialog box. The **ShowWindow()** function accepts a single parameter, which can be any of a number of predefined values, that specifies how the window is to be shown. The values generally used with a modeless dialog box are SW_SHOW to display the dialog box, and SW_HIDE to hide it.

Note If you need to remind yourself of the inheritance hierarchy of the **CDialog** class, refer to Figure 3.1 in Chapter 3.

Because modal dialog boxes take control of an application interface, they are usually created as they are needed. An object that represents a modal dialog box will be declared just before it is used, and will be allowed to go out of scope once the dialog box has been closed and the user responses have been processed.

Modeless dialog boxes tend to exist for the lifetime of the application and are simply shown or hidden in response to user commands. Modeless dialog boxes are often created early on in the application, usually as members of one of the application classes. SW_SHOW and SW_HIDE are used to show or hide the dialog box as the application demands. Modeless dialog boxes are similar to application toolbars in this respect. Toolbar objects are created at application startup as members of the **CMainFrame** class and are always available to be shown or hidden as the user selects or clears the **Toolbar** menu option.

You will learn more about how to use modal and modeless dialog boxes in Chapter 5. In the following exercise, you will see how to make the **Connect** menu option of the MyApp application display the **Connect to Data Source** dialog box.

▶   **To display the Connect to Data Source dialog box**

1. In the MyApp project, click the **ClassView** tab and expand the **CMyAppApp** class icon.

2. Double-click the **OnUpdateConnect**() function icon to locate the user-interface update command handler.

3. Remove the single line of implementation code that reads:

   ```
   pCmdUI->SetCheck(m_isDatabaseConnected);
   ```

4. Locate the **OnConnect**() handler function. Replace the current line of implementation code that reads

   ```
   m_isDatabaseConnected = m_isDatabaseConnected ? FALSE : TRUE;
   ```

   with the following lines:

   ```
   CConnectDialog aCD;
   aCD.DoModal();
   ```

5. At the top of the MyApp.cpp file, along with the other #include statements, add the following line:

   ```
   #include "ConnectDialog.h"
   ```

6. Build and run the MyApp application. On the **Data** menu, click **Connect**, and verify that the **Connect to Data Source** dialog box appears. Note that although we have changed the **OK** command button caption to *Connect*, it retains the **IDOK** ID and will therefore call the default **OnOK**() handler to close the dialog box.

At present, you cannot do much with this dialog box. In the next chapter, you will add code to set and retrieve dialog box data and process messages from controls.

Common Dialog Classes

MFC supplies several classes derived from **CDialog** that encapsulate the "common dialog boxes" supplied as part of the Windows common dialog library COMMDLG.DLL. These dialog boxes simplify common Windows application tasks such as locating and opening files or specifying print job information. Common dialog boxes should always be used where appropriate to ensure that your application presents a standard interface to the users and complies with the Windows Logo requirements.

The five common dialog classes provided by MFC are listed in Table 4.2.

Table 4.2   Windows Common Dialog Boxes

Dialog Class	Description
CColorDialog	Used to select colors.
CFileDialog	Used to select a filename to open or save.
CFindReplaceDialog	Used to initiate a find or replace operation in a text file.
CFontDialog	Used to specify a font.
CPrintDialog	Used to specify information for a print job.

For more information on these classes, refer to the MFC class documentation in the Visual C++ online Help.

Lesson Summary

A dialog box is a child window of the main application. It is used to display application status information or to get input from the user. A dialog box contains controls, which are small, standardized window objects that can be manipulated by the user to perform an action, or used by the application to display information to the user.

There are two types of dialog boxes. Modal dialog boxes require the user to supply information or cancel the dialog box before returning control to the application. Modeless dialog boxes do not take control of an application interface, but allow you to work on other areas of the application without closing the dialog box. A property sheet is a special kind of dialog box that presents the user with a tabbed, index card-like selection of property pages. Property sheets can be modal or modeless.

The first stage in creating a dialog box is to use the Visual C++ dialog editor to create a *dialog box template*. A dialog box template is a reusable application resource that is a binary description of a dialog box and the controls it contains. The next stage is to create a class, derived from the MFC class **CDialog**, to represent the dialog box in your code. The task of creating a dialog box class is greatly simplified by automatic features of ClassWizard.

Once you have created a dialog class, you can display a modal dialog box by creating an instance of the dialog class in your code and calling the **CDialog::DoModal()** function. To display a modeless dialog box, you call the **CDialog::Create()** function, passing the resource ID of the dialog box template as a parameter. Use the **CWnd::ShowWindow()** with a parameter of SW_SHOW or SW_HIDE to display or hide the modeless dialog box.

MFC supplies several classes derived from **CDialog** that encapsulate common Windows dialog boxes. These dialog boxes simplify common Windows application tasks and should always be used where appropriate to ensure that your application presents a consistent interface to the users.

Lab 4: Creating the STUpload User Interface

In this lab, you will develop the user interface for the STUpload application. You will create menu commands, edit the toolbar, and create dialog box templates. It is assumed that you have completed the exercises in this chapter and are familiar with the operation of the resource editors.

We have provided application icons and toolbar button bitmaps for you. To ensure that your project corresponds to this lab, replace your current development folder with a copy of the Chapter4\Lab\Partial\STUpload folder (and its subfolders) found on the companion CD.

Editing the STUpload Application Menu

In the first part of this lab, you will design the STUpload application menu in accordance with the customer requirements, as described in Lab 1. At this point, you should think about the functionality that the application is going to offer. Use the AppWizard-generated menus as a basis to plan how that functionality will be presented to the user as a set of menu choices.

You will recall that the user is able to load ASCII text files into the application and can save the data that these files contain in the application's document format. You will also implement the standard printing facilities offered by an MFC document/view application. Therefore, you will want to retain the **File** menu in the STUpload application interface.

The STUpload application will display a graph of the data that is loaded in from the text file. Users will not be able to interact with the data, and the graph will not contain selectable elements; therefore, you do not need to implement the **Edit** menu.

▶ **To remove the Edit menu**

1. Open the STUpload project in Visual C++.
2. Click the **ResourceView** tab and expand the STUpload resources.
3. Expand the Menu folder.
4. Double-click the **IDR_MAINFRAME** menu resource to open the menu editor.
5. On the menu bar, click **Edit**, press DELETE, and then press ENTER to confirm removal of the **Edit** menu.

In place of the **Edit** menu you will create the **Data** menu, which provides options for importing data from a text file, uploading imported data to the central database, and querying and browsing the central database.

► **To add the Data menu**

1. Click the blank menu command to the right of the title bar.

2. Drag the blank command and drop it between the **File** and **View** menu commands.

3. Double-click the blank menu command to display its properties. Type **&Data** as the **Caption** property.

► **To add the Import menu command to the Data menu**

1. Click the blank command under the **Data** menu title.

2. Type the string **&Import...\tCTRL+I**. As you start typing, the **Menu Item Properties** dialog box will appear, and your text will be entered into the **Caption** box.

3. In the **Prompt** box, type **Import data from file\nImport from file**.

4. Click the thumbtack icon in the upper-left corner of the **Menu Item Properties** dialog box to keep the dialog box open while you edit different menu commands.

5. Click on another command, then click again on the **Import** menu command. Confirm that the editor has constructed the menu command ID **ID_DATA_IMPORT**.

6. Repeat the process just outlined to add the commands listed in Table 4.3 below the **Import** command on the **Data** menu.

Table 4.3   Data Menu Commands

Caption	Prompt	ID (Generated by editor)
&Upload\tCTRL+U	Upload data to central database\nUpload Data	ID_DATA_UPLOAD
&Query Database...\tCTRL+Q	Query the central database\nQuery Database	ID_DATA_QUERYDATABASE

Recall that the application loads text files that contain data from a number of different funds, and that the user should be able to select which fund to view. In a subsequent exercise, you will be implementing a Select Fund window—a modeless dialog box that contains a list of funds from which the user can select. In this exercise, you will create a menu command to allow the user to show or hide the Select Fund window. You will create this command on the **View** menu because this command is similar in function to the standard **Toolbar** and **Status Bar** options provided for the **View** menu by default.

► **To add the Select Fund command to the View menu**

1. Select the **View** menu title.

2. Drag the empty command at the bottom of the menu to the top of the menu, above the **Toolbar** command.

3. Type the caption and prompt as indicated in Table 4.4.

Table 4.4   Select Fund Caption and Prompt ID

Caption	Prompt	ID (Generated by editor)
&FundSelection	View Select Fund window\nFund Selection	ID_VIEW_FUNDSELECTION

Adding New Shortcut Keys

You will now add shortcut keys for your new menu commands.

► **To define shortcut keys**

1. In ResourceView, expand the Accelerator folder.
2. Double-click the IDR_MAINFRAME accelerator resource to open the accelerator editor.
3. Double-click the blank entry at the bottom of the list of accelerator entries. The **Accelerator Properties** property page should appear.
4. In the **ID** list, click **ID_DATA_IMPORT**.
5. Type **I** in the **Key** box and select the **Ctrl** modifier check box. Clear the **Shift** check box if it is selected.
6. Close the property page. The accelerator is added to the table.
7. Repeat this process to add the two shortcut keys in Table 4.5.

Table 4.5   Accelerator Table Entries

ID	Shortcut Key
ID_DATA_UPLOAD	CTRL+U
ID_DATA_QUERYDATABASE	CTRL+Q

Editing the STUpload Application Toolbar

If you open the **IDR_MAINFRAME** toolbar resource for the STUpload application, you will see that we have supplied a new toolbar bitmap for your use. The bitmap contains icons for the **Import**, **Upload**, and **Query Database** commands. The new toolbar is illustrated in Figure 4.14.

Figure 4.14   The STUpload application toolbar

Your next task will be to associate the toolbar buttons with the command IDs that you created for the new menu commands.

▶ **To associate a toolbar button with a command ID**

1. In ResourceView, expand the Toolbar folder.
2. Double-click the IDR_MAINFRAME toolbar resource to open the toolbar editor.
3. Click the **Import** toolbar button.
4. Press ENTER to open the **Toolbar Button Properties** dialog box. You will see that the button is still associated with the **ID_EDIT_CUT** ID.
5. In the **ID** list, click **ID_DATA_IMPORT**. This is the ID that was generated when you created the **Import** menu command.
6. Click the thumbtack icon to keep the **Properties** dialog box open. Following the procedure just outlined, change the command IDs of the other new buttons as specified in Table 4.6.

Table 4.6   Toolbar Button Command IDs

Button	Old ID	New ID
Upload	ID_EDIT_COPY	ID_DATA_UPLOAD
Query	ID_EDIT_PASTE	ID_DATA_QUERYDATABASE
Select Fund	ID_APP_ABOUT	ID_VIEW_FUNDSELECTION

Creating STUpload Application Dialog Boxes

In this portion of the lab, you will be creating two dialog boxes for the STUpload application: the **Conflicting Record** dialog box and the **Select Fund** dialog box.

Conflicting Record Dialog Box

The **Conflicting Record** dialog box will contain a *rich edit* control—an edit control that can display rich text format (RTF) text, and three buttons labeled **Yes**, **No**, and **Abort**. The dialog box will warn the user of conflicting data records during the import process. The edit control will display details of the existing and new records, which have the same fund and date values, but different price values. The user will decide whether to replace the existing record, leave the existing record and discard the new record, or abort the import process altogether.

The **Conflicting Record** dialog box is shown in Figure 4.15. You can use this illustration as a guide when following through this section of the lab.

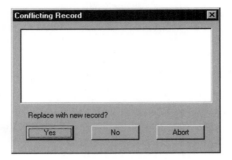

Figure 4.15   The **Conflicting Record** dialog box

► **To create the Conflicting Record dialog box**

1. In ResourceView, expand the STUpload resources folder.
2. Right-click the Dialog folder. Click **Insert Dialog**. A new blank dialog box appears.
3. Resize the dialog box so that it measures 3 inches tall by 4 inches wide.
4. Press ENTER to edit the properties.
5. On the **General** tab, change the dialog resource ID by typing **IDD_CONFLICT_DIALOG** in the **ID** box.
6. In the **Caption** box, type **Conflicting Record**.
7. Change the **OK** button caption to read **Yes**, but do not change the IDOK command ID. Change the **Cancel** button caption to read **No**, but do not change the IDCANCEL command ID.
8. Copy the **Cancel** button to create a new button. Click the new button and type **Abort** to set the caption. In the **ID** list, click **IDABORT**. Close the **Properties** dialog box.
9. Reorganize the buttons so that they appear as in Figure 4.15.

► **To add a static text control to the dialog box**

1. Locate and click the **Static Text** drawing tool.
2. Just above the **Yes** button, draw a static text box that extends across the dialog box but is no deeper than a single line of text.
3. With the static text box selected, type **Replace with new record?**
4. Close the **Text Properties** dialog box that has appeared. Using Figure 4.15 as a guide, ensure that the text item is in an appropriate position and the text displays fully.

▶ **To add a rich edit control to the dialog box**

1. Using the ToolTips feature, click the **Rich Edit** tool on the **Controls** toolbar. Do not confuse this with the regular Edit Box tool.

2. With the crosshair pointer, draw a rich edit control box as shown in Figure 4.15. This should be as wide as the dashed drawing guides in the editor and deep enough to take six lines of text.

3. Press ENTER to edit the properties.

4. On the **General** tab, change the control ID by typing **IDC_CONFLICT_ RICHEDIT** in the **ID** box.

5. On the **Styles** tab, select the **Multiline** and **Read Only** check boxes.

6. Close the **Rich Edit Properties** dialog box.

7. From the **Layout** menu of the Visual Studio main window, click **Tab Order**.

8. Click first on the **Yes** button, then on the **No** button, and then on the **Abort** button to set the tab order.

9. Press CTRL+T to test the operation of the dialog box.

Select Fund Window

As mentioned in the *Editing the STUpload Application Menu* section earlier in this lab, the Select Fund window will be implemented as a modeless dialog box. This dialog box will contain a list box control that allows the user to select from all the fund names currently loaded into the application.

The **Select Fund** dialog box is shown in Figure 4.16.

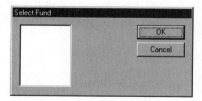

Figure 4.16   The **Select Fund** dialog box

▶ **To create the Select Fund dialog box**

1. In ResourceView, right-click the Dialog folder.

2. Click **Insert Dialog**. A new blank dialog box appears. Use the center bottom resize handle to shrink the height of the dialog box to about 1.75 inches.

3. Press ENTER to edit the properties.

4. Type **IDD_FUNDDIALOG** in the **ID** text box.

5. Type **Select Fund** in the **Caption** text box.

6. On the **Styles** tab, clear the **System menu** check box.

7. On the **Extended Styles** tab, select the **Tool window** check box.

8. Close the **Dialog Properties** sheet.

▶ **To add a list box control**

1. Click **List Box** on the **Controls** toolbar.

2. Use the crosshair pointer to draw a list box to fit the height of the drawing guides. The list box should be about 1 inch wide, as shown in Figure 4.14.

3. Press ENTER to edit the properties.

4. On the **General** tab, type **IDC_FUNDLIST** in the **ID** box.

5. Close the list box property sheet.

You will now add dialog classes for your **Conflicting Record** and **Select Fund** dialog boxes. In Lesson 2 of this chapter, you learned that you could create dialog classes automatically by invoking ClassWizard from within the dialog editor. In the following exercises, you will use ClassWizard to create the class without having the dialog editor open. This will demonstrate how ClassWizard automates the creation of *any* class that is derived from an MFC class.

▶ **To create the dialog classes**

1. On the **Window** menu, click **Close All**.

2. On the **ClassView** tab, press CTRL+W to open ClassWizard.

3. Click **Add Class**. Select **New** from the pop-up menu.

4. The **New Class** dialog box appears as shown in Figure 4.17.

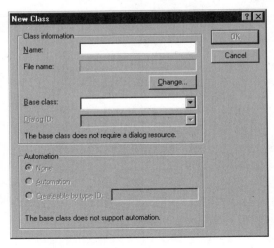

Figure 4.17   The **New Class** dialog box

5. In the **Name** box, type **CConflictDialog**.

6. In the **Base Class** list, click **CDialog**. Note that you can derive your class from any MFC class. Note, too, that the selection of the **CDialog** class enables the **Dialog ID** list box.

7. In the **Dialog ID** list, click **IDD_CONFLICT_DIALOG**.

8. Click **OK** to create the new class.

9. Repeat the procedure to add a dialog class for the **Select Fund** dialog box. The class name should be **CFundDialog**, the class should be derived from the **CDialog** class, and the class should be based on the **IDD_FUNDDIALOG** dialog ID.

10. Click **OK** to close ClassWizard. Note that the new classes have been added to the **MyApp classes** tree.

Using Common Dialog Boxes

In the final part of this lab, you will learn how to use a Windows common file dialog box by creating an instance of the MFC class **CFileDialog**. The **Import** command of the STUpload application is used to locate and open a text file to import into the application. You will create a handler for the **Import** command that will (for now) simply display a Windows common file dialog box with the file type filter set to show only files with a .dat extension. Because the task of the handler function is to load the application data, you will create the function as a member of the application's document object **CSTUploadDoc**.

▶ **To create the Import command handler function**

1. Press CTRL+W to open ClassWizard.

2. In the **Class Name** list, click **CSTUpload**.

3. In the **Object IDs** list, click **ID_DATA_IMPORT**.

4. In the **Messages** list, click **COMMAND**.

5. Click **Add Function**, and then click **OK** to accept the name **OnDataImport**.

▶ **To implement the OnDataImport() function**

1. Click **Edit Code** to edit the function implementation.

2. In Windows Explorer, locate the \Chapter 4\Code folder on the companion CD.

3. Double-click the CH4_01.cpp file to edit it in Visual C++. The file contains the following code:

```
// String to customize File Dialog
CString strFilter = Data Files (*.dat)|*.dat|All Files (*.*)|*.*||";
CFileDialog aFileDialog(TRUE, NULL, NULL,
    OFN_HIDEREADONLY | OFN_OVERWRITEPROMPT, strFilter);
int nID = aFileDialog.DoModal();
```

This code creates an object of the MFC class **CFileDialog**. The filter string passed to the constructor specifies that the Windows common file dialog box will be created with a filter set to show only files with a .dat extension, although the user will also be able to select the "all files" *.* filter. The dialog box is activated by a call to the base class method **CDialog::DoModal()**.

4. Select all the text in the CH4_01.cpp file and press CTRL+C to copy the code to the clipboard. Close the CH4_01.cpp file.

5. Return to the implementation of the **OnDataImport()** function. Select the entire // TODO comment line.

6. Press CTRL+V to replace this line with the code on the clipboard.

You can now build and run the STUpload application. Test the menu and toolbar prompt and ToolTip features. Click **Import** on the **Data** menu to ensure that the common file dialog box appears as expected. You can browse to find the file Ch4Test.dat in the \Chapter 4\Data folder on the companion CD. You will provide further implementation of the **Import** command in Lab 5.

You will not be able to see the dialog boxes that you have created at this point. Although you have created templates and classes for them, you have not yet created instances of those classes within your application code. We will create these instances in Lab 5.

Review

1. Which icons should you supply for an application that meets the Windows 98/Windows NT logo requirements?

2. How do you implement ToolTip text for your toolbar buttons?

3. How can you dynamically change the text of a menu command from within your application code?

4. What is the recommended way to update a status bar indicator?

5. How would you make an edit control in a dialog box read-only? Why might you want to do this?

6. You have created a dialog box template using the dialog editor. How would you display a modal dialog box, based on this template, in your application?

C H A P T E R   5

Implementing Application Behaviors

About This Chapter

In Chapter 4, you learned how you could use features of the Microsoft Visual C++ programming environment to construct a user interface for your application without writing more than a few lines of code. One of the advantages of a visual programming environment is that you can quickly and easily implement the user interface you have designed.

In this chapter, you will learn about some MFC programming techniques you can use to implement the operational behavior of an application. You will learn how to use of the dialog box classes that you constructed in Chapter 4 and how to take advantage of the multithreading capabilities of the Win32 platform. You will also learn more about the techniques used to send application data to an on-screen window or a printer, and how to implement Help for an MFC application.

Before You Begin

Before you start this chapter, you should have read Chapters 2 through 4, and completed the exercises in the text.

Lesson 1: Working with Dialog Boxes

In Lesson 2 of Chapter 4, you learned how to create a dialog class, based on a dialog template, that could be used to display a dialog box within your application. In this lesson, you will learn how to work with the dialog class in your application code. You will pass data between the dialog box controls and your application, which will process messages that originate from the controls. You will also learn how to implement dialog templates as pages in a property sheet.

After this lesson, you will be able to:

- Describe how to implement dialog data exchange and dialog data validation.
- Use ClassWizard to add member variables to represent dialog data.
- Use ClassWizard to add a function that handles a message from a dialog box control.
- Describe how to implement a property sheet.

Estimated lesson time: 60 minutes

Dialog Data Exchange and Validation

Dialog data exchange (DDX) is an easy way to initialize the controls in your dialog box and to gather data input by the user. Dialog data validation (DDV) provides an easy way to validate data entry in a dialog box.

DDX and DDV are implemented within the dialog class and use a code architecture similar to the message map architecture you saw in Chapter 3. Member variables within the dialog class correspond to the controls in your dialog template. Global MFC functions are used to transfer data between the member variables and the controls and to validate data input by the user.

When ClassWizard creates a dialog class, it adds code to the class to implement the basic DDX/DDV architecture. You can then use ClassWizard to add to the dialog class member variables that correspond to controls in your dialog template, and to specify simple validation rules for the data that is entered into the controls.

When you use ClassWizard to add DDX member variables, ClassWizard performs the following tasks for you:

- The member variables are added to the class definition.
- The member variables are initialized in the class constructor.
- DDX functions are added to the class to handle the transfer of data between the DDX member variables and the dialog box controls.

- If you use ClassWizard to specify validation criteria for your variables, DDV functions are added to the class to validate the data input by the user to the dialog box controls before saving that data to the DDX member variables.

The DDX and DDV functions are global MFC functions that are provided to perform the task of transferring data between controls and dialog class variables (DDX functions), and to validate data (DDV functions). MFC defines a number of DDX functions to correspond to the various types of common controls. The most commonly used functions are **DDX_Text()**, which transfers data between an edit control and a CString member variable of the dialog class; and **DDX_Check()**, which transfers the select state of a check box control to or from a BOOL member variable of the dialog class. MFC defines a number of DDV functions to correspond to the kinds of validation that you might want to apply to string or numeric values. Example functions are **DDV_MaxChars()** and **DDV_MinMaxInt()**. You can find a complete list of these functions by going to the **Index** tab of the Visual C++ Help file and typing **DDX_** (or **DDV_**) in the **Keyword** box.

Typically, you will define a member variable (and thus a DDX function) for every control in your dialog box that accepts user input to set its data content or its state. You need to specify validation only where it is necessary to control the range of the input data.

The following exercise shows you how to use ClassWizard to add DDX member variables and to specify validation criteria.

▶ **To add DDX member variables using ClassWizard**

1. Return to the MyApp project.
2. Press CTRL+W to open ClassWizard. Click the **Member Variables** tab.
3. In the **Class name** box, click the **CConnectDialog** class.
4. In the **Control IDs** box, click **IDC_USERID**.
5. Click **Add Variable**. The **Add Member Variable** dialog box appears.
6. In the **Member variable name** box, type **m_strUserID**.
7. Make sure that the **Category** box shows **Value** and the **Variable type** box shows **CString**.
8. Click **OK** to add the variable. The variable name and type will appear selected in the **Control IDs** box next to the IDC_USERID. This variable will be used to set the text that appears in the User ID edit control and retrieve the text entered into the control by the user.
9. Beneath the **Control IDs** list box is the **Maximum Characters** edit box. Type **15** to create a validation function that will limit the length of the input string to 15 characters.

10. Repeat the above process to add a CString value variable named
   m_strPassword, with a maximum length of 15 characters, that is associated
   with the **IDC_PASSWORD** control ID.

11. Add an **int** value variable named **m_nAccess**, which is associated with the
   IDC_ACCESS control ID. Note that for an integer variable you are able to
   specify the minimum and maximum values that can be input. In the **Minimum value** box, type **1**, and in the **Maximum value** box, type **5**.

12. Add a BOOL value variable named **m_bConnect**, which is associated with the
   IDC_CHECKCONNECT control ID. This will set the control state to selected
   (TRUE) or cleared (FALSE), and retrieve the control state set by the user.

13. Click **OK** to close ClassWizard. You can now build and run the MyApp application.

14. Choose the **Connect** command from the **Data** menu and type a username
   and password. See how the validation rule that you specified in step 9 makes
   it impossible to enter more than 15 characters for a user name. To achieve
   this behavior, the **DDV_MaxChars()** function sends a EM_LIMITTEXT
   message to the control as it is initialized. This method of validation is more
   immediate and user-friendly than the alternative method of checking the
   value in the field after the user has clicked **OK** (or **Connect** in our case).

15. As an example of the usual form of validation, type **6** in the **Access level** edit
   box and click **Connect**. The validation function that has been assigned to this
   field should display a message box warning you of the invalid value, and return you to the offending control. In a real-world application, you would
   probably implement the access level selection as a combo box with a limited
   set of values from which the user could select one—thus eliminating the need
   for a validation function.

16. Click **Cancel** to close the dialog box.

How ClassWizard Implements Dialog Data Exchange and Validation

To see the code that ClassWizard has added to implement the DDX/DDV architecture, open the ConnectDialog.h file and inspect the class declaration. You will
see that ClassWizard has added the following member variables:

```
//{{AFX_DATA(CConnectDialog)
enum {IDD = IDD_CONNECTDIALOG};
CString m_strUserID;
CString m_strPassword;
BOOL    m_bConnect;
int     m_nAccess;
//}}AFX_DATA
```

Like all code maintained by ClassWizard, these declarations are enclosed within a special //{{AFX_ comment block.

Locate the class constructor in the ConnectDialog.cpp file, which contains the following ClassWizard code to provide default initialization for the variables:

```
//{{AFX_DATA_INIT(CConnectDialog)
m_strUserID = _T("");
m_strPassword = _T("");
m_bConnect = FALSE;
m_nAccess = 0;
//}}AFX_DATA_INIT
```

The function that actually does the work of passing data between the dialog box controls and the application is **CWnd::DoDataExchange()**. An overloaded version of this function is automatically provided for you when you use ClassWizard to derive a class from **CDialog**. ClassWizard updates the overloaded **DoDataExchange()** function by adding DDX and DDV functions.

Your **CConnectDialog::DoDataExchange()** function can be found in the ConnectDialog.cpp file, and at present it should look as follows:

```
void CConnectDialog::DoDataExchange(CDataExchange* pDX)
{
    CDialog::DoDataExchange(pDX);
    //{{AFX_DATA_MAP(CConnectDialog)
    DDX_Text(pDX, IDC_USERID, m_strUserID);
    DDV_MaxChars(pDX, m_strUserID, 15);
    DDX_Text(pDX, IDC_PASSWORD, m_strPassword);
    DDV_MaxChars(pDX, m_strPassword, 15);
    DDX_Check(pDX, IDC_CHECKCONNECT, m_bConnect);
    DDX_Text(pDX, IDC_ACCESS, m_nAccess);
    DDV_MinMaxInt(pDX, m_nAccess, 1, 5);
    //}}AFX_DATA_MAP
}
```

The *pDX* parameter that is passed to the DDX and DDV functions is an object of the MFC class **CDataExchange**, which represents the context of the current data exchange. The **CDataExchange** class contains a member variable m_bSaveAndValidate, which indicates the direction of the data exchange. If m_bSaveAndValidate is TRUE, then data is being passed from the controls to be validated and stored in the dialog class member variables. If m_bSaveAndValidate is FALSE, data is being passed to the onscreen dialog box to initialize the controls.

Dialog Data Exchange and Validation Process

The **DoDataExchange()** function is called by the **CWnd::UpdateData()** function. **UpdateData()** creates the **CDataExchange** object that **DoDataExchange()** receives as a parameter and passes to the DDX/DDV functions.

The **UpdateData()** function takes a single BOOL parameter that indicates the direction of the data exchange. The **CDialog::OnInitDialog()** function, which is called when a dialog box is created, calls the **UpdateData()** function with a *FALSE* parameter to initialize the controls in the dialog box with the values held in the dialog class member variables. When a user clicks **OK** in a dialog box, the default **CDialog::OnOK()** handler calls the **UpdateData()** function with a *TRUE* parameter to perform any data validation and to save the values in the controls to the dialog class. The process is illustrated in Figure 5.1.

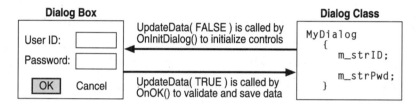

Figure 5.1   Dialog data exchange and validation

Your code might call **CWnd::UpdateData()** at any time to perform data exchange and validation. For example, suppose you have an image viewing application that allows the user to alter the image resolution and color depth with controls in a modeless dialog box. The updated image is displayed as soon as the user changes the values in the controls. In such a case, you might call **UpdateData()** every time the settings are changed so that they would be saved by the dialog class, and thus made accessible to the application drawing functions.

▶ **To set initial values for dialog box controls**

1. Return to the MyApp project.
2. On the **ClassView** tab, expand the **CMyAppApp** class icon.
3. Double-click the **OnDataConnect()** icon to edit the function.
4. Between the declaration of the **CConnectDialog** object and the call to the **DoModal()** function, add the following lines of code:

```
aCD.m_nAccess = 1;
aCD.m_bConnect = TRUE;
```

The complete function should now look as follows:

```
void CMyAppApp::OnDataConnect()
{
    CConnectDialog aCD;
    aCD.m_nAccess = 1;
    aCD.m_bConnect = TRUE;
    aCD.DoModal();
}
```

5. Build and run the MyApp application. On the **Data** menu, click **Connect**. Confirm that the values you assigned to the member variables of the dialog object are displayed in the dialog box controls.

▶ **To set the values of dialog box controls**

1. Return to the **OnDataConnect()** function.

2. Remove the following line:

```
aCD.DoModal();
```

3. In its place, add the following code:

```
if(aCD.DoModal() == IDOK)
{
    CString strMessage;
    strMessage.Format("User %s logged in", aCD.m_strUserID);
    AfxMessageBox(strMessage);
}
```

An IDOK return value from the **DoModal()** function signifies that the user has clicked the **OK** button to close the dialog box and that the data entered into the controls has passed the associated validation functions. The data entered by the user is stored in the dialog class's DDX member variables—in our case, the value entered into the **User ID** edit control is now contained in the CConnectDialog::m_strUserID variable.

4. Build and run the MyApp application and test the **Connect** command on the **Data** menu to ensure that the User ID value that you entered is displayed in the message box.

Custom Dialog Data Exchange and Validation

You can define your own DDX and DDV functions. DDX functions take the pointer to a **CDataExchange** object, the ID of the dialog box control, and the dialog class member variable as parameters. DDV functions also take the pointer to a **CDataExchange** object and the dialog class member variable. They might also specify extra parameters to set the validation constraints, just as **DDV_MinMaxInt()** takes parameters to specify the minimum and maximum values. DDV functions must *always* be placed directly after the DDX functions to which they refer. For more information on creating custom DDX/DDV functions, refer to the Technical Note "TN026: DDX and DDV Functions" in the Visual C++ Help file.

You might also need to add your own DDV functions if you want to set validation parameters by using variable, rather than constant, values; or if you want to perform conditional validation. As an example, consider the following code. It applies a different validation function according to whether or not the IDC_FEMALE check box control is selected. The maximum age for females and males is passed as a variable.

```
//{{AFX_DATA_MAP(CMyClass)
DDX_Check(pDX, IDC_FEMALE, m_bFemale);
DDX_Text(pDX, IDC_EDIT1, m_age);
//}}AFX_DATA_MAP
if (m_bFemale)
    DDV_MinMax(pDX, m_age, 0, m_maxFemaleAge);
else
    DDV_MinMax(pDX, m_age, 0, m_maxMaleAge);
```

This code sample also illustrates the important point that all custom DDX/DDV functions must be placed *outside* the //{{AFX_ comment block that delimits code maintained by ClassWizard.

In the following exercise, you will add a custom validation function that will require the user to enter a value for the **UserID** field.

▶ **To add custom validation to the MyApp application**

1. Add the following global function declaration to the ConnectDialog.h file, *outside* the **CConnectDialog** class defintion:

```
void PASCAL DDV_Required(CDataExchange * pDX, CString str);
```

2. Add the **DDV_Required()** function definition as follows to the bottom of the ConnectDialog.cpp file:

```
void PASCAL DDV_Required(CDataExchange * pDX, CString str)
{
    if(pDX->m_bSaveAndValidate && str.IsEmpty())
    {
        AfxMessageBox("Please enter the User ID.");
        pDX->Fail();
    }
}
```

Note how the CDataExchange::m_bSaveAndValidate member variable is queried to affirm that data validation is taking place. Note, too, how the function **CDataExchange::Fail()** is used to abandon the validation process and restore the focus to the control that has failed the validation.

3. Locate the **CConnectDialog::DoDataExchange()** function implementation in the ConnectDialog.cpp file. Select the following two lines:

```
DDX_Text(pDX, IDC_USERID, m_strUserID);
DDV_MaxChars(pDX, m_strUserID, 15);
```

4. Press CTRL+X to remove these two lines from their current position in the //{{AFX_DATA_MAP comment block and place them on the Clipboard.

5. Use CTRL+V to paste the two lines to a new location beneath the //{{AFX_DATA_MAP comment block, but still inside the **DoDataExchange()** function.

6. Immediately following these two lines, add the following line to call your new **DDV_Required()** function:

```
DDV_Required(pDX, m_strUserID);
```

Your **DoDataExchange()** function should now look as follows:

```
void CConnectDialog::DoDataExchange(CDataExchange* pDX)
{
    CDialog::DoDataExchange(pDX);
    //{{AFX_DATA_MAP(CConnectDialog)
    DDX_Text(pDX, IDC_PASSWORD, m_strPassword);
    DDV_MaxChars(pDX, m_strPassword, 15);
    DDX_Check(pDX, IDC_CHECKCONNECT, m_bConnect);
    DDX_Text(pDX, IDC_ACCESS, m_nAccess);
    DDV_MinMaxInt(pDX, m_nAccess, 1, 5);
    //}}AFX_DATA_MAP

    DDX_Text(pDX, IDC_USERID, m_strUserID);
    DDV_MaxChars(pDX, m_strUserID, 15);
    DDV_Required(pDX, m_strUserID);
}
```

7. Build and run the MyApp application and test the **Connect** command on the **Data** menu. See what happens if you try to click the **Connect** button without entering a User ID.

Using OnInitDialog() to Initialize Controls

Certain types of controls require more than the standard initialization provided by the MFC-supplied DDX functions, or more than can be easily achieved by writing a custom DDX function. An example is the **Connect to Data Source** dialog box in the MyApp application, which displays a list of available data sources in a list box control. The data that the list box displays can vary as data sources are added or removed from the system. MFC provides the functions **DDX_LBIndex** and **DDX_LBString** so that you can set the initial selection and retrieve the user selection, but you cannot use these functions to set up the list box items.

The usual way to set up list box items is to provide an overloaded version of the **CDialog::OnInitDialog**() virtual function for your class. **OnInitDialog**() is the function that calls **CWnd::UpdateData**() (and ultimately the DDX/DDV functions) when your dialog class is initialized. **OnInitDialog**() is the appropriate place to perform custom initialization of dialog box controls because it is called after the control windows have been created but before they are displayed.

MFC provides classes to correspond to each of the Windows common controls. Using ClassWizard, you can create objects of these control classes as data members of your dialog class. These objects are associated with the controls in your dialog box by means of a **DDX_Control**() function placed in the **DoDataExchange**() function. You can use these control objects to initialize or update the dialog box controls.

The following exercises show you how to add an object of the MFC class **CListBox** to your dialog class that corresponds to the **Data Source** list box, and how to use the member object to initialize the list and set the initial selection.

▶ **To add a CListBox member variable**

1. Press CTRL+W to open ClassWizard. Click the **Member Variables** tab.
2. In the **Class name** box, click **CConnectDialog**.
3. In the **Control IDs** box, click **IDC_DSNLIST**.
4. Click **Add Variable**. The **Add Member Variable** dialog box appears.
5. In the **Member variable name** box, type **m_lbDSN**.
6. In the **Category** box, click **Control**.
7. Click **OK** to add the variable. The variable name and type will appear selected in the **Control IDs** box next to IDC_DSNLIST.
8. Click **OK** to close ClassWizard.

▶ **To overload the OnInitDialog() function**

1. Press CTRL+W to open ClassWizard. Click the **Message Maps** tab.
2. In the **Class name** box, click **CConnectDialog**.

3. With the **CConnectDialog** class name selected in the **Object IDs** box, click **WM_INITDIALOG** in the **Messages** box.

4. Click the **Add Function** button.

5. Click the **Edit Code** button. Notice that ClassWizard will include a call to the base class where it is necessary. **CDialog::OnInitDialog()** is called so that **CWnd::UpdateData()** will be called to initialize the controls. Replace the // TODO comment in the function implementation with the following code:

```
m_lbDSN.AddString("Accounts");
m_lbDSN.AddString("Admin");
m_lbDSN.AddString("Management");
```

Note how the m_lbDSN variable that you added is used to set up the members of the list box.

You can also use your **CListBox** member object to retrieve the choice made by the user. You can use the **CListBox::GetCurSel()** function to get the zero-based index that indicates the user's selection. You can then pass the index to the **CListBox::GetText()** function to retrieve the item text. In the following exercise, you will retrieve the data source name that the user selects and save it to the CMyAppApp::m_strDSN variable. This variable is used to store the name of the data source displayed on the status bar. The best place to implement this code is in a handler for the **OK** button for your dialog class because users click the **OK** button to indicate that they want to commit their selections. You must be sure to call the default **CDialog::OnOK()** handler as it is this function that calls the **CWnd::UpdateData()** function.

▶ **To retrieve the user list box choice**

1. Press CTRL+W to open ClassWizard. Click the **Message Maps** tab.

2. In the **Class name** box, click **CConnectDialog**.

3. In the **Object IDs** box, click **IDOK**. In the **Messages** box, click **BN_CLICKED**.

4. Click the **Add Function** button. Accept **OnOK** as the name for the function.

5. Click the **Edit Code** button. Replace the // TODO comment in the function implementation with the following code:

```
CMyAppApp * pApp = dynamic_cast<CMyAppApp *>(AfxGetApp());
ASSERT_VALID(pApp);
int nChoice = m_lbDSN.GetCurSel();

if(nChoice != LB_ERR)
{
    m_lbDSN.GetText(nChoice, pApp->m_strDSN);
    pApp->m_isDatabaseConnected = TRUE;
}
```

You can now build and run the MyApp application. Test your dialog box to ensure that the list box choices appear correctly. Select a data source name and click **OK**. The data source name that you choose should appear in the status bar pane.

Handling a Control Message

The **OnOK()** function that you have just implemented is an example of a control notification message handler. Recall from Lesson 3 of Chapter 3 that control notification messages are sent by controls and other child windows to notify the parent window of an interaction between the user and the control. The **OnOK()** function handles the BN_CLICKED message that is sent to the dialog box window (as a parameter to a WM_COMMAND message) when the user clicks the **OK** button once.

Different sets of notification messages are associated with the different types of controls. The **Message Maps** tab of ClassWizard provides a convenient quick-reference for the notification messages associated with any control that is placed in your dialog box. If you select your dialog class in the **Class Name** box and click on the control ID in the **Object IDs** box, the set of notification messages that can be generated by the control will appear in the **Messages** box. Selecting one of these message IDs will cause a brief explanation of the message to appear in the **Description** field at the bottom of the property page.

Figure 5.2 shows the **Message Maps** tab of the **MFC ClassWizard** dialog box and the list of control notification messages that it supports for an edit control (in this case, **IDC_USERID**).

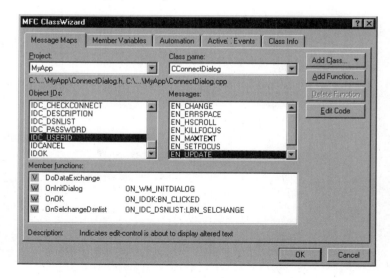

Figure 5.2   Using ClassWizard to handle control notification messages

For more detailed documentation about control notification messages, you can search for the message IDs in the Visual C++ Help index. Control notification message IDs are prefixed by an abbreviation of the control type followed by *N_*, as illustrated in Table 5.1.

Table 5.1   Control Notification Message ID Prefixes

Notification message ID prefix	Control type
BN_	Button
CBN_	Combo box
CLBN_	Check list box
EN_	Edit control
LBN_	List box
STN_	Static text control

ClassWizard will insert entry macros into the message map to handle notification messages from each of these control types. These macros are constructed by prefixing the message ID with *ON_*. For example, if you use ClassWizard to create a handler for the EN_UPDATE notification message from the IDC_USERID edit control (as illustrated by Figure 5.2), ClassWizard will insert a message map entry similar to the following:

```
ON_EN_UPDATE(IDC_USERID, OnUpdateUserid)
```

Note BN_CLICKED notification messages for the **IDOK** and **IDCANCEL** buttons will be mapped directly to overridden versions of the **CDialog::OnOK()** and **CDialog::OnCancel()** virtual functions. Message map entry macros are not used unless you specify the name of a different function to handle the messages. In most cases, you should use the **OnOK** and **OnCancel** functions.

MFC provides the generic **ON_CONTROL** and **ON_NOTIFY** macros to allow for the handling of custom messages. ClassWizard uses the **ON_NOTIFY** macro for notifications from the newer common controls that became available with Windows NT and Windows 95/98.

In the following exercise, you will add a handler function for the notification message that is sent when the user changes the selection in the **Data Source** box. You will use the handler function to display Help text for the current selection in the read-only edit control beneath the list box. First, you will need to create a CEdit variable to represent the edit control in your code.

▶ **To add a CListBox member variable**

1. Press CTRL+W to open ClassWizard. Click the **Member Variables** tab.

2. In the **Class name** box, click **CConnectDialog**.

3. In the **Control IDs** box, click **IDC_DESCRIPTION**. Click **Add Variable**.

4. In the **Member variable name** box, type **m_editDesc**.

5. In the **Category** box, click **Control**. Click **OK** to add the variable.

6. Click **OK** to close ClassWizard.

▶ **To add the OnSelChangeDsnlist() control notification message handler**

1. Press CTRL+W to open ClassWizard. Click the **Message Maps** tab.

2. In the **Object IDs** box, click **IDC_DSNLIST**. In the **Messages** box, click **LBN_SELCHANGE**.

3. Click **Add Function**. Accept **OnSelchangeDsnlist** as the name for the function.

4. Click **Edit Code**. Replace the // TODO comment in the function implementation with the following code:

```
int nCursel = m_lbDSN.GetCurSel();

switch(nCursel)
{
    case 0 : m_editDesc.SetWindowText("Accounting Data");
        break;

    case 1 : m_editDesc.SetWindowText("Administration Data");
        break;

    case 2 : m_editDesc.SetWindowText("Management Data");
        break;
}
```

Note the use of the **CWnd::SetWindowText()** function to set the text in the edit control.

5. Build and run the MyApp application. Test the **Connect to Data Source** dialog box to ensure that the description text changes as you select different items in the **Data Source** box.

Enabling and Disabling Controls

In our discussion of user interface design in Lesson 1 of Chapter 4, we stated that menu and toolbar commands that were not able to perform their function should not be available for selection. The same applies to dialog box controls.

The **Connect to Data Source** dialog box currently allows the user to attempt to connect to a data source even if no data source is currently selected and no logon ID has been supplied. Rather than use validation functions to handle this situation, it would be better to ensure that the **Connect** button is not available until sufficient information has been provided. The following exercise shows you how to use the **CWnd::EnableWindow()** function to make a control available or unavailable, and how control notification handler functions can be used to update the status of a control as the dialog box data is amended by the user.

▶ **To enable or disable the Connect button**

1. On the **Member Variables** tab of ClassWizard, click the **IDOK** control ID for the **CConnectDialog** class. Add a CButton member variable called **m_bnConnect**.

2. On the **Member Variables** tab of ClassWizard, click the **IDC_USERID** control ID for the **CConnectDialog** class. Add a CEdit control member variable called **m_editUserID**. Click **OK** to close ClassWizard.

3. To the bottom of the **CConnectDialog::OnSelchangeDsnlist()** function, just before the final closing brace, add the following lines of code to make the **Connect** button available when a data source is selected and a User ID value has been supplied. (**CWnd::GetWindowText()** returns the number of characters copied.)

```
char tempbuf[8];
if(m_editUserID.GetWindowText(tempbuf, 7))
    m_bnConnect.EnableWindow(TRUE);
```

4. On the **Message Maps** tab of ClassWizard, select the **IDC_USERID** control ID for the **CConnectDialog** class. Select the **EN_UPDATE** message and add the **OnUpdateUserid()** control notification function. Click **Edit Code** to edit the function implementation.

5. Add the following lines of code to the **OnUpdateUserid()** function:

```
char tempbuf[8];
if(m_lbDSN.GetCurSel() != LB_ERR)
{
    if(m_editUserID.GetWindowText(tempbuf, 7))
        m_bnConnect.EnableWindow(TRUE);
    else
        m_bnConnect.EnableWindow(FALSE);
}
```

6. To the bottom of the **CConnectDialog::OnInitDialog()** function, just before the return statement, add the following line of code to ensure that the **Connect** button appears correctly when the dialog box is first displayed:

```
OnUpdateUserid();
```

7. As the validation function for this field is no longer necessary, remove the **DDV_Required()** function from the ConnectDialog.cpp file, along with its declaration in the ConnectDialog.h file. Remove the call to **DDV_Required()** from the **CConnectDialog::DoDataExchange()** function in the ConnectDialog.cpp file. Move the following lines back within the

scope of the //{{AFX_DATA_MAP comment block to make them maintainable by ClassWizard (making sure that they are kept together):

```
DDX_Text(pDX, IDC_USERID, m_strUserID);
DDV_MaxChars(pDX, m_strUserID, 15);
```

8. Build and run the MyApp application. Test the **Connect to Data Source** dialog box to ensure that the **Connect** button is available only when a data source is selected and an entry is in the **UserID** edit field.

Using a Dialog Box to Edit Application Data

In this practice exercise, you will add some member variables to the MyApp application's document class. Remember that in an MFC application, the document class is the proper container for the application data. You will create a dialog box where you can edit the values of the application data variables. You should complete this practice before you proceed, as it lays the foundation for examples and practices in this and subsequent chapters.

▶ **To add application data variables**

1. Open the MyApp project. In ClassView, right-click the **CMyAppDoc** class and click **Add Member Variable**. Add a public int variable named **m_nLines**.

2. Double-click the **CMyAppDoc** constructor to edit the code.

3. Initialize the m_nLines variable with a value of **20**. Assign a string of 60 characters to the m_string variable so that the constructor looks something like this:

```
CMyAppDoc::CMyAppDoc()
{
    m_nLines = 20;
    m_string =
        "This is a very long string designed to take up lots of space";
}
```

4. Using the menu editor, add a new command to the top of the **Data** menu. This command should have the caption **&Edit** and the prompt string should be "Edit document data." Accept the **ID_DATA_EDIT** ID that is created by default.

5. Use the dialog editor to create a new dialog template with a resource ID of **IDD_EDITDATA**. The dialog box should be titled **Edit Document Data** and contain two static text items with the captions **Line text:** and **Number of lines:**, which correspond to the edit controls IDC_EDIT_LINETEXT and IDC_EDIT_NUMLINES. The controls should be arranged as illustrated in

Figure 5.3. For the IDC_EDIT_NUMLINES control, select the **Number** checkbox on the **Styles** property page.

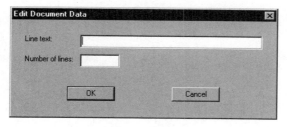

Figure 5.3   The **Edit Document Data** dialog box

6. Use ClassWizard to create a dialog class for the **IDD_EDITDATA** dialog box. The class should be called **CEditDataDialog,** and be derived from the **CDialog** class. Add two value member variables to correspond to the edit controls: a CString variable named **m_strLineText** and a UINT variable named **m_nLines**.

7. Add the following line of code to the top of the MyAppDoc.cpp file with the rest of the #include statements:

```
#include "EditDataDialog.h"
```

8. Use ClassWizard to add a handler function **OnDataEdit()** for the **ID_DATA_EDIT** object ID. The function should handle the COMMAND message and be added to the **CMyAppDoc** class.

9. Add the following code to the body of the **OnDataEdit()** function:

```
CEditDataDialog aDlg;

aDlg.m_nLines = m_nLines;
aDlg.m_strLineText = m_string;

if(aDlg.DoModal())
{
    m_nLines = aDlg.m_nLines;
    m_string = aDlg.m_strLineText;
    UpdateAllViews(NULL);
}
```

10. Build and run the MyApp application. Click **Edit** on the **Data** menu to check that the **Edit Document Data** dialog box appears correctly.

Implementing Property Sheets

In Chapter 4, you learned that a property sheet is a special kind of dialog box that is generally used to modify the attributes of an object, such as the application or the current selection in a view. The property sheet has three main parts: the containing dialog box, one or more property pages shown one at a time, and a tab at the top of each page that the user clicks to select a page. Property sheets are useful for situations in which you have a number of similar groups of settings or options to change. A property sheet allows a large amount of information to be grouped in an easily understood fashion. A good example of a property sheet is the **Project Settings** dialog box in the Visual C++ development environment.

MFC implements property sheets through two classes: the **CPropertySheet** class, which represents the containing dialog box; and the **CPropertyPage** class, which represents the individual pages of the property sheet. The procedure to create a property sheet using these classes is as follows:

1. Create a dialog template resource for each property page. These need not be all the same size, but try as much as possible to maintain a consistent layout for each page to make the property sheet intuitive and easy to use. Dialog template resources for property pages should be created with a **Thin** style border and should have the **Child** and **Disabled** properties set. The caption that you enter will appear on the page tab.

2. Use ClassWizard to create a class derived from **CPropertyPage** corresponding to each property page dialog template.

3. Use ClassWizard to create member variables to hold the values for this property page and set up DDX and DDV functions.

4. Create a **CPropertySheet** object in your source code. Usually, you construct the **CPropertySheet** object in the handler for the command that displays the property sheet. Create one object of each of your property page classes.

5. For each page to be added to the property sheet, call the function **CPropertySheet::AddPage()** and pass the address of each property page as a parameter.

6. Create a modal property sheet with the **CDialog::DoModal()** function, or a modeless property sheet with the **CDialog::Create()** function.

For modal property sheets, the framework supplies **OK**, **Cancel**, and **Apply** buttons by default, and handles DDX and DDV for the controls on each of the property pages. For a modal property sheet, it is generally sufficient to create a temporary object on the stack, add the **CPropertyPage** objects, and call **DoModal()**. If you need to add additional controls to the property sheet, you will need to use ClassWizard to create your own class derived from **CPropertySheet**. This step is necessary for modeless property sheets because the **Create()** function does not add any default controls that could be used to close the property sheet.

For more information on this topic, search for the title "Adding Controls to a Property Sheet" in Visual C++ Help. Be sure to select the **Search titles only** check box at the bottom of the **Search** tab so that only the topic with the desired title is returned.

In the following exercises, you will create the **MyApp Settings** property sheet for the MyApp application. This property sheet, illustrated in Figure 5.4, has two pages. The pages will contain mock controls—you will not work with their data in this exercise.

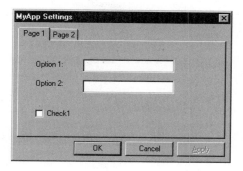

Figure 5.4   The **MyApp Settings** property sheet

► **To create the Page 1 dialog template**

1. In the MyApp project, click **ResourceView** and expand the MyApp resources folder.
2. Right-click the Dialog folder. Click **Insert Dialog**.
3. A new blank dialog box appears. Remove the **OK** and **Cancel** buttons by selecting them and pressing DELETE.
4. Press ENTER to edit the Dialog Properties. In the **ID** box, type **IDD_PPAGE1**. In the **Caption** edit box, type **Page 1**.
5. Click the **Styles** tab. In the **Style** box, click **Child**.
6. In the **Border** box, click **Thin**.
7. Ensure that the **Title bar** check box is selected.
8. Click the **More Styles** tab. Select the **Disabled** check box.
9. Add a few controls to the page—you can use Figure 5.4 as a guide. Include at least one edit control and give it the ID **IDC_EDIT_PP1**.

► **To create the CPage1 class**

1. With the **IDD_PPAGE1** dialog box open in the dialog editor, press CTRL+W to open ClassWizard.
2. Click **OK** to open the **New Class** dialog box.
3. In the **Name** edit box, type **CPage1**.

4. In the **Base Class** box, click **CPropertyPage**.

5. Click **OK** to create the **CPage1** dialog class.

6. Click **OK** to close ClassWizard. Close the dialog editor.

Create a second property page template. To visually distinguish this template from the first, change its size and add different controls. Give this template an ID of **IDD_PPAGE2** and the caption **Page 2**. Make sure that it has the same style settings as the first page. From this template, create the **CPage2** class, derived from **CPropertyPage**.

You will now set up the property sheet to contain the two property pages that you have created. The property sheet will be displayed by means of a new **Settings** command on the **View** menu.

▶ **To create the Settings command to display the property sheet**

1. Using the menu editor, create a new command under the **View** menu title. Type **Setti&ngs** as a caption and **Application settings** as a prompt. Allow the editor to create the ID **ID_VIEW_SETTINGS**. Close the menu editor.

2. Open ClassWizard. To the **CMainFrame** class, add a command handler named **OnViewSettings()** for the **ID_VIEW_SETTINGS** ID.

3. Add the following code to the body of the **OnViewSettings()** function:

```
CPropertySheet PropSheet;
CPage1 pp1;
CPage2 pp2;

PropSheet.AddPage(&pp1);
PropSheet.AddPage(&pp2);

PropSheet.SetTitle("MyApp Settings");
PropSheet.DoModal();
```

4. Add the following code to the top of the CMainFrame.cpp file:

```
#include "Page1.h"
#include "Page2.h"
```

5. Build and run the MyApp application. Click **Settings** on the **View** menu to test the property sheet. Note how the pages are sized to fit the property sheet, and how the captions are used as tab labels. Note, too, how the framework automatically adds an **Apply** button.

Handling the Apply Button on a Property Page

The **OK** button closes the property sheet and exchange and validate data from all the controls on all of the property pages. The **Apply** button, on the other hand, allows users to exchange and validate the changes that they have made without closing the property sheet. This is useful if users want to save the settings made on one page before proceeding to another.

The **Apply** button appears unavailable by default. To make the **Apply** button become available after the user has entered data or changed the state of one of the controls, use a call to **CPropertyPage::SetModified(TRUE)**. Clicking the **Apply** button will call the **CPropertyPage::OnApply()** handler function to perform data exchange and validation without closing the property sheet.

If you decide not to use the **Apply** button on your property pages, you do not have to remove it. Microsoft's design guidelines state that you can leave it available.

The following exercise shows you how to make the **Apply** button available when the user enters data in an edit control.

► **To make the Apply button available**

1. Open ClassWizard and click the **Message Maps** tab. Click **CPage1**.
2. In the **Object IDs** box, click **IDC_EDIT_PP1**. In the **Messages** box, click **EN_UPDATE**.
3. Click **Add Function**. Accept **OnUpdateEditPp1** as the name for the function.
4. Click **Edit Code**. Replace the // TODO comment in the function implementation with the following line of code:

```
SetModified(TRUE);
```

5. Build and run the MyApp application. Type some characters into the edit control that corresponds to the IDC_EDIT_PPI resource. Check that the **Apply** button is available as you type. Click the **Apply** button and note how it is automatically made unavailable.

Lesson Summary

You use DDX to set the initial values displayed by the controls in your application's dialog boxes, and to retrieve the data that the user enters into the controls so that you can use it in your application code. DDV allows you to validate the data input by the user before it is passed to the application. The implementation of DDX and DDV is largely automated by the use of ClassWizard.

Standard DDX functionality is added by using ClassWizard to create a member variable in your dialog class that corresponds to the data entered into the dialog box control. Simple DDV functionality can be added by using ClassWizard to specify simple validation criteria as you create the variable. As you add variables and validation rules, ClassWizard will add calls to predefined MFC global functions to the overloaded **DoDataExchange()** function to perform the tasks of data validation and exchange.

The **DoDataExchange()** function is called by the **CWnd::UpdateData()** function. **UpdateData()** is called by **CDialog::OnInitDialog()** to initialize the controls, and by **CDialog::OnOK()** to retrieve data from the controls and perform validation.

You can extend the DDX/DDV functionality by writing your own custom functions. Custom DDX and DDV functions should be placed outside of the blocks of code that are maintained by ClassWizard. All DDX and DDV functions take a parameter to a **CDataExchange** object, which represents the context of the current data exchange. The **CDataExchange** class includes a member variable m_bSaveAndValidate, which indicates the direction of the data exchange; and the **Fail()** function, which is used to abandon the validation process and restore the focus to the control that has failed the validation.

Control initialization that cannot easily be achieved by a DDX function can be performed by overloading the **CDialog::OnInitDialog()** function in the dialog class. Retrieval of dialog data can also be achieved through an overload of the **CDialog::OnOK()** function.

MFC provides classes to correspond to each of the Windows common controls. Using ClassWizard, you can create objects of these control classes as data members of your dialog class. These objects are associated with the controls in your dialog box by means of a **DDX_Control()** function placed in the **DoDataExchange()** function. You can use these control objects to initialize or update the dialog box controls.

You can use ClassWizard to create functions to handle notification messages that are sent by controls to their parent window (the dialog box). These control notification message handlers are usually implemented as members of the dialog class. A common use of these handler functions is to make controls available or unavailable while the user is interacting with the dialog box.

Property sheets are multi-tabbed dialog boxes that allow information to be grouped in an easily understood fashion. MFC implements property sheets through two classes. The **CPropertySheet** class represents the containing dialog box, and the **CPropertyPage** class represents the individual pages of the property sheet. To implement a property sheet, for each page, or tab, you first create a dialog template, and then you create a dialog class derived from **CPropertyPage**. Create a **CPropertySheet** object in your source code and add each property page object with a call to **CPropertySheet::AddPage()**. Usually you create your **CPropertySheet** object on the stack, in the handler for the command that displays the property sheet.

By default, the framework creates a property sheet with an **Apply** button that is initially unavailable. The **Apply** button allows users to exchange and validate the changes that they have made without closing the property sheet. If you choose to implement the **Apply** button for your application, you should make it become available as soon as the user alters any data in the dialog box controls. You can make the **Apply** button available with a call to **CPropertyPage::SetModified(TRUE)**.

Lesson 2: Displaying and Printing Application Data

In Lesson 4 of Chapter 3, you learned how a class derived from the MFC **CView** class is used to render an image of your application data. You learned how MFC provides a **CDC** class, which encapsulates a device context and a set of drawing functions that operate upon the device context, to render output on a device. You also learned how the framework passes a **CDC**-derived device context object, which corresponds to the current output device, to the **CView::OnDraw()** function. In this way, the **OnDraw()** function provides a centralized location for your application drawing code. The same code is used whether the output target is an application window, a print preview window, or a page on a printing device.

In this lesson, you will learn more about how to use classes derived from **CView** and **CDC**. You will also learn about MFC's drawing tool classes, which you use to send your application's data to the screen or to a printing device.

After this lesson, you will be able to:

- Describe how to set up a logical coordinate system to make your application output appear correctly on any device that conforms to the Windows Graphical Device Interface (GDI).
- Describe the Windows coordinate mapping modes and explain how they are used.
- Describe how to implement scrolling for an MFC application.
- Describe how to use the MFC drawing tool classes to draw in a device context.
- Understand the printing and print preview processes, and how you can implement custom printing functions.

Estimated lesson time: 40 minutes

Before you proceed with this lesson, you will need to modify the application drawing function so that it displays the application data rather than "Hello World!"

► **To modify the OnDraw() function**

1. Locate the implementation of the **CMyAppView::OnDraw()** function. Replace the current implementation with the following code:

```
void CMyAppView::OnDraw(CDC* pDC)
{
    CMyAppDoc* pDoc = GetDocument();
    ASSERT_VALID(pDoc);

    CFont aFont;
    aFont.CreateFont(16, 0, 0, 0, 0, 0, 0, 0, 0, 0, 0, 0,
        FF_ROMAN, 0);
```

```
    CFont * pOldFont = pDC->SelectObject(&aFont);

    CSize TextSize = pDC->GetTextExtent(pDoc->m_string);
    int nLinePos = 10;

    for(int i = 0; i < pDoc->m_nLines; i++)
    {
        pDC->TextOut(10, nLinePos, pDoc->m_string);
        nLinePos += TextSize.cy;
    }

    pDC->SelectObject(pOldFont);
}
```

2. Build and run the MyApp application.

3. On the **Edit** menu, click **Data**.

4. In the **Edit Document Data** dialog box, type a string 60 characters long into the **Line text** edit control, and the number **20** into the **Number of lines** edit control.

5. Click **OK** to close the dialog box. The line of text that you entered should appear 20 times, as shown in Figure 5.5.

Figure 5.5   MyApp application test output

Understanding Coordinate Mapping

Graphical devices render their output across a two-dimensional coordinate system. Screen output is mapped to a pixel grid; printers work with a two-dimensional array of dots on the printed page. The GDI drawing functions that are used by Windows applications specify their output in a similar manner. GDI drawing is measured and scaled in abstract units of measure known as *logical units*.

For example, the following line from our **OnDraw**() function initializes a font object for outputting text into the device context. The font will be created with a height of 16 logical units.

```
aFont.CreateFont(16, 0, 0, 0, 0, 0, 0, 0, 0, 0, 0, 0, FF_ROMAN, 0));
```

The following code moves to the point in the application drawing space with the coordinates (100,200), and draws a horizontal line 200 logical units long to the point (300,200).

```
pDC->MoveTo(100, 200);
pDC->LineTo(300, 200);
```

Logical units have no intrinsic value. It is up to you to specify the actual value, in terms of units of measure on the device, of a logical unit. To provide a standard interface to the many different types of screens, printers, and other output devices that an application might encounter, the GDI implements a coordinate mapping system. You can specify a *mapping mode*, which determines how the logical units of the application drawing space are to be mapped to the drawing space of the hardware device (specified in *device units*). The GDI ensures that the mapping will produce consistent output on whatever hardware device is attached.

The GDI defines a set of eight mapping modes that specify the ratio between logical coordinates and device coordinates. The default mapping mode is identified by the value MM_TEXT. This maps a logical unit to a single pixel on the device, regardless of the device resolution. This can cause problems with printed output, as illustrated by the following exercise.

► **To view the effects of the default MM_TEXT mapping mode**

1. Run the MyApp application.

2. On the **Data** menu, click **Edit**, and type a string of about 60 characters to be displayed 20 times.

3. If you have a printer installed, click **Print** on the **File** menu to print the application data. If you don't have a printer installed, click **Print Preview** on the **File** menu to view the data as it would appear on a printed page.

Notice how the printer output appears extremely small. This is due to the difference in resolution between the screen and printer. The drawing functions are scaling their output in terms of the resolution of the target device. So a character that is 16 pixels high is about 0.21 inches tall on an 800 x 600 monitor. On a 600 x 600 dots per inch printer, it is only about 0.026 inches tall.

MM_TEXT is one of six *fixed* mapping modes, which establish predefined mappings between logical units and device units. Other fixed mapping modes map logical units to units of measure on the device. MM_LOENGLISH for example, specifies that a logical unit will correspond to 0.01 inches on the output device. The fixed mapping modes are shown in Table 5.2.

Table 5.2   Fixed Mapping Modes

Mapping mode	One unit maps to
MM_TEXT	1 device pixel
MM_LOENGLISH	0.01 inch
MM_HIENGLISH	0.001 inch
MM_LOMETRIC	0.1 millimeter
MM_HIMETRIC	0.01 millimeter
MM_TWIPS	1/1440 inch

Note There is no true physical measurement for displays in Windows because a display driver has no knowledge of the actual physical size of the target monitor. Thus the inches and millimeters in the preceding table are really logical values based on the physical size of an idealized monitor. Printer measurements, on the other hand, are physically accurate.

In addition to the fixed mapping modes, you can use one of the unconstrained mapping modes MM_ISOTROPIC or MM_ANISOTROPIC. These modes do not set up a predefined mapping and so require you to specify the ratio between logical units and device units. When the MM_ISOTROPIC mode is set, the GDI will continually adjust the mapping to ensure that one logical unit maps to the same physical distance in both x and y directions. The MM_ANISOTROPIC mode allows the x and y coordinates to be adjusted independently.

To specify the ratio between logical units and device units, you must describe two rectangles that specify the relative dimensions of the logical space (the *window*) and the device space (the *viewport*). Window dimensions are specified in logical units using the **CDC::SetWindowExt()** function. Viewport extents are set using **CDC::SetViewportExt()** and are specified in device units. Information about the current device dimensions can be obtained by using the **CDC::GetDeviceCaps()** function.

The following code sets up a mapping mode similar to MM_LOENGLISH:

```
pDC->SetMapMode(MM_ANISOTROPIC);
pDC->SetViewPortExt(pDC->GetDeviceCaps(LOGPIXELSX),
    pDC->GetDeviceCaps(LOGPIXELSY);
pDC->SetWindowExt(100, -100);
```

The *LOGPIXELSX* and *LOGPIXELSXY* parameters to the **GetDeviceCaps()**
function return the number of pixels per logical inch along the width and height
of the display. The code specifies that a 1 x 1-inch square on the device is to
correspond to a square in the application drawing space that is 100 x 100 logical
units. Or to put it another way, one logical unit will correspond to 0.01 inch on
the output device.

Note that the *y* parameter of the **SetWindowExt()** function has a negative value.
By default, device coordinates follow the Windows convention that the origin is
located in the upper left corner of the window and *y* values increase downward.
By specifying an inverse ratio between the window and the viewport *y* values, you
can allow your drawing functions to describe output using the traditional mathematical coordinate system, with *y* values that increase upward. Be aware that
because the origin of the onscreen display window (the position *(0, 0)*) is set by
default to the top left corner of the window, your drawing will not be visible if you
use *y* coordinates that increase upward. You will be drawing in the space above
the top of the visible window. Either invert the values of your *y* coordinates or use
the **CDC::SetViewportOrg()** function to offset the device window origin to a
point that corresponds to the bottom left corner of your logical window.

The fixed mapping modes follow the mathematical convention that *x* coordinates
increase in value toward the right and that *y* coordinates increase as they go up.
The MM_TEXT mapping mode follows the Windows convention that *y* coordinate values increase as they go down.

After you have set up a suitable mapping mode for your view, you simply use
the GDI drawing functions to render output using logical coordinates. The conversion between logical coordinates and physical (device) coordinates is handled
for you. At times, you will need to convert coordinates yourself using the **CDC**
methods **LPtoDP()** and **DPtoLP()** because certain types of information are supplied to you only in device coordinates. For example, the location of a mouse-
click is supplied as a parameter to the **CView::OnLButtonDown()** handler
function as a pair of physical coordinates. You would have to convert the coordinates if you needed to determine whether the location of the mouse click corre-
sponded to a significant region of your logical drawing space.

Scrolling Views

When drawing your application output in logical space, you are limited only by the size of the coordinate range. Drawing coordinates in a Windows 95 or 98 application must lie within the range –32,768 through 32,767. Using the MM_LOENGLISH mapping mode, this range maps to nearly 3000 square feet of physical drawing space—considerably larger than any output device that you are likely to encounter.

Windows that are not able to display all of the application output in a single frame should implement scroll bars. Scroll bars should be implemented wherever the user can resize the window, and they should appear at the point where the window frame starts to clip the output in the client area.

Fortunately, MFC makes it easy to add scrolling to your document/view application. You will recall from Lesson 1 of Chapter 2 that the view class for the MyApp application was derived from the **CScrollView** class. You can implement scrolling yourself in any view class by using the **CWnd** scrolling functions and handling the WM_VSCROLL and WM_HSCROLL messages, but **CScrollView** makes it easy for you to implement scrolling by:

- Managing window and viewport sizes and mapping modes.
- Scrolling automatically in response to scroll-bar messages.

The following exercise introduces the scrolling capabilities offered by **CScrollView**.

▶ **To view the default scrolling behavior of the MyApp application**

1. Run the MyApp application.
2. On the **Data** menu, click **Edit,** and then type a string of about 60 characters to be displayed 20 times.
3. Resize the window so that it resembles Figure 5.6.

Figure 5.6   Testing the MyApp scrolling capabilities

Notice that although scrolling is invoked automatically, it doesn't behave quite as it should. In Figure 5.6, you can see that the right side of the data lines is out of the view and that a horizontal scroll bar has not appeared. You would expect the scroll bars to appear as soon as the frame edges clip the data displayed in the window. Also notice that when you shrink the window further so that a horizontal scroll bar appears, you cannot scroll across to see an entire data line.

The reason for this behavior is that it is your responsibility to specify a logical size and a mapping mode for a scrolling view. When an AppWizard application is created with a view derived from **CScrollView**, the AppWizard adds the following code to the overloaded **CView::OnInitialUpdate()** method:

```
CSize sizeTotal;
// TODO: calculate the total size of this view
sizeTotal.cx = sizeTotal.cy = 100;
SetScrollSizes(MM_TEXT, sizeTotal);
```

The **CScrollView::SetScrollSizes()** function is used to specify the logical size and a mapping mode for the scrolling view. The default **OnInitialUpdate()** method will set up the view window with dimensions of 100 x 100 logical units. Under the MM_TEXT mapping mode, this corresponds to an onscreen viewport that is 100 x 100 pixels—about a square inch on an 800 x 600 monitor. The **SetScrollSizes()** function has additional parameters that specify the *line size* and the *page size*. The line size is the horizontal and vertical distance to scroll in each direction when the user clicks on a scroll arrow. The page size is the distance to scroll when the user clicks in the scroll bar, but not on a scroll arrow. These last two parameters have default values that are calculated to be in proportion to the total size of the window.

When the MyApp application window is large enough, you can see all the text. If the window is resized so that the view becomes smaller than the size set in the **SetScrollSizes()** function, the scroll bars are displayed. The scroll bar scale and positions are also calculated on the basis of the size of the scrolling view. This is why, when you were experimenting with the default scrolling behavior of the MyApp application, it was impossible to scroll to see data that lay outside the 100 x 100 logical window area.

To set up a simple scrolling view for a document/view application, you need to decide how large a logical drawing space is required to render your document data. Then determine a suitable mapping mode to scale your drawing to an output device, and set the values with a call to **SetScrollSizes()** in the view class's **OnInitialUpdate()** function. The following code snippet illustrates how you might set up a view of 8.5 x 11 inches:

```
sizeTotal.cx = 850;
sizeTotal.cy = 1100;
SetScrollSizes(MM_LOENGLISH, sizeTotal);
```

This approach is appropriate if you can determine a fixed size for your document data. However, consider an application such as a word processing application, which does not place a constraint on the length of a document. As the user adds lines of text, you will be required to resize the logical window and to recalculate the scale of the scroll bars. In such a case, you will need to call the **SetScrollSizes()** function frequently as the size of the document data changes.

In the following exercise, you will use the **SetScrollSizes()** function to adjust the CMyAppView view so that the scroll bars will appear as the displayed data is obscured by the window frame. The **SetScrollSizes()** function will be called from within the drawing function so that the scroll sizes will be adjusted according to the size of the string that is displayed. The function will also set the mapping mode to MM_LOENGLISH so that the output will appear consistently on the screen and the printer.

▶ **To set the scroll sizes for the MyApp application**

1. In ClassView, expand the **CMyAppView** class icon.

2. Double click the **OnDraw()** icon to edit the method.

3. Beneath the following line,

    ```
    CSize TextSize = pDC->GetTextExtent(pDoc->m_string);
    ```

    add these lines:

    ```
    CSize scrollArea =
        CSize(TextSize.cx, TextSize.cy * pDoc->m_nLines);

    // Allow a margin
    scrollArea += CSize(20, 20);

    SetScrollSizes(MM_LOENGLISH, scrollArea);
    ```

The scroll sizes are set relative to the size of the data that will be displayed and are specified by the length of the string and the number of lines that are to be displayed.

When the MM_TEXT mapping mode is used, the y coordinate values increase downward and the other fixed mapping modes follow the mathematical convention, with y values that increase upward. As you have changed the mapping mode from the default MM_TEXT to MM_LOENGLISH, you will need to invert the y coordinates in your display code so that their values decrease as you proceed down the page.

▶ **To invert the *y* coordinates in your display code**

1. Locate the following lines of code in the **OnDraw()** function:

```
int nPos = 10;

for(int i = 0; i < pDoc->m_nLines; i++)
{
    pDC->TextOut(10, nPos, pDoc->m_string);
    nPos += TextSize.cy;
}
```

2. Change the initial value of **nPos** to **–10**.

3. Change the operator that increments **nPos** in the loop to **– =**. The entire function should now look as follows:

```
void CMyAppView::OnDraw(CDC* pDC)
{
    CMyAppDoc* pDoc = GetDocument();
    ASSERT_VALID(pDoc);

    CFont aFont;
    aFont.CreateFont(16, 0, 0, 0, 0, 0, 0, 0, 0, 0, 0, 0,
        FF_ROMAN, 0);

    CFont * pOldFont = pDC->SelectObject(&aFont);

    CSize TextSize = pDC->GetTextExtent(pDoc->m_string);

    CSize scrollArea =
        CSize(TextSize.cx, TextSize.cy * pDoc->m_nLines);

    // Allow a margin
    scrollArea += CSize(20, 20);

    SetScrollSizes(MM_LOENGLISH, scrollArea);

    int nPos = -10;

    for(int i = 0; i < pDoc->m_nLines; i++)
    {
        pDC->TextOut(10, nPos, pDoc->m_string);
        nPos -= TextSize.cy;
    }

    pDC->SelectObject(pOldFont);
}
```

4. Build and run the MyApp application.

5. On the **Data** menu, click **Edit** and make 20 long lines of text appear.

6. Resize the application window and check that the scroll bars appear as the view area becomes smaller than the data display. Try changing the size of the string and the number of lines that are displayed, and notice how the scroll bars automatically scale to fit the size of the data display.

7. Print the document, or use Print Preview to check that the printed output is a reasonable size.

Drawing in a Device Context

The framework passes to your **OnDraw()** function a pointer to a device context object, which represents the client area of your application window. The **CDC** class, the base class for all MFC device context objects, provides a number of functions that enable you to draw lines, shapes, and fill areas; output text; and manipulate bitmap patterns. You have met a few of these functions, such as **LineTo()**, **Rectangle()**, and **TextOut()**, in the examples throughout this chapter.

The drawing functions work together with the MFC drawing tool classes, which include **CPen** (for drawing lines), **CBrush** (for filling areas), **CFont**, and **Cbitmap**, among others. A drawing tool of each type is *selected into* the device context for use with the drawing functions. Thus the **CDC::Rectangle()** function will draw a rectangle in the device context using the current **CPen** and fill it using the current **CBrush**.

The recommended procedure for using the drawing tool graphic objects is as follows:

1. Use a two-stage creation process to create a graphic object. First declare the object and then initialize it with the type-specific create function, such as **CPen::CreatePen()**.

2. Using the **CDC::SelectObject()** function, select the object into the current device context. The **SelectObject()** function is overloaded in several ways to correspond to the different types of graphic objects that can be selected.

3. The **SelectObject()** function returns a pointer to the graphic object that was originally selected. Create a pointer of the appropriate type to save this pointer value.

4. When done with the current graphic object, use the saved pointer to select the old graphic object back into the device context to restore its state. You should leave the device context just as you found it.

The **OnDraw()** function that you implemented for the MyApp application provides a good example of the procedure. The following lines declare and create a new font and select it into the current device context:

```
CFont aFont;
aFont.CreateFont(16, 0, 0, 0, 0, 0, 0, 0, 0, 0, 0, 0, FF_ROMAN, 0);
CFont * pOldFont = pDC->SelectObject(&aFont);
```

The *aFont* font is used in subsequent calls to the **CDC::TextOut()** function to display text in the device context. When the function has finished with the font, it discards the **aFont** object and uses the following line of code to restore the object stored in the **pOldFont** pointer:

```
pDC->SelectObject(pOldFont);
```

Tip Rather than saving and restoring each individual object in the device context, you can use the **CDC** methods **SaveDC()** and **RestoreDC()** to save and restore the entire device context.

In this courseware, we will only describe how to implement a passive display of application data. A fair amount of work needs to go into developing views that support features such as object selection, cut, copy, and paste, the manipulation of on-screen objects by the user, drawing with the mouse, and so forth. The DRAWCLI sample application that is provided with Visual C++ gives a good example of how to implement many of these features.

Printing Process

In Lesson 4 of Chapter 3, you learned that the process of rendering an image of your application data on a printed page is simple because the same **OnDraw()** function is used for both screen and printer output. The functions **CView::OnPrint()** and **CWnd::OnPaint()** both call the **OnDraw()** function to render output.

When printing, the framework will perform the following tasks:

- Display the **Print** dialog box.
- Create a device context object for the printer.
- Call the **CDC::StartDoc()** function to notify the printer that all subsequent pages should be spooled under the same job until a **CDC::EndDoc()** call occurs. This ensures that documents longer than one page will not be interspersed with other jobs.
- Repeatedly call the **CDC::StartPage()** and **CDC::EndPage()** functions to inform the printer driver of the beginning and end of each page.
- Call overridable functions in the view at the appropriate times.

Several of the functions, including those for implementing pagination for the printed document, allocating GDI resources for printing, and sending escape codes to change the printer mode before printing a given page, can be overridden. You can use these functions to customize the printing process. Table 5.3 lists the printing functions that can be overridden (all members of the **CView** class).

Table 5.3   Printing Functions That Can Be Overridden

Name	Function
OnPreparePrinting()	Allows you to modify a **CPRINTIINFO** structure to insert values into the **Print** dialog box—commonly used to set the length of the document. Passes the **CPRINTIINFO** structure to the **CView::DoPreparePrinting()** method, which displays the dialog box and creates the printer device context object.
OnBeginPrinting()	Allows you to allocate fonts or other GDI resources used for printed output.
OnPrepareDC()	Allows you to adjust attributes of the device context for a given page. If the length of the document hasn't been specified, a check for the end of the document is performed.
OnPrint()	Allows you to print a given page. By default, this function simply calls **OnDraw()** to render the output, although you can override **OnPrint()** to provide printed output that is significantly different to the screen display.
OnEndPrinting()	Allows you to disconnect GDI resources.

Figure 5.7 illustrates the full printing cycle and shows the order in which these functions are called.

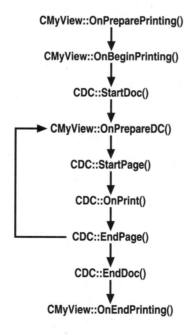

Figure 5.7   The MFC printing cycle

The **Print** dialog box in the MyApp application currently allows you to select a range of pages to print. This feature should be made unavailable for an application that allows you to print only one page of data. In the following exercise, you will add code to the **CMyAppView::OnPreparePrinting**() function to set the maximum number of document printer pages to 1. This has the effect of making the page range selection feature in the **Print** dialog box unavailable.

▶ **To set the maximum number of printer pages**

1. Run the MyApp application. On the **File** menu, click **Print** to verify that the page range feature is available.

2. In ClassView, expand the **CMyAppView** class icon.

3. Double-click the **OnPreparePrinting**() icon to edit the method.

4. To the body of the function, before the return statement, add the following line:

```
pInfo->SetMaxPage(1);
```

5. Build and run the MyApp application. Click **Print** on the **File** menu to verify that the page range feature has been made unavailable.

Print Preview

When the user selects the **Print Preview** command from the **File** menu, the framework creates a **CPreviewDC** object. Whenever your application performs an operation that sets a characteristic of the printer device context, the framework also performs a similar operation on the preview device context. For example, if your application selects a font for printing, the framework selects a font for screen display that simulates the printer font. Whenever your application sends output to the printer, the framework sends the output to the screen.

Print Preview differs from printing in the order that the pages of a document are drawn. During printing, the framework loops until a certain range of pages has been rendered. During Print Preview, one or two pages are displayed and then the application waits. No further pages are displayed until the user clicks **Next Page** or **Previous Page**. During Print Preview, the application must also respond to WM_PAINT messages, just as it does during ordinary screen display.

The **OnPreparePrinting**() function is called when preview mode is invoked, just as it is when beginning a print job. The **CPRINTINFO** structure passed to the function contains several members whose values you can set to adjust certain characteristics of the print preview operation. For example, you can set the **m_nNumPreviewPages** member to specify whether you want to preview the document in one-page or two-page mode.

Modifying Print Preview

You can rather easily modify the behavior and appearance of print preview in a number of ways. Some of the modifications you can make include those listed on the next page.

- Causing the print preview window to display a scroll bar for easy access to any page of the document.
- Causing print preview to maintain the user's position in the document by beginning its display on the current page.
- Causing different initialization to be performed for print preview and printing.

Lesson Summary

The Windows GDI provides a layer of abstraction between applications and the many different types of output devices upon which an application can display output. The graphical output of applications is measured and scaled in logical units. The GDI implements a coordinate mapping system, which determines how the logical units of the application output are to be mapped to the drawing space of the hardware device. This ensures consistent application output on whatever hardware device is attached.

The GDI defines a set of eight mapping modes that specify the ratio between logical coordinates and device coordinates. You can choose one of the six fixed mapping modes that establish predefined mappings between logical units and units of measure on the device, or one of the two unconstrained mapping modes that allow you to specify the ratio between logical units and device units.

Scroll bars should be implemented for a window whenever the window is not able to display all of the application output in a single frame. MFC makes it easy to add scrolling to your document/view application by allowing you to derive your application view class from the MFC class **CScrollView**. It is your responsibility to specify a size and a mapping mode for a scrolling view so that the framework knows when and how to implement scrolling capabilities.

MFC provides a number of drawing tool classes, which are used in conjunction with the GDI drawing functions to render application output in a device context. Generally, you create and configure drawing tool objects to suit the needs of your application. You select these objects into the device context using the **CDC::SelectObject**() function, which returns a pointer to the previously selected object. You should always use this pointer to restore the object at the end of your drawing function to preserve the original state of the device context.

When printing a document, the framework calls a sequence of functions. All the functions are virtual member functions of the **CView** class. You can override these functions to customize the printing process. The most common task is to implement pagination for the printed document. Other tasks include the allocation of any GDI resources needed for printing, and sending escape codes to change the printer mode before printing a given page. You can also use some of these functions to perform customizations that are specific to the display of application data in a print preview window.

Lesson 3: Using Multiple Threads

In Lesson 2 of Chapter 4, you learned that a *process* is an instance of an executing program. A *thread* is a path of execution within a process and is the smallest piece of code that can be scheduled to run on the processor. A thread runs in the address space of the process and uses resources allocated to the process. All processes have at least one thread of execution, known as the *primary thread*. You can create additional *secondary threads* to take advantage of the multitasking capabilities of Windows 32-bit operating systems.

In this lesson, you will learn how to enhance the capabilities and the performance of your application by creating secondary threads of execution using MFC classes and global functions.

After this lesson, you will be able to:

- Describe when to use multithreaded programming techniques.
- Describe the two different types of thread that you can implement using MFC.
- Describe the role of the MFC class **CWinThread** in the implementation of secondary threads.
- Describe how to create and terminate secondary threads in an MFC application.
- Describe how to use the MFC synchronization classes to control thread access to shared data and resources.

Estimated lesson time: 60 minutes

Multithreaded Applications

You can use multiple threads in your application wherever an improvement in performance can be gained by running separate tasks concurrently. As an example, consider a word processing application that automatically backs up the current document every five minutes. The user's input to the document, via the main application window, is handled by the primary thread. The application code can create a separate secondary thread that is responsible for scheduling and performing the automatic backups. Creating a secondary thread prevents the backing up of lengthy documents from interfering with the responsiveness of the application's user interface.

Situations where using multiple threads can deliver performance benefits to your application include:

- **Scheduled (timer-driven) activities** The thread that runs the automatic backup feature in the word processor example is blocked for five-minute intervals between backups. Thread schedules can be set with millisecond precision in Win32 applications.

- **Event-driven activities** The threads can be triggered by signals from other threads. An example is a monitoring system, in which an error-logging thread is inactive until one of the other threads alerts it to an error condition.

- **Distributed activities** When data must be collected from (or distributed to) several computers, it makes sense to create a thread for each request so that these tasks can proceed in parallel, in their own time frame.

- **Prioritized activities** Win32 threads can be assigned *priorities* to determine the proportionate amount of execution time that is assigned to a thread by the thread scheduler. To improve a program's responsiveness, it is sometimes useful to divide its work into a high-priority thread for the user interface and a low-priority thread for background work.

Multithreading with MFC: CWinThread Class

All threads in MFC applications are represented by **CWinThread** objects. This includes the primary thread of your application, which is implemented as a class derived from **CWinApp**. **CWinApp** is directly derived from **CWinThread**.

Although the Win32 API provides the **_beginthreadex** function, which allows you to launch threads at a low level, you should always use the **CWinThread** class to create threads that use MFC functionality. This is because the **CWinThread** class uses thread-local storage to manage information specific to the context of the thread in the MFC environment. You can declare **CWinThread** objects directly, but in many cases, you will allow the global MFC function **AfxBeginThread**() to create a **CWinThread** object for you.

The **CWinThread::CreateThread**() function is used to launch the new thread. The **CWinThread** class also provides the functions **SuspendThread**() and **ResumeThread**() to allow you to suspend and resume the execution of a thread.

Worker Threads and User Interface Threads

MFC distinguishes between two types of threads: *worker* threads and *user interface* threads. This distinction is made solely by MFC; the Win32 API does not distinguish between threads.

Worker threads are commonly used to complete background tasks that do not require user input. Examples could include database backup functions or functions that monitor the current state of a network connection.

User interface threads are able to handle user input, and they implement a message loop to respond to events and messages generated by user interaction with the application. The best example of a user interface thread is the application primary thread represented by your application's **CWinApp**-derived class. Secondary user interface threads can be used to provide a means to interact with an application without degrading the performance of other application features. For example, consider an application that allows anesthetists to monitor the condition of a patient undergoing surgery. A user interface thread could be used to allow the anesthetists to enter details of the drugs that they have administered without interrupting the threads that handle the monitoring of a patient's vital signs.

You create secondary threads in an MFC application by calling the global function **AfxBeginThread**(). There are two overloaded versions of **AfxBeginThread**(), one for creating worker threads, and one for creating user interface threads. The following sections demonstrate how these two versions are used.

Creating Worker Threads

Creating a worker thread is simply a matter of implementing a controlling function that performs the task your thread is to perform, and passing the address of the controlling function to the appropriate version of the **AfxBeginThread**() function.

The controlling function should have the following syntax:

```
UINT MyControllingFunction(LPVOID pParam);
```

The parameter is a single 32-bit value. The parameter can be used in a number of ways, or it can be ignored. It can pass a simple value to the function or a pointer to a structure containing multiple parameters. If the parameter refers to a structure, the structure can be used not only to pass data from the caller to the thread, but also to pass data back from the thread to the caller.

The worker-thread version of **AfxBeginThread**() is declared as follows:

```
CWinThread* AfxBeginThread(AFX_THREADPROC pfnThreadProc,
    LPVOID pParam,
    int nPriority = THREAD_PRIORITY_NORMAL,
    UINT nStackSize = 0,
    DWORD dwCreateFlags = 0,
    LPSECURITY_ATTRIBUTES lpSecurityAttrs = NULL);
```

The first two parameters are the address of the controlling function and the address of the parameter that is to be passed to it. The remaining parameters (which all have default values) allow you to specify the thread priority, its stack size, whether it is to be created in a suspended state, and whether it is to run immediately. The final parameter allows you to specify the security attributes for the thread—the default value NULL means that the thread will inherit the attributes of the calling thread.

AfxBeginThread() creates a new **CWinThread** object, calls its **CreateThread**() function to start executing the thread, and returns a pointer to the thread. Checks are made throughout the procedure to make sure all objects are deallocated properly should any part of the creation fail. To end the thread, you call the global function

AfxEndThread() from within the thread or simply return from the controlling function of the worker thread. The return value of the controlling function is commonly used to indicate the reason for termination. Traditionally, the exit code is 0 if the function was successful. Nonzero values are used to indicate specific types of errors.

Creating a Worker Thread

The following exercises illustrate how to create a worker thread for the MyApp application. You will create a simple timer function that displays a message box when the system time reaches the timer setting. The user will set the timer using a dialog box. After the timer has been set, a worker thread will monitor the system clock once every second. After the timer time has been reached, the thread will display the message box and terminate.

You will create the **CTimer** class to encapsulate the timer. This class will contain a protected MFC **CTime** variable to store the timer time. It will also contain a public **CWinThread** pointer, which will be used to determine whether the **CTimer** object is currently referenced by an active thread.

► **To create the CTimer class**

1. Open the CMyApp project. Then in FileView, double-click the **MainFrm.cpp** file icon.

2. To the top of the file, beneath the #include statements, add the following code:

```
class Ctimer
{
protected:
    CTime m_time;

public:
    CWinThread * m_thread;

    CTimer() {Reset();}

    CTime GetTime() {return m_time;}
    void  SetTime(CTime time) {m_time = time;}

    void  Reset() {
        m_time = CTime::GetCurrentTime();
        m_thread = NULL;
    }
};
```

The **GetCurrentTime()** function is a static member function of the **CTime** class that returns the current system time in **CTime** format.

3. Directly beneath the class declaration, add the following line to declare a global **CTimer** object:

```
CTimer g_timer;
```

You will now implement a controlling function for the worker thread. This function will compare the system time to the timer time at one-second intervals. After the timer time is reached, the function will display a message box and reset the timer.

▶ **To add the DoTimer() function**

1. In the MainFrm.cpp file, directly beneath the class declaration, add the following function definition:

```
UINT DoTimer(LPVOID pparam)
{
    CTime currenttime = CTime::GetCurrentTime();

    while(currenttime < g_timer.GetTime())
    {
        Sleep(1000);
        currenttime = CTime::GetCurrentTime();
    }

    AfxMessageBox("Time's up!");

    g_timer.Reset();

    return 0;
}
```

The **Sleep()** function causes the thread on which the function is called to be suspended for the specified number of milliseconds.

2. Your next step is to implement the dialog box that is used to set the timer time. Use the dialog editor to create a dialog box like the one shown in Figure 5.8.

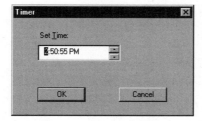

Figure 5.8   The **Timer** dialog box

The dialog box as a whole should have the ID **IDD_TIMER**. The control that looks similar to a combo box is a **Date Time Picker** control, which is available on the control toolbar. This control should be given the ID **IDC_DTPSETTIME** and should be set to display the time only.

▶ **To set the IDC_DTPSETTIME control to display the time only**

1. In the dialog editor, select the **IDC_DTPSETTIME** control. Press ENTER to edit the control properties.

2. Click the **Styles** tab. In the **Format** box, click **Time**.

3. Click outside the property sheet to close it.

You will now create a dialog class for the **Timer** dialog box.

▶ **To create the CTimerDialog class**

1. With the dialog editor open, press CTRL+W to open ClassWizard. When instructed, create the **CTimerDialog** class.

2. Click the **Member Variables** tab. Create a Value member variable for the **IDC_DTPSETTIME** ID. This should be a variable of type CTime and be named **m_settime**.

3. Click **OK** to close ClassWizard.

Now all you have to do is add a command and handler function to set the timer time and start the timer thread.

▶ **To add the Timer option to the View menu and the OnViewTimer() handler function**

1. Use the menu editor to create the **Timer** command on the **View** menu. Accept the **ID_VIEW_TIMER** ID that is created by default.

2. Use the **Message Maps** tab on ClassWizard to add a command handler for the **ID_VIEW_TIMER** object ID to the **CMainFrame** class. Name the function **OnViewTimer()**.

3. After the handler has been added, click the **Edit Code** button to locate the **CMyAppApp::OnViewTimer()** implementation. Add the following code to the body of the function:

```
CTimerDialog aTDlg;

aTDlg.m_time = g_timer.GetTime();

if(aTDlg.DoModal() == IDOK)
{
    g_timer.SetTime(aTDlg.m_time);
```

```
        // Only one timer running per instance
        if(!g_timer.m_thread)
            g_timer.m_thread = AfxBeginThread(DoTimer, 0);
    }
```

4. To the top of the MainFrm.cpp file, along with the other #include statements, add the following line of code:

```
#include "TimerDialog.h"
```

5. Now compile and build the MyApp application. Test the timer operation by choosing the **Timer** command from the **View** menu. The **Timer** dialog box appears with the current time displayed in the Date Time Picker control. Use the control to set the timer time to a minute or two later than the current time. Click **Start** to close the **Timer** dialog box and start the timer.

While waiting for the timer, experiment with the other features of the MyApp interface. You will notice that their performance is not affected by the independent worker thread checking the system clock every second.

When the system clock catches up with the time set in the **Timer** dialog box, the message box appears and the worker thread terminates.

Creating User Interface Threads

As we stated earlier, all threads in an MFC application are represented by objects of the **CWinThread** class, which are created by the **AfxBeginThread()** function. When you create a worker thread, **AfxBeginThread()** creates a generic **CWinThread** object for you, and assigns the address of your controller function to the CWinThread::m_pfnThreadProc member variable. To create a user interface thread, you must derive your own class from **CWinThread** and pass run-time information about the class to the user interface version of **AfxBeginThread()**.

The following code snippet, taken from the MFC source code, shows how the framework distinguishes between a worker thread and a user interface thread. The code is taken from _AfxThreadEntry(), the entry-point function for all MFC threads.

```
// First -- check for simple worker thread
DWORD nResult = 0;
if (pThread->m_pfnThreadProc != NULL)
{
    nResult = (*pThread->m_pfnThreadProc)(pThread->m_pThreadParams);
    ASSERT_VALID(pThread);
}
// Else -- check for thread with message loop
else if (!pThread->InitInstance())
{
    ASSERT_VALID(pThread);
    nResult = pThread->ExitInstance();
}
```

```
else
{
    // Will stop after PostQuitMessage called
    ASSERT_VALID(pThread);
    nResult = pThread->Run();
}
// Clean up and shut down the thread
threadWnd.Detach();
AfxEndThread(nResult);
```

If m_pfnThreadProc points to a controller function, the code knows that it is dealing with a worker thread. The controller function is called and the thread is terminated. If m_pfnThreadProc is NULL, the function assumes that it is dealing with a user interface thread. The thread object's **InitInstance()** function is called to perform thread initialization—to create the main window and other user interface objects, for example. If **InitInstance()** returns successfully (i.e., by returning TRUE), the **Run()** function is called. **CWinThread::Run()** implements a message loop to process messages directed to the thread's main window.

The **InitInstance()** and the **Run()** functions should sound familiar to you. They are two of the key virtual functions that are inherited by **CWinApp**, which was described in Lesson 3 of Chapter 3, in connection with the MFC implementation of the Win32 application architecture.

You are obliged to provide an overloaded version of **InitInstance()** for your thread class. Very often you will provide class-specific cleanup functions in an overloaded version of **CWinThread::ExitInstance()**. Generally, you will use the base class version of the **Run()** function.

The following exercise demonstrates the easiest way to create a **CWinThread**-derived class.

▶ **To create the CMyUIThread class**

1. From within the CMyApp project, press CTRL+W to open ClassWizard.

2. Click the **Add Class** button and choose **New** from the drop-down menu. The **New Class** dialog box appears.

3. In the **Name** box, type **CMyUIThread**. Choose **CWinThread** from the **Base class** drop-down menu.

4. Click **OK** to create the class, and then click **OK** to close ClassWizard.

Open the MyUIThread.h and the MyUIThread.cpp files to inspect the source code for your thread class. Note that ClassWizard has provided stub implementations of the **InitInstance()** and **ExitInstance()** functions, to which you should add your class-specific implementation code. Note, too, that a message map is implemented for your thread class. The **DECLARE_DYNCREATE** and **IMPLEMENT_DYNCREATE** macros play an important role here, as they implement the run-time class information for **CObject**-derived classes that is required by the user interface thread version of **AfxBeginThread()**.

After you have completed the implementation of your thread class, you call the user interface thread version of **AfxBeginThread()**, passing your thread class's run-time class information as a pointer as follows:

```
AfxBeginThread(RUNTIME_CLASS(CMyUIThread));
```

The **RUNTIME_CLASS** macro returns a pointer to the **CRuntimeClass** structure that maintains run-time type information for all **CObject**-derived classes declared with the **DECLARE_DYNAMIC, DECLARE_DYNCREATE**, or **DECLARE_SERIAL** macros. This enables **AfxBeginThread()** to create a thread object of the correct type.

The user interface thread version of **AfxBeginThread()** has the same set of default parameters as the worker thread version. It also returns a pointer to the thread object that it creates.

Thread Synchronization

Secondary threads are generally used to implement *asynchronous* processing. An asynchronous operation is one that executes independently of other events or actions. Consider our timer thread, which runs along its own path of execution, checking the system clock once every second. It does not need to wait upon events in the application primary thread, and the application can proceed without waiting for the thread to finish its task.

There are a number of situations where these asynchronous activities will need to *synchronize*, or coordinate their operations. As an example, consider a print scheduler thread that queues print job threads created by different applications. The print job threads will need to notify the scheduler that they want to join the queue, and the scheduler will send a message to each print job in the queue when its turn comes to print.

Another scenario that typically requires thread synchronization is the updating of global application data. Consider a monitoring application with a sensor thread that updates a data structure with readings from a sensor device. Another thread is used to read the structure and display a representation of its state on the screen. Now suppose that the display thread tries to obtain a reading at the very millisecond that the data structure is being updated by the sensor thread. The result is likely to be corrupted data, which could have serious consequences if the application was, for example, monitoring a nuclear power plant. Thread access to global data needs to be synchronized to ensure that only one thread can read or modify a thread at any time.

One way to implement thread synchronization is to use a global object to act as an intermediary between threads. MFC provides a number of synchronization classes, listed in Table 5.4. These synchronization classes, derived from the base class **CSyncObject**, can be used to coordinate asynchronous events of any kind.

Table 5.4   MFC Synchronization Classes

Name	Description
CCriticalSection	A synchronization class that allows only one thread from within the current process to access an object.
CMutex	A synchronization class that allows only one thread from any process to access an object.
CSemaphore	A synchronization class that allows between one and a specified maximum number of simultaneous accesses to an object.
CEvent	A synchronization class that notifies an application when an event has occurred.

The synchronization classes are used in conjunction with the synchronization access classes **CSingleLock** and **CMultiLock** to provide thread-safe access to global data or shared resources. The recommended way to use these classes is as follows:

- Wrap global data objects or resource access functions inside a class. Protect the controlled data and regulate access through the use of public functions.

- Within your class, create a synchronization object of the appropriate type. For example, you would use a **CCriticalSection** object to ensure that your global data is updated by only one thread at a time, or you might include a **CEvent** object to signify that a resource was ready to receive data.

- In the member functions that give access to the data or resource, create an instance of a synchronization access object. Use **CSingleLock** when you need to wait on only one object at a time. Use **CMultiLock** when there are multiple objects that you could use at a particular time.

- Before the function code attempts to access the protected data, call the **Lock()** member function of the synchronization access object. The **Lock()** function can be instructed to wait for a specified amount of time (or to wait indefinitely) for the associated synchronization object to become available. For example, a **CCriticalSection** object is available if it successfully manages to secure exclusive execution access for the current thread. The availability of an event is set in the program code by calling the **CEvent::SetEvent()** function.

- After the function has finished accessing the protected data, call the access object's **Unlock()** function or allow the object to be destroyed.

Encapsulating global resources and synchronization code inside a thread-safe class helps you centralize and control access to the resource and protect against a *deadlock* situation. A deadlock is a condition in which two or more threads wait for one another to release a shared resource before resuming their execution. Deadlock conditions are notoriously difficult to reproduce or to track down, so you are strongly advised to analyze your multithreaded application for possible deadlock conditions and take steps to prevent their occurrence.

The following exercise illustrates the procedure for providing thread-safe access to global data. You will use a **CCriticalSection** object and a **CSingleLock** object to protect access to the **CTime** object contained within the **CTimer** class that you created in the previous exercise.

▶ **To implement thread-safe access to the CTimer class data**

1. At the top of the MainFrm.cpp file, with the other #include statements, add the following line:

```
#include <afxmt.h>
```

2. Add this line of code to the **protected** section of the **CTimer** class definition:

```
CCriticalSection m_CS;
```

3. Remove the inline definitions of the **CTimer::GetTime()** and **CTimer::SetTime()** functions (remember to add semicolons in their place).

4. Beneath the **CTimer** class definition, add the **CTimer::GetTime()** function definition as follows:

```
CTime CTimer::GetTime()
{
    CSingleLock csl(&m_CS);
    csl.Lock();
    CTime time = m_time;
    csl.Unlock();
    return time;
}
```

5. Add the following **CTimer::SetTime()** function definition beneath the lines of code you added in step 4:

```
void CTimer::SetTime(CTime time)
{
    CSingleLock csl(&m_CS);
    csl.Lock();
    m_time = time;
    csl.Unlock();
}
```

The calls to **CSingleLock::Unlock()** in these functions are not strictly necessary—we just consider them good programming style.

You can now build and run the application. You will not notice any difference in the operation of the program, but you can rest assured that the data encapsulated in any instance of the **CTimer** class can safely be accessed by any number of threads.

Lesson Summary

Multiple threads can be used in an application wherever an improvement in performance might be gained by running separate tasks concurrently. Asynchronous operations that run in their own time frame, operations scheduled by a timer, and operations that need to wait on events triggered by other threads are all possible candidates for implementation as secondary threads in an application process.

All threads that use MFC functionality should be created by an instance of the MFC **CWinThread** class. MFC provides the global function **AfxBeginThread()** to assist you in the process of creating threads in an MFC application. MFC distinguishes between two types of threads. Worker threads are commonly used to complete background tasks that do not require user input. User interface threads are able to handle user input, and they implement a message loop to respond to events and messages generated by the user interaction with the application.

To create a worker thread, you implement a controlling function that performs the task that your thread is to perform, and then pass the function address to the worker-thread version of **AfxBeginThread()**. To create a user interface thread, you derive your own class from **CWinThread**, provide overloads for key member functions, and pass run-time information about the class to the user interface thread version of the **AfxBeginThread()** function.

Secondary threads are generally used to implement *asynchronous* processing. However, there are a number of situations where threads will need to synchronize their activity. They might need to wait on a signal from another thread, or send signals to other threads. Thread access to global data needs to be synchronized to ensure that simultaneous access attempts do not result in data corruption.

MFC provides a number of synchronization classes derived from the base class **CSyncObject**, which can be used to coordinate asynchronous thread activity. These classes are used in conjunction with the synchronization access objects **CSingleLock** and **CMultiLock**.

When controlling thread access to a shared resource, the recommended practice is to encapsulate the resource inside a class, and to implement synchronization objects as protected members of the same class. Use the synchronization access objects within the class member functions to ensure that the resources are accessed in only a thread-safe manner—so that not more than one thread is allowed at any given time.

Lesson 4: Context-Sensitive Help

Windows applications usually provide context-sensitive Help, allowing the user to get help on a particular feature of an application, such as a dialog box, a command, or a toolbar button.

Currently, Windows provides two distinct Help authoring environments: the traditional Windows Help system *WinHelp*, based on rich text format (RTF) documents; and the newer *HTML Help* system, based on compiled HTML documents.

In this chapter, you will learn how to provide context-sensitive Help for your applications using application framework features provided by the MFC AppWizard. You will also learn the basic steps required to implement HTML Help for an application.

After this lesson, you will be able to:

- Describe how a Windows application implements context-sensitive Help.
- Describe how to add context-sensitive Help to an MFC AppWizard application.
- Describe the components of WinHelp development.
- Describe how to display HTML-based Help for an application.

Estimated lesson time: 40 minutes

WinHelp

Applications that use the Windows Help system respond to user requests for Help by loading the WinHelp application (Winhlp32.exe) located in the system folder.

WinHelp displays pages from the application Help file. The application Help file resides in the same directory as the application executable file and has the same file name but with an .hlp extension. The page that is displayed is determined by the *help context*, a parameter passed to WinHelp by the application.

The user can access the application Help in the following ways:

- **Pressing the F1 key** The user can press the F1 key from an active window, dialog box, or message box, or with a command or toolbar button selected, to invoke a Help topic relevant to the selected item. For commands, Help is summoned for the item currently selected.

  Note that although you can define any key as a Help key, the F1 key is the accepted standard.

- **Entering Help mode** From within an active application, the user can press SHIFT+F1 or click the **Help** button to activate "Help mode."

  In Help mode, the mouse pointer changes to an arrow with a question mark. While the application is in this mode, the user can click any window, dialog box, message box, command, or toolbar button to summon Help specific to the item. Help mode ends when Help is displayed. Pressing ESC or switching away from the application and then back to the application ends Help mode.

- **Using the Help menu** Most applications provide Help support through one or more commands. For instance, most Windows applications include a **Help** command that invokes the application's Help file when chosen. Additional commands on the **Help** menu might display a **Search** dialog box or provide a link to a Web site for more information.

AppWizard Support for Context-Sensitive Help

The MFC application framework provides extensive support for the implementation of WinHelp. Selecting the context-sensitive Help option when using the MFC AppWizard will set up your project with everything you need to create WinHelp for your application with minimal effort.

The following exercises show you how to use the AppWizard to create a project that provides support for context-sensitive Help, and they demonstrate how application Help pages are displayed.

▶ **To create the MyHelpApp project**

1. Use the **New** command on the **File** menu to create a new MFC AppWizard (exe) project named **MyHelpApp**.

2. On the Step 1 screen of the MFC AppWizard, select **Single document**.

3. Select the default options for Steps 2 and 3. For Step 4, select the **Context-sensitive Help** check box as shown in Figure 5.9.

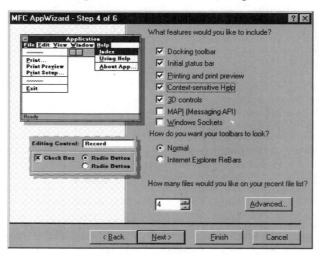

Figure 5.9 The AppWizard context-sensitive Help option

4. Select the default options for the remaining AppWizard steps and create the MyHelpApp project.

In the following exercises, you will view the default Help application that is created for your application.

▶ **To view MyHelpApp Help**

1. Press F7 to build the MyHelpApp application.

2. Press CTRL+F5 to run the application.

3. On the **Help** menu, click **Help Topics**. The MyHelpApp application Help appears.

4. Click the **Contents** tab. Double-click **Menus** so that the Help screen appears as shown in Figure 5.10.

Figure 5.10   The MyHelpApp application Help window

5. Select the **File menu** Help topic. The **Close** button changes to the **Display** button.

6. Click **Display** to view the Help topic about the **File** menu. The **File** menu Help page appears as shown in Figure 5.11 on the following page.

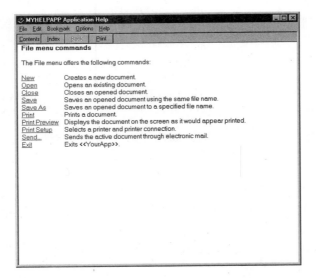

Figure 5.11 The **File** menu Help page

Take some time to explore the Help system. Try selecting some of the hyperlinks and experiment with some of the toolbar and menu options. When you have finished, close the Help application.

▶ **To invoke context-sensitive Help**

1. Click **File** in the MyHelpApp application to open the **File** menu. Highlight the **Print** command with the mouse, but do not select it.

2. Press the F1 key. The Help application will open and display the **Print** command topic.

3. Close the Help application. Click in the application window client area to close the **File** menu. Position the pointer over the **Context Help** button so that the button appears raised and the ToolTip text is displayed. The **Context Help** button, which is on the far right of the toolbar, depicts a black cursor arrow next to a blue question mark.

4. Press the F1 key. The Help application will open and display the **Context Help** command topic.

5. Close the Help application.

▶ **To view Help-mode Help**

1. Click the **Context Help** button. Notice how the pointer changes to inform you that you are in Help mode.

2. Click any command or toolbar button to view its Help information.

3. Close the Help application.

Help Development Components

When you choose the context-sensitive Help option for your application, AppWizard creates an extra subfolder named *hlp* beneath your main project folder. This subfolder contains files that are used in the development of your application's Help file. Figure 5.12 shows Windows Explorer displaying the contents of the hlp folder for the MyHelpApp project (after the project has been built).

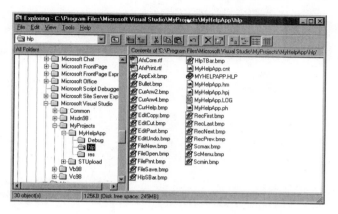

Figure 5.12 The MyHelpApp\hlp folder

The following sections explain how these files are used in the Help file development process.

.hpj Files

A .hpj file is a *Help project* file that provides the information the Windows Help compiler needs to build a Help file for your application. Help project files are maintained by the Microsoft Help Workshop, which is an application that allows you to visually develop application Help—.hpj files are to Help Workshop what .dsw files are to Visual Studio. Like Visual Studio, Help Workshop is capable of hosting several different types of files.

The Microsoft Help Workshop (*hcw.exe*) is installed in the \Program Files\ Microsoft Visual Studio\Common\Tools folder as part of a standard installation of Visual Studio. You can launch Help Workshop by double-clicking a Help project file. Figure 5.13 on the following page shows the MyHelpApp.hpj file open in Help Workshop.

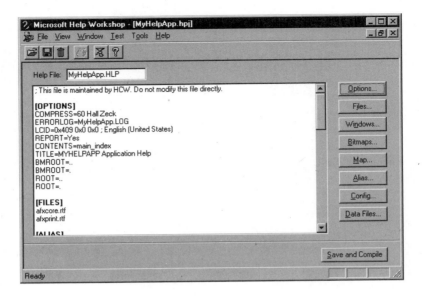

Figure 5.13   Help Workshop displaying MyHelpApp.hpj

The .hpj file contains several sections that can be modified by using the buttons on the right side of the pane. Options used by the Help compiler are specified in the Options section displayed in Figure 5.13. Other sections contain references to other types of files that can be included in the Help project build.

.rtf Files

An .rtf file is a rich text format file that forms the pages in the Help file. The .rtf files that are to be included in a Help file are listed in the [FILES] section of the project's .hpj file.

AppWizard supplies skeleton .rtf files that contain Help topics for common elements of the Windows user interface, such as the **File** and **Edit** menus. You can edit these files to revise the supplied text and add your own application-specific Help information. To edit .rtf files, you will need to install a word processor, such as Microsoft Word, that is capable of editing the rich text format.

.bmp Files

The .rtf files can contain references to .bmp files to be used as illustrations.

.hm Files

An .hm file is created by the MakeHm tool. MakeHm reads your Resource.h file and creates Help context IDs to correspond to the application resource IDs so that each dialog box, command, or other resource has a Help context ID associated with it. Be aware that MakeHm is not guaranteed to generate unique IDs and that this can sometimes result in name collisions.

Your project's .hpj file contains a statement in its [MAP] section that includes the project's .hm file, as well as the standard .hm file included with MFC. The Help compiler uses the Help context IDs in these .hm files to determine which Help topic is associated with each dialog box, command, or other resource.

When adding new resource IDs, you should be careful to use the standard prefixes for resource IDs so that MakeHm can create the mappings correctly. The names suggested for your resources by the Visual C++ resource editor use the correct prefixes. For more information, search for "Preferred Resource ID Prefixes" in the Visual C++ Help file.

Whenever you add new resources to your project, you must add new Help topics for those resources to your .rtf files. AppWizard creates custom build rules for your project to so that your Help file is rebuilt when its source files are changed. This includes a call to MakeHm.exe when the Resource.h file is changed.

.cnt Files

A .cnt file contains the information needed to create the Help file's Contents screen. You use Help Workshop to visually edit a .cnt file, as shown in Figure 5.14.

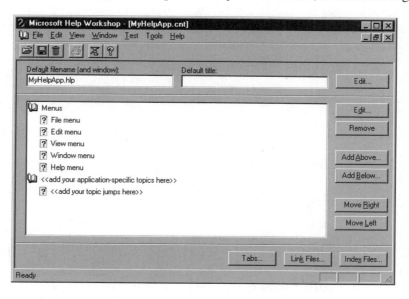

Figure 5.14   Help Workshop displaying MyHelpApp.cnt

.ph Files

A .ph file is a key-phrase table file created by the Help compiler when the compression option is specified.

.hlp Files

As mentioned earlier, .hlp files are the application Help files, the output of the Windows Help compiler. The Help compiler creates the .hlp file in your application's main source code folder. If an output folder (i.e. a Debug or Release folder) exists, the .hlp file is copied there so that an up-to-date copy of the application Help is always available when you run the application.

.log Files

A .log file contains messages generated by the Help compiler. They can be viewed with Help Workshop.

Source Code Components

In addition to creating the files required to build a Help file for your application, AppWizard adds features to your application source code to implement context-sensitive Help. The **Help Topics** option (resource **ID_HELP_FINDER**) is added to the **Help** menu, and the **Context Help** button (help-mode help, which has the resource **ID_CONTEXT_HELP**) is added to the application toolbar. The application's accelerator table defines F1 as the context-sensitive help key (resource **ID_HELP**), and SHIFT+F1 as the help-mode help key.

These resource IDs are mapped to base class handler functions in the main frame window's message map, as illustrated by the following code:

```
BEGIN_MESSAGE_MAP(CMainFrame, CFrameWnd)
    //{{AFX_MSG_MAP(CMainFrame)
    ON_WM_CREATE()
    //}}AFX_MSG_MAP
    // Global Help commands
    ON_COMMAND(ID_HELP_FINDER, CFrameWnd::OnHelpFinder)
    ON_COMMAND(ID_HELP, CFrameWnd::OnHelp)
    ON_COMMAND(ID_CONTEXT_HELP, CFrameWnd::OnContextHelp)
    ON_COMMAND(ID_DEFAULT_HELP, CFrameWnd::OnHelpFinder)
END_MESSAGE_MAP()
```

The handler functions all eventually call the **CWnd::WinHelp()** function, which starts the WinHelp application. **OnContextHelp()** generates a Help context ID from the resource ID, which it passes to WinHelp as a parameter to the **WinHelp()** function. If the framework fails to generate a valid Help context ID, an **ID_DEFAULT_HELP** command message is sent to the application.

Creating Help Topics

In the following exercises, you will add a new menu to the MyHelpApp application menu and add Help topics for the menu and its item. You will learn how to add Help context information so that the context-sensitive Help features function correctly.

To complete these exercises, you will need to install a word processor that is capable of editing rich text format files. In our examples, we have used Microsoft Word.

▶ **To add the ID_IMPORT_TEXTFILE command**

1. From the ResourceView of the MyHelpApp project, open the **IDR_ MAINFRAME** menu in the menu editor. Add a new menu title with the caption **&Import**. Under this title, create a command with the caption **&Text File**. Close and re-open the Menu Item Properties to ensure that the editor has created the ID **ID_IMPORT_TEXTFILE** for the command.

2. Build the MyHelpApp application. Note that the following messages appear in the output window:

```
Making Help include file...
Making Help file...
```

3. Locate the MyHelpApp.hm file in the hlp subfolder. Use Notepad to view this file, and confirm that the MakeHm utility has added the Help context ID **HID_IMPORT_TEXTFILE**. Close the MyHelpApp.hm file.

In the next exercise, you will add topics to the application's .rtf file. To help you understand the file format, open AfxCore.rtf in your rich text editor. If the editor contains an option that allows you view hidden text, make that option available. In Word, this is achieved by choosing **Options** from the **Tools** menu and selecting the **Hidden text** check box on the **View** tab. Also, make footnote editing available—in Word, choose **Footnotes** from the **View** menu.

Figure 5.15 on the following page shows how AfxCore.rtf looks in Word's Normal view.

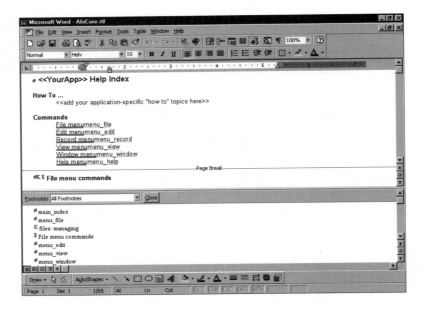

Figure 5.15 Microsoft Word displaying AfxCore.rtf

Each Help topic in the .rtf file begins with a hard page break. Each topic might contain hypertext links to other Help topics. Links are formatted as double-underlined text and are followed immediately by the link destinations formatted as hidden text. The link destinations are signified by a pound (#) footnote mark. The footnote text contains the context name, which can either be a name internal to the Help file or one of the context IDs specified in the Help project's .hm file. Help uses embedded context IDs to locate the correct Help topic for context-sensitive Help.

The other special footnote marks identify keywords for searching (K) and for topic names ($).

The text in double angle-brackets (for example, <<YourApp>> in Figure 5.15) is generic placeholder text generated by the AppWizard, which you replace with text specific to your application.

In the following exercise, you will create a Help topic for the **Import** menu that you added to the MyHelpApp application.

▶ **To create the Import menu Help topic**

1. In the AfxCore.rtf file, replace all instances of <<YourApp>> with **MyHelpApp**.

2. In the Help Index topic (the first in the file), change the hypertext link item **Record menu** to **Import menu**. (The **Record** menu is not implemented by MyHelpApp, so there is no Help topic for it.)

3. Change the associated link destination text (the hidden text immediately after the link text) to **menu_import**.

4. At an appropriate location, add a new topic titled **Import Menu Commands**. Ensure that the topic is on its own page. The title should be marked with a # footnote that points to the text **menu_import**. The topic page should contain a hypertext link named **Text File**, followed by a reference to the jump location **HID_IMPORT_TEXTFILE**. The hyperlink should be followed by a brief explanation formatted as plain text, as shown in Figure 5.16.

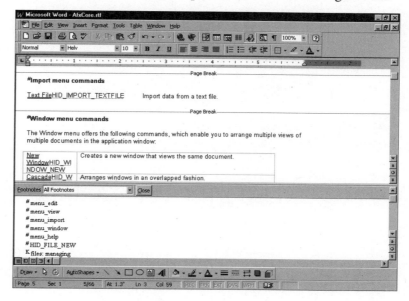

Figure 5.16   The **Import** menu Help topic

5. At an appropriate location, add another topic titled **Text Files command (Import menu)**. The title should be marked with a # footnote that points to the text **HID_IMPORT_TEXTFILE**. Add a K footnote that points to the text **Text Files**, and a $ footnote that points to the text **Importing Text Files.** Add a brief explanation of the topic. Use Figure 5.17, shown on the following page, as a guide.

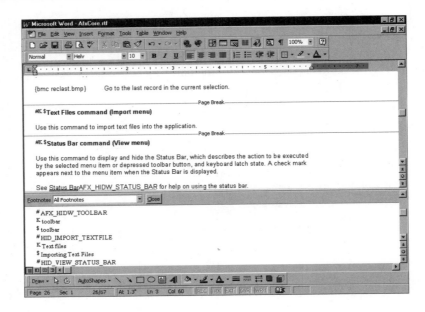

Figure 5.17   The Importing Text Files Help topic

6. Save and close the AfxCore.rtf file.

Note In a real-world development situation, you would probably want to re-name the AfxCore.rtf and AfxPrint.rtf files once they become specific to your application. You'd then need to alter the file references in the Visual Studio and the Microsoft Help Workshop projects. We have omitted this step from the exercises for the sake of brevity.

---

7. Rebuild and run the MyHelpApp application. Press F1 to view your modified MyHelpApp index page. Search for "Import menu", and then "Text files" to locate the Importing Text Files topic. Close the MyHelpApp application Help file.

8. Check that the context-sensitive Help feature works properly for the **Text Files** option on the **Import** menu.

9. Open the **Help Topics** dialog box and search for the "Text files" topic on the **Index** tab, and perform a keyword search for the topic on the **Find** tab.

Note You are able to do this because of the K and $ footnotes you added to the AfxCore.rtf file.

HTML Help

HTML Help, Microsoft's next-generation Help development platform, uses the underlying components of Microsoft Internet Explorer to display Help content. You can use HTML, ActiveX, Java, scripting (JavaScript and Microsoft Visual Basic Scripting Edition), and HTML image formats (.jpeg, .gif) to give your application Help system the power and appearance of a fully featured Web site. Your Help system can provide your customers with links to external resources such as your company's technical support Web site.

The viewer used by HTML Help contains a toolbar and a contents/index control to help the user navigate through the Help pages. You should be very familiar with the HTML Help interface by now, as it is used by the Visual C++ 6.0 Help system.

At some point, Microsoft will likely provide the same kind of support in the MFC application framework for HTML Help as it has already provided for WinHelp. In the meantime, if you require an HTML Help system for your application, you will need to implement it manually. However, your task is made easier because the HTML Help Workshop, the development environment used to develop HTML Help files, bears a strong resemblance to WinHelp's Help Workshop. Best of all, the HTML Help Workshop allows you to convert a WinHelp project (a .hpj file) into an HTML Help project (a *.hhp* file). The WinHelp project's rich text files are converted to HTML files, .bmp files are converted to .gif files, and the WinHelp contents files (.cnt files) are converted to the HTML Help equivalent *.hhc* files. The output of the HTML Help compiler is a *.chm* file—a compressed HTML file format.

It is not our intention for this book to cover HTML Help development in depth. However, we have provided a couple of exercises to get you started. The first exercise shows you how to use the HTML Help Workshop to convert the WinHelp project that you created for MyHelpApp into an HTML Help project named MyHHelp.hhp. You will then build the MyHHelp Help file and add code to the MyApp application to display it.

Before you can complete these exercises, you will need to install HTML Help on your computer.

▶ **To install HTML Help**

1. Run **Htmlhelp.exe**, which is located in the \HtmlHelp subfolder on Disc 1 of your Visual C++ or Visual Studio CDs.

2. Follow the setup instructions to install HTML Help to this default location: **c:\Program Files\HTML Help Workshop**.

▶ **To convert the MyHelpApp WinHelp project**

1. Close any Visual Studio projects that you have open. Using Windows Explorer, create a subfolder named **hlp** inside your MyApp development folder.

2. On the **Start** menu, point to **Programs**, point to **HTML Help Workshop**, and click **HTML Help Workshop**.

3. On the **File** menu of HTML Help Workshop, click **New**.

4. Specify that you want to create a new project by clicking **OK**.

5. On the first screen of the New Project Wizard, select the **Convert WinHelp Project** check box and click **Next**.

6. On the second screen of the New Project Wizard, type the full path to the MyHelpApp.hpj WinHelp project file into the first edit box (for example, **c:\Program Files\Microsoft Visual Studio\MyProjects\MyHelpApp\hlp\ MyHelpApp.hpj**).

7. In the second edit box, type the full path of the new **hlp** folder that you created in Step 1. Use **MyHHelp** as the name of the HTML Help project file that you want to create (for example, **c:\Program Files\Microsoft Visual Studio\MyProjects\MyApp\hlp\MyHHelp**).

8. Click **Next** to continue and then click **Finish**. The MyHHelp.hhp file is created and opened in HTML Help Workshop, as shown in Figure 5.18.

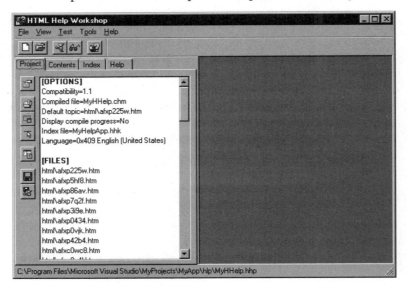

Figure 5.18   HTML Help Workshop

9. Click the **Save all project files and compile** button to create the Help file. This is the bottom button on the vertical toolbar to the left of the project information window.

When the Help compiler has finished, close the HTML Help Workshop. Using Windows Explorer, locate the MyHHelp.chm file from the ..\MyApp\hlp folder. Double click the MyHHelp.chm file to run it inside the HTML Help application. You will see how the WinHelp file that you created for MyHelpApp has been nicely converted into the HTML Help format, as shown in Figure 5.19.

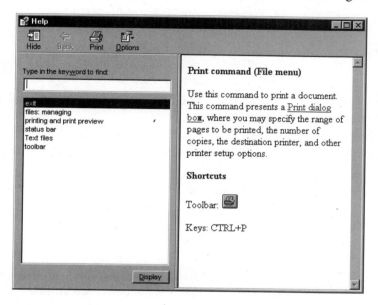

Figure 5.19 The MyHHelp.chm file

In the next exercise, you will learn how to use the HTML Help API to call the MyHHelp.chm Help file from within the MyApp application. To be able to do this, you will need to link the HTML Help library to your application.

▶ **To invoke HTML Help from the MyApp application**

1. In Visual C++, open the MyApp project. On the **Project** menu, click **Settings**.
2. Click the **Link** tab. In the **Category** box, click **Input**.
3. In the **Object/library modules** box, type **htmlhelp.lib**.
4. In the **Additional library path** box, type the path to the directory where the htmlhelp.lib file is installed (for example, **c:\Program Files\HTML Help Workshop\lib**).
5. Click the **C/C++** tab. In the **Category** box, click **Preprocessor**.
6. In the **Additional include directories** box, type the path to the directory where the htmlhelp.h file is installed (for example, **c:\Program Files\HTML Help Workshop\include**).
7. Click **OK** to save the settings.

8. In FileView, locate and open the StdAfx.h file. Add the following line of code after the other #include statements:

```
#include <htmlhelp.h>
```

9. Open the **IDR_MAINFRAME** menu in the menu editor. Add a new item with the caption **&Help Topics** to the **Help** menu. Close and re-open the **Menu Item Properties** dialog box to ensure that the command has been created with the ID **ID_HELP_HELPTOPICS**.

10. Use ClassWizard to create an **OnHelpHelptopics**() handler function for the **ID_HELP_HELPTOPICS** command message in the **CMainFrame** class.

11. Add the following line of code to the function implementation:

```
::HtmlHelp(NULL,
    C:\\Program Files\\Microsoft Visual
    Studio\\MyProjects\\MyApp\\hlp\\MyHHelp.chm",
    HH_DISPLAY_TOPIC, 0);
```

Your code will differ slightly if the path to the .chm file is not the same. Notice that backslash characters embedded in strings need to be represented by the escape character sequence \\. If you break the string across a line, make sure that you add a \ continuation character.

The **HtmlHelp**() function is the core of the HTML API. You can use it to display .chm files, HTML files, URL destinations, or plain text inside a pop-up window. There are many parameters to the **HtmlHelp**() function that specify the features of the display window and what should be displayed, For more information, see "HTML Help API reference" in the Visual C++ Help files.

12. Build the MyApp application. Don't worry if you get a linker warning message about library conflicts—this is a side effect of linking to the htmlhelp.lib library and will not affect your application. Run the application and choose **Help Topics** from the **Help** menu. The HTML Help application should appear, displaying the MyHHelp.chm Help file.

Lesson Summary

Applications written in Windows usually provide context-sensitive Help, which you can use to get help on features of the application user interface.

Windows applications are now moving from the WinHelp traditional Windows Help system, which is based on RTF documents, to the newer HTML Help, which is based on compiled HTML documents. Although Visual C++ ships with a development environment for producing HTML Help files, the automatic features of the MFC AppWizard, which provide Help systems for your programs, still employ the WinHelp system.

By convention, users access context-sensitive Help by pressing the F1 key. If a feature of the user interface, such as a command, toolbar button, or dialog box control, is currently selected when F1 is pressed, the application should display context-sensitive Help for the selected feature. An application should also implement Help mode Help. An application is put into Help mode when the user presses SHIFT+F1 or selects **Help** from the toolbar. When in Help mode, the user can gain information about a user interface element simply by clicking it with the mouse.

The MFC application framework provides extensive support for the implementation of WinHelp. Selecting **Context-sensitive Help** in Step 4 of the MFC AppWizard will set up your project with everything you need to create WinHelp for your application with a minimum of effort. The AppWizard creates a folder named hlp beneath your project folder and generates a Help project file and source files for your application Help file. These source files include .rtf files that contain Help topics for the common elements of the Windows user interface, such as the **File** and **Edit** menus. You can edit these files to revise the supplied text and add your own application-specific Help information.

Help project files are managed by the Microsoft Help Workshop, which is installed in the \Program Files\Microsoft Visual Studio\Common\Tools folder as part of a standard installation of Visual Studio. AppWizard creates custom build rules for your project to so that your Help file is rebuilt when its source files are changed.

User interface features are linked to topics in the application's Help file by Help context IDs. These are created from the application resource IDs by the MakeHm tool and stored in files with the .hm extension as part of the Help project.

An application's Help file is distributed with an .hlp extension. Help is invoked from within an application source code with a call to the **CWnd::WinHelp()** function. The application framework generates an appropriate Help context ID that it passes to the Help system as a parameter to the **WinHelp()** function.

HTML Help is Microsoft's next-generation Help development platform, which uses the underlying components of Microsoft Internet Explorer to display Help content. You can use the power of HTML, ActiveX, Java, scripting, and HTML image formats to implement your application's Help system, which can include links to intranet and Internet-based resources.

Currently, the AppWizard cannot automatically generate an HTML Help system for your application. You can manually create a system using the HTML Help development environment that ships with Visual C++ 6.0. This includes the HTML Help Workshop, which bears a strong resemblance to the Microsoft Help Workshop, and which allows you to convert a WinHelp project into an HTML Help project. The WinHelp project's rich text files are converted to HTML files. An application's HTML Help is contained in a .chm file—a compressed HTML file format. HTML Help is invoked from within the application source code with a call to the HTML Help API function **HTMLHelp()**.

Lab 5: Enhancing the STUpload Data Display

In Lab 3, you learned how to implement a very simple **OnDraw()** function for the STUpload application, which outputs the data records held in the application document object as lines of text. The application displays all the records that are stored in the document—currently a hard-coded set of records representing data from three different stock funds.

In Lab 5, you are going to enhance the application in two ways. First, you are going to implement the **Select Fund** dialog box, a modeless dialog box that allows the user to select from a list of funds currently stored in the application document object. Then you will create a new **CSTUploadView::OnDraw()** function to display data for the currently selected fund in a graph format.

Displaying the Select Fund Dialog Box

To create the **Select Fund** dialog box, you will use the dialog template IDD_FUNDDIALOG and the class **CFundDialog** that you created for Lab 4. At this point, the dialog box design is not complete. The final version will not have **OK** and **Cancel** buttons because you are going to allow the user to show and hide the dialog box using only the **Select Fund** command option on the **View** menu (or by using the toolbar button). However, you will need to overload the **OnOK()** and **OnCancel()** handler functions. Because IDOK and IDCANCEL messages will be generated when the user presses the ENTER or ESC keys, you will need to create versions of the handler functions for the **Select Fund** dialog class that do nothing; otherwise, the base class (**CDialog**) versions will be called. Remember that the base class versions call the **EndDialog()** function to dismiss the dialog box.

It is much easier to add handlers for the **OK** and **Cancel** messages when the buttons are still defined as part of the dialog box, so you will create **OnOK()** and **OnCancel()** handlers at this point.

▶ **To create the OnOk() handler**

1. Press CTRL+W to open ClassWizard. In the **Class name** box, click **CFundDialog**.

2. In the **Object IDs** box, click **IDOK**.

3. In the **Messages** box, click **BN_CLICKED**.

4. Click **Add Function** and then click **OK** to accept the suggested handler name **OnOK**.

5. Click **Edit Code** to jump to the **CFundDialog::OnOK()** implementation code.

6. From the body of this function remove the following line:

```
CDialog::OnOK();
```

7. Repeat the process to add an empty **OnCancel()** function to handle the BN_CLICKED message for the IDCANCEL item. Now you can remove the **OK** and **Cancel** buttons from the dialog template.

▶ **To complete the Select Fund dialog template**

1. Open the **IDD_FUNDDIALOG** resource with the dialog editor.
2. Click **OK**. Press the DELETE key to remove the button.
3. Click **Cancel**. Press DELETE.
4. Resize the dialog box so the list box fits just inside the dashed blue edit guide. Your dialog box should look as shown in Figure 5.20.

Figure 5.20   The **Select Fund** dialog box

Now you will write code to control the behavior of the **Select Fund** dialog box. You will create a single **CFundDialog** object early on in the application, as the m_wndFundDialog member of the application main frame window object **CMainFrame**. The dialog window will be a child window of the application main window, and it will be shown or hidden according to the status of m_bFundsVisible, a Boolean member variable of the **CMainFrame** class. The status of m_bFundsVisible will be set by menu and toolbar commands.

▶ **To create the m_wndFundDialog member object**

1. In ClassView, right-click the **CMainFrame** class icon.
2. On the shortcut menu, click **Add Member Variable**.
3. In the **Add Member Variable** dialog box, type **CFundDialog** into the **Variable Type** box.
4. Type **m_wndFundDialog** in the **Variable Name** box.
5. Set the access specifier to **Protected**. Click **OK** to add the variable.
6. Repeat the process to add a protected BOOL member variable **m_bFundsVisible** to the **CMainFrame** class.
7. Double-click the **CMainFrame** class icon in ClassView to open the header file and jump to the top of the class declaration.
8. Check that ClassView has added the following line of code to the top of the file:

```
#include "FundDialog.h"
```

▶ **To initialize the m_bFundsVisible member in the class constructor**

1. Double-click the icon that represents the **CMainFrame** class constructor.

2. Add the following line of code to the body of the function:

```
m_bFundsVisible = FALSE;
```

▶ **To create accessor functions for the m_bFundsVisible member variable**

1. Return to the **CMainFrame** class declaration in **MainFrm.h**. Add the following lines of code to the public section:

   (This code can be found in CH5_01.cpp, installed from the companion CD.)

```
BOOL AreFundsVisible() {return m_bFundsVisible;}
void SetFundsVisible(BOOL bSet)
{
    m_bFundsVisible = bSet;
    if(bSet)  m_wndFundDialog.ShowWindow(SW_SHOW);
    else  m_wndFundDialog.ShowWindow(SW_HIDE);
}
```

2. You will now need to initialize your dialog object by calling its **Create()** function and passing the resource ID as a parameter. The **Create()** function takes a second parameter with which you can specify the dialog box's parent window. You will use the default setting **NULL**, which sets the parent window to be the main application window.

▶ **To initialize the m_wndFundDialog object**

1. In ClassView, expand the **CMainFrame** class icon.

2. Double-click the **OnCreate()** member function icon to jump to the function implementation.

3. At the end of the function, *before* the return statement, add the following lines of code:

```
// Create the fund dialog window
m_wndFundDialog.Create(IDD_FUNDDIALOG);
```

Remember that the dialog box does not have the WS_VISIBLE style property, so it will need to be displayed explicitly with a call to the **CWnd::ShowWindow()** function.

Hiding and showing the dialog box is going to be controlled by the handler for the **Selection Fund** command on the **View** menu. In the following exercises, you will create a command handler and a user interface update command handler for the **ID_VIEW_FUNDSELECTION** command ID.

▶ **To add the CMainFrame::OnViewFundselection() function**

1. Press CTRL+W to invoke ClassWizard. Click the **Message Maps** tab.

2. In the **Class Name** box, click **CMainFrame**.

3. In the **Object IDs** box, click **ID_VIEW_FUNDSELECTION**.

4. In the **Messages** box, click **COMMAND**.

5. Click **Add Function**. Click **OK** to accept the suggested handler function name **OnViewFundselection()**.

6. Click **Edit Code**. The MainFrm.cpp file is opened. and the insertion point is positioned at the top of the function implementation.

7. Add the following line to the body of the **OnViewFundselection()** function:

```
SetFundsVisible(m_bFundsVisible ? FALSE : TRUE);
```

▶ **To implement the CMainFrame::OnUpdateViewFundselection() function**

1. Using ClassWizard, create the **OnUpdateViewFundselection** function for the **UPDATE_COMMAND_UI** message and the **ID_VIEW_FUNDSELECTION** object ID.

2. Select **Settings** from the **Project** menu. On the **C/C++** page, click **C++ Language** in the **Category** box. Ensure that **Enable Run-Time Type Information (RTTI)** is selected. Click **OK** to close the **Project Settings** dialog box.

3. Add the following lines of code to the body of the function **OnUpdateViewFundselection()**:

(This code can be found in CH5_02.cpp, installed from the companion CD.)

```
// Enable the View Funds Selection dialog if
// the document CStockDataList is not empty.
// If enabled, then toggle button state checked/unchecked
// according to whether the window is displayed or hidden
BOOL bEnable = FALSE;
CSTUploadDoc * pDoc =
    dynamic_cast<CSTUploadDoc *>(GetActiveDocument());
if(pDoc)
    bEnable = pDoc->GetDocList().GetCount() ? TRUE : FALSE;
pCmdUI->Enable(bEnable);
if(bEnable)
    pCmdUI->SetCheck(m_bFundsVisible ? 1 : 0);
```

4. Add the following line of code to the top of the MainFrm.cpp file:

```
#include "STUploadDoc.h"
```

5. You can now build and run the STUpload application. Experiment with showing and hiding the **Select Fund** dialog box by using the command and the toolbar button.

Displaying Fund Names in the Funds List Box

Now that you have displayed the **Select Fund** dialog box, you will write a function to load the names of the funds into the list box control. Because the list of fund records held in the **CSTUploadDoc::m_DocList** object will be created in fund sort order, it is not a difficult matter to iterate across the list and extract a unique list of fund names.

Before you can write this function, you will have to create a variable with the MFC type CListBox.

▶ **To add the CFundDialog::m_listBox member variable**

1. Press CTRL+W to open ClassWizard and click the **Member Variables** tab.

2. In the **Class Name** list, click the **CFundDialog** class.

3. Click **Add Variable**. In the **Member variable name** box, type **m_listBox**.

4. In the **Category** box, click **Control**. The **Variable Type** box displays **CListBox**.

5. Click **OK** to create the variable, and then click **OK** again to close ClassWizard.

You are now going to add the **UpdateFundList()** member function to the **CMainFrame** class to perform the task of loading the fund name items into the list box. The function will take two parameters—a reference to a *CStockDataList*, which will be the source of the fund names; and a string to specify the fund name that should be selected initially. If the second parameter contains an empty string (the default value), or the provided string is not found in the list box, no item is selected.

▶ **To implement the CMainFrame::UpdateFundList() function**

1. In FileView, expand the Header Files folder and double-click the **CMainFrm.h** file icon to open the file.

2. At the top of the file, with the other #include statements, add the following line:

```
#include "StockDataList.h"
```

3. Switch to ClassView and right-click the **CMainFrame** icon. Use the **Add Member Function** option to add the function declaration to the **public** section of the class declaration, and to add a function stub. The function should have the following signature:

```
void UpdateFundList(const CStockDataList & pList,
    CString strCurrentFund = "");
```

4. Add the following code to the body of the **UpdateFundList()** function:

(This code can be found in CH5_03.cpp, installed from the companion CD.)

```
// Function to add one entry per fund to fund view list box.
// CStockDataLists are sorted by fund name so this is easy.
CListBox *pListBox = &m_wndFundDialog.m_listBox;
// Empty current contents of list box
pListBox->ResetContent();
CString strLastFund;
POSITION pos = pList.GetHeadPosition();
while(pos)
{
    CStockData sd = pList.GetNext(pos);
    CString strFund = sd.GetFund();
    if(strFund != strLastFund)
        pListBox->AddString(strFund);
    strLastFund = strFund;
}
// Set list box selection to strCurrentFund parameter.
// No selection if parameter empty or not found.
int iPos = pListBox->FindStringExact(-1, strCurrentFund);
pListBox->SetCurSel(iPos);
```

Look through the code and make sure that you understand how the function achieves its objectives.

The **UpdateFundList()** function will be called from the **LoadData()** function. Eventually the **LoadData()** function will handle the loading of data records from a text file. For now, you will create a temporary version that simply adds some hard-coded records.

▶ **To implement the STUploadDoc::LoadData() function**

1. Right-click the **STUploadDoc** icon in ClassView and use the **Add Member Function** dialog box to add the function declaration to the **protected** section of the class declaration, and to add a function stub. The function should have the following signature:

```
BOOL LoadData(CStdioFile & infile)
```

2. To the body of the **LoadData()** function, add the code from CH5_04.cpp (installed from the companion CD), part of which is shown below:

```
m_DocList.AddTail(CStockData(_T("ARSC"),
COleDateTime(1999, 4, 1, 0, 0, 0), 22.33));
// ... more records added here
m_DocList.AddTail(CStockData(_T("COMP"),
COleDateTime(1999, 4, 5, 0, 0, 0), 19.77));

// Update main window

UpdateAllViews(NULL);

// Update Fund Selection dialog box
CMainFrame * pWnd =
    dynamic_cast<CMainFrame *> (AfxGetMainWnd());
if(pWnd)
{
    pWnd->UpdateFundList(m_DocList);
    // Show fund window after loading new funds
    pWnd->SetFundsVisible(TRUE);
}

return TRUE;
```

3. Add the following to the top of the CSTUploadDoc.cpp file:

```
#include "MainFrm.h"
```

4. Locate the CSTUploadDoc constructor. Remove all the implementation code to leave an empty function stub so that the constructor appears as follows:

```
CSTUploadDoc::CSTUploadDoc()
{
}
```

5. Locate the **CSTUploadDoc::OnDataImport()** function. To the bottom of the function, before the closing brace, add the following code to call the **LoadData()** function:

```
if(nID == IDOK)
{
    CStdioFile aFile;
    LoadData(aFile);
}
```

You can now build the STUpload application. Choose **Import** from the **Data** menu. Using the **Open** dialog box, open the Ch5Test.dat file from the ..\Chapter 5\Data folder. Records should be displayed for the ARSC, BBIC and COMP funds, and the **Select Fund** dialog box should display these three funds.

Handling Notification Messages from the Select Fund Dialog Box

The purpose of the **Select Fund** dialog box is to allow the user to limit the display of fund price data so that records for only the currently selected fund are displayed. You have already filled the list box with options—you now have to act upon the user's selection.

To start, you will add the m_strCurrentFund variable to record the fund name currently selected by the user. In the next chapter, you will be making this variable persistent so that you can save the current user selection as part of the document data. Thus the m_strCurrentFund variable will be a member of the **CSTUploadDoc** class.

To ensure that this variable always represents the current selection of the **Select Fund** dialog box, you will handle notification messages from the list box control. The list box sends a LBN_SELCHANGE message to its parent window (the **CFundDialog** object) every time the selection changes. You can use ClassWizard to provide a handler for this message.

You will also change the **CSTUploadView::OnDraw()** function so that it refers to the "currently selected fund" variable held by the document object to ensure that it displays records that pertain to the currently selected fund only.

▶ **To add the CDocument::m_strCurrentFund member**

Right-click the **CDocument** icon in ClassView and add a protected member variable of type CString named **m_strCurrentFund**.

▶ **To initialize the m_strCurrentFund member in the class constructor**

1. Double-click the icon that represents the **CSTUploadDoc** class constructor.
2. Add the following line of code to the body of the function:

```
m_strCurrentFund = "";
```

▶ **To create accessor functions for the m_strCurrentFund member variable**

Add the following lines of code to the **public** section of the **CDocument** class declaration:

```
CString GetCurrentFund () {return m_strCurrentFund;}
void SetCurrentFund (CString strSet){m_strCurrentFund= strSet;}
```

▶ **To add a method to the CFundDialog class to handle the LBN_SELCHANGE message**

1. Press CTRL+W to open ClassWizard. Click the **Message Maps** tab.

2. In the **Class Name** box, click **CFundDialog**.

3. In the **Object IDs** box, click **IDC_FUNDLIST**.

4. In the **Messages** box, click **LBN_SELCHANGE**.

5. Click **Add Function**. Click **OK** to accept the suggested handler function name **OnSelchangeFundlist()**.

6. Click **Edit Code**. The FundDialog.cpp file is opened and the insertion point is positioned at the top of the function implementation.

▶ **To implement the CMainFrame::OnSelchangeFundlist() function**

1. Add the following lines of code to the body of the **OnSelchangeFundlist()** function:

   (This code can be found in CH5_05.cpp, installed from the companion CD.)

```
CMainFrame * pWnd =
    dynamic_cast<CMainFrame *> (AfxGetMainWnd());
ASSERT_VALID(pWnd);

CSTUploadDoc * pDoc =
    dynamic_cast<CSTUploadDoc *>(pWnd->GetActiveDocument());
ASSERT_VALID(pDoc);

CString strCurFund;

int sel = m_listBox.GetCurSel();

if(sel == LB_ERR) sel = 0;

m_listBox.GetText(sel, strCurFund);

pDoc->SetCurrentFund(strCurFund);

pDoc->UpdateAllViews(NULL);
```

2. Add the following lines of code to the top of the FundDialog.cpp file:

```
#include "MainFrm.h"
#include "STUploadDoc.h"
```

► **To alter the CSTUploadView::OnDraw() function**

1. Locate the display loop at the bottom of the **CSTUploadView::OnDraw()** function. Just after the call to **CStockDataList::GetNext()**, add this code:

```
if(sd.GetFund() != pDoc->GetCurrentFund()) continue;
```

The entire loop section should now look as follows:

```
while(pos)
{
    CStockData sd = pData.GetNext(pos);

    if(sd.GetFund() != pDoc->GetCurrentFund())continue;

    pDC->TextOut(10, yPos, sd.GetAsString());
    yPos += nTextHeight;
}
```

2. Build and run the STUpload application. Test loading the data as before. You will now see that no records appear initially, but as soon as you select a fund from the **Select Fund** dialog box, the appropriate records will appear.

Making the Select Fund Dialog Box a Topmost Window

The **Select Fund** dialog box is a key element of the STUpload application user interface. It will be constantly in use to switch from fund to fund as the operator checks through the data held on file. In its current implementation, however, it is easily hidden if the user clicks on the main application window—to access the main menu, for example. The **Select Fund** dialog box is so small that it is inconvenient to retrieve once it is hidden behind the larger window.

The solution to this problem is to make the **Select Fund** dialog box a *topmost* window—that is, a window that is always on top of other windows in the application. A topmost window will appear even if it does not have input focus.

A topmost window has the style WS_EX_TOPMOST. In an MFC application, you can set this by calling the **CWnd::SetWindowPos()** function with the address of the **wndTopMost** constant as the first parameter.

► **To set the Select Fund dialog box as a topmost window**

1. In ClassView, double-click the **CMainFrame::OnCreate()** function icon to edit the code.

2. At the bottom of the function, directly after the following line:

```
m_wndFundDialog.Create(IDD_FUNDDIALOG);
```

and *before* the return statement, add the line shown on the next page.

```
m_wndFundDialog.SetWindowPos(&wndTopMost, 0, 0, 0, 0,
    SWP_NOMOVE | SWP_NOSIZE);
```

This is all you need to do to make the **Select Fund** dialog box stay on top of the application main window. Unfortunately, it has the undesirable side effect of making the dialog box stay on top of *all other* application windows—even when the STUpload application is not active. If you build and run the application and test its behavior at this point, you will see that the **Select Fund** dialog box remains visible even when the STUpload application is minimized.

To solve this problem, you need to hide the dialog box (if it is visible) at the point where the application *as a whole* loses focus, and then re-display it when the user switches focus back to the application. To do this, you need to provide a handler for the WM_ACTIVATEAPP message, which is called when the user switches between applications. You will use ClassWizard to create a handler that is an overload of the **CWnd::OnActivateApp()** method. This function is called by the framework with a Boolean parameter that indicates whether the application is being activated or deactivated.

▶ **To add a handler for the WM_ACTIVATEAPP message**

1. Press CTRL+W to open ClassWizard. Click the **Message Maps** tab.
2. In the **Class Name** box, click **CMainFrame**.
3. In the **Object IDs** box, click **CMainFrame**.
4. In the **Messages** box, click **WM_ACTIVATEAPP**.
5. Click **Add Function**.
6. Click **Edit Code**. The MainFrm.cpp file is opened, and the insertion point is positioned at the top of the function implementation.

▶ **To implement the CMainFrame::OnActivateApp() function**

1. To the body of the **OnActivateApp()** function, after the call to the base-class version, add the following code:

   (This code can be found in CH5_15.cpp, installed from the companion CD.)

```
if(bActive)
{
    if(AreFundsVisible())
        m_wndFundDialog.ShowWindow(SW_SHOW);
}
else
{
    if(AreFundsVisible())
        m_wndFundDialog.ShowWindow(SW_HIDE);
}
```

2. Build the application and test to ensure that the **Select Fund** dialog box remains on top of the STUpload application window, but that it is hidden when other applications have focus.

Displaying STUpload Application Data

You are now ready to implement the graphical display of price data for the currently selected fund. The first task is to determine the document size so that the scroll bars provided by **CScrollView** will appear correctly. In the STUpload application, although the size of the application data changes as text files are loaded into the document, the size of the display output remains constant. Only one graph is displayed at any time. You will fix the size of the graph to the size of a standard laser printer page in landscape orientation—that is, 11 inches wide by 8.5 inches tall.

▶ **To set up scroll sizes for the STUpload application**

1. In ClassView, expand the **CSTUploadView** class icon.

2. Double click the **OnInitialUpdate()** icon to edit the function.

3. Edit the following lines:

```
sizeTotal.cx = sizeTotal.cy = 100;
SetScrollSizes(MM_TEXT, sizeTotal);
```

so that they appear as follows:

```
sizeTotal.cx = 1100;
sizeTotal.cy = 850;
SetScrollSizes(MM_LOENGLISH, sizeTotal);
```

You will now replace the **CView::OnDraw()** function with a provided version. This function collects the data currently held on file for a particular fund into a temporary array. It uses the data to calculate a suitable scale for the dates (x-axis) and the prices (y-axis). The data is presented as a line graph, which should enable the operator to spot any erratic data easily, with the exact values displayed at the graph points. Look through the code to see how the MFC drawing tool classes and the GDI drawing functions are used to display output in a device context.

▶ **To implement the OnDraw() method**

1. In ClassView, expand the **CSTUploadView** class icon.

2. Double click the **OnDraw()** icon to edit the method.

3. Replace the *entire* method with the following code:

   (This code can be found in CH5_07.cpp, installed from the companion CD.)

```cpp
void CSTUploadView::OnDraw(CDC* pDC)
{
    CSTUploadDoc* pDoc = GetDocument();
    ASSERT_VALID(pDoc);

    // Save the current state of the device context
    int nDC = pDC->SaveDC();

    const CStockDataList & pData = pDoc->GetDocList();

    // Make a small array containing the
    // records for the current fund.
    // We use an array to take advantage of indexed access.
    CArray<CStockData, CStockData &> arrFundData;

    POSITION pos = pData.GetHeadPosition();

    while(pos)
    {
        CStockData sd = pData.GetNext(pos);

        if(sd.GetFund() == pDoc->GetCurrentFund())
            arrFundData.Add(sd);
    }

    int nPrices = arrFundData.GetSize();
    if(nPrices == 0)
        return;

    // Some constant sizes (in device units)
    const int AXIS_DIVIDER_LENGTH = 6;
    const int AXIS_FONT_HEIGHT = 24;
    const int HEADING_FONT_HEIGHT = 36;

    // Create font for axis labels
    CFont AxisFont;
    if(AxisFont.CreateFont(AXIS_FONT_HEIGHT, 0, 0, 0, 0, 0, 0, 0, 0,
        0, 0, 0, FF_ROMAN, 0))

        pDC->SelectObject(&AxisFont);
    else
    {
        AfxMessageBox("Unable to create Axis font");
        return;
    }
```

```
CPen AxisPen;
if(AxisPen.CreatePen(PS_SOLID, 1, RGB(0,0,0)))
    pDC->SelectObject(&AxisPen);
else
{
    AfxMessageBox("Unable to create Axis Pen");
    return;
}

// Array to graph coordinates as we go
CArray<CPoint, CPoint&> CoordArray;
for(int i = 0; i < nPrices; i++)
    CoordArray.Add(CPoint(0, 0));

// Set viewport origin to bottom left corner of window
CPoint ptBottomLeft(0, -850);
pDC->LPtoDP(&ptBottomLeft);
pDC->SetViewportOrg(ptBottomLeft);

// Base coordinates for axes
const CPoint ORIGIN(100, 100);
const CPoint Y_EXTENT(ORIGIN.x, ORIGIN.y + 650);
const CPoint X_EXTENT(ORIGIN.x + 900, ORIGIN.y);

// Draw axes
pDC->MoveTo(Y_EXTENT);
pDC->LineTo(ORIGIN);
pDC->LineTo(X_EXTENT);

int nLabelPos = Y_EXTENT.y + ((ORIGIN.y - Y_EXTENT.y) / 2);
pDC->TextOut(ORIGIN.x - 50, nLabelPos, '$');

// Divide x-axis into number of prices held in the file
int nXIncrement = (X_EXTENT.x - ORIGIN.x) / nPrices;

double nMaxPrice = 0;
double nMinPrice = 0;

for(i = 0; i < nPrices; i++)
{
    int xPoint = (ORIGIN.x + (i * nXIncrement));
    CoordArray[i].x = xPoint;

    pDC->MoveTo(xPoint, ORIGIN.y);
    pDC->LineTo(xPoint, ORIGIN.y + AXIS_DIVIDER_LENGTH);

    COleDateTime aDate = arrFundData[i].GetDate();
    double aPrice = arrFundData[i].GetPrice();
```

```cpp
            nMaxPrice = max(nMaxPrice, aPrice);
            nMinPrice = nMinPrice == 0 ?
                nMaxPrice :
                min(nMinPrice, aPrice);

            CString strDate = aDate.Format("%m/%d/%y");

            if(i == 0 || i == (nPrices-1))
                pDC->TextOut(xPoint-2,
                    ORIGIN.y - AXIS_FONT_HEIGHT / 2, strDate);
            else
            {
                CString strDay = strDate.Mid(
                    strDate.Find('/') + 1);
                strDay = strDay.Left(strDay.Find('/'));
                pDC->TextOut(xPoint-6,
                    ORIGIN.y - AXIS_FONT_HEIGHT / 2, strDay);
            }
        }

        // Divide y-axis into suitable scale based on
        // the difference between max and min prices on file
        nMaxPrice += 2.0;
        nMinPrice -= 1.0;
        int iScale = int(nMaxPrice) - int(nMinPrice);

        int nYIncrement = (ORIGIN.y - Y_EXTENT.y) / iScale;

        for(i = 0; i < iScale; i++)
        {
            int yPoint = (ORIGIN.y - (i * nYIncrement));
            pDC->MoveTo(ORIGIN.x, yPoint);
            pDC->LineTo(ORIGIN.x - AXIS_DIVIDER_LENGTH, yPoint);

            int iCurrentPrice = int(nMinPrice) + i;

            for(int j = 0; j < nPrices; j++)
            {
                double aPrice = arrFundData[j].GetPrice();
                if(aPrice >= double(iCurrentPrice) &&
                    aPrice < double(iCurrentPrice) + 1.0)
                {
                    double dFraction = aPrice -
                        double(iCurrentPrice);
                    CoordArray[j].y =
                        yPoint - int(dFraction *
                            double(nYIncrement));
                }
            }
        }
```

```
    CString strPrice;
    strPrice.Format("%d", iCurrentPrice);

    int nTextSize = pDC->GetTextExtent(strPrice).cx;
    nTextSize += 10;

    pDC->TextOut(ORIGIN.x - nTextSize, yPoint+12, strPrice);
}

// Graph figures stored in CoordArray
CPen GraphPen;
if(GraphPen.CreatePen(PS_SOLID, 1, RGB(255,0,0)))  // Red pen
{
    pDC->SelectObject(&GraphPen);
}
else
{
    AfxMessageBox("Unable to create Graph Pen");
    return;
}

// Draw Graph
// Label graph points with price value (in blue)
COLORREF crOldText = pDC->SetTextColor(RGB(0,0,255));

pDC->MoveTo(CoordArray[0]);

for(i = 0; i <nPrices; i++)
{
    pDC->LineTo(CoordArray[i]);
    CPoint TextPoint;
    if((i+1) <nPrices)
    {
        if(CoordArray[i + 1].y >= CoordArray[i].y)
            TextPoint = CoordArray[i] + CPoint(5, 0);
        else
            TextPoint = CoordArray[i] + CPoint(5,
                AXIS_FONT_HEIGHT);
    }
    else
        TextPoint = CoordArray[i] + CPoint(5, 0);

    CString strPrice;
    strPrice.Format("%.2f", arrFundData[i].GetPrice());

    pDC->TextOut(TextPoint.x, TextPoint.y, strPrice);
}

pDC->SetTextColor(crOldText);
```

```
// Create heading
CFont HeadingFont;
if(HeadingFont.
    CreateFont(HEADING_FONT_HEIGHT, 0, 0, 0, FW_BOLD, 1, 0, 0,
    0, 0, 0, 0, FF_ROMAN, 0));

    pDC->SelectObject(&HeadingFont);
else
{
    AfxMessageBox("Unable to create Heading Font");
    return;
}

CString strHeading = pDoc->GetCurrentFund();
strHeading += " - Closing Prices ";

COleDateTime aDate = arrFundData[0].GetDate();
strHeading += aDate.Format("%m/%d/%y");
strHeading += " to ";
aDate = arrFundData[nPrices - 1].GetDate();
strHeading += aDate.Format("%m/%d/%y");

CSize sizeText = pDC->GetTextExtent(strHeading);

pDC->TextOut(X_EXTENT.x - sizeText.cx,
    Y_EXTENT.y + sizeText.cy, strHeading);

// Restore the original device context
pDC->RestoreDC(nDC);
}
```

4. Build and run the STUpload application. Test loading the data as before. The application data should now appear as shown in Figure 5.21.

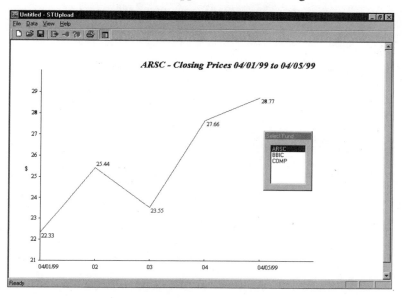

Figure 5.21   The STUpload application

Review

1. How is the **DoDataExchange()** function called? How does it determine the direction of the data exchange?

2. How do you make controls unavailable in a dialog box?

3. Which two functions are used to specify coordinate mapping for an unconstrained mapping mode?

4. Which function associates a drawing tool object with a device context?

5. What kinds of threads must be created by using a **CWinThread** object?

6. What is the difference between a **CCriticalSection** object and a **CMutex** object?

7. How are Help context IDs specified in a Help project file?

8. How do you create a hyperlink in a Help project .rtf file?

C H A P T E R   6

Persistent Data

About This Chapter

Persistent data is data saved on a storage device, typically a hard drive, which preserves (persists) changes made to the data between application sessions.

In this chapter, you will learn ways to make your application data and settings persistent. You will learn how to use the MFC **CFile** class for general file input/output (I/O) operations; how to use the serialization facilities of the MFC framework to save and restore structured application data; and how to save individual data items, such as application settings, in the system registry.

Persistent data can also be stored in a database external to the application. Connections to databases will be covered in Chapter 7.

Before You Begin

Before you start this chapter, you should have read Chapters 2 through 5, and completed the exercises in the text.

Lesson 1: File I/O

In this lesson, you will learn about the file I/O classes provided by MFC. You will also learn about the basic file services offered by the **CFile** class and how to use its derived class **CStdioFile**, which provides buffered stream file access.

After this lesson, you will be able to:

- Create new files and open existing files using member functions of the **CFile** class.
- Read and write binary files and text files using the **CStdioFile** class.
- Handle errors that might occur while attempting file I/O.

Estimated lesson time: 25 minutes

CFile Class

The MFC **CFile** class provides access to binary disk files by encapsulating an operating system file handle and providing member functions for opening, reading from, writing to, and closing a file. The **CFile** class provides direct, unbuffered access to files. Derived from **CFile**, the **CStdioFile** class implements buffered stream files in MFC.

CFile is the base class for the **CMemFile** and the **CSharedFile** classes. **CMemFile** provides support for *in-memory files*, which are stored in RAM rather than on a disk for increased performance. **CSharedFile** provides support for shared in-memory files.

Opening and Closing Files

There is more than one way to open a file using the **CFile** class. The class provides a constructor that allows you to specify the file to open. This constructor lets you declare a **CFile** object and associate that object with a disk file in a single statement. Specifying the file in the constructor is risky. If the file doesn't exist, errors will result.

It is generally better to use a two-stage approach. First, create a **CFile** object; second, associate this object with a disk file. This approach gives you more flexibility in handling errors, and also helps clarify the logical distinction between the file object in your code and the physical disk file.

To open a disk file using the two-stage approach, first declare a **CFile** object without any parameters. Next, call the **CFile::Open()** function for the object, specify the path to the disk file, and provide flags that specify the access and sharing modes. For example, note the following code, which uses the two-stage approach:

```
CString strPath = "MyFile.bin";
CFile MyFile;
BOOL bResult = MyFile.Open(strPath, CFile::modeRead);
if(!bResult)
    AfxMessageBox(strPath + " could not be opened");
```

Specifying a file name without any path information will result in the **Open** command searching for the file in the current folder first, and in the folders within the system path next. You can also specify paths relative to the current folder and paths using a Universal Naming Convention (UNC) name. A UNC name provides a computer-independent means of locating the file, and has the format *Server Name\Network Share\File Path.*

When specifying a path name for the file to be opened, don't make any assumptions about the file's location. For example, specifying the path name as follows assumes that the MyFile.bin file will be found in the C:\\Program Files\\MyApp folder:

```
CString strPath = C:\\Program Files\\MyApp\\MyFile.bin;
```

This assumption might not be valid if your application has been installed on a drive other than drive C. Your application or setup program can create environment variables or registry entries (see Lesson 3 of this chapter) to record the location of the files that it uses.

The second parameter to the **Open()** function allows you to specify a bitmask that defines the file's access and sharing modes. The bitmask values are declared as enumerated constants within the scope of the **CFile** class, which means that the flags must be qualified with the class scope. The access mode determines whether the file will be open for reading only, writing only, or both reading and writing. The sharing mode determines the access to this file granted to other processes while you have the file open. You can create a new file by specifying the **CFile::modeCreate** value.

The bitmask values passed to the **Open()** function can be combined by using the bitwise **OR** operator (|). Generally, you should specify an access mode as well as a sharing mode. For example, the following code will open the MyFile.bin file for reading and writing:

```
MyFile.Open("MyFile.bin", CFile::modeReadWrite|CFile::shareDenyWrite);
```

If the file MyFile.bin is successfully opened by this function call, all other processes will be denied write permissions to the file. If MyFile.bin cannot be found, it will not be created.

Table 6.1 summarizes the access and sharing modes defined by the **CFile** class.

Table 6.1   Access and Sharing Modes

Flag Value	Action
CFile::modeCreate	Creates a new file. If the specified file already exists, it is truncated to zero length.
CFile::modeNoTruncate	Can be combined with **CFile::modeCreate** to ensure that, if the specified file already exists, it is opened without being truncated to zero length. Thus, the file is guaranteed to open, either as an existing file or as a newly created file. This value might be useful when opening a settings file that might or might not already exist.
CFile::modeRead	Opens the file as read-only.
CFile::modeReadWrite	Opens the file as read/write.
CFile::modeWrite	Opens the file as write-only.
CFile::shareDenyNone	Does not deny other processes read or write permissions to the file.
CFile::shareDenyRead	Denies other processes read permissions to the file.
CFile::shareDenyWrite	Denies other processes write permissions to the file.
CFile::shareExclusive	Denies other processes both read and write permissions to the file.

File Errors

It is not difficult to see that a number of factors might cause the **CFile::Open()** function to fail. Attempting to open a file that does not exist (without specifying the **CFile::modeCreate** flag) will cause the **Open()** function to fail. Attempting to open a file already opened exclusively by another process will also result in failure. Numerous environmental factors can cause errors when working with files.

In the example code showing how to use **CFile::Open()**, the function returned a Boolean value indicating success or failure. If there was a failure, you will usually want to retrieve information about *why* the operation failed. You can then relay such information to the user, and suggest steps they can take to remedy the problem.

MFC provides the **CFileException** class (derived from the **CException** base class) to represent a file error condition. The MFC exception classes contain member data and functions that allow you to retrieve information about the error that generated the exception.

The version of the **CFile** constructor that attempts to open a file will throw the exception **CFileException** upon failure. If you use this constructor, you should enclose it in a *try/catch* exception handling block, as follows:

```
try
{
    CFile MyFile("MyFile.old", CFile::modeRead);
}
catch(CFileException * fx)
{
    TCHAR buf[255];
    fx->GetErrorMessage(buf, 255);
    CString strPrompt(buf);
    AfxMessageBox(strPrompt);
}
```

To learn more about exception handling and MFC exceptions, refer to Lesson 1 of Chapter 13.

The **CFile::Open()** function does not throw an exception. Instead, it takes an optional third parameter that is a pointer to a **CFileException** object. If the file open operation fails, the **CFileException** object is filled with information about the error's nature. This information can be used by subsequent code to provide information to the user, as shown in the following code:

```
CFile MyFile;
CFileException fx;

if(!MyFile.Open("MyFile.old", CFile::modeRead, &fx))
{
    TCHAR buf[255];
    fx.GetErrorMessage(buf, 255);
    CString strPrompt(buf);
    AfxMessageBox(strPrompt);
}
```

Closing Files

CFile provides the **Close()** member function to close an open disk file. The following code provides an example of how to use the **Close()** function:

```
BOOL MyFileFunction()
{
    CFile MyFile;
    if(!MyFile.Open("MyFile.old", CFile::modeRead))
    {
        AfxMessageBox("Cannot open MyFile.old");
        return FALSE;
    }
    // Do something with the file . . .
    MyFile.Close();
    return TRUE;
}
```

In this example, the call to **MyFile.Close()** is not strictly necessary. The **CFile** destructor, which is called as the object loses scope, will call the **Close()** function for you if it detects that you have not done so already. However, it is good programming style to always match a call to **CFile::Open()** with a corresponding call to **CFile::Close()**.

You can use the **Close()** function to disassociate your **CFile** object from a file before reusing the object to access a different file. For example, the following code will create three empty files named file1.txt, file2.txt, and file3.txt in the current application folder. All three files are created using the same **CFile** object:

```
CString  strFiles[3] = { "file1.txt", "file2.txt", "file3.txt" };
CFile file;

for(int i = 0; i < 3; i++)
{
    file.Open(strFiles[i], CFile::modeCreate);
    file.Close();
}
```

Reading and Writing Files

CFile supplies the **Read()** and **Write()** functions, which call the Microsoft Windows API functions **ReadFile()** and **WriteFile()**, to provide direct, unbuffered read and write operations to disk files. Because direct file access is quite tricky to use, the C run-time library provides *stream I/O* functions. (For example, buffers and pointer offsets must be specified in units that are integer multiples of the disk volume's sector size.)

Stream I/O functions allow you to process data from disk files and other sources in formats ranging from single characters to large data structures. These functions also provide I/O buffering, which can improve performance. Examples of stream I/O functions include **fopen()**, **fseek()**, **fread()** and **fwrite()**. As a C++ programmer, you might be familiar with stream I/O through the **iostream** classes.

MFC provides access to stream file I/O through the **CStdioFile** class. The **CStdioFile** versions of **Read()** and **Write()** use the run-time stream I/O functions. Unless you have a specific need for low-level direct access to a disk file, you should use the **CStdioFile** class, which is flexible and easy to use.

Disk files associated with a **CStdioFile** object can be opened in *text mode* or in *binary mode*. Text mode provides special processing for carriage return/linefeed (CR/LF) pairs. When you write a newline character (0x0A) to a text-mode **CStdioFile** object, the byte pair for a CR/LF (0x0D, 0x0A) is sent to the file. When you read a text-mode file, the byte pair 0x0D, 0x0A is translated to a single 0x0A byte. To open a **CStdioFile** object as a text-mode file, supply the **CFile::typeText** flag to the **Open()** function as follows:

```
CStdioFile inFile("MyFile.txt", CFile::modeRead | CFile::typeText);
```

Use the **CFile::typeBinary** flag to open a **CStdioFile** in binary mode. Newline characters are not converted in binary mode.

To read data from a **CStdioFile** file object, you can use either the **Read()** function or the **ReadString()** function.

Read() takes a pointer to a buffer that will contain the data read from the file, and an unsigned integer (UINT) value that specifies the number of bytes to read. The **Read()** function returns the number of bytes that were read. If the required number of bytes could not be read because the end of the file was reached, the actual number of bytes read is returned.

If a read error occurs, a **CFileException** exception is thrown. When writing to a text mode file, use the **ReadString()** function, which is similar to **Read()** except that:

- Reading stops when a newline character is encountered.
- A terminating null is appended to the text in the buffer.
- A pointer to the buffer is returned. This pointer will contain a NULL if the end of the file was reached without reading any data.

ReadString() provides a simple way to read a single line from a text file into a string by providing a version that returns a BOOL value, which indicates success or failure.

Write() is similar to **Read()**, taking a buffer containing the bytes to be written and a value that specifies the number of bytes to read. The number of bytes written is not returned with the use of **Write()**. If a write error occurs, including not writing all bytes specified, **CFileException** is thrown. When writing to a text mode file, use **CStdioFile::WriteString()**, which writes a newline character.

The following code illustrates how to use the **CStdioFile** class to read and write disk files. The code opens the MyFile.bin file in binary mode and reads its data in blocks of 10 bytes. Each block is written to a new line in the newly created Output.txt file, as demonstrated in the following code example:

```
try
{
    CStdioFile inFile("MyFile.bin", CFile::modeRead |
        CFile::typeBinary);
    CStdioFile outFile("outfile.txt", CFile::modeCreate |
        CFile::modeWrite | CFile::typeText);

    const UINT linelength = 10;
    TCHAR strBuf[16];

    while(inFile.ReadString(strBuf, linelength))
    {
        _tcscat(strBuf, _T("\n"));
        outFile.WriteString(strBuf);
    }
}

catch(CFileException * fx)
{
    TCHAR buf[255];
    fx->GetErrorMessage(buf, 255);
    AfxMessageBox(buf);
}
```

Random File Access

Text files are generally read and written sequentially, a line at a time. When reading binary files, you often need to perform *random access*. Random access allows you to jump directly to a specific location, then immediately access data stored at that location.

An open file maintains a *file pointer* that specifies the next byte to be read, or the location to receive the next byte written. When a file is opened, the file pointer is placed at the beginning of the file. You can position the file pointer by using the **CFile::Seek()** function. **CFile::Seek()** moves the file pointer to a specified offset from the beginning or end of the file, or from the current file pointer position. A read or write operation will advance the file pointer by the number of bytes read or written.

Lesson Summary

The MFC class **CFile** provides direct, unbuffered I/O to disk files. **CFile** is also the base class for the **CStdioFile** class, which allows access to files through the buffered stream I/O provided by the C run-time library. The **CStdioFile** class allows you to open files in *text mode* (in which newline characters are converted to CR/LF pairs) or in *binary mode* (in which newline characters are not converted). If you need specific direct access to disk files, you can use the **CFile** class. For general-purpose disk file I/O, you should use the **CStdioFile** class.

Objects derived from **CFile** are either associated with a disk file at creation time (by using the appropriate constructor), or created using a two-stage process, in which a **CFile**-derived object is created and its **Open()** function is called. The **Open()** function accepts a path to the file to be opened, and also accepts flag values that specify the access and sharing modes to be used. The access mode determines whether the file will be open for read-only, write-only, or read/write permissions, and whether a new file should be created. The sharing mode determines the level of access to this file that is granted to other processes while the file is open.

Many of the **CFile** member functions throw MFC exceptions of the type **CFileException**. **CFileException** objects can be queried to provide information about the error that caused the exception condition. The **Open()** function takes an exception object as a parameter.

To read and write an open disk file, you can use the **Read()** and **Write()** functions provided by **CFile**, or you can use **CStdioFile::ReadString()** and **CStdioFile::WriteString()**. Both **Read()** and **ReadString()** place characters read from the file into a buffer that you supply to the function. **ReadString()** stops reading when a newline character is encountered, and appends a terminating null character to the text in the buffer.

Use the **Write()** function to write text in a buffer into a file. When writing to a text mode file, use **CStdioFile::WriteString()**, which writes a newline character as a CR/LF pair.

A file opened for random access maintains a *file pointer* that specifies the next byte to be read or the location to receive the next byte written. Use the **CFile::Seek()** function to move the file pointer to a specified offset within the file before performing a read or write operation.

Lesson 2: Serialization of Application Data

Implementing persistence presents special problems in development of object-oriented applications. A development team must consider how to preserve the structure and relationships of application objects when storing and retrieving persistent data. This consideration can be troublesome, since data in a file is typically stored as an unstructured binary stream. To address this problem, the MFC application framework implements *serialization*, which enables you to preserve your application data's object structure when saving it to, and restoring it from, a persistent archive.

After this lesson, you will be able to:

- Understand how the MFC application framework implements serialization.
- Use the overloaded << and >> operators to serialize built-in types and MFC types to an archive.
- Make a class serializable.
- Serialize an MFC collection.

Estimated lesson time: 50 minutes

MFC Support for Serialization

MFC provides built-in support for serialization through the **CObject** class. All classes that implement serialization must derive from **CObject** and must also provide an overload of the **CObject::Serialize()** function. The **Serialize()** function's task is to archive selected data members of the class, and save them to or restore them from an object of the MFC class **CArchive**.

A **CArchive** object acts as an intermediary between the object to be serialized and the storage medium. Also, a **CArchive** object is always associated with a **CFile** object. The **CFile** object usually represents a disk file, but it can also represent a memory file. For example, you could associate a **CArchive** object with a **CSharedFile** object to serialize data to and from the Windows Clipboard. Additionally, a **CArchive** object provides a type-safe buffering mechanism for reading and writing serializable objects to and from a **CFile** object.

A given **CArchive** object is used either to store data or to load data, but never both. The life of a **CArchive** object is limited to one pass, through either writing objects *to* a file or reading objects *from* a file. Separately created **CArchive** objects are required to serialize data to a file, and also to restore data back from a file. The status of a **CArchive** object, whether used for storing or loading, can be determined by querying the Boolean return value of the **CArchive::IsStoring()** function.

The **CArchive** class defines both the insertion operator (**<<**) and the extraction operator (**>>**). These operators are used in a manner similar to the insertion and extraction operators defined for the standard C++ stream classes, as illustrated by the following code:

```
if (ar.IsStoring())
{
    ar << m_string;
}
else
{
    ar >> m_string;
}
```

You can use the insertion and extraction operators to store data to, and retrieve data from, a **CArchive** object. Table 6.2 lists the data types and objects that can be used with the insertion and extraction operators.

Table 6.2 Data Types and Objects Used with Insertion and Extraction Operators

CObject*	SIZE and CSize	float
WORD	CString	POINT and CPoint
DWORD	BYTE	RECT and CRect
double	LONG	CTime and CTimeSpan
int	COleCurrency	COleVariant
COleDateTime	COleDateTimeSpan	

Serialization Process

In Lesson 4 of Chapter 3, you learned that the application data is stored in the application's document object. Application data is serialized to a document file on disk, then restored from the document file into the document object. A document file type is associated with an application by specifying a filename extension in the **Advanced Options** dialog box, in Step 4 of the AppWizard (see Lesson 1 of Chapter 2).

The document object begins application data serialization in response to file commands selected by the user. A **CArchive** object of the appropriate type (according to whether data is to be saved to or restored from the archive) is created by the framework, and passed as a parameter to the document object's **Serialize()** function.

The AppWizard creates a stub **Serialize()** function for your document class. You must add code to this function to store or retrieve persistent data members to or from the archive. You can store and retrieve simple data members using the **<<** and **>>** operators. If the document object contains more complex objects that implement their own serialization code, you must call the **Serialize()** function for those objects, and forward a reference to the current archive.

As an example, consider an application TestApp that maintains a document class with three data members, as shown by the following code sample:

```
Class CtestAppDoc
{
    CString m_string;
    DWORD m_dwVar;
    MyObj m_obj;
}
```

Assume that the **MyObj** class is a serializable class.

The following code illustrates a **Serialize()** function that might be written for the **TestApp** document class:

```
void CTestAppDoc::Serialize(CArchive& ar)
{
    if (ar.IsStoring())
    {
        ar << m_string;
        ar << m_dwVar;
    }
    else
    {
        ar >> m_string;
        ar >> m_dwVar;
    }
    m_obj.Serialize(ar);
}
```

Note how the **MyObj::Serialize()** function is called outside of the conditional branching code, as it contains its own branch condition to determine whether data is being stored or retrieved. Figure 6.1 illustrates how you can apply this technique to serialize objects recursively.

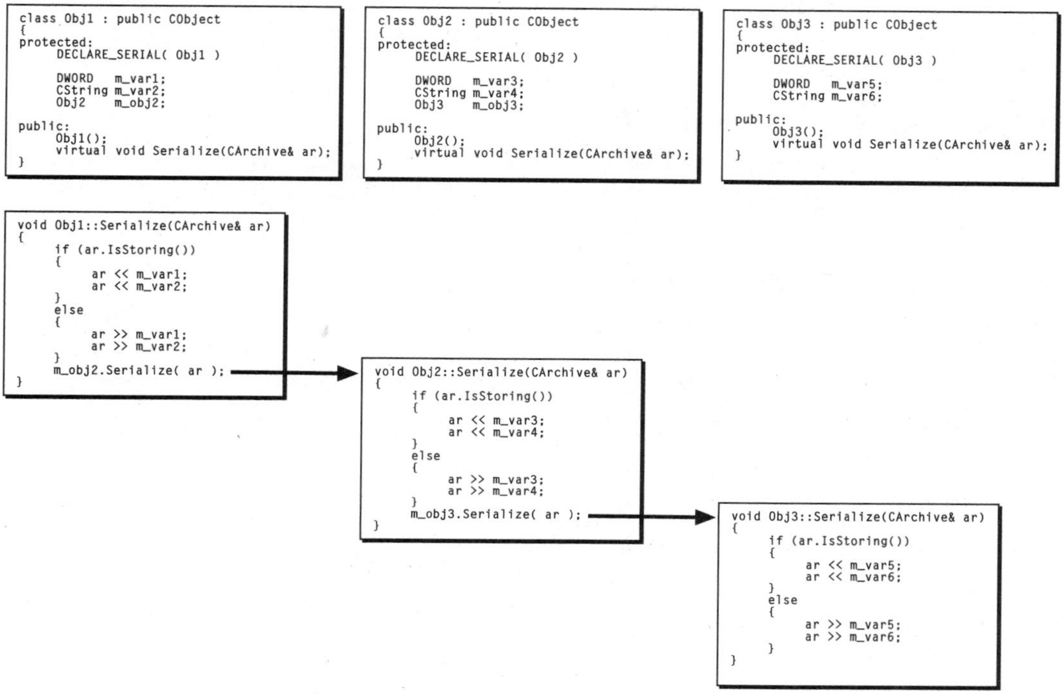

```
class Obj1 : public CObject
{
protected:
    DECLARE_SERIAL( Obj1 )

    DWORD   m_var1;
    CString m_var2;
    Obj2    m_obj2;

public:
    Obj1();
    virtual void Serialize(CArchive& ar);
}
```

```
class Obj2 : public CObject
{
protected:
    DECLARE_SERIAL( Obj2 )

    DWORD   m_var3;
    CString m_var4;
    Obj3    m_obj3;

public:
    Obj2();
    virtual void Serialize(CArchive& ar);
}
```

```
class Obj3 : public CObject
{
protected:
    DECLARE_SERIAL( Obj3 )

    DWORD   m_var5;
    CString m_var6;

public:
    Obj3();
    virtual void Serialize(CArchive& ar);
}
```

```
void Obj1::Serialize(CArchive& ar)
{
    if (ar.IsStoring())
    {
        ar << m_var1;
        ar << m_var2;
    }
    else
    {
        ar >> m_var1;
        ar >> m_var2;
    }
    m_obj2.Serialize( ar );
}
```

```
void Obj2::Serialize(CArchive& ar)
{
    if (ar.IsStoring())
    {
        ar << m_var3;
        ar << m_var4;
    }
    else
    {
        ar >> m_var3;
        ar >> m_var4;
    }
    m_obj3.Serialize( ar );
}
```

```
void Obj3::Serialize(CArchive& ar)
{
    if (ar.IsStoring())
    {
        ar << m_var5;
        ar << m_var6;
    }
    else
    {
        ar >> m_var5;
        ar >> m_var6;
    }
}
```

Figure 6.1   Serializing contained objects

As long as your serialization routines are kept consistent, complex object structures can be saved to disk and restored to an application. You need to ensure that the storing and restoring branches of your **Serialize()** functions match—in other words, that they store and restore the same objects in the same order.

The serialization routines handle proper reconstruction of an object structure when this structure is restored from a disk file. Serialization accomplishes this by writing information about the object's type as well as its state (data member values) into the disk file. When an object is restored, this information is used to determine what type of object needs to be created to receive the data. The serialization routine automatically performs the object creation. However, to ensure that this action works properly, you must provide a default constructor (one with no arguments) for your serializable class.

In the following practice exercise, you will learn the steps required to implement simple serialization of application data.

Serializing Application Data

In Lesson 1 of Chapter 5 you added two member variables, CMyAppDoc::m_nLines and CMyAppDoc::m_string, as application data for the MyApp application. You will now add code to this project to serialize these data items to a document file.

▶   **To serialize the MyApp application data**

1. Locate the **Serialize**() function created by the AppWizard for your document class **CMyApp**. The generated code for the **Serialize**() function is shown in the following code example:

```
void CMyApp::Serialize(CArchive& ar)
{
    if (ar.IsStoring())
    {
        // TODO: add storing code here
    }
    else
    {
        // TODO: add loading code here
    }
}
```

2. Replace the //TODO comments with code to store and restore the document data members. The completed code should look as follows:

```
void CMyAppDoc::Serialize(CArchive& ar)
{
    if (ar.IsStoring())
    {
        ar << m_nLines;
        ar << m_string;
    }
    else
    {
        ar >> m_nLines;
        ar >> m_string;
    }
}
```

3. Locate the **CMyAppDoc::OnDataEdit**() function. At the end of the function, directly beneath the call to **UpdateAllViews**(), add the following line:

```
SetModifiedFlag();
```

Thus, the entire function looks as follows:

```
void CMyAppDoc::OnDataEdit()
{
    CEditDataDialog aDlg;

    aDlg.m_nLines = m_nLines;
    aDlg.m_strLineText = m_string;

    if(aDlg.DoModal())
    {
        m_nLines = aDlg.m_nLines;
        m_string = aDlg.m_strLineText;

        UpdateAllViews(NULL);
        SetModifiedFlag();
    }
}
```

The **CDocument::SetModifiedFlag**() function is called to notify the application framework that the application data has been modified. This function causes the framework to prompt the user to save changes before closing a document.

4. Use ClassWizard to overload the **CDocument::DeleteContents**() function for the **CMyAppDoc** class. Replace the comment code in the generated code with the following lines:

```
m_nLines = 0;
m_string = "";
```

Thus, the entire function looks as follows:

```
void CMyAppDoc::DeleteContents()
{
    m_nLines = 0;
    m_string = "";

    CDocument::DeleteContents();
}
```

Unlike multiple-document interface (MDI) applications, which create a new document object each time a new document is created or an existing document file is opened, single-document interface (SDI) applications create only one document object, which is reused each time a document is created or opened. The **DeleteContents()** function clears the application data held in the document object before the object is reused. When developing an SDI application, you must implement a **DeleteContents()** function that sets all document object data members to zero or null values. Otherwise, you will find data from previous editing sessions in your current document.

▶ **To test MyApp serialization**

1. Build and run the MyApp application.

2. Using the **Edit** option on the **Data** menu, type a string to display, and also type the number of times you want it displayed. Click **OK** to close the **Edit Document Data** dialog box.

3. On the **File** menu, choose **New**. A message box appears, prompting you to save changes to your untitled MyApp document before opening the new document. This dialog box appears because your code called the **SetModifiedFlag()** function after you modified the application data.

4. Click **Yes**. Use the **Save As** dialog box to save your document as **MyFile.mya** in the current directory.

5. Another untitled document now appears on your screen. The **DeleteContents()** function that you provided has cleared the data from your MyFile.mya document.

6. Open the MyFile.mya file by choosing **Open** from the **File** menu, or by selecting **MyFile.mya** from the **Most Recently Used** list on the **File** menu.

7. Your application data is now restored and displayed as it originally was, both in the application window and in the **Edit Document Data** dialog box's edit controls.

Making a Serializable Class

You have already seen how a document object can contain objects that implement their own serialization code. To create a serializable class, perform the following steps:

1. Derive the class from **CObject** or a class derived from **CObject**.

2. Provide a default constructor (one with no arguments) for your class.

3. Add the MFC macro **DECLARE_SERIAL** to the class declaration in the header file. **DECLARE_SERIAL**, and its partner **IMPLEMENT_SERIAL**,

provide MFC run-time class information for your class. These macros also provide a global extraction operator (>>), which uses the run-time class information to restore objects of your class from an archive. **DECLARE_SERIAL** takes the name of your class as a parameter.

The following code illustrates a serializable class declaration:

```
// MyClass.h
class CMyClass : public CObject
{
    DECLARE_SERIAL(CMyClass)

public:
    CMyClass() {;}  // Default constructor

    virtual void Serialize(CArchive& ar);

};
```

4. Add the **IMPLEMENT_SERIAL** macro to your class implementation (.cpp) file. The **IMPLEMENT_SERIAL** macro takes three parameters: the name of the class being serialized, the name of its parent class, and a schema number, as shown here:

```
IMPLEMENT_SERIAL(CMyClass, CObject, 1)
```

The schema number allows you to implement a versioning system for your document files. You will likely change your application documents' object structure between releases. These changes will most likely cause errors for a user that tries to use a new version of your application to open a document created with an older version.

You can assign a different schema number to an object's **IMPLEMENT_SERIAL** macro for each release that changes the object's structure. This action allows you to add code that detects discrepancies between application and document versions, and takes appropriate actions, such as displaying an error message or running a document format conversion routine.

5. Provide an override of the **CObject::Serialize()** function for your class.

Serializing MFC Collection Classes

MFC's templated collection classes **CArray**, **CList** and **CMap**, implement their own versions of the **Serialize()** function that serialize all of the elements in the collection.

Suppose your document class contains a collection of integer values as shown in the following code sample:

```
CList<int, int &> m_intList;
```

This collection can be serialized by adding the following line to the document's **Serialize()** function:

```
m_intList.Serialize(ar);
```

This line of code is all that is required to serialize a collection of simple types. **CList::Serialize()** calls the global helper function template **SerializeElements()**, which has the following signature:

```
template<class TYPE> void AFXAPI SerializeElements(CArchive& ar, TYPE*
pElements, int nCount);
```

The compiler generates an appropriate instantiation of this template for the collection class element type. The **SerializeElements()** function's default behavior is to perform a bitwise copy of the data contained in the collection (referenced by the pointer **pElements**) to or from the archive.

This default behavior is fine for simple objects, but is problematic for more complicated object structures. Suppose that your document class contains the member as shown in the following example code:

```
CList<CMyClass, CMyClass &> m_objList;
```

CMyClass would be defined as follows:

```
class CmyClass
{
    DECLARE_SERIAL(CMyClass)

public:
    CMyClass() {;}
    int m_int;
    DWORD m_dw;
    CString m_string;
    virtual void Serialize(CArchive& ar);
}
```

Attempting to serialize the m_objList collection by adding the following line to the document object's **Serialize()** function will cause errors:

```
m_objList.Serialize(ar);
```

Such errors will result because the **CMyClass** objects contain **CStrings**; which are complex objects that use custom memory allocation and reference-counting techniques.

The default **SerializeElements**() function generated for the m_objlist collection will attempt to read or write a bitwise copy of the collection elements to or from the archive, therefore bypassing the custom serialization routines built in the << and >> operators defined for the **CString** class.

In this case, you must write your own version of the **SerializeElements**() function. Assuming that **CMyClass** has been properly constructed as a serializable class, the corresponding **SerializeElements**() function might look as follows:

```
template <> void AFXAPI SerializeElements <CMyClass>
    (CArchive& ar, CMyClass * pNewMC, int nCount)
{
    for (int i = 0; i < nCount; i++, pNewMC++)
    {
        // Serialize each CMyClass object
        pNewMC->Serialize(ar);
    }
}
```

Note You do not have to provide your own version of **SerializeElements**() for a simple collection of **CString** objects, as MFC provides one as part of the **CArchive** source code.

Lesson Summary

The MFC application framework implements a technology called serialization that enables you to preserve your application data's object structure when saving it to, and restoring it from, a persistent archive. All classes that implement serialization must be derived from the **CObject** class, and additionally must overload the **CObject::Serialize**() function.

The **Serialize**() function stores and retrieves persistent data members to and from a **CArchive** class object. This object acts as an intermediary between the object to be serialized and the storage medium, which is usually a disk file encapsulated as a **CFile** class object. In addition, a **CArchive** object provides a type-safe buffering mechanism for writing and reading serializable objects to or from a **CFile** object. Separate **CArchive** objects must be used for storing and retrieving data. Once the archive object has been created, its role (determined by whether the **CArchive::IsStoring**() function returns TRUE or FALSE) cannot be changed.

The document object begins application data serialization in response to user commands to load or save files. A **CArchive** object is created by the framework, and passed as a parameter to the document object's **Serialize()** function.

The AppWizard creates a stub **Serialize()** function for your document class. You must add code to this function to store or retrieve persistent data members to, or from, the archive. The **CArchive** class defines the **<<** insertion operator and the **>>** extraction operator, which can be used to store or retrieve various C++ and MFC data types. If an object contains other serializable objects, you call the **Serialize()** function for these objects. To make a class serializable, you must:

- Derive the class from **CObject**.
- Provide a default constructor for your class.
- Add the **DECLARE_SERIAL** macro to the class declaration and the **IMPLEMENT_SERIAL** macro to your class implementation file.
- Provide an override of the **CObject::Serialize()** function for your class.

To serialize an instance of an MFC collection template class, simply call the collection object's serialize function. It is important to be aware that the collection template classes implement serialization by calling the instantiation of the **SerializeElements()** function template that is generated for the element type of the collection class. The default behavior of the **SerializeElements()** function is to perform a bitwise copy of the data contained in the collection to or from the archive. If this behavior is not appropriate for the element type of your collection, you should provide your own implementation of the **SerializeElements()** function template.

Lesson 3: Accessing the Registry

The Windows registry is a central, hierarchically organized database that holds persistent configuration information for the operating system and for applications. On Windows NT, Windows 95, and Windows 98, the registry provides a secure alternative to the .ini configuration files used by 16-bit Windows platforms. In this lesson, you will learn how to use the registry to save and retrieve user settings for a Windows application.

After this lesson, you will be able to:

- Recognize the registry's basic organizational structure.
- Understand how MFC supports programmatic access to the registry and how you can use these features to store and retrieve application settings.
- Describe the circumstances under which you might use the Win32 API to access the registry, and the principal functions that enable you to perform this action.

Estimated lesson time: 40 minutes

Registry Data

The registry is used to store configuration information for the operating system and settings for applications. It is used to store everything from the IP address of installed network cards to the Regional Settings found in the Control Panel to the view mode (Scientific or Standard) of the Windows calculator. As a result, the registry typically contains at least several megabytes of data.

To facilitate manipulating such large amounts of data, the logical view of the registry is that of a hierarchy. While the underlying physical structure of the files constituting the registry is different under Windows NT than under Windows 95 and Windows 98, the Win32 API hides these differences from users and developers by providing a consistent interface for storing and retrieving registry settings. However, before attempting to programmatically manipulate the registry, you should become familiar with the registry hierarchy. A good way to do that is through the *registry editor*.

The registry editor for Windows 95 and Windows 98 is *regedit.exe*, which can be found in the Windows directory. Windows NT users will find an additional registry editor—*regedt32.exe*—in the Winnt\System32 directory. Regedt32.exe has some additional features useful under Windows NT. (It is able to set security for registry keys and to view or edit the **REG_EXPAND_SZ** and **REG_MULTI_SZ** data types.) Most users prefer the search features of regedit, but for exploration under Windows NT, the read-only mode of regedt32 affords the beginning programmer an added level of protection against accidentally corrupting the registry.

Caution Improper editing of your registry entries could cause your applications to stop working, and could even permanently cause your operating system to become unavailable. Before editing the registry, you should first back up the registry files. With Windows 95, you should make copies of System.dat and User.dat, both of which are hidden files in the Windows folder. With Windows NT, you should create an updated Emergency Repair Disk. Consult your operating system documentation for more details.

▶ **To explore the registry (Windows NT)**

1. On the **Start** menu, click **Run**.

2. In the **Open** box, type **regedt32** and click **OK**.

   The registry editor opens as shown in Figure 6.2.

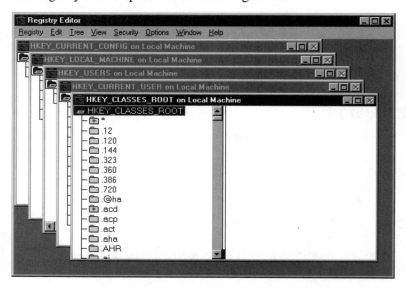

Figure 6.2   Exploring the registry using RegEdt32

3. On the registry editor **Options** menu, select **Read Only Mode**.

▶ **To explore the registry (Windows 95 and Windows 98)**

1. On the **Start** menu, click **Run**.

2. In the **Open** box, type **regedit** and click **OK**.

   The registry editor opens as shown in Figure 6.3.

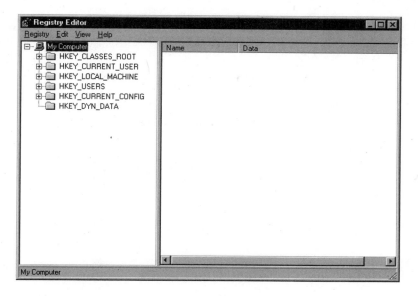

Figure 6.3   Exploring the registry using RegEdit

Registry Organization

The registry is organized as a hierarchically structured database. At the root of the hierarchy is a set of predefined subtrees, which correspond to the most general categories of the system's organization. Notice how the two editors differ in the way they display the subtrees. **RegEdit** displays all of the subtrees in a single window, descended from a common root. **RegEdit32** displays each subtree in its own window.

Table 6.3 illustrates the five subtrees common to the Windows platforms.

Table 6.3   Windows 95, Windows 98, and Windows NT Subtrees

Key name	Purpose
HKEY_CLASSES_ROOT	Contains software configuration information. Includes file name extension/application associations, drag and drop protocols, printing configurations, and COM configuration information.
HKEY_CURRENT_USER	Contains user-specific settings for the system. This subtree is created when the user logs on, loaded with information from the user's entry in **HKEY_USERS**, and deleted when the user logs off.
HKEY_LOCAL_MACHINE	Contains specifications for the computer, drivers and other system settings for installed hardware. Entries in this section are shared by all users of the computer.
HKEY_USERS	Contains information about all users who log on to the computer. Includes both user-specific information and generic user information. Generic system settings are available to all users of the system.
HKEY_CURRENT_CONFIG	Contains configuration data for the hardware profile currently in use on the computer.

If you are working on a Windows 95 or Windows 98 computer, you will see the additional subtree **HKEY_DYN_DATA**, used to store dynamic data such as performance statistics and plug and play information.

The subtrees contain *keys* that can act as containers for other keys. Keys are similar to directory folders in the way that they can be nested, and are referenced using a similar notation. Figure 6.4 shows RegEdt32 being used to view the **HKEY_CURRENT_USER\Software\MyCompany\MyApp\Settings** key.

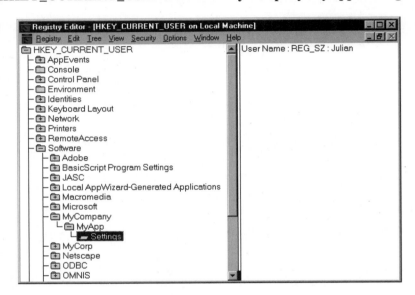

Figure 6.4   Exploring registry keys

Keys can contain values as well as subkeys. Values are terminating leaf nodes in the registry hierarchy which are used to store registry data. Figure 6.4 shows the *User Name* value contained within the **Settings** key.

A value has three parts—the name, the data type, and the value itself. A key might contain a single unnamed value that serves as the default value for the key. For the sake of clarity however, you should give your registry values names that give a clear indication of their function.

Windows defines a special set of registry data types. Some of the more commonly used registry data types are shown in Table 6.4.

Table 6.4   Registry Data Types

Data type	Use
REG_DWORD	A 32-bit number.
REG_BINARY	Binary data in any form.
REG_SZ	A null-terminated string.
REG_MULTI_SZ	An array of null-terminated strings, terminated by two null characters.
REG_EXPAND_SZ	A null-terminated string that contains unexpanded references to environment variables.

You can see the complete list of registry data types by searching for "RegSetValueEx"—the Windows API function used to set the value and data type of a registry value—in the Visual C++ Help file.

MFC Support for the Registry

A document/view application generated by the MFC AppWizard creates the following registry entries:

- An entry that enables the Windows file manager to associate the application document type with the application. This enables the user to launch an application by double-clicking on a document icon.

- An entry that determines the location of the application *user profile*. The user profile is used to store a user's application settings in the registry, so that the user settings can be preserved between application sessions.

The following sections explain how these registry entries are created, and how they can be used.

Registering Document Types

To register an application's document type with the Windows file manager, the AppWizard adds the following line of code to your application object's **InitInstance()** function:

```
RegisterShellFileTypes(TRUE);
```

CWinApp::RegisterShellFileTypes() iterates through the list of document templates that the application maintains and adds file association entries to the **HKEY_CLASSES_ROOT** registry subtree for each document template. **RegisterShellFileTypes()** also adds an entry specifying a default icon for the document type.

Since the shell identifies a document type on the basis of its file name extension, you must be sure to specify a document file name extension for your application on the Advanced Options screen in Step 4 of the AppWizard. If you fail to specify an extension, **RegisterShellFileTypes()** will not be called.

RegisterShellFileTypes() is called with a TRUE parameter to specify that registry entries should be added for the shell commands **Print** and **Print To**, allowing a user to print files directly from the shell, or by dropping the file on a printer object.

The AppWizard creates a registry file (with a .reg extension) that you can use in conjunction with a setup program to perform registry updates at installation time. Using a registry file in this manner is advantageous because you can instruct the setup program to remove its registry entries if the program is uninstalled, which contributes to more efficient application management. If you omit a file name extension for your document type, no .reg file is created.

Note If you specify that your application should be Compound Document Server, additional code is added to your application's **InitInstance()** function to create OLE-related registry entries.

Application User Profile

To specify the location of the application's user profile settings, the AppWizard adds the following code line to your application object's **InitInstance()** function:

```
SetRegistryKey(_T("Local AppWizard-Generated Applications"));
```

CWinApp::SetRegistryKey() is called with a parameter that specifies the name of the key under which your application settings will be stored. This key will be created under the **HKEY_CURRENT_USER\Software** key. You should replace the default key name (**Local AppWizard-Generated Applications**) with a suitable name for a key containing user profile settings for all of your applications. Typically, this name is the name of the company developing the application.

Note If you remove the call to **SetRegistryKey()** from your **InitInstance()** function, the framework will create an .ini file in the Windows directory and use it to store (non user-specific) profile information. The .ini files are a feature of 16-bit Windows, and should not be used for 32-bit applications.

In the following exercise, you will specify a registry key for use in storing application user profile settings for the MyApp application.

▶   **To set the name of the user profile registry key**

1. Open the MyApp project.

2. In ClassView, expand the **CMyAppApp** class icon.

3. Double-click the **InitInstance()** member function to edit the code.

4. Approximately 20 lines into the function, locate the code that reads:

```
SetRegistryKey(_T("Local AppWizard-Generated Applications"));
```

5. Edit the line so that it reads:

```
SetRegistryKey(_T("MyCompany"));
```

6. Build and run the MyApp application.

Complete the following steps to check that the application has created the key correctly.

▶ **To locate the user profile registry key**

1. Ensure that you have built and run the MyApp application at least once after specifying a user profile registry key.

2. Close the MyApp application. On the **Start** menu, click **Run**.

3. In the **Open** box, type **RegEdt32** if you are using Windows NT or **RegEdit** if you are using Windows 95 or Windows 98. Click **OK**.

4. Locate the **HKEY_CURRENT_USER** subtree.

5. Double-click the **Software** key to expand it. Verify that the following key has been created by the MyApp application:

```
HKEY_CURRENT_USER\Software\MyCompany\MyApp\Settings
```

Note The **SetRegistryKey()** function creates a registry key with the same name as the application to serve as a root location for the application settings.

MFC applications write to the application user profile using the MFC profile management functions. These functions, all members of the **CWinApp** class, are:

- **WriteProfileString()**
- **GetProfileString()**
- **WriteProfileInt()**
- **GetProfileInt()**

These functions store and retrieve string and integer values to and from your application's profile key in the registry. All of these functions take a section name (a subkey of your profile key), and a value name as the first two arguments. If the section or value names do not exist, they are created.

WriteProfileString() creates a REG_SZ value. **WriteProfileInt()** creates a REG_DWORD value. Both functions return a BOOL value to indicate the success or failure of the write operation. Both functions take a third argument specifying the actual value to be written.

For example, the following line:

```
WriteProfileString("Settings", "User Name", "Julian");
```

will create the **HKEY_CURRENT_USER\Software\MyCompany\MyApp\ Settings\User Name** value, which is assigned the string "Julian." This value is illustrated in Figure 6.4.

GetProfileString() and **GetProfileInt()** return a specified value from the registry. Both functions take a third argument that specifies a default value to be returned if the requested registry value cannot be found.

Working with Application User Profile Settings

In this exercise, you will learn how to use the MFC profile management functions to save MyApp application settings to the **HKEY_CURRENT_USER\ Software\MyCompany\MyApp** profile key that you created in the previous exercise. This exercise will work with the **Connect to Data Source** dialog box that you created by completing the exercises in Chapters 4 and 5.

The **Connect to Data Source** dialog box contains a check box option that allows users to specify if they want to attempt to connect at application startup.

▶ **To implement the Connect at Application Startup option**

1. Save the Data Source Name, the User ID, the Access level and the status of the **Attempt to connect at application startup** check box to the registry. These settings will be saved after the user clicks the **Connect** button.

2. Use the settings saved in the registry to initialize the **Connect to Data Source** dialog box controls.

3. Alter the **InitInstance()** function to retrieve the **Attempt to connect at application startup** check box status. If this check box has been selected, display the **Connect to Data Source** dialog box to allow the user to connect to the database.

▶ **To save the dialog box settings**

1. In the MyApp project, locate the **CMyAppApp::OnDataConnect()** function.

2. Inside the code branch that reads:

```
if(aCD.DoModal() == IDOK)
```

add the following lines beneath the call to **AfxMessageBox()**:

```
WriteProfileString("Settings", "User ID", aCD.m_strUserID);
WriteProfileInt("Settings", "Access Level", aCD.m_nAccess);
WriteProfileInt("Settings", "Connect at Startup",
    aCD.m_bConnect ? 1 : 0);
WriteProfileString("Settings", "DSN", m_strDSN);
```

m_strDSN is a member variable of the **CMyAppApp** class, which is set by the **CConnectDialog::OnOK()** function.

▶ **To initialize the Connect to Data Source dialog box controls**

1. Delete the following lines from the top of the **CMyAppApp:: OnDataConnect()** function:

```
aCD.m_nAccess = 1;
aCD.m_bConnect = TRUE;
```

2. Replace the deleted lines with the following code:

```
aCD.m_nAccess = GetProfileInt("Settings", "Access Level", 1);
aCD.m_strUserID = GetProfileString("Settings", "User ID", "");
aCD.m_bConnect = BOOL(GetProfileInt("Settings",
    "Connect at Startup", 0));
```

The entire **OnDataConnect()** function should look as follows:

```
void CMyAppApp::OnDataConnect()
{
    CConnectDialog aCD;

    aCD.m_nAccess = GetProfileInt("Settings", "Access Level", 1);
    aCD.m_strUserID = GetProfileString("Settings", "User ID", "");
    aCD.m_bConnect = BOOL(GetProfileInt("Settings", "
        Connect at Startup", 0));

    if(aCD.DoModal() == IDOK)
    {
        CString strMessage;
        strMessage.Format("User %s logged in", aCD.m_strUserID);
        AfxMessageBox(strMessage);

        WriteProfileString("Settings", "User ID", aCD.m_strUserID);
        WriteProfileInt("Settings", "Access Level", aCD.m_nAccess);
        WriteProfileInt("Settings", "Connect at Startup",
            aCD.m_bConnect ? 1 : 0);
        WriteProfileString("Settings", "DSN", m_strDSN);
    }
}
```

3. Locate the **CConnectDialog::OnInitDialog()** function. Add the code indicated in bold text in the following code example:

```
BOOL CConnectDialog::OnInitDialog()
{
    CDialog::OnInitDialog();

    m_lbDSN.AddString("Accounts");
    m_lbDSN.AddString("Admin");
    m_lbDSN.AddString("Management");
    CMyAppApp * pApp = dynamic_cast<CMyAppApp *>(AfxGetApp());
    ASSERT_VALID(pApp);
    CString strDSN = pApp->GetProfileString("Settings", "DSN", "");
    int index = m_lbDSN.FindStringExact(-1, strDSN);
    m_lbDSN.SetCurSel(index);
    OnUpdateUserid();
    return TRUE;
    // return TRUE unless you set the focus to a control
    // EXCEPTION: OCX Property Pages should return FALSE
}
```

This code retrieves the data source name from the profile settings, and uses it to set the list selection to the appropriate item.

▶ **To display the Connect to Data Source dialog box (if required)**

1. Locate the **CMyAppApp::InitInstance()** function. Add the following code just before the return statement near the end of the function string:

```
if(GetProfileInt("Settings", "Connect at Startup", 0))
    OnDataConnect();
```

2. Build and run the MyApp application.

3. Select the **Connect** option from the **Data** menu, and fill in the **Connect to Data Source** dialog box, making sure that the **Attempt to connect at application startup** check box is selected.

4. Save the settings by clicking **Connect**.

5. Quit and restart the application to ensure that the **Attempt to connect at application startup** dialog box appears as soon as the application has started, and that the saved settings have been correctly restored. You can also use the registry editor to check that the profile registry values have been created as expected.

Registry Support in the Win32 API

The MFC registry functions make storing information in the registry easy, but they are probably not flexible enough to meet all of your needs. The MFC profile functions allow you to write only to a specified profile key under the **HKEY_CURRENT_USER** subtree. If you wanted to store values at other registry locations, you have to use the Win32 API registry functions. For example, you might want to store application settings common to all users of a computer. To do this, you would need to create a registry key under the key **HKEY_LOCAL_ MACHINE\SOFTWARE**.

Also, the MFC functions allow you to store only string or integer values. The Win32 API functions allow you to store information using any of the registry data formats.

Table 6.5 lists some of the Win32 API registry functions. You can search for the functions in the Visual C++ Help file to find out more about how they are used.

Table 6.5   Win32 API Registry Functions

Function	Purpose
RegCreateKeyEx()	Creates a registry key. If the key already exists in the registry, the function will open it.
RegOpenKeyEx()	Opens an existing registry key.
RegCloseKey()	Closes an open handle to a registry key that has been returned by the **RegCreateKeyEx()** or the **RegOpenKeyEx()** function.
RegDeleteKey()	In Windows 95, deletes a subkey and all its descendants. In Windows NT, deletes a single subkey that cannot have descendants.
RegSetValueEx()	Sets the data and type of a value under an open registry key.
RegQueryValueEx()	Retrieves the type and data for a value associated with an open registry key.
RegDeleteValue()	Removes a named value from a registry key.

Lesson Summary

The Windows registry is a central, hierarchically organized database that holds persistent settings and configuration information for the operating system and applications. Your applications can use Win32 API functions to store and retrieve registry settings. You can use the registry editor to view and edit data stored in the registry.

The registry is logically organized around five predefined subtrees that correspond to the most general categories of the system's organization. These categories are:

- **HKEY_CLASSES_ROOT**
- **HKEY_CURRENT_USER**
- **HKEY_LOCAL_MACHINE**
- **HKEY_USERS**
- **HKEY_CURRENT CONFIG**

Subtrees contain keys that can act as containers for other keys and for *values*, which are leaf nodes used to store registry data. A value has three parts: a name, its data type, and the value itself. Windows defines a special set of data types for registry values. These data types include:

- **REG_DWORD**
- **REG_BINARY**
- **REG_SZ**
- **REG_MULTI_SZ**
- **REG_EXPAND_SZ**

A document/view application generated by the MFC AppWizard calls **CWinApp::RegisterShellFileTypes()** to add an entry to the registry to associate the application document type with the application. **RegisterShellFileTypes()** also adds an entry to specify a default icon for the document type; and entries for the shell commands **Print** and **Print To**, to allow a user to print files directly from the shell.

The application calls the **CWinApp::SetRegistryKey()** function to add a registry entry to specify the location of the application's *user profile*. The user profile is used to store a user's application settings in the registry so that the user settings can be preserved between application sessions. You should change the name of the key specified by **SetRegistryKey()** to a name that is suitable for a key that contains user profile settings for all of your applications—the name of your company, for example. The **SetRegistryKey()** function creates a registry key under your profile key with the same name as the application, to serve as a root location for the application settings.

MFC applications write to the application user profile using the following MFC profile management functions:

- **WriteProfileString()**
- **GetProfileString()**
- **WriteProfileInt()**
- **GetProfileInt()**

These functions are used to store and retrieve string and integer values to and from your application's profile key in the registry.

In cases where the MFC profile management functions are not flexible enough for your needs, you can use the Win32 API registry functions. For example, use these functions when you need to write to a registry location not under the specified profile key. You can also use these functions to create and delete registry keys, and to store and retrieve values. The most commonly used Win32 API registry functions are:

- **RegCreateKeyEx()**
- **RegOpenKeyEx()**
- **RegCloseKey()**
- **RegDeleteKey()**
- **RegSetValueEx()**
- **RegQueryValueEx()**
- **RegDeleteValue()**

Lab 6: Working with Persistent Data

In this lab, you will enable the STUpload application to work with persistent data contained in files on your local hard disk. You will modify the application in two sections. First, you will finish implementing the **CSTUploadDoc:: LoadData()** function that you created in Chapter 5. The **CSTUploadDoc:: OnDataImport()** function calls the **LoadData()** function to load data from a text file into the application.

Second, you will implement standard MFC serialization for the STUpload application so that the application data imported from the text file can be saved as an STUpload document file.

Importing Data from a Text File

In Lab 5, you created a temporary implementation of the **CSTUploadDoc:: LoadData()** function. Currently, this function simply adds some hard-coded stock price records to the **CStockDataList** object **CSTUploadDoc::m_DocList**. You will finish implementing the **LoadData()** function to load records into **m_DocList** from the **CStdioFile** object passed in from the **CSTUploadDoc:: OnDataImport()** function. Your first task is to use the **CStdioFile** object to open the text file selected by the user.

▶   **To open the text file**

1. Edit the **CSTUploadDoc::OnDataImport()** function. Locate the code branch that begins with the line of code:

   ```
   if(nID == IDOK)
   ```

2. After the **CStdioFile** object declaration, add the following code:

   (This code can be found in CH6_01.cpp, installed from the companion CD.)

   ```
   CFileException fx;
   if(!aFile.Open(aFileDialog.GetPathName(), CFile::modeRead |
       CFile::typeText, &fx))
   {
       TCHAR buf[255];
       fx.GetErrorMessage(buf, 255);
       CString strPrompt(buf);
       AfxMessageBox(strPrompt);
       return;
   }
   ```

The entire function should now look as follows:

```
void CSTUploadDoc::OnDataImport()
{
    // String to customize File Dialog
    CString strFilter =
        Data Files (*.dat)|*.dat|All Files (*.*)|*.*||";

    CFileDialog aFileDialog(TRUE, NULL, NULL, OFN_HIDEREADONLY |
        OFN_OVERWRITEPROMPT, strFilter);

    int nID = aFileDialog.DoModal();

    if(nID == IDOK)
    {
        CStdioFile aFile;

        CFileException fx;
        if(!aFile.Open(aFileDialog.GetPathName(),
            CFile::modeRead | CFile::typeText, &fx))
        {
            TCHAR buf[255];
            fx.GetErrorMessage(buf, 255);
            CString strPrompt(buf);
            AfxMessageBox(strPrompt);
            return;
        }
        LoadData(aFile);
    }
}
```

Before you replace the old **LoadData()** function with a new version, you will make a couple of changes to enable the new function to use the **Conflicting Records** dialog box. First, you must call the **AfxInitRichEdit()** function to initialize rich edit controls for your application.

► **To enable the use of rich edit controls by an application**

1. Edit the **CSTUploadApp::InitInstance()** function. Add the following line just before the return statement near the end of the function:

   ```
   AfxInitRichEdit();
   ```

2. Add a DDX CConflictDialog::m_REditText member variable. This variable will be a CString variable used to set the data displayed in the rich edit control.

▶   **To add the CConflictDialog::m_REditText variable**

1. Open ClassWizard.

2. Click the **Member Variables** tab.

3. Add a **CString** variable m_REditText to the **CConflictDialog** class, which is associated with the **IDC_DUPL_RICHEDIT** resource ID.

Now you are ready to implement the new **LoadData()** function.

▶   **To replace the LoadData() function**

1. To the top of the STUploadDoc.cpp file, with the other #include statements, add the following line:

```
#include "ConflictDialog.h"
```

2. Locate the **CSTUploadDoc::LoadData()** function. Delete the entire function and replace it with the following code:

(This code can be found in CH6_02.cpp, installed from the companion CD.)

```
BOOL CSTUploadDoc::LoadData(CStdioFile &infile)
{
    // Check for NULL
    ASSERT(infile.m_hFile != NULL);

    // Hold data in temporary list of CStockData objects,
    // which we assign to CSTUploadDoc::m_DocList only
    // when we are sure load has been completed successfully
    CStockDataList TempList;
    // Additions are cumulative, so we need to copy in existing data
    TempList.AddHead(&m_DocList);

    // Line buffer
    CString strTemp;

    // Today's date
    COleDateTime Today = COleDateTime::GetCurrentTime();
    COleDateTime FileDate;
    CString strFileHeader;

    int addedCtr = 0; // Count added items
    int discardedCtr = 0; // Count discarded items

    BOOL bFirstLine = TRUE;
```

```
while(infile.ReadString(strTemp))
{
    BOOL bValidDate = FALSE;
    CString strFund;
    CString strDate;

    // Exclude blank lines
    if(strTemp.GetLength() == 0) continue;

    if(bFirstLine)
    {
        // Get Header information
        strFileHeader = strTemp.Left(18);
        strFileHeader.TrimRight();
        strDate = strTemp.Mid(18, 10);
    }
    else
    {
        strFund = strTemp.Left(8);
        strFund.TrimRight();
        strDate = strTemp.Mid(8, 10);
    }

    int nYear = atoi(strDate.Right(4));
    int nMonth = atoi(strDate.Left(2));
    int nDay = atoi(strDate.Mid(3, 2));

    COleDateTime aDate(nYear, nMonth, nDay, 0, 0, 0);

    if(aDate.GetStatus() != COleDateTime::valid)
    {
        if(bFirstLine)
        {
            // Cannot read file date - assume invalid
            AfxMessageBox("Invalid File Format");
            return FALSE;
        }
        else
        {
            // Cannot read record date - discard line
            discardedCtr++;
            continue;
        }
    }
```

```
if(bFirstLine)
{
    // Get file date - loop back to top
    FileDate = aDate;
    bFirstLine = FALSE;
    continue;
}

double dPrice = atof(strTemp.Mid(19));

// Make a CStockData object and add it
// to our temporary array
CStockData aStData(strFund, aDate, dPrice);
CStockDataList::errorstatus err;
POSITION CurPos = TempList.AddSorted(aStData, err);

switch(err)
{
    // Discard identical entry
    case CStockDataList::duplicate_entry :

        discardedCtr ++ ;
        continue;

    // Same record, different price value
    case CStockDataList::conflicting_entry :
    {
        // Query if user wants to discard duplicate,
        // replace, or abort
        CConflictDialog aDialog;

        // Construct text to appear in rich edit
        // control
        CString strText = "Existing entry:\n\n";

        CStockData SDTemp = TempList.GetAt(CurPos);

        strText += SDTemp.GetAsString();
        strText += "\n\nReplacement entry:\n\n";
        strText += aStData.GetAsString();

        // Assign text to control variable
        aDialog.m_REditText = strText;
```

```
                        switch(aDialog.DoModal())
                        {
                            case IDABORT : // Abandon
                            return FALSE;

                            case IDCANCEL : // Discard new record
                            discardedCtr++ ;
                            continue;

                            case IDOK : // Replace existing record
                            TempList.SetAt(CurPos, aStData);
                        }
                    }

            default:  // Ok
                addedCtr++ ;
        }
    }

    // If we got this far then this is a valid record

    CString strPrompt;
    strPrompt.Format(
        "Import of file %s complete:\nRecords loaded: %d \
        \nRecords discarded: %d  \
        \n\nHit OK to load data into document.",
        strFileHeader, addedCtr, discardedCtr);

    if(AfxMessageBox(strPrompt, MB_OKCANCEL) == IDOK)
    {
        // Update document data
        m_DocList.RemoveAll();
        m_DocList.AddHead(&TempList);

        // Update fund view
        CMainFrame * pWnd =
            dynamic_cast<CMainFrame *> (AfxGetMainWnd());

        if(pWnd)
        {
            pWnd->UpdateFundList(m_DocList);
            // Show fund window after loading new funds
            pWnd->SetFundsVisible(TRUE);
        }

        return TRUE;
    }
    else
        return FALSE;
}
```

3. Look through the code, and make sure that you understand how:

- A temporary list is used to hold the data that is loaded so that the application data is not modified until the load process has completed successfully, and the user has approved the import.

- The routine distinguishes between a header line and a data line.

- The header line is parsed to ensure that the correct type of document is being loaded.

- **CString** member functions are used to extract data from a data line.

- The routine deals with invalid lines, duplicate lines and conflicting entries (same fund and date, different price). You might want to pay close attention to the **CStockDataList::AddSorted()** function.

4. Build and run the STUpload application. Try using the **Import** option from the **Data** menu to load the Ch6Test.dat file from the ..\Chapter 6\Data folder on the companion CD-ROM. Make sure that the data loads as expected. Close the application and run it again. This time load the conflict.dat file from the ..\Chapter 6\Data folder. This file contains a conflicting record to allow you to test the conflict handling routine.

Implementing STUpload Serialization

STUpload application data consists of a single **CStockDataList** object that is a collection of **CStockData** objects. The **CStockData** object encapsulates a fund name, a date and a price. The document also contains a CString variable that records the currently selected fund name. This variable should also be serialized, so that the fund that was currently selected when the document file was saved will still be selected when the file is restored.

To serialize the STUpload application data, you will need to:

- Make **CStockData** a serializable class.

- Provide an implementation of the **SerializeElements()** function template for the **CStockData** element type (This is necessary because **CStockData** contains a **CString**).

- Implement the **CSTUploadDoc::Serialize()** function.

- Implement the **CSTUploadDoc::DeleteContents()** function to clear out the data held in the document object before it is reused.

- Add calls to **CDocument::SetModifiedFlag()** wherever the application data is altered so that the framework will prompt the user to save changes before closing a modified document.

Making CStockData a Serializable Class

The **CStockData** class that we have provided is directly derived from the **CObject** class, and it includes a default constructor. You will need to add the serialization macros and the **Serialize()** function.

▶ **To add the serialization macros**

1. Open the StockData.h file to edit the **CStockData** class definition.

2. To the top of the class declaration, in the **public** section, add the following line:

```
DECLARE_SERIAL(CStockData)
```

3. Open the StockData.cpp file. At the top of the file, below the preprocessor statements, add the following line:

```
IMPLEMENT_SERIAL(CStockData, CObject, 1)
```

▶ **To add the Serialize() function**

1. Switch back to the StockData.h file.

2. Add the following declaration to the **public** section of the **CStockData** class definition:

```
virtual void Serialize(CArchive& ar);
```

3. Switch back to the StockData.cpp file. At the end of the file, add the following code:

(This code can be found in CH6_03.cpp, installed from the companion CD.)

```
void CStockData::Serialize(CArchive& ar)
{
    if (ar.IsStoring())
    {
        ar << m_strFund;
        ar << m_date;
        ar << m_dblPrice;
    }
    else
    {
        ar >> m_strFund;
        ar >> m_date;
        ar >> m_dblPrice;
    }
}
```

Overriding SerializeElements()

You will now implement the function template **SerializeElements()** for the **CStockData** element type. The function will simply iterate across the collection data and call **Serialize()** for each **CStockData** object.

▶ **To override the SerializeElements() function**

1. Open the StockDataList.h file.

2. At the end of the file, before the #endif statement and *after* the end of the **CStockDataList** class declaration, add the following line:

```
template <> void AFXAPI SerializeElements <CStockData>
    (CArchive& ar, CStockData* pNewSD, int nCount);
```

3. Open the StockDataList.cpp file.

4. At the end of the file, add the following code:

(This code can be found in CH6_04.cpp, installed from the companion CD.)

```
template <> void AFXAPI SerializeElements <CStockData>
    (CArchive& ar, CStockData* pNewSD, int nCount)
{
    for (int i = 0; i < nCount; i++, pNewSD++)
    {
        // Serialize each CStockData object
        pNewSD->Serialize(ar);
    }
}
```

Implementing the CSTUploadDoc::Serialize() Function

At this point, you are ready to implement the document serialization code.

▶ **To implement the CSTUploadDoc::Serialize() function**

1. Locate the **CSTUploadDoc::Serialize()** function.

2. Replace the function with the following version:

(This code can be found in CH6_05.cpp, installed from the companion CD.)

```
void CSTUploadDoc::Serialize(CArchive& ar)
{
    m_DocList.Serialize(ar);

    if (ar.IsStoring())
    {
        ar << m_strCurrentFund;
    }
```

```
else
{
    ar >> m_strCurrentFund;

    // Update Select Fund window
    CMainFrame* pWnd = dynamic_cast<CMainFrame *>
        (AfxGetMainWnd());

    if(pWnd)
    // Will fail if running from icon or from
    // command line with file name argument
    {
        // Update and show fund window
        pWnd->UpdateFundList(m_DocList, m_strCurrentFund);
        pWnd->SetFundsVisible(TRUE);
    }
}
}
```

All the stock data records are serialized in a single call to **CStockDataList::
Serialize()**. The **CSTUploadDoc::m_strCurrentFund** data member is also
serialized.

Displaying the Select Fund Window

Take note of the code that displays the fund window when a document file is
loaded. This is not possible here when the application is launched by double-
clicking a document file icon, as the pointer to the main window is not available
at this point. However, you can instruct the application to display the fund window after the main window has been created, if it detects that a document has
already been loaded.

▶ **To display the Select Fund window at application startup**

1. Locate the **CSTUploadApp::InitInstance()** function.

2. At the end of the function, just before the return statement, add the following code:

   (This code can be found in CH6_06.cpp, installed from the companion CD.)

```
CMainFrame * pFrameWnd =
    dynamic_cast<CMainFrame *> (m_pMainWnd);

ASSERT_VALID(pFrameWnd);
```

```
CSTUploadDoc * pDoc =
    dynamic_cast<CSTUploadDoc *>(pFrameWnd->GetActiveDocument());

ASSERT_VALID(pDoc);

if(pDoc->GetDocList().GetCount() > 0)
// Non-empty document at main window creation time means we are
// running from icon or from command line with file name argument
{
    pFrameWnd->UpdateFundList(pDoc->GetDocList(),
      pDoc->GetCurrentFund());
    pFrameWnd->SetFundsVisible(TRUE);
}
```

Implementing DeleteContents()

Because STUpload is an SDI application, any data contained in the document object must be cleared out by the **DeleteContents()** function.

▶ **To implement the CSTUploadDoc::DeleteContents() function**

1. Use ClassWizard to overload the **DeleteContents()** function for the **CSTUploadDoc** class.

2. Edit the function code. Replace the //TODO comment line with the following code:

   (This code can be found CH6_07.cpp, installed from the companion CD.)

```
m_DocList.RemoveAll();

CMainFrame * pWnd =
    dynamic_cast<CMainFrame *> (AfxGetMainWnd());

if(pWnd)
{
    pWnd->UpdateFundList(m_DocList);
    // No funds on file, so hide fund window
    pWnd->SetFundsVisible(FALSE);
    // And reset current fund value
    SetCurrentFund("");
}
```

Notifying Document Data Modification

Finally you must add calls to **CDocument::SetModifiedFlag()** whenever the persistent document data is changed. In the STUpload application the data is modified in two places:

- In the **CSTUploadDoc::OnDataImport()** function, after the **LoadData()** function has returned with a TRUE value, to indicate that records have been successfully imported from a text file.

- In the **CFundDialog::OnSelchangeFundlist()** function, when the user changes the currently selected fund.

▶ **To modify the CSTUploadDoc::OnDataImport() function**

1. Locate the line in the **OnDataImport()** function that reads:

```
LoadData(aFile);
```

2. Replace this line with the following code:

```
if(LoadData(aFile))
{
    SetModifiedFlag();
    UpdateAllViews(NULL);
}
```

▶ **To modify the CFundDialog::OnSelchangeFundlist() function**

Locate the **CFundDialog::OnSelchangeFundlist()** function. At the end of the function string, before the closing brace, add the line:

```
pDoc->SetModifiedFlag();
```

Testing Serialization

▶ **To build and test the STUpload application**

1. Run the application, then use the **Import** option from the **Data** menu to load data from the ..\Chapter 6\Data\Test.dat file on the companion CD.

2. Select a fund to view, then close the application. When prompted, save the document as **MyFile.stu**.

3. Restart the application. From the **File** menu, choose **Open**, then select and open the MyFile.stu file.

4. Select a new fund to view and close the application, saving your changes.

5. Use Windows Explorer to locate the MyFile.stu file, and launch the STUpload application by double-clicking the file icon.

6. Check that the file is restored correctly.

Review

1. How do you open a file in text mode?

2. What kind of exception is thrown by the **CFile::Open()** function?

3. What steps are necessary to make a class serializable?

4. What does the default implementation of the **SerializeElements()** function do?

5. Which registry key should be used to store application settings that are common to all users of the computer on which the application is installed?

6. Where do the MFC profile management classes **WriteProfileString()** and **WriteProfileInt()** store profile settings?

C H A P T E R   7

Adding Database Support

About This Chapter

Most applications work with large amounts of data, often shared, that is frequently stored in a relational database management system (RDBMS). An RDBMS is an application that allows you to organize large amounts of data in linked tables. RDBMS applications usually provide you with a query language, which you can use to quickly retrieve data from the database. Examples of an RDBMS include Oracle and Microsoft SQL Server. Smaller, single-user applications might use desktop database applications, such as Microsoft Access, to store and retrieve data. Desktop databases generally work with concepts similar to those employed by larger RDBMS applications.

In this chapter, you will learn about a variety of data access interfaces available to Microsoft Visual C++ application developers. These interfaces include features of the Microsoft Foundation Classes (MFC), which provide support for data access, and ActiveX Data Objects (ADO), which is Microsoft's standard interface to essentially all forms of external data.

Before You Begin

Before you start this chapter, you should have read Chapters 2 through 6, and completed the exercises in the text.

Lesson 1: Data Access with Visual C++

This lesson will explain the different data access interfaces available to the Visual C++ application developer, and also explain circumstances in which each interface should be used. Because these technologies can connect to relational databases, you should have a basic understanding of relational database theory and Structured Query Language (SQL), the host language for controlling and interacting with an RDBMS. This lesson provides only a cursory introduction to relational database theory and SQL.

After this lesson, you will be able to:

- Describe the development of Microsoft's strategy for data access.
- Describe the data access interfaces available and determine the appropriate technology to use for a given situation.
- Describe the basic architecture of a relational database and how to use simple SQL statements to retrieve data from tables within an RDBMS.

Estimated lesson time: 40 minutes

Data Access Interfaces

The number of data access interfaces available for Microsoft Windows applications can seem overwhelming. Which of the cryptically named technologies— DAO, ODBC, RDO, UDA, OLE DB or ADO—should you use to meet your specific application requirements?

Your decision may be made easier by an explanation of the historical context of these technologies. Microsoft's data access strategy was previously based on Data Access Objects (DAO), for access to desktop databases; and Remote Data Objects (RDO), which use the Open Database Connectivity (ODBC) architecture, for access to client/server databases. This strategy is now being replaced by a single model, Universal Data Access (UDA), which provides access to all types of data.

The goal of Microsoft's UDA strategy is to provide high-performance access to non-relational data sources as well as relational databases through an easy-to-use programming interface that is tool- and language-independent. UDA is implemented through ADO, which provides a high-level interface to OLE DB, Microsoft's newest Component Object Model (COM)–based data access technology.

While you can still use any of the earlier C++ data access technologies, you should always use UDA technology when developing a new application. Generally, you should use ADO for all of your data access because ADO is easy to use, has many powerful features, and performs well. Experienced COM developers can use the OLE DB interfaces directly to gain optimum performance and efficiency benefits. Visual C++ 6.0 provides the *OLE DB Templates*, a set of templated classes that implement many of the commonly used OLE DB interfaces, to make the OLE DB technology easier to use.

If you are considering migrating an existing DAO/ODBC application to ADO, you will have to consider whether the benefits of ADO justify the cost of the conversion. Code written in DAO or RDO will not directly map to ADO code. However, a solution implemented using other data access technologies will most likely be achievable using ADO. Eventually, you should look towards converting all your code to ADO because it implements a simpler, more flexible object model.

Data Access Objects

DAO, the native programming interface to the Microsoft Jet database engine, was originally designed for use with Microsoft Visual Basic and Microsoft Visual Basic for Applications. DAO uses the Microsoft Jet engine to provide a set of data access objects that encapsulate common database objects such as tables, queries, and *recordsets* (objects that contain a set of rows returned as a result of a query against a database).

DAO is generally used to access local desktop data sources such as Microsoft Access, Microsoft FoxPro, and Paradox, but it can also be used to access remote data sources.

At the lowest level, DAO exposes its objects through COM interfaces. However, C++ programmers are more likely to access them through the MFC DAO database classes (described in Lesson 2 of this chapter), or through the **dbDAO** classes. The **dbDAO** classes provide C++ with the same DAO functionality available through Visual Basic and also use a similar syntax.

Open Database Connectivity

ODBC provides a common application programming interface (API) to access client/server data sources, usually an RDBMS, such as SQL Server or Oracle. ODBC's consistent interface provides maximum interoperability; a single application can access different RDBMS platforms through a common set of code.

This ability enables developers to build and distribute a client/server application without targeting a specific RDBMS or having to know specific details of the different database server platforms that the application may access. All that is needed to connect to a RDBMS is an ODBC driver. These drivers are supplied by RDBMS vendors or third-party developers, and developed according to the ODBC open standard.

Because the capabilities of different RDBMS platforms vary, and because ODBC driver developers might choose to limit the number of features they implement, ODBC defines three levels of driver *conformance* that provide the application with information about what features are available to the application from the driver:

- *Core* conformance, which all ODBC drivers must meet.
- *Level 1* conformance, which includes the Core interface conformance level functionality plus additional features, like transactions, that are usually available in a RDBMS.
- *Level 2* conformance, which includes the Level 1 interface conformance level functionality plus advanced features like the asynchronous execution of ODBC.

For more information about ODBC conformance levels, search for "Interface conformance levels" in the Visual C++ Help file.

You can install and configure ODBC drivers on your computer using the ODBC Data Sources applet in Control Panel. The ODBC Data Sources applet is also used to register a *Data Source Name* (DSN). A DSN is a uniquely named collection of information used by the ODBC Driver Manager to connect your application to a particular ODBC database. A DSN must be registered on the specific system that will use it. DSNs can be stored in a file (a *file DSN*) or in the registry (a *machine DSN*). Machine DSNs are either installed for a particular user (a *user DSN*), or are accessible to all users of a computer (a *system DSN*). Figure 7.1 shows the ODBC Data Source Administrator being used to inspect system DSNs.

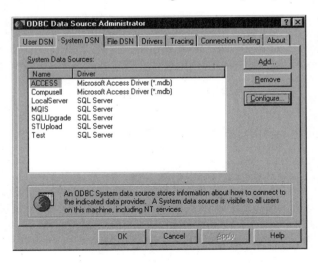

Figure 7.1   The ODBC Data Source Administrator

ODBC is based on SQL as a standard for accessing data. When an application needs to get data from a data source, the application sends an SQL statement to the ODBC Driver Manager, which then loads the ODBC driver required to inter-face with the data. The driver then translates the SQL sent by the application into the SQL used by the DBMS, and finally sends it to the database server. The DBMS retrieves the data and passes it back to the application via the driver and the Driver Manager.

ODBC provides a *cursor library*, which provides scrollable cursors for any driver that meets the minimum level of ODBC conformance. You can use cursors to iterate across a set of rows selected from a database.

C++ developers can use the ODBC API to connect to a database, send SQL statements, retrieve results, get errors, disconnect, and so on. The ODBC API is a well-documented way of writing client/server applications but is fairly difficult and involves a lot of code. As a result, object models such as ADO or RDO, or the MFC ODBC database support classes, are more commonly used.

Remote Data Objects

RDO is a thin objectified layer over the ODBC API. RDO depends on the ODBC driver and the database engine for much of its functionality. Data access using RDO is intended to provide access to an ODBC data source through an object model similar to that used by DAO, without additional memory require-ments necessitated by supporting a local database. The RDO object model pro-vides additional features such as server-side cursors, disconnected recordsets, and asynchronous processing.

Like DAO, RDO exposes its objects through COM interfaces. RDO provides the *Data Source Control*, an ActiveX control that encapsulates a database query and the retrieved recordset. The Data Source Control provides controls that al-low you to browse through the recordset, displaying the data that it contains in one of Microsoft's data-bound ActiveX controls, such as the *DBGrid* or *DBList* controls.

OLE DB

OLE DB is a set of COM interfaces that provides applications with uniform ac-cess to data stored in diverse information sources, regardless of location or type. OLE DB is an open specification designed to build on the success of ODBC by providing an open standard for accessing all types of data. Whereas ODBC was created to access relational databases, OLE DB is designed for both relational and non-relational information sources, including but not limited to mainframe, server, and desktop databases; e-mail and file system stores; spreadsheets and project management tools; and custom business objects.

Conceptually, OLE DB has three types of components: *data consumers*, *service components,* and *data providers,* as illustrated in Figure 7.2.

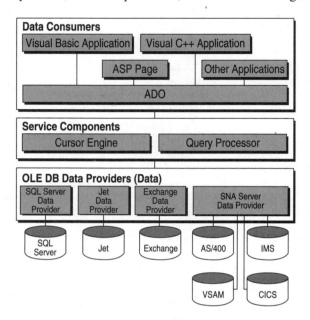

Figure 7.2   Components of OLE DB

Data consumers are applications or components that use the data exposed by data providers. Any application that uses ADO is an OLE DB data consumer.

Service components are elements that process or transport data to extend the functionality of data providers. Examples of service components include query processors that generate or optimize queries; or cursor engines that consume data from a sequential, forward-only data source to produce scrollable data.

Data providers are applications such as SQL Server or Microsoft Exchange, or system components such as file systems or document stores, which expose their data to other applications. Data providers expose OLE DB interfaces that data consumers or service components can access directly. An OLE DB provider is available for ODBC; this provider makes the many existing ODBC data sources available to OLE DB data consumers.

ActiveX Data Objects

ADO is designed as a high-performance, easy-to-use application-level interface to OLE DB. ADO is implemented with a small footprint, minimal network traffic, and a minimal number of layers between the application and the data source, all contributing to a lightweight, high-performance interface. ADO exposes a

COM Automation interface, which makes it accessible by all leading Rapid Application Development tools, database tools, application development environments, and scripting languages.

Since ADO was designed to combine the best features of, and eventually replace, RDO and DAO, it uses similar conventions with simplified semantics to make it easy to learn. ADO provides the *ADO Data Control*, an improved version of the RDO Data Source Control.

A feature of ADO, *Remote Data Service* (RDS) manages the transport of disconnected recordsets to clients over HTTP as well as over *Distributed COM* (DCOM), making it possible to develop full-featured, data-centric Web applications. ADO will be covered in greater detail in Lesson 3 of this chapter.

Using the ODBC Data Source Administrator

In this practice exercise, you will use the ODBC Data Source Administrator to register a system DSN for the *pubs* sample database that is included as part of a standard SQL Server installation. You will use this DSN in subsequent exercises to access ODBC data.

▶ **To add a data source using the ODBC Administrator**

1. On the **Start** menu, click **Control Panel**. Open the **ODBC Data Sources** applet.

2. On the **System DSN** tab, click **Add**. Select the SQL Server driver from the list of drivers that are displayed, and then click **Finish**.

Note If the SQL Server driver is not displayed in the list, you will need to install the SQL Server ODBC Driver from your Visual C++ CD-ROM. Select **Add/Remove** from the installation screen, and install the driver from the **Data Access** option group.

---

3. Type **MyDSN** as the name of the data source. You can leave the **Description** box empty.

4. Select **(local)** as the SQL Server to connect to, and click **Next**.

5. If you have installed the Desktop version of SQL Server, select **SQL Server authentication using a login ID and password entered by the user**. Enter the login ID and password on this screen, and click **Next**.

Note Use the default login ID, **sa**, and leave the password box blank unless you have assigned a password for this account. (On a default installation, the **sa** account has no password.)

If you have installed the SQL Server Standard version, select **Windows NT authentication using the network login ID**, and click **Next**.

6. Select the check box to make the **Change the default database to:** option available. Select **pubs** from the drop-down list, and click **Next**.

Note If the pubs database does not appear, you will need to install it on your SQL Server. To do this, use the SQL Server Query Analyzer to load and execute the *MSSQL7\ Install\InstPubs.sql* script.

---

7. On the following screen, maintain the default options, and click **Finish**.

8. Test the data source by clicking **Test Data Source**. The last line returned should read TESTS COMPLETED SUCCESSFULLY! Click **OK** to dismiss the **SQL Server ODBC Data Source Test** dialog box, then click **OK** again to complete the registration procedure.

You will see that the DSN has been added to the list of system DSNs. Close the ODBC Data Source Administrator, and then close Control Panel.

Relational Database Concepts

While there are database system types other than relational databases, and while ADO is intended to provide access to non-relational data as well as relational data, the relational model is currently dominant. For that reason, before working with a data source, you should have a basic understanding of relational database theory.

A *relational database* stores and presents data as a collection of tables. (Tables are covered in greater detail later in this section.) A logical structure is defined for this type of database by establishing relationships between tables. The *relational database model* offers the following benefits in that it:

- Organizes data into a collection of tables to make the design easy to understand.

- Provides a relationally complete language for data definition, retrieval, and update.

- Provides data integrity rules that define consistent database states to improve data reliability.

Elements of a Relational Database

A relational database presents data as a collection of tables. For example, the SQL Server sample database *pubs* contains business information of the type that might be held by a publishing house. The pubs database contains one table that lists all authors, and another that lists all book titles. Figure 7.3 shows a portion of the *authors* table.

au_id	au_lname	au_fname
172-32-1176	White	Johnson
213-46-8915	Green	Marjorie
238-95-7766	Carson	Cheryl
267-41-2394	O'Leary	Michael
274-80-9391	Straight	Dean
341-22-1782	Smith	Meander
409-56-7008	Bennet	Abraham
427-17-2319	Dull	Ann
472-27-2349	Gringlesby	Burt
486-29-1786	Locksley	Charlene
527-72-3246	Greene	Morningstar
648-92-1872	Blotchet-Halls	Reginald
672-71-3249	Yokomoto	Akiko

Figure 7.3   The authors table from the pubs database

Tables are logical groupings of related information made up of *rows* and *columns*. A row (sometimes called a *record*) contains information about a single entry in a table. For example, a row in the authors table would contain information about a single author.

A row is composed of multiple columns (sometimes called *fields*). Each column contains a single piece of information about the row. For example, a row in the authors table has columns for the author ID, the author's first name, and the author's last name. If you look at the portion of the authors table shown in Figure 7.3, you will see that these columns are named *au_id*, *au_lname* and *au_fname*.

Unlike columns, table rows are not named. To uniquely identify rows within a table, you must define a *primary key* for the table. A primary key is a column, or a combination of columns, which has a unique value for each row in the table. The **au_id** column shown in Figure 7.3 is an example of a primary key. Once a column or columns have been defined as the primary key for a table, the data integrity rules built into the RDBMS ensure that rows with duplicate keys cannot be added to the table.

A table can also define *foreign keys* to specify relationships between tables. A foreign key points to a primary key field in a related table. For example, the pubs database contains the *titles* table, which lists published titles. The titles table defines one of its columns as a foreign key, containing a primary key value from the *publishers* table to designate the publisher of a particular title. Figure 7.4 shows this relationship as portrayed in the Visual Studio database diagram tool.

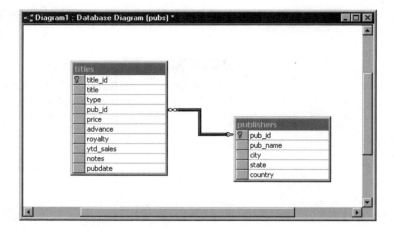

Figure 7.4   The relationship between the titles table and the publishers table

The symbols used to qualify the relationship depicted by this diagram indicate that a *one-to-many* relationship exists between the publishers table and the titles table. In other words, the titles table can contain any number of rows with the same value in the **pub_id** column; or to put it another way, the titles table can contain many titles from the same publisher. Because the **pub_id** column in the publishers table is defined as the table's primary key, each row in the publishers table will have a unique value in the **pub_id** column.

Structured Query Language

Structured Query Language (SQL) is a well-defined, standard language used for querying, updating, and managing relational databases. Approved as a standard by the International Standards Organization (ISO), SQL can retrieve, sort, and filter specific data from a database. In addition, you can change and delete data in a database using SQL statements.

It is important to have a fundamental understanding of SQL so that your applications will communicate effectively with your database. By using SQL, an application can ask the database to perform tasks rather than requiring application code and processing cycles to perform them. More importantly, effective use of SQL can minimize the amount of data that must be read from and written to a remote database server. Effective use of SQL can also minimize the amount of data sent across the network. Minimizing disk and network input/ output (I/O) are important factors in improving application performance.

You must be aware that, in different environments, databases have different implementations of the same SQL functionality, both syntactically and semantically.

Each implementation of SQL has its own support for different data types, integrity rules, and query optimization.

SQL SELECT Statement

The SQL **SELECT** statement returns information from the database as a set of selected rows. The **SELECT** statement is divided into three major sections:

- **SELECT** The **SELECT** list allows you to specify which columns will be returned from the query.

- **FROM** The **FROM** clause allows you to specify which tables will be used to get the columns specified in the **SELECT** list.

- **WHERE** The optional **WHERE** clause allows you to specify filter criteria to limit the selection of rows. You can filter queries based on multiple columns.

The minimum syntax for a **SELECT** statement is:

```
SELECT columns FROM tables
```

To perform this operation, the database engine searches the specified table or tables and extracts the chosen columns. You can select all columns in a table by using an asterisk (*). For example, the following SQL statement will return all columns and rows from the authors table:

```
SELECT *
FROM authors
```

It might not be efficient to return all data from a table. By adding a **WHERE** clause to the end of the statement, you can specify that only rows meeting a certain condition are to be returned. The following example will return all columns from all rows in the authors table having a last name equal to Ringer:

```
SELECT *
FROM authors
WHERE au_lname = 'Ringer'
```

Note the use of apostrophes (') surrounding the name Ringer in this example. Apostrophes are used when the value in the **WHERE** clause is a string. In this case, au_lname is defined by the database as a string value. When a numeric value is specified in the **WHERE** clause, apostrophes are not used, as shown in the following example:

```
SELECT *
FROM titles
WHERE royalty = 10
```

IN Operator

By using the IN operator in a **WHERE** clause, you can return only those rows in which a **WHERE** clause parameter is contained in a specified list. For example, you can use the IN operator to return last names and state codes of all authors living in Utah or Tennessee, as illustrated in the following example and in Figure 7.5.

```
SELECT au_lname, state
FROM authors
WHERE state IN ('UT', 'TN')
```

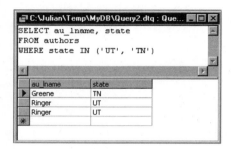

Figure 7.5   Using the IN operator with a **WHERE** clause to filter rows

BETWEEN Operator

This operator returns a selection of rows in which the **WHERE** parameter is between two given criteria. Note that dates are specified in the *'yyyymmdd'* string format.

```
SELECT title_id, title, pubdate
FROM titles
WHERE pubdate BETWEEN '19910601' AND '19910630'
```

LIKE Operator

You can use the **LIKE** operator to find values in a column that match a pattern you specify. You can specify the complete value, as in **LIKE 'Smith'**, or you can use wildcard characters to find a range of values (for example, **LIKE 'Sm%'**). In the following example, also illustrated in Figure 7.6, all rows where the author's last name starts with the letter S are returned.

```
SELECT au_lname
FROM authors
WHERE au_lname LIKE 'S%'
```

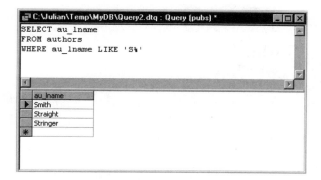

Figure 7.6   Syntax and results of an SQL statement using the **LIKE** operator

ORDER BY Clause

By default, rows are returned in the order they were entered in the database. The optional **ORDER BY** clause will sort a query's resulting rows on a specified column or columns, in ascending or descending order. The ASC option indicates ascending order; the DESC option indicates descending order. The default sort order is ascending (A to Z, 0 to 9). The following example selects all columns from the authors table and sorts them in descending order, by last name:

```
SELECT *
FROM authors
ORDER BY au_lname DESC
```

Lesson Summary

A number of different interfaces are available to allow your Visual C++ application to access persistent data from an externally managed source. Over the last few years, Microsoft's data access strategy has moved from a model based on the DAO and the ODBC-based RDO, to a newer, single model known as UDA. UDA is based on OLE DB, which is a set of COM interfaces that provide high-performance access to all types of data—both relational databases and nonrelational sources such as e-mail and file-system stores. Although you can use the OLE DB interfaces directly, Microsoft recommends that you use ADO, which is a powerful, easy-to-use, high-level interface to OLE DB data sources.

Visual C++ still supports DAO and RDO, so you can support and maintain earlier applications that use these technologies. However, you should always use UDA technology when creating a new application.

DAO uses the Microsoft Jet database engine to provide a set of data access objects to access local desktop data sources. The DAO object model encapsulates common database objects such as tables, queries, and recordsets. DAO exposes its objects through COM interfaces, but Visual C++ programmers generally use the DAO database classes provided by MFC.

RDO provides access to ODBC data sources through an object model similar to that used by DAO. ODBC has been widely used as a low-level API to client/server data sources. RDO provides many powerful features such as server-side cursors, disconnected recordsets, and asynchronous processing.

Based on SQL as a standard for accessing data, ODBC is an important technology—a large number of ODBC-based applications have been written. ODBC-based applications interface with a database through ODBC drivers, which are supplied by RDBMS vendors or third-party developers, and developed according to the ODBC open standard. You can use the ODBC Data Source Administrator to install and configure ODBC drivers on your computer and register a DSN with the operating system.

Visual C++ developers can use the ODBC API to connect to a database, send SQL statements, retrieve results, get errors, disconnect, and so on. However, it is easier to use one of the object models such as ADO or RDO, or to use the MFC ODBC database support classes.

OLE DB is an open specification, designed to build on the success of ODBC by providing an open standard for accessing all kinds of data. Conceptually, OLE DB has three types of components: *data consumers*, *service components,* and *data providers*.

- Data providers are applications that expose their data to other applications. They also expose OLE DB interfaces that service components or data consumers can access directly. The OLE DB provider for ODBC makes the many existing ODBC data sources available to OLE DB data consumers.

- Data consumers are applications or components that use the data exposed by data providers. Any application that uses ADO is an OLE DB data consumer.

- Service components are elements that process or transport data to extend the functionality of data providers.

ADO is designed as a high-performance, easy-to-use application-level interface to OLE DB. ADO exposes a COM Automation interface, which makes it accessible by a wide variety of development tools and scripting languages.

So that you can use ODBC and ADO efficiently, you should have a basic understanding of relational database theory and SQL, the language that controls and interacts with an RDBMS.

A relational database presents data as a collection of *tables* made up of *rows* and *columns*. A row contains information about a single record in a table. Each column contains a single piece of information about the record.

To uniquely identify rows within a table, you should define a *primary key* for the table. A primary key is a column or a combination of columns whose value is guaranteed to be unique for each row in the table. You can also define *foreign keys* to specify relationships between tables. A foreign key "points to" a primary key field in a related table.

Remember that SQL is a standard language used for querying, updating, and managing relational databases. SQL can both retrieve and update data in a database. You should have a fundamental understanding of SQL so your applications will communicate effectively with your database. The proper use of SQL can ensure that the database server, on behalf of your application, executes processing; and also that your data is retrieved efficiently, without generating unnecessary network traffic and disk I/O.

You should be aware that, in different environments, databases have different implementations of the same SQL functionality.

The SQL **SELECT** statement returns information from the database as a set of records. The **SELECT** statement is divided into three major sections: **SELECT**, **FROM**, and **WHERE**.

- **SELECT** allows you to specify which columns will be returned from the query.
- **FROM** allows you to specify which tables will be used to get the columns specified in the **SELECT** section of the SQL statement.
- **WHERE** allows you to specify filter criteria to limit the selection of rows. You can filter queries based on multiple columns. The **WHERE** clause can be further qualified with **IN**, **BETWEEN**, or **LIKE** operators.

You can also specify an **ORDER BY** clause to sort a query's resulting rows on a specified column or columns, in ascending or descending order.

Lesson 2: MFC Database Support

MFC provides classes to support database access through DAO or through ODBC. This lesson shows you how to use these classes to create applications that allow you to retrieve and manipulate data stored in an external database.

After this lesson, you will be able to:

- Describe the MFC DAO and ODBC database classes and how they work together to provide access to desktop and client/server databases.
- Describe how to use the AppWizard to create a database application based on the **CRecordView** or **CDaoRecordView** class.
- Describe how to use MFC database objects to query a database from within your application code.
- Describe how to filter a recordset based on parameters supplied at run time.

Estimated lesson time: 50 minutes

MFC Database Classes

MFC provides two distinct sets of classes for database access: one to allow access through DAO, the other through ODBC. DAO is generally used to access desktop databases and ODBC to connect to relational database servers through a named data source.

Both sets of classes are similar, and are based on a common programming model. The DAO and ODBC database classes often differ only in name and a few relatively minor implementation details. Table 7.1 lists the core ODBC classes, their DAO equivalents, and a brief description of their functions:

Table 7.1   ODBC Classes and Their DAO Equivalents

ODBC class	DAO class	Function
CDatabase	CDaoDatabase	Encapsulates a connection to a remote data source or desktop database
CRecordset	CDaoRecordset	Encapsulates a set of records selected from a table in a database
CRecordView	CDaoRecordView	Provides a dialog-based form view directly connected to a recordset object

These classes work together to enable you to retrieve data from a data source so that the data can be displayed in a dialog-based view for browsing or updating. The following sections explain the role of each class. Bear in mind that, because the ODBC and DAO versions of the classes are so similar, we might often discuss the classes in general terms rather than naming them specifically. We will draw your attention to significant differences between the classes where they occur.

CDatabase and CDaoDatabase

The **CDatabase** class typically establishes a connection to an ODBC data source such as a SQL Server database. The **CDaoDatabase** class usually establishes a connection to a desktop data source such as an Access database.

Establishing a connection to a database is a two-stage process. You first create a database object, then call that object's **Open()** member function. Both classes provide similar **Open()** functions. For **CDatabase::Open()**, you specify a DSN or a connection string; for **CDaoDatabase::Open()**, you specify a database file name. The **Open()** functions take arguments to allow you to specify whether the connection should be opened for exclusive or for read-only access.

For ODBC connections, use the **CDatabase::OpenEx()** function. The syntax for the **OpenEx()** function is as follows:

```
CDatabase::OpenEx (LPCTSTR lpszConnectString,
    DWORD dwOptions = 0);
```

The *lpszConnectString* parameter is the connection string that specifies the DSN. If Windows NT authentication is not used on the data source, you can supply user and password information in the connection string. If you pass **NULL** to the *lpszConnectString* parameter, a dialog box will appear at run time that will prompt you to enter the DSN, user ID, and password.

The second parameter, *dwOptions*, is a bitmask value that determines the mode in which the data source is opened. The default value is **0**, which specifies that the data source will be opened in the shared mode, with write access. Other values that can be used are combinations of those shown in Table 7.2.

Table 7.2   Optional Parameters for the CDatabase::OpenEx Member Function

dwOptions parameter	Meaning
CDatabase::openReadOnly	Opens the data source in a read-only mode
CDatabase::useCursorLib	Loads the ODBC cursor library
CDatabase::noOdbcDialog	Does not display the ODBC connection dialog box irrespective of whether insufficient information was provided in the connection string
CDatabase::forceOdbcDialog	Always displays the ODBC connection dialog box

This code shows how you might call **OpenEx()** to open a connection to the *pubs* DSN, using the **sa** account with a password of *password*.

```
CDatabase db;
db.OpenEx("DSN=pubs;UID=sa;PWD=password",0);
```

The **CDaoDatabase** class contains several features that allow you to make use of functionality specific to the Microsoft Jet database engine. For example, you can associate a collection of **CDaoTableDef** objects with a **CDaoDatabase** object. These are table definition objects that you can use to create and modify tables within a Jet-compatible database file.

You should always use the **Close()** function to close your database objects when you have finished with them. Connections to data sources are expensive resources that should be conserved.

CRecordset and CDaoRecordset

A recordset encapsulates a set of records selected from a database. A recordset is comparable to a document in the document/view architecture, in that it holds the data that a record view object displays.

Recordsets enable scrolling from record to record, updating records (adding, editing, and deleting records), qualifying the selection with a filter, sorting the selection, and parameterizing the selection with information obtained or calculated at run time. **Recordset** objects contain member variables that correspond to columns selected from the database table. These member variables are updated with values from the corresponding database row, as the user moves through the recordset.

The exchange of data between data members of a recordset object and the corresponding table columns on the data source is implemented by a mechanism called *Record Field Exchange* (RFX). RFX is similar to the DDX mechanism used to transfer data between dialog box controls and dialog classes.

Note In the DAO world, RFX is called *DFX*—short for DAO Record Field Exchange.

Recordset objects are created in association with a database object. You should pass the address of an existing database object to your recordset constructor, as shown in the following example that uses the ODBC classes:

```
CDatabase db;
db.OpenEx("DSN=pubs;UID=sa;PWD=password",0);
CRecordset rs(&db);
```

If you derive a recordset class from **CRecordset** or **CDaoRecordset**, you can overload member functions to specify connection information, and pass a NULL value to the constructor when creating an object instance. If you use this method, MFC will create a temporary database object to associate with your recordset, using the connection information that you specify.

Once you have created your recordset object, you call the **Open()** member function to submit a query and populate the recordset with the records returned from the query. The following code shows how to call the **Open()** function for the **CRecordset** object created in the previous example:

```
rs.Open(CRecordset::dynaset, "SELECT * FROM authors",
    CRecordset::none);
```

The first parameter of the **CRecordset::Open()** function determines the type of cursor that will be created for the data that is returned, as shown in Table 7.3.

Table 7.3   Cursor Types for the CRecordset::Open Member Function

Parameter	Meaning
CRecordset::dynaset	Creates a recordset that is dynamic in nature and can be scrolled in both directions. However, the ordering of data is determined when the record set is opened. Dynasets are applicable for most database operations because they use minimal memory by storing the keys from the result set only, and they show most changes by other users. The only changes that cannot be seen are record insertions.
CRecordset::snapshot	Creates a recordset that does not display the changes made by other users to the data source; also can be scrolled in both directions. Snapshots are useful when you need to ensure the result set does not change while you are using it, for example, when generating reports.
CRecordset::dynamic	Creates a recordset that is truly dynamic in nature. You can scroll through the recordset in both directions and every time a user makes a change, the data source content reflects that change. The dynamic cursor consumes the greatest amount of resources. The dynaset is useful for situations where the result set must be constantly up to date.
CRecordset::forwardonly	Creates a read-only recordset that can be scrolled in the forward direction only. The forward-only cursor is the fastest and least memory-consumptive cursor. Many database tasks involve making a single pass through the result set, making this cursor useful for those tasks.

The **Open** function's second parameter is an SQL command string. The last parameter is a bitmask value that allows you to specify whether the recordset will be append-only or read-only, whether it will allow processing of multiple rows of records, and so on. The value **CRecordset::none** indicates that none of the options have been set. For a complete list of values that this parameter can take, search for "**CRecordset::Open**" in the Visual C++ Help file.

CDaoRecordset::Open() is similar to **CRecordset::Open()**. The **CDaoRecordset** class allows you to create only a dynaset, a snapshot, or a *Table* recordset. A **Table** recordset is an updateable recordset that represents records from a single database table. Snapshot recordsets are read-only for the **CDaoRecordset** class.

You must call the **Close()** member function once you have finished with a recordset object. Make sure that you close a recordset *before* you attempt to close the database object with which it is associated.

CRecordView and CDaoRecordView

The record view classes provide the means of displaying the data in a recordset. **CRecordView** and **CDaoRecordView** are derived from *CFormView*, a view class that provides an application with a client area based on a dialog template resource. This kind of application is often referred to as a *forms-based* application.

The record view classes add the ability to connect dialog box controls to member variables of an associated recordset. The user can view the current record through the controls on the form, as illustrated in Figure 7.7.

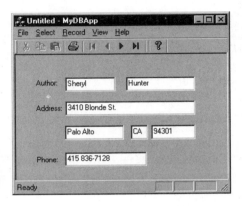

Figure 7.7   A **CRecordView**-based application

The exchange of data between the current record of the recordset and the controls of the record view is handled by the dialog data exchange/dialog data validation (DDX/DDV) mechanism, which is implemented for the record view classes. **CWnd::UpdateData()** is called from within the record view class's **OnMove()** function, which is called when the user moves from the current record. If the recordset is not read-only, the current record in the recordset is updated with the values from the record view controls. The RFX/DFX mechanism propagates these changes to the tables on the data source. Figure 7.8 illustrates the relationships between the ODBC database objects and the data exchange mechanisms.

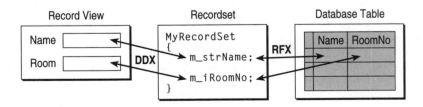

Figure 7.8   DDX and RFX

Database Errors

Accessing an external resource such as a database carries a high risk of failure. The database might be offline, or a user might not have adequate permissions to access the database. Calls to open a database connection or a recordset should be protected by a **try... catch...** block to catch any exceptions that might occur. MFC provides special database exception classes, similar to the **CFileException** class, which provide information about the nature of the database error.

The **CDatabase::Open()** and the **CRecordset::Open()** functions throw a **CDBException** upon failure. The **CDaoDatabase::Open()** and the **CDaoRecordset::Open()** functions throw a **CDaoException**. An example of how to handle database exceptions is given later in this lesson.

Creating a Database Application with AppWizard

To give you a better understanding of how the database, recordset, and record view classes work together, you will use AppWizard to create a database application. You will create a form-based application to retrieve and update data on the SQL Server sample database *pubs*, using the ODBC data source from Lesson 1. Although the ODBC classes are used throughout the following examples, the techniques demonstrated can easily be applied to a project based around the DAO classes.

▶   **To create the MyDBApp application**

1.   On the Visual C++ **File** menu, click **New** to create an **MFC AppWizard (exe)** project. Name the project **MyDBApp**.

2.   In Step 1 of the AppWizard, select **Single document**. Click **Next** to display Step 2 as shown in Figure 7.9.

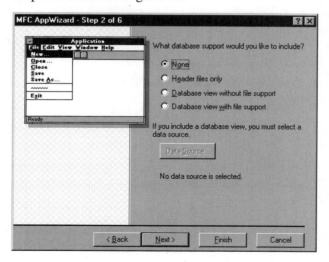

Figure 7.9   AppWizard database options

Step 2 lets you choose between four options to specify the level of database support to include in the application. Choose the first option if you do not need to include database support. Select the second option to include the database header files in your project; this allows you to use the database classes and manually create your own recordsets. Select the third or fourth option to create a document/view-based application in which the document class contains a recordset; the view class is derived from **CRecordView** or **CDAORecordView**. The third option does not provide serialization routines, and is typically used when you want to create a simple form-based application that views and/or updates data held in a database. Use the fourth option if you require serialization support.

3. Select the **Database view without file support** option. Because you have selected a database view for your application, you must select a data source for the recordset class created for the project. Click **Data Source**. The **Database Options** dialog box appears as shown in Figure 7.10.

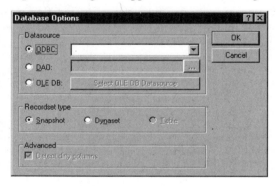

Figure 7.10   The **Database Options** dialog box

4. Ensure that the **ODBC** option is selected. Click the drop-down list to see all the DSNs registered on your computer. Click **MyDSN**.

5. Ensure that the **Snapshot** recordset type is selected, and click **OK**. Note that the SQL Server service must be running for this step to be completed successfully. The **Select Database Tables** dialog box appears.

6. Click **dbo.authors** and then click **OK** (**dbo** is the *owner name* assigned to the table by SQL Server).

7. Click **Finish** to accept the default values on the remaining AppWizard screens. In the **New Project Information** dialog box, click **OK** to create the project.

The new project opens with the **IDD_MYDBAPP_FORM** dialog template displayed in the dialog editor. **IDD_MYDBAPP_FORM** is the dialog template on which your record view class **CMyDBAppView** is based. The template is opened at this point as a hint that you need to add controls to your record view before you can display any recordset data.

Before you create the dialog template for your record view, you should take a brief look at the code generated for you by AppWizard, to help you understand how a database application is implemented.

► To view the generated code

1. Open MyDBAppSet.h to view the recordset class definition. Note that AppWizard has added a set of RFX member variables, one for each column in the authors table, to the class.

2. Open **MyDBAppSet.cpp** and locate the **CMyDBAppSet::DoFieldExchange()** function. Note that this is similar to the **DoDataExchange()** function used by DDX. AppWizard adds a call to an RFX function of the appropriate type to this function for each column in the authors table.

3. The **GetDefaultSQL()** member function, just above the **DoFieldExchange()** function, defines the **FROM** section of the **SELECT** statement on which the recordset is based:

```
CString CMyDBAppSet::GetDefaultSQL()
{
    return _T("[dbo].[authors]");
}
```

Note that the ODBC object names are enclosed in square brackets. Although this is required only when the object names contain spaces, the generated code always contains them by default.

To define a filter for your recordset, assign a string specifying a **WHERE** clause to the m_strFilter data member of your recordset class. You can also sort the records in your recordset by assigning a string specifying an **ORDER BY** clause to the m_strSort data member.

4. The **GetDefaultConnect()** member function, just above the **GetDefaultSQL()** function, returns a connection string that specifies the data source to be used by the recordset.

```
CString CMyDBAppSet::GetDefaultConnect()
{
    return _T("ODBC;DSN=MyDSN");
}
```

The framework does not create a **CDatabase**-derived object for your project. The recordset constructor receives a **NULL** parameter, causing a temporary **CDatabase** object to be created and used.

If you have used SQL Server authentication for your data source, you can prevent a **SQL Server Login** dialog box from appearing when you run the application by including authentication information in the following connection string:

```
CString CMyDBAppSet::GetDefaultConnect()
{
    return _T("ODBC;DSN=MyDSN;UID=sa;PWD=");
}
```

The connection string shown assumes that the **sa** account has no password.

5. Finally, open the MyDBAppDoc.h file to view the document class definition. Notice that the **CMyDBAppDoc** class contains the m_myDBAppSet public member variable. The **CMyDBApp** application conforms to the document/view model—the document class contains the application data that is displayed by the view class (the **CMyDBAppView** class).

You can make your recordset class more efficient by deleting the RFX member variables and functions for the columns in the authors table that are not used by your application. The next exercise shows you how to use ClassWizard to do this.

▶ **To remove unwanted fields from your recordset class**

1. Press CTRL+W to open ClassWizard, and select the **Member Variables** tab.
2. Select the **CMyDBAppSet** class name. In the list of member variables, click **m_au_id,** which corresponds to the [au_id] column. Click **Delete Variable**.
3. Repeat the process to remove the **m_contract** variable that corresponds to the [contract] column. Click **OK** to save the changes.

You will now return to the IDD_MYDBAPP_FORM dialog template to add the controls to display the data held in these recordset variables.

▶ **To modify the record view dialog template**

1. Use the dialog editor to add controls the IDD_MYDBAPP_FORM dialog template. Add three static text controls and seven edit controls as shown in Figure 7.11.

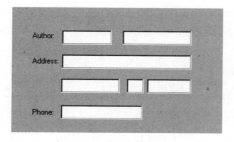

Figure 7.11   The IDD_MYDBAPP_FORM dialog template

2. Assign the following control IDs to the edit controls:

- **IDC_AU_FNAME**
- **IDC_AU_LNAME**
- **IDC_AU_ADDRESS**
- **IDC_AU_CITY**
- **IDC_AU_STATE**
- **IDC_AU_ZIP**
- **IDC_AU_PHONE**

You will now use ClassWizard to associate member variables of the recordset class with these control IDs.

▶   **To associate recordset variables with the record view dialog control IDs**

1. On the ClassWizard **Member Variables** tab, select the **CMyDBAppView** class.

2. In the **Control IDs** box, click **IDC_AU_ADDRESS**. Click **Add Variable**.

3. Expand the **Member variable name** drop-down list to see a list of recordset class data members that can be associated with the controls in this record view. Select the **m_pSet->m_address** variable.

4. Ensure that **Value** is selected in the **Category** box, and that **CString** is selected in the **Variable** type box, and click **OK**.

5. Repeat the previous steps to associate the corresponding recordset variable with each of the control IDs. For the IDC_AU_STATE control, create a validation rule to specify that a maximum of two characters can be entered.

6. Click **OK** to close ClassWizard and save your work.

Look through the MyDBAppView.h and MyDBAppView.cpp files to see the changes ClassWizard has made. Note that you have not added any member variables to the **CMyDBAppView** class. You have merely associated the controls with existing member variables from the **CMyDBAppSet** class. ClassWizard implements the association by using the **DDX_FieldText()** function inside the record view's **DoDataExchange()** function, as shown here:

```
void CMyDBAppView::DoDataExchange(CDataExchange* pDX)
{
    CRecordView::DoDataExchange(pDX);
    //{{AFX_DATA_MAP(CMyDBAppView)
    DDX_FieldText(pDX, IDC_AU_ADDRESS, m_pSet->m_address, m_pSet);
    DDX_FieldText(pDX, IDC_AU_CITY, m_pSet->m_city, m_pSet);
    DDX_FieldText(pDX, IDC_AU_FNAME, m_pSet->m_au_fname, m_pSet);
    DDX_FieldText(pDX, IDC_AU_LNAME, m_pSet->m_au_lname, m_pSet);
    DDX_FieldText(pDX, IDC_AU_PHONE, m_pSet->m_phone, m_pSet);
    DDX_FieldText(pDX, IDC_AU_STATE, m_pSet->m_state, m_pSet);
    DDV_MaxChars(pDX, m_pSet->m_state, 2);
    DDX_FieldText(pDX, IDC_AU_ZIP, m_pSet->m_zip, m_pSet);
    //}}AFX_DATA_MAP
}
```

Note that a standard DDV validation function can still be used.

Build and run the MyDBApp application. The application should appear as shown in Figure 7.12, although you might see a different record displayed.

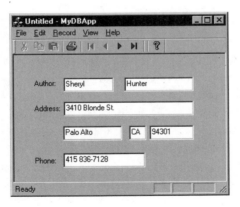

Figure 7.12   The MyDBApp application

Note that the **CRecordView** class provides a set of VCR-style navigation buttons on the toolbar that allows you to move forward and backward through the recordset, and jump to the beginning or to the end. The framework maps the control IDs for these buttons to the record view's **OnMove()** function. The base class implementation of the **OnMove()** function calls **CWnd::UpdateData(TRUE)** to save changes made to the record as you move off a record; and calls **CWnd::UpdateData(FALSE)** to update the record view with values from the recordset as you move on to a record. **UpdateData** updates the view by calling its **DoDataExchange()** function.

Filtering a Recordset

We mentioned earlier that you could filter a recordset by assigning a string specifying a **WHERE** clause to the recordset's m_strFilter data member. The following exercises show you how to apply this technique so that the MyDBApp application displays records on the authors table filtered by state of residence. You will create a menu option that allows the users to select from a list of state codes from the authors table. The selected state code will be used to filter the recordset.

▶ **To update the MyDBApp user interface**

1. In the MyDBApp project, open the **IDR_MAINFRAME** menu in the menu editor. Delete the **Edit** menu, since it is not used by the MyDBApp application.

2. In place of the **Edit** menu, create a new menu with the caption **&Filter**. To this menu, add a single item with the caption **&State**. This menu command should be assigned the ID **ID_FILTER_STATE**. Close the menu editor.

3. Using the toolbar editor, delete the buttons on the **IDR_MAINFRAME** toolbar that correspond to the deleted **Edit** menu options (**ID_EDIT_CUT**, **ID_EDIT_COPY** and **ID_EDIT_PASTE**). Remember that you delete toolbar buttons by dragging them off the toolbar. Close the toolbar editor.

4. Open ClassWizard and select the **Message Maps** tab. Select the **CMyDBAppDoc** class and create a command handler function for the **ID_FILTER_STATE** ID. Accept the default name **OnFilterState()** for the function.

5. Click **OK** to close ClassWizard and save your changes.

Next, you will create the **Select State** dialog box, which will display a list of state codes from the authors table.

▶ **To create the Select State dialog box**

1. In ResourceView, right-click the Dialog folder. On the shortcut menu, select the **Insert Dialog** option to create a new dialog template resource. This resource should be assigned the ID **IDD_STATEDIALOG**, and the caption **Select State**.

2. Add a list box control to the dialog box, and assign it the ID **IDC_ STATELIST**. Arrange the controls so that the dialog box resembles the one shown in Figure 7.13 on the following page.

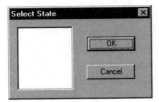

Figure 7.13   The **Select State** dialog box

3. Press CTRL+W to open ClassWizard, and create a dialog class for the
   IDD_STATEDIALOG template. Name the dialog class **CStateDialog**.

4. On the ClassWizard **Member Variables** tab, select the **IDC_STATELIST**
   control ID. Click **Add Variable** to add a **CString** variable named m_strState
   and store the value selected from the list box. Click **Add Variable** again to
   add a **CListBox** variable named m_statelist, to represent the list box control.

5. On the ClassWizard **Message Maps** tab, select **CStateDialog** in the **Object
   IDs** box and **WM_INITDIALOG** in the **Messages** box. Click **Add Function**
   to create an overload of the **OnInitDialog()** virtual function for your class.

6. Click **Edit Code** to edit the function implementation. Replace the // TODO
   comment line with the following code:

```
CDatabase aDB;

try
{
    aDB.OpenEx("DSN=MyDSN");
    // Specify login information if using SQL Server authentication,
    // e.g., aDB.OpenEx("ODBC;DSN=MyDSN;UID=sa;PWD=");

    CRecordset aRS(&aDB);

    aRS.Open(CRecordset::forwardOnly,
        "SELECT DISTINCT state FROM authors");

    while(! aRS.IsEOF())
    {
        CString strValue;
        aRS.GetFieldValue(short(0), strValue);
        m_statelist.AddString(strValue);
        aRS.MoveNext();
    }

    m_statelist.InsertString(0, "All records");
```

```
        aRS.Close();
        aDB.Close();
    }

    catch(CDBException * ex)
    {
        TCHAR buf[255];
        ex->GetErrorMessage(buf, 255);
        CString strPrompt(buf);
        AfxMessageBox(strPrompt);
    }
```

Notice that this function uses locally created **CDatabase** and **CRecordset** objects to retrieve information from the database. The code creates a *forward-only* recordset, as it needs to make only a single pass through the records. The **SELECT** statement that is used to open the recordset is qualified by the **DISTINCT** keyword, which specifies that only unique rows can appear in the recordset. This means that the recordset will contain one record per state for each state found in the table.

The **CRecordset::MoveNext()** function moves through the recordset until **CRecordset::IsEOF()** returns true. The value of the state column in each row is retrieved by the **CRecordset::GetFieldValue()** function. This function allows you to dynamically retrieve data from a recordset field by specifying a zero-based numeric index. Because the recordset in this function returns only one column, we know that the value we require can be accessed by the index value 0. Note how this function enables you to use the **CRecordset** class directly, without deriving your own class and specifying RFX variables.

Values retrieved from the recordset rows are added to the dialog box's list box control. The **CListBox::InsertString()** function is use to insert an "All records" item at the top of the list.

Notice that the database code is enclosed within a *try* block, and that the *catch* handler extracts information from the **CDBException** object to display to the user.

Finally, you will implement the **OnFilterState()** function to handle the **State** option from the **Filter** menu. This function will display the **Select State** dialog box and use the state code chosen by the user to filter the records displayed by the application.

▶   **To implement the OnFilterState() function**

1. Add the following line to the top of the MyDBAppDoc.cpp file:

```
#include "StateDialog.h"
```

2. Locate the **CMyDBAppDoc::OnFilterState()** function that you created earlier. Replace the // TODO comment line with the following code:

```
CStateDialog aSD;

if(aSD.DoModal() == IDOK)
{
    if(aSD.m_strState == "All records")
        m_myDBAppSet.m_strFilter = "";
    else
        m_myDBAppSet.m_strFilter.Format("state = '%s'",
            aSD.m_strState);

    m_myDBAppSet.Requery();

    POSITION pos = GetFirstViewPosition();
    if (pos != NULL)
    {
        CView* pView = GetNextView(pos);
        ASSERT_VALID(pView);
        pView->UpdateData(FALSE);
    }
}
```

The **CRecordset::Requery()** function refreshes the recordset after the filter has been changed. After a requery, the first record of the new set of records becomes the current record. It is important to make sure that you call **UpdataData()** on the record view to refresh the values displayed by the controls with data from the new current record.

You can parameterize your recordset by including question marks (?) as parameter placeholders in your filter string like this:

```
m_myDBAppSet.m_strFilter = "state = ?";
```

You can then use the RFX mechanism to replace the parameter placeholders with run-time values. To learn how to parameterize a recordset in this way, refer to the article "Recordset: Parameterizing a Recordset (ODBC)" in the Visual C++ Help file. Using a parameter in this way is more efficient than simply replacing the filter string. For a parameterized recordset, the database must process an SQL **SELECT** statement only once. For a filtered recordset without parameters, the **SELECT** statement must be processed each time you requery with a new filter value.

Lesson Summary

MFC provides two distinct sets of classes for database access: one to allow access through DAO, the other through ODBC. Both sets of classes are similar and are based on a common programming model.

A set of three core classes work together to enable you to retrieve data from a data source so that it can be displayed in a dialog-based view for browsing or updating. These classes are:

- **CDatabase/CDaoDatabase**
- **CRecordset/CDaoRecordset**
- **CRecordView/CDaoRecordView**

The database classes are used to establish a connection to a data source or database file. This is achieved by creating an object of the appropriate type, and calling the object's **Open()** function. The **Open()** functions allow you to supply connection information using a connection string, and to specify whether the connection should be opened for exclusive or for read-only access.

For ODBC connections, Microsoft recommends that you use the **CDatabase::OpenEx()** function. This function allows you to specify flags to pass additional ODBC information.

You should always use the **Close()** functions to close your database objects when you have finished with them.

A recordset encapsulates a set of records selected from a database. Recordsets enable scrolling from record to record, updating records, filtering and sorting records. Recordset objects contain member variables that correspond to columns selected from the database table. As the user moves through the recordset, the member variables are updated with values from the corresponding database row, by RFX.

Recordset objects are created in association with a database object. You should pass the address of an existing database object to your recordset constructor. For derived recordset classes, you can pass a NULL value to the constructor when creating an object instance, and the framework will create a temporary database object for the recordset to use. Overload the **GetDefaultConnect()** member function to supply connection information for the temporary database object.

After you have created your recordset object, you call the **Open()** member function to submit a query and populate the recordset with the records returned from the query.

The **Open()** function specifies the type of cursor to be created for the recordset. For a **CRecordset** object, this recordset can be one of the following:

- **dynaset** A recordset that is dynamic in nature and can be scrolled in both directions.
- **snapshot** A recordset that does not display the changes made by other users to the data source and can be scrolled in both directions.

- **dynamic** A recordset that is truly dynamic in nature. The recordset can be scrolled on both directions, and is reordered every time a user makes a change to the data source content.
- **forwardonly** A read-only recordset that can be scrolled in the forward direction only.

CDaoRecordset objects support read-only snapshot recordsets, dynasets, and table recordsets, based on an entire table in an .mdb database.

The recordset **Open()** functions take an SQL command string to select records for the recordset. **CDaoRecordset** objects can take the name of a DAO table definition or query definition object.

Use the **Close()** functions to close your recordset objects when you have finished with them.

The record view classes provide the means of displaying recordset data in a view based on a dialog template resource. Controls in a record view are connected to member variables of an associated recordset. The exchange of data between the current record of the recordset and the controls of the record view is handled by the DDX/DDV mechanism.

The **CDatabase::Open()** and the **CRecordset::Open()** functions will throw a **CDBException** upon failure. The **CDaoDatabase::Open()** and the **CDaoRecordset::Open()** functions throw a **CDaoException**.

Step 2 of the **MFC AppWizard (.exe)** option allows you to specify the level of database support to include in an application. You can simply include the database header files in your project, and use the database and recordset classes manually. Alternatively, you can create a document/view-based application in which the document class contains a recordset, and the view class is derived from **CRecordView** or **CDaoRecordView**. You can create an application with serialization routines, or a simple form-based application that views and/or updates data held in a database.

When you select a database view for your application, you must specify a data source for your application's recordset class. AppWizard creates recordset and record view classes for your project, and a blank dialog template to which you add controls to display the recordset data. The record view class supplies a set of VCR-style buttons on the toolbar that allows you to navigate the recordset.

You can filter a recordset by assigning a string specifying a **WHERE** clause to the m_strFilter data member of your recordset class. You can also sort the records in a recordset by assigning a string specifying an **ORDER BY** clause to the m_strSort data member. For maximum efficiency, you can parameterize the m_strFilter string and use the RFX mechanism to specify parameters.

Lesson 3: Introduction to ADO

Microsoft now recommends the use of ADO as a standard interface to all kinds of external data. Because ADO is based on COM technology, you will not learn how to use the ADO API directly until you have learned more about COM. Chapter 10, *COM Clients*, shows you how to create and use ADO objects within your C++ application code.

As an introduction to using ADO technology, this lesson shows you how to use the ADO Data Control to display records from an OLE DB data provider in a dialog-based application.

After this lesson, you will be able to:
- Describe the advantages of using ADO objects.
- Describe the components and the structure of the ADO object model.
- Describe how to use the ADO Data Control and data-bound ActiveX controls to display records from an OLE DB data provider.

Estimated lesson time: 30 minutes

Advantages of Using ADO

ADO is designed as an easy-to use application interface to OLE DB. ADO is easy to use because it exposes Automation objects that abstract the OLE DB interfaces. This allows the programmer to focus on the tasks to accomplish rather than the complexity of OLE DB. Any development platform that supports COM and Automation, which includes scripting languages such as Microsoft Visual Basic Scripting Edition (VBScript) and Microsoft JScript, can use ADO objects. This means that ADO can be used in Web-based development, using technologies such as Active Server Pages (ASP); as well as in desktop application development environments such as Visual C++ and Visual Basic.

For more information about Automation technology, see Lesson 3 of Chapter 8.

ADO recordsets are unique because they can be disconnected from the data source. Disconnected recordsets can be passed to other applications; and updates can be made to the data in the recordset, without requiring any network trips or connections to the data source. This feature is particularly useful in Web-based applications.

The ADO object model has fewer objects and is easier to use when compared to other data access objects such as DAO or RDO.

ADO Object Model

The ADO object model is designed to present the most commonly used features of OLE DB. As illustrated in Figure 7.14, the ADO object model has three main components, the **Connection** object, the **Command** object, and the **Recordset** object:

- The **Connection** object makes a connection between your application and an external data source, such as SQL Server. The **Connection** object also provides a mechanism for initializing and establishing the connection, executing queries, and using transactions. It is the highest-level object in the ADO object model.

- The **Command** object builds queries, including user-specific parameters, to access records from a data source. Typically, these records are returned in a **Recordset** object. **Command** objects are created from a database table, or an SQL query. You can also create relationships between **Command** objects to retrieve a set of related data in the form of a hierarchy.

- The **Recordset** object accesses records returned from an SQL query. You can use **Recordset** objects to permit users to edit, add, or delete records in the data source.

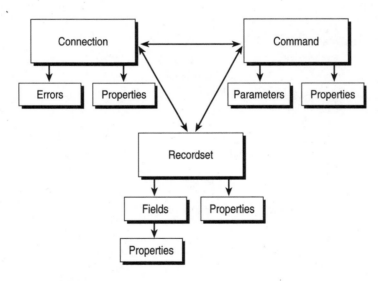

Figure 7.14   The ADO object model

The ADO object model differs from the DAO and RDO object models in that many of the objects can be created independently of one another. ADO objects are stored in a hierarchical format, but the hierarchy is de-emphasized so that you create only the objects that you need for your solution. You can create a **Recordset**, **Connection**, or **Command** object directly, without having to create their parent objects. For example you can create a **Recordset** object without first explicitly creating a **Connection** object. ADO implicitly creates the required **Connection** object for you.

ADO Collections

In addition to the three main objects, ADO supports three collections that can provide additional functionality to your applications:

- **Errors Collection** Any operation involving ADO objects can generate one or more provider errors. As each error occurs, one or more error objects are placed in the **Errors** collection of the **Connection** object. Each **Error** object represents a specific provider error, not an ADO error.

- **Parameters Collection** A **Command** object has a **Parameters** collection made up of **Parameter** objects. The **Parameters** collection is used to pass specific data to the parameterized query or stored procedure encapsulated by the **Command** object. It is particularly useful if you need to retrieve the value of output parameters from a stored procedure.

- **Fields Collection** A **Recordset** object has a **Fields** collection made up of **Field** objects. Each **Field** object corresponds to a column in the recordset. You use the **Fields** collection to access specific fields in an existing **Recordset** object.

In addition to their inherent object properties, ADO objects support the *Properties* collection. This is a collection of **Property** objects, which contain provider-specific information about the object. For example, the **Properties** collection of the **Connection** object contains **Property** objects that specify the maximum number of columns or the maximum row size of the current provider.

Using the ADO Data Control

The ADO Data Control is a graphical ActiveX control, complete with record navigation buttons, which provides an easy-to-use interface to help you create database applications with a minimum of code. The ADO Data Control uses

ADO to quickly create connections between data-bound controls and data providers. Data-bound controls are ActiveX user-interface controls that have two important characteristics:

- A *DataSource* property, which can be set to the ID of an ADO Data Control
- The ability to display data retrieved by the ADO Data Control to which they are bound

When you bind controls to an ADO Data Control, each field is automatically displayed and updated when navigating through records. This behavior is implemented by the controls themselves—you do not have to write any code.

Visual C++ includes several data-bound ActiveX controls such as the Microsoft DataGrid and Microsoft DataList Controls. You can also create your own data-bound controls or purchase controls from other vendors.

In the following exercises, you will create a simple dialog-based application, which uses the ADO Data Control and the DataGrid Control to display records from the *authors* table of the *pubs* database. You will also learn how to set the properties of these controls from within your application source code.

► **To create the ViewDB Application**

1. Start a new **MFC AppWizard (.exe)** project to create an application named **ViewDB**.
2. In Step 1 of the AppWizard, select **Dialog based**, and then click **Finish**.
3. Click **OK** to confirm the selection.

A dialog-based application is the simplest form of application that can be created by the AppWizard; such an application is not a document/view application. The application main window is a modal dialog box, and the application terminates when this dialog box is closed.

The AppWizard creates a dialog template and a dialog class for the main window dialog box. For the ViewDB application it has created the **IDD_VIEWDB_DIALOG** template and the **CViewDBDlg** class. The **IDD_VIEWDB_DIALOG** template resource should be currently open in the dialog editor.

The ADO Data Control and the DataGrid Control are installed as part of a standard installation of Visual C++. However, before you can place them in your application dialog box, you must use the Components and Controls Gallery to insert the controls into your project.

Inserting an ActiveX control into your project makes it available for you to use by:

- Placing an icon on your **Controls** toolbar so that you can use the mouse to place the control when editing a dialog template.
- Creating C++ classes for your project that wrap the Automation interfaces exposed by the control. You can use these classes to get and set the control properties, and to call the methods that the control provides.

▶ **To insert ActiveX controls into a project**

1. From the **Add to Project** option on the **Project** menu, select **Components and Controls**.
2. In the **Components and Controls Gallery**, double-click the **Registered ActiveX Controls** folder to display all ActiveX controls registered on your system.
3. Click **Microsoft ADO Data Control, version 6.0 (OLE DB)** and then click **Insert**.
4. Click **OK** to insert the component. Click **OK** to confirm that you want to generate classes for the control.
5. Repeat the process to insert the **Microsoft DataGrid Control, Version 6.0 (OLE DB)** into the project.
6. Click **Close** to close the Components and Controls Gallery.

You will now see that icons for the ADO Data Control and the DataGrid Control have been added to your **Controls** toolbar.

Using Figure 7.15 on the following page as a guide, edit the IDD_VIEWDB_ DIALOG template by taking the following steps:

▶ **To edit the IDD_VIEWDB_DIALOG template**

1. Remove the static text control that reads **TODO: Place dialog controls here**.
2. Set the dialog box caption to read **View Database**.
3. Place an ADO Data Control as shown in Figure 7.15. Edit the properties to remove the caption. Leave the control ID as **IDC_ADODC1**.
4. Place a DataGrid Control as shown in Figure 7.15. Change the caption to read **Authors**. Leave the control ID as **IDC_DATAGRID1**. On the Control page of the DataGrid Control **Properties**, clear the **AllowUpdate** checkbox to make the control read-only.

5. Add a static text control that displays the text **Order by:**. Next to this add a list box control that is tall enough to take two lines of text, as shown in Figure 7.15. Assign the list box the ID **IDC_ORDERLIST**.

6. Reorganize the **OK** and **Cancel** buttons as shown in Figure 7.15.

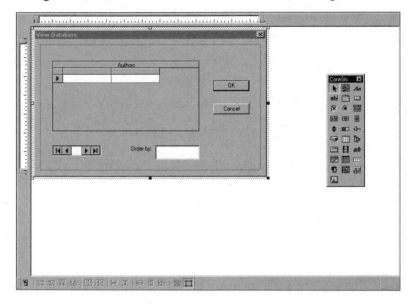

Figure 7.15   Editing the IDD_VIEWDB_DIALOG template

▶   **To connect the ADO Data Control to the data source**

1. Edit the properties of the **IDC_ADODC1** ADO Data Control. On the **Control** page, make sure that **Use Connection String** is selected. Click **Build** to create a connection string.

2. The **Data Link Properties** dialog box appears. On the **Provider** page, select **Microsoft OLE DB Provider for SQL Server**. Click **Next** to proceed to the **Connection** page.

3. Type **(local)** as the server name. Select **Use Windows NT integrated security**, or enter a SQL Server account name and password, as appropriate.

4. Select the **pubs** database on the server.

5. Click **Test Connection**. If the test is successful, click **OK** to save the **Data Link** properties.

6. Reopen the **ADO Data Control Properties** dialog box. Select the **RecordSource** page.

7. From the **Command Type** drop-down list select **1 – adCmdText,** which is an ADO-defined constant that specifies that you will supply a textual definition of an SQL command. Notice the other options that indicate that you will specify a table name or a stored procedure name.

8. In the **Command Text (SQL)** box, type the following command:

```
SELECT au_fname,au_lname,state FROM authors
```

9. Close the **ADO Data Control Properties** dialog box.

▶ **To bind the DataGrid Control to the ADO Data Control**

1. Edit the properties of the **IDC_DATAGRID1** DataGrid Control. Select the **All** page, which displays a list of all available control properties. To see this page, you might have to scroll to the right by using the arrow key to the top right of the **Properties** dialog box.

2. Click in the **Value** column of the **DataSource** property (currently displaying the text **<Not bound to a DataSource>**). As you click here, a drop-down list control appears. From this list, select the ID of the ADO Data Control: **IDC_ADODC1.**

   You can test your dialog box by pressing CTRL+T or by clicking the light-switch icon to the left of the **Dialog** toolbar. The dialog box should appear as shown in Figure 7.16, with the selected columns from the authors table displayed in the DataGrid Control. You can use the navigation buttons on the ADO Data Control to move through the recordset, or you can select the DataGrid Control and browse the records using the mouse and the cursor keys.

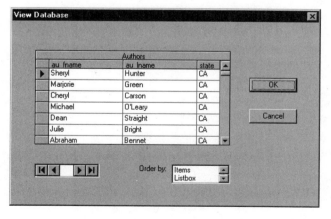

Figure 7.16   Testing the **IDD_VIEWDB_DIALOG** dialog box

3. Build and run the ViewDB application to verify that it behaves as expected.

Setting Control Properties from Your Source Code

If you look at the ViewDB project ClassView, you will see that it shows all the classes that were created for your project when you inserted the ADO Data Control and the DataGrid Control. Of particular interest are the **CAdodc** and the **CDataGrid** classes, which represent the controls themselves. If you expand these classes in ClassView, you will see that they provide member functions that allow you to get and set the control properties. The names of these functions are simply the names of the properties prefixed by **Get** or **Set**. The classes also provide member functions that wrap the methods exposed by the control.

In the following exercise, you will learn how to use these functions from within your application source code to set control properties and to call control methods. You will add two items to the **Order By** list box control, which will allow the user to specify whether they want to see the records ordered by author last name or by state. When the user changes the selection, the order of the records selected from the data source and the caption of the DataGrid Control will be updated.

▶ **To add member variables for the dialog box controls**

1. Open ClassWizard. Click the **Member Variables** tab.
2. Select the **CViewDBDialog** class. Add the member variables shown in Table 7.4.

Table 7.4   CViewDBDialog Member Variables

Resource ID	Category	Variable type	Variable name
IDC_ADODC1	Control	CAdodc	m_adodc
IDC_DATAGRID1	Control	CDataGrid	m_datagrid
IDC_ORDERLIST	Value	CString	m_lbOrder
IDC_ORDERLIST	Control	CListBox	m_strOrder

3. Click **OK** to close ClassWizard and save your changes.

▶ **To initialize the Order By list box**

Locate the **CViewDBDlg::OnInitDialog**() function. At the bottom of the function, just before the **return** statement, add the following code:

```
m_lbOrder.AddString("By last name");
m_lbOrder.AddString("By state");
m_lbOrder.SetCurSel(0);
OnSelchangeOrderlist();
```

This code adds the two items to the list box and sets the current selection to the first item in the list. You will now create the **OnSelchangeOrderlist**() function to handle the **LBN_SELCHANGE** control notification message that is fired when the user changes the selection in the list box.

► **To create the OnSelchangeOrderlist() function**

1. Open ClassWizard. Click the **Message Maps** tab.

2. Select the **CViewDBDlg** class. Select the **IDC_ORDERLIST** object ID.

3. Select the **LBN_SELCHANGE** message. Click **Add Function** and specify the name **OnSelchangeOrderlist**.

4. Click **Edit Code** to edit the function. Replace the // TODO comment with the following code:

```
if(m_lbOrder.GetCurSel() == 0)
{
        m_adodc.SetRecordSource("SELECT  au_fname,au_lname,\
        state FROM authors ORDER BY au_lname");
        m_datagrid.SetCaption("Authors by name");
}
else
{
        m_adodc.SetRecordSource("SELECT  au_fname,au_lname,\
        state FROM authors ORDER BY state");
        m_datagrid.SetCaption("Authors by state");
}

m_adodc.Refresh();
```

Note how member functions of the **CAdodc** and the **CDataGrid** classes are used to set properties and call methods of the ADO Data Control and the DataGrid Control. The code sets the **RecordSource** property of the ADO Data Control and the **Caption** property of the DataGrid Control. The code also calls the **Refresh()** method of the ADO Data Control.

Build and run the DBView application. Change the selection in the **Order By** list box. Check that the caption of the DataGrid Control and the order of the records it displays are updated as expected.

Lesson Summary

ADO is designed as an easy-to use application interface to OLE DB. ADO exposes Automation objects that abstract the OLE DB interfaces. This means that scripting languages such as VBScript and JScript as well as desktop application development environments such as Visual C++ and Visual Basic can use it. ADO supports disconnected recordsets that can be edited while disconnected from the data source and passed to other applications.

ADO presents a simple object model that organizes objects in a de-emphasized hierarchy. This means that you create only the objects that you need for your solution. If other objects are needed, they are created implicitly.

The three principal components of the ADO object model are:

- The **Connection** object makes a connection between your application and an external data source.
- The **Command** object builds queries, including user-specific parameters, to access records from a data source.
- The **Recordset** object accesses records returned from an SQL query.

In addition to the three main objects, ADO supports three collections that can provide additional functionality to your applications:

- The **Errors** collection is attached to the **Connection** object. Stores provider errors.
- The **Parameters** collection is attached to the **Command** object and stores parameters to be passed to a query or stored procedure.
- The **Fields** collection is attached to the **Recordset** object and provides access to columns in the recordset.

ADO objects support an additional **Properties** collection, which contains provider specific information about the object.

The ADO Data Control is a graphical ActiveX control that provides an easy-to-use interface to help you create database applications with a minimum of code. The ADO Data Control creates connections between data-bound controls and data providers. Data-bound controls are ActiveX user-interface controls that can connect to an ADO Data Control and automatically display the data that it retrieves.

The ADO Data Control and a set of data-bound controls are supplied with Visual C++. As with any ActiveX controls, you must insert them into your project before you can use them; use the Components and Controls Gallery to perform this action. Inserting a control enables you to use the dialog editor to place the ActiveX control just like any other control. Inserting a control will also create C++ classes for your project that wrap the Automation interfaces exposed by the control. You can use these classes to get and set the control properties, and to call the methods that the control provides.

Lab 7: Querying a Database

In this lab, you will implement the **Query Database** option for the STUpload application. This option allows the user to submit a simple ad hoc query to the central database. The user specifies a fund name, a start date, and an end date in a **Query** dialog box; and is returned price history data for the specified fund between the two dates. The user browses the query results in the **Results** dialog box, which contains a read-only DataGrid Control bound to an ADO Data Control.

The **Query Database** option is available only if the STUpload application is currently displaying price history data for a fund. The **Query Database** option is generally used to check that the records the user is about to upload do not already exist on the server. Therefore, the **Query** dialog box appears displaying the current fund and date range as default values.

This lab assumes that you have installed SQL Server and set up the Stocks database as directed in the "Getting Started" section of *About This Book*.

Implementing the Query Dialog Box

Your first task is to create the dialog template and the dialog class for the **Query** dialog box.

▶ **To create the Query dialog template**

1. Using Figure 7.17 as a guide create the **Query Database** dialog box template. The resource has the ID **IDD_QUERYDIALOG**, and contains a combo box control and two **Date Time Picker** controls. (Use the ToolTip feature to locate the buttons for these controls on the **Controls** toolbar.)

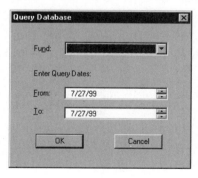

Figure 7.17   The **Query Database** dialog box

2. Assign the combo box control the ID **IDC_QUERY_FUND**. On the **Styles** page, ensure that the **Sort** check box is selected. In the **Type** box, select **Drop List**.

3. Click the drop-down arrow of the combo box. The selection handles change to show the extent of the drop-down list. Drag the handle of the drop-down list so that it extends to just above the **OK** and **Cancel** buttons.

4. Name the first **Date Time Picker** control **IDC_FROMDATE**. On the **Styles** page, set the **Format** option to **Short Date**. Select the **Use Spin Control** check box.

5. Repeat the procedure for the second **Date Time Picker** control, naming it **IDC_TODATE**.

▶ **To create the CQueryDialog dialog class**

1. Press CTRL+W to open ClassWizard. When prompted, create the **CQueryDialog** dialog class.

2. On the **Member Variables** tab, add the member variables shown in Table 7.5.

Table 7.5   CQueryDialog Member Variables

Resource ID	Category	Variable type	Variable name
IDC_FUND	Value	int	m_nFund
IDC_FUND	Control	CComboBox	m_dtFund
IDC_FROMDATE	Value	CTime	m_fromdate
IDC_FROMDATE	Control	CDateTimeCtrl	m_dtFrom
IDC_TODATE	Value	CTime	m_todate
IDC_TODATE	Control	CDateTimeCtrl	m_dtTo

You will now implement the **CQueryDialog::OnInitDialog()** function to initialize the **Query Dialog** box. This function will fill the combo box with the funds currently on file, and set the current selection. It will also initialize the **Date Time Picker** controls with the first and last dates on file.

▶ **To initialize the Query Dialog box**

1. Your first task is to make the **Select Fund** dialog box available to the **CQueryDialog::OnInitDialog()** function. Open the **Mainfrm.h** file. To the public section of the **CMainFrame** class definition, add the following inline function:

```
const CFundDialog * GetFundDialog()
{return &m_wndFundDialog;}
```

2. Add the following lines to the top of the QueryDialog.cpp file:

```
#include "Mainfrm.h"
#include "STUploadDoc.h"
#include "FundDialog.h"
```

3. Use ClassWizard to create the **CQueryDialog::OnInitDialog**() function (handle the **WM_INITDIALOG** message in the **CQueryDialog** class). Replace the // TODO comment in the generated function with the following code:

(This code can be found in CH7_01.cpp, installed from the companion CD.)

```
CMainFrame * pWnd =
dynamic_cast<CMainFrame *>
(AfxGetAPP()->m pMainWnd();

ASSERT_VALID(pWnd);

CSTUploadDoc * pDoc =
    dynamic_cast<CSTUploadDoc *>(pWnd->GetActiveDocument());

ASSERT_VALID(pDoc);

const CFundDialog * pFD = pWnd->GetFundDialog();

ASSERT_VALID(pFD);

// Fill combo box with current fund names
for(int n = 0; n < pFD->m_listBox.GetCount(); n++)
{
    CString strBuf;
    pFD->m_listBox.GetText(n, strBuf);
    m_cbFund.AddString(strBuf);
}

// Set listbox selection to strCurrentFund parameter
int iPos =
    m_cbFund.FindStringExact(-1, pDoc->GetCurrentFund());
    m_cbFund.SetCurSel(iPos);

// Setup Date Time Pickers
m_dtFrom.SetFormat("d MMM yyy");
m_dtTo.SetFormat("d MMM yyy");
```

You will need to overload the **OnOK**() function for the **CQueryDialog** class to retrieve the fund selected by the user:

▶ **To implement the CQueryDialog::OnOK() function**

1. Open the QueryDialog.h file, and add the following variable to the **public** section of the **CQueryDialog** class definition:

```
CString m_strFund;
```

2. Use ClassWizard to create the **OnOK()** function to handle the **BN_CLICKED** message for the **IDOK** object ID. Replace the // TODO comment with this code:

```
int nChoice = m_cbFund.GetCurSel();

if(nChoice >= 0)
    m_cbFund.GetLBText(nChoice, m_strFund);
```

Implementing the Query Results Dialog Box

You will now create the dialog template and dialog class for the **Query Results** dialog box.

▶   **To create the Query Results dialog template**

1. Using the Components and Controls Gallery, insert the **Microsoft ADO Data Control, version 6.0 (OLEDB)** and the **Microsoft DataGrid Control, Version 6.0 (OLEDB)** into the project. Make sure that you create all the classes associated with these controls.

2. Using Figure 7.18 as a guide, create the **Results** dialog box template. The resource has the ID **IDD_RESULTSDIALOG**, and contains an ADO Data Control with the default ID **IDC_ADODC1**, and a DataGrid Control with the default ID **IDC_DATAGRID1**. The **OK** button has been given the caption **Close**. The **Cancel** button has been removed.

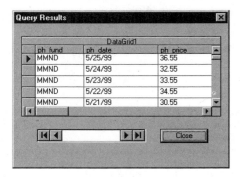

Figure 7.18   The **Query Results** dialog box

3. On the **Control** page of the **ADO Data Control Properties** dialog box, build a connection string to connect to the **Microsoft OLE DB Provider for SQL Server**. On the **Connection** page, specify the **(local)** SQL Server and select the **Stocks** database.

4. Reopen the **ADO Data Control Properties** dialog box. On the **RecordSource** page, select **1 – adCmdText** from the **Command Type** drop-down list. In the **Command Text (SQL)** box, type the following command:

```
SELECT * FROM pricehistory
```

5. Edit the DataGrid Control properties. On the **Control** page, deselect the **AllowUpdate** check box. On the **All** page, set the **DataSource** property to the ID of the ADO Data Control **IDC_ADODC1**.

Press CTRL+T to test the **Query Results** dialog box. Check that records from the price history table of the Stocks database are displayed.

▶ **To create the CResultsDialog dialog class**

1. Press CTRL+W to open ClassWizard. When prompted, create the **CResultsDialog** dialog class.

2. On the **Member Variables** tab, add the member variables shown in Table 7.6.

Table 7.6   CResultsDialog Member Variables

Resource ID	Category	Variable type	Variable name
IDC_ADODC1	Control	CAdodc	m_adodc
IDC_DATAGRID1	Control	CDataGrid	m_datagrid

3. Close ClassWizard. Open the ResultsDialog.h file, and add the following variables to the **public** section of the **CResultsDialog** class definition:

```
CString m_strQuery;
CString m_strCaption;
```

You will now implement the **CResultsDialog::OnInitDialog()** function to initialize the **Query Results** dialog box. This function will fill the combo box with the funds currently on file, and set the current selection. It will also initialize the **Date Time Picker** controls with the first and last dates on file.

▶ **To initialize the Query Results Dialog box**

1. Add the following line to the top of the ResultsDialog.cpp file, to include the **C_Recordset** class, which was generated by inserting the ADO Data Control into the project:

```
#include "_recordset.h"
```

2. Use ClassWizard to create the **CResultsDialog::OnInitDialog()** function. Replace the // TODO comment in the generated function with the following code: (This code can be found in CH7_02.cpp, installed from the companion CD.)

```
m_adodc.SetRecordSource(m_strQuery);
m_adodc.Refresh();

C_Recordset cRS = m_adodc.GetRecordset();
```

```
long lRecs = cRS.GetRecordCount();

if(lRecs < 1)
{
    AfxMessageBox("No records match this query");
    EndDialog(IDCANCEL);
}

m_datagrid.SetCaption(m_strCaption);
```

Handling the Query Database Menu Command

You will now add the command handler function and the user-interface update
handler function for the **Query Database** option on the **Data** menu.

▶ **To add the OnDataQuerydatabase() command handler**

1. To the top of the STUploadDoc.cpp file, add the following:

```
#include "QueryDialog.h"
#include "StockDataList.h"
#include "ResultsDialog.h"
```

2. Use ClassWizard to add a command handler for the **ID_QUERY_
   DATABASE** ID to the **CSTUploadDoc** class. The function should be called
   OnDataQuerydatabase().

3. Replace the // TODO comment with the following code:

   (This code can be found in CH7_03.cpp, installed from the companion CD.)

```
CQueryDialog aQDlg;

// Set the default values for the Date Time Picker controls
// with first and last date on file (all funds)
CStockData sdFirst = m DocList.GetHead();
CStockData sdLast = m DocList.GetTail();

aQDlg.m fromdate = sdFirst.GetDate();
aQDlg.m todate = sdLast.GetDate();

if(aQDlg.DoModal() == IDOK)
{
    // Construct query
    CString strQuery =
        "select * from PriceHistory where ph_fund = '";
    strQuery += aQDlg.m strFund;
    strQuery += "' and ph date between '";
    strQuery += aQDlg.m fromdate.Format("%Y/%m/%d");
```

```
strQuery += "' and '";
strQuery += aQDlg.m todate.Format("%Y/%m/%d");
strQuery += "'";

// Construct caption string
CString strCaption = aQDlg.m strFund;
strCaption += " Prices ";
strCaption += aQDlg.m fromdate.Format("%d/%m/%Y");
strCaption += " - ";
strCaption += aQDlg.m todate.Format("%d/%m/%Y");

CResultsDialog rd;
rd.m strQuery = strQuery;
rd.m strCaption = strCaption;

rd.DoModal();
}
```

The user-interface update command handler will ensure that the **Query Database** option is available only if the application is currently displaying price history data for a fund.

▶ **To add the user-interface update command handler**

1. Use ClassWizard to add an **UPDATE_COMMAND_UI** handler for the **ID_QUERY_DATABASE** ID to the **CSTUploadDoc** class. The function should be called **OnUpdateDataQuerydatabase()**.

2. Replace the // TODO comment with the following code:

   (This code can be found in CH7_04.cpp, installed from the companion CD.)

```
// Enable the Query Database command only if there is
// data on file and a fund currently selected for viewing

BOOL bEnable = FALSE;
bEnable = m strCurrentFund.IsEmpty() ? FALSE : TRUE;

pCmdUI->Enable(bEnable);
```

You can now build and run the STUpload application. Import the Ch7Test.dat file from the \Chapter 7\Data folder. Select a fund to view and select the **Query Database** command that is now enabled. The values in the Ch7Test.dat file correspond to records that have already been uploaded to the Stocks database. Accept the default values in the controls and click **OK** to browse the records on the database. You can experiment by submitting queries that will retrieve some of the records or none of them.

Review

1. How can you connect an ADO application to an ODBC data source?

2. What is wrong with the following SQL statement?

   ```
   SELECT * FROM authors WHERE au_lname LIKE M%
   ```

3. You need to open a **CRecordset** object so that you can list all the records in a database table to the printer. What value should you supply to the first parameter of the **Open()** function?

4. What does the **CRecordset::GetDefaultConnect()** function specify?

5. With which ADO object is the **Errors** collection associated? What does it contain?

6. Which property of the ADO Data Control is used to specify an SQL command to retrieve records from the data source?

C H A P T E R   8

Introducing the Component Object Model

About This Chapter

When developing with Microsoft Visual C++, a thorough understanding of the Component Object Model (COM) will enable you to simplify the construction of applications by utilizing reusable software components. The use of reusable components speeds development and results in more reliable applications.

This chapter provides a conceptual introduction to COM and discusses ActiveX controls, which are self-registering COM components designed to be placed in an ActiveX control container such as an application dialog box or a Web page. This chapter provides the necessary background for Chapters 9 through 11, which deal with the practical implementation of COM components.

Before You Begin

Before you start this chapter, you should have read Chapters 2 through 7, and completed the exercises in the text.

Lesson 1: COM Architecture

COM is a binary standard that defines a way for software objects, developed in different languages or operating on different platforms, to communicate. A COM component is a reusable software object that conforms to COM specifications.

In this lesson, you will learn about the basic architecture of Win32 operating systems, which allows you to create and use COM components in your programs. You will learn about the essential features of the COM specification, and how COM components are registered on a computer so that client programs can identify and make use of the functionality they offer.

After this lesson, you will be able to:

- Describe the architecture that enables a client to use a COM object.
- Describe the role of interfaces in COM.
- Describe the purpose of the **IUnknown** interface.
- Describe how globally unique identifiers (GUIDs) uniquely identify components and interfaces.
- Describe the registry entries required to register a COM object.
- Describe how to use the **CoCreateInstance**() function to create COM objects.

Estimated lesson time: 50 minutes

Using COM Objects

COM objects allow you to construct an application comprising a set of distinct cooperating components. One benefit of using COM objects is that they make interoperability available, irrespective of where the binary object is physically located. An important aspect of COM objects is that a program may attach dynamically to the object during execution.

For example, an application hosted in an executable file may link dynamically to a COM component hosted in a DLL. Because the component and executable are dynamically linked, they do not need to reside in the same location. To dynamically link to a binary object during execution, a program and the operating system cooperate to locate the object. COM defines all elements that both you and the operating system use in cooperation to ensure that the dynamic linking process works correctly.

Figure 8.1 shows the elements that participate in the dynamic linking process.

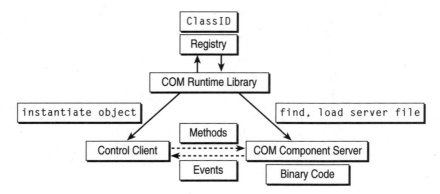

Figure 8.1   COM elements used to support dynamic linking

COM objects are implemented as .dll or .exe files. Every COM object that resides on your system must be registered with the Windows operating system. Registration information appears in the Windows registry. In the registry, you find a class identifier (ClassID) that identifies the object uniquely across all computers. The ClassID is a specially formatted globally unique identifier, or *GUID*. You will learn more about GUIDs later in this lesson.

When your client wants to link dynamically to a registered COM object, the client program uses the ClassID to identify the binary object. The COM run-time libraries, an integral component of the Windows operating system, provide the means for clients to locate and instantiate COM objects.

Once the COM libraries receive a ClassID, they search the **HKEY_CLASSES_ ROOT** portion of the registry in an attempt to find the location of the COM object that owns that ClassID. If the search is successful, the COM libraries create an instance of the object and return a pointer to the object's interface. The client uses this pointer to call the methods that the object provides. Otherwise, an error is reported to the client. An application will typically interact with this dynamically linked binary object by executing methods listed in its interface pointer. If the object needs to initiate interaction with your client program, you register event handler methods with the object. Under appropriate and well-defined conditions, the object fires events that are processed by these handler methods.

One of the features of COM is *location transparency*. Client applications can be written without concern as to whether the objects used run within their process, in a different process on the same computer, or in a process on a separate computer.

COM Interfaces

Your COM object provides access to its services through one or more interfaces. A COM interface is a logical grouping of related methods identified by a GUID, known as an Interface Identifier (IID). COM components are often described in terms of the client/server model, wherein a COM server is a component that provides services to client programs through the methods it exposes. Using this model, an interface can be understood as a description of the services provided by a component.

You gain access to the methods provided by the interface by obtaining a pointer to the interface, which references a table of function pointers known as the *vtable*. Each function pointer in the vtable enables you to access a single method provided by the interface.

Figure 8.2 shows a COM server object named **Encoder** that exposes three interfaces. **IUnknown** (discussed in the following section) is the interface that must be implemented by every COM component. The **IEncoder** and **ICommunicate** interfaces are specified by the designer of the component to expose the **Encoder** object's services. Figure 8.2 illustrates the default notation for illustrating COM components. We have shown the methods provided by the interfaces to the left of the diagram.

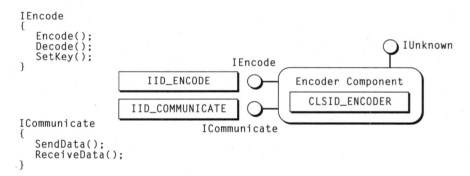

Figure 8.2   Components and interfaces

Figure 8.2 shows that components and interfaces have separate GUIDs. The names of the GUIDs shown illustrate the kind of #defined IDs that you use in your code to refer to the different types of GUIDs. As you will learn later in this chapter, GUIDs are large hexadecimal numbers.

An *interface* is a logically separate entity from the component that implements the component. In other words, the same interface can be implemented by many different components. An interface is analogous to a C++ abstract class definition. The identity of an interface is established by its unique IID. Once you publish your interface specification to the world, you are guaranteeing to anyone who might want to use or implement your interface that it *will not change*. The number and order of the methods, and the data types of the arguments and return values, are guaranteed to remain the same. If you want to add or alter methods, you must define a new interface with a different IID.

The fact that an interface is obtained as a pointer to a function table (the vtable), would seem to imply that a COM object could provide only methods to client applications. However, many languages that support COM (Microsoft Visual Basic, for example) support the notion of *properties*—public data members of components that are analogous to the member variables of a C++ class. Components written in C++ implement properties as pairs of methods used to set and get the value of encapsulated class data. This technique is illustrated in Chapter 9.

Note In this book we use the terms *property* and *method* to refer specifically to features of a COM interface. For regular C++ objects we use the terms *member variable* and *member function*.

IUnknown

The **IUnknown** interface, illustrated in Figure 8.3, must be implemented by every COM component.

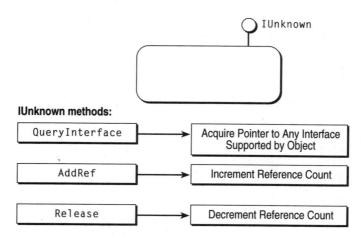

Figure 8.3   The **IUnknown** interface

IUnknown contains three methods that you implement for your COM object. When you implement the **QueryInterface()** method, you provide a mechanism for a client program to access any of the interfaces supported by your COM object.

Because a single instance of a component may service requests from a number of different clients, you must implement a reference counter for your COM object. This private data member serves to track the number of connected client applications. The **AddRef()** and **Release()** methods operate on the reference counter. When the reference counter reaches zero, the component terminates itself.

You must implement your COM components so that the **IUnknown** methods are always the first three methods in the vtable. The methods exposed by the other interfaces are listed sequentially after these methods.

Figure 8.4 illustrates a possible vtable layout for the **Encoder** object illustrated in Figure 8.2.

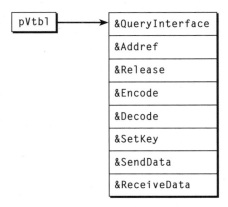

Figure 8.4   The structure of a vtable

At the beginning of the vtable are the **IUnknown** methods, followed by the methods exposed by the **IEncoder** interface, and then followed by the **ICommunicate** methods. When the COM run-time library instantiates the **Encoder** object, it obtains a pointer to the beginning of the vtable (shown as **pVtbl** in Figure 8.4). This pointer can be used to call the first function in the table—the **QueryInterface()** function. Your object's implementation of the **QueryInterface()** function must return a pointer to the requested interface.

GUIDs

GUIDs are 128-bit numeric identifiers that uniquely distinguish each COM object and the specific interfaces supported by COM objects. GUIDs are guaranteed to be unique across the world and to remain unique for a very long time. You use the Windows command-line utility UUIDGEN.EXE (or the graphical user-interface version GUIDGEN.EXE) to generate GUIDs for your components and interfaces.

A detailed characterization of a GUID appears in Figure 8.5.

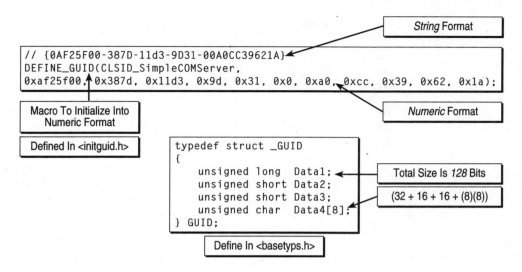

Figure 8.5   The construction of a GUID

A GUID actually exists in two formats: string and numeric. A string format appears in various locations in the registry. Numeric representations of GUIDs are necessary when using the GUID within client applications and within the actual COM object implementation.

As you can see in Figure 8.5, the numeric representation of a GUID is 128 bits in length. Within the structure _GUID, an unsigned long field named **Data1** is 32 bits long. The fields named **Data2** and **Data3** are unsigned short values, each consuming 16 bits. Eight unsigned **char** values each require 8 bits. If you add all of this together, you find that the numeric representation of a GUID consists of a 128-bit representation.

When you use the numeric representation within your COM object or within C++ client code, you declare a variable and use a specific macro to initialize the variable to the associated numeric value. The macro that you use is named **DEFINE_GUID** and appears in the header file initguid.h. Typically, the variable name that you use begins with either the prefix *CLSID* or *IID*. These prefixes indicate whether the GUID refers to a COM object or to an interface supported by a COM object.

COM Registry Entries

When you install a COM object onto a computer, you must register the object by creating entries in the computer's registry.

Figure 8.6 on the following page illustrates the registry entries required for a typical COM object.

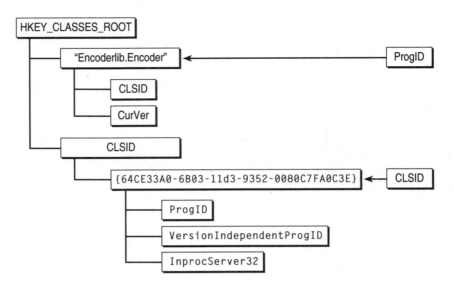

Figure 8.6   Registering the COM object

To register your COM object, you create entries under the **HKEY_CLASSES_ ROOT** subtree, under the predefined **CLSID** key. These entries enable the COM libraries to locate your COM object and load it into memory. Beneath the **CLSID** key, you type a subkey that is the string form of your **CLSID** COM object. Beneath this subkey, you attach the subkey that provides COM with the path to the component server, as shown here:

```
HKEY_CLASSES_ROOT\CLSID\{64CE33A0-6B03-11d3-9352-0080C7FA0C3E}\
    InprocServer32 = c:\Encoder\debug\Encoder.dll
```

The name of the subkey—**InprocServer32**—indicates that the component server is a DLL on the local computer.

Immediately beneath **HKEY_CLASSES_ROOT**, you can provide a key value representing a string name for your COM object. This string name is a version-independent programmatic identifier (ProgID). Associated with this string name, you type a subkey explicitly named **CLSID** whose value indicates the GUID for your COM object in its string format. A path representation for this entry looks like this:

```
HKEY_CLASSES_ROOT\Encoder\CLSID = {64CE33A0-6B03-11d3-9352-
0080C7FA0C3E}
```

By using a function named **CLSIDFromProgID()**, a client application can retrieve the CLSID from the ProgID. By providing the ProgID, you enable a client application developer to create an instance of your COM object without having to go through the error-prone process of typing a CLSID into the source code. Visual Basic client code will always specify COM objects as ProgIDs, so you will need to register a ProgID if you are intending to use your objects with non-C++ clients.

Creating Objects Using CoCreateInstance()

Once the CLSID is obtained using the **CLSIDFromProgID**() function, a client application submits the CLSID to the COM run-time library to load the COM object and retrieve an interface pointer. The function used to perform this operation is **CoCreateInstance**(). Using the CLSID and the registry, **CoCreateInstance**() locates the specified object, creates an instance of that object, and returns an interface pointer to that object.

The signature of the **CoCreateInstance**() function is shown below:

```
STDAPI CoCreateInstance (REFCLSID rclsid,
    LPUNKNOWN pUnkOuter,
    DWORD dwClsContext,
    REFIID riid,
    LPVOID * ppv) ;
```

The first argument to the function is the CLSID of the object. The second argument is used to aggregate the object as part of another object. Aggregation is explained in detail in Lesson 2 of Chapter 10.

The third argument specifies the execution context of the object. The possible values for this argument are:

```
CLSCTX_INPROC_SERVER
CLSCTX_INPROC_HANDLER
CLSCTX_LOCAL_SERVER
CLSCTX_REMOTE_SERVER
```

Execution contexts are discussed in the following lesson.

The *riid* argument is the IID of the requested interface. If the COM object is created successfully and supports the interface requested by the client, an interface pointer is returned through the *ppv* argument.

A detailed operational analysis of COM object creation that results from executing the **CoCreateInstance**() function appears in Figure 8.7, shown on the following page.

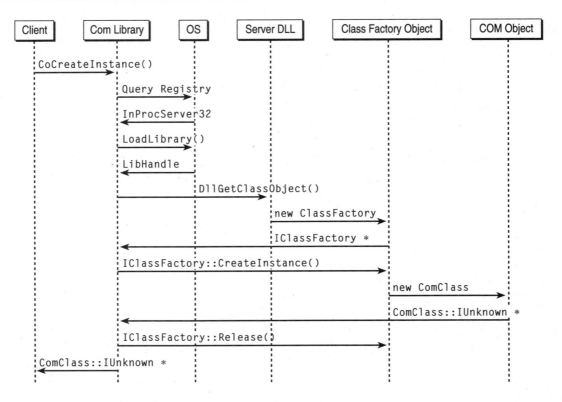

Figure 8.7   The COM object creation sequence

This sequencing diagram shows the elements used in the COM object creation process. The specific entities involved in COM object creation are across the top of the diagram. The sequence of interactions among the participating entities proceeds from the top of the diagram down to the bottom of the diagram.

A client application requests access to a specific interface supported by the COM object using the **CoCreateInstance**() function. This function accesses the COM library, requesting that the COM object be loaded. The COM library queries the registry along the indicated path, obtaining the path to and the name of the component server (in this case, a DLL).

When the component server is initialized, a class factory object is instantiated. A class factory is an object that creates other objects of a specific class, which you implement as part of your COM component. A class factory implements the **IClassFactory** interface. A pointer to the class factory interface then propagates all the way back to the COM library. Using this interface pointer, the COM library executes the **CreateInstance**() method supported by the class factory object. Your implementation of this method creates an instance of the COM class that actually provides all the methods that might be accessed by a client application. The act of creating this class initializes the vtable so a client application can execute the supported methods. A pointer to the **IUnknown** interface is returned to the COM library. When the COM library receives this interface pointer, it releases the class factory object and returns the **IUnknown** pointer to the client application. This pointer now references the component vtable, enabling the client to execute the methods provided by the COM object.

The entity interaction sequence outlined previously occurs in its entirety only the first time a client instantiates a COM object. If another client wants to use methods supported by this COM object, an interface pointer to the same COM object returns to the new client, and the server increments the reference count by calling **IUnknown::AddRef()**. When the client has finished using the component interface, it *must* call the **IUnknown::Release()** method to decrement the reference count. If any client fails to perform this action, the reference count will never reach zero, and the component will not be destroyed, leading to serious memory leakage problems.

Lesson Summary

COM allows dynamic linking of binary software components that can reside on a local computer or on a computer across a network. The COM run-time library uses registry entries to locate and to load a COM object. Every COM object supports the **IUnknown** interface and additional component-specific interfaces. Each interface is a collection of one or more methods. Separate GUIDs identify the COM object and every interface exposed by the object. Within your class implementation you provide an object known as a class factory that creates an instance of your COM object.

Lesson 2: Interface Marshaling

COM servers are not required to load into the same process as the client that makes use of their services. The client and the server do not even have to reside on the same computer. This has implications for the way that data is passed between client and server. You have to ensure that when a COM client calls a method, the COM server will receive the parameters in a format that it can understand, no matter where the server is running, or on which platform.

The transferring of data across process boundaries is called *marshaling*. In this lesson, you will learn about the different ways in which COM components marshal data passed to and from methods defined by the component interfaces.

After this lesson, you will be able to:

- Describe the different execution contexts in which COM components can be run.
- Describe the different techniques that can be used to marshal your interfaces.

Estimated lesson time: 30 minutes

Component Execution Contexts

A COM component can be run in one of three ways—as an in-process server, as an out-of-process server, or as a remote server. Figure 8.8, shown on the next page, summarizes the characteristics and implementations of using each of these execution environments.

An in-process COM server is implemented as a DLL, and executes within the same process address space as the object's client application. Since the COM object resides in the same address space, your COM server responds more quickly than either an out-of-process server or a remote server can. In-process servers can be developed more quickly since you have less code to implement. However, with this server, you must register a copy of the COM object on every computer on which you intend to run the client application.

Out-of-process COM servers are implemented as .exe files that reside on the same computer as the client application, but execute in a different process address space. As a result, you have to ensure that the arguments passed to a method transfer correctly across process boundaries—that is to say, you have to marshal your interfaces. Since you have to write some extra code to accomplish the marshaling of interfaces, your COM object is going to take a little more time to respond to method calls. Developing the extra code to pass arguments across process boundaries does require a bit more coding. Since the COM object executes on the same computer as the application client, you must also store and register a copy of the COM object on every client computer.

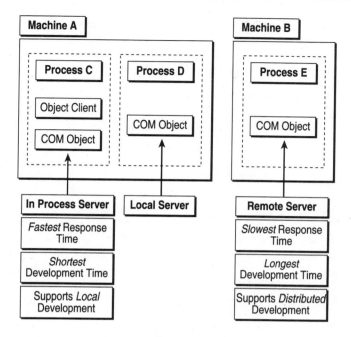

Figure 8.8   Execution contexts for COM objects

You can also implement your out-of-process COM object so it executes on a remote computer. This kind of object is known as a *remote server*. In this case, you transmit from the client computer to the server computer across a network. Response times for executing server methods are considerably longer. Executing a method across a network connection is a non-deterministic process. Every time you invoke a remote method, even if it is the same method, your client application experiences a different response time. If the network is clogged with traffic, your client application may experience longer response times. The code that you generate to support marshaling of method arguments for a local server also supports marshaling of method arguments for a remote server. If you use a remote server, then you need to have only a single copy of the server loaded and registered on the server computer. Many remote clients can use this single COM server copy. Since only one server exists, updating the behavior of the COM component is a relatively painless, low-effort process.

Marshaling Technologies

The act of marshaling data between a client and a server is a key issue when implementing a COM object or server. Depending upon the relationship between the client and the server, you use different programming technologies to marshal data for method calls between a client application and a COM server.

Table 8.1 identifies the programming technologies employed to perform marshaling of data for method calls on a COM object, and also shows the types of marshaling, the boundaries across which you marshal the data, and the specific approach for marshaling the data.

Table 8.1   Marshaling Technologies for Data Transfer to COM Objects

Type of marshaling	Boundaries	Approach
No marshaling	DLL	Global addressing
Standard marshaling	Process	Interface Definition Language
Automation marshaling	Programming language	Automation marshaler
Custom marshaling	Process	Special software, protocol

When you host your COM object as an in-process server, you package the COM object in a DLL, which means that the COM object loads into the process space of the client. All of the COM object's methods can be called directly by the client, and data can be passed freely to and from the object.

Standard Marshaling

When a client calls interface methods from a COM component hosted on a local or a remote server, data is transferred across process boundaries or between computer nodes on a network. To accomplish this transfer, you must implement marshaling code to ensure that the client and server know how to communicate. Visual C++ provides a utility—the *MIDL compiler*—that enables you to produce a DLL that implements standard marshaling between an out-of-process object and its client. To implement standard marshaling, you specify your interfaces using the Interface Definition Language (IDL). IDL is a strongly typed language, similar to Visual C++ in its syntax, that allows you to define your interfaces precisely.

The MIDL compiler compiles your IDL code and generates C source code that implements two components, a proxy and a stub. The proxy attaches to the client application, and the COM server uses the stub. You compile this code to create a *proxy/stub DLL*, which is used by COM to handle the mechanics of moving data between the client application and the COM server across process or computer boundaries.

Using the Automation Marshaler

The Automation marshaler is a COM server (oleaut32.dll) that provides marshaling services for the COM-based technology known as Automation (formerly known as OLE Automation). Automation allows client code written in languages other than C++ to access COM components. Automation is implemented by the COM interface **IDispatch**, which is discussed in greater detail in the next lesson. To use the Automation marshaler, you do not have to implement a dispatch interface. You can specify that your component interfaces use the Automation marshaler by defining them with the IDL attribute **oleautomation**, as shown in the following code:

```
[
    oleautomation,
    object,
    uuid(A84DA762-6486-11D3-9347-0080C7FA0C3E),

    helpstring("IHello Interface"),
    pointer_default(unique)
]
interface IHello : IUnknown
{
    [propget, helpstring("property String")] HRESULT
    String([out, retval] BSTR *pVal);
};
```

To make communication available between different languages, Automation defines a standard set of data types that can be packaged into a union data structure called a **VARIANT**. When you use the Automation marshaler, you must use Automation-compatible data types. The **BSTR** data type used in the previous code snippet is a string type used by Automation.

The Automation marshaler is not as efficient as the standard marshaling code generated by MIDL.

Custom Marshaling

In some cases, standard marshaling may not be appropriate for an application. In such cases, a server object can provide support for custom marshaling.

To support custom marshaling, your server should implement the **IMarshal** interface. When a server supports custom marshaling, it does not use the standard marshaling infrastructure. Instead, COM requests that the server object form a packet, containing the data to be marshaled, and transmit the packet to the client context. COM instantiates an object-specified handler to receive the packet and act as a smart proxy to the client. The smart proxy unmarshals the packet to the client.

Communication can now occur across process boundaries just as with standard marshaling. The client is never aware that custom marshaling (or any form of marshaling) is occurring.

In general, marshaling is not an issue for developers of COM objects. MIDL generates marshaling code for standard COM interfaces, and the Automation marshaler provides marshaling for objects that implement dispatch interfaces. However, there are times when you may have specific reasons to enable an object to support custom marshaling, which include the following:

- **Shared memory** Standard marshaling always copies data back and forth between client and server. By using custom marshaling, you can create shared memory that both the client and server can use to avoid repeated copies of data and improve performance.

- **Marshaling by value** Marshaling by value instead of by reference enables you to make copies of objects locally so that all subsequent calls are local.

- **Smart proxy** Depending on the state of an internal cache, a proxy can make an intelligent decision about whether or not to go remote. Some methods can be implemented directly by the proxy to avoid making calls on the server. A smart proxy can also boost performance by enabling asynchronous calls. To allow for asynchronous calls, a smart proxy can create a new thread to make the call, and then let the calling thread return while the server is processing the call.

- **Bypassing native COM threading models** You may not want to be bound by the standard threading models. For a discussion of COM threading models, see Lesson 4 of this chapter.

Lesson Summary

Every COM object executes within a specific context. In-process servers execute with the process address space of the client application. When you perform method calls from client to server, you marshal these calls from the client context to the server context. Standard marshaling consists of using an interface definition language and the MIDL compiler to generate a proxy/stub DLL to perform marshaling from a client in one process to a server in another process. Marshaling across languages employs the Automation marshaler. When you use the Automation marshaler you must use Automation-compatible data types. By implementing the **IMarshal** interface, you can create a custom marshaling mechanism to meet program-specific needs.

Lesson 3: Dispatch Interfaces

In Lesson 2, you learned that dispatch interfaces implement Microsoft's Automation technology. Automation allows components written in different languages to communicate with one another.

In this lesson, you will learn more about how the **IDispatch** interface and the VARIANT data type are used to allow other languages to access COM components. You will also learn how clients written in Microsoft development languages such as Visual Basic or Microsoft Visual J++ can access component interfaces directly without using the dispatch mechanism.

After this lesson, you will be able to:

- Describe how a dispatch interface invokes methods on behalf of a client.
- Describe the structure of the VARIANT data type.
- Describe how type libraries enable Visual Basic clients to access component interfaces directly.
- Describe how a dual interface exposes component methods.

Estimated lesson time: 30 minutes

IDispatch Interface

Dispatch interfaces enable client applications written in different languages to access your COM objects. For example, consider a scripting language such as Microsoft Visual Basic Scripting Edition (VBScript), which is used to create an instance of a COM component written in C++. VBScript does not enforce strict type checking and does not know about many of the C++ data types. To enable the VBScript client to communicate successfully with the server component, you must provide your component with a *dispatch interface*. This is achieved by implementing the standard COM interface **IDispatch**.

In certain development situations, you will only want to create COM objects that are going to be used exclusively by C++ clients. For example, objects created by a software development company for in-house use might fall into this category. In such a case you would not need to incur the overhead of implementing **IDispatch**. However, if you want your COM object to be accessible from a wider range of languages, you must implement the **IDispatch** interface. Clients written in other Microsoft development languages such as Visual Basic can use COM components written in C++ that do not implement the **IDispatch** interface. However, Visual Basic clients can only use interfaces that pass *automation-compatible* parameters to and from their methods. Automation-compatible data types are those that can be packaged into the **VARIANT** standard data format. A VARIANT is a COM-defined union data type, described in detail later in this lesson.

Figure 8.9 provides a simple illustration of how the **IDispatch** interface might be implemented for the **Encoder** class.

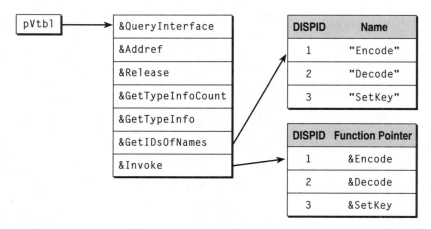

Figure 8.9   Implementing the **IDispatch** interface

The **Encoder** object vtable contains entries that point to the implemented **IDispatch** functions. A client application executes the **GetIDsOfNames()** method, providing the method name "Encode" as a string value, for example. The **GetIDsOfNames()** method implements an internal table, which maps the name of each method into a numerical dispatch identifier, known as a Dispatch ID, or DISPID. The DISPID is simply a numerical value—in the example illustrated in Figure 8.9, the DISPID of the **Encode** function is 1.

Once the client application has retrieved the DISPID of the method it wants to call, it can call the **Invoke()** method to execute the method. The Dispatch ID returned from **GetIDsOfNames()** is passed as an argument to the **Invoke()** method. Also passed to **Invoke()** are the parameters to the requested methods, packaged as an array of **VARIANT**s. **Invoke()** also takes a pointer to a **VARIANT** to hold any value returned by the requested method.

Note   This is a simplified account of the dispatch process. For example, parameters to invoked methods can be named and can also have Dispatch IDs.

Your implementation of the **Invoke()** method calls the requested method on behalf of the Automation client. Your implementation must maintain some kind of table to map DISPIDs to component methods. It must also unpack the arguments from the array of **VARIANT**s and pass them to the requested component method in the correct form. Any return values must be packed into the object referenced by the **VARIANT** pointer for return to the client.

VARIANT Data Type

The **VARIANT** data type is defined in the file OAIDL.IDL as follows:

```
struct tagVARIANT {
    union {
        struct __tagVARIANT {
            VARTYPE vt;
            WORD    wReserved1;
            WORD    wReserved2;
            WORD    wReserved3;
            union {
                LONG            lVal;       // VT_I4
                BYTE            bVal;       // VT_UI1
                SHORT           iVal;       // VT_I2
                FLOAT           fltVal;     // VT_R4
                DOUBLE          dblVal;     // VT_R8
                VARIANT_BOOL    boolVal;    // VT_BOOL
                _VARIANT_BOOL   bool;       // (obsolete)
                SCODE           scode;      // VT_ERROR
                CY              cyVal;      // VT_CY
                DATE            date;       // VT_DATE
                BSTR            bstrVal;    // VT_BSTR
                IUnknown *      punkVal;    // VT_UNKNOWN
                IDispatch *     pdispVal;   // VT_DISPATCH
                SAFEARRAY *     parray;     // VT_ARRAY
                BYTE *          pbVal;      // VT_BYREF|VT_UI1
                SHORT *         piVal;      // VT_BYREF|VT_I2
                LONG *          plVal;      // VT_BYREF|VT_I4
                FLOAT *         pfltVal;    // VT_BYREF|VT_R4
                DOUBLE *        pdblVal;    // VT_BYREF|VT_R8
                VARIANT_BOOL *  pboolVal;   // VT_BYREF|VT_BOOL
                _VARIANT_BOOl * pbool;      // (obsolete)
                SCODE *         pscode;     // VT_BYREF|VT_ERROR
                CY *            pcyVal;     // VT_BYREF|VT_CY
                DATE *          pdate;      // VT_BYREF|VT_DATE
                BSTR *          pbstrVal;   // VT_BYREF|VT_BSTR
                IUnknown **     ppunkVal;   // VT_BYREF|VT_UNKNOWN
                IDispatch **    ppdispVal;  // VT_BYREF|VT_DISPATCH
                SAFEARRAY **    pparray;    // VT_BYREF|VT_ARRAY
                VARIANT *       pvarVal;    // VT_BYREF|VT_VARIANT
                PVOID           byref;      // Generic ByRef
                CHAR            cVal;       // VT_I1
```

```
        USHORT         uiVal;      // VT_UI2
        ULONG          ulVal;      // VT_UI4
        INT            intVal;     // VT_INT
        UINT           uintVal;    // VT_UINT
        DECIMAL *      pdecVal;    // VT_BYREF|VT_DECIMAL
        CHAR *         pcVal;      // VT_BYREF|VT_I1
        USHORT *       puiVal;     // VT_BYREF|VT_UI2
        ULONG *        pulVal;     // VT_BYREF|VT_UI4
        INT *          pintVal;    // VT_BYREF|VT_INT
        UINT *         puintVal;   // VT_BYREF|VT_UINT
        struct __tagBRECORD {
            PVOID    pvRecord;
            IRecordInfo * pRecInfo;
        } __VARIANT_NAME_4;        // VT_RECORD
      } __VARIANT_NAME_3;
    } __VARIANT_NAME_2;
    DECIMAL decVal;
  } __VARIANT_NAME_1;
};
```

The **VARIANT** data structure contains two fields (if you discount the reserved fields). The **vt** field describes the type of data in the second field. To allow multiple data types to appear in the second field, a union structure is declared. Therefore, the name of the second field varies, depending on the value typed into the **vt** field. The constants used to specify the value of the **vt** field are indicated by a comment on the corresponding line of the union declaration.

Using the **VARIANT** and **VARIANTARG** data structure requires that you follow a two-step process. As an example, consider the following code:

```
long lValue = 555;
VARIANT vParam;

VParam.vt = VT_I4;
vParam.lVal = lValue ;
```

In the first line, you specify a data type indicator. The **VT_I4** constant states that a long data value appears in the second element. From the definition of the **VARIANT** type, you can see that the second field uses the name **lVal** when you store a long data value into the **VARIANTARG** data structure.

Using **VARIANT**s to pass parameters means that less strongly typed languages, such as VBScript, can invoke methods implemented in strongly typed languages such as C++. The implementation of the **Invoke**() method can check to see if the value encapsulated in a **VARIANT** parameter is of the correct type. If it is, then the type can be extracted and passed to the invoked method. If not, then the **Invoke**() method can attempt to coerce the value to the correct type using the **VariantChangeType**() API function.

Type Libraries

You might appreciate, from the previous discussion of the dispatch mechanism, that it is a relatively slow way of passing data between a server and a client. Also, the packing and unpacking of parameters into **VARIANT**s is not type-safe. High-performance development languages, such as Visual Basic 6.0, need to be able to access interface methods directly, through the vtable.

To make this possible, the Visual Basic client must know the number and types of parameters expected by the interface methods. This information is supplied to clients as a *type library*—a binary description of the interface properties and methods—and the method arguments. Type libraries can be thought of as a compiled, language-independent version of a C++ header file.

The Visual Basic environment reads the type library and presents a description of the interface to a programmer. The programmer creates an instance of the component using the Visual Basic syntax that allows direct access to the component's vtable. The information from the type library allows the programmer to pass the correct argument types to the interface methods. In this way, the Visual Basic programmer can bypass the dispatch mechanism and improve performance when using an in-process server. Remember that to make a component usable by a Visual Basic client, you must use only the Automation data types. A type library is described using IDL. The MIDL compiler outputs a type library file with a .tlb extension. This file is often linked to the .dll or .exe server that hosts the COM component.

For clients such as Visual Basic to access your type library, you must place additional entries into the registry for your COM object. These entries provide the COM run-time library with information about the location of your type library.

Figure 8.10 is a map of the registry entries associated with a COM object that supports a type library.

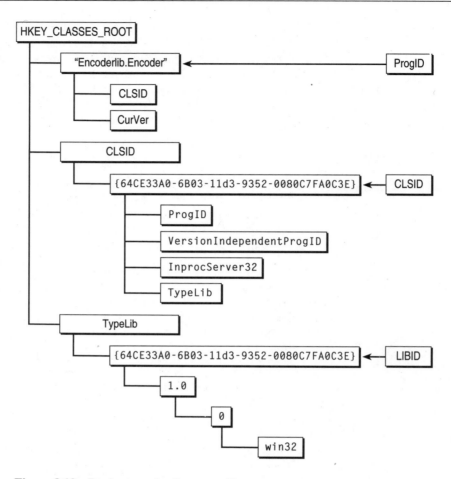

Figure 8.10   Registry entries for a type library

In fact, you only need two additional entries to locate the type library. Beneath the **CLSID** subkey for your COM object, you add the **TypeLib** subkey. The value that you assign to this subkey is the type library's *LIBID*—the GUID defined for the type library in the IDL file.

This LIBID is used as the second registry entry for your type library, which you place beneath the predefined **HKEY_CLASSES_ROOT \TypeLib** key. As shown in Figure 8.10, several other subkeys are found beneath your LIBID key. The **win32** subkey specifies a path to the file containing your type library as shown here:

```
win32 = c:\Encoder\debug\Encoder.dll
```

The value that follows the equal sign is a path to the physical location of the type library file. In this case, it is linked to the COM server DLL. Applications that use type libraries know how to read them from .dll and .exe files.

When you instruct Visual Basic to reference a COM component, it uses this information to retrieve a path to the actual type library file. Once the file path is obtained, Visual Basic reads and parses the type library, constructs the programmatic representation, and enables Visual Basic programmers to write and execute code that uses the services of a COM server.

Dual Interfaces

The preferred way to implement a dispatch interface is as a *dual interface*. Dual interfaces make all of the **Invoke()** methods available directly, as entries in the component's vtable. Figure 8.11 illustrates a possible implementation of a dual interface—it shows how the addresses of the **IEncoder** methods are included in the vtable, as well as in the table consulted by the **Invoke()** function.

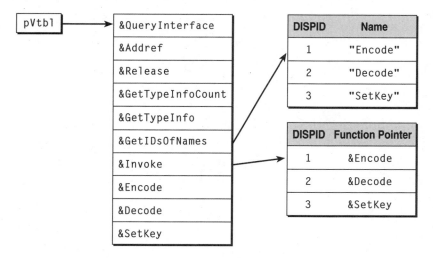

Figure 8.11   Implementation of a dual interface

If you implement a dual interface, properties and methods exposed by a component can still be accessed through a dispatch interface by languages such as VBScript; while languages such as Visual C++ can access methods directly through the vtable. Visual Basic can use either the dispatch interface or the vtable. Implementing a dual interface allows clients that can access the vtable to make faster method calls, but still supports those clients that require a dispatch interface.

Lesson Summary

The **IDispatch** interface enables a client environment such as VBScript to use a common entry point, the **Invoke()** method, to use your COM object. Arguments passed to the **Invoke()** method are packed into **VARIANT** data structures. These data structures contain one field that describes the type of data and a second field that stores the actual data.

To enable a development language such as Visual Basic to create a programmatic interface to your COM object, you generate a type library. The type library is a binary file that contains a description of your COM object's methods, properties, and the data types used. Visual Basic can use the type library information when making direct calls to methods using function pointers obtained from a COM component's vtable.

A dual interface allows calls through the dispatch interface or through the vtable, according to the capabilities of the client.

Lesson 4: Threading Models

In Chapter 5, you learned how you can improve the performance of an application by running concurrent tasks on multiple threads. Because a single instance of a COM object can be accessed simultaneously by any number of client threads, you must make sure that access to your COM object is properly synchronized.

Generally, object synchronization is handled by the operating system. It is important to know how the operating system handles object synchronization so that you can create components that perform efficiently in a multithreaded environment. COM defines four *threading models* that simplify the issues surrounding multithreaded component development.

After this lesson, you will be able to:
- Describe the four COM threading models.
- Describe the advantages and disadvantages of using each of the threading models.
- Identify the registry keys used to identify component threading models.

Estimated lesson time: 30 minutes

COM Threading Models

A threading model describes the type and degree of thread safety implemented by a component. A COM component can support one of the following four threading models:

- The single-threading model
- The apartment-threading model
- The free-threading (multi-threaded) model
- The mixed-threading model (supports both apartment and free-threading)

Before a client thread can use a COM object, it must initialize the COM libraries by calling the **CoInitializeEx()** API function. When it does this, it can specify the model it uses for calls to the objects that it creates. A client thread can specify that it will use the apartment-threading model or the free-threading model.

Any client application, regardless of its own threading arrangement, can safely access a COM component built from any threading model. If a client's threading is not compatible with that of the server, the COM run-time library takes steps to ensure that the client and server communicate in a thread-safe manner. However, these measures can adversely affect the performance of the application.

Single-Threading Model

A COM server that supports the single-threading model requires that all client requests for object services are queued on a single thread. Single-threaded COM servers are suitable for use with only single-threaded applications—which means legacy code. Access to a single-threaded component is very efficient for the thread that actually creates the component. The thread that first creates the component can obtain direct pointers to the interfaces exposed by the component. However, subsequent requests from other threads cannot directly access the interface pointers because the server process only supports a single thread. All subsequent threads must marshal interface requests between a proxy on the client and a stub on the server main thread. Calls made by external threads through the proxy/stub are placed in the server message queue. External threads experience poor performance as a result of the overhead involved in marshaling, and because the direct interface requests made by the creator thread take priority over the requests waiting in the message queue.

Apartment-Threading Model

The apartment-threading model enables all clients to obtain a direct pointer to a component interface, without going through proxy and stub services. An apartment is a conceptual entity that provides a logical structure for thread concurrency. An apartment is created when a thread calls the **CoInitializeEx()** API function to initialize the COM libraries. An apartment is associated with one or more threads, and one or more COM object instances. As long as the objects created within an apartment support the apartment-threading model, all threads in an apartment can obtain direct interface pointers to all objects in the apartment.

The terminology surrounding apartment threading can be confusing because there are two types of apartments: *single-threaded apartments* (STAs) and *multithreaded apartments* (MTAs). The distinction between the two is as follows:

- STAs implement the apartment-threading model.
- MTAs implement the free-threading model.

A process can contain any number of STAs (each one containing a single thread) but only one MTA to which any number of threads can belong.

Single-Threaded Apartments

STAs have only one thread that creates and calls objects. Because only one thread can access those objects in the apartment, the objects are effectively synchronized.

Components that support STAs perform better than those that support the single-threaded model. You can use the STA model to write more efficient code. At the same time a thread in one STA waits for an operation to finish, another STA can allow the interim execution of a thread in still another STA.

When a thread calls **CoInitializeEx()** with the *COINIT_APARTMENTTHREADED* parameter, the thread creates an STA. A thread that is initialized as an STA is known as an STA thread type. A COM object that is instantiated by an STA thread type can be accessed by that thread only. This protects COM objects from being accessed by multiple threads simultaneously.

Synchronizing Threads

Threads that want to use a COM object residing in another apartment must have the interface pointers of the COM object marshaled to them. The threads cannot have a direct interface pointer because this would allow multiple threads to access the object, which violates the STA model rules.

By marshaling an interface pointer to other threads, COM uses window messages to synchronize multiple threads. Each STA thread type has a message loop that receives marshaled calls from other processes and other apartments in the same process. When a client makes a call to a server object, the marshaling code places a corresponding window message in the server thread's message queue. Multiple thread calls are queued in the message queue while the object's STA thread type process each message, one at a time.

Passing Interface Pointers

When interface pointers are passed between apartments, the pointers must be marshaled. You use the **CoMarshalInterThreadInterfaceInStream()** COM API function to marshal interface pointers between threads in the same process. For more information about the **CoMarshalInterThreadInterfaceInStream()** function, refer to the Visual Studio Help file.

Multithreaded Apartments

MTAs are also called free-threading models. This model differs from an STA in that multiple threads can reside in one apartment. MTAs provide the highest performance.

Note The MTA model was introduced in Windows NT 4.0 and is also available in Windows 95 with DCOM95 installed.

All threads that call **CoInitializeEx()** with the *COINIT_MULTITHREADED* parameter live in a single MTA and are known as MTA thread types. Unlike the STA model, there is only one MTA per process. When additional MTA threads are initialized as MTA thread types, they live in the same apartment. In addition, there is no need to marshal between threads.

COM objects created by MTA thread types must be thread safe and must provide their own synchronization code. By removing the bottleneck created by marshaling, MTAs provide the highest performance and throughput on the server side.

In the MTA model, any thread can call a COM object concurrently, and COM does not synchronize the calls. Because synchronization is not provided, COM objects written for an MTA must be thread safe. Therefore, synchronization objects such as events, mutexes, and semaphores (as described in Lesson 3 of Chapter 5) must be used to protect a component's static and global data.

Threading-Model Registry Keys

In-process servers must enter their threading model in the registry because in-process servers typically do not call **CoInitializeEx()**. When a client creates an in-process server COM object, COM uses the threading-model registry key to determine if marshaling code is necessary for the returned interface pointer.

To indicate the type of threading model in the registry, the named ThreadingModel value is created under the following key:

```
HKEY_CLASSES_ROOT\CLSID\[component CLSID]\InProcServer32
```

ThreadingModel can contain one of the following values:

- **None** Supports the single-threading model only
- **Apartment** Supports the STA model
- **Free** Supports the MTA model only
- **Both** Supports both the STA and MTA model

Lesson Summary

COM defines four threading models that simplify the issues surrounding the synchronization of access to components in a multithreaded environment. The single-threading model requires that all client requests for object services are queued on a single thread. The apartment-threading model uses an STA to define a logical grouping of components that are only accessed by a single thread. The free-threading model groups thread-safe components together in a single MTA. If a component supports the mixed-threading model, threads in a single or a multi-threaded apartment can safely access it.

An apartment is created when a thread calls the **CoInitializeEx()** API function to initialize the COM libraries. Use arguments to the **CoInitializeEx()** function to specify an STA or an MTA type thread. In-process servers typically do not call **CoInitializeEx()**—they specify their threading model in a registry entry.

COM ensures that communication between clients and objects with different threading models is conducted in a thread-safe manner, marshaling the data if necessary. When you pass interface pointers between apartments, you must marshal the interface using the **CoMarshalInterThreadInterfaceInStream()** COM API function.

Lesson 5: ActiveX Controls

An ActiveX control is a COM object that is designed to be placed in an ActiveX control container, such as an application dialog box or on a Web page, to perform a self-contained function. ActiveX controls frequently present a graphical user interface.

This lesson gives a brief introduction to ActiveX controls and some of the considerations faced by the control developer.

After this lesson, you will be able to:

- Describe the interaction between ActiveX controls and ActiveX control containers.
- Describe the interfaces that an ActiveX control must implement to meet the requirements of commonly used control containers.
- Describe some common features of ActiveX controls.

Estimated lesson time: 20 minutes

ActiveX Controls and Containers

An ActiveX control is any COM object that implements the **IUnknown** interface and is hosted by a self-registering server that can be a DLL or an .exe file. We refer to the client of an ActiveX control as a *container*. ActiveX controls are located, or *sited*, within an ActiveX control container. Figure 8.12 on the facing page shows the Microsoft Chart ActiveX control located within the ActiveX Control Test Container.

ActiveX controls usually display a user interface. In fact, many people consider the implementation of a user interface to be a defining characteristic of an ActiveX control. As we move into an age of distributed applications, there are good reasons why regular COM components should not display a user interface. For example, if your COM component displays a message box to alert you of an error condition, and the component happens to be installed on a remote server in the next building, you will not be aware that an error occurred. Most ActiveX controls, on the other hand, are tightly coupled to a container that implements a user interface. The container expects the control to participate as part of the user interface.

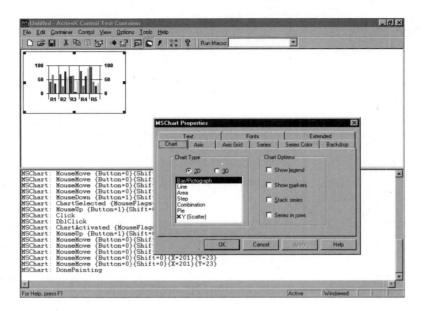

Figure 8.12   The ActiveX Control Test Container

Although the definition of ActiveX controls requires only that the control supports the **IUnknown** interface, different containers have different requirements. Some containers require certain interfaces for a control to work, while others do not. If you want your control to work with a particular container, your control must implement the interfaces required by the container.

Most of the commonly used control containers expect a control to maintain a set of data, fire events, and support enough interfaces so that a client application can successfully interact with it. Table 8.2 on the following page defines the minimum set of interfaces that the ActiveX Control Test Container (and most other user-interface containers) expects an ActiveX control to support.

Although the number of interfaces listed might imply that implementing an ActiveX control involves a lot of hard work, both MFC and ATL provide wizards that generate the basic framework of an ActiveX control. Such wizards allow you to concentrate on the implementation of the functionality specific to your control.

Table 8.2   Minimum set of interfaces to be supported by the ActiveX control

Interface	Description
IOleObject	Required for communication with a control's client site, except through events. Events are handled through the **IConnectionPointContainer** interface described later.
IOleInPlaceObject	Implemented by controls that can be activated in place and provide their own user interface. Requires support for **IOleObject**.
IOleInPlaceActiveObject	Required only by controls that provide a user interface and that support **IOleInPlaceObject**.
IDataObject	Required by controls that transfer data to a container in some way, as through shared memory or a file. **IDataObject** provides the means for COM's Uniform Data Transfer, a protocol that sets the rules for the exchange of data of any type.
IViewObject2	Implemented by visible controls that display a window.
IDispatch	Required by controls with custom methods or properties that a client can access through **IDispatch::Invoke()**
IConnectionPointContainer	Required by controls that fire events. This interface enumerates for a client the events that a control object can fire.
IConnectionPoint	Required by controls that support **IConnectionPointContainer**.
IProvideClassInfo	Implemented by controls that contain type library information, which means most ActiveX controls. Through its **GetClassInfo()** method, the interface provides a pointer to an **ITypeInfo** implementation from which a client can extract the control's type information.
IPersistStorage	Required by controls that can save and load from an **IStorage** instance provided by the container.
IClassFactory	Instantiates a requested class object and returns a pointer to it. The object is identified by a CLSID registered in the system registry.
IClassFactory2	Same as **IClassFactory**, but adds support for licensing.

Features of ActiveX Controls

ActiveX controls support properties, methods, and events to make the control programmable. ActiveX controls usually support a dispatch interface to enable a wide variety of programming languages and scripting languages to work programmatically with the control.

Stock Properties

The ActiveX standards define a set of stock properties that are common to many controls. Examples of stock properties include the font used for text displayed by the control, and its foreground and background colors. Stock properties are distinguished from *custom* properties: custom properties are specific to the functionality of a control.

Ambient Properties

Ambient properties provide information to the control about the appearance of the control container. A control's properties should be set so that it appears integrated with the environment of the container. For example, the **BackColor** ambient property represents the background color of the container. The control can set its own **BackColor** stock property to this color so that the control appears to be part of the container. Control developers are encouraged to write ActiveX controls that detect and respond to the ambient properties of the container.

Events

Controls can also respond to actions by generating *events*. Events are notifications from the control to the container. The event interface is defined by the control, but is implemented by the container, which makes the event interface an outgoing interface.

As with properties, a distinction is made between stock events and custom events. Stock events result from common actions such as mouse clicks or key presses. Custom events are control-specific.

Property Pages

Most ActiveX controls implement property pages to provide users with a graphical interface to change the properties of a control. Figure 8.12 shows the property page of the Microsoft Chart ActiveX control. Each property page is based on a dialog box template resource, and is a separate COM object with its own CLSID.

Property Persistence

One capability of ActiveX controls is *property persistence* (or serialization), which allows the ActiveX control to read or write property values to and from a file or stream. A container application can use serialization to store a control's property values even after the application has destroyed the control. The property values of the ActiveX control can then be read from the file or stream when a new instance of the control is created at a later time.

Lesson Summary

ActiveX controls are regular COM objects located within an ActiveX control container. ActiveX controls implement interfaces to meet the requirements of the container. This usually involves implementing a user interface, so that the control can participate as part of the container's user interface.

ActiveX controls typically support properties, methods, and events to make the control programmable.

Lab 8: Using the OLE/COM Object Viewer

In this lab, you will become familiar with aspects of implementing COM objects and ActiveX controls. You will use the OLE/COM Object Viewer to browse through the registry and you will inspect both a COM object and an ActiveX control.

▶ **To open the OLE/COM Object Viewer**

1. Start Visual Studio.

2. On the **Tools** menu, click **OLE/COM Object Viewer**.

3. On the **View** menu, click **Expert Mode**. Then scroll down the list of folders at the left of the Viewer until you find the folder labeled **All Objects**.

4. Click the plus sign at the left of this folder to obtain a list of all the COM objects and ActiveX controls appearing in the registry. Some entries appear as GUIDs. Other entries use string names.

▶ **To browse a COM object**

1. Scroll down the list of entries until you find **ADODB.Connection**. This object is the **ADO Connection** object that you will use in Lab 10.

2. Click the **ADO Connection** object. Information about the object's registry entries appears in the right pane. Note the **InprocServer32** entry, which contains the path to the DLL that implements the object.

3. Click the plus sign at the left of this folder to obtain a list of all the interfaces supported by this COM object. The viewer should look like Figure 8.13.

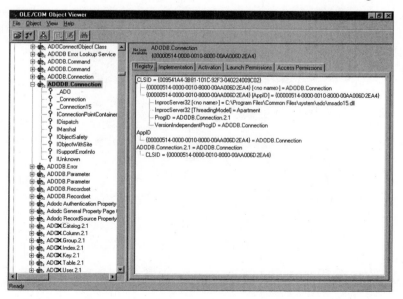

Figure 8.13   The OLE/COM Object Viewer

Several interfaces appear in this list. The **IUnknown** interface supports interface pointer retrieval. By implementing the **IDispatch** interface, scripting languages, such as VBScript, can access this COM object. The interface that clients use most frequently is the **_Connection** interface. This interface contains methods that allow you to connect to a data source.

4. Click the **_Connection** interface. This action causes information about the interface to appear in the panel at the right.

   If you look under the **CLSID** entry in the panel at the right, you see that the **InprocServer32** entry is *oleaut32.dll*—the Windows Automation marshaler. The use of the Automation marshaler to marshal this interface means that you have to use Automation-compatible types (types that can be packaged as a **VARIANT**) when passing arguments to and return values from any method supported by this interface.

   Below the **TypeLib** entry, you find the **win32** key set to "C:\Program Files\ Common Files\ADO\MSADO15.DLL". This indicates that the type library is linked to the server DLL.

   Double click the **_Connection** interface. In response, you see the **Default Interface Viewer** dialog box.

5. In the **Default Interface Viewer** dialog box, click **View Type Info**.

6. In the **ITypeInfo Viewer** dialog box, click the plus sign at the left of the Methods folder.

7. Scroll down the list of methods until you find the **Open** method.

8. Click the **Open** method.

9. In the panel at the right, you see detailed information about the method, as shown in Figure 8.14.

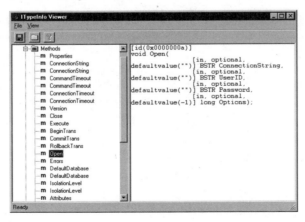

Figure 8.14   The ITypeInfo Viewer

The first entry that you see is the dispatch identifier. Next, you see the arguments that your client application provides for this method. Note the use of Automation-compatible data types.

10. Close the **ITypeInfo Viewer** dialog box.

11. In the **Default Interface Viewer** dialog box, click **Close**.

12. Click the minus sign to the left of the **ADODB.Connection** entry in the OLE/ COM Object Viewer.

▶ **To browse an ActiveX control**

1. Scroll down the entries at the left of the OLE/COM Object Viewer until you find the **Microsoft ADO Data Control**.

2. Click the entry named **Microsoft ADO Data Control**. At the right side of the Viewer, you see detailed information about this control.

3. Under the CLSID, you see the **InprocServer32** defined as "[system directory]\MSADODC.OCX". ActiveX controls typically reside in files that end with the extension .ocx. (However, these files are DLLs.)

4. At the right side of the Viewer, you should see the key name **Control**. The inclusion of this key is another strong indicator that you are viewing an ActiveX control.

5. Click the plus sign at the left of the **Microsoft ADO Data Control** entry in the left panel of the Viewer.

6. You see a large number of interfaces supported by this entry. This list includes all the interfaces that most ActiveX control containers expect an ActiveX control to support.

7. Double click the **IAdodc** interface beneath the **Microsoft ADO Data Control** entry.

8. In the **Default Interface Viewer** dialog box, click **View Type Info**.

9. Click the plus sign at the left of the Methods folder in the **ITypeInfo Viewer** dialog box to expand the Methods folder.

10. Click any of the methods in the Methods folder. The dispatch identifier and the method signature appear in the panel at the right of the **ITypeInfo Viewer** dialog box.

11. Close the **ITypeInfo Viewer** dialog box.

12. On the **Default Interface Viewer** dialog box, click **Close**.

13. Close the OLE/COM Object Viewer.

Review

1. What is a COM interface?

2. What is a GUID, and what role does it play in COM?

3. What are the differences among in-process, local, and remote server COM objects?

4. How do you implement standard marshaling?

5. What is a type library, and how is it used?

6. What are the implications of declaring your COM object to be free-threaded?

7. What issues must you consider when implementing an ActiveX control?

C H A P T E R   9

Creating COM Components

About This Chapter

In this chapter, you will learn how to create a simple COM component using the Microsoft ActiveX Template Library (ATL). You will review aspects of the source code generated for your COM object by the ATL wizards and learn about other approaches to generating COM components.

Before You Begin

Before you start this chapter, you should have read Chapters 2 through 8, and completed the exercises in the text.

Lesson 1: Creating COM Components with ATL

ATL is a set of templated C++ classes with which you can easily create efficient COM components. It has special support for key COM features including the **IUnknown** and **IDispatch** interfaces, and dual interfaces. ATL can also be used to create ActiveX controls. ATL code can also be used to create single-threaded, apartment-threaded, or free-threaded objects.

In addition to ATL, Microsoft Visual Studio supplies wizards that simplify the process of using ATL as the basis of your development framework.

This lesson shows you how to create simple COM components using ATL.

After this lesson, you will be able to:

- Describe how to use the ATL COM AppWizard to create a COM server to host COM objects.
- Describe how to use the ATL Object Wizard to create a COM object.
- Describe how to create and implement a property for an ATL COM object.
- Describe how to create and implement a method for an ATL COM object.

Estimated lesson time: 30 minutes

Using ATL

A significant amount of boilerplate code can be used when creating COM objects. With ATL, Visual Studio provides an easily tailored approach to generating and implementing COM objects. A number of ATL wizards generate boilerplate code, leaving you free to concentrate on the component-specific methods that perform the real work of your COM object.

The code generated by the ATL wizards is based around the core set of templated classes and macros that form ATL. The use of templates (as opposed to the kind of deep inheritance structure used by MFC) enables ATL to produce fast, light-weight code that is suitable for developing components and controls.

A COM object is created using ATL by the following process:

1. Create an ATL COM project using the ATL COM AppWizard. The type of project you create will determine the type of server (in-process or out-of-process) that will host your COM objects.
2. Insert a new ATL object using the ATL Object Wizard.

3. Add methods to your object using the Add Method to Interface Wizard.

4. Add properties to your object using the Add Property to Interface Wizard.

5. Provide the implementation of your object's methods.

In this lesson, you will follow these steps to construct a simple ATL-based COM object that provides encryption services. This COM object, called **Encoder**, supports a single interface named **IEncoder**. This interface exposes a single method, named **EncodeString()**, which returns an encoded version of a single string through the use of a simple encryption algorithm that increases or decreases the value of each character by a specified number. This number is specified as a configurable property named **Key**.

Creating an ATL COM Project

In this exercise, you will use the ATL COM AppWizard to create an ATL COM project for your COM server.

▶   **To create the EncodeServer project**

1. On the **File** menu, click **New**, and then click the **Projects** tab.

2. The project category options are listed in the window on the left side of the dialog box. Click **ATL COM AppWizard**.

3. In the **Project name** box, type **EncodeServer**. Click **OK**.

4. In the **ATL COM AppWizard** dialog box, ensure that **Dynamic Link Library (DLL)** is selected as shown in Figure 9.1, and then click **Finish**.

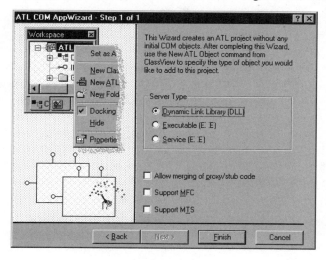

Figure 9.1   The **ATL COM AppWizard** dialog box configured to create a DLL

If you choose to create a DLL to host your COM components, you are indicating that you want to create an in-process COM server. If you select the **Executable (EXE)** option, you will create a server that can be an out-of-process server or a remote server, depending on how it is implemented. These terms are defined in Lesson 2 of Chapter 8. The **Service** option allows you to create a *Windows NT service*—a program that runs in the background when Windows NT starts up.

5. The **New Project Information** dialog box describes the files generated for your COM project, as shown in Figure 9.2. Click **OK** to continue.

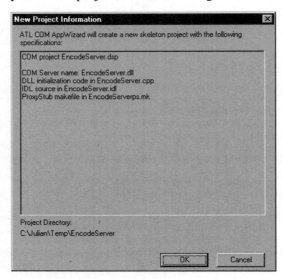

Figure 9.2   The **New Project Information** dialog box

You have now created the DLL host environment for an in-process COM server, as well as all the code necessary to register your COM object in the system registry. This type of COM object is known as a *self-registering* component.

Inserting a New COM Component

Now that you have the hosting environment defined and configured, you can add an actual COM object. You use the ATL Object Wizard to perform this task.

▶ **To add the Encoder COM component**

1. On the **Insert** menu, click **New ATL Object**.

2. In the **Category** list, click **Objects**.

3. In the **Objects** box, click the **Simple Object** icon shown in Figure 9.3, and then click **Next**.

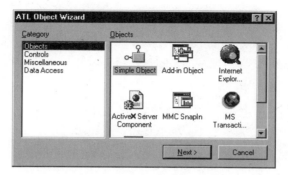

Figure 9.3   The **ATL Object Wizard** dialog box

4. In the **ATL Object Wizard Properties** dialog box, click the **Names** tab.

5. In the **Short Name** box, type the name of your server class—**Encoder**. All remaining fields will update automatically based on the contents of the **Short Name** box, as shown in Figure 9.4.

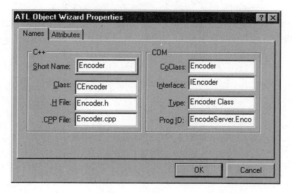

Figure 9.4   The **ATL Object Wizard Properties** dialog box

The left pane of this dialog box indicates that the wizard will create a C++ class named **CEncoder** (defined in the Encoder.h and the Encoder.cpp files). You will add code to this class to provide the implementation of your COM component. The pane on the right indicates that the name of the component will be **Encoder**, and that it will expose the default interface **IEncoder**. Note also the ProgID **EncodeServer.Encoder**. This is the name you can use to retrieve the object's GUID using the **CLSIDFromProgID()** function.

6. In the **ATL Object Wizard Properties** dialog box, click the **Attributes** tab. Set the following attributes as shown in Figure 9.5:

   ▪ Under **Threading Model**, select **Single**.

   ▪ Under **Interface**, select **Custom**.

   ▪ Under **Aggregation**, select **No**.

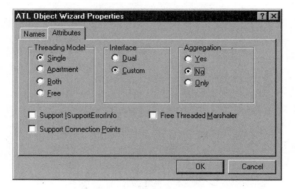

Figure 9.5   The **Attributes** tab of the **ATL Object Wizard Properties** dialog box

ATL follows the recommended practice of implementing dispatch interfaces as dual interfaces. By selecting a custom interface, you are choosing *not* to implement a dispatch interface for your COM component. Only clients that are capable of attaching directly to the component's vtable will be able to call the interface methods. (Aggregation is discussed in Lesson 3 of Chapter 11.)

7. Ensure that all check boxes are cleared, and then click **OK** to add the Encoder object.

In ClassView you will see that you have inserted the **CEncoder** component class and the **IEncoder** interface, as shown in Figure 9.6 on the facing page.

Figure 9.6   ClassView displaying the **CEncoder** class and **IEncoder** interface

With the **CEncoder** component class, you acquire a templated version of a class factory, which will be used to create your COM component when it is instantiated. You also inherit default implementations for the **IUnknown** methods **QueryInterface()**, **AddRef()**, and **Release()**, which manage client access to interface pointers and control the lifetime of your COM object.

Adding Methods to the Component Interface

After you have the host environment, a class factory, and the **IUnknown** methods added to your COM component, you insert component-specific methods. A client can execute these methods to use the services of your COM object. When adding a method to your component, you use the Add Method to Interface Wizard.

► **To add the EncodeString() method**

1. In ClassView, right-click the **IEncoder** interface.

2. On the shortcut menu, click **Add Method**. The **Add Method to Interface** dialog box appears.

3. In the **Return Type** box, select **HRESULT**.

4. In the **Method Name** box, type **EncodeString**.

5. Insert the following code into the **Parameters** box.

```
[in] const BSTR instring, [out, retval] BSTR * outstring
```

In the **Implementation** box, the Add Method to Interface Wizard shows a complete MIDL listing of the method signature based upon the data you entered, as shown in Figure 9.7 on the following page.

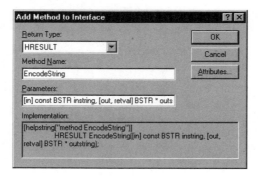

Figure 9.7   The **Add Method to Interface** dialog box

When you specify parameters using the Add Method to Interface Wizard, you must provide the parameter list in the format used by the Interface Definition Language (IDL). This format requires that you use attributes to indicate the direction of data transfer. By indicating the direction [**in**], you establish that the first parameter passes data into the method. The [in] parameter is passed by value.

The **EncodeString**() function will take the [in] parameter and create an encoded string using a simple encryption algorithm. A pointer to the encoded string will be passed to the client as the [out] parameter.

Note the use of the Automation string data type BSTR. Using Automation-compatible data types for your interface method parameters means that languages such as Microsoft Visual Basic or Microsoft Visual J++ will be able to use the services provided by your component.

Most COM interface methods return an HRESULT—a COM-specific 32-bit value that indicates a success or failure condition. HRESULTS are explained in detail in Lesson 2 of Chapter 13. Some client languages (Visual Basic, for example) are not capable of using the HRESULT data type directly. The [**retval**] attribute indicates the parameter that is used as a return value in such a case. The Visual Basic run-time error-handling system will process the HRESULT returned by the function, but as far as the Visual Basic code is concerned, the return value of the **EncodeString**() function is the value referred to by the [retval] parameter. Thus the following piece of Visual Basic code will cause the encrypted form of "Hello" to be displayed in a message box:

```
Dim comobj As Encoder

Set comobj = New Encoder

MsgBox comobj.EncodeString("Hello")
```

Click **OK** to add the **EncodeString**() method. The Add Method to Interface Wizard places an entry in your project's IDL file based on the descriptive information you entered. The wizard also adds a C++ method to the **CEncoder** component class.

Adding Properties to the Component Interface

Properties are public data members of a COM object. Languages that support COM properties can get and set the value of an object property in much the same way that you set member variables of a C++ class. For example, the following piece of Visual Basic code displays the current value of the **Key** property in a message box, and assigns it a new value of 3:

```
Dim comobj As Encoder

Set comobj = New Encoder

MsgBox comobj.Key

comobj.Key = 3
```

Because a COM interface is essentially a table of pointers to functions, C++ implements COM properties as a pair of functions—one to set the value of the function and another to get the value. The Add Property to Interface Wizard automatically creates **Get** and **Put** methods for each property you define, although you can choose not to implement a **Put** method and thus create a read-only property.

▶ **To add the Key property**

1. In ClassView, right-click the **IEncoder** interface.
2. On the shortcut menu, click **Add Property**.
3. In the **Return Type** box, select **HRESULT**, and in the **Property Type** box, select **short**.
4. In the **Property Name** box, type **Key**. Note the MIDL signatures of the **get_Key** and **put_Key**() functions that appear in the **Implementation** box.
5. Click **OK** to create the functions that implement the property.

In the class that implements your COM object, you must define a member variable to hold the data. You must also provide implementations of the **Get** and **Put** methods to pass data to and from this member variable.

▶   **To implement the Key property**

1. Add a **short** protected member variable named **m_Key** to the **CEncoder** class.

2. Add the following line to the constructor **CEncoder::CEncoder()** to initialize the m_Key variable to a default value:

```
m_Key = 1;
```

3. In ClassView, expand the **IEncoder** interface under the **CEncoder** class item to locate the **get_Key()** and **put_Key()** functions. Implement these functions as shown in the following code:

```
STDMETHODIMP CEncoder::get_Key(short *pVal)
{
    *pVal = m_Key;

    return S_OK;
}

STDMETHODIMP CEncoder::put_Key(short newVal)
{
    newVal = newVal > 5 ? 5 : newVal;
    newVal = newVal < -5 ? -5 : newVal;
    m_Key = newVal;

    return S_OK;
}
```

Note the simple bounds-checking code incorporated into the **put_Key()** function.

Implementing Component Methods

Now that you have implemented the **Key** property, you can add code to implement the **EncodeString()** method.

▶   **To implement the EncodeString() method**

1. On the **View** menu, click **Workspace**, and then click the **ClassView** tab.

2. Click the plus sign next to **CEncoder** to expand the contents of this class.

3. Click the plus sign next to **IEncoder**, within the **CEncoder** class, to expand the contents of this interface as shown in Figure 9.8 on the facing page.

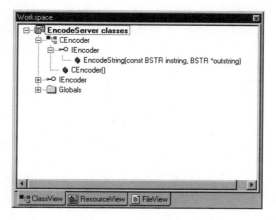

Figure 9.8   ClassView displaying the methods of the **IEncoder** interface

4. Double-click the **EncodeString()** method underneath the **IEncoder** interface, which is subordinate to the **CEncoder** class. This opens an edit window into the body of the **EncodeString()** implementation function within the Encoder.cpp file.

5. Add code to the body of the **EncodeString()** function so that it appears as follows:

```
STDMETHODIMP CEncoder::EncodeString(const BSTR instring, BSTR
*outstring)
{
    BSTR tempstring = ::SysAllocString(instring);
    wcscpy(tempstring, instring);

    for(UINT i = 0; i < ::SysStringLen(tempstring); i++)
        tempstring[i] += m_Key;

    *outstring = ::SysAllocString(tempstring);

    ::SysFreeString(tempstring);

    return S_OK;
}
```

It may help you to understand the function above if you know a little more about BSTRs. A BSTR is essentially a pointer to a wide-character string (*wchar_t*). You can see how the code just shown uses a BSTR as a parameter to the **wscpy()** standard library function. However, a BSTR is more than just an array of characters—it is prefixed with a 4-byte integer that indicates the number of bytes that the string contains. This means that you *must* allocate space for a BSTR using the Win32 function **SysAllocString()**. The example on the previous page allocates a BSTR from an existing BSTR. Alternatively, you can allocate a BSTR from a *wchar_t* array as shown here:

```
wchar_t wszPeas[] = L"Visualize Whirled Peas";
BSTR bstrPeas = ::SysAllocString(wszPeas);
```

When you have finished with a BSTR, deallocate it using **SysFreeString()**. Note that the BSTR *outstring* in our example is not deallocated because it needs to be passed back to the client. In COM, it is the client's responsibility to free resources allocated by a server at a client's request.

You will also notice that the **EncodeString()** function makes use of the **SysStringLen()** function to discover the length (in characters) of the BSTR.

You can now build your EncodeServer project. If compilation and linking are successful, Visual Studio takes the additional step of registering your **Encoder** object on the local computer so that client applications will be able to use the services of the **Encoder** object. In Chapter 11, you will develop a client program that does just that.

Lesson Summary

When you want to create COM objects, the simplest approach is to employ ATL. This framework provides several wizards to aid you, including the ATL COM AppWizard, the ATL Object Wizard, the Add Method to Interface Wizard, and the Add Property to Interface Wizard. These wizards let you harness ATL to generate all the COM-specific boilerplate code necessary to implement a COM object. Your focus can thus be on the implementation of the interface properties and methods exposed by your COM object. The net result is higher productivity.

Lesson 2: Understanding ATL COM Component Code

In this lesson, you will review aspects of the source code generated by the ATL wizards for your COM object. You will review specific code segments including the class declaration, the class body, the global entry-point functions, the registry script resource, and the interface definition language (IDL) file. After you get familiar with the code involved with the ATL approach, you learn about some alternative approaches to developing a COM object.

After this lesson, you will be able to:

- Describe the functionality provided for a component by the **CComObjectRootEx** and the **CComCoClass** templated base classes.
- Describe the global entry-point functions provided for a COM server.
- Describe features of the registry script file created for an ATL project.
- Describe features of the IDL file created for an ATL project.
- Describe some of the alternative approaches to COM component development.

Estimated lesson time: 30 minutes

Component Class Definition

The definition for your component class appears in the Encoder.h file. This definition is a standard C++ class specification that uses multiple inheritance.

```
class ATL_NO_VTABLE CEncoder :
    public CComObjectRootEx<CComSingleThreadModel>,
    public CComCoClass<CEncoder, &CLSID_Encoder>,
    public Iencoder
{
public:
    CEncoder()
    {
        m_Key = 1;
    }

DECLARE_REGISTRY_RESOURCEID(IDR_ENCODER)
DECLARE_NOT_AGGREGATABLE(CEncoder)

DECLARE_PROTECT_FINAL_CONSTRUCT()

BEGIN_COM_MAP(CEncoder)
    COM_INTERFACE_ENTRY(IEncoder)
END_COM_MAP()
```

```
// IEncoder
public:
    STDMETHOD(get_Key)(/*[out, retval]*/ short *pVal);
    STDMETHOD(put_Key)(/*[in]*/ short newVal);
    STDMETHOD(EncodeString)(/*[in]*/ const BSTR instring,
    /*[out, retval]*/ BSTR * outstring);
protected:
    short m_Key;
};
```

Your class inherits from three base classes: **CComObjectRootEx**, **CComCoClass**, and **IEncoder**. The first two of these classes are ATL templated base classes. The remaining class is your interface, which has been declared in the EncodeServer.h file as an abstract base class. The interface methods you define are added to the **IEncoder** class as pure virtual functions. The derived-class versions of these functions that you provide implement the specific services of your COM server. In a public section at the end of the class definition, you can see the declaration of the **EncodeString()** implementation.

The **CComObjectRootEx** class provides a default implementation for the **IUnknown** interface methods **QueryInterface()**, **AddRef()**, and **Release()**. When you derive from this class, your client can use **QueryInterface()** to acquire an interface pointer to any interface that your COM object supports. The methods **AddRef()** and **Release()** perform reference counting to hold your COM object in memory while clients are using interface pointers.

Deriving from the **CComCoClass** base class provides you with a default implementation of a class factory. The class factory creates an instance of your COM server. You provide the name of the server class (**CEncoder**) and a reference to its GUID (**CLSID_Encoder**) as arguments to this templated base class. The ATL wizards use the UUIDGEN.EXE utility to generate all the GUIDs in this project.

Another important element of your class declaration is the COM map. This map contains a list of the interfaces that your COM object supports. You add an entry to the COM map by using the macro **COM_INTERFACE_ENTRY**. Behind the scenes, the framework maintains a corresponding array of **ATL_INTMAP_ENTRY** structures that associate interface GUIDs with functions that retrieve interface pointers. The COM map is used by the default **QueryInterface()** method that you inherited from the templated base class **CComObjectRootEx**. Whenever a client application executes **QueryInterface()**, the default implementation searches this map for a matching interface GUID. If a match is found, the associated function returns the corresponding interface pointer.

Component Method Implementation

The Encoder.cpp file contains the body of the **EncodeString()** method that you implemented in the previous lesson.

```
#include "stdafx.h"
#include "EncodeServer.h"
#include "Encoder.h"

STDMETHODIMP CEncoder::EncodeString(const BSTR instring, BSTR
*outstring)
{
    BSTR tempstring = ::SysAllocString(instring);
    wcscpy(tempstring, instring);

    for(UINT i = 0; i < ::SysStringLen(tempstring); i++)
        tempstring[i] += m_Key;

    *outstring = ::SysAllocString(tempstring);

    ::SysFreeString(tempstring);

    return S_OK;
}
```

This code contains a couple of COM-specific features that were automatically added to the method on your behalf by the Add Method to Interface Wizard.

This method uses the macro **STDMETHODIMP** as the return data type. You can find this macro defined in the header file BASETYPS.H as:

```
HRESULT export stdcall
```

Because you have specified that the return value is to be an HRESULT, the Add Method to Interface Wizard automatically inserts a line of code to return the constant S_OK. This intrinsic constant meets the data structure format of an HRESULT and contains a success return code embedded within that structure. For more information on the HRESULT type, see Lesson 2 of Chapter 13.

Global Entry-Point Functions

On the **ClassView** tab of the Workspace view, you find a folder named Globals. If you expand this folder, you will see several global functions (with the prefix *Dll*) and a single global object named **_Module**. These elements appear in the file EncodeServer.cpp, and are added to your project by the ATL COM AppWizard to provide entry point functions that are exported by the DLL and

called by COM and other system utilities. The following code is contained in
EncodeServer.cpp:

```cpp
#include "stdafx.h"
#include "resource.h"
#include <initguid.h>
#include "EncodeServer.h"

#include "EncodeServer_i.c"
#include "Encoder.h"

CComModule _Module;

BEGIN_OBJECT_MAP(ObjectMap)
OBJECT_ENTRY(CLSID_Encoder, CEncoder)
END_OBJECT_MAP()

/////////////////////////////////////////////////////////////////////////////
//////
// DLL Entry Point

extern "C"
BOOL WINAPI DllMain(HINSTANCE hInstance, DWORD dwReason, LPVOID /
*lpReserved*/)
{
    if (dwReason == DLL_PROCESS_ATTACH)
    {
        _Module.Init(ObjectMap, hInstance, &LIBID_ENCODESERVERLib);
        DisableThreadLibraryCalls(hInstance);
    }
    else if (dwReason == DLL_PROCESS_DETACH)
        _Module.Term();
    return TRUE;    // ok
}

/////////////////////////////////////////////////////////////////////////////
//////
// Used to determine whether the DLL can be unloaded by OLE

STDAPI DllCanUnloadNow(void)
{
    return (_Module.GetLockCount()==0) ? S_OK : S_FALSE;
}

/////////////////////////////////////////////////////////////////////////////
//////
// Returns a class factory to create an object of the requested type
```

```
STDAPI DllGetClassObject(REFCLSID rclsid, REFIID riid, LPVOID* ppv)
{
    return _Module.GetClassObject(rclsid, riid, ppv);
}


/////////////////////////////////////////////////////////////////////////
//////
// DllRegisterServer - Adds entries to the system registry

STDAPI DllRegisterServer(void)
{
    // registers object, typelib and all interfaces in typelib
    return _Module.RegisterServer(TRUE);
}


/////////////////////////////////////////////////////////////////////////
//////
// DllUnregisterServer - Removes entries from the system registry

STDAPI DllUnregisterServer(void)
{
    return _Module.UnregisterServer(TRUE);
}
```

Near the beginning of the file you can see the declaration of a single **CComModule** object named **_Module**. The **CComModule** class implements a COM server module, allowing a client to access the module's components. **CComModule** supports both in-process and out-of-process modules. Out-of-process (EXE) servers use an application-specific object that is *derived* from **CComModule**.

A **CComModule** instance uses a table called an *object map* to maintain a set of class object definitions. Behind the scenes, this object map creates and maintains an array of **_ATL_OBJMAP_ENTRY** structures, which include information used by the framework to:

- Instantiate objects through a class factory.
- Establish communication between a client and the root object in the component.
- Perform lifetime management of class objects.
- Enter and remove object descriptions in the system registry.

An **OBJECT_ENTRY** macro is placed in the object map for each COM object in the DLL. The **OBJECT_ENTRY** macro takes two parameters. The first parameter is a GUID that uniquely identifies the COM object. The second parameter is the name of the class that implements the COM object. Using this information, the macro expansion creates a corresponding **_ATL_OBJMAP_ENTRY** for the specified object.

When loading your DLL in response to a client request, COM executes your **DllGetClassObject()** function. This function calls the **CComModule:: GetClassObject()** base class function provided by the _Module global object to access the class factory of the specified object. **CComModule::GetClassObject()** accesses the table maintained by the object map to retrieve a pointer to the **CreateInstance()** method of the class factory. The **GetClassObject()** function uses the pointer to create a COM object, executes the COM object's **QueryInterface()** function, and returns the interface pointer to COM.

EXE servers do not implement the *Dll...* functions; they call the COM run-time function **CoRegisterClassObject()** on startup for each of the class factories that the function implements. Pointers to the class factories are cached in an internally maintained table.

The **DllRegisterServer()** and the **DllUnregisterServer()** functions provide an in-process COM object with its self-registering capability. These functions can be called by programs such as the command-line utility RegSvr32.exe to add or remove information about your COM object to or from the registry. EXE servers check for the command-line switches—RegServer or UnregServer—to determine whether they should register or unregister the server. Both EXEs and DLLs end up calling the **CComModule::RegisterServer()** and **CComModule:: UnregisterServer()** functions. These functions register or unregister all objects declared in the object map using information contained in a registry script resource, which is described in the following section.

Registry Script Resource

When a client application attempts to load a COM object, the COM run-time looks in the registry for specific information. This information appears in the registry under **HKEY_CLASSES_ROOT (HKCR)**. The ATL wizards create a registry script for your COM component that contains the required information.

The registry script is included as a resource in your project. The script file has an .rgs extension, and can be found in your project folder. The following is the Encoder.rgs file:

```
HKCR
{
    EncodeServer.Encoder.1 = s 'Encoder Class'
    {
        CLSID = s '{69F4B917-6641-11D3-934B-0080C7FA0C3E}'
    }
    EncodeServer.Encoder = s 'Encoder Class'
    {
        CLSID = s '{69F4B917-6641-11D3-934B-0080C7FA0C3E}'
        CurVer = s 'EncodeServer.Encoder.1'
```

```
    }
NoRemove CLSID
{
    ForceRemove {69F4B917-6641-11D3-934B-0080C7FA0C3E}
        = s 'Encoder Class'
    {
        ProgID = s 'EncodeServer.Encoder.1'
        VersionIndependentProgID = s 'EncodeServer.Encoder'
        InprocServer32 = s '%MODULE%'
        {
        }
        'TypeLib' = s '{69F4B91A-6641-11D3-934B-0080C7FA0C3E}'
    }
    }
    }
```

The registry script just shown places data into the registry subtree **HKEY_ CLASSES_ROOT**. Entries are created for the CLSID, the ProgID (both versioned and version-independent forms), and the type library. As the Encoder object is hosted in a DLL server, an InprocServer32 entry is created. This entry contains a variable called %MODULE%. When the registry script is processed by Visual Studio, the actual name of the project executable is inserted in place of this variable.

IDL File

An IDL file is compiled by the Microsoft IDL compiler (MIDL). MIDL creates the following files in your project folder:

- Proxy/stub source code to implement standard marshaling.
- A type library file.
- A C file that defines the component and interface GUIDs.
- A C/C++ header file that declares the interface methods exposed by the component.

The proxy/stub code generated for the **Encoder** object is contained in the files DllData.c and EncodeServer_p.c. You compile this code to create a *proxy/stub DLL* which is used by COM to marshal data across process boundaries. The type library file EncodeServer.tlb is linked to the DLL when you build the component.

The GUID definition file (EncodeServer_i.c) and the interface declaration header file (EncodeServer.h) are both used by the EncodeServer project. However, it is important to know about these files because they can be included (using #include) in C/C++ client code to create and use instances of the COM component. The CLSID **CLSID_Encoder** and the IID **IID_IEncoder** declared in EncodeServer_i.c can be used as parameters in a call to **CoCreateInstance()**. The EncodeServer.h file declares a class that represents the **IEncoder** interface, which provides the compiler with the signatures of the interface methods. You use an instance of this class to call the **IEncoder** methods when the **Encoder** object is instantiated.

You will learn how these files are used by client programs in Lesson 1 of Chapter 10.

The EncodeServer.idl file is as follows:

```
import "oaidl.idl";
import "ocidl.idl";
    [
        object,
        uuid(69F4B926-6641-11D3-934B-0080C7FA0C3E),
        helpstring("IEncoder Interface"),
        pointer_default(unique)
    ]
    interface IEncoder : Iunknown
    {
        [helpstring("method EncodeString")] HRESULT
        EncodeString([in] const BSTR instring,
            [out, retval] BSTR * outstring);
        [propget, helpstring("property Key")]
            HRESULT Key([out, retval] short *pVal);
        [propput, helpstring("property Key")]
            HRESULT Key([in] short newVal);
    };

[
    uuid(69F4B91A-6641-11D3-934B-0080C7FA0C3E),
    version(1.0),
    helpstring("EncodeServer 1.0 Type Library")
]
library ENCODESERVERLib
{
    importlib("stdole32.tlb");
    importlib("stdole2.tlb");

    [
        uuid(69F4B917-6641-11D3-934B-0080C7FA0C3E),
        helpstring("Encoder Class")
    ]
    coclass Encoder
    {
        [default] interface IEncoder;
    };
};
```

This IDL file defines the **Encoder** COM object (coclass), the **IEncoder** interface, and the ENCODESERVERLib type library. You can see from this example that IDL syntax is very similar to C++, with the most noticeable difference being the inclusion of attributes in square brackets in front of each object declaration.

MIDL attributes specify the characteristics of interfaces, coclasses, and libraries. For example, [**uuid**] is a required attribute that specifies the unique identifier (GUID) for each of these objects. The GUIDs that appear in this file are generated by the ATL wizards. Notice the [**propput**] and [**propget**] attributes, which inform languages such as Visual Basic that a method is to be treated as a property.

Notice that the coclass definition is enclosed within the type library definition. This means that a description of the COM object will be included in the type library. By declaring a coclass *outside* the library block you can prevent information about the COM object appearing in the type library. You might want to do this if you create COM objects that are used only internally—by other objects in the same DLL, for example.

Alternative Approaches To Development

In addition to ATL, there are several other approaches to developing COM objects. You can implement an object from scratch using C++. You can also use the Microsoft Foundation Classes (MFC).

C++

Implementing a COM object from scratch in C++ requires extensive coding. To achieve this you would perform the following process:

1. Create a DLL for hosting an in-process COM server.
2. Derive an interface class from the **IUnknown** class.
3. Generate GUIDs for the object (CLSID) and the interface (IID).
4. Declare a component class derived from the interface class.
5. Implement the **IUnknown** methods for managing the lifetime of the COM object.
6. Implement the component-specific methods for performing the real work of the COM object.
7. Implement a class factory for creating the server inside the memory space of the DLL.
8. Implement the methods **DllGetClassObject()** and **DllCanUnloadNow()** to interface the DLL in-process server to COM.

9. Export the **DllGetClassObject()** and **DllCanUnloadNow()** methods to the operating system.

10. Generate a registry script containing the object class and class interface GUIDs.

11. Register the object using the registry script.

Most of this process is concerned with the mechanics of generating the equivalent of the COM boilerplate code that ATL provides automatically. While you can generate this boilerplate by editing existing code, it's a tedious and error-prone task. Using ATL saves you a lot of time, and generates efficient components that perform extremely well.

MFC

It is perfectly possible to use MFC to generate a COM object. However, MFC is really geared towards the creation of applications, and its COM support is framed in the context of OLE. OLE (now largely rebranded as ActiveX) is the COM-based technology that allows applications to export feature sets (aspects of their functionality) to other applications. For example, it is OLE technology that allows you to embed a Microsoft Excel spreadsheet inside a Microsoft Word document.

Because OLE features are generally implemented using dispatch interfaces, MFC COM support is based around dispatch mapping technologies implemented by the **CCmdTarget** class. If you want to create a component that exposes a custom interface, you have to resort to using raw C++ code.

Another drawback of MFC COM is that you have to distribute the weighty MFC libraries with your component. If you are distributing the component along with an application that already installs the MFC DLLs, this is not such a big issue, but having to check for and install the libraries for the sake of a single small component is tiresome. In certain situations, statically linking the MFC libraries to your component can make them unacceptably large. One of the reasons for the development of ATL was that MFC components and controls were not found to be suitable for deployment and activation in an Internet environment.

However, MFC is a perfectly good tool for the development of Automation-based components in environments where the MFC libraries can be easily deployed. You can use MFC to easily create ActiveX controls that can be reused many times in your MFC applications. This will be the subject of Chapter 11.

Lesson Summary

When you implement a COM server using the ATL wizards, you are provided with a framework based on ATL templates and macros. Your component class inherits from two base classes: **CComObjectRootEx** and **CComCoClass**. These classes are templated base classes that provide you with the methods of **IUnknown** and a class factory. The ATL wizards provide you with a set of global entry point functions that register your component and allow COM to create instances of your component to service client requests. An IDL file is created that is compiled by the MIDL compiler; this generates proxy/stub code, a type library, and C/C++ header files that define your component's GUIDs and declare the interfaces exposed by your component. These header files can be used by clients to create instances of your COM object and call its interface methods.

Although you can use straight C++ to implement your COM objects, the easiest and safest approach is to use ATL and the ATL wizards. MFC COM support is more geared towards the creation of larger-scale ActiveX applications and Automation-based components operating in an MFC environment.

Lab 9: Creating the STUpload Database Access Component

In this lab you will return to the STUpload project. You will create an in-process COM server called STLoadData.dll, which hosts the **UploadStockData** component. This component exposes the **IUploadStockData** interface, which contains three methods: **ConnectToDatabase()**, **Disconnect()**, and **UploadRecord()**.

Start by creating the STLoadData project within the STUpload workspace.

▶ **To create the STLoadData project**

1. Open the STUpload workspace. From the **File** menu, select **New**.

2. In the **New** dialog box, click the **Projects** tab. Select the **ATL COM AppWizard** project category.

3. Type **STLoadData** in the **Project name** box. Select **Add to current workspace** and click **OK**.

4. In Step 1 of the ATL COM AppWizard click **Finish**, and then click **OK** to create the new project.

5. The STLoadData project appears in ClassView. The project name appears in bold text, signifying that STLoadData is the active project. Make sure that you have the full **Build** toolbar displayed rather than the **Build** minibar. This enables you to switch between projects easily by using the project drop-down list box.

6. Right-click the **STLoadData** project in ClassView. On the shortcut menu, select **New ATL Object**.

7. In the **ATL Object Wizard** dialog box, select the **Objects** item in the **Category** list. In the **Objects** box, select the **Simple Object** icon, and then click **Next**.

8. In the **ATL Object Wizard Properties** dialog box select the **Names** tab. In the **Short Name** box, type **UploadStockData**.

9. On the **Attributes** page, set the following attributes:

   ▪ Under **Threading Model**, select **Apartment**.

   ▪ Under **Interface**, select **Dual**.

   ▪ Under **Aggregation**, select **No**.

10. Ensure that all check boxes are cleared, and then click **OK** to add the **UploadStockData** object.

► **To add the IUploadStockData methods**

1. In ClassView, expand the **STLoadData classes** item. Right-click the **IUploadStockData** interface.

2. On the shortcut menu, click **Add Method**.

3. In the **Return Type** box, select **HRESULT**.

4. In the **Method Name** box, type **UploadRecord**.

5. In the **Parameters** box, enter the following code:

```
[in] BSTR fund, [in] DATE date, [in] double price, [in] BSTR uplBy,
[in] DATE uplDate
```

6. Repeat the procedure to add methods with the following signatures:

```
HRESULT ConnectToDatabase()
```

and

```
HRESULT Disconnect()
```

You will implement these methods in Lab 11 because they themselves are clients of other COM components (the ADO library).

Take a look at the STLoadData.idl file. Note particularly the interface definition:

```
[
    object,
    uuid(241A7771-6888-11D3-934F-0080C7FA0C3E),
    dual,
    helpstring("IUploadStockData Interface"),
    pointer_default(unique)
]
interface IUploadStockData : Idispatch
{
    [id(1), helpstring("method UploadRecord")]
    HRESULT UploadRecord([in] BSTR fund, [in] DATE date,
        [in] double price, [in] BSTR uplBy,
        [in] DATE uplDate);
    [id(2), helpstring("method ConnectToDatabase")]
    HRESULT ConnectToDatabase();
    [id(3), helpstring("method Disconnect")]
    HRESULT Disconnect();
};
```

Note how the **IUploadStockData** interface inherits from the **IDispatch** interface. This is how ATL implements a dual interface. Scripting clients will be able to use the **UploadStockData** component through the dispatch interface. Visual C++ and Visual Basic clients will be able to connect directly to the component's vtable.

Review

1. Describe the features provided by the templated base class **CComObjectRootEx**.

2. Describe the features provided by the templated base class **CComCoClass**.

3. What is a COM map and how is it used?

4. What is an object map and how is it used?

5. How are the keywords **interface**, **coclass**, and **library** used in IDL, and how do they relate to each other?

C H A P T E R   1 0

COM Clients

About This Chapter

In this chapter, you will learn how applications and components can act as clients of COM server components and how they can make use of the services that the component provides. You will learn how the Microsoft Visual C++ compiler simplifies the creation of COM client code. You will also learn techniques that allow you to create COM objects that contain instances of other COM objects.

Before You Begin

Before you start this chapter, you should have read Chapters 2 through 9, and completed the exercises in the text.

Lesson 1: COM Client Applications

In this lesson, you will create a simple application that uses the Encoder COM component you created in the exercises in Chapter 9. The application will use the header files generated by the MIDL compiler from the EncodeServer.idl file. In the latter part of the lesson, you will learn about the features of the Visual C++ compiler that support the creation of COM client applications and components, and you will use these features to re-implement the EncodeClient application.

After this lesson, you will be able to:

- Describe how the header files generated by the MIDL compiler can be used by a client application.
- Describe the features of the Visual C++ COM compiler support.
- Describe how to import a type library into a project.

Estimated lesson time: 30 minutes

COM Server Header Files

In Chapter 9, you learned how the MIDL compiler generates header files that make a COM server's interface and GUID definitions available to C and C++ clients. The files generated for the Encoder component are named EncodeServer.h and EncodeServer_i.c.

The EncodeServer_i.c file contains the following code, which declares the GUIDs defined by the Encoder component as easy to read (and easy to type!) constants:

```
const IID IID_IEncoder =
{0x69F4B926,0x6641,0x11D3,{0x93,0x4B,0x00,0x80,0xC7,0xFA,0x0C,0x3E}};

const IID LIBID_ENCODESERVERLib =
{0x69F4B91A,0x6641,0x11D3,{0x93,0x4B,0x00,0x80,0xC7,0xFA,0x0C,0x3E}};

const CLSID CLSID_Encoder =
{0x69F4B917,0x6641,0x11D3,{0x93,0x4B,0x00,0x80,0xC7,0xFA,0x0C,0x3E}};
```

The IID and CLSID types are defined earlier in the file as C structures that represent a GUID.

At the heart of the EncodeServer.h file is the following C++ declaration (comments have been removed for clarity):

```
MIDL_INTERFACE("69F4B926-6641-11D3-934B-0080C7FA0C3E")
IEncoder : public Iunknown
```

```
{
    public:
    virtual HRESULT STDMETHODCALLTYPE EncodeString(
        const BSTR instring, BSTR __RPC_FAR *outstring) = 0;

    virtual HRESULT STDMETHODCALLTYPE get_Key(
        short __RPC_FAR *pVal) = 0;

    virtual HRESULT STDMETHODCALLTYPE put_Key(
        short newVal) = 0;
};
```

This code defines an abstract class named **IEncoder** (derived from the abstract class **IUnknown**), which contains member functions corresponding to the methods exposed by the **IEncoder** COM interface. The **MIDL_INTERFACE** macro uses the Microsoft specific **__declspec(uuid())** declarator to associate the interface GUID with the class. The keyword **__uuidof()** can be applied to retrieve a constant GUID attached to a class in this way.

Client programs use the definitions contained in these header files to create pointers to the **IEncoder** class, which can be passed to the **CoCreateInstance()** function, as shown in the following example:

```
IEncoder * pServer;
HRESULT hr = ::CoCreateInstance(CLSID_Encoder, NULL,
    CLSCTX_INPROC_SERVER,
    IID_IEncoder,
    (void **) &pServer);
```

If this function call succeeds in creating an **Encoder** COM object, the pServer variable receives a pointer to the vtable of the COM object. The **pServer** pointer can then be used to call the methods of the **IEncoder** interface.

To demonstrate the use of the EncodeServer.h and EncodeServer_i.c header files, you will develop a simple console application, EncodeHello, that uses an **Encoder** COM object to display an encoded "Hello World" string.

► **To create the EncodeHello application**

1. On the Visual C++ **File** menu, click **New**. Choose **Win32 Console Application** as the project type and enter **EncodeHello** as the project name. Click **OK**.

2. In Step 1 of the Win32 Console Application Wizard, select **A simple application** and click **Finish**. Click **OK** to create the project.

3. Using Windows Explorer, copy the files EncodeServer.h and EncodeServer_i.c from the EncodeServer project folder to the EncodeHello project folder.

4. In FileView, locate and open the EncodeHello.cpp file. At the top of the file, add the following lines:

```
#include <iostream.h>
#include "EncodeServer.h"
#include "EncodeServer_i.c"
```

5. Add code to the body of the **Main()** function so that it appears as follows: (This code can be found in CH10_01.cpp, installed from the companion CD.)

```
int main(int argc, char* argv[])
{
    ::CoInitialize(NULL);

    IEncoder * pServer;

    HRESULT hr = ::CoCreateInstance(CLSID_Encoder, NULL,
        CLSCTX_INPROC_SERVER,
        IID_IEncoder,
        (void **) &pServer);

    if(SUCCEEDED(hr))
    {
        short nKey = 1;
        cout << "Enter a code key between -5 and 5: ";
        cin >> nKey;

        wchar_t wstrHello[16] = L"Hello World!";
        BSTR bstrHello = ::SysAllocString(wstrHello);
        BSTR bstrCodedHello;

        HRESULT hr = pServer->put_Key(nKey);
        if(FAILED(hr)) goto ComError;

        hr = pServer->EncodeString(bstrHello, &bstrCodedHello);
        if(FAILED(hr)) goto ComError;

        char strOut[16];
        wcstombs(strOut, bstrCodedHello, 16);
        cout << "\n" << strOut << "\n\n";

    ComError:
        if(FAILED(hr)) cout << "COM Error" << "\n\n";

        ::SysFreeString(bstrHello);
        ::SysFreeString(bstrCodedHello);

        pServer->Release();
    }
```

```
        ::CoUninitialize();

        return 0;
    }
```

The **CoInitialize()** function calls the **CoInitializeEx()** function with the *COINIT_APARTMENTTHREADED* parameter. In Lesson 4 of Chapter 8, you learned how the **CoInitializeEx()** function must be called to initialize the COM libraries on the current thread and specify the threading model to use for the COM objects that are created. Each call to **CoInitialize()** or to **CoInitializeEx()** must be balanced with a call to the **CoUninitialize()** function, which closes the COM library on the current thread.

The code contained in EncodeHello.cpp is pretty straightforward—an instance of the **Encoder** COM object is created, the **Key** property is set to a value supplied by the user, and the **EncodeString()** method is called to encode the "Hello World!" string.

Notice the call to **IUnknown::Release()** toward the end of the function. In Lesson 1 of Chapter 8, you learned that when **CoCreateInstance()** is used to obtain a pointer to an interface, the server reference count is incremented. It is the client's responsibility to call **Release()** to decrement the reference count after the client has finished with the interface pointer.

6. Build and run the EncodeHello application to ensure its performance.

Visual C++ COM Compiler Support

With Visual C++ 5.0, Microsoft introduced a number of classes and C++ language extensions that simplified the creation of COM client programs. These include **_com_ptr_t**, a smart pointer class that encapsulates a COM interface pointer; and the **_bstr_t** and **_variant_t** classes, which encapsulate the **BSTR** and **VARIANT** data types. Also provided is a COM exception class, **_com_error**. You can use these classes by including (using #include) the comdef.h file. Another new feature introduced with Visual C++ 5.0 is the #import directive, which generates C++ header files from information contained in a COM server object's type library. These header files make extensive use of the **_com_ptr_t** class and use **_bstr_t** and **_variant_t** where the **BSTR** and **VARIANT** data types are used.

The features of the Visual C++ COM compiler support are described briefly in the following sections.

_com_ptr_t

The **_com_ptr_t** class is a templated class that encapsulates a COM interface pointer. The class provides some extra code that helps simplify reference counting. A **_com_ptr_t** object calls the **IUnknown::AddRef()** and **IUnknown:: Release()** methods of the encapsulated interface on your behalf to ensure that the lifetime of the COM object that provides the interface is managed properly. **AddRef()** is called automatically when a **_com_ptr_t** object is created as a copy from an existing interface pointer, and **Release()** is called automatically when a **_com_ptr_t** object goes out of scope.

Although this "smart pointer" behavior makes for more readable source code, you shouldn't let the **_com_ptr_t** class lull you into a false sense of security. You should always be aware of the current usage of COM objects in your code, and know when you should be calling **AddRef()** and **Release()**—even if you employ a smart pointer to do this for you.

The simplest way to instantiate a **_com_ptr_t** template to a specific interface type is to create the **_com_ptr_t** object with the **_COM_SMARTPTR_ TYPEDEF** macro. This macro takes an interface name and the unique GUID for a specific interface and declares a specialization of **_com_ptr_t** with the name of the interface plus a suffix of *Ptr*. For example, in a file that includes the EncodeServer.h and EncodeServer_i.c header files, the following line will declare the **_com_ptr_t** specialization **IEncoderPtr**:

```
_COM_SMARTPTR_TYPEDEF(IEncoder, __uuidof(IEncoder));
```

Instances of the instantiated type can then call the **com_ptr_t** member function **CreateInstance()** to obtain an interface pointer from a COM server, as follows:

```
IEncoderPtr pEnc ;
pEnc.CreateInstance(CLSID_Encoder);
```

This pointer can then be used to call the methods of the interface using the **com_ptr_t** overload of the -> operator as follows:

```
int n = 3;
HRESULT hr = pEnc->put_Key(n);
```

Note that the **_com_ptr_t** member functions are called by using the **dot** operator (as in the call to **CreateInstance()**); and that the methods of the interface are called through the overloaded -> operator (as in the call to the **put_Key()** method just shown).

It is also possible for **_com_ptr_t** objects to be created from an existing pointer to a COM interface, or copied from another **_com_ptr_t** object. The Visual C++ Help file gives details on how the **AddRef()** and **Release()** methods are called by the assignment operators and copy constructors.

_bstr_t

A **_bstr_t** object encapsulates the **BSTR** data type. The class manages resource allocation and de-allocation through internal calls to **SysAllocString()** and **SysFreeString()**, and uses reference counting for efficient use of memory. The class provides a number of operators that enable you to use a **_bstr_t** object as easily as you would use a **CString** object. One object that isn't provided, however, is the **&** **"address of"** operator, so you cannot pass the address of a **_bstr_t** object to a function that expects a **BSTR*** object.

_variant_t

A **_variant_t** object is a thin wrapper for the **VARIANT** data type. The class manages creation and destruction of an encapsulated **VARIANT** through internal calls to the API functions **VariantInit()** and **VariantClear()**. A **_variant_t** object provides constructors and operators that allow easy creation and manipulation of a **VARIANT**.

_com_error

A **_com_error** object represents a COM exception condition and encapsulates the HRESULT code returned by nearly all COM interface methods. A **_com_error** object can be thrown by the **_com_raise_error()** function. For more information on **_com_error**, see Lesson 2 of Chapter 13.

Import Directive

The #import preprocessor directive enables you to generate C++ header information about the COM object and its interfaces from a type library. This is very useful if you don't have access to the MIDL-generated header files; the type library is nearly always available because it is usually bound to the server DLL or EXE file. The #import preprocessor also generates a set of smart pointers that enable you to access the COM object interfaces.

When you use #import, the Visual Studio C compiler preprocessor creates two header files that reconstruct the type library contents as C++ source code. The primary header file is similar to that produced by MIDL in that it defines C++ functions that can be used to call methods of the interface exposed by the COM object. However, it also declares additional functions that wrap the direct interface methods to provide properties and methods similar to those expected by a Visual Basic client. Properties can be accessed as member variables of the class, and the methods are wrapped so that an *[out, retval]* parameter is passed back as a return value. The HRESULT value is intercepted—if it reports an error condition, it is thrown as a **_com_error** exception. The **_bstr_t** and **_variant_t** classes are used as argument types and return types for these wrapper functions wherever it is appropriate.

The primary header file has the same name as the type library or the dynamic link library, with a .tlh extension. The secondary header file has the same name as the type library, with a .tli extension. The secondary header file contains the implementations for compiler-generated wrapper functions, and is included (using #include) in the primary header file.

Both header files are placed in the output directory. They are read and compiled by the compiler as if the primary header file was named by a #include directive.

The primary type library header file includes smart pointer declarations for the interfaces exposed by the COM object. The **_COM_SMARTPTR_TYPEDEF** macro is used to instantiate a **_com_ptr_t** template for every interface defined in the type library. The file comdef.h, which contains the definitions of the compiler support classes, is included in the .tlh file.

In the following exercise, you will learn how to use the #import directive to import a type library, and how to use the generated smart pointer types and wrapper functions in your client application code. You will modify the EncodeHello application that you created earlier in this chapter.

▶ **To import the EncodeServer type library**

1. Return to the EncodeHello project. In FileView, locate and open the StdAfx.h file.

2. Just before the //{{AFX_INSERT_LOCATION}} comment, add a line similar to the following:

```
#import "C:\EncodeServer\Debug\EncodeServer.dll" no_namespace
```

Make sure that you type the correct path to the EncodeServer.dll file. It will probably be different on your computer from the one shown above. You should specify the **no_namespace** attribute. This ensures that the classes generated from the type library will be defined within the global namespace.

3. Save and close the StdAfx.h file. In FileView, right-click the **StdAfx.cpp** file, and click **Compile StdAfx.cpp** on the shortcut menu.

4. When the compilation is complete, locate the files EncodeServer.tlh and EncodeServer.tli in the EncodeServer\Debug folder. Inspect the contents of the .tlh file. Note the declaration of the **IEncoderPtr** smart pointer provided by the following line:

```
_COM_SMARTPTR_TYPEDEF(IEncoder, __uuidof(IEncoder));
```

Also note the following member functions declared within the **IEncoder** structure definition:

```
// Property data
__declspec(property(get=GetKey,put=PutKey))
short Key;
```

```
// Wrapper methods for error-handling
_bstr_t EncodeString (_bstr_t instring);
short GetKey ();
void PutKey (short pVal);

// Raw methods provided by interface
virtual HRESULT __stdcall raw_EncodeString (BSTR instring, BSTR *
    outstring) = 0;
virtual HRESULT __stdcall get_Key (short * pVal) = 0;
virtual HRESULT __stdcall put_Key (short pVal) = 0;
```

The "raw" methods at the bottom are similar to those in the EncodeServer.h file
generated by the MIDL compiler. The wrapper methods, however, look much
more like the kind of member functions provided by a regular C++ class. Note
that the declaration of the Key member variable uses the __declspec(property)
declarator. This allows the user of the class to access the **Get** and **Put** functions
by using the Key variable on the left and right sides of an assignment statement.
Also note that these functions use the **_bstr_t** class for argument types and
return values.

The implementation of the wrapper functions can be found in the
EncodeServer.tli file. The implementation of the **GetKey()** function, which
follows, demonstrates how an *[out, retval]* parameter is passed back as a return
value and the HRESULT value is intercepted and potentially thrown as an
exception.

```
inline short IEncoder::GetKey ()
{
    short _result;
    HRESULT _hr = get_Key(&_result);
    if (FAILED(_hr)) _com_issue_errorex(_hr, this, __uuidof(this));
    return _result;
}
```

Now that you have imported the type library, you can alter the application code
to take advantage of the classes generated by importing the type library.

▶ **To alter the EncodeHello application code**

1. Remove the following **#include** directives from the top of the
   EncodeHello.cpp file:

   ```
   #include "EncodeServer.h"
   #include "EncodeServer_i.c"
   ```

2. Re-implement the **Main()** function of the EncodeHello application as follows:

(This code can be found in CH10_02.cpp, installed from the companion CD.)

```
int main(int argc, char* argv[])
{
    CoInitialize(NULL);
    {
        IEncoderPtr pServer;

        HRESULT hr = pServer.CreateInstance(__uuidof(Encoder));

        if(SUCCEEDED(hr))
        {
            short nKey = 1;
            cout << "Enter a code key between -5 and 5: ";
            cin >> nKey;

            _bstr_t bstrHello = "Hello World!";
            _bstr_t bstrCodedHello;

            try
            {
                pServer->Key = nKey;
                bstrCodedHello = pServer->EncodeString(bstrHello);

                cout << "\n" << (const char *)
                bstrCodedHello << "\n\n";
            }
            catch(_com_error e)
            {
                cout << e.ErrorMessage() << "\n\n";
            }
        }
    }
    ::CoUninitialize();

    return 0;
}
```

Note that in this example, the application code is placed within its own code block between the calls to **CoInitialize()** and **CoUninitialize()**. This ensures that the *pServer* variable goes out of scope before the **CoUninitialize()** function is called to close the COM libraries. When *pServer* goes out of scope, the **_com_ptr_t** destructor calls the **Release()** method on the encapsulated **IEncoder** pointer. If this occurs *after* the COM libraries have been closed, disaster will ensue.

Notice that this code is much easier to read than the previous version, and that it closely resembles regular C++ code that does not use COM. Don't be fooled by appearances, however—it is impossible to write efficient, error-free COM code without a thorough understanding of the underlying technology.

Lesson Summary

The MIDL compiler generates header files that make a COM server's interface and GUID definitions available to C and C++ client application source code. These files define structures that can be used to access the interface methods of the instantiated COM objects. Readable definitions of GUIDs are also provided.

Visual C++ COM compiler support provides the **#import** statement, which allows you to generate C++ header information about the COM object and its interfaces from a type library. The generated files make extensive use of the **_com_ptr_t** smart pointer class, the **_com_error** exception class, and other Microsoft-specific C++ language extensions to wrap the COM interface methods and simplify client development. The **_bstr_t** and **_variant_t** classes simplify the use of **BSTR** and **VARIANT** data types.

Lesson 2: Reusing COM Objects

One of the principal benefits of object-oriented software development is that it provides a structure that enables code reuse. After you have created an object that performs a well-defined service in an efficient and error-free manner, you will probably want to reuse that object many times. In this lesson, you will learn about the different ways in which COM objects can use the services of other COM objects. In particular, this includes a discussion of two common reuse techniques, containment and aggregation. These techniques allow you to embed existing COM objects within the COM objects you develop, exposing the interfaces of the embedded objects as interfaces of the containing object.

After this lesson, you will be able to:

- Describe the difference between implementation inheritance and interface inheritance.
- Describe the difference between containment and aggregation as methods of object reuse.
- Describe how to implement the **IUnknown** interface of an aggregatable object.
- Describe how aggregation is implemented by ATL.

Estimated lesson time: 30 minutes

Object Reuse in C++ and COM

C++ programmers generally reuse existing class definitions using either the *containment* or *inheritance* techniques. Containment involves the declaration of an object within a class scope, as shown in the following example:

```
#include "Acme.h" // Contains AcmeViewer class definition
        // Defines the member functions SetFile() and Display()
class MyViewer
{
protected:
    AcmeViewer m_obj;

public:
    MyViewer() {m_obj.SetFile("C:\images\scully.gif", AV_TYPE_GIF);}
    DisplayGif() {m_obj.Display();}
}
```

This code defines a simple class called **MyViewer**, which contains an instance of the pre-existing **AcmeViewer** class. **MyViewer** reuses the code contained in the **AcmeViewer** class. The **MyViewer** constructor initializes the contained **AcmeViewer** object, and the **MyViewer::DisplayGif()** function uses services provided by the **AcmeViewer** object. The **MyViewer** class can control access to the **AcmeViewer** object and the way in which the object's services are used.

Inheritance is a powerful reuse technique that is central to the C++ language. Given what you already know about the **AcmeViewer** class, it should be obvious that the following declaration:

```
#include "Acme.h"

class MyViewer : public AcmeViewer
{
public:
    MyViewer() {SetFile("C:\images\scully.gif", AV_TYPE_GIF);}
}
```

will allow you to call public or protected member functions of the **AcmeViewer** class as member functions of a **MyViewer** object, as follows:

```
MyViewer aViewer;
aViewer.Display();
```

COM supports containment, but it does not support inheritance in the same way that C++ does. In the example just given, the **MyViewer** class inherits functionality implemented by the **AcmeViewer** class. The public or protected member functions of the **AcmeViewer** class are available to the **MyViewer** class. This kind of inheritance is known as *implementation* inheritance.

COM does not support implementation inheritance. COM makes a strict logical distinction between the interface that a COM object provides and the object's implementation of that interface. A published COM interface, which is identified around the world by its GUID, is *immutable*—it is guaranteed never to change. Although there might be many COM objects that implement the functionality described by the interface in many different ways, clients will always know how to communicate with any of these objects. An interface represents a contract between a COM server and a client that specifies what kind of data the object is expecting and what kind of data it will return.

Implementation inheritance causes the implementation of a derived class to be dependent on the implementation of its base class. If the implementation of the base class changes, the derived classes might cease to function properly and would, therefore, need to be re-implemented. This can cause serious problems in large-scale development, particularly if you do not have access to the source code of the base classes. The separation between interface and implementation that COM provides helps to alleviate these kind of problems; but it also means that you cannot reuse COM components by deriving one from another as you can with C++ classes.

COM does support a form of inheritance known as *interface* inheritance. Interfaces in C++ are implemented as abstract classes containing only pure virtual functions that specify, but do not implement, the interface methods. By deriving one interface from another, you specify the structure of the vtable that will hold pointers to the instantiated methods. For example, the following definition will create a properly structured vtable that contains pointers to the three **IUnknown** methods, followed by pointers to the methods defined by **IEncoder**:

```
IEncoder : public IUnknown
{
    // IEncoder methods declared here
}
```

It is the immutability of COM interfaces that makes interface inheritance possible. You can derive your COM interface from any other COM interface and be assured that no one will change the definition of the parent interface without your knowledge and thus mess up your vtable.

Containment and Aggregation

Developers of COM objects reuse existing COM objects by using either *containment* or *aggregation* techniques. Containment and aggregation depend on a relationship in which one object (referred to as the *outer object*) reuses another object (referred to as the *inner object*).

Containment

COM containment works in a similar manner to the C++ containment technique discussed at the beginning of this lesson. The outer object creates an inner object (typically by calling **CoCreateInstance**()) and stores a reference to the inner object as a data member. The outer object implements the interfaces of the inner object through stub interfaces that forward method calls to the inner object.

Figure 10.1 shows how a COM object with the **ICar** interface contains a COM object with the **IVehicle** interface and how the outer object can expose both interfaces.

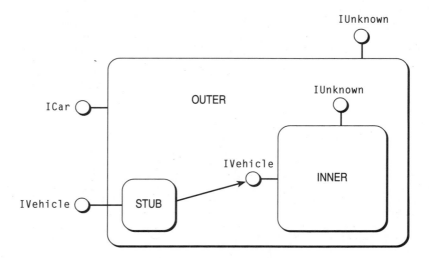

Figure 10.1 COM containment

The outer object is not required to expose all interfaces of the inner object. Just as with C++ containment, the interface on the outer object can control access to the inner object, and can also control the way in which the inner object's services are used. The outer object does not forward calls to any of the **IUnknown** interface methods of the inner object because the inner object does not have any knowledge of the interfaces exposed by the outer object. For example, if a client of the object depicted in Fig 10.1 requested an **IUnknown** pointer, it would expect to be able to use this pointer to access the **ICar** interface as well as the **IVehicle** interface. A pointer to the **IUnknown** interface of the inner object would not be able to service requests for an **ICar** pointer.

Aggregation

As with containment, the outer object stores a reference to the **IUnknown** interface of the inner object. Unlike containment, however, the outer object exposes interfaces of the inner object directly to the client, rather than implementing interface stubs for them. This means that aggregation does not incur the overhead of forwarding method calls imposed by containment.

Figure 10.2 on the following page shows how the interface of an inner object is exposed through aggregation.

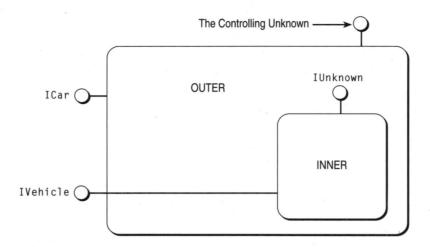

Figure 10.2   COM aggregation

For aggregation to work, the inner object must be *aggregatable*—it must be written to support aggregation. Because clients of the outer object can now obtain interface pointers exposed by the inner object, they are able to call the **IUnknown** interface methods of the inner object. Because the inner object will not be able to service calls to **QueryInterface()**, **AddRef()** and **Release()** on behalf of the outer object, client calls to the inner object's **IUnknown** interface must be delegated to the outer object's **IUnknown** interface (the *controlling unknown*).

Note Bear in mind that a client of an aggregated object knows nothing of the aggregation, which as far as the client is concerned, is implementation detail. The client sees a single COM object that exposes a single **IUnknown** pointer. If the client receives pointers to interfaces of the inner object, it will assume that they are interfaces exposed by the outer object.

When the outer object creates the inner object, it uses the second argument of the **CoCreateInstance()** function to pass the address of the controlling unknown to the inner object's class factory. If this address is not NULL, the inner object knows that it is being aggregated and delegates **IUnknown** method calls from external clients to the controlling unknown.

However, the inner object must be able to handle **IUnknown** method calls from external clients (which are intended for the controlling unknown) differently from **IUnknown** method calls that originate from the controlling unknown (which are used by the outer object to discover the interfaces and control the lifetime of the aggregated object). This means that an aggregatable COM object must provide two versions of the **IUnknown** interface: a *delegating* version and a *non-delegating* version. The outer component calls the non-delegating

IUnknown methods; external clients call the delegating **IUnknown** methods. The delegating methods redirect the calls to the controlling unknown (if the object is aggregated), or to the non-delegating unknown (if the object is not aggregated).

Implementing Aggregation Using ATL

ATL provides you with a number of macros and base-class methods that facilitate the implementation of component aggregation. To create an aggregatable (inner) object, you use the ATL Object Wizard to add a new COM object to an ATL project and specify that the component is to support aggregation. You select the appropriate option on the **Attributes** page, as shown in Figure 10.3.

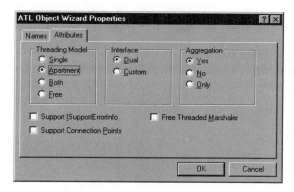

Figure 10.3 ATL Object Wizard aggregation options

By default, ATL COM objects are created as aggregatable. Selecting the **No** option in the aggregation group will create a non-aggregatable object. The **Only** option will create an object that can be used only as an aggregatable object.

▶ **To implement an outer object:**

1. Add an **IUnknown** pointer to your class object and initialize it to NULL in the constructor. For the purposes of this example, we will refer to this pointer as **m_pUnkInner**.

2. Inside your class definition, declare the macro **DECLARE_GET_CONTROLLING_UNKNOWN**. This macro defines a function named **GetControllingUnknown()**.

3. Override the methods **FinalConstruct()** and **FinalRelease()**. These are methods of the **CComObjectRootBase** base class, which are called as the last steps for creating and destroying a COM object.

4. In **FinalConstruct()**, you call **CoCreateInstance()**, passing the CLSID of the inner object you want to create as the first argument. Pass the return value of the **GetControllingUnknown()** function as the second argument to supply

the inner class with the controlling **IUnknown** pointer. Pass the address of the **m_pUnkInner** pointer as the fifth argument, to receive a pointer of the inner object's **IUnknown** interface. An example of an overridden **FinalConstruct()** function follows:

```
HRESULT FinalConstruct()
{
    return CoCreateInstance(CLSID_InnerObject,
        GetControllingUnknown(), CLSCTX_ALL,
        IID_IInnerObject, &m_pUnkInner);
}
```

5. In **FinalRelease**, call **IUnknown::Release()** on the inner object.

6. Using the **COM_INTERFACE_ENTRY_AGGREGATE** macro, add an entry to the outer object's COM map for the interface of the inner object. This is a specialization of the **COM_INTERFACE_ENTRY** macro that handles aggregated objects. **COM_INTERFACE_ENTRY_AGGREGATE** takes an extra **IUnknown *** argument that points to the inner unknown.

7. Add the interface definition for the inner object to the .idl file of the outer object, and reference that interface in the [coclass] section.

Lesson Summary

C++ developers are accustomed to using implementation inheritance as a code reuse technique. COM makes a strict logical distinction between interface and implementation and insists that interfaces remain immutable around the world. This means that COM can support only interface inheritance (reuse of the interface specification) and not implementation inheritance.

COM supports two forms of object reuse: aggregation and containment. These techniques depend on a relationship in which an outer object reuses an inner object. When an inner object is contained, its interfaces are not exposed directly to a client but instead are mediated through stub interfaces implemented by the outer object. An aggregated object exposes its interfaces directly to the client. When aggregating objects, you must implement the inner and outer objects so that a client will be able to access only the controlling unknown—a pointer to the **IUnknown** interface of the outer object. ATL provides you with a number of macros and base-class methods that facilitate the implementation of component aggregation.

Lab 10: Implementing the UploadStockData Component

In this lab, you will provide the implementation for UploadStockData, the
component you created for Lab 9. You will add code to implement the
ConnectToDatabase(), **Disconnect()**, and **UploadRecord()** methods of the
IUploadStockData interface. These methods use the ADO library to connect
to the Stocks database. To refresh your memory about ADO, refer back to
Lesson 3 of Chapter 7.

In this Lab, you will also write code to implement the **Upload** command on the
Data menu of the STUpload application. The user will select this command to
upload the data in the currently loaded document to the Stocks database.

This Lab assumes that you have installed SQL Server and have set up the Stocks
database as directed in the "Getting Started" section of the introduction.

Creating a Data Link File

The UploadStockData component creates an ADO **Connection** object to
connect to the Stocks database. You provide the **Connection** object with information about which provider, database, and security settings to use by specifying
the details in a connection string. For example, the connection string used by the
ADO data control in my version of the STUpload application is as follows:

```
Provider=SQLOLEDB.1;Integrated Security=SSPI;Persist Security
Info=False;Initial Catalog=Stocks;Data Source=(local)
```

When distributing an application, it is not advisable to hard-code connection information into the application source code because this might mean that changes
to the database and network configuration will require you to recompile and redistribute your application. To avoid problems of this kind, you can specify the
connection information in a special disk file known as a *data link file*. A data
link file has a .udl extension. When OLE DB is installed on your computer, you
can configure the data link file using a simple user interface. After the data link
file has been configured, you simply set the connection string to refer to the file
as follows:

```
File Name=C:\DataLinks\STLink.udl
```

The configuration in the data link file can easily be redistributed or reconfigured
on the client computer if the database or network configuration changes.

▶ **To create a data link file**

1. Using Windows Explorer, create a new folder beneath the root of your hard
   drive. Name the folder **DataLinks**.
2. Click the **DataLinks** folder in the left pane of Windows Explorer. Right-click
   in the right pane and on the **New** menu, click **Microsoft Data Link**.

3. Rename the new data link file **STLink.udl**.

4. Double-click the **STLink.udl** file to edit the configuration information.

5. On the **Provider** page of the **Data Link Propertie**s dialog box, click **Microsoft OLE DB Provider for SQL Server**.

6. On the **Connection** page (shown in Figure 10.4), select your local computer name as the Server name. Click **Use Windows NT Integrated security**, or enter a SQL Server account name and password as appropriate.

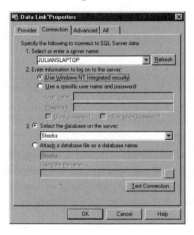

Figure 10.4   Editing the data link file

7. Click the **Stocks** database on the server. Test your connection by clicking **Test Connection**.

8. Click **OK** to close the message box, and **OK** again to save the connection information to the data link file.

Implementing the IUploadStockData Interface Methods

In this section of the lab, you will return to the STLoadData project and implement the **ConnectToDatabase()**, **Disconnect()**, and **UploadRecord()** methods of the **IUploadStockData** interface exposed by the UploadStockData component. In the course of completing these exercises, you will learn how a client can use the COM interfaces supplied by ADO to work with an OLE DB data provider.

The first step is to import the ADO type library to make the GUID definitions available to the project, and to generate smart pointers for the ADO interfaces.

▶ **To import the ADO type library**

1. Open the **STUpload.dsw** workspace file in Visual Studio. Make sure that the full **Build** toolbar is displayed and then click the **STLoadData** project in the drop-down list.

2. In FileView, expand the Header Files folder under the **STLoadData Files** item. Double-click the **StdAfx.h** file.

3. At the end of the file, just before the //{{AFX_INSERT_LOCATION}} comment, add the following line:

```
#import "C:\Program Files\Common Files\System\ado\msado15.dll" \
    no_namespace rename("EOF", "adoEOF")
```

The path to the msado15.dll file might be different on your computer. Check that the version in your code points to the correct location. Note, also, that in the example just given, a continuation character \ is used to break the statement over two lines.

4. Save and close the StdAfx.h file.

5. In FileView, right-click the **StdAfx.cpp** file in the Source Files folder. On the shortcut menu, click **Compile StdAfx.cpp**.

The compiler processes the #import statement in the StdAfx.h file and creates the msado15.tlh and msado15.tli files in your Debug folder. These files contain the GUID definitions and smart pointer declarations for the ADO interfaces, which are now available for use in the STLoadData project.

The UploadStockData component will connect to the database through a single ADO **Connection** object, which will be used by successive calls to the **UploadRecord()** method. This **Connection** object will be implemented as a member variable of the component class and will be opened and closed by the **ConnectToDatabase()** and **Disconnect()** methods.

▶ **To implement the Connection object**

1. Add the following **protected** data member to the definition of the **CUploadStockData** class in the UploadStockData.h file:

```
_ConnectionPtr m_pConnection;
```

2. In the same file, add the following line to the **CUploadStockData** class constructor:

```
m_pConnection = NULL;
```

3. In the UploadStockData.cpp file, locate the **CUploadStockData:: ConnectToDatabase**() function. Add code to the function so that it appears as follows:

```
STDMETHODIMP CUploadStockData::ConnectToDatabase()
{
    // Test to see if we're connected already
    if(m_pConnection) return S_OK;

    HRESULT hr = m_pConnection.CreateInstance(__uuidof(Connection));
    if(FAILED(hr)) return hr;

    hr = m_pConnection->Open(L"File Name=C:\\STLink.UDL",
        L"", L"", -1);

    if(FAILED(hr)) return hr;

    return S_OK;
}
```

Remember that the m_pConnection variable is a **_com_ptr_t** smart pointer type that points to the interface exposed by the ADO **Connection** object.

4. Locate the **CUploadStockData::Disconnect**() function. Add code to the function so that it appears as follows:

```
STDMETHODIMP CUploadStockData::Disconnect()
{
    if(m_pConnection)
    {
        m_pConnection->Close();
        m_pConnection = NULL;
    }
    return S_OK;
}
```

You can now add code to implement the **IUploadStockData::UploadRecord**() method.

▶ **To implement the UploadRecord() method**

1. On the **Project** menu, click **Settings**. Make sure the STLoadData project is selected in the left pane. On the **C/C++** page of the **Project Settings** dialog box, click **C++ Language** in the **Category** drop-down list. Click the **Enable exception handling** option and click **OK**.

2. In the UploadStockData.cpp file, locate the **CUploadStockData::
   UploadRecord()** function. Add code to the function so that it appears
   as follows:

   (This code can be found in CH10_03.cpp, installed from the companion CD.)

```cpp
STDMETHODIMP CUploadStockData::UploadRecord(BSTR fund, DATE date,
    double price, BSTR uplBy, DATE uplDate)
{
    // Test for live connection to data source
    if(m_pConnection == NULL)
        return E_FAIL;

    // Create recordset
    _RecordsetPtr pRecordset;

    HRESULT hr = pRecordset.CreateInstance(__uuidof(Recordset));
    if(FAILED(hr)) return hr;

    try
    {
        // Open recordset
        _variant_t vConnection = m_pConnection.GetInterfacePtr();
        hr = pRecordset->Open(L"pricehistory", vConnection,
            adOpenForwardOnly, adLockOptimistic, adCmdTableDirect);

        if(FAILED(hr)) return hr;

        // Add new record, set fields to new values and update
        hr = pRecordset->AddNew();
        if(FAILED(hr)) throw _com_error(hr);

        pRecordset->Fields->GetItem(L"ph_fund")->Value = fund;
        pRecordset->Fields->GetItem(L"ph_date")->Value = date;
        pRecordset->Fields->GetItem(L"ph_price")->Value = price;
        pRecordset->Fields->GetItem(L"ph_uploadedby")->Value = uplBy;
        pRecordset->Fields->GetItem(L"ph_uploaddate")->
            Value = uplDate;

        hr = pRecordset->Update();
        if(FAILED(hr)) throw _com_error(hr);
    }
    catch(_com_error e)
    {
        // very unsophisticated error handling
        try
        {
            pRecordset->Close();
        }
```

```
                    catch(...) // Close() may throw another exception
                    {
                    }
                    return E_FAIL;
              }
              pRecordset->Close();

              return S_OK;
        }
```

Note that the existing Connection object **m_pConnection** is passed as an argument to the Recordset **Open()** method. For details of the other arguments to **Open()**, look up "*ADO*" in the Visual C++ Help file.

Note, too, that the **AddNew()** and **Update()** methods of the ADO **Recordset** object are used together to add a new record. A new record is added to the recordset with **AddNew()**, the field values (accessed through the **Recordset** object's *Fields* collection) are set to the new values, and the **Update()** method is called to update the database.

3. You can now build the STLoadData project to re-create and re-register the STLoadData.dll COM server.

Implementing the Upload Data Command for the STUpload Application

In the next section of the lab, you will implement the **Upload** command on the **Data** menu of the STUpload application. You will also add a user-interface update command handler to make the menu and toolbar command available when a document is currently loaded into the application.

▶   **To implement the Upload Data command**

1. Close all documents currently displayed in the Visual Studio editor.

2. On the **Build** toolbar, click the **STUpload** project in the drop-down list.

3. Press CTRL+W to open ClassWizard. On the **Message Maps** tab, click the **CSTUploadDoc** class in the **Class name** drop-down list.

4. Create COMMAND and UPDATE_COMMAND_UI handlers named **OnDataUpload()** and **OnUpdateDataUpload()** for the **ID_DATA_UPLOAD** ID. Click the **OnUpdateDataUpload()** function in the **Member functions** list and click **Edit Code** to jump to the function implementation.

5. Implement the **CSTUploadDoc::OnUpdateDataUpload**() function as follows:

(This code can be found in CH10_04.cpp, installed from the companion CD.)

```
void CSTUploadDoc::OnUpdateDataUpload(CCmdUI* pCmdUI)
{
    // Enable the UploadData command only if there is
    // data on file and a fund currently selected for viewing

    BOOL bEnable = GetCurrentFund().IsEmpty() ? FALSE : TRUE;

    pCmdUI->Enable(bEnable);
}
```

6. At the top of the STUploadDoc.cpp file, add the following directives:

```
#include <comdef.h>     // for Compiler COM support
#include <lmcons.h>     // for the UNLEN constant
#include ".\STLoadData\STLoadData.h"
#include ".\STLoadData\STLoadData_i.c"
```

7. Locate the **CSTUploadDoc::OnDataUpload**() function and add code to implement the function as follows:

```
void CSTUploadDoc::OnDataUpload()
{
    if(AfxMessageBox("Upload current file to database?",
        MB_OKCANCEL) == IDCANCEL)
        return;

    ::CoInitialize(NULL);

    _COM_SMARTPTR_TYPEDEF(IUploadStockData,
        __uuidof(IUploadStockData));

    IUploadStockDataPtr pServer;

    HRESULT hr = pServer.CreateInstance(CLSID_UploadStockData);

    if(SUCCEEDED(hr))
        hr = pServer->ConnectToDatabase();

    if(SUCCEEDED(hr))
    {
        try
        {
            POSITION pos = m_DocList.GetHeadPosition();

            while(pos)
```

```
            {
                CStockData sd = m_DocList.GetNext(pos);

                BSTR fund = sd.GetFund().AllocSysString();
                DATE date = sd.GetDate().m_dt;
                double price = sd.GetPrice();

                DWORD dwLen = UNLEN + 1;
                TCHAR cUser[UNLEN + 1];
                ::GetUserName(cUser, &dwLen);
                CString strUser(cUser);

                BSTR uplBy = (strUser.Left(10)).AllocSysString();
                COleDateTime dtToday =
                    COleDateTime::GetCurrentTime();
                DATE uplDate = dtToday.m_dt;

                HRESULT hr = pServer->UploadRecord(fund,
                    date, price, uplBy, uplDate);

                ::SysFreeString(fund);
                ::SysFreeString(uplBy);

                if(FAILED(hr))
                {
                    CString strPrompt = "Upload of:\n";
                    strPrompt += sd.GetAsString();
                    strPrompt += "\nfailed";

                    if(AfxMessageBox(strPrompt,
                        MB_OKCANCEL) == IDCANCEL)
                        break;
                }
            }
            if(!pos) // We got to the end of the loop
                AfxMessageBox("Upload completed successfully");
        }
        catch(_com_error e)
        {
            ::MessageBox(NULL, e.ErrorMessage(), NULL, MB_OK);
        }
        pServer->Disconnect();
    }
    ::CoUninitialize();
}
```

Look through the code to make sure you understand how the code creates and uses an instance of the UploadStockData component to add to the database records contained in the document's **m_DocList** member. Note that the Windows API function **GetUserName()** is used to get the name of the currently logged-on user. The first 10 characters of this name are placed in the **ph_uploadedby** field in the pricehistory table of the Stocks database.

You can now build the STUpload application.

▶ **To test the Upload Data command**

1. Run the STUpload application. On the **Data** menu, click **Import**, and load the Ch10Test.dat file from the Chapter 10\Data folder.

2. Click any fund in the Select Fund window to make the **Upload Data** command available.

3. On the **Data** menu, click **Upload**. Click **OK** to upload the data in the file to the pricehistory table of the Stocks database. When the upload has completed, click **OK**.

4. Re-run the **Upload** command from the **Data** menu. Notice now that each record in the file will fail. This is because the Primary Key constraint on the pricehistory table will not allow duplicate records to be added. Click **Cancel** to abort the upload process. Close the STUpload application.

5. Click the **Start** menu, point to **Programs**, point to **Microsoft SQL Server 7.0**, and open the Query Analyzer application. Connect to your **(local)** database.

6. Click **Stocks** in the **DB** drop-down list on the toolbar.

7. In the Query Analyzer main window, type the following:

```
select * from pricehistory
```

8. Press CTRL+E to execute the SQL query.

The results of the query will appear in the lower half of the Query Analyzer window as shown in Figure 10.5. Check to see that the rows that you added appear at the bottom of the table with your user name and the current date in the ph_uploadedby and ph_uploaddate columns.

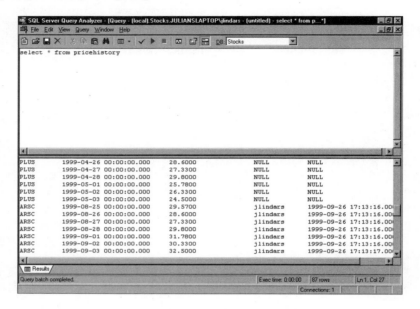

Figure 10.5　The Query Analyzer displaying the pricehistory table

Review

1. What kind of class represents a COM interface in C++?

2. How does a **_com_ptr_t** object help you control the lifetime of a COM server?

3. What are the advantages and disadvantages of COM containment?

4. What is the purpose of the second argument to **CoCreateInstance()**?

C H A P T E R   1 1

Creating ActiveX Controls

About This Chapter

In Chapter 8, you learned about some of the characteristics of ActiveX controls that distinguish the controls from other COM objects, and you were introduced to the ActiveX control container. Recall that a container generally implements a user interface and expects the control to participate as part of this user interface. A control exposes a dispatch interface that allows the container to get and set properties and call methods. A control communicates with its container by firing events. ActiveX controls usually implement a property sheet that allows users to change the properties of the control. Control containers are usually capable of persisting the properties of the ActiveX controls they contain.

In this chapter, you will learn about the two most popular methods of Microsoft Visual C++ ActiveX control development. In Lesson 1, you will develop a simple ActiveX control using MFC. In Lesson 2, you will develop the same control using ATL. By creating the same control, you will be able to compare the two development methods and assess which method might be most appropriate in a particular development scenario.

Before You Begin

Before you start this chapter, you should have read Chapters 2 through 10, and completed the exercises in the text.

Lesson 1: Creating ActiveX Controls with MFC

MFC simplifies the process of creating an ActiveX control. Using the MFC ActiveX ControlWizard, you can easily create a fully featured ActiveX control. In this lesson, you will use MFC to create an ActiveX control that implements a dispatch interface, fires events, and provides a property page that can be used to get and set persistent properties.

After this lesson, you will be able to:

- Describe how to use the MFC ActiveX ControlWizard to create an ActiveX control.
- Describe how to use ClassWizard to add properties, methods, and events to your control.
- Describe how to implement a control property page.
- Describe how to make properties persistent.
- Describe how to use the ActiveX Control Test Container to test your control.

Estimated lesson time: 50 minutes

Creating an MFC ActiveX Control Project

In this lesson, you will develop the OneArmedBandit ActiveX control, a software version of a Las Vegas-style slot machine. The control provides the single method **Play()**, which causes a random combination of symbols to appear in the control's three "reels." When the control displays three identical symbols, the **Jackpot** event is fired. When the user clicks inside the control, the **Click** event is fired. Figure 11.1 on the facing page shows the OneArmedBandit control inside the ActiveX Control Test Container.

The OneArmedBandit control provides a property page that allows a user to set the values of the **ForeColor** and **BackColor** properties, and to set the custom control-specific **NumberOfSymbols** property. This property is used to set the number of possible symbols that the control can display, and thus increase or decrease the odds of winning the jackpot. All three of the control properties are persistent.

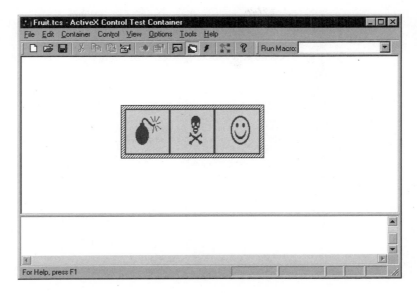

Figure 11.1   The OneArmedBandit ActiveX control

As with all MFC development, the first stage in creating an ActiveX control is to create a development project. In the following exercise, you will create the OneArmedBandit project.

► **To create the OneArmedBandit project**

1. On the **File** menu, click **New,** and then click the **Projects** tab.

2. Click **MFC ActiveX ControlWizard**. In the **Project name** box, type **OneArmedBandit** and click **OK**.

3. Step 1 of the ControlWizard appears. Review the options and click **Next** to accept the default settings.

4. In Step 2 of the ControlWizard, clear the **Has an "About" box** option. Click **Finish**.

5. The **New Project Information** dialog box appears as shown in Figure 11.2 on the following page.

Figure 11.2   Creating the OneArmedBandit project

There are a couple of interesting things to note about the information displayed in this dialog box. First, the DLL is created with an .ocx extension. The use of the .ocx extension is not required for ActiveX controls; it is simply a convention left over from the days when ActiveX controls were called OLE controls. OLE controls replaced the older Visual Basic Extension (VBX) controls. Second, the type library source code is in a file named OneArmedBandit.odl. This file contains Object Description Language (ODL) code. ODL was the predecessor to Interface Definition Language (IDL), and it is very similar to IDL in syntax. The Microsoft IDL (MIDL) compiler is capable of compiling ODL code.

6. Click **OK** to create the OneArmedBandit project. Expand the ClassView items to view the classes created for your project, as shown in Figure 11.3 on the facing page.

The ActiveX ControlWizard creates classes to implement the control's DLL server, the control itself, and the control's property page. The **COneArmedBanditCtrl** control class is derived from the MFC class **COleControl**. This powerful class inherits all the functionality of the **CWnd** and **CCmdTarget** classes and provides a large number of member functions related to the operation of an ActiveX control. Using these functions, you can get and set a control's stock properties, retrieve ambient properties from the container, fire stock events, implement property persistence, and perform a number of operations related to siting and displaying a control.

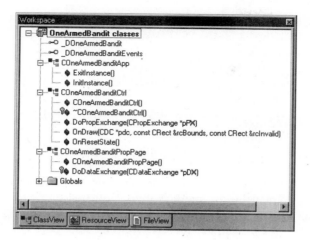

Figure 11.3 OneArmedBandit project classes

Defining the Control Interface

The ControlWizard also defines two dispatch interfaces for your control: **_DOneArmedBandit** and **_DOneArmedBanditEvents**. You add methods and properties to the first of these and events to the second. Although you can make these additions by right-clicking the interface items and choosing the appropriate command from the shortcut menu, the preferred method is to use ClassWizard.

Adding Properties

In the following exercises, you will be adding the stock **ForeColor** and **BackColor** properties and the custom **NumberOfSymbols** property to the **COneArmedBanditCtrl** class.

▶ **To add properties to an ActiveX control**

1. Press CTRL+W to open ClassWizard. Select the **Automation** tab.

2. Click **Add Property** to display the **Add Property** dialog box.

3. Expand the **External name** drop-down list to display a list of stock properties supported by the **COleControl** class. From this list, select **BackColor**.

4. Note that the **Stock** radio button in the **Implementation** group is selected automatically. The dialog box also indicates that the **GetBackColor()** and **SetBackColor()** functions will be created. Click **OK** to implement the **BackColor** stock property and create the **Get** and **Set** functions.

5. Repeat the process to create the **ForeColor** stock property.

6. To create the custom property, open the **Add Property** dialog box and type the name **NumberOfSymbols** into the **External name** list. Note that ClassWizard will create the m_numberOfSymbols member variable to store the property value, and that it will also create a notification function **OnNumberOf SymbolsChanged**() that is called when the property is changed.

7. From the **Type** drop-down list, select **short**, and then click **OK** to create the custom property.

8. Click **OK** to finish creating the properties.

In ClassView, you will be able see the new properties listed underneath the **_DOneArmedBandit** interface item. Notice also that the member variable and the notification function have been added to the **COneArmedBanditCtrl** class. Double-click the **OnNumberOfSymbolsChanged**() function to view the source code in the OneArmedBanditCtl.cpp file. The default version of the function simply calls the **COleControl::SetModifiedFlag**() function.

Toward the top of the OneArmedBanditCtl.cpp file, you will find this code:

```
BEGIN_DISPATCH_MAP(COneArmedBanditCtrl, COleControl)
    //{{AFX_DISPATCH_MAP(COneArmedBanditCtrl)
    DISP_PROPERTY_NOTIFY(COneArmedBanditCtrl, "NumberOfSymbols",
        m_numberOfSymbols, OnNumberOfSymbolsChanged, VT_I2)
    DISP_STOCKPROP_BACKCOLOR()
    DISP_STOCKPROP_FORECOLOR()
    //}}AFX_DISPATCH_MAP

END_DISPATCH_MAP()
```

This code, along with the corresponding **DECLARE_DISPATCH_MAP** macro in the header file, implements an MFC *dispatch map* for the class. The dispatch map is very similar to the message map you learned about in Chapter 3, but instead of mapping Windows messages to class handler functions, the dispatch map maps Automation client requests to your control class's implementation of the properties and methods. For example, when a Visual Basic client requests the **NumberOfSymbols** property with the following code, the control uses the dispatch map (specifically the **DISP_PROPERTY_NOTIFY** macro) to retrieve the value contained in the m_numberOfSymbols variable and pass it back to the client:

```
Dim myobj As OneArmedBandit
Set myobj = New OneArmedBandit
MsgBox myobj.NumberOfSymbols
```

As you can see from the dispatch map code, stock properties are supported with their own specific macros.

Property Persistence

MFC makes it easy to make control properties persistent. The **COleControl:: DoPropExchange()** function serializes the control properties to and from a storage medium—usually the control's container. The ActiveX ControlWizard overloads the **DoPropExchange()** function for your control class. The framework passes this function a pointer to a **CPropExchange** object, which encapsulates the context of the property exchange, including its direction. The overloaded version of **DoPropExchange()** calls the base class version to serialize the stock properties implemented by the control. It is your responsibility to add code to serialize any custom properties you want to make persistent.

MFC provides a number of functions that allow you to serialize properties of different types. The names of these functions begin with the prefix *PX_*. To serialize your **NumberOfSymbols** property, replace the //TODO comment in your control class's **DoPropExchange()** function with a call to the **PX_Short()** function, as follows:

```
void COneArmedBanditCtrl::DoPropExchange(CPropExchange* pPX)
{
    ExchangeVersion(pPX, MAKELONG(_wVerMinor, _wVerMajor));
    COleControl::DoPropExchange(pPX);

    PX_Short(pPX, "NumberOfSymbols", m_numberOfSymbols, 3);

}
```

The fourth argument to the **PX_Short()** function specifies a default value for the property that is used if the function is unable to retrieve a value from storage medium. The example code above ensures that the **NumberOfSymbols** property of a new control instance will be initialized with a default value of 3.

Adding Methods

As well as providing access to control properties, the dispatch map also maps client method calls to class member function implementations. You use ClassWizard to add a method.

▶ **To add a method to an ActiveX control**

1. In ClassWizard, click the **Automation** tab and click **Add Method** to display the **Add Method** dialog box.
2. In the **External name** list, type **Play**.
3. In the **Return type** drop-down list, click **void**.
4. Click **OK**, and then click **OK** in ClassWizard to create the method.

Notice that the **Play()** function has been added to the **COneArmedBanditCtrl** class. If you inspect the dispatch map, you will see that the following line has been added:

```
DISP_FUNCTION(COneArmedBanditCtrl, "Play", Play, VT_EMPTY, VTS_NONE)
```

Adding Events

ClassWizard also automates the process of defining events fired by the control. In the following exercise, you will implement the **Click** stock event and the **Jackpot** custom event.

▶   **To define an ActiveX control event**

1. In ClassWizard, click the **ActiveX Events** tab. Click **Add Event** to display the **Add Event** dialog box.

2. From the **External name** drop-down list, choose the **Click** stock event. Click **OK** to add the event.

3. Click **Add Event** once again. In the **Add Event** dialog box, type **Jackpot** into the **External name** list. Click **OK**.

4. In ClassWizard, click **OK** to finish creating events.

In ClassView, notice that the **FireJackpot()** function has been added to the **COneArmedBanditCtrl** class. You can use this function from within your code to fire the **Jackpot** event. ClassWizard has also added entries to the class's *event map*. The event map is a structure very similar to the dispatch map that is used to implement ActiveX control events. The following is the event map implementation for the **COneArmedBanditCtrl** class:

```
BEGIN_EVENT_MAP(COneArmedBanditCtrl, COleControl)
    //{{AFX_EVENT_MAP(COneArmedBanditCtrl)
    EVENT_CUSTOM("Jackpot", FireJackpot, VTS_NONE)
    EVENT_STOCK_CLICK()
    //}}AFX_EVENT_MAP
END_EVENT_MAP()
```

Creating Property Pages

Now that you have implemented your ActiveX control's interface, you can add property pages to allow users of the control to get and set its properties. The framework uses the **PROPPAGEID** series of macros to specify an array of property page IDs for your control's property sheet. The default code generated by the ActiveX ControlWizard for the OneArmedBandit project can be found in the OneArmedBandit.cpp file, and is as follows:

```
BEGIN_PROPPAGEIDS(COneArmedBanditCtrl, 1)
    PROPPAGEID(COneArmedBanditPropPage::guid)
END_PROPPAGEIDS(COneArmedBanditCtrl)
```

Note that this structure, unlike the dispatch and event maps, is not maintained by ClassWizard. You have to maintain the code yourself.

Custom Property Pages

In the code that is shown above, the single **PROPPAGEID** entry in the table refers to the default property page that is created for your control. The ActiveX ControlWizard creates a dialog template resource and a dialog class (based on the **COlePropertyPage** class) that you can edit and compile to create a property page that allows access to your control's custom properties.

In the following exercises, you will create a property page that allows a user to set the **NumberOfSymbols** custom property.

▶ **To implement the custom property page**

1. In ResourceView, expand the Dialog folder. Double-click **IDD_PROPPAGE_ ONEARMEDBANDIT** to edit the dialog template resource.

2. Delete the //TODO static text. Add a static text control and an edit control so that the dialog template appears as shown in Figure 11.4.

Figure 11.4   Implementing the custom property page

Give the edit control the ID **IDC_NUMSYMBOLS**. On the **Styles** tab of the **Edit Properties** dialog box, select the **Number** check box.

3. Press CTRL+W to open ClassWizard. Select the **Member Variables** tab.

4. Click **Add Variable** to add a Value category member variable named **m_numsymbols**. The variable type should be **short**. In the **Optional property name** box, type **NumberOfSymbols** and then click **OK**.

5. Specify the range validation by entering a minimum value of **3** and a maximum value of **7**. Click **OK**.

Look at the **DoDataExchange()** function of the **COneArmedBanditPropPage** class. Notice that in addition to the DDX and DDV functions, ClassWizard has added the following line:

```
DDP_Text(pDX, IDC_NUMSYMBOLS, m_numsymbols, _T("NumberOfSymbols"));
```

This is one of a number of functions with the *DDP_* prefix that is provided by MFC to transfer data between an ActiveX Control property page and the control properties. Note that the dispatch name of the control property is used, so you do not have to provide an additional code link between the **COneArmedBanditPropPage** class and the **COneArmedBanditCtrl** class.

Stock Property Pages

Because you have added the **ForeColor** and **BackColor** properties to your control, you will need to implement a property page to allow the user to set them. MFC provides three stock property pages for use with ActiveX controls: **CLSID_ CColorPropPage**, **CLSID_CFontPropPage**, and **CLSID_CPicturePropPage**. These pages display a user interface for stock color, font, and picture properties, respectively. To add a stock property page, add another **PROPPAGEID** macro to the code in the OneArmedBandit.cpp file, as shown here:

```
BEGIN_PROPPAGEIDS(COneArmedBanditCtrl, 2)
    PROPPAGEID(COneArmedBanditPropPage::guid)
    PROPPAGEID(CLSID_CColorPropPage)
END_PROPPAGEIDS(COneArmedBanditCtrl)
```

Note that the second argument to the **BEGIN_PROPPAGEIDS** macro must be altered to match the number of property pages specified for the ActiveX control.

OnDraw() Function

Controls created with the MFC ActiveX ControlWizard are user-interface controls. This means that much of the control-specific implementation that you provide is drawing code. As with an MFC document/view application, all the drawing code for a control is placed within a single function named **OnDraw()**. The following is the default implementation generated by the ControlWizard:

```
void COneArmedBanditCtrl::OnDraw(
    CDC* pdc, const CRect& rcBounds, const CRect& rcInvalid)
{
    // TODO: Replace the following code with your own drawing code.
    pdc->FillRect(rcBounds,
    CBrush::FromHandle((HBRUSH)GetStockObject(WHITE_BRUSH)));
    pdc->Ellipse(rcBounds);

}
```

The **COleControl::OnDraw()** function receives a pointer to an MFC device context object, and a rectangle that represents the control's on-screen area, specified in logical units. You should avoid using fixed values in your drawing code, and you should scale all drawing output to the dimensions of the bounding rectangle. In this way, you ensure that the entire control is always visible and that its internal proportions are always maintained. The **OnDraw()** function also receives a rectangle that represents the invalidated area of the control and can be used to optimize your drawing code.

► **To implement the COneArmedBanditCtrl::OnDraw() function**

Replace the code in your project with the following code:

(This code can be found in CH11_01.cpp, installed from the companion CD.)

```cpp
void COneArmedBanditCtrl::OnDraw(
    CDC* pdc, const CRect& rcBounds, const CRect& rcInvalid)
{
    // Get colors of stock properties
    COLORREF colorBack = TranslateColor(GetBackColor());
    COLORREF colorFore = TranslateColor(GetForeColor());

    // Get dimensions of control
    float ctrlWidth = float(rcBounds.Width());
    float ctrlHeight = float(rcBounds.Height());

    // Setup DC
    CBrush brush(colorBack);
    CBrush * pOldBrush = pdc->SelectObject(&brush);

    CPen pen(PS_SOLID, 3, colorFore);
    CPen *pOldPen = pdc->SelectObject(&pen);

    CFont SymbolFont;
    CFont *pOldFont;

    if(SymbolFont.
        CreateFont(long(ctrlHeight / 1.1), long(ctrlWidth/6),
        0, 0, 0, 0, 0, 0, SYMBOL_CHARSET, 0, 0, 0,
        0,"WingDings"));

        pOldFont = pdc->SelectObject(&SymbolFont);
    else
        pOldFont = SelectStockFont(pdc);

    // Draw bounding rectangle
    pdc->Rectangle(rcBounds);
    pdc->SetBkMode(TRANSPARENT);
```

```
// Draw text
pdc->SetTextColor(colorFore);
RECT rect;
::CopyRect(&rect, rcBounds);
CString strDisplay;
strDisplay.Format("%c %c %c",
    m_symbols[0], m_symbols[1], m_symbols[2]);

pdc->DrawText(strDisplay, &rect, DT_SINGLELINE | DT_CENTER
    | DT_VCENTER );

// Draw vertical bars
long onethird = long(ctrlWidth / 3);
CPoint ptTop(rcBounds.TopLeft());
CPoint ptBtm(rcBounds.left, rcBounds.bottom);

ptTop.x += onethird; ptBtm.x += onethird;
pdc->MoveTo(ptTop);
pdc->LineTo(ptBtm);

ptTop.x += onethird; ptBtm.x += onethird;
pdc->MoveTo(ptTop);
pdc->LineTo(ptBtm);

// Restore device context
pdc->SelectObject(pOldFont);
pdc->SelectObject(pOldPen);
pdc->SelectObject(pOldBrush);
}
```

This function simulates the slot machine window by displaying three characters
from the Wingdings symbol font, as shown in Figure 11.1. The characters themselves are contained in the fixed-length string **m_symbols**, which is a member
variable of the **COneArmedBanditCtrl** class. You will need to add this member
before your code will compile.

▶   **To implement the COneArmedBanditCtrl::m_symbols string**

1. In ClassWizard, right-click the **COneArmedBanditCtrl** class. Click **Add
   Member Variable**. Create the following protected member variable:

   ```
   TCHAR m_symbols[3];
   ```

2. Locate the **COneArmedBanditCtrl** constructor and add the following line to
   initalize the string:

   ```
   _tcscpy(m_symbols, _T("JJJ"));
   ```

Implementing the Control Method

All that remains is to implement the **Play()** method that simulates the spinning of the slot machine reels, displaying a random symbol in each window. You created a stub for the **Play()** implementation function when you added the method to the interface. Now you need to add code to randomly alter each of the characters in the **COneArmedBanditCtrl::m_symbols** string.

▶ **To implement the COneArmedBanditCtrl::Play() function**

1. Locate the **Play()** function stub and then replace the stub with the code that follows:

   (This code can be found in CH11_02.cpp, installed from the companion CD.)

```
void COneArmedBanditCtrl::Play()
{
    srand((unsigned)time(NULL));

    _tcscpy(m_symbols, _T("JJJ"));

    for(int i = 0; i < 3; i++)
        m_symbols[i] += UINT(rand() % m_numberOfSymbols);

    InvalidateControl(); // repaints control

    if(m_symbols[0] == m_symbols[1] &&
        m_symbols[1] == m_symbols[2])
        FireJackpot();

}
```

The use of the modulus operator (%) ensures that each character in the m_symbols string is incremented by a random number between zero and *m_numberOfSymbols*. When all three characters are the same, the **Jackpot** custom event is fired.

2. Press F7 to build the OneArmedBandit ActiveX control. The compiler and linker create a DLL with an .ocx extension in your output directory. If the build is successful, the control is registered on your computer.

Testing the Control

The ActiveX Control Test Container is a useful tool provided by Visual Studio that allows you to run and test any ActiveX control registered on your computer. In the following exercises, you will learn how to use the ActiveX Control Test Container to test the property pages, the events, and the **Play()** method of the OneArmedBandit ActiveX control.

▶ **To test the OneArmedBandit ActiveX control**

1. On the **Tools** menu in Visual C++, click **ActiveX Control Test Container**. On the Test Container's **Edit** menu, click **Insert New Control**.

2. In the **Insert Control** dialog box, click **OneArmedBandit Control** and then click **OK**.

3. Using the resize handles around the edge of the control, make the control a suitable size.

4. On the **Edit** menu, simply click **Properties**. On the **General** tab of the **OneArmedBandit Control Properties** dialog box, change the **Number of symbols** property to **5**.

5. Click the **Colors** tab and choose **BackColor** and **ForeColor** values for the control.

6. Click **OK**, and then check that the control displays the correct colors.

7. Click inside the control area and verify that the **Click** event is notified in the lower half of the Test Container window.

8. On the **Control** menu, click **Invoke Methods**. If necessary, move the **Invoke Methods** dialog box so that you can see the entire control and the output in the lower half of the Test Container window.

9. With **Play (Method)** selected in the **Method Name** drop-down list, click **Invoke** to play the one-armed bandit game. Keep playing until you get three symbols that are the same. When this happens, you should see the **Jackpot** event notified in the lower half of the Test Container window.

▶ **To test property persistence**

1. Close the ActiveX Control Test Container. When prompted, save the session as **oab.tcs**.

2. Re-open the ActiveX Control Test Container. On the **File** menu, simply click **oab.tcs** from the recently used file list. The OneArmedBandit control should display with the size and colors saved from the previous session. (The **COleControl** class implements the serialization of the control dimensions, without requiring any coding on your part).

3. Click the control border to select the control. View the control properties to check that the **NumberOfSymbols** property is still set to **5**.

4. Close the ActiveX Control Test Container.

Lesson Summary

In this lesson, you have seen just how easy it is to develop ActiveX controls using MFC. The ActiveX ControlWizard creates a set of classes that implement a DLL, a control and a property page. The ControlWizard defines dispatch interfaces for your control's properties, methods, and events. You use ClassWizard to design these interfaces. An MFC ActiveX control is based on the **COleControl** class, which provides many member functions that allow you to implement stock properties and events, retrieve ambient properties from the container, implement property persistence, and connect a control's properties to a property page. Apart from the implementations of the custom methods, most of the code that you need to write for your control is drawing code, placed within the control's **OnDraw()** function.

Lesson 2: Creating ActiveX Controls with ATL

In this lesson, you will re-implement the OneArmedBandit ActiveX control using ATL. By doing this, you will be able to compare the differences between MFC and ATL control development techniques and assess which technology is most suited to your needs.

After this lesson, you will be able to:

- Describe how to develop ActiveX controls using ATL.
- Describe how to add properties and methods to your control.
- Describe how to implement a control property page and make properties persistent.
- Describe how to use ATL's implementation of the COM connection point architecture to add events to your control.

Estimated lesson time: 50 minutes

Adding Controls to an ATL COM Project

As with any ATL COM development, you start by creating an ATL project and then add individual COM objects using the ATL Object Wizard. In the following exercises, you will create a DLL project to host your control, and then you'll add your ATL ActiveX control.

▶ **To create the OneArmedBanditATL project**

1. On the **File** menu, click **New**. On the **Projects** tab, click **ATL COM AppWizard**.
2. In the **Project name** box, type **OneArmedBanditATL** and click **OK**.
3. In the **ATL COM AppWizard** dialog box, ensure that **Dynamic Link Library (DLL)** is selected and click **Finish**.
4. Review the **New Project Information** dialog box and click **OK**.

▶ **To add the ATLBandit ActiveX control**

1. On the **Insert** menu, click **New ATL Object**.
2. In the **Category** list, click **Controls**. The **ATL Object Wizard** should appear as shown in Figure 11.5 on the facing page.

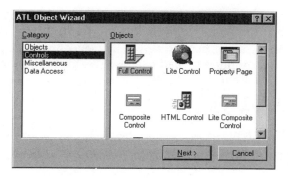

Figure 11.5   ATL Object Wizard control options

The ATL Object Wizard displays a number of different types of controls that you can create, including:

- **Full controls** Controls that can be embedded in any container that complies with ActiveX guidelines.

- **Lite controls** Controls that can be embedded in Internet Explorer, but that do not support interfaces required by many other containers.

- **Composite controls** Controls such as dialog boxes that are capable of containing other ActiveX controls.

- **HTML controls** Controls that use an embedded Web-browser control to display an HTML page. You'll learn more about these in Chapter 12.

3. In the **Objects** list, click **Full Control**. Click **Next**.
4. Click the **Names** tab. In the **Short Name** box, type **ATLBandit**.
5. On the **Attributes** tab, select the **Support Connection Points** option.
6. On the **Stock Properties** tab, use the **>** button to move the **Background Color** and the **Foreground Color** stock properties from the **Not Supported** list to the **Supported** list, as shown in Figure 11.6.

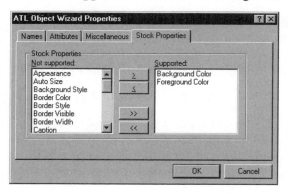

Figure 11.6   Selecting stock properties in the ATL Object Wizard

7. Click **OK** to add the **ATLBandit** ActiveX control to the project.

In ClassView, you see that the wizard has added the **IATLBandit** interface and the **CATLBandit** implementation class. The **CATLBandit** class is derived from the ATL **CComControl** class (as well as many others). Open the ATLBandit.h file and locate the COM map structure. You see that the **CATLBandit** class supports the many interfaces that are required by ActiveX control containers.

Directly beneath the COM map, you will see this property map structure:

```
BEGIN_PROP_MAP(CATLBandit)
    PROP_DATA_ENTRY("_cx", m_sizeExtent.cx, VT_UI4)
    PROP_DATA_ENTRY("_cy", m_sizeExtent.cy, VT_UI4)
    PROP_ENTRY("BackColor", DISPID_BACKCOLOR, CLSID_StockColorPage)
    PROP_ENTRY("ForeColor", DISPID_FORECOLOR, CLSID_StockColorPage)
    // Example entries
    // PROP_ENTRY("Property Description", dispid, clsid)
    // PROP_PAGE(CLSID_StockColorPage)
END_PROP_MAP()
```

ATL creates the property map structure to make implementing property persistence easy. You can see in the code just shown that entries for the stock properties, including the dimensions of the control, have already been added to the property map. Note that the **PROP_ENTRY** macros allow you to associate a property page with a property, and that the color stock property page has already been specified for your **ForeColor** and **BackColor** properties.

Adding Properties

You will now add the **NumberOfSymbols** custom property to the control class.

▶ **To add the NumberOfSymbols property**

1. In ClassView, right-click the **IATLBandit** interface item. Click **Add Property**.

2. In the **Add Property To Interface** dialog box, select **short** for the property type. In the **Property Name** box, enter **NumberOfSymbols**.

3. Click **OK** to create the functions that implement the property.

Remember that when you are working with ATL, you must define a member variable to hold the data and provide implementations of the **Get** and **Put** functions so that you can pass data to and from this member variable.

▶   **To implement the NumberOfSymbols property**

1. Add a protected member variable named **m_numberOfSymbols** of type **short** to the **CATLBandit** class.

2. In ClassView, expand the **IATLBandit** interface under the **CATLBandit** class item to locate the **get_NumberOfSymbols()** and **put_NumberOfSymbols()** functions. Implement these functions as shown in the following code:

```
STDMETHODIMP CATLBandit::get_NumberOfSymbols(short *pVal)
{
    *pVal = m_numberOfSymbols;

    return S_OK;
}

STDMETHODIMP CATLBandit::put_NumberOfSymbols(short newVal)
{
    newVal = newVal < 3 ? 3 : newVal;
    newVal = newVal > 7 ? 7 : newVal;

    m_numberOfSymbols = newVal;
    SetDirty(TRUE);

    return S_OK;
}
```

You should note that the **put_ NumberOfSymbols()** function ensures that the **NumberOfSymbols** property is set to a valid value. Note also the call to the **SetDirty()** function. This function should be called when the value of a persistent property is changed, so that the container can ask the user whether to save or abandon changes to the control's state. You will implement persistence for the **NumberOfSymbols** property after you have added a property page that allows access to the property value.

Adding Events

You will now implement the **Click** and **Jackpot** events for your control. To help you understand how COM events are implemented, open the project IDL file, OneArmedBanditATL.idl, and look at the type library definition, which is shown on the following page.

```
[
    uuid(39623002-6FAA-11D3-935D-0080C7FA0C3E),
    version(1.0),
    helpstring("OneArmedBanditATL 1.0 Type Library")
]
library ONEARMEDBANDITATLLib
{
    importlib("stdole32.tlb");
    importlib("stdole2.tlb");

    [
        uuid(39623010-6FAA-11D3-935D-0080C7FA0C3E),
        helpstring("_IATLBanditEvents Interface")
    ]
    dispinterface _IATLBanditEvents
    {
        properties:
        methods:
    };

    [
        uuid(3962300F-6FAA-11D3-935D-0080C7FA0C3E),
        helpstring("ATLBandit Class")
    ]
    coclass ATLBandit
    {
        [default] interface IATLBandit;
        [default, source] dispinterface _IATLBanditEvents;
    };
};
```

The definition of the ONEARMEDBANDITATLLib type library contains the
definition of a dispatch interface named **_IATLBanditEvents**. This interface
is declared inside the **ATLBandit** coclass block—indicating that the ATLBandit
control exposes the **_IATLBanditEvents** interface. Notice, however, that the interface is declared with the *[source]* IDL attribute, which indicates that the
_IATLBanditEvents interface is a source of events. This kind of interface is
known as a *connection point*. COM objects that expose connection points implement the **IConnectionPointContainer** interface, which manages the connection
of source interfaces to a corresponding client object known as a *sink*. A sink object implements methods defined by the source object. Through the connection
point mechanism, a pointer to the sink object's interface is passed to the source
object. This pointer provides the source with access to the sink's implementation
of its methods. To fire an event, the source object calls the corresponding
method on the sink interface.

The first stage of defining an event is to add a method to the source interface to
represent the event.

► **To add the Click() and Jackpot() event methods**

1. In ClassView, right-click the **_IATLBanditEvents** interface item. Click **Add Method** on the shortcut menu.

2. Select **void** as the return type. Enter **Click** as the method name.

3. Repeat the process to create a **void** method with the name **Jackpot**.

After you have added the event methods to the source interface, you use an ATL Wizard to implement a connection point. ATL uses information from the type library to achieve this implementation, which means that the type library must first be compiled.

► **To compile the type library**

1. Switch to FileView and locate the OneArmedBanditATL.idl file.

2. Right-click **OneArmedBanditATL.idl** and then click **Compile OneArmedBanditATL.idl**.

3. When the compile is completed, switch back to ClassView.

Now you can use the ATL Wizard to implement the connection point.

► **To implement a connection point for the ATLBandit control**

1. Right-click the **CATLBandit** class item and then click **Implement Connection Point**. The Implement Connection Point Wizard displays as shown in Figure 11.7.

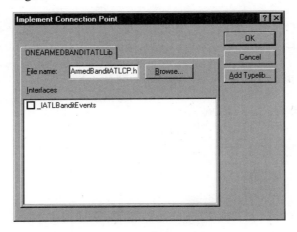

Figure 11.7   The Implement Connection Point Wizard

2. In the Implement Connection Point Wizard, select the **_IATLBanditEvents** checkbox and click **OK**.

The wizard creates a *proxy class* (nothing to do with the proxy objects used in marshaling), which contains proxy functions that implement the event methods you added to your event interface. If you look in ClassView, you will see that the **CProxy_IATLBanditEvents** class has been added to your project, and that it provides the functions **Fire_Click()** and **Fire_Jackpot()** that you use to fire control events. ATL alters the definition of the **CATLBandit** class so that it derives from the **CProxy_IATLBanditEvents class**, making the **Fire_Click()** and **Fire_Jackpot()** methods accessible as members of your control class.

The Implement Connection Point Wizard also creates the following connection point map within your class.

```
BEGIN_CONNECTION_POINT_MAP(CATLBandit)
    CONNECTION_POINT_ENTRY(IID_IPropertyNotifySink)
    CONNECTION_POINT_ENTRY(DIID__IATLBanditEvents)
END_CONNECTION_POINT_MAP()
```

Make sure that the connection point map appears exactly as just shown—ATL sometimes fails to implement this map correctly, causing compilation errors.

You are now in a position to use the event proxy functions to fire events from your control. To demonstrate this, you will implement a handler function that fires a **Click()** event when you click inside the control.

▶ **To implement the OnLButtonDown() handler function**

1. In ClassView, right-click the **CATLBandit** class item. On the shortcut menu, click **Add Windows Message Handler**.
2. In the **New Windows messages/events** list, click **WM_LBUTTONDOWN**.
3. Click **Add and Edit** to add the **OnLButtonDown()** function and jump to the implementation code, which is declared inline in the **CATLBandit** class definition. Note that ATL maintains its own kind of message map, which is located just below the connection point map.
4. Replace the //TODO comment inside the **OnLButtonDown()** function implementation with the following single line of code:

```
Fire_Click();
```

Adding Methods

You will now add the **Play()** method to the control interface and provide the code to implement the method.

▶ **To add the Play() method**

1. In ClassView, right-click the **IATLBandit** interface. Click **Add Method** on the shortcut menu.

2. In the **Add Method to Interface** dialog box, type **Play** in the **Method Name** box.

3. Click **OK** to create the method.

► **To implement the Play() method**

1. As you did with the MFC OneArmedBandit control in Lesson 1, add the following protected member variable to the **CATLBandit** class:

```
TCHAR m_symbols[3];
```

To the CATLBandit constructor, add the following line to initialize the string:

```
_tcscpy(m_symbols, _T("JJJ"));
```

2. In ClassView, expand the **IATLBandit** interface beneath the **CATLBandit** class item.

3. Double-click the **Play()** method underneath the **IATLBandit** interface item to edit the **CATLBandit::Play()** implementation function.

4. Add code to the body of the **CATLBandit::Play()** function so that it appears as follows:

(This code can be found in CH11_03.cpp, installed from the companion CD.)

```
STDMETHODIMP CATLBandit::Play()
{
    srand((unsigned)time(NULL));

    _tcscpy(m_symbols, _T("JJJ"));

    for(int i = 0; i < 3; i++)
        m_symbols[i] += UINT(rand() % m_numberOfSymbols);

    // repaint control
    m_spInPlaceSite->InvalidateRect(NULL, TRUE);

    if(m_symbols[0] == m_symbols[1] &&
        m_symbols[1] == m_symbols[2])
        Fire_Jackpot();

    return S_OK;
}
```

5. To the top of the ATLBandit.cpp file, add the following line:

```
#include <time.h>
```

Creating Property Pages

You will now implement the **Symbols** property page, which will enable users to set the value of the **NumberOfSymbols** custom property. ATL sets up each page of a control's property sheet as a separate object, implemented by a class derived from **IPropertyPage**. In the following exercise, you will insert a new property page class into your project.

▶ **To add the Symbols property page**

1. On the **Insert** menu, click **New ATL Object**. In the **Category** list, click **Controls**.

2. In the **Objects** list, click **Property Page**. Click **Next**.

3. Click the **Names** tab. In the **Short Name** box, type **BanditPP**.

4. On the **Strings** tab, type **Symbols** in the **Title** box. Delete the text in the other two boxes.

5. Click **OK** to add the property page. A dialog template for the page opens in the dialog editor.

6. Create the dialog template just as you did for the MFC control (refer back to Figure 11.4). Add a static text control and a numeric edit control with the ID **IDC_NUMSYMBOLS**.

If you switch back to ClassView, you will see that the **CBanditPP** class has been added to the project. The ATL Object Wizard has provided an implementation of the **IPropertyPageImpl::Apply()** function for this class. **Apply()** is executed when the user of the property page clicks the **OK** or **Apply** button. You will add code to provide an implementation of this function.

▶ **To implement the CBanditPP::Apply() function**

Locate the **CBanditPP::Apply()** function in the BanditPP.h file. Replace the example code with the following implementation:

```
STDMETHOD(Apply)(void)
{
    CComQIPtr<IATLBandit> pIBandit(m_ppUnk[0]);

    pIBandit->put_NumberOfSymbols(GetDlgItemInt(IDC_NUMSYMBOLS));

    m_bDirty = FALSE;
    return S_OK;
}
```

This function sets the control's **NumberOfProperties** property with the integer value retrieved from the edit control. Notice the use of the ATL smart pointer class **CComQIPtr** to retrieve an **IATLBandit** pointer. The member variable m_ppUnk is an array of **IUnknown** pointers to the objects associated with the property page.

The **Apply()** function stores the value in the edit control to the persistent **IATLBandit::NumberOfSymbols** property. You will also need to create a function to initialize the edit control with the property value. This function is essentially the **Apply()** function in reverse.

▶ **To implement the CBanditPP::OnInitDialog() function**

1. In ClassWizard, right-click the **CBanditPP** class item. Click **Add Windows Message Handler** on the shortcut menu.
2. In the **New Windows messages/events** list, click the **WM_INITDIALOG** message.
3. Click **Add and Edit** to add the **OnInitDialog()** function and jump to the implementation code.
4. Implement the function as shown in the following code:

```
LRESULT OnInitDialog(UINT uMsg, WPARAM wParam, LPARAM lParam,
    BOOL& bHandled)
{
    CComQIPtr<IATLBandit> pIBandit(m_ppUnk[0]);

    short i = 0;
    pIBandit->get_NumberOfSymbols(&i);
    SetDlgItemInt(IDC_NUMSYMBOLS, i);
    return 0;
}
```

At this point, you should also add a notification function to indicate that the property page has been modified. This function should handle the **EN_CHANGE** event that fires when the user changes the value in the edit control.

▶ **To implement the CBanditPP::OnChangeNumsymbols() function**

1. In ClassWizard, right-click the **CBanditPP** class item. Click **Add Windows Message Handler** on the shortcut menu.
2. In the **Class or object to handle** list, click the **IDC_NUMSYMBOLS** object.
3. In the **New Windows messages/events** list, click the **EN_CHANGE** event.
4. Click **Add and Edit** and then click **OK** to add the **OnChangeNumsymbols()** function and jump to the implementation code.
5. Replace the //TODO comment with the following line of code:

```
SetDirty(TRUE);
```

Now that you have fully implemented the property page, you can add an entry to the control class property map to make the **NumberOfSymbols** property persistent.

▶ **To make the NumberOfSymbols property persistent**

1. Locate the property map in the ATLBandit.h file.

2. Add a new entry for the **NumberOfSymbols** property so that the property map appears as follows:

```
BEGIN_PROP_MAP(CATLBandit)
    PROP_DATA_ENTRY("_cx", m_sizeExtent.cx, VT_UI4)
    PROP_DATA_ENTRY("_cy", m_sizeExtent.cy, VT_UI4)
    PROP_ENTRY("NumberOfSymbols", 1, CLSID_BanditPP)
    PROP_ENTRY("BackColor", DISPID_BACKCOLOR, CLSID_StockColorPage)
    PROP_ENTRY("ForeColor", DISPID_FORECOLOR, CLSID_StockColorPage)
END_PROP_MAP()
```

The second parameter to the **PROP_ENTRY** macro is the *DISPID*, which can be found in the IDL file. The **CLSID_BanditPP** constant is defined in the OneArmedBanditATL_i.c file.

Drawing the Control

All that remains is to implement the drawing code. Like the MFC **COleControl** class, the **CComControl** class provides an **OnDraw()** function to contain all the drawing code. The **CComControl::OnDraw()** function receives a reference to an **ATL_DRAWINFO** structure that contains, among other things, a handle to a device context and a pointer to a **RECT** structure that denotes the bounding rectangle of the control. The device context is an **HDC**, the raw Windows data type that is wrapped by the MFC class **CDC**. This means that you have to use the GDI API functions to render your control. The GDI functions are similar to their **CDC** counterparts, the main difference being that they receive the **HDC** as the first argument. If you compare the implementation of **CATLBandit::OnDraw()** with the **COneArmedBanditCtrl::OnDraw()** function in the previous lesson, you will get a pretty good idea of how it all works.

▶ **To implement the CATLBandit::OnDraw() function**

Replace the function in ATLBandit.h with the following version:

(This code can be found in CH11_04.cpp, installed from the companion CD.)

```
HRESULT OnDraw(ATL_DRAWINFO& di)
{
    const RECT& rc = *reinterpret_cast<const RECT*>(di.prcBounds);
    HDC dc = di.hdcDraw;
```

```
COLORREF colorBack, colorFore;
OleTranslateColor(m_clrForeColor, NULL, &colorFore);
OleTranslateColor(m_clrBackColor, NULL, &colorBack);

// Get dimensions of control
float ctrlWidth = float(rc.right - rc.left);
float ctrlHeight = float(rc.bottom - rc.top);

// Set up DC
HBRUSH brush = CreateSolidBrush(colorBack);
HBRUSH oldBrush = static_cast<HBRUSH>(SelectObject(dc, brush));

HPEN pen = CreatePen(PS_SOLID, 3, colorFore);
HPEN oldPen = static_cast<HPEN>(SelectObject(dc, pen));

HFONT SymbolFont = CreateFont(long(ctrlHeight / 1.1),
    long(ctrlWidth/6), 0, 0, 0, 0, 0, 0, SYMBOL_CHARSET, 0, 0, 0,
    0,"WingDings");

HFONT oldFont = static_cast<HFONT>(SelectObject(dc, SymbolFont));

// Draw bounding rectangle
Rectangle(dc, rc.left, rc.top, rc.right, rc.bottom);
SetBkMode(dc, TRANSPARENT);

// Draw text
SetTextColor(dc, colorFore);
RECT rect;
CopyRect(&rect, &rc);

TCHAR strDisplay[5];
_stprintf(strDisplay, "%c %c %c",
    m_symbols[0], m_symbols[1], m_symbols[2]);

DrawText(dc, strDisplay, 5, &rect, DT_SINGLELINE | DT_CENTER |
    DT_VCENTER );

// Draw vertical bars
long onethird = long(ctrlWidth / 3);
POINT ptTop = { rc.left, rc.top };
POINT ptBtm = { rc.left, rc.bottom };

ptTop.x += onethird; ptBtm.x += onethird;
MoveToEx(dc, ptTop.x, ptTop.y, NULL);
LineTo(dc, ptBtm.x, ptBtm.y);

ptTop.x += onethird; ptBtm.x += onethird;
MoveToEx(dc, ptTop.x, ptTop.y, NULL);
LineTo(dc, ptBtm.x, ptBtm.y);
```

```
// Restore device context
SelectObject(dc, oldFont);
SelectObject(dc, oldPen);
SelectObject(dc, oldBrush);

DeleteObject(brush);
DeleteObject(pen);
DeleteObject(SymbolFont);

return S_OK;
}
```

You can now build the **ATLBandit** control. Load the control into the ActiveX Control Test Container to test the control display, the property pages, the property persistence, the **Play**() method, and the **Click** and **Jackpot** events.

MFC or ATL?

By now you should have a good idea of the differences between MFC and ATL ActiveX control development. MFC makes it very easy to develop controls, shielding you from most of the complexities of COM programming. Although developing controls with ATL involves more work, as your COM expertise develops you might come to appreciate the greater degree of control that ATL affords.

ActiveX controls written in ATL are smaller than their MFC counterparts, and if written properly will perform better. A self-contained (MinDependency) build of the ATLBandit project results in a control that is 100 KB in size. The OneArmedBandit.ocx, when statically linked to the MFC libraries, is about 264 KB. When the component is dynamically linked to the MFC libraries, its size drops to about 36 KB, making MFC an attractive proposition when developing for target platforms where you can expect the MFC DLLs to be installed.

Lesson Summary

ATL can be used to create small, high-performance ActiveX controls that are suitable for use in any ActiveX control container. In ATL, ActiveX controls are implemented by a class that inherits from the **CComControl** class. ActiveX controls also implement the many COM interfaces that are required by ActiveX control containers. ATL control classes implement a property map structure to implement property persistence, a message map to handle Windows messages, and COM connection points to implement ActiveX events. You can insert a property page COM object into your project to implement a property page for your control. You draw your control using GDI API functions inside the **CComControl::OnDraw**() function.

Lab 11: Using an ActiveX Control in an Application

In Lab 7, you saw how the STUpload application uses two ActiveX controls—the Microsoft ADO Data Control and the Microsoft DataGrid Control—as part of its user interface. You are not going to implement any additional ActiveX controls for the STUpload application. Instead, you will learn how to use the OneArmedBandit control that you created in this chapter as part of a Windows application. This application, named VirtualSlot, is shown in Figure 11.8.

Figure 11.8   The VirtualSlot application

This application calls the **Play()** method exposed by the OneArmedBandit control, and handles the **Jackpot** event. While designing the application, you will use the property page to set the number of symbols displayed and the control colors.

If you have not completed the exercises in this chapter, you can use the OneArmedBandit control located in the Chapter 11\Lab folder. Take the following steps to register this control on your computer:

1. Copy the OneArmedBandit.ocx file to a suitable location on your hard drive.

2. From the **Start** menu, open a command prompt and change to the directory that contains the OneArmedBandit.ocx file.

3. Enter the following command to register the control on your computer:

```
regsvr32 onearmedbandit.ocx
```

You are now ready to create the VirtualSlot application.

▶ **To create the VirtualSlot project**

1. In Visual C++, choose **New** from the **File** menu.

2. Select the **MFC AppWizard (exe)** to create a new project named **VirtualSlot**. Click **OK**.

3. In Step 1 of the AppWizard, click **Dialog Based** and then click **Finish**.

4. Click **OK** to confirm the selection.

The IDD_VIRTUALSLOT_DIALOG dialog template appears in the dialog editor. You will modify this to create the VirtualSlot application interface, which will consist of an instance of the OneArmedBandit control, a **Play** button, and a **Close** button.

▶ **To modify the IDD_VIRTUALSLOT_DIALOG dialog template**

1. Delete the //TODO static text.
2. Change the **OK** button caption to **Close**. Assign a new ID, **ID_PLAY**, to the **Cancel** button and change the caption to **Play**.
3. Rearrange the buttons as shown in Figure 11.8.

▶ **To insert the OneArmedBandit control into the project**

1. On the **Project** menu, click **Add to Project**, and then click **Components and Controls**.
2. In the Components and Controls Gallery, double-click the **Registered ActiveX Controls** folder to display all ActiveX controls registered on your system.
3. Click the OneArmedBandit Control, and then click **Insert**.
4. Click **OK** to insert the component. Click **OK** to confirm that you want to generate the **COneArmedBandit** class for the control.
5. Click **Close** to close the Components and Controls Gallery.

Note that the generic **OCX** icon for the OneArmedBandit control is placed on the **Controls** toolbar. The MFC OneArmedBandit project you created in this chapter contained a bitmap resource **IDB_ONEARMEDBANDIT** that you could have modified to create a distinctive toolbar button.

In ClassView, you see the **COneArmedBandit** class that has been created by the Components and Controls Gallery. This class contains wrapper functions that provide access to your control properties and methods. The **Create()** function allows you to dynamically create an instance of the control (within a **CView** object for example).

▶ **To place an instance of the COneArmedBandit control**

1. Click the **OneArmedBandit** button on the **Controls** toolbar and place the control on the dialog box. Resize the control and the dialog box so that they appear as shown in Figure 11.8.
2. With the OneArmedBandit control selected, press ENTER to edit the control properties. Your familiar property pages will appear, along with the **General** and **All** pages that are implemented by the container.

3. On the **Control** page, change the **Number of Symbols** to **7**.

4. On the **Colors** page, select colors for your **ForeColor** and **BackColor** properties.

You will now modify the **CVirtualSlotDlg** dialog class to implement the **Play** button and handle the **Jackpot** event.

▶ **To implement the Play button**

1. Press CTRL+W to open ClassWizard. On the **Member Variables** tab, click the **IDC_ONEARMEDBANDIT1** control ID. Click **Add Variable** to create a **Control** member variable of type **COneArmedBandit**, named **m_bandit**.

2. On the **Message Maps** page, click the **ID_PLAY** object ID. Add a handler for the BN_CLICKED message named **OnPlay()**.

3. Click **Edit Code**. In the **OnPlay()** function implementation, replace the //TODO comment with the following line of code:

```
m_bandit.Play();
```

▶ **To handle the Jackpot event**

1. On the **Message Maps** tab of ClassWizard, simply click the **IDC_ ONEARMEDBANDIT1** control ID.

2. Click the **Jackpot** message, and then click **Add Function** to create the **OnJackpotOnearmedbanditctrl1()** function.

3. Click **Edit Code**. In the function implementation, replace the //TODO comment with the following line of code:

```
AfxMessageBox("Jackpot!");
```

4. You can now build and run the VirtualSlot application. Click the **Play** button to spin the one-armed bandit. Keep playing until you hit the jackpot!

Review

1. How do you implement property persistence for an MFC ActiveX control?

2. What is the purpose of the DDP functions, and where are they used?

3. What is a connection point?

4. How does an object derived from **CComControl** handle Windows messages?

5. What situations are best suited to using MFC to implement your ActiveX control?

CHAPTER 12

Internet Programming

About This Chapter

This chapter introduces you to some of the features of Microsoft Visual C++ 6.0 that allow you to create Internet-based applications. You will learn how to use Dynamic HTML (DHTML) to create application user interfaces, and how to add Web browsing capabilities to your applications and components. You will learn how you can develop an application that creates *ActiveX documents*—documents that can be hosted by Microsoft Internet Explorer—for viewing and editing over the Web. You will also learn how to create Internet Server API (ISAPI) DLLs that enhance the services provided by Microsoft's Web servers: Internet Information Server (IIS) and Personal Web Server (PWS).

Before You Begin

Before you start this chapter, you should have read Chapters 2 through 11, and completed the exercises in the text. You should have Internet Explorer 4.0 or higher installed on your system, and should have installed IIS 4.0 (if you are running Microsoft Windows NT Server) or PWS (on Windows NT Workstation or Microsoft Windows 95/98), as described in the *About This Book* section of the introduction.

Lesson 1: Working with Dynamic HTML

Hypertext Markup Language (HTML) is a system of marking up, or tagging, a document so that it can be published on the World Wide Web. Dynamic HTML (DHTML) is an extension of HTML supported by Internet Explorer 4.0 that exposes a Web page and all the elements on it as scriptable objects. In this lesson, you will learn how you can display HTML documents and work with the DHTML object model from within your Visual C++ applications.

After this lesson, you will be able to:

- Describe some of the benefits of using DHTML as an application user interface.
- Describe the DHTML object model and how you can access DHTML objects from within your code.
- Describe how to use the **DHTMLView** class to display HTML documents in an MFC application.
- Describe how to use the ATL HTML control to display HTML documents.
- Describe the function of DHTML scriptlets and how they can be incorporated into a Visual C++ application.

Estimated lesson time: 50 minutes

Review of the Internet, Intranets, and HTML

The Internet is a global, distributed network of computers that use the TCP/IP protocol. An intranet is also a network of computers operating on the TCP/IP protocol, but it is not global. Generally, an intranet is restricted to a particular set of users. An organization might run an intranet to provide information to employees only, and run a separate Internet site for the general public. Employees of the company can access both, but non-employees can access only the company's Internet site.

Note In this chapter, we will use the term Internet to include both the global network of computers and intranet networks.

Most people's experience of the Internet comes from browsing the *World Wide Web* (the Web). The Web is the portion of the Internet that uses the Hypertext Transfer Protocol (HTTP) to connect pages and resources in a way that lets you reach any page from any other page. If you are connected to the Internet, a Web browser like Internet Explorer lets you explore the Web to view pages on Web servers across the world.

The Web operates on a client/server model. The browser running on a desktop computer acts as the client, and a Web server acts as the server by providing the HTTP pages in response to a user's request.

Web pages viewed in a Web browser appear as a collection of text, pictures, sounds, digital movies; and as links to other Web pages. Web pages are created using HTML, which tags an ASCII document so that it includes formatting tags; references to graphics, sound, or animation files; and hyperlinks to Web pages or other resources.

Users of an intranet also use a Web browser to browse Web pages located on the company's Web servers. Additionally, users can use a Web browser to access resources or run applications on remote servers on your local area network (LAN), or on your desktop computer. You can use HTML to develop applications that present a rich and consistent interface and provide seamless access to resources on a desktop computer, on remote company servers, and on global Web servers.

HTML Documents

HTML defines a standard set of formatting tags that all Web browsers recognize. For example, this is the code for a simple HTML page:

```
<!-- MyPage.htm -->
<HTML>
<HEAD>
<TITLE>
A basic HTML Page
</TITLE>
</HEAD>
<BODY>
<H1> This is some text with H1
</H1>
<H3> This is some text with H3
</H3>
<P>Here is a new paragraph with normal text in
<B>Bold</B> and <I>Italic</I>
</P>
<P>Here is a <A HREF= "SecondPage.htm">
link to a local page </A>
</P>
</P>
<P>Here is a <A HREF= "http://www.microsoft.com/visualc/">
link to a page on the World Wide Web </A>
</P>
</BODY>
</HTML>
```

HTML formatting tags divide a document into discrete sections known as *elements*. The HTML document just shown is composed of two main elements enclosed by the <HEAD> and <BODY> tag pairs. The <HEAD> element contains header information that does not affect the rendering of the document, but might be of use to the browser. The <BODY> element specifies the content of the page that is displayed by the browser. Our example demonstrates some simple tags that define elements of the document. These tags specify whether text is to be displayed in one of the pre-defined heading formats such as <H1> or <H3>, or as bold or italic text. The <A> (anchor) element specifies a hypertext link.

Most of the HTML tags define attributes that are used to supply additional information about the element. In the example just shown, the elements defined within <A> tags contain *HREF* attributes, which are assigned strings that specify the link destination as a Uniform Resource Locator (URL) address. You can also assign the name of a local file to the HREF attribute by prefacing the path with "file:\\".

The MyPage.htm file can be found in the Chapter 12\Exercises folder that is installed from the companion CD. Double-click the MyPage.htm file so that it displays in Internet Explorer, as shown in Figure 12.1. You can experiment by following the link to the SecondPage.htm file and, if you have a live Internet connection, to the Visual C++ home page at www.microsoft.com/visualc/.

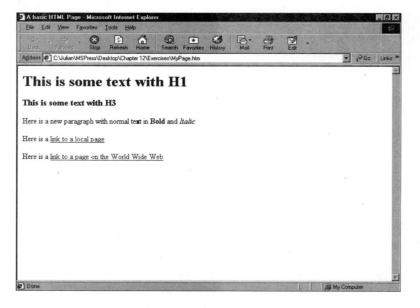

Figure 12.1   MyPage.htm, as displayed by Internet Explorer 5

Dynamic HTML

DHTML is an exciting technology that was introduced as part of Internet Explorer 4.0. Using DHTML, you can create dynamic, interactive Web pages, thereby presenting users of your Web site with the kind of user interface they have come to expect from desktop applications.

For example, with DHTML you can:

- Modify the text of your Web page.
- Modify elements of a style sheet that specify how text is displayed (the font or the text color, for example).
- Animate text and images on your Web page.
- Respond to user-initiated actions such as mouse movements or clicks.
- Validate user input to a form before it is submitted to a server.

DHTML achieves these effects by automatically reformatting and redisplaying the current document to show changes. It does not need to reload the document or load a new document, nor does it require a distant server to generate new content, as HTML would require. Instead, it uses the power of the user's computer to calculate and carry out changes. This means a user does not have to wait for text and data to complete potentially time-consuming round-trips to and from a server before seeing results.

Furthermore, DHTML does not require additional support from applications or embedded controls to carry out changes. Typically, DHTML documents are self-contained, using HTML styles to specify the format and appearance of the document; and using small blocks of script to process user input and directly manipulate the HTML tags, attributes, styles, and text in the document.

The HTML elements, attributes, and styles in DHTML are based on existing HTML specifications. Microsoft is working with the World Wide Web Consortium (W3C) toward a DHTML standard. Some of the dynamic and interactive features that you add to your documents might not be fully functional when viewed with a browser that does not support DHTML. However, by following some basic guidelines, you can ensure that the content of your document will still be viewable in other browsers.

DHTML Object Model

When Internet Explorer 4.0 (or later versions) loads an HTML page, it creates an internal representation of the page that is accessible through the DHTML object model.

Using the DHTML object model, you can access and manipulate virtually anything within a document. The HTML elements in the document are available as individual objects, which means you can examine and modify an element and its attributes by reading and setting properties and by calling methods. Elements of a document are contained in *collections*—similar to the MFC collections or the linked lists you use in C++ programming. You can iterate across a DHTML collection to gain access to the elements it contains.

Figure 12.2 shows several sub-objects of the document object. Most of these are collections, including the *all* collection that contains all of the document's HTML elements.

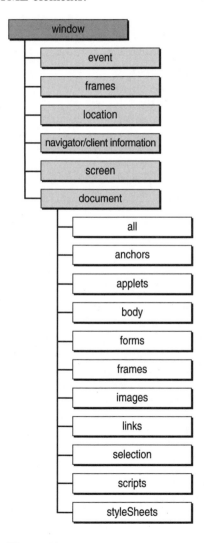

Figure 12.2   The DHTML object model

The object model also makes user actions, such as pressing a key or clicking the mouse, available as events. You can intercept and process these and other events by creating event handler functions and routines.

As an example, consider the following simple DHTML document:

```
<!-- MyDynPage.htm -->
<HTML>
<HEAD><TITLE>Welcome!</TITLE></HEAD>
<SCRIPT LANGUAGE="JavaScript">
function changeMe() {
    document.bgColor = "hotpink";
    MyHeading.style.color = "green";
    MyText.innerText = "Color effects courtesy of DHTML";
}
</SCRIPT>
<BODY onclick="changeMe()">
<H3 ID=MyHeading>Welcome to Dynamic HTML!</H3>
<P ID=MyText>Click anywhere in this document.</P>
</BODY>
</HTML>
```

This document changes the color of the background and heading font, and also changes a line of text when the user clicks the mouse in the document. You can test this behavior by viewing the page (Chapter 12\Exercises\MyDynPage.htm) in Internet Explorer.

Note that you can identify individual elements on a page by setting the ID attribute inside the element tag. In the example, the heading is named *MyHeading* and the paragraph is named *MyText*. You can use these IDs to access the page elements, and then write scripts to get and set the element properties. Scripts are defined with the <SCRIPT> tag.

In the example, notice that the JavaScript scripting language is used to define the **changeMe()** handler function, which is associated with the **onClick** event inside the document's <BODY> tag. The function sets the **bgColor** property of the **document** object's **body** object to change the document's background color. The function also changes the color of the heading by setting the **color** property of the **style** object of the **MyHeading** element. It replaces the text in the paragraph element by setting the **innerText** property of the **MyText** element.

Note The scripting examples in this chapter will use the JavaScript language. Because it is syntactically very similar to C++, it will probably be your scripting language of choice. Most browsers use JavaScript as their default language, but it is good practice to always specify the language used in the LANGUAGE attribute of the <SCRIPT> tag. In the MSDN documentation and in other books, you might see *JScript* used. JScript is Microsoft's version of JavaScript, and it includes some Internet Explorer-specific extensions.

It is not the intention of this book to give you more than a brief introduction to DHTML. If you would like to know more about DHTML, refer to one of the several books available on the subject, such as *Inside Dynamic HTML* by Scott Isaacs (Microsoft Press, 1997). This brief introduction to the capabilities of DHTML is intended to help you appreciate that HTML—a simple markup language used to render hypertext documents—is evolving into a powerful development tool capable of providing a dynamic, interactive user interface for applications.

Microsoft WebBrowser Control

To help you incorporate Web browser elements into your applications, Microsoft provides the WebBrowser ActiveX control. This control is the component of Internet Explorer that implements the Internet Explorer main window. The WebBrowser control supports Web browsing through hyperlinks and URL navigation and maintains a history list that allows the user to browse forward and backward through previously browsed sites, folders, and documents. The control also handles security and lists of "favorite" Web sites. The WebBrowser control is itself an ActiveX control container that can host any ActiveX control.

The following sections show you how you can use the MFC **CHtmlView** class (which encapsulates the WebBrowser control) to create a Web browser–style application that uses HTML as the primary interface. You will learn how to use ATL to create an ActiveX control that hosts the WebBrowser control.

You will also learn how you can access the DHTML object model from within your C++ code to access and manipulate elements of the HTML document displayed by your application or control.

MFC Web Browser-Style Applications

The Microsoft WebBrowser control is a standard ActiveX control, which means you can insert the control into your MFC project using the Components and Controls Gallery. Inserting the control will create the **CWebBrowser2** class, which wraps the **IWebBrowser2 Automation** interface exposed by the WebBrowser control. You can use the **CWebBrowser2** class to get and set properties and call methods using C++ types rather than Automation types.

However, the preferred method of creating a Web browser–style application is to use the MFC AppWizard and specify **CHtmlView** as the view class. The **CHtmlView** class is derived from **CView** and provides the functionality of the WebBrowser control within the context of MFC's document/view architecture. **CHtmlView** provides member functions to allow you to access the browser functionality from within your code.

Note that you must have installed Internet Explorer 4.0 (or a later version) before you can use the **CHtmlView** class or the WebBrowser control.

The following exercise shows you how to create a Web browser–style application using the MFC AppWizard.

▶ **To create the MyHtmlApp application**

1. On the **File** menu, click **New** to create a new **MFC AppWizard (exe)** project named **MyHtmlApp**.

2. In Step 1 of the MFC AppWizard, select the **Single document** option.

3. Select the default options for steps 2 through 5.

4. In Step 6, click **CHtmlView** in the **Base class** box. Click **Finish** and then click **OK** to create the project.

After the project is created, expand the **CMyHtmlAppView** class in ClassView. Double-click the **OnInitialUpdate** function to view the code. The code should be as follows:

```
void CMyHtmlAppView::OnInitialUpdate()
{
    CHtmlView::OnInitialUpdate();

    // TODO: This code navigates to a popular spot on the Web.
    // Change the code to go where you'd like.
    Navigate2(_T("http://www.microsoft.com/visualc/"),NULL,NULL);
}
```

The **OnInitialUpdate** function uses the **CHtmlView::Navigate2()** function to locate and display Microsoft's Visual C++ home page in the application main window. If you do not have a live Internet connection, you might want to alter the **Navigate2()** function call to make the application display the MyPage.htm file instead. Supposing that MyPage.htm file is located in the c:\DAVC\Chapter 12\Exercises folder, you might want to alter the line to be as follows:

```
Navigate2(_T("c:\\DAVC\\Chapter 12\\Exercises\\MyPage.htm") ,NULL,NULL);
```

Before you build and run the MyHtmlApp application, complete the following exercise to add **Forward** and **Back** navigation options.

▶ **To add navigation menu and toolbar options**

1. In ResourceView, open the **IDR_MAINFRAME** menu resource from the **Menu** folder.

2. Delete the **Edit** menu, and in its place add a new menu with the caption **&Go**.

3. Add two commands to this menu with the captions **&Back** and **&Forward**. Add suitable prompt strings for the options. Allow the editor to create the default IDs **ID_GO_BACK** and **ID_GO_FORWARD**.

4. Close the menu editor. Open the **IDR_MAINFRAME** toolbar resource. Delete the **Cut**, **Copy**, and **Paste** toolbar buttons by dragging them off the toolbar.

5. Create toolbar buttons for the **ID_GO_BACK** and **ID_GO_FORWARD** command IDs as shown in Figures 12.3 and 12.4.

Figure 12.3   The **ID_GO_BACK** toolbar button

Figure 12.4   The **ID_GO_FORWARD** toolbar button

6. Close the toolbar editor. Open ClassWizard and click the **Message Maps** tab.

7. To the **CMyHtmlAppView** class, add command handlers for the **ID_GO_BACK** and **ID_GO_FORWARD** command IDs, named **OnGoBack()** and **OnGoForward()**. Click **Edit Code** to locate the function implementations.

8. To each of the handler functions, add the corresponding **CHtmlView** navigation member function, as follows:

```
void CMyHtmlAppView::OnGoBack()
{
    GoBack();
}

void CMyHtmlAppView::OnGoForward()
{
    GoForward();
}
```

9. Build and run the application. Figure 12.5 on the facing page shows the MyHtmlApp application displaying the Microsoft Visual C++ home page, as specified by the default implementation of the **CMyHtmlAppView:: OnInitialUpdate()** function.

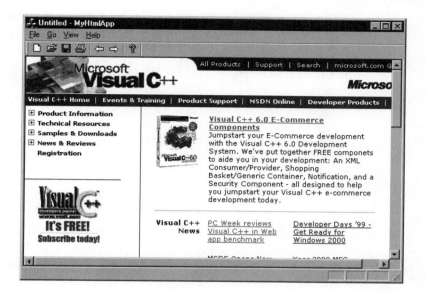

Figure 12.5   The MyHtmlApp application

Explore the browser features that are provided to your application by **CHtmlView**. Notice that the application status bar displays information about the hyperlinks, and about the progress of a page download operation. After you have moved to other pages using hyperlinks on the page, you can move through your history list by using the **Go Back** and **Go Forward** menu and toolbar options that you created.

Accessing the DHTML Object Model

You will remember that access to DHTML objects such as **window** or **document** is very easy when you are writing a piece of script in an HTML document. You can simply refer to objects by name, as shown in the following piece of JavaScript:

```
document.bgColor = "hotpink";
```

This ability is made possible by the fact that the Internet Explorer script interpreter is parsing your lines of script and converting them into calls to the Internet Explorer Automation interfaces. In C++, you access the DHTML object model by using the Automation interfaces directly.

The DHTML object model is exposed through a set of COM interfaces with the prefix IHTML (**IHTMLDocument**, **IHTMLWindow**, **IHTMLElement**, and so on). The **CHtmlView** class provides the **GetHtmlDocument()** function, which returns an **IDispatch** pointer of the HTML document that is currently displayed. You can call **QueryInterface()** on this **IDispatch** pointer to obtain pointers to the IHTML interfaces. After you have obtained pointers to these interfaces, you can use the properties and methods they provide to manipulate the document.

The following exercise demonstrates how you can access elements of an HTML page displayed in the MyHtmlApp application. You will write code to retrieve all of the anchor elements (links) in the current page, and display their HREF attribute values (URLs or file paths) in a dialog box. The user will be able to select a link to view in the browser.

▶ **To create the View Links dialog box**

1. Using the dialog editor, create the **View Links** dialog box as illustrated in Figure 12.6. This dialog box should be given the resource ID **IDD_LINK_DIALOG**, and it should contain a large list box control named **IDC_LINK_LIST** as well as the standard **OK** and **Cancel** buttons. The **OK** button should display the caption **Go to link**.

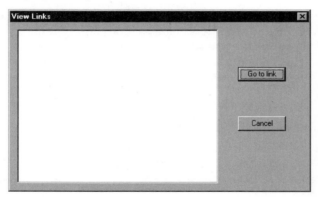

Figure 12.6   The **View Links** dialog box

2. From within the resource editor, press CTRL+W to create a dialog class named **CLinkDialog** for the **View Links** dialog box. On the **Member Variables** page of ClassWizard, add the variables listed in Table 12.1.

Table 12.1   Variables for the View Links Dialog Box

Resource ID	Category	Variable type	Variable name
IDC_LINK_LIST	Value	CString	m_strLink
IDC_LINK_LIST	Control	CListBox	m_lbLinkList

3. On the **Message Maps** tab of ClassWizard, create an overload of the **OnInitDialog()** function for the **CLinkDialog** class (to handle the WM_INITDIALOG message). Click **Edit Code** to locate the function implementation.

4. Replace the stub function with the following code, which can be found in the InitLnkDlg.cpp file in the Chapter 12\Exercises folder.

```cpp
BOOL CLinkDialog::OnInitDialog()
{
    CDialog::OnInitDialog();

    // Get pointer to view
    CFrameWnd * pFrame =
        dynamic_cast<CFrameWnd *>(AfxGetMainWnd());
    ASSERT_VALID(pFrame);

    CHtmlView * pHtmlView =
        dynamic_cast<CHtmlView *>(pFrame->GetActiveView());
    ASSERT_VALID(pHtmlView);

    // Get pointer to the document object dispatch interface
    IDispatch * pDisp = pHtmlView->GetHtmlDocument();

    if(pDisp != NULL)
    {
        // Get pointer to IHTMLDocument2 interface to
        // access document object's properties and methods
        IHTMLDocument2 * pHTMLDocument2;
        HRESULT hr;

        hr = pDisp->QueryInterface(IID_IHTMLDocument2,
            (void**)&pHTMLDocument2);

        if(hr == S_OK)
        {
            // Get pointer to the anchors collection
            IHTMLElementCollection * pColl = NULL;
            hr = pHTMLDocument2->get_anchors(&pColl);

            if(hr == S_OK && pColl != NULL)
            {
                LONG nElem;
                hr = pColl->get_length(&nElem);

                if(hr == S_OK)
                {
```

```
                        // Iterate across anchors collection
                        for(long i = 0; i < nElem; i++)
                        {
                            _variant_t vIndex(i);
                            _variant_t vName = vIndex;

                            IDispatch * pDisp2;

                            hr = pColl->item(
                                vName, vIndex, &pDisp2);
                            if(hr == S_OK)
                            {
                                // Retrieve pointer to each
                                // Anchor element so that you can
                                // retrieve the URL text and add
                                // it to the list box
                                IHTMLAnchorElement * pAnchElem;

                                hr = pDisp2->QueryInterface(
                                    IID_IHTMLAnchorElement,
                                    (void**) &pAnchElem);
                                if(hr == S_OK)
                                {
                                    BSTR bstrHref = 0;
                                    pAnchElem->get_href(&bstrHref);

                                    CString strLink(bstrHref);

                                    if(!strLink.IsEmpty())
                                        m_lbLinkList.AddString(strLink);

                                    SysFreeString(bstrHref);
                                    pAnchElem->Release();
                                }
                                pDisp2->Release();
                            }
                        }
                    }
                    pColl->Release();
                }
                pHTMLDocument2->Release();
            }
            pDisp->Release();
        }
        return TRUE; // return TRUE unless you set the focus to a control
            // EXCEPTION: OCX Property Pages should return FALSE
    }
```

Look through this function to understand how it really works. A pointer to the HTML document's dispatch interface is obtained by calling the **CHtmlView::GetHtmlDocument**() function. This pointer is used to obtain an **IHTMLDocument2** interface pointer, and the **IHTMLDocument2:: get_anchors**() function is called to get a pointer to the DHTML anchors collection. The **InitDialog**() function iterates across the *anchors* collection and, on each iteration, retrieves an **IHTMLAnchorElement** pointer to the current element. From this element, the value of the HREF attribute is obtained and inserted into the list box.

5. To the top of LinkDialog.cpp, along with the other #include statements, add the following lines:

```
#include <mshtml.h>
#include <comdef.h>
```

The mshtml.h file contains the definitions for the IHTML interfaces. Comdef.h contains the definition of the **_variant_t** COM helper class.

6. Create a new menu command with the caption **Links** under the **View** menu. This should have the default command ID **ID_VIEW_LINKS**. Using ClassWizard, create a command handler function for this ID in the **CMyHtmlAppView** class. This function should be named **OnViewLinks**.

7. To the body of the **CMyHtmlAppView::OnViewLinks**() function, add the following code:

```
CLinkDialog aDlg;
if(aDlg.DoModal() == IDOK)    // ("Go to link" button)
{
    // If a link was selected, go there!
    if(!aDlg.m_strLink.IsEmpty())
        Navigate2(aDlg.m_strLink, NULL, NULL);
}
```

8. To the top of the MyHtmlAppView.cpp file, with the other #include statements, add the following line:

```
#include "LinkDialog.h"
```

9. You can now build and run the application. Using the Web or the local HTML files, test to see that all of the links on a particular page are displayed in the dialog box when the **Links** option is selected from the **View** menu. Select a link from the list and click **Go to link** to check that you moved to the destination successfully. Figure 12.7 shows the **View Links** dialog box displaying all the URLs for links on the Microsoft Visual C++ home page.

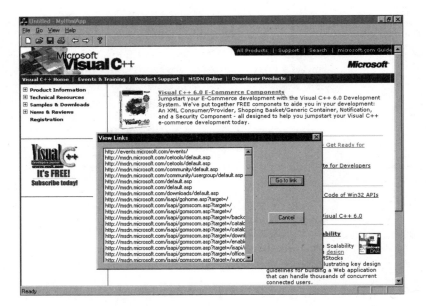

Figure 12.7   The **View Links** dialog box in action

Note You will find that URLs containing spaces, such as c:\DAVC\Chapter 12\
Exercises\MyPage.htm, will appear in the **View Links** dialog box with escape
sequences in place of the spaces. This is because Internet Explorer uses the
InternetCanonicalizeUrl() API function to convert the URLs into a safe format
for resolution. You can use the **InternetCanonicalizeUrl()** function to decode
the URLs for display purposes. See the Internet Explorer Platform SDK for
more information.

HTML Resources

You can include HTML pages as resources in your project, just as you can include bitmaps or dialog templates. HTML resources can be stored as .htm files
in your project's res subfolder, or defined inline in your project's resource script
(.rc) file. In either case, you edit the HTML resource using the Visual C++
editor. Because HTML resources are compiled into your program executable,
their use provides a safe and convenient way to distribute HTML pages used by
your application.

In the following exercise, you will include the MyPage.htm and SecondPage.htm files, which you saw earlier in this chapter, as resources in your application.

▶ **To add HTML resources to the MyHtmlApp project**

1. In ResourceView, right-click the top-level **MyHtmlApp Resources** folder. On the shortcut menu, click **Import**.

2. Using the **Import Resource** dialog box, click **HTML files (.htm; .html)** in the **Files of type** box. Locate the Chapter 12\Exercises\MyPage.htm file and click **Import**.

3. The HTML source opens in the editor window. Note the HTML-aware color syntax highlighting.

4. Right-click the **IDR_HTML1** resource that has been added and then click **Properties**.

5. Rename the resource **IDR_MYPAGE**. Note the **External file** check box, which allows you to specify whether the resource is stored as a file in your project's res folder or in your .rc file. Leave this check box selected.

6. Repeat the process to add the Chapter 12\Exercises\SecondPage.htm file as an application resource. Name the resource **IDR_SECONDPAGE**.

To make your application display an HTML resource, use the **CHtmlView:: LoadFromResource()** function as shown in the following exercise.

▶ **To display an HTML resource**

1. Locate the **CMyHtmlAppView::OnInitialUpdate()** function. Comment out the following line:

```
Navigate2(_T("http://www.microsoft.com/visualc/"),NULL,NULL);
```

Beneath this line, add the following:

```
LoadFromResource(IDR_TITLEPAGE);
```

2. Build and run the MyHtmlApp application. Check that the **IDR_TITLEPAGE** HTML resource displays as expected.

Note that what you are seeing is a compiled version of the TitlePage.htm file. This means that any changes you make to the HTML code in the TitlePage.htm file will not display unless you rebuild the application. This also means that your **View Links** dialog box will not be able to retrieve and display the link on this page.

Additionally, you will notice that you are not able to follow the *local page* link. This is because the link is defined as follows to point to an external .htm file:

```
<A HREF= "SecondPage.htm"> link to a local page </A>
```

You will need to redefine this link to point to the **IDR_SECONDPAGE** resource. Internet Explorer provides the *res:* protocol, which is similar to the HTTP protocol. It allows you to define a URL to locate a resource that is bound to an executable or DLL file. The res: protocol has the following format:

```
res://resource_file/[resource_type]/resource_id
```

In this protocol, *resource_file* indicates the name of the executable or DLL file that contains the resource, and *resource_type* is an optional numeric value that indicates the type of the resource—two values most commonly used here are 23 (an HTML page) and 2 (a bitmap). The numeric identifier of the resource is indicated by *resource_id*. The winuser.h file in the Microsoft Visual Studio\Vc98\Include folder gives a complete list of resource types as a list of constants with the RT_ prefix. If you do not specify the type, the default value 23 is used.

In the following exercise, you will amend the links on your HTML resource pages to use the res: protocol.

▶   **To create a link to another resource**

1. In ResourceView, right-click the **MyHtmlApp resources** folder. On the shortcut menu, click **Resource Symbols**. The **Resource Symbols** dialog box will appear.

2. Write down the numeric values assigned to the **IDR_MYPAGE** and the **IDR_SECONDPAGE** resource IDs. Close the **Resource Symbols** dialog box.

3. Double-click the **IDR_MYPAGE** resource to edit the HTML source. Replace the following hyperlink definition:

```
<A HREF= "SecondPage.htm"> link to a local page </A>
```

with the new hyperlink definition:

```
<A HREF= "res://MyHtmlApp.exe/n">
```

where *n* is the number assigned to the **IDR_SECONDPAGE** resource ID.

4. Edit the **IDR_SECONDPAGE** resource. Replace the following hyperlink definition:

```
<A HREF="MyPage.htm"> Here </A>
```

with the new hyperlink definition:

```
<A HREF="res://MyHtmlApp.exe/n"> Here </A>
```

where *n* is the number assigned to the **IDR_MYPAGE** resource ID.

5. Build and run the MyHtmlApp application. Check that you can use the links to move between the MyPage and the SecondPage pages.

Creating HTML Controls with ATL

Using ATL, you can create a control that is capable of displaying HTML pages. An ATL *HTML control* hosts the WebBrowser control and provides a pointer to the **IWebBrowser2 Automation** interface, which gives you access to the DHTML object model.

As with any other control created with ATL, the HTML control provides an empty dispatch interface to which you can add methods and properties to define how your control will interact with a container. In addition, the HTML control provides another dispatch interface that is used to communicate between the C++ code and the HTML user interface. The HTML user interface calls into C++ code using this interface, enabling you to write C++ methods that are callable from script within your HTML page.

The ATL HTML control provides an HTML resource as an example user interface for the control, and a method that demonstrates how you can write functions that are callable from the HTML user interface.

The following exercises show you how to create a simple HTML control using ATL.

▶   **To create the MyHtmlControl project**

1. On the Visual C++ **File** menu, click **New**. Create an **ATL COM AppWizard** project named **MyHtmlControl**.

2. In Step 1 of the ATL COM AppWizard, accept the default settings and click **Finish**. Click **OK** to create the project.

▶   **To insert an HTML control**

1. In ClassView, right-click **MyHtmlControl classes** and then click **New ATL Object**. In the ATL Object Wizard, click the **Controls** category and the **HTML Control**, as shown in Figure 12.8 on the following page.

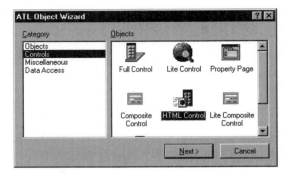

Figure 12.8 The ATL Object Wizard

2. Click **Next**. On the **Names** page of the **ATL Object Wizard Properties** dialog box, type **MyHtmlCtrl** in the **Short Name** box. The other boxes will be filled automatically and will appear as shown in Figure 12.9.

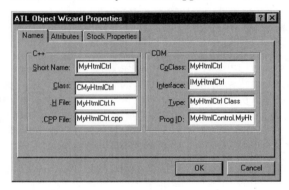

Figure 12.9 The **ATL Object Wizard Properties dialog** box

3. Click **OK** to add the HTML control to the project.

4. In ResourceView, double-click the **IDH_MYHTMLCTRL** resource in the HTML resources folder to view the source code for the example HTML page that is created as the user interface for the MyHtmlCtrl control. The HTML code displays as follows:

```
<HTML>
<BODY id=theBody>
<BUTTON onclick='window.external.OnClick(theBody, "red");'>Red
</BUTTON>
<BR>
```

```
<BR>
<BUTTON onclick='window.external.OnClick(theBody, "green");'>Green
</BUTTON>
<BR>
<BR>
<BUTTON onclick='window.external.OnClick(theBody, "blue");'>Blue
</BUTTON>
</BODY>
</HTML>
```

This simple piece of DHTML defines three buttons on the page that all respond to the **onclick** event by calling a function named **OnClick()**. The **OnClick()** function takes two parameters; the name of an element ID, and a string that specifies one of the colors in the Internet Explorer color table.

The **OnClick()** function is not part of the DHTML object model. It is a method of the **IMyHtmlCtrlUI** interface defined for your project by the ATL Object Wizard. You define properties and methods for the **IMyHtmlCtrlUI** interface that are callable from your control's DHTML code via the *window.external* object.

If you look in MyHtmlCtrl.h, you will find the implementation of **IMyHtmlCtrlUI::OnClick()** as follows:

```
// Example method called by the HTML to change the <BODY>
   background color
STDMETHOD(OnClick)(IDispatch* pdispBody, VARIANT varColor)
{
    CComQIPtr<IHTMLBodyElement> spBody(pdispBody);
    if (spBody != NULL)
        spBody->put_bgColor(varColor);
    return S_OK;
}
```

The **OnClick()** function takes the **IDispatch** pointer of the DHTML page element and a VARIANT that contains the color string. The function uses the ATL **CComQIPtr** class to obtain a smart pointer to the **IHTMLBodyElement** interface from the element's dispatch interface. If the **IHTMLBodyElement** interface pointer is obtained correctly (a BODY element has been passed as expected), then the **put_bgColor()** method is called to set the background color of the document body.

5. Build the MyHtmlControl project to create the MyHtmlControl.dll and to register the MyHtmlCtrl ActiveX control. Take the steps on the following page to test the operation of the MyHtmlCtrl control.

► **To test the MyHtmlCtrl control**

1. On the Visual C++ **Tools** menu, click **ActiveX Control Test Container**.

2. On the **Edit** menu of the ActiveX Control Test Container, click **Insert New Control**. In the **Insert Control** dialog box, click **MyHtmlCtrl Class** and then click **OK** to place the control in the container.

3. Experiment with the control buttons to see that they change the background color as expected.

Note This control does not function properly with some versions of Internet Explorer 5. You may need to install Internet Explorer 4.0 to see the correct behavior.

In the following exercises, you will add a button and a handler function that will move to and display a Web page in your HTML control.

► **To add the WWW button**

1. Open the **IDH_MYHTMLCONTROL** HTML resource in the editor.

2. Add the following lines to the bottom of the BODY section of the document:

```
<BR>
<BR>
<BUTTON  onclick='window.external.GoToWeb();'>WWW</BUTTON>
```

► **To add the GoToWeb() method**

1. In ClassView, expand the **CMyHtmlCtrl** item.

2. Right-click the **IMyHtmlCtrlUI** interface item that is a sub-item of the **CMyHtmlCtrl** item. Select **Add Method**.

3. In the **Add Method to Interface** dialog box, add **GoToWeb** to the **Method Name** box. Leave the **Parameters** box blank and click **OK** to add the method.

4. Expand the **IMyHtmlCtrlUI** interface item and double-click the **GoToWeb()** function to open the MyHtmlCtrl.cpp file and edit the **GoToWeb()** function implementation.

5. Replace the //TODO comment in the **GoToWeb()** function with the following line of code:

```
m_spBrowser->Navigate(CComBSTR("http://www.microsoft.com/visualc/"),
    NULL, NULL, NULL, NULL);
```

CMyHtmlCtrl::m_spBrowser is a smart pointer to the **IWebBrowser2** interface, the Automation interface of the WebBrowser control. This member variable is supplied for your control class by the ATL Object Wizard.

6. Build the MyHtmlControl project and test the MyHtmlCtrl control by loading it into the ActiveX Control Test Container. Check that when you click the **WWW** button, the control displays the Visual C++ home page, as illustrated in Figure 12.10.

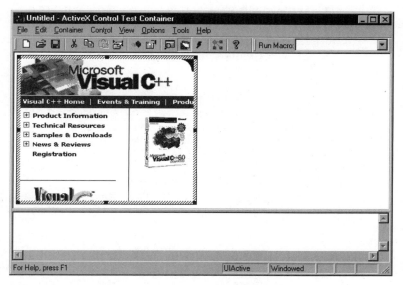

Figure 12.10 The MyHtmlCtrl ActiveX control

Dynamic HTML Scriptlets

DHTML scriptlets were introduced in Internet Explorer 4.0 to allow you to develop simple user interface controls using DHTML. Scriptlets are reusable DHTML objects that expose a well-defined public interface—a list of properties and methods that are accessible to clients. Scriptlets are also capable of firing events.

One of the most interesting features of scriptlets is that they can be used like an ActiveX control. For example, they can be placed on a Web page or on a form in a desktop application. This behavior is made possible by the fact that scriptlets are run inside the *Microsoft Scriptlet Component*, an ActiveX control that is installed along with Internet Explorer. Internally, the Scriptlet Component hosts an instance of the DHTML parsing engine to interpret the scriptlet code. Externally, it presents a standard ActiveX control interface to allow interaction with a control container.

The Scriptlet Component exposes the scriptlet's public interface to the control container. It acts as a bridge so that the container application can access the public properties and methods defined in the scriptlet's DHTML code.

The Scriptlet Component provides an internal interface, which is accessible from the scriptlet code. Scriptlet code can query the **window.external** object to gain run-time information about the current state of its host; and to access services of the Scriptlet Component, such as the forwarding of events fired by the scriptlet to the containing application.

Because scriptlets run as interpreted DHTML, they execute more slowly than compiled ActiveX controls. But if all you need is a simple lightweight control, scriptlets provide you with an easy way of developing reusable components.

Elements of a DHTML Scriptlet

A DHTML scriptlet is a normal DHTML document that contains <BODY> and <SCRIPT> elements. The <BODY> element defines the visual interface of the control, which you create as you would for a regular Web page.

Within the <SCRIPT> element, you define the properties, methods, and events that allow you to use the scriptlet as a control. By following certain naming conventions, you can distinguish between the public properties and methods that are exposed to clients through the control interface; and the private properties and methods that are used only internally by the scriptlet.

Declaring Scriptlet Properties and Methods

Within a scriptlet, all properties and methods that are not explicitly declared public are considered private. As with any other HTML document, the <SCRIPT> elements are local to the document in which they are defined.

There are two ways of declaring public properties and methods. The first way simply involves adding the *public_* prefix to the names of all public properties and methods. You can also specify properties by declaring them as functions with the *public_get_* and *public_put_* prefixes. This allows you finer control over the property—for example, you could make a property read-only by speci-fying a **public_get()** function and not a **public_put()** function.

The following example shows a simple scriptlet containing a paragraph named *p1*. The script block following the paragraph exposes a property called **text** and another called **color**, which is defined using **get** and **set** functions. The scriptlet also exposes a function called **animate()**.

```
<HTML><HEAD></HEAD>
<BODY>
<FONT ID="f1" color="black">
<P ID="p1">This is a paragraph of text.</P>
</FONT>

<SCRIPT LANGUAGE="JavaScript">
var public_text = p1.innerText;
function public_get_color()
{
    return f1.color;
}
function public_put_color(color)
{
    f1.color = color;
}
function public_animate()
{
    // Code to perform animation
}
</SCRIPT>
</BODY></HTML>
```

If a client page were to declare an instance of this scriptlet object (you will see how this is done later), naming it **MyScriptlet**, any of the following JavaScript operations would be legal:

```
MyScriptlet.text = "Hello";
...
MyScriptlet.animate();
...
var OldColor = MyScriptlet.color;
...
MyScriptlet.color ="blue";
```

The second method of defining the public interface of a scriptlet is to use the JavaScript **public_description** object. You create a JavaScript constructor function that declares your scriptlet's public properties and methods, and you assign this function to the scriptlet's **public_description** object. Properties and methods within the scriptlet document that are not declared within the constructor function are private.

Using the **public_description** method, the scriptlet from our previous example would look as follows:

```
<HTML><HEAD></HEAD>
<BODY>
<FONT ID="f1" color="black">
<P ID="p1">This is a paragraph of text.</P>
</FONT>

<SCRIPT LANGUAGE="JavaScript">
public_description = new CreateScriptlet();
function CreateScriptlet()
{
this.text = p1.innerText; // text property
this.put_color = putcolor;   // color property (write)
this.get_color = getcolor;   // color property (read)
this.animate = doAnimation;  // animate() method
}
function getcolor()
{
    return f1.color;
}
function putcolor(color)
{
    f1.color = color;
}
function doAnimation()
{
    // Code to perform animation
}
</SCRIPT>
</BODY></HTML>
```

The name of the constructor function (it can have any name) is assigned to the **public_description** object. In the example just given, the **CreateScriptlet()** constructor function specifies the **text** and **color** properties, assigning a value for the text property and specifying the names of the private functions **getcolor()** and **putcolor()** used to get and set the color property values. The function also specifies the **animate()** method and the name of the private function **doAnimation()** that implements the method.

Using the **public_description** object is the preferred method of seasoned object-oriented software developers. This technique creates a clear distinction between interface and implementation, and it allows you to neatly define the interface of the scriptlet in a single location—usually at the beginning of a <SCRIPT> block.

Scriptlet Events

An application containing a scriptlet can be notified about events that occur in the scriptlet. A DHTML scriptlet can expose two types of events:

- **Standard DHTML events** include the **onclick** event and the **onkeypress** event.
- **Custom events** are events that you define or DHTML events not provided as standard events. For example, the scriptlet can fire an event when a property value changes.

► **Handling Standard Events**

A DHTML scriptlet can expose any of these standard DHTML events:

- onclick
- ondblclick
- onkeypress
- onkeydown
- onkeyup
- onmousemove
- onmousedown
- onmouseup

You will recall from our introduction to DHTML scriptlets that one of the services provided by the Scriptlet Component is to forward events fired by the scriptlet to the control container. For example, suppose a user double-clicks the mouse in the scriptlet body. The DHTML **ondblclick** event is intercepted by the Scriptlet Component, and it might react by passing on a corresponding event of the appropriate type to its container. However it is important to understand that it will do this *only if* it is specifically instructed to do so by an element of the scriptlet code.

To pass an event from the scriptlet to the container application, you must provide an event handler for the event you want to pass, and call the **bubbleEvent** method from the event handler. The **bubbleEvent** method is provided by the Scriptlet Component, and is accessed through the **window.external** object.

To continue with our example, you would handle mouse double-clicks in the scriptlet body by specifying the body as follows:

```
<BODY ondblclick = passthru()>
...
</BODY>
```

To forward the event to the container, you would define the **passthru()** function as follows:

```
function passthru()
{
    if(!window.external.frozen)
        window.external.bubbleEvent();
}
```

Note that before it attempts to forward the event, the routine checks the Scriptlet Component's *frozen* property to ensure that it is ready to handle events.

► **Creating and Handling Custom Events**

It addition to handling the standard DHTML events, you can make your scriptlet fire custom events. You can use custom events to:

- Send more detail about a standard event that occurred—for example, which of several buttons in the scriptlet was clicked.
- Notify the host application about non-standard changes in the scriptlet, such as when the value of a property changes.
- Notify the host application about DHTML events that are not among the standard events handled by the **bubbleEvent** method.

You can fire custom events from anywhere in your scriptlet code by using the **raiseEvent** method. The following example shows how you can use a custom event to notify the container application that the scriptlet's background color has been changed:

```
<SCRIPT LANGUAGE="JavaScript">
function public_put_backgroundColor(value)
{
    window.document.bgColor = value;
    if(!window.external.frozen)

    window.external.raiseEvent("onbgcolorchange",
        value);
}
</SCRIPT>
```

You will notice that the **raiseEvent** method takes two parameters. The first parameter specifies a name for the event so that it can provide a standard interface to its container. The Scriptlet Component routes all custom scriptlet events through a single event named **onscriptletevent**. You can query the *name* parameter to identify which event has been fired. The second parameter can be used to pass data associated with the event.

The following code below illustrates how Internet Explorer could handle the **onbgcolorchange** event raised in the previous example:

```
<SCRIPT LANGUAGE="JavaScript"
    FOR="MyScriptlet"
    EVENT="onscriptletevent (event, obj)">
    if(event == "onbgcolorchange")
    {
        msg = "Scriptlet background changed to " + obj;
        alert(msg);
    }
</SCRIPT>
```

Scriptlet Example

To help you understand how scriptlets work, and how you can use them in your applications, we have included the **ColorSelector** scriptlet—a simple control that allows you to browse through a set of colors and select one. The source code for the scriptlet is available from Chapter 12\Exercises\ColorSelector.htm on the companion CD:

```
<!-- ColorSelector.htm -->
<HTML><HEAD></HEAD>
<BODY style="border:2px solid black;
    color:white; background-color:white "
    ondblclick = passthru()>

<DIV ID=d1 style="position:relative; border:1px solid black;
top:5; left:5; width:130; height:50">
</DIV>

<P ID=p1 style="position:relative; left:13">
<BUTTON ID=BackButton onclick = cycle("back")> < </BUTTON>.
<BUTTON ID=ForwardButton onclick = cycle("forward")> > </BUTTON>
<BUTTON ID=SelectButton onclick = doSelect()> Select </BUTTON>
</P>
</BODY>
```

```
<SCRIPT LANGUAGE="JavaScript">
public_description = new colorselector();
var colors = new Array("white", "red", "green", "blue", "black") ;
var numcolors = colors.length;
var curcolor = 0;

// Object description
function colorselector()
{
    this.get_color = getcolor;
}

// Public property access function
function getcolor()
{
    return colors[curcolor];
}

// Events
// Standard
function passthru()
{
    if(!window.external.frozen)
        window.external.bubbleEvent();
}

// Custom
function doSelect()
{
    if(!window.external.frozen)
        window.external.raiseEvent("onClickSelect", colors[curcolor]);
}

// Private methods
function cycle(direction)
{
    if(direction == "back")
    {
        curcolor -- ;
        if(curcolor < 0)
            curcolor = numcolors-1;
    }
    if(direction == "forward")
    {
        curcolor++;
        if(curcolor >= numcolors)
            curcolor = 0;
```

```
    }
    d1.style.backgroundColor = colors[curcolor];
}
</SCRIPT>
</HTML>
```

By examining the **colorselector()** function assigned to the scriptlet's **public_ description** object, you will be able to see that the scriptlet exposes a single read-only property named **color**. Note that the scriptlet exposes the standard **ondblclick** event and raises a custom event named **onClickSelect**.

Hosting Scriptlets in a Web Page

Like regular ActiveX controls, scriptlets can be placed in a Web page by using the HTML <OBJECT> tag. Unlike regular ActiveX controls, scriplets are not identified using a ClassID. Instead, you assign the scriptlet **MIME** type to the **TYPE** attribute, and a URL that points to the scriptlet source file to the **DATA** attribute. MIME (Multipurpose Internet Mail Extensions) is an Internet protocol that allows a Web browser to identify the type of file that it is displaying. The **b** type that identifies a scriptlet is *text/x-scriptlet*.

The following example shows you how to place a scriptlet defined in the MyScriptlet.htm file.

```
<OBJECT ID="MyScriptlet" TYPE="text/x-scriptlet"DATA="MyScriptlet.htm">
</OBJECT>
```

This code assumes that the MyScriptlet.htm file can be found in the same directory as the current file.

With the **ColorSelector** scriptlet, we have included a simple HTML page that allows you to test the scriptlet. *TestScriptlet.htm* is located in the Chapter 12\Exercises folder and is also listed as follows:

```
<!-- TestScriptlet.htm -->
<HTML>
<HEAD>
<TITLE>
Scriptlet Test
</TITLE>
</HEAD>
<BODY>
<H1> Scriptlet Test
</H1>
<P>
<OBJECT ID="MyScriptlet" TYPE="text/x-scriptlet"
    DATA="ColorSelector.htm">

</OBJECT>
```

```
</P>
<P>
<BUTTON ID="Btn1" onclick="UseScriptlet()"> Display </BUTTON>
</P>
</BODY>

<SCRIPT LANGUAGE="JavaScript">
function UseScriptlet()
{
    alert(MyScriptlet.color);
}
</SCRIPT>

<SCRIPT LANGUAGE="JavaScript"
    FOR="MyScriptlet"
    EVENT="onscriptletevent(event, obj)">
    if(event == "onClickSelect")
        document.body.bgColor = obj;
</SCRIPT>

<SCRIPT LANGUAGE="JavaScript"
    FOR="MyScriptlet"
    EVENT=ondblclick>
    alert("double-clicked in scriptlet");
</SCRIPT>
</HTML>
```

This page tests the scriptlet functionality in the following ways:

- The scriptlet is hosted in Internet Explorer. You can test the internal functions of the scriptlet by clicking its arrow buttons to cycle through its colors.

- When you click the test page's **Display** button, the scriptlet retrieves the current value of the scriptlet's **color** property and displays it in an alert box.

- When you click the scriptlet's **Select** button, the scriptlet fires an **onClickSelect** event. The event handler uses the color passed as an event parameter to set the background color of the test page.

- The test page provides a handler to trap a standard **ondblclick** event from the scriptlet.

Open the TestScriptlet.htm file in Internet Explorer and test the scriplet. Figure 12.11 on the facing page shows the scriptlet in action.

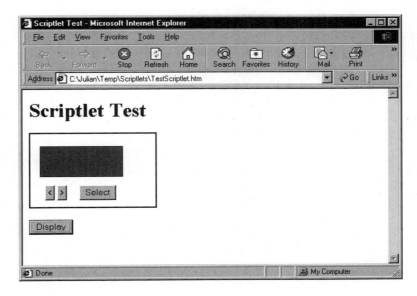

Figure 12.11 Testing the **ColorSelector** scriptlet

Hosting Scriptlets in a Visual C++ Application

Although scriptlets can be placed on a form in a Microsoft Visual Basic application and used like a regular ActiveX control, this functionality is not yet available for Visual C++ containers such as dialog boxes. The theory is that you should use the Components and Controls gallery to insert the Scriptlet Component into the container, generating the **CWebBridge** class to wrap the **IWebBridge** interface exposed by the component. You can use this class to set the **url** property of the Scriptlet Component to the URL of the scriptlet's HTML document, and you can access the **event** property to handle custom events from the scriptlet.

Although you can successfully insert the Scriptlet Component into the project, and generate the **CWebBridge** class, you are not currently able to place a control in a dialog box. If you try, you will receive the message shown in Figure 12.12.

Figure 12.12 Scriptlet Component error message

Users who try to use the **CWebBridge** class to create an instance of the Scriptlet Component control programmatically face similar difficulties, as documented in the Knowledge Base article Q190838. The article suggests that you might be able to create an instance of the Scriptlet Component by importing (with #import) the type library. Until the functionality to place the Scriptlet Component in a dialog box becomes available, you will be best off hosting scriptlets in an HTML page, and hosting the page in a **CHtmlView**-based application or an ATL HTML control.

Lesson Summary

The rapid growth of the Internet in recent years has led to many changes in the way we think about application development. Web browsers such as Internet Explorer are now used not just to view pages on the World Wide Web or on company intranets, but to access resources and run applications on your local area network servers, or on your desktop computer. You can develop Web browser–style applications that use HTML to present a rich and consistent interface; providing seamless access to resources on the desktop computer, on remote company servers, and on Web servers across the world.

HTML is a system of marking up or tagging an ASCII document so that it includes formatting tags; references to graphics, sound, or animation files; and hyperlinks to Web pages or other resources. HTML defines a standard set of formatting tags that all Web browsers recognize. These tags divide an HTML document into discrete sections known as elements. Some elements denote a format to be applied to text within the document; others are used to include an external resource such as an image file, or to define a hyperlink to another document. Most of the HTML tags define attributes, which you can use to supply additional information about the element.

DHTML allows you to create dynamic, interactive Web pages. For example, using DHTML, you can modify the content and style of your Web page and process user input. DHTML achieves these effects by using the user's computer to modify the current document, automatically reformatting and redisplaying the document to show changes.

DHTML documents use HTML styles to specify the format and appearance of the document; and small blocks of script to process user input and directly manipulate the HTML tags, attributes, styles, and text in the document. Scripts in your DHTML document use the DHTML object model to access and manipulate elements of the current page.

Microsoft provides the WebBrowser ActiveX control to help you incorporate the functionality of the Internet Explorer Web browser into your applications. The MFC class **CHtmlView** incorporates the WebBrowser control into MFC's document/view architecture. The **CHtmlView** class provides the **GetHtmlDocument()**

function, which returns a pointer to the dispatch interface of the HTML document that is currently displayed. You can use this pointer access the Automation interfaces of the DHTML object model, and thus manipulate the document.

Using ATL, you can create a control that is capable of displaying HTML pages. The ATL HTML control defines a dispatch interface to which you can add methods and properties to define how your control will interact with a container. The ATL HTML control defines an additional dispatch interface that is used to communicate between the C++ code and the HTML user interface. Script in the HTML page displayed by your control can access properties and methods defined for this interface via the DHTML **window.external** object.

You can include HTML pages as resources in your project, just as you can include bitmaps or dialog templates. HTML resources are compiled into your program executable, and this provides a safe and convenient way to distribute HTML pages used by your application. You can use the res: protocol in a URL to locate a resource that is bound to an executable or DLL file.

DHTML scriptlets are reusable DHTML objects that expose properties and methods that can be accessed by clients. Scriptlets can be used as ActiveX controls—for example, they can be placed in a Web page, or within a dialog box in a Visual C++ application. Scriptlets are run inside the Scriptlet Component, an ActiveX control that is installed along with Internet Explorer. The Scriptlet Component acts as a bridge so that the container application can access the public properties and methods defined in the scriptlet's DHTML code.

The Scriptlet Component provides an internal interface, which is accessible from the scriptlet code. Scriptlet code can query the **window.external** object to gain run-time information about the current state of its host; and to access services of the Scriptlet Component, such as the forwarding of events fired by the scriptlet to the containing application.

Lesson 2: Creating ActiveX Documents

ActiveX documents, also known as *Active documents,* are document files created by *ActiveX document server* applications. ActiveX documents can be viewed and edited not only by the server application that created them, but also by any *ActiveX document container* application.

Microsoft Word documents are an example of ActiveX documents. Users of Internet Explorer (an ActiveX document container application) can view and edit Word documents using the full functionality of Word (an ActiveX document server application) from within the Internet Explorer browser window.

ActiveX documents have come to be a powerful feature of Web sites for users of Microsoft applications, extending the functionality of the Internet Explorer browser to provide a versatile, feature-rich alternative to simple HTML Web pages.

After this lesson, you will be able to:

- Describe how to use ActiveX documents.
- Describe some of the advantages of using ActiveX documents on your Web site.
- Describe how to use the MFC AppWizard to create an ActiveX document server.
- Describe how to deploy an ActiveX document on a Web site, and how to view the ActiveX document using Internet Explorer.

Estimated lesson time: 30 minutes

Using ActiveX Documents

In Chapter 6, you learned how a document/view application can save its data to disk as a document file. Generally speaking, you can view or edit a document file only by launching the application that created it. However, with very little extra work, you can make your application into an ActiveX document server so that any ActiveX document container application can be used to view or edit your documents using the functionality of the server application.

When a container application loads an ActiveX document, it also loads menu, toolbar, and status bar resources from the associated server application. The menus and toolbars are merged with those of the container frame window to make the functionality of the server application available from within the container application. In effect, the server temporarily "takes over" the container when an ActiveX document is displayed.

If you have Internet Explorer and Word installed, you can easily try out ActiveX document technology.

▶ **To view an ActiveX document located on your local hard drive**

1. Start Internet Explorer.
2. Start Windows Explorer and use it to locate a Word .doc file.
3. Move the Word document file from Windows Explorer to the Internet Explorer window using a drag-and-drop operation. Your Word document should open in Internet Explorer as an ActiveX document, as shown in Figure 12.13.

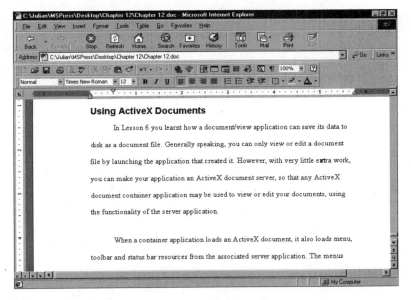

Figure 12.13   Viewing an ActiveX document using Internet Explorer 5

Notice that Internet Explorer displays the Word menus and toolbars in addition to its own. Try editing the Word document from within Internet Explorer, and try using some of the features provided by the Word menus. Click the **Back** button to return to the previously displayed page. Note that Internet Explorer asks whether you want to save the edited ActiveX document before proceeding.

Note There are some differences between the way that versions 4.0 and 5 of Internet Explorer handle ActiveX documents. In Internet Explorer 4.0, you can load an ActiveX document by specifying it as a *file://* URL in the address bar. Internet Explorer 5, however, will load a separate instance of the Word application to view the document rather than loading it as an ActiveX document.

Using ActiveX Documents on a Web Site

Internet Explorer is not the only ActiveX document container application (the Microsoft Office Binder is another), but it is the container that is of interest to us in this chapter because we are demonstrating Internet programming. The example just given portrays a somewhat artificial situation. Internet Explorer is not generally used to view an ActiveX document on your local computer—it is much more efficient to use the document's parent application to do this.

Internet Explorer uses its ActiveX container capabilities to view ActiveX documents that are deployed on a Web server. This means that Word documents, Microsoft Excel spreadsheets, and any of your custom-built ActiveX documents can be included on your Web site and made available for viewing and editing by anyone who has the corresponding ActiveX document server applications installed on their computer. An ActiveX document server won't let you save any changes you make to the document back to the Internet host, but it will let you save them in a new version on your own hard disk. In other words, the **Save** command on the **File** menu is unavailable, but the **Save As** command is available.

A common use for ActiveX documents is to create a "forms" center on a company intranet site. An area of the intranet site can contain Word or Excel versions of forms—such as training request forms or expense claim forms—that are regularly submitted by employees. This means that employees, whether they are in the office, at home, or halfway across the world, can browse to the intranet site and load a blank form into their Web browser. Using ActiveX document technology, they can fill out the form online, and then save a local copy that can be faxed or e-mailed to the personnel department.

You can provide a much richer interface to Web site data using ActiveX document technology than you can using standard HTML pages. When you view an Excel spreadsheet over the Web, you have access to all of the powerful features of Excel to organize and display your data. The fact that you need to have the ActiveX document server application installed on your local computer before you can view ActiveX documents on a remote Web site could be perceived as a limitation. To address this issue, you could develop different versions of your server application. You could, for example, create a fully featured version that is used to create and maintain ActiveX documents deployed on your Web site, and a lightweight viewer application that can be downloaded to Internet clients for use in conjunction with the Web browser. Microsoft takes this approach with its Word document viewer application, which allows you to view Word documents deployed on a Web site without having a full version of Word installed on your computer.

One potential drawback of using ActiveX document technology on your Web site is that users of your site are compelled to use a browser that supports ActiveX documents. They must also have a copy of your ActiveX document server application installed on their computer, which assumes that they are running Windows. This means that ActiveX documents are best used in a situation where you are in a position to specify the platform and configuration of the client computers. When you want to create a public Web site that is accessible from many different unknown clients, you should use HTML.

Creating an ActiveX Document Server

Visual C++ 6.0 makes creating ActiveX documents extremely easy. Selecting the appropriate option in the AppWizard will generate all the code and resources necessary to make your application an ActiveX document server.

► **To create an ActiveX document server application**

1. Use AppWizard to create a new .exe project named **MyADSApp**. In Step 1, click the **Single document** option.

2. Accept the default options for Step 2. In Step 3, click the **Full-server** and the **Active document server** options, as shown in Figure 12.14.

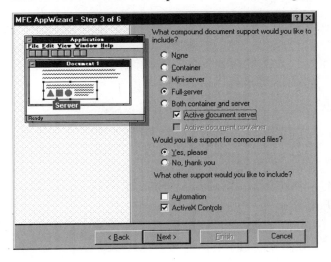

Figure 12.14   MFC AppWizard compound document options

3. In Step 4, click **Advanced** and enter **ads** as the file extension. Close the **Advanced Options** dialog box.

4. Click **Finish** and then click **OK** to create the project.

In the following exercises, you will create a simple application that displays a line of text in the application's main window. First you will create a dialog box to allow the user to specify the text to be displayed.

▶ **To create the Set Display String dialog box**

1. Create a dialog template containing a single edit control, as shown in Figure 12.15. The dialog ID should be **IDD_EDITSTRING** and the edit control ID should be **IDC_NEWSTRING**.

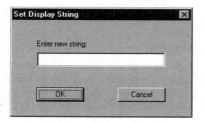

Figure 12.15   The **Set Display String** dialog box

2. Create a dialog class named **CEditStringDlg**. On the ClassWizard **Member Variables** page, create a **Value** category **CString** member variable named m_newstring.

Next you will create the application data (the string to be displayed) by adding a data member to the document class. You will also implement the **Serialize()** function to store and retrieve this data member to the ActiveX document file.

▶ **To create the CMyADSApp application data**

Add a public **CString** member variable named m_strDisplay to the **CMyADSAppDoc** class. Modify the **CMyADSAppDoc::Serialize()** function to serialize the m_strDisplay variable, as shown in the following code:

```
void CMyADSAppDoc::Serialize(CArchive& ar)
{
    if (ar.IsStoring())
    {
        ar << m_strDisplay;
    }
    else
    {
        ar >> m_strDisplay;
    }
}
```

Now you will modify the application menu and toolbar to create the **Edit String** command. You will also create a handler function for this command.

▶ **To create and implement the Edit String menu command**

1. Edit the **IDR_MAINFRAME** menu resource. On the **Edit** menu, delete the **Undo** command. Replace it with a new command with the caption **&String**. Provide a suitable prompt string. Accept the default command ID **ID_EDIT_STRING** for the command.

2. Edit the **IDR_MAINFRAME** toolbar. Create a simple toolbar button to represent text entry. Assign the **ID_EDIT_STRING** command ID to the new toolbar button.

3. Add the following line to the top of the MyADSAppDoc.cpp file:

```
#include "EditStringDlg.h"
```

4. Create a command handler in the **CMyADSAppDoc** class for the **ID_EDIT_STRING** command ID. Name the function **OnEditString()** and implement the function as follows:

```
void CMyADSAppDoc::OnEditString()
{
    CEditStringDlg myDialog;
    myDialog.m_newstring = m_strDisplay;

    if(myDialog.DoModal() == IDOK &&
        myDialog.m_newstring != m_strDisplay)
    {
        m_strDisplay = myDialog.m_newstring;
        UpdateAllViews(NULL);
        SetModifiedFlag();
    }
}
```

This function displays the **Set Display String** dialog box to allow the user to specify the string displayed by the application. The string is stored in the CMyADSAppDoc::m_strDisplay variable.

▶ **To implement the application drawing function**

Locate the **CMyADSAppView::OnDraw()** function. Replace the //TODO comment line with the following code:

```
CFont HeadingFont;
if(HeadingFont. CreateFont(64, 0, 0,
    0, FW_NORMAL, 1, 0, 0, 0, 0, 0, 0, FF_DECORATIVE, 0))

    pDC->SelectObject(&HeadingFont);

pDC->TextOut(10, 10, pDoc->m_strDisplay);
```

If you build and run the CMyADSApp application at this point, it will function perfectly well as a stand-alone application. You will be able to choose the **String** command from the **Edit** menu and add a string to be displayed in the application main window. You will be able to save the string in a document file with an .ads extension.

If you try and load the saved .ads file into an ActiveX document container such as Internet Explorer, you will be able to see the string displayed, but you will not be able to access the **String** command on the **Edit** menu. This is because an ActiveX document container does not load menu commands and toolbar buttons from the **IDR_MAINFRAME** resources.

When you use AppWizard to create an ActiveX document server, additional menu and toolbar resources, both with the ID **IDR_SRVR_INPLACE**, are created for the project. The commands on the **IDR_SRVR_INPLACE** menu are merged into the container menu; and the **IDR_SRVR_INPLACE** toolbar is added to the toolbars displayed by the container application.

You will need to edit the **IDR_SRVR_INPLACE** menu and toolbar to make the the **String** command on the **Edit** menu available from the menu of the ActiveX document container.

▶   **To edit the IDR_SRVR_INPLACE menu and toolbar resources**

1. In ResourceView, double-click the **IDR_SRVR_INPLACE** menu item. Edit the menu item properties for the **Undo** command on the **Edit** menu. Change the menu item caption to **&String** and the ID to **ID_EDIT_STRING**. The prompt string will change automatically when the **Menu Item Properties** dialog box is closed.

2. Edit the **IDR_SRVR_INPLACE** toolbar resource. Create a new button identical to the button you created for the **IDR_MAINFRAME** resource (you can copy and paste from one edit window to another). Assign the button the **ID_EDIT_STRING** ID.

3. Build and run the CMyADSApp application. Use the **String** command on the **Edit** menu to display the string "Hello World!" in the application's main window. Close the application and, when prompted, save the file as **Hello.ads**.

4. Start Internet Explorer. Use Windows Explorer to locate the Hello.ads file and drag the file onto the Internet Explorer window. If the **File Download** message box appears, click **Open this file from the current location** and click **OK**. The file should appear as shown in Figure 12.16 on the facing page.

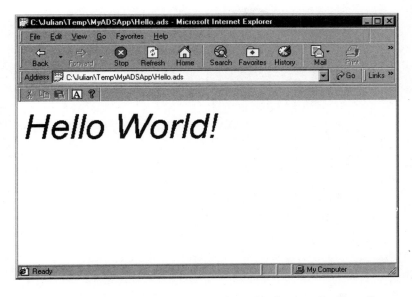

Figure 12.16   The Hello.ads document hosted in Internet Explorer 5

5. Check that you can use the **String** command on the **Edit** menu to change the string displayed in the document. Click the Internet Explorer **Back** button to go back to the previous page that was displayed in the browser. In the message box that asks whether you want to save your changes, click **No**.

Deploying an ActiveX Document on a Web Site

The following exercises show you how to deploy the Hello.ads file on a Web site so that it can be accessed across the Internet using HTTP. Instructions are provided for IIS 4.0 and PWS.

Web Site Organization

A new installation of IIS 4.0 or PWS will create a default Web site for your computer, which is accessible by specifying your computer name as a URL. For example, if you enter the following URL into your Internet Explorer **Address** box, the browser will display the Web server's default welcome page:

```
http://[your computer name]/
```

The trailing slash after the computer name (which will be added by the browser if you do not type it yourself) signifies that you wish to go to your home directory. The Windows NT Option Pack welcome page appears because it is designated as the default document for the home directory.

You can organize your Web site into a hierarchy of *virtual directories*, which are organizational subdivisions of your Web site that are conceptually similar to the subdirectories, or folders, of your hard disk's file system. All virtual directories are subdirectories of the Web site's home directory. They are known as virtual directories because the structure you define is not directly related to the organization of folders on your hard disk. Each virtual directory points to a folder on a hard disk that stores the Web pages, ActiveX documents, and other files that make up the *content* of the virtual directory. These content folders do not even need to be on the same computer as the Web server.

When specifying virtual directories in a URL, use the UNIX-style forward slash. For example, entering the following URL into your Web browser's **Address** box will take you to the visualc virtual directory on Microsoft's Web site:

```
http://www.microsoft.com/visualc/
```

If you do not name a specific Web page in the URL, as just shown, the Web server will display the default document specified for the virtual directory.

Deploying Content on a Microsoft IIS 4.0 Web Server

The Microsoft Internet Service Manager is a utility installed with IIS that is used to administrate a Web server, as well as the other Internet services that IIS provides, such as mail and FTP servers. Using the Internet Service Manager, you can configure the content, security and performance of a Web site.

In the following exercise, you will use the Internet Service Manager to create the *docs* virtual directory on the default Web site. The docs virtual directory will host the Hello.ads ActiveX document.

▶ **To deploy the Hello.ads ActiveX document**

1. Using Windows Explorer, create a new folder under the \InetPub\WWWRoot folder and name it **MyActiveXDocs**. Then place a copy of the Hello.ads file in this folder.

2. On the **Start** menu, point to **Programs**, point to **NT 4.0 Option Pack**, point to **Microsoft Internet Information Server**, and click **Internet Service Manager**.

3. In the left pane, expand the **Internet Information Server** item. Expand the item that is labeled with your computer name so that the application looks similar to Figure 12.17.

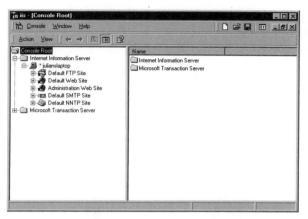

Figure 12.17   Internet Service Manager

4. Right-click **Default Web Site**. On the **New** submenu, click **Virtual Directory**.

5. In the New Virtual Directory Wizard, type the name **docs** and then click **Next**.

6. Click **Browse** and then locate the \InetPub\WWWRoot\MyActiveXDocs folder. Click **OK** to specify that this folder will contain the content for the docs virtual directory. Click **Next**.

7. Accept the default options on the last page of the wizard by clicking **Finish**. If you click **Default Web Site** in the left pane, you will see the docs virtual directory displayed in the right pane.

8. Close the Internet Service Manager. Open Internet Explorer and enter the following URL into the address box:

```
http://[your computer name]/docs/hello.ads
```

The Hello.ads file should display in the browser as shown in Figure 12.16.

Deploying Content on a Microsoft IIS Personal Web Server

PWS provides the Personal Web Manager utility, which you use to administer a Web site.

In the following exercise, you will use the Personal Web Manager to create the *docs* virtual directory on the default Web site. The docs virtual directory will host the Hello.ads ActiveX document.

► **To deploy the Hello.ads ActiveX document**

1. Using Windows Explorer, create a new folder under the \InetPub\WWWRoot folder named **MyActiveXDocs**. Place a copy of the Hello.ads file in this folder.

2. On the **Start** menu, click **Programs** and then click **Microsoft Personal Web Server** to start the Personal Web Manager.

3. Personal Web Manager appears with the **Main** page displayed. Click **Advanced** in the left pane so that the application looks similar to Figure 12.18.

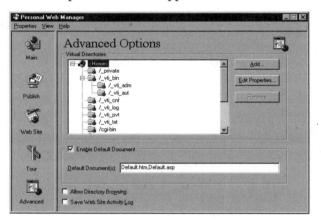

Figure 12.18   Personal Web Manager

4. With the home directory item selected, as shown in Figure 12.18, click **Add**.

5. The Add Directory Wizard appears. In the **Alias** box, type **docs**. Click **Browse** to locate the \InetPub\WWWRoot\MyActiveXDocs folder. Click **OK** to add this folder to the **Directory** box. Click **OK** to create the virtual directory.

6. Check that the docs virtual directory has been added beneath the home directory in the Virtual Directories window. Close the Personal Web Manager.

7. Launch Internet Explorer and enter the following URL into the address box:

```
http://[your computer name]/docs/hello.ads
```

The Hello.ads file should display in the browser as shown in Figure 12.16.

Lesson Summary

ActiveX documents are created by an ActiveX document server application. ActiveX documents can be viewed and edited by the server application that created them, and by any ActiveX document container application. When a container application loads an ActiveX document, it loads resources from the associated server application. The menus and toolbars are merged with those of the container frame window to make the functionality of the server application available from within the container application.

Internet Explorer is the most widely used ActiveX document container application. Internet Explorer is frequently used to view and edit ActiveX documents deployed on Web sites. You can use ActiveX documents to provide a much richer interface to Web site data than you can with standard HTML pages.

You are required to have the ActiveX document server application installed on your local computer before you can view ActiveX documents over the Internet. This means that ActiveX documents are best used in a situation where you are in a position to specify the platform and configuration of the client computers, such as on a corporate intranet.

The MFC AppWizard that comes with Visual C++ 6.0 provides options that make it easy to create an ActiveX server application.

Lesson 3: Programming the Web Server

In Lesson 2, you were introduced to Microsoft's Web server applications: IIS 4.0 and PWS. You learned how to use these applications to organize and deploy content such as HTML pages and ActiveX documents on a Web site.

In this lesson you will learn how to write programs that extend the functionality of a Microsoft Web server using ISAPI. You will learn about two types of programs: ISAPI *server extensions* and ISAPI *filters*, both of which are implemented as DLLs. ISAPI server extensions are programs that run within the Internet server process. ISAPI filters intercept data travelling to and from the server, and thus can perform specialized logging, encryption and other tasks.

After this lesson, you will be able to:
- Describe how to create an ISAPI server extension using MFC.
- Describe how to make an ISAPI server extension generate customized content based on parameters submitted from an HTML form.
- Describe how to create an ISAPI filter using MFC.
- Describe how to install an ISAPI filter.

Estimated lesson time: 30 minutes

ISAPI Server Extensions

An ISAPI server extension is a server-side program that runs in response to requests from a Web browser. A server extension is implemented as a DLL, which is loaded by IIS. The browser can run the program by specifying the name of the .dll file in a URL like this:

```
http://myserver/apps/charts.dll
```

The ISAPI server extension implements functions that can be called by the browser. To call a function, you append the function name to the URL as follows:

```
http://myserver/apps/charts.dll?GetChart
```

This example references the *charts.dll* server extension and calls the **GetChart()** function. All ISAPI server extensions must define a default function that is called if the client does not specify a function. Server extension functions can take parameters, which can be specified in the URL as follows:

```
http://myserver/apps/charts.dll?GetChart?Fund=ARSC
```

An ISAPI server extension can be linked to an HTML form by assigning the extension's URL to the *action* attribute inside a <FORM> tag, as follows:

```
<FORM action="myextension.dll?GetColor" method=POST>
<!-- form controls go here -->
</FORM>
```

Values that the user enters into the form's controls are automatically passed as parameters to the ISAPI server extension when the user submits the form. ISAPI server extension functions typically send back customized HTML code based on these parameter values.

ISAPI server extensions are based on the Common Gateway Interface (CGI) standard. CGI is part of the HTTP, which was developed as a way to allow browser programs to interact with scripts or separate executable programs running on a Web server. Without altering the HTTP/CGI specifications, Microsoft developed IIS to allow any browser to load and run a server extension DLL. Because DLLs run as part of the process that loads them, server extensions are faster than scripts that might need to load separate executable programs.

CGI shifts the programming burden to the server. Using CGI parameters, the browser sends small amounts of information to the server. The server can do absolutely anything with this information, including access a database, generate images, and control peripheral devices. The server sends a file (HTML or otherwise) back to the browser, which can be read from the server's disk or generated by the program.

Creating an ISAPI Server Extension Using MFC

To see a basic ISAPI server extension in action, you will now use the MFC ISAPI Extension Wizard to create one of your own.

▶ **To create the MyExtension ISAPI server extension DLL**

1. On the **File** menu in Visual C++, click **New**. On the **Projects** page of the **New** dialog box, click **ISAPI Extension Wizard**. Enter **MyExtension** as a project name and click **OK**.

2. The ISAPI Extension Wizard appears as shown in Figure 12.19.

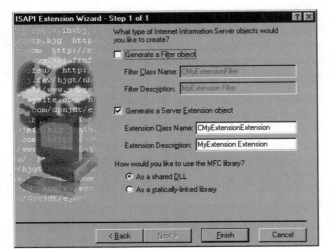

Figure 12.19   The ISAPI Extension Wizard

3. Click **Finish** to accept the default settings, and then click **OK** to create the project.

4. Build the project to create the MyExtension.dll ISAPI server extension.

5. Using Windows Explorer, create a new folder under the \InetPub\WWWRoot folder named **MyISExtensions**. Place a copy of the MyExtension.dll file in this folder.

6. Using your Web server management program, create a virtual directory beneath your Web site's home directory, and name it **apps**. Specify that the content from this directory will be placed in the C:\INetPub\WWWRoot\ MyISExtensions folder. Make sure that you allow **Execute** access to this directory.

7. Start Internet Explorer and enter the following URL into the **Address** box:

```
http://[your computer name]/apps/myextension.dll
```

This request will call the default function of MyExtension.dll. The output of this should appear in the browser as shown in Figure 12.20 on the facing page.

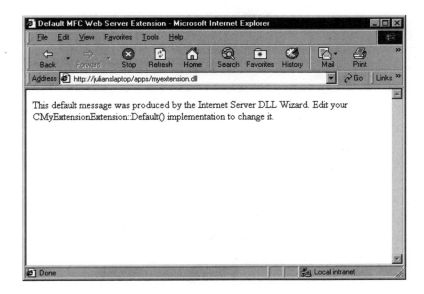

Figure 12.20   Internet Explorer 5 displaying output from MyExtension.dll

Examining the MyExtension Code

If you look at the source code in the MyExtension project, you will see that
the ISAPI Extension Wizard has created a single class for you named
CMyExtensionExtension. This class is derived from the MFC base class
CHttpServer. You can add member functions to this class to implement the
functions exported by the DLL.

MFC provides a code construct called a *parse map* to define the DLL functions
and map them to member functions of your **CHttpServer**-derived class. The parse
map is declared in the header file with the **DECLARE_PARSE_MAP** macro,
and implemented with **BEGIN_PARSE_MAP** and **END_PARSE_MAP** macros, as shown in the following example from your MyExtension.cpp file:

```
BEGIN_PARSE_MAP(CMyExtensionExtension, CHttpServer)
    // TODO: insert your ON_PARSE_COMMAND() and
    // ON_PARSE_COMMAND_PARAMS() here to hook up your commands.
    // For example:

    ON_PARSE_COMMAND(Default, CMyExtensionExtension, ITS_EMPTY)
    DEFAULT_PARSE_COMMAND(Default, CMyExtensionExtension)
END_PARSE_MAP(CMyExtensionExtension)
```

You can see that the ISAPI Extension Wizard has added the **DEFAULT_PARSE COMMAND** macro to specify the name of the default function as **Default()**. The Wizard provides a simple implementation of this function that can be found further down the file:

```
void CMyExtensionExtension::Default(CHttpServerContext* pCtxt)
{
    StartContent(pCtxt);
    WriteTitle(pCtxt);

    *pCtxt << _T("This default message was produced by the Internet");
    *pCtxt << _T("
        Server DLL Wizard. Edit your CMyExtensionExtension::Default()");
    *pCtxt << _T(" implementation to change it.\r\n");

    EndContent(pCtxt);
}
```

The output from this function is shown in Figure 12.20.

The **Default()** function, like all ISAPI extension functions, takes a pointer to a **CHttpServerContext** object. One **CHttpServerContext** object is created by **CHttpServer** for each HTTP client/server transaction. As the server extension DLL processes requests, it uses **CHttpServerContext** member functions to perform tasks such as retrieving details contained in the header of the HTTP client request (using **CHttpServerContext::GetServerVariable()**), or inserting HTML text into the response file that is sent back to the client (using the overloaded << operator).

The server extension's **CHttpServer** object creates a **CHttpServerContext** object for each client request. Each object is created on a separate thread to allow multiple simultaneous calls to the **CHttpServer** object by different client connections. You must be careful to perform synchronization for global variables, or for any data members of your **CHttpServer** class.

Adding a Function to Your Server Extension

You will now add a simple function named **GetColor()** to your ISAPI server extension. **GetColor()** takes any one of the HTML color names as a parameter and generates a page with an appropriately colored background.

▶   **To add the GetColor() function**

1. Add the following lines to the Parse Map in the MyExtension.cpp file:

   ```
   ON_PARSE_COMMAND(GetColor, CMyExtensionExtension, ITS_PSTR)
   ON_PARSE_COMMAND_PARAMS("color")
   ```

The **ON_PARSE_COMMAND** macro specifies the name of the function—the class name to map the function to. The parameters received by the function are specified as the third (and subsequent) parameters of the **ON_PARSE_COMMAND** macro. The parameter types are specified by the **ON_PARSE_COMMAND_PARAMS** macro. The lines in the example just shown specify that the **GetColor()** function will have a single string parameter named *color*.

2. Use the ClassView **Add Member Function** feature to add a function with the following signature to the **CMyExtensionExtension** class:

```
void GetColor(CHttpServerContext *pCtxt, LPCTSTR pstrColor)
```

3. Implement the function as follows:

```
void CMyExtensionExtension::GetColor(CHttpServerContext *pCtxt,
LPCTSTR pstrColor)
{
    StartContent(pCtxt);
    WriteTitle(pCtxt);

    *pCtxt << _T("You have chosen the ");
    *pCtxt << pstrColor << _T(" page.\r\n");
    *pCtxt << _T("<SCRIPT language=\"JavaScript\">
        document.bgColor = \"");
    *pCtxt << pstrColor << _T("\" </SCRIPT>\r\n");

    EndContent(pCtxt);

}
```

4. Build and run the MyExtension project. You will need to copy the new DLL to the \INetPub\WWWRoot\MyISExtensions folder so that it replaces the previous version. Before you can do this, you will have to stop the Web (WWW) service on your computer. This is because ISAPI server extension DLLs are loaded into the IIS process when a client first requests them, and stay loaded until the WWW service is stopped. The easiest way to stop the WWW service on a computer using IIS is to open a system command prompt and type the following:

```
net stop w3svc
```

5. After you have copied the DLL, restart the service by typing the following:

```
net start w3svc
```

The revised DLL will be loaded at the first client request.

On a computer running Windows 95 or Windows 98, you can stop and start the Web service from the **Properties** menu of the Personal Web Manager. To gain access to the DLL, you might have to restart your computer after stopping the service.

The following HTML document called *Form.htm* allows you to test your new extension function. This document implements a simple form that allows the user to pick a color from a drop-down list box. The user clicks a **Submit** button to retrieve a page of the chosen color from the server.

```
<!-- Form.htm -->
<HTML>
<HEAD>
    <TITLE>
        Color Form
    </TITLE>
</HEAD>
<BODY>
    <H3> Choose a color from the list box and click SUBMIT</H3>

    <FORM action="myextension.dll?GetColor" method=POST>
    <SELECT name="color">
        <option> pink
        <option> green
        <option> yellow
        <option> blue
    </SELECT>
    <P>
    <input type="submit">
    </FORM>
</BODY>
</HTML>
```

Form.htm can be found in the Chapter 12\Exercises folder. Place a copy of Form.htm in the \INetPub\WWWRoot\MyISExtensions folder.

6. Start Internet Explorer and enter the following URL into the address box:

```
http://[your computer name]/apps/form.htm
```

You will see the page appear as shown in Figure 12.21 on the facing page.

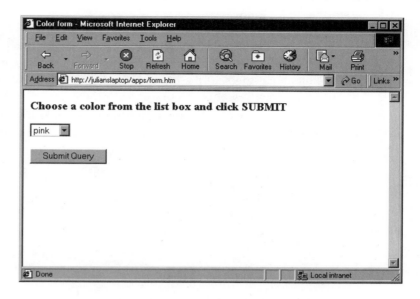

Figure 12.21   Form.htm displayed in Internet Explorer 5

7. Select a color from the list box and click **Submit Query**. A page with the background color you have chosen will be returned to your browser.

ISAPI Filters

ISAPI filters sit between the network connection to the clients and the HTTP server. They can be used to enhance Internet servers with custom features such as the enhanced logging of HTTP requests or custom encryption and compression schemes, or to implement alternative authentication methods. Filters are implemented as DLLs that are loaded when the WWW service is started. You can use the Internet Service Manager to assign filters to your IIS 4.0 Web sites. Personal Web Server does not support ISAPI filters.

Filters can be set to receive notification when selected server events occur. For example, the server might notify the filter that it is processing raw data from a client request, or that it is sending data to the client, or that it has just written to the log or closed a transaction. As the filter processes these notifications, it has access to the server data related to the notification event. For example, a filter that is notified that the server is sending raw data to the client has access to the data being sent so that the filter can modify the data, perhaps applying a compression or encryption algorithm.

The following exercises demonstrate a simple ISAPI filter that is built using the ISAPI Extension Wizard.

▶ **To create the MyFilter ISAPI filter**

1. On the **Projects** tab of the **New** dialog box, click **ISAPI Extension Wizard**. Enter **MyFilter** as a project name and click **OK**.

2. On the first screen of the ISAPI Extension Wizard, clear the **Generate a Sever Extension object** option and select the **Generate a Filter object** option.

3. In Step 2 of the ISAPI Extension Wizard, select **Incoming raw data and headers**. Leave **End of connection** selected so that the dialog box looks as shown in Figure 12.22.

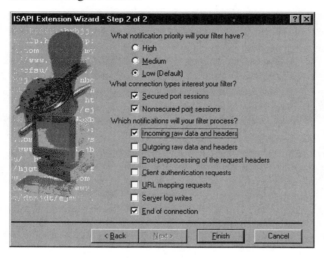

Figure 12.22   Creating an ISAPI filter

4. Click **Finish**, and then click **OK** to create the MyFilter project.

If you examine the generated code, you will see that the ISAPI Extension Wizard has created a single class **CMyFilterFilter** that is derived from the MFC class **CHttpFilter**. A handler function has been added to this class for each notification that you specified in Step 2 of the ISAPI Extension Wizard, as shown in this extract from the **CMyFilterFilter** class definition:

```
virtual DWORD OnReadRawData(CHttpFilterContext* pCtxt,
    PHTTP_FILTER_RAW_DATA pRawData);
virtual DWORD OnEndOfNetSession(CHttpFilterContext* pCtxt);
```

These functions are overloaded versions of **CHttpFilter** member functions. The Wizard provides stub functions in the .cpp file. You define your filter behavior by implementing these functions.

Note that another overloaded function, **GetFilterVersion()**, is implemented for your class. This function is called by the server to learn which notifications the filter will handle. To make the filtering process more efficient, the server sends notifications only for the events specified in this function. The following line from the **MyFilter::GetFilterVersion()** function shows how to specify the events:

```
pVer->dwFlags |= SF_NOTIFY_ORDER_LOW | SF_NOTIFY_SECURE_PORT |
    SF_NOTIFY_NONSECURE_PORT | SF_NOTIFY_READ_RAW_DATA |
    SF_NOTIFY_END_OF_NET_SESSION;
```

Be aware that if you add handler functions for additional notification events, you must also add the corresponding flags to this line. Although you can use ClassWizard to add notification event handler functions, ClassWizard does not update the **GetFilterVersion()** function for you, so you must remember to do this manually.

Notification handler functions receive data structures that contain information about the event they are handling. They also receive a pointer to a **CHttpFilterContext** object, which like the **CHttpServerContext** object, contains information about the current client connection and provides methods to retrieve information about the connection or to write data into the client response.

In the following exercises, you will provide a simple implementation of the **MyFilter::OnReadRawData()** function. This will use the **CHttpFilterContext:: GetServerData()** function to retrieve the IP address of the remote server that is currently connected, and then write it to a log file.

▶ **To implement the MyFilter::OnReadRawData() function**

1. Locate the **MyFilter::OnReadRawData()** function and replace it with the following implementation:

```
DWORD CMyFilterFilter::OnReadRawData(CHttpFilterContext* pCtxt,
PHTTP_FILTER_RAW_DATA pRawData)
{
    char pchVar[64];
    DWORD dwSize = 64;

    CStdioFile logfile("C:\\iislog.txt",
        CFile::modeCreate | CFile::modeWrite);

    BOOL bRet = pCtxt->GetServerVariable(
        "  REMOTE_HOST", pchVar, &dwSize);

    if(bRet)
        logfile.Write(pchVar, dwSize);

    logfile.Close();

    return SF_STATUS_REQ_NEXT_NOTIFICATION;
}
```

2. Build the MyFilter project. Copy the MyFilter.dll file to the c:\Winnt\System32\inetsrv folder.

▶ **To install the filter on an IIS 4.0 Server**

1. Open the Internet Service Manager. Right-click your local server icon (the icon is labeled with the name of your computer) and select **Properties**.

2. In the **Master Properties** box, make sure the **WWW Service** option is selected and click **Edit**.

3. In the **WWW Service Master Properties** dialog box, click the **ISAPI Filters** tab. This tab is shown in Figure 12.23.

Figure 12.23   Installing ISAPI filters on a Web server

4. Click **Add**. Type **MyFilter** as the filter name. Use the **Browse** button to locate the MyFilter.dll file in the c:\Winnt\System32\inetsrv folder and enter the full path to the file into the **Executable** box.

5. Click **OK** to close the **WWW Service Master Properties** dialog box, and then click **OK** again to close the Server Properties.

6. Open a system command prompt and type:

```
net stop w3svc
```

followed by:

```
net start w3svc
```

7. Open Internet Explorer and browse to a page on your local server Web site—for example, the http://[*your computer name*]/apps/form.htm page from the previous exercises.

8. Close Internet Explorer. If you look in the root directory of your c:\ drive you will find the *iislog.txt* file has been created. Double-click this file to view it in Notepad. You will see that the IP address of your computer has been added to the log file.

Lesson Summary

ISAPI allows you to write programs that extend the functionality of IIS 4.0 and its desktop counterpart, PWS.

There are two types of ISAPI programs: server extensions and filters, both of which are implemented as DLLs. ISAPI server extensions are compiled server-side programs that can be launched by an Internet client request. ISAPI filters intercept data travelling to and from the server and thus can perform specialized logging, encryption and other tasks.

ISAPI server extensions are based on the CGI standard and can be invoked from a URL by specifying the name of the DLL. Server extensions expose functions that can take parameters. You can specify the function name and parameter values as part of a URL, or you can connect the extension to an HTML form so that it receives parameters from the form controls. You use the ISAPI Extension Wizard to create a server extension project based around the **CHttpServer** and **CHttpServerContext** classes.

ISAPI filters sit between the network connection to the clients and the HTTP server, and they add custom features such as enhanced logging or encryption and compression to your Internet server. The filter is implemented as a DLL that is loaded when the WWW service is started. You can use the Internet Service Manager to assign filters to your IIS 4.0 Web sites. PWS does not support ISAPI filters.

Filters receive notification when selected server events occur. As the filter processes these notifications, it has access to the server data related to the notification event. You use the ISAPI Extension Wizard to create an ISAPI filter project based around the **CHttpFilter** and **CHttpFilterContext** classes.

Lab 12: Creating STUpload as an ActiveX Document Server

In this lab, you will see how a fully featured MFC application can easily be created as an ActiveX document server. You will see how the functionality of the STUpload application can be made available to allow Internet Explorer users to view STUpload document files deployed on a Web site.

To make the examples clearer, the STUpload projects that you have been working with throughout this book have not been created with ActiveX document server support. The Chapter 12\Partial folder contains a copy of the STUpload project that has been created with ActiveX document server support. The ActiveX document server support, as you recall, is added by selecting the **Full-server** and the **Active document server** options in Step 3 of the MFC AppWizard. You should use a copy of this project as a starting point for the exercises in this lab.

▶ **To view the ActiveX document server classes**

1. Open your copy of the Chapter 12\Partial\STUpload project. If you look at the classes displayed in ClassView, you will see that the ActiveX document server version of the project has some extra classes. The **CInPlaceFrame** class represents the frame window that encloses the document when it is edited "in place"—that is, when it is edited in a container. The **CSTUploadServerItem** class provides the server interface to the container.

2. Double click the **CSTUploadDoc** item. Look at the class definition and notice that it is derived from the **COleServerDoc** class.

You will now modify the **IDR_SRVR_INPLACE** menu and toolbar to make STUpload menu commands available from the menu of the ActiveX document container.

▶ **To edit the IDR_SRVR_INPLACE menu**

1. In ResourceView, double-click the **IDR_SRVR_INPLACE** menu item. Select the **Edit** submenu and press **DEL** to delete the menu. Confirm the deletion by clicking **OK**.

2. Double-click the **IDR_MAINFRAME** menu item. On the **Window** menu, click **Tile Horizontally** to view both menus together.

3. Copy the **Data** submenu from the **IDR_MAINFRAME** menu to the former location of the **Edit** submenu on the **IDR_SRVR_INPLACE** menu. Copy by dragging the menu while holding down the CTRL key.

4. From the **Data** submenu on the **IDR_SRVR_INPLACE** menu, delete the **Import** menu comand. Close both menu editor windows.

You delete the **Import** menu command because the ActiveX document elements of the STUpload application will be used only to view and upload existing documents deployed on a Web server. You will not offer the capability to create new documents over the Web.

▶ **To edit the IDR_SRVR_INPLACE toolbar**

1. In ResourceView, double-click the **IDR_SRVR_INPLACE** toolbar item. Remove the **Cut, Copy** and **Paste** toolbar buttons by dragging them off the toolbar.

2. Double-click the **IDR_MAINFRAME** toolbar item. From the **Window** menu, select **Tile Horizontally** to view both toolbars together.

3. Copy the **ID_DATA_UPLOAD** and the **ID_DATA_QUERYDATABASE** toolbar buttons from the **IDR_MAINFRAME** menu to the **IDR_SRVR_ INPLACE** menu. Copy by holding down the CTRL key while dragging the buttons across. Close both toolbar editor windows.

Build the STUpload project. Once the build has completed successfully, complete the following steps to test the ActiveX document server functionality of the STUpload application.

▶ **To create and deploy an STUpload ActiveX document**

1. Press CTRL+F5 to run the STUpload application. Using the **Import** command on the **Data** menu, load the Ch12Test.dat file from the Chapter 12\ Data folder. Use the **Select Fund** window to choose a fund to view.

2. Close the STUpload application, saving the current document as **ADTest.stu**.

3. Deploy the **ADTest.stu** document to the **Docs** virtual directory that you created for the exercises in this chapter.

▶ **To test the STUpload ActiveX document server**

1. Open Internet Explorer and enter the following URL into the **Address** box:

```
http://[your computer name]/docs/ADTest.stu
```

The ADTest.stu file should display in the browser. If you do not have a Web site set up on your machine, you can simulate this step by dragging the ADTest.stu file icon from Windows Explorer and dropping it onto the browser.

2. On the **Data** menu, click the **Upload** command. Click **OK** to upload the file to the database.

3. Once the upload has completed, use the **Query Database** command on the **Data** menu to check that the items you uploaded are now on the database.

4. Close Internet Explorer.

Review

1. What is the preferred method of creating a Web browser–style application?

2. In an ATL HTML control, how do you define methods to be accessible to the HTML source code of the document displayed by the control?

3. How does the Microsoft Scriptlet Component handle scriptlet custom events?

4. How can you save changes to ActiveX documents deployed on a Web server?

5. How do you specify which menu commands of the ActiveX server application are displayed by an ActiveX document container when it loads an ActiveX document?

6. How do you specify the default function for an ISAPI server extension?

7. How do ISAPI server extensions and ISAPI filters differ in the way they are loaded?

CHAPTER 13

Error Handling, Debugging, and Testing

About This Chapter

In this chapter, you will learn about error handling, debugging, and testing. Cutting corners on these essential but "unglamorous" final steps to development is usually false economy; a poorly tested application can incur significant costs through lost revenue, waste productivity, and strained relations with users.

Before You Begin

To complete the lessons in this chapter, you should have read Chapters 2 through 12, and completed the exercises in the text. In addition, you must install the Microsoft Visual C++ development tools as described in Lesson 2 of Chapter 1.

Lesson 1: Error Handling

Experienced developers treat *error handling* as a natural part of the coding process; appropriate error handling is an essential component of a robust application. This lesson explains some of the common techniques used in error handling. This lesson also presents a broad discussion of how to incorporate code that not only detects a problem when it occurs but reacts appropriately (for example, by displaying a message box to users). It's far easier to address error handling during the coding process than to try retrofitting the code later.

After this lesson, you will be able to:

- Write code that effectively handles errors as they occur in a running program.
- Understand exceptions and use exception-handling techniques in your code.
- Keep a running record of a program's progress using the **TRACE** macro.

Estimated lesson time: 30 minutes

Anticipating Program Errors

Most experienced programmers have a healthy skepticism about whether code will perform as intended. Your code might contain logical errors that affect your program in ways that are not instantly apparent. Even code that is *logically* error free might have unexpected effects within certain environmental circumstances. As you write code, develop the habit of questioning every assumption. Try to anticipate things that might go wrong and incorporate additional code to react gracefully to such problems. These added lines of code might execute only rarely, if ever, but are present in case they are needed to solve problems.

Failing to properly anticipate environmental contingencies catches many developers off guard. Consider the following typical scenario, in which a function allocates a buffer in memory, then fills it with text. Using the **new** operator, this function receives a pointer to a block of memory, then immediately proceeds to write to it. Throughout the development process, the function performs flawlessly because the development computer has ample resources to provide free store memory. After the program is released, the program's developer begins receiving calls from irate users who have lost a day's work because the program has failed as a result of the users' computers not having adequate memory to perform the task.

Experienced programmers take a more conservative approach when allocating memory. They add code that checks the value of the pointer returned by **new** and will only use the pointer if it holds a non-zero value. If **new** returns a **NULL** pointer—meaning that the allocation failed—code should react appropriately. The result should resemble the following code:

```
int  *ptr = new int[BLOCK_SIZE];
if (ptr)
{
    // Memory block successfully allocated, so use it
    .

    .

    .
    delete[] ptr;
}
else
{
    // Allocation failed -- take appropriate steps
}
```

Anticipation of potential problems and implementation of proper contingency procedures lead to more robust code with increased stability under adverse circumstances, which in turn leads to reduced failure rates. Programmed robustness is considered to be *fault-tolerant*, referring to the degree to which code can accommodate problems without failure. You might think of this anticipatory approach as *inline error handling*, in which possible errors are dealt with immediately in the body of the code.

Handling errors by continually checking return values can make code difficult to read and maintain because of constant interruptions of the program's logic flow. This method of error checking can often lead to a long series of nested **IF-ELSE** blocks, in which the **IF** blocks contain the code as it is intended to run, and the **ELSE** blocks contain the code that deals with errors. Following is a pseudocode illustration of how such nested tests can move closer to the right side of the screen. If the nested tests contain long lines of code, the intended flow might be difficult to follow:

```
if (condition1 == TRUE)
{
    // Compute condition2
    if (condition2 == TRUE)
    {
        // Compute condition3
        if (condition3 == TRUE)
        {
            // Other nested conditions
            .

            .

            .
        }
        else
        {
```

```
                // Failure for condition3
        }
    }
    else
    {
        // Failure for condition2
    }
}
else
{
    // Failure for condition1
}
```

Microsoft Windows and Visual C++ offer another approach to handling errors inline: *exception handling*. Exception handling allows developers to separate a function logically into two sections: one for normal execution and the other for trapping errors. Seemingly oblivious to potential errors, code in the normal execution section does not check return values and executes as though no problems exist. The second code section traps errors as they occur.

Exceptions

An *exception* is any condition that the operating system considers to be an error. When an application raises an exception, the operating system attempts to notify the offending application that it has caused an error by calling the application's exception handler code (assuming such code exists). If the application does not provide an exception handler, the operating system resolves the problem itself, often by terminating the application abruptly with a terse message to its user such as "This program has performed an illegal operation and will be shut down."

Two levels of exception handling exist:

- **Structured exception handling (SEH)** pertains exclusively to operating system errors.
- **C++ exception handling** pertains to errors in Visual C++ applications.

Structured Exception Handling

Although this chapter primarily examines C++ exception handling, Structured Exception Handling (SEH) merits attention for two reasons. First, though they are quite distinct, the two types of exception handling are often confused. Second, although the C language cannot use C++ exception handling, it can implement SEH.

All exception handling is based on the SEH mechanism. SEH initiates the beginning of a communication chain that winds its way up to the application level. An application incorporates SEH through the **__try**, **__except**, and **__finally** keywords. A **__try** block must be matched with either an **__except** block or a **__finally** block, but not both. The syntax is as follows:

```
__try
{
    // Normal code goes here
}
__except (filter)
{
    // Errors that occur in the try block are trapped here
}
```

Note that SEH keywords are preceded by two underscores, not one. The **__except** block executes only if code in the **__try** block causes an exception. If the **__try** block finishes successfully, execution resumes at the next instruction following the **__except** block, thus bypassing the **__except** block entirely.

Through its *filter* parameter, the **__except** block specifies whether it is able to deal with the exception. The **filter** parameter must evaluate to one of the values described in Table 13.1.

Table 13.1   Filter Parameter Evaluation Values

Value	Meaning
EXCEPTION_CONTINUE_SEARCH	The **__except** block declines the exception and passes control to the handler with the next highest precedence.
EXCEPTION_CONTINUE_EXECUTION	The **__except** block dismisses the exception without executing, forcing control to return to the instruction that raised the exception.
EXCEPTION_EXECUTE_HANDLER	The body of the **__except** block executes.

A filter such as EXCEPTION_CONTINUE_EXECUTION might seem odd in that it apparently renders the **__except** block useless. Why have an exception handler if it never executes, but merely requests that the statement causing the exception be repeated? An **__except** block usually calls a helper function that returns a value for the *filter* parameter, as shown in the following code:

```
__except (GetFilter())
{
    // Body of __except block
}
    .
    .
    .
long GetFilter()
{
    long lFilter;
    // Determine the filter appropriate for the error
    return lFilter;
}
```

The helper function must analyze current conditions and attempt to fix the problem that triggered the exception. If it succeeds, the helper function returns EXCEPTION_CONTINUE_EXECUTION, thus causing control to bypass the __except block and return to the original instruction in the __try block for another attempt. However, such techniques must be employed with care; if the helper function does not truly fix the problem, the program enters an infinite loop in which the statement in the __try block continually executes, raising over and over an exception that is never properly solved.

Although nominally part of SEH, the __finally keyword has little to do with the operating system. Rather, it defines a block of instructions that the compiler guarantees will execute when the __try block finishes. Even if the __try block contains a **RETURN** or **GOTO** statement that jumps beyond the __finally block, the compiler ensures that the __finally block executes before returning or jumping. The __finally keyword does not take a parameter.

C++ Exception Handling

C++ exception handling is at the higher end of the command chain initiated by SEH. Whereas SEH is a system service, C++ exception handling is code that you write to implement that system service. C++ exception handling is more sophisticated and offers more options than SEH. Use of the low-level __try and __except keywords of SEH is discouraged for Visual C++ applications.

In much the same way that a C application uses SEH, a Visual C++ application provides exception handler code that executes in response to an error. This code resolves the problem and retries the instruction that caused the error, ignores the problem completely, or passes the notification further along the chain of potential handlers. C++ provides the **try**, **catch**, and **throw** keywords for this purpose. Unlike their SEH counterparts, these keywords do not have a double-underscore prefix.

To see a simple example of C++ exception handling, consider again the scenario in which a program attempts to write to unowned memory after the **new** operator fails. Previously, we saw how an application can prevent failure by testing the value of a returned pointer. Exception handling offers a somewhat more sophisticated solution in which code is separated into **try** and **catch** blocks instead of a series of nested **IF-ELSE** blocks, as demonstrated in the following code:

```
try
{
    int  *iptr = new int[BLOCK_SIZE];
    .
    .        // If we reach this point, allocation succeeded
    .
    delete[] iptr;
}
```

```
catch(CMemoryException* e)
{
    // Allocation failed, so address the problem
    e->Delete();
}
```

If the **new** command fails to allocate the requested memory, it triggers an exception that causes the **catch** block to execute. In this example, the **catch** block accepts as its parameter a pointer to an MFC **CMemoryException** object, which contains information about out-of-memory conditions caused by the **new** operator. C++ programs that do not use MFC can design their own class for this purpose, or even use a pointer to a standard type, such as a pointer to a string. The block's parameter list can also be an ellipsis (...), which indicates to the compiler that the **catch** block handles all types of exceptions, not exclusively memory exceptions.

If the **catch** block can fix the problem, it retries the instruction that caused the exception by executing the **throw** command. Notice that this option is much more flexible than using the EXCEPTION_CONTINUE_EXECUTION filter of SEH, because it allows the **catch** block to execute. If the **catch** block does not retry (or *rethrow*) the exception, program flow continues to the next statement following the **catch** block.

MFC Exception Macros

Early versions of MFC provided macros as substitutes for the C++ exception handling commands, naming them **TRY**, **CATCH**, and **THROW**. For various reasons, the macros have fallen out of favor; since MFC 3.0, these macros have simply become aliases for the original C++ keywords **try**, **catch**, and **throw**. Thus, while MFC still supports the uppercase macro names, the names are no longer recommended because there is no advantage to using them.

Benign Exceptions

Some exceptions are benign and consequently do not show up as errors in an application. For example, a benign exception can occur when a program accesses an uncommitted page of its stack memory. The operating system confronts this situation transparently by trapping the invalid access, committing another page to the stack, and then allowing the access to continue using the committed page. The application does not recognize that the exception has occurred. The only external evidence of such an exception is a momentary delay while the operating system sets up a new page.

Logging Errors

The first two sections of this lesson describe how errors can be handled inline as they occur. Because not all errors can be anticipated and caught by developers, it is important to keep a record of unexpected errors as they occur. This section presents a third technique in which an executing program simply compiles a record of errors (an error log) without stopping to confront them. Developers can then read through the resulting error log after the program terminates, and revise the program's code to ensure that the errors do not occur again.

MFC programs use the **TRACE** macro and its variations to achieve this "offline" approach to error handling. Many C programmers employ a similar technique by the liberal use of **printf**() statements throughout their code, which provide a running commentary as the code progresses by displaying brief messages such as these:

```
Entering Function1
Allocating memory block
Block successfully allocated
.
.
.
Leaving Function1
```

The **TRACE** macro logs errors by displaying messages at the location specified by **AfxDump**, which by default is the **Debug** tab of the Visual C++ Output window. **TRACE** operates only for a project's debug build (described in Lesson 3 of this chapter). For release builds, the macro does nothing. Because it does not expand into code, the **TRACE** macro does not increase the size of a program's release version.

TRACE accepts the same string formatting commands as **printf**(), so you can display variables in a **TRACE** line as demonstrated in the following code:

```
int  iFileSize = 10;
char sz[] = "kilobytes";
// Display the string "File size is 10 kilobytes"
TRACE("File size is %d %s\n", iFileSize, sz);
```

The maximum string length after formatting cannot exceed 512 characters, including the terminating **NULL**. MFC also offers the macros **TRACE0**, **TRACE1**, **TRACE2**, and **TRACE3**, which take fixed numbers of variables (0, 1, 2 or 3). The only advantage offered by these variations over **TRACE** is that they expand into code that is a bit more compact.

Lesson Summary

In this lesson, you've learned some of the many ways an application can anticipate and respond to errors as they occur during execution.

The operating system's structured exception handling mechanism is the foundation on which C++ exception handling is built. Visual C++ implements C++ exception handling through the **try**, **catch**, and **throw** keywords. The MFC macro equivalents for these keywords are no longer used in C++ programming.

Testing for return values is an excellent programming habit, but can often be replaced by exception handling. **TRACE** statements provide a convenient way to create a running record of a program's logic flow, which you can examine to make sure your program is executing as expected.

The philosophy of error handling can be summed up in two words: "Don't assume!" Errors have a habit of occurring when least expected. Proper error-handling techniques enable your program to gracefully respond to the unexpected, without terminating abnormally—or worse, continuing to execute in an unstable state.

Lesson 2: COM Errors

COM applications and components can use the error handling techniques discussed in Lesson 1, but must also confront COM's preferred method of communicating error information through values known as HRESULT codes.

This lesson describes HRESULT codes in detail and points out various pitfalls to avoid when dealing with COM errors. Keep in mind that, with COM, success and failure are not always black and white concepts. COM allows for the idea that success and failure might be only partial, not complete.

You will also learn how a COM component can notify its client of an error through the **Error** event, one of the several stock events defined in COM.

After this lesson, you will be able to:

- Understand and create HRESULT codes used in COM programming.
- Compensate for applications that do not properly receive error codes from COM servers.
- Understand when to use the COM **Error** event.

Estimated lesson time: 15 minutes

HRESULT Codes

In COM, interface methods return HRESULT codes to report success or failure. Despite its "H" prefix, an HRESULT code is not a handle, but merely a 32-bit value indicating a success or failure condition.

COM predefines many HRESULT codes such as **S_OK** for success, **S_FALSE** for failure, and various error codes such as **E_INVALIDARG** and **E_NOTIMPL**. The "E" prefix stands for error. The "S" prefix identifies the first two codes as status code (SCODE) values. Under 32-bit Windows, HRESULT and SCODE mean the same thing.

COM allows your own programs to define new HRESULT values, as explored in the next section. However, to prevent confusion, you should use COM's predefined values whenever appropriate. For example, the **E_OUTOFMEMORY** code, already defined by the COM library, communicates a common error condition without ambiguity. You can find a list of predefined HRESULT values and their meanings in the WinError.h file under the heading "OLE Error Codes."

Anatomy of an HRESULT Code

An HRESULT code consists of four bit fields, as illustrated in Figure 13.1. Table 13.2, which follows the figure, describes the fields in the figure from left to right.

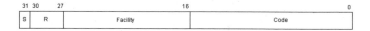

Figure 13.1   Bit fields of an HRESULT value

Table 13.2   Bit Field Descriptions

Field ID	Bits	Description
S	31	Severity code. A value of 0 indicates success, and a value of 1 indicates an error. Because the severity bit is also the value's sign bit, a severity value of 1 makes the HRESULT code a negative number.
R	27-30	Reserved bits of the facility code. Should be zero.
Facility	16-26	Facility code that indicates a general category to which the error code belongs.
Code	0-15	A 16-bit WORD value that identifies the condition.

Facility codes are defined as part of the COM specification. Error codes within most facility categories (for example, FACILITY_NULL, FACILITY_RPC) are specified by COM and have universal meaning. COM defines the FACILITY_ ITF category to contain developer-specified error codes that have their meanings determined by the interface member functions from which they are returned.

When defining your own HRESULT codes, use FACILITY_ITF as shown in the following code:

```
#define MY_SUCCESS_CODE ((0 << 31) | (FACILITY_ITF << 16) | 0x200)
#define E_MY_ERROR_CODE ((1 << 31) | (FACILITY_ITF << 16) | 0x201)
```

The WinError.h file defines FACILITY_ITF as 4, so the first example creates a positive value of 0x00040200. The second example produces a negative value of 0x80040201. WinError.h also defines the **MAKE_HRESULT** macro to simplify forming HRESULTs on the fly:

```
// Set HRESULT value 0x80040202
HRESULT hr = MAKE_HRESULT(SEVERITY_ERROR, FACILITY_ITF, 0x202);
```

A further wrinkle to keep in mind when dealing with HRESULT codes is that COM assumes that a value of zero indicates success, not failure. The manifest constant **S_OK**, for example, has a value of zero. As Table 13.1 illustrates, COM also assumes that any positive value indicates success, though perhaps qualified.

To save developers the trouble of memorizing these rules, COM provides two macros, named **SUCCEEDED** and **FAILED**, which are often used to test HRESULT codes. The macros are not a required addition to your COM programs, but they help make code more readable, as demonstrated in the following code:

```
HRESULT hr;

hr = pUnk->QueryInterface(IID_SomeObject, (PVOID*) &pObj);
if (SUCCEEDED(hr))
{
    // Use the pObj value
    .
    .
    .
    pObj->Release();
}
```

The macro definitions in the WinError.h file show that **SUCCEEDED** returns **TRUE** for any expression that evaluates to zero or greater; in contrast, **FAILED** evaluates to **TRUE** for any negative expression, as demonstrated in the following code:

```
#define SUCCEEDED(Status) ((HRESULT)(Status) >= 0)
#define FAILED(Status) ((HRESULT)(Status) < 0)
```

When dealing with an HRESULT not of your making, be careful how your code interprets it. Generally, you can rely on any constant with an "E" prefix having a negative value; other than that, you have no assurances. When unsure, consult the appropriate header file to determine a defined constant's true numeric value.

_com_error Support Class

Visual C++ provides the **_com_error** support class, which encapsulates an HRESULT code and helps hide the details behind COM error codes. The **_com_error** class provides several member functions that retrieve information about the encapsulated error. The most important of these functions are listed in Table 13.3, shown on the facing page.

Table 13.3   Important _com_error Member Functions

Member function	Return value
Error	The HRESULT code from which the **_com_error** object is constructed.
ErrorInfo	A pointer to an associated **IErrorInfo** (described later), or NULL if no **IErrorInfo** item exists. The caller must call **Release()** on the returned **IErrorInfo** object when finished using it.
Wcode	The HRESULT minus 0x80040200 if the HRESULT uses FACILITY_ITF. Otherwise, the function returns zero.
ErrorMessage	A **TCHAR** pointer to a system message describing the error. If no system message is available, the returned string is "Unknown error" followed by the hexadecimal HRESULT value.

If the encapsulated HRESULT has an associated **IErrorInfo** object, **_com_error** can access the contextual error information that the object contains. For example, the **HelpFile()** and **HelpContext()** member functions access the **IErrorInfo** object and return information about context-sensitive help pertaining to the error, which the caller can then display to the user through the familiar Windows Help system.

Because **_com_error** represents an exception condition, it often serves as the object passed to a **catch** block. Following is a simple program that illustrates how to trap errors with **_com_error**, using the **E_OUTOFMEMORY** error code as an example:

```
#include <comdef.h>
#include <stdio.h>

void main()
{
    try
    {
        _com_error e(E_OUTOFMEMORY);  // Construct the object
        throw(e);                     // Force an exception
    }

    catch(_com_error& e)
    {
        printf("Error   = %08lx\n", e.Error());
        printf("WCode   = %04x\n",  e.WCode());
        printf("Meaning = %s\n\n",  e.ErrorMessage());
    }
}
```

When the program runs, it displays the following lines:

```
Error   = 8007000e
WCode   = 0000
Meaning = Not enough storage is available to complete this operation.
```

Client Access to HRESULT Codes

After all this, you might be disappointed to learn that many client applications cannot even receive the HRESULT codes that a server's methods return. Thus, your carefully constructed and expressive codes often go to waste. The blame can be traced to limitations inherent in the **IDispatch** interface.

For example, the MFC client applications discussed in Chapter 11 do not receive HRESULT codes from their embedded COM components. The reason for this is because the wrapper class that Visual C++ creates for a component communicates through the **IDispatch** interface rather than calling component methods directly through a vtable. During its circuitous connections with the server, **IDispatch** loses the method's return value, which never makes its way back to the client. The MFC client using **IDispatch** can only infer when an error occurs in a COM server because a negative HRESULT value returned from a method generates an exception. By enclosing code that accesses the server in **try-catch** blocks, the client can respond in a general way to errors, though it cannot tell precisely what error occurred.

A Microsoft Visual Basic client fares no better. Like the MFC client, a program written in Visual Basic cannot receive HRESULT return values. The Visual Basic client can only react to negative error codes, usually through an **On Error** statement.

Before closing this section, we should point out that some C++ clients do properly receive HRESULT return codes. Whether it uses MFC or not, an application written in C++ does not need to rely on **IDispatch** and can receive a server's return values by bypassing the wrapper class that Visual C++ creates. However, such a technique is beyond the scope of this course.

Error Event

When a COM component method returns an HRESULT code to the client application, the notification is said to be *synchronous*. A synchronous notification forms part of the normal flow of communication between server and client: the client calls the server, the server detects an error, the server returns an HRESULT code explaining the problem, and the client reacts to the error. These steps occur in ordered progression; the client learns of the error only after the component ceases its task and returns.

In some cases, the component might encounter an error of which the client should be immediately apprised. In such a case, the component can fire an event and continue working. In another scenario, a component might have worker threads operating simultaneously with the client. If a worker thread detects an error, its only means of notifying the client is by firing an event. COM defines a stock event named **Error** that allows this type of asynchronous error notification.

The **Error** event has the predefined dispatch identifier **DISPID_ERROREVENT**. An ActiveX control using MFC and derived from **COleControl** can invoke the **FireError()** member function.

Lesson Summary

This lesson described how to deal with COM error codes, with particular attention paid to creating and using HRESULT codes in servers such as ActiveX controls. HRESULT codes are not handles, but simply 32-bit values containing four bit fields. The bit fields describe an error's severity, its facility category, and its code within a category. Negative HRESULT codes indicate failure, and generate exceptions in MFC and Visual Basic clients. The HRESULT and SCODE type definitions are interchangeable under 32-bit Windows programming.

By encapsulating an HRESULT value, the **_com_error** support class can make dealing with COM errors easier. A **_com_error** object is often passed as the exception parameter to a **catch** block.

Although developers of COM servers have an obligation to ensure that their products return accurate and expressive error codes, most client applications cannot or do not receive those codes. This will undoubtedly change in the future.

The stock **Error** event provides a COM component with the means of immediately notifying the client when an error occurs. The **Error** event should be used in asynchronous programming situations, where it is neither possible nor practical to use returned HRESULT values to indicate errors.

Lesson 3: Introduction to Debugging

This lesson presents a general introduction to the Visual C++ integrated debugger. Coverage of the extensive subject of debugging is best begun with an overview, rather than with an immediate jump into specifics about the debugger. After attaining a solid foundation about the debugger's purpose, as well as its advantages and limitations, you will be better prepared to use the debugger, which is described in the next lesson.

After this lesson, you will be able to:

- Understand the general manner in which a debugger works.
- Understand specific features of the Visual C++ integrated debugger.
- Use various macros, provided by the MFC framework that facilitate the task of debugging.

Estimated lesson time: 20 minutes

What Is a Debugger?

Debugging is a general term for finding and correcting program logic errors. It is necessary to master the art of debugging to develop applications successfully. A debugger is an application that facilitates the debugging process. The debugger runs a program under tight control, and can freeze operations at any point to allow you to check the program's status during execution.

The Visual C++ debugger is incorporated into the Visual Studio environment, and has its own menu and toolbar commands. Before using the debugger, you must create a debug build of your project. You cannot begin using the debugger until your code compiles into an executable file without syntactic error.

► **To create a debug build**

1. Right-click in the toolbar area and display the full **Build** toolbar (not the **Build** minibar). On the **Build** toolbar, make sure the Win32 Debug build configuration is selected as shown in Figure 13.2.

Figure 13.2   The Win32 Debug build configuration

2. On the same toolbar, click the **Build** button.

A debug operation consists of several steps, typically beginning in the text editor. To begin the debug operation, identify in the source code of a failing program the section where you suspect the problem originates, and then mark the first instruction of that section. Start the debugger, which executes the program until control reaches the mark you set at the start of the questionable section. When the debugger suspends the program's execution, you can then step through each instruction. This process gives you the opportunity to check current data values while the program is suspended, and ensure that the flow of control is proceeding along an expected path.

Debug vs. Release

The debug version of a product is the version with which you work during development and testing while you strive to make the program error-free. The debug version contains symbol information that the compiler places in the object file. By reading both the original source files and the project's symbol information, the debugger can associate each line of the source code with the corresponding binary instructions in the executable image. The debugger runs the executable but uses the source code to show the program's progress.

Note Code that has been optimized by the compiler can cause the debugger to behave in an unexpected manner. If strange errors occur when you step through code in the debugger, check that the debug configuration of your project has compiler optimization set to unavailable. Optimization is set on the **C/C++** page of the **Project Settings** dialog box.

The release version of a product is a more tightly compiled version that is distributed to your customers. The release version contains only executable instructions optimized by the compiler, without the symbol information. You can execute a release version inside the debugger; however, if you do, the debugger informs you that the file has no symbol data. Conversely, you can execute the debug version of a program normally, without the debugger. These execution processes have practical consequences as a result of a Visual C++ feature known as just-in-time debugging. If the program encounters an unhandled exception, the system's SEH mechanism causes control to be returned to Visual C++, which then executes the debugger. The debugger shows the instruction that caused the fault and displays data values as they existed when the program stopped.

MFC Debug Macros

MFC provides several macros that serve as debugging aids and affect only debug builds. We have already examined the **TRACE** macro and its variations, and seen how it's possible to use **TRACE** to log a program's actions and state. This section examines several other MFC macros, including **ASSERT** and its variants **VERIFY** and **DEBUG_NEW**.

The **ASSERT** macro offers a convenient way to test assumptions during application development without adding permanent error-checking code. For example, you might want to check a pointer for a non-zero value before using it. One way you can perform this action is to add a specific **if** test, as demonstrated in the following code for a function that accepts a **CButton** pointer as its parameter:

```
void SomeFunction(CButton* pbutton)
{
    if (pbutton)
    {
        // Use the pbutton pointer
        ...
    }
}
```

While such checks are good programming practices that help avoid potential problems, they might no longer be warranted in a program's release version. Including hundreds of such checks throughout a program can add unnecessary code to the finished product—code that increases the program's size and slows its execution. This unneeded code can be avoided by using an **ASSERT** macro, as demonstrated in the following code:

```
void SomeFunction(CButton* pbutton)
{
    ASSERT(pbutton);   // Make sure that pbutton is non-zero
    // Use the pbutton pointer
    ...
}
```

If the expression passed to **ASSERT** evaluates to zero, the program halts with a system message alerting you to the problem. As shown in Figure 13.3, the message gives you the choice of terminating the application, ignoring the problem, or debugging the application to learn more about the problem.

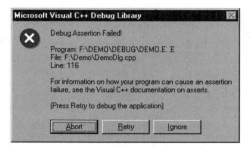

Figure 13.3   ASSERT failure message

The **ASSERT** macro creates code only for debug builds and evaluates to nothing in release builds. You can therefore insert hundreds of **ASSERT** statements in your code without increasing the size of the final product. If you prefer to leave a check in place for both debug and release builds, use the **VERIFY** macro instead, which functions regardless of the build configuration.

ASSERT can be used with any expression that yields a Boolean result, such as **ASSERT**(x < y) and **ASSERT**(i > 10), but its variants are more specialized. The similar **ASSERT_VALID** macro, for example, is used only with pointers to an object derived from the MFC **CObject** class. This macro does everything **ASSERT** does, but also calls the object's **AssertValid** member function to verify the object.

The **ASSERT_KINDOF** macro applies only to pointers to objects derived from **CObject**. **ASSERT_KINDOF** tests that the pointer represents an object of a specified class, or is an object of a class derived from the specified class. For example, this line verifies that **pDoc** points to an object derived from **CDocument**:

```
ASSERT_KINDOF(CMyDocument, pDoc)
```

The **DEBUG_NEW** macro helps you find memory leaks that can result when a **new** statement is not properly matched to a **delete** statement. The macro is easy to use and requires the addition of only a single line to your source code:

```
#define new DEBUG_NEW
```

With this definition in place, the compiler interprets every **new** statement in your code as **DEBUG_NEW**, and MFC takes care of the rest. For debug builds, **DEBUG_NEW** keeps track of the file name and line number where each **new** statement occurs. Your program can then call the **CMemoryState:: DumpAllObjectsSince()** member function, which displays a list of **new** allocations in the Visual C++ Output window, together with the file name and line number where the allocation occurs. This type of information can aid in pinpointing leaks. In release builds, **DEBUG_NEW** simply resolves to **new**.

Lesson Summary

This lesson introduced the concepts of the important process of debugging, in which the developer locates and corrects logical errors in an application. It described in general terms how a debugger works and the differences between release and debug versions of a project, and explained some of the macros that MFC provides as aids to debugging.

The **ASSERT** macro provides an effective means of alerting you to errors without becoming a permanent part of your program's release version. Its variants **ASSERT_VALID** and **ASSERT_KINDOF** are used with pointers to objects derived from the MFC **CObject** class. The **ASSERT** macro is used with a Debug build of an application. The **VERIFY** macro may be used with both debug and release builds. The **DEBUG_NEW** macro finds cases where free store memory is allocated but not properly returned to the system.

Lesson 4: Using the Integrated Debugger

Armed with the general overview of debugging provided in Lesson 3, you are now ready to use the Visual C++ debugger. As you will see, the debugger greatly facilitates the debugging process and can help you find nearly any bug you are likely to encounter in Windows software development.

After this lesson, you will be able to:

- Use the Visual C++ integrated debugger and understand the extensive information presented in the debugger windows.
- Monitor a running program and set breakpoints to interrupt the program.
- Single-step through a program.
- Use the debugger's **Edit and Continue** feature to correct code on the fly while debugging.
- Debug COM-based programs and components.
- Use the Test Container utility to monitor ActiveX controls.

Estimated lesson time: 40 minutes

Breakpoints

The debugger does not interrupt the program being debugged. Rather, the program interrupts itself when it locates a marker set in the text editor. The marker is called a *breakpoint*. As the program executes, the debugger sleeps. It regains control when the executing program triggers a breakpoint.

The debugger recognizes two different types of breakpoints, one based on location in the code, and the other based on program data. A *location breakpoint* is a marker attached to a particular instruction in your source code, similar to using a bookmark in the Visual C++ text editor. A *data breakpoint* depends on data instead of code. Use a data breakpoint to suspend execution of your program when the value of a variable changes. A data breakpoint can be useful if you suspect a variable is being incorrectly altered in your program, but you aren't sure in which location. The data breakpoint triggers the debugger to interrupt execution when the variable changes or becomes a certain value (for example, when a pointer is reassigned or when the variable x exceeds a value of 500).

Setting Breakpoints

The text editor is the best place to begin debugging. Location breakpoints are by far the most commonly used breakpoints, and are easy to set in the Visual C++ debugger. You simply need to have a general idea of where you think your program is going wrong.

▶ **To set a location breakpoint**

1. Open the program's source files and locate the line where you want to interrupt the execution of the program.

2. Click anywhere on the line to place the insertion point there, then press F9 to set a location breakpoint. The editor marks the line by placing a small red dot in the selection margin to the left of the line.

3. To remove a location breakpoint, press F9 again to toggle the breakpoint off.

4. You can also set or remove a location breakpoint by right-clicking the line. On the shortcut menu that appears (shown in Figure 13.4), select the **Insert/Remove Breakpoint** command to set or clear a breakpoint.

Figure 13.4   The **Insert/Remove Breakpoint** command

Though less convenient, you can also set a location breakpoint through the **Breakpoints** dialog box. This dialog box provides the only means for setting data breakpoints and two other variations, called *conditional breakpoints* and *message breakpoints*. Conditional breakpoints trigger as soon as a variable is set to a specified value. Message breakpoints trigger as soon as a specified message is received by a window.

Breakpoints Dialog Box

To invoke the **Breakpoints** dialog box shown in Figure 13.5, press CTRL+B or click the **Breakpoints** command on the **Edit** menu. The three tabs in the dialog box let you set location, data, conditional, and message breakpoints.

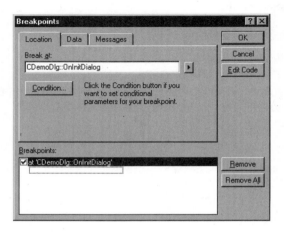

Figure 13.5   The **Breakpoints** dialog box

Location Breakpoints

The **Breakpoints** dialog box provides several enhancements for location breakpoints that often prove useful. For instance, you can type the name of a function in the **Break At** text box to set a location breakpoint at the first line of the function, or type the name of a label to set a breakpoint at the labeled line. The text in the **Break At** control is case-sensitive, so it must match the function name or label exactly. A C++ function name must include the class name and scope resolution operator. Thus, the entry **OnInitDialog**() does not specify a valid breakpoint location, but **CDemoDlg::OnInitDialog**() does.

Data Breakpoints

The **Breakpoints** dialog box provides the only means for setting a data break-point. On the **Data** tab in the **Breakpoints** dialog box, enter the name of the variable or the expression you want the debugger to monitor. Type an ex-pression in the form of a standard C/C++ conditional expression, such as the following:

```
i == 100 or nCount > 25
```

The debugger can monitor a range of variables identified by a pointer, such as an array or structure name, provided you dereference the pointer in the expression.

► **To set a data breakpoint for an array or structure**

1. In the **Breakpoints** dialog box, click the **Data** tab.

2. For an array, type the array name followed by **[0]** to dereference the pointer—**iArray[0]**, for example.

3. To monitor more than just the first element of the array, set the number of elements to monitor in the text box labeled **Enter the number of elements in an array or structure**. Notice that this is the number of elements, not the number of bytes.

4. To set a data breakpoint for a structure, precede the pointer variable with the asterisk dereference operator, as in **pStruct**.

Similarly, to monitor a string of character bytes that the variable pString points to, type ***pString** in the **Enter The Expression** text box. In the **Enter the number of elements** text box, type the number of bytes that you want the debugger to monitor. Typing **pString** without the asterisk dereference operator will result in the breakpoint being triggered only if pString is changed to point somewhere else. In this case, the debugger monitors pString itself, not the contents of the string to which it points.

Your program's execution speed can slow significantly if you set more than four data breakpoints, or if any of the data breakpoints are set on a variable residing on the stack.

Conditional Breakpoints

The debugger responds to a conditional breakpoint only if a specified condition is TRUE when control reaches the marked instruction. Each time an instruction marked as a conditional breakpoint executes, the debugger evaluates the expression and suspends program flow only if the expression does not evaluate to zero.

► **To set a conditional breakpoint**

1. In the **Breakpoints** dialog box, click the **Location** tab.

2. Specify the source code instruction at which to set the breakpoint.

3. Click the **Condition** button (shown in Figure 13.5) to display the **Breakpoint Condition** dialog box.

4. In the **Enter the expression to be evaluated** text box, type the breakpoint condition in the form of a C/C++ conditional expression.

Message Breakpoints

A message breakpoint attaches to a window procedure. Execution breaks when the window procedure receives a specified message, such as WM_SIZE or WM_COMMAND. Message breakpoints are not always useful in C++ programs that use MFC, since window procedures usually lie buried inside the MFC framework. To trap a specific message in an MFC program, set a location breakpoint for the function that handles the message, which is identified in the class's message map.

Running the Debugger

Once you have created a debug build and have established where and under what conditions you want your program to stop, you are ready to execute your program.

▶ **To start the debugger**

1. On the **Build** menu, click **Start Debug**. You will be presented with four choices: **Go**, **Step Into**, **Run to Cursor**, and **Attach to Process**.

2. When you have set at least one breakpoint in the source code, click **Go**. The debugger runs the program, suspending execution when the flow of execution in your program reaches a location breakpoint or triggers a data breakpoint.

3. Click **Step Into** to start program execution, and stop at the first command.

4. Click the **Run to Cursor** command to run the program and break at the source line containing the insertion point. If no source file is open in the text editor, the **Run to Cursor** command is unavailable. Otherwise, it allows you to quickly jump into a program without setting a breakpoint.

5. Click the **Attach to Process** command to launch the debugger and attach it to a program that is currently executing.

The debugger provides shortcut keys for the first three subcommands of **Start Debug**, so you don't have to pull down the **Build** menu to begin debugging. The shortcut keys are F5 for **Go**, F11 for **Step Into**, and CTRL+F10 for **Run to Cursor**.

Debugger Windows

When the program you are debugging stops at a breakpoint, the debugger updates its windows with information about the program's current state. The most important debugger window is the source window, which shows the source code where the program stopped. A small yellow arrow, the *instruction pointer*, appears in the selection margin to the left of the interrupted instruction. The instruction pointer identifies the instruction that has not yet executed, but is next in line to do so when the program resumes execution.

When control is returned to the debugger, the **Debug** toolbar appears on the screen. The six buttons identified in Figure 13.6 as debugger windows act as toggles that expose or hide dockable windows containing information about the current state of the program. Table 13.4 describes the type of information displayed in the debugger windows.

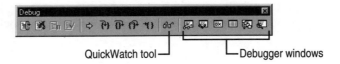

Figure 13.6   Debugger windows buttons

Table 13.4   Information Displayed by the Debugger Windows Buttons

Window	Information displayed
Watch	Current values of variables and expressions tracked by the debugger
Variables	Current values of variables accessed at or near the break location
Registers	Current contents of the CPU registers
Memory	Memory contents at a specified address
Call Stack	List of called functions that have not yet returned
Disassembly	Assembly language translation of the compiled code that supplements the source window on the screen

Variables Window and Watch Window

The Variables window displays information about variables relevant to the location where the program flow has been suspended. Variables referenced by the instruction that last executed, and usually one or two previous instructions, appear in the Variables window. You can change the value of a variable by double-clicking it in the Variables window and typing a new value.

The Watch window shows the current values of specified variables no matter where they are referenced in the program. To add a variable to the Watch window, double-click the dotted new-entry box in the window and type the variable name. The QuickWatch tool shown in Figure 13.6 lets you query for a current value without adding the variable to the Watch window. If the variable name appears on the screen, the debugger offers a more convenient way to query for its current value. Simply position the mouse pointer over the variable name in the Source window to see a ToolTip showing the current value.

Memory Window and Registers Window

The Memory window shows the contents of memory at a given address. The Memory window is useful for examining buffers that might not appear in the Variables window. Determine the value of the buffer pointer by locating it in the Variables or Watch window, then type or paste the address into the text box in the Memory window and press ENTER.

The Registers window shows the state of the processor's registers as they existed when the program was suspended. The Registers window is generally used only when the Disassembly window is active, showing the code in assembly language.

Call Stack Window

The Call Stack window shows the route the program has taken to reach the point you are examining. It answers the question, "How did I get here?"

A *call stack* is a list of nested functions, each of which have been called and none of which have yet returned. The list begins with the current function that contains the point of interruption, and continues in reverse order toward the oldest parent function. MFC programs often wind through many nested functions hidden in the framework, so the call stack for these programs can be lengthy.

Stepping Through Code

The **Debug** toolbar holds a group of four buttons (shown in Figure 13.7) that allow you to step through a suspended program. You can recognize the Step tools by the arrows and curly braces on them. In the order shown, the buttons activate the **Step Into**, **Step Over**, **Step Out**, and **Run To Cursor** commands. We've already discussed the **Run To Cursor** command; this section covers the **Step Into**, **Step Over**, and **Step Out** commands.

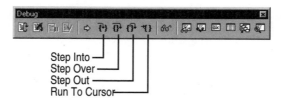

Figure 13.7   The **Debug** toolbar Step tools

The **Step Into** and **Step Over** commands (or their respective shortcut keys F11 and F10) let you single-step through the program. When you select **Step Into** or **Step Over**, the debugger allows the program to resume execution, but for only one instruction. After the instruction finishes, the debugger again suspends execution. If the Disassembly view is available, the **Step** tools act on individual assembly instructions instead of the high-level C/C++ instructions. If applied to an instruction that calls a function, **Step Over** halts at the instruction following the call, whereas **Step Into** halts at the first instruction of the function called. For instructions that do not call a function, **Step Into** and **Step Over** have the same effect.

The **Step Out** command is useful for leaving a function. The command executes the rest of the current function, then stops at the next statement following the function call. In other words, when applied to a function call, the **Step Into** and **Step Out** commands together have the same effect as **Step Over**.

Edit and Continue

Through its **Edit and Continue** feature, Visual C++ lets you permanently fix many problems directly in the debugger's source window, without having to exit the debugger and recompile. When you continue running the program after editing the source, Visual C++ first compiles the revised code and replaces the affected module with the corrected version.

Edit and Continue has certain limitations; this feature does not recognize source changes that are impossible, impractical, or unsafe to compile while debugging, such as:

- Alterations to exception handler blocks.
- Wholesale deletions of functions.
- Changes to class and function definitions.
- Changes to static functions.
- Changes to resource data in the project's resource (.rc) file.

Attempting to resume execution through **Edit and Continue** after making any of these changes causes the debugger to display an error message in the status bar that explains the problem. You have the option of continuing to debug using the original code, or closing the debugger and recompiling the revised code normally.

Debugging COM Components

The Visual C++ debugger easily handles in-process COM components such as ActiveX controls, though such components require a container application to run them. If you have written the component's container as another project, it does not matter where you begin debugging, whether in the container's project or in the component's project. The debugger crosses the boundary between projects transparently as execution flow moves from client to server and back again.

To begin debugging in the component's project, first specify the container application in which you want to embed the component. On the **Debug** tab of the **Project Settings** dialog box, type the container's path and file name in the text box labeled **Executable For Debug Session**. You can also browse for the container by clicking the arrow next to the text box. This action displays a small menu of choices, one of which is **ActiveX Control Test Container**.

ActiveX Control Test Container

The Test Container utility shown in Figure 13.8 is a general-purpose container utility for ActiveX controls. Visual C++ provides the Test Container so that you can debug and test ActiveX controls without having to write a corresponding container for them.

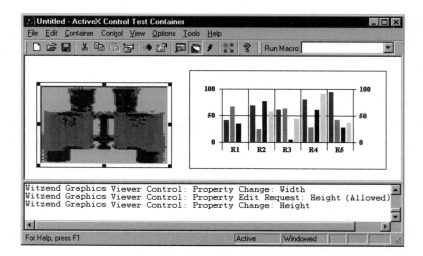

Figure 13.8   The ActiveX Control Test Container

The first step is to set breakpoints in your project's source files. If you have chosen the Test Container as the host for your component during debugging, the debugger launches the utility automatically, as it would any other container. When a breakpoint in the method triggers, focus returns to the Visual C++ debugger, ready for you to single-step through your source code.

You can also execute the Test Container without the debugger, as the next practice exercise demonstrates.

Executing ActiveX Controls in the Test Container

In this practice exercise, you will launch the Test Container utility manually, without starting the debugger. You will learn how to open an ActiveX control in the Test Container and program it through its methods and properties.

▶ **To start the Test Container**

1. On the **Tools** menu, click **ActiveX Control Test Container**.

2. When the Test Container appears, click **New Control** on the toolbar, which displays a list of registered ActiveX controls.

3. If you have built your own ActiveX control and it has been properly registered, locate it in the list. Otherwise, double-click any control in the list to activate it, such as the **Calendar** control that comes with Internet Explorer.

4. Once the control appears in the Test Container window, click the **Invoke Methods** tool to display the **Invoke Methods** dialog box.

5. Click the **Method Name** box to expose a list of methods that the control exports. If you have activated the **Calendar** control or a similar object, select the **BackColor (PropPut)** property method in the list. Methods identified as **PropPut** write a control property; **PropGet** methods read a property.

6. Enter the new property value in the **Parameter Value** box. To set a color, enter the decimal equivalent of an RGB value, such as **255** for bright red.

7. Click the **Invoke** button to call the method with the new value. If the property affects the control's appearance (as does the **BackColor** property), you should see the control change accordingly.

8. Press DELETE to delete the selected control, then close the Test Container.

Debugging Out-of-Process COM Servers

Many out-of-process COM servers can run as stand-alone programs, and thus do not technically require an executing container. However, as a server's methods and events execute only when activated by a client, you should specify a path to the client instead of the server on the **Debug** tab of the **Project Settings** dialog box. Set breakpoints in the server's source code as you want them, then launch the debugger to automatically start the client application. When both the client and server are active, switch to the client and invoke the commands necessary to activate the server's functions that contain the breakpoints. As with an in-process server, the Visual C++ debugger becomes active when execution reaches a breakpoint. You can then examine the server's code.

Lesson Summary

This lesson presented the Visual C++ debugger, an invaluable tool for locating the causes of errors in a program. You learned how to set both location and data breakpoints through the **Breakpoints** dialog box, how to launch the debugger, and how to single-step through code when the debugged program halts at a breakpoint. The lesson also described the debugger's **Edit and Continue** feature, which allows you to correct source code without having to exit the debugger and recompile.

A typical debugging session begins in the text editor. You can set breakpoints in the project source code, at those sections of your program that you want to interrupt, before you start the debugger. The debugger in turn automatically starts your program and gains control when a breakpoint is triggered. The debugger displays six dockable windows:

- **Watch** displays the values of selected data.
- **Variables** displays information pertaining to the current instruction.
- **Call Stack** contains a list of nested function calls.
- **Registers** displays the current contents of the CPU registers.
- **Memory** displays any area of accessible memory.
- **Disassembly** translates source code into equivalent assembly instructions.

In-process ActiveX controls are DLLs and therefore are debugged with the same ease as normal DLLs. Visual C++ also provides the Test Container utility, which serves as a general-purpose container application for running ActiveX controls. The Test Container enables you to debug and test your ActiveX control without having to develop a separate container for it.

Lesson 5: Using the Dependency Walker

Visual C++ provides other utilities in addition to the debugger that can help you look inside an application or DLL module. In this lesson, you will learn how to use the Dependency Walker utility, sometimes referred to by its file name Depends.exe.

After this lesson, you will be able to:

- Explain why Windows programs depend on other modules to run.
- Execute the Dependency Walker utility to examine a program's dependencies.

Estimated lesson time: 15 minutes

What Is a Dependency?

A Windows program is not as self-sufficient as it might appear on the surface. Even the simplest "Hello, world" program requires the presence of several DLLs provided by the system, such as Kernel32 and GDI32. Because the elementary MyApp program (seen in examples throughout this book) links to MFC, the program depends on the help of other module files, such as MFC42.dll. In turn, MFC cannot run without other files, such as the C run-time library MSVCRT.dll. This string of required modules must all be present and available to the operating system before a program can execute. Together, they form a program's *dependencies*.

Each executing Windows module, whether application or DLL, keeps a list of its dependencies in a header area within the executable file. When the operating system loads a module, it reads the list of dependencies and loads each required module. Only when all dependencies are loaded does the original program run.

Dependency Information

Ordinarily, a program's dependencies are invisible to users. A dependency usually makes itself known to users only when it is missing. In that case, Windows displays a message explaining that the requested program cannot run because a required file cannot be found.

The Dependency Walker utility reads the dependency list in a program's header and displays information about each dependency. The results are illustrated in Figure 13.9 on the next page, which shows the dependencies for a typical program named Demo.exe.

Module dependency tree   Parent import function list

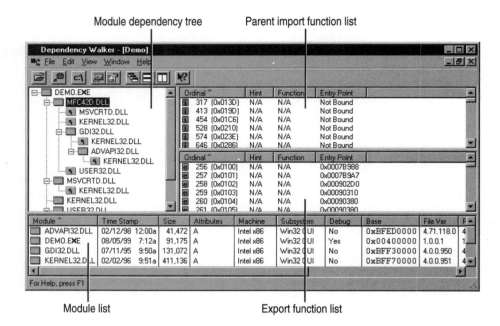

Module list   Export function list

Figure 13.9   The Dependency Walker utility

The Dependency Walker reveals such information as:

- The name and location of each file required to run an application or DLL.
- The base address of each dependency module.
- Version information about each dependency module.
- Whether each dependency module contains debug information.

▶ **To start the Dependency Walker**

1. On the **Start** menu, click **Programs**.

2. Click **Microsoft Visual Studio 6.0**, click **Microsoft Visual Studio 6.0 Tools**, and then click **Depends**. As with any utility, you can also add a command to the Visual C++ **Tools** menu to invoke the Dependency Walker.

3. When the utility appears, click **Open** on the **File** menu and browse to the application or DLL that you would like to examine.

The Dependency Walker is an MDI application, so you can open several views, each showing the dependencies for a different executable file. As Figure 13.9 reveals, the Dependency Walker displays four panes separated by split bars. Table 13.5 describes the four panes identified in Figure 13.9.

Table 13.5   The Four Panes Displayed in the Dependency Walker

Pane	Description
Module dependency tree	A hierarchical tree showing the program's dependencies. The tree often contains duplicate names because several modules can have the same dependencies.
Parent import function list	A list of parent import functions for the module selected in the Module dependency tree. Parent import functions are those functions (in the selected module) that are called by its parent module. The selected module must export every function that the parent is importing from it. If the selected module does not export one of the functions that the parent module expects to call, an unresolved external error occurs when the module is loaded.
Export function list	A list of functions exported by the module selected in the Module dependency tree. Export functions are functions that a module exposes to other modules.
Module list	A list of all required dependencies for the opened program. This list defines the minimum set of files needed for the program to execute.

Lesson Summary

This lesson introduced the Dependency Walker, a utility that provides information about the modules a Windows program requires to run. Such modules are known as dependencies. The Dependency Walker displays:

- A tree view of modules forming a program's dependencies.
- A list of import functions called by a module's parent.
- A list of functions that a module exports.
- A list of a program's dependencies.

Lesson 6: Using Spy++

In this lesson, you will learn how to use Spy++, another Visual C++ utility. This useful, popular utility can display information about all current processes, their threads, and all open windows—even hidden windows.

After this lesson, you will be able to:

- Execute the Spy++ utility and use it to display a graphical tree of relationships among system objects, including processes, threads, and windows.
- Use Spy++ to search for specified windows, threads, processes, or messages.
- View the properties of selected windows, threads, and processes.
- Use the Spy++ Finder tool to select a window for monitoring.
- View a real-time record of messages that a window sends and receives.

Estimated lesson time: 15 minutes

Spy++ Views

Start Spy++ the same way as you would the Dependency Walker, by selecting it from the **Microsoft Visual Studio 6.0 Tools** menu. The utility displays four main views:

- **Windows view** shows a list of open windows.
- **Processes view** lists current processes.
- **Threads view** lists all current threads.
- **Message log** lists the messages that a window receives.

These four views are activated by commands in the **Spy** menu, or by the first four buttons on the toolbar. Each time a command is invoked, it creates a view as a new child window, so the tool buttons do not toggle between existing views. Instead, you should create a view only once, and thereafter switch between views by making a selection in the **Window** menu. Like the Dependency Walker, Spy++ is an MDI program, so you can tile views within the client area.

Figure 13.10 shows how the Windows and Processes views might look when arranged in the Spy++ window. The views show that Visual C++ is currently running (named **MSDEV** in the Processes view) and has created several child windows.

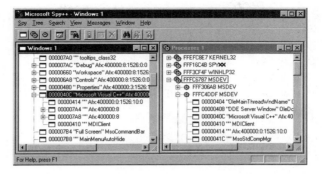

Figure 13.10   Windows and Processes views in the Spy++ window

A Spy++ view represents a snapshot, so applications that begin running after Spy++ are not automatically added to the lists. Similarly, applications that terminate while Spy++ is executing are not automatically removed from the list. To update a view, give the view focus and click the **Refresh** command on the **Window** menu.

Windows View

The Windows view displays a list of all windows currently open. It does not matter if the window is hidden or not; many open windows in a typical Windows session are invisible, serving their various applications only as message receivers. When Spy++ begins or when the view is refreshed, the utility compiles a list of all windows and displays the list in the Windows view.

The list is a normal tree view with small plus and minus icons that collapse or expand the list into levels. The tree's hierarchy indicates window parentage—that is, the relation between windows in which one window can create others as child windows. Click any plus icon adjacent to a window to expand the list to include that window's children. If the plus icon does not appear next to a window, it means that the window does not have any children.

A typical list in the Windows view can include many windows, so it's sometimes difficult to locate the entry for a particular window. In these cases, use the Window Finder tool.

▶ **To use the Window Finder tool**

1. Arrange the screen so that Spy++ and the window you want to investigate are both visible on the screen.

2. On the Spy++ toolbar, click **Find Window**, or choose **Find Window** from the **Search** menu.

3. Drag the **Finder Tool** icon (shown in Figure 13.11) out of the **Find Window** dialog box. As the dragged icon passes over an exposed window, the window appears framed in thick black lines, and the **Find Window** dialog box notes the window's handle. Drop the icon over the window you want, and close the **Find Window** dialog box. You can then locate the window's entry in the list by scanning for its window handle.

Figure 13.11   The **Finder Tool** icon

Processes View and Threads View

Each process running in the Windows multitasking environment creates one or more threads; each thread can create any number of windows. Use the Processes view to examine a particular process, which usually corresponds to an executing program. Processes are identified by module names, or are designated *system processes*.

The Threads view lists all currently executing threads along with the names of their owner processes. Expand a thread entry to see a list of its associated windows.

Message Log

For debugging purposes, the message log is perhaps the most useful of Spy++'s capabilities. It keeps a record in real-time of all messages that a window sends or receives. This allows you to examine a list of messages to see in what order they arrive, which is particularly useful for capturing window initialization messages.

A convenient way to begin message logging for a window is by using the Window Finder tool described earlier.

► **To log messages using Window Finder**

1. Drag and drop the **Finder Tool** icon over a target window as you did previously. In this instance, click the **Messages** radio button at the bottom of the **Find Window** dialog box before closing the dialog box.

   As you work in the target window, Spy++ compiles a list of messages the window sends and receives, as shown in Figure 13.12.

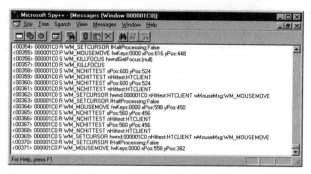

Figure 13.12   Spy++ message log

The Spy++ message log is divided into four columns, which are described in Table 13.6.

Table 13.6   The Four Columns of the Spy++ Message Log

Column	Description
1	Index number showing the message count
2	Window handle
3	Message code: either S (sent), R (received), P (posted), or s (message was sent, but security prevents access to the return value)
4	Message, parameters, and return values

By default, the list includes all messages, including mouse movement and keystroke messages such as WM_KEYDOWN and WM_KEYUP. This means the list can get crowded in a hurry, but Spy++ can filter the log to only those messages that interest you most.

2. On the **Messages** menu, click **Options**, then click the **Messages** tab.

3. Click the **Clear All** button to clear all the check boxes, then select only those check boxes for the messages you want to investigate.

4. End message tracking either by clicking the button with the stoplight icon on the **Spy++** toolbar, or by clicking **Stop Logging** on the **Messages** menu.

Viewing Window Messages in Spy++

In this practice exercise, you will launch the Spy++ utility and use it to spy on another application. By turning on the utility's message logging feature, you can view in real time the messages belonging to a selected window.

▶   **To start Spy++**

1. On the **Programs** menu, click **Start**.

2. Click **Microsoft Visual Studio 6.0**, click **Microsoft Visual Studio 6.0 Tools**, and then click **Spy++**.

3. When the utility appears, click the **Find Window** tool on the toolbar and drag the **Finder Tool** icon and drop it onto another window. If no other application is running, drop the **Finder Tool** icon onto the desktop.

4. Click the **Messages** radio button at the bottom of the **Find Window** dialog box, and then close the dialog box.

5. Experiment by moving the mouse pointer over the selected window. You will see the many messages that the window sends and receives pertaining to mouse movement, such as WM_MOUSEMOVE and WM_SETCURSOR.

Lesson Summary

This lesson described Spy++, a Visual C++ utility that reports information about executing programs. Spy++ can provide invaluable insight into an application's behavior that is not available through the Visual C++ debugger.

Spy++ displays four main views that show a list of windows, processes, threads, and messages pertaining to a particular window. The Window Finder tool aids in associating any exposed window with the list of windows that Spy++ displays. The message tracking feature intercepts and logs all messages that enter and leave a window, showing chronological order and the values of message parameters. The message log can be filtered to monitor messages of particular interest only.

Lesson 7: Testing Your Application

Application testing ensures that your application actually performs as specified. When your application is viewed as nearly complete and reasonably stable, debugging and testing should begin in earnest—testing to detect errors, and debugging to fix them. This lesson examines some of the techniques of testing.

As much as possible, testing should be conducted under widely different scenarios that mimic real-life conditions under which an application might have to function. For example, a program designed to run under Microsoft Windows 95 and Microsoft Windows NT should be tested under both operating systems. Whereas developers try to create code that can't be broken, testers concentrate on breaking the code—that is, finding the weak points. Developers who must wear both hats should bring equal zeal to both tasks.

After this lesson, you will be able to:

- Understand terminology pertaining to testing.
- Design an effective test plan.
- Employ common techniques for testing your application.

Estimated lesson time: 15 minutes

Glossary of Testing Terms

Like any rigorous field, testing has a unique lexicon. This section defines some of the terms that pertain to testing, making subsequent discussions in the lesson more meaningful. The glossary is arranged by level, starting with the simplest type of testing and proceeding to more involved testing practices.

- **Unit testing** verifies a discrete piece of code, such as a loop, a block, a subroutine, or an event. In formal terms, a unit test applies to the smallest piece of code for which a practical test can be conducted.

- **Integration testing** is the next highest level of testing, and is concerned with confirming that no problems arise from combining units of code into more complex processes. For example, two functions might test successfully as units, but the effects of providing one function with the output of the other should also be considered. Threads must be subjected to stringent integration testing to ensure that they perform as expected when running simultaneously.

- **System testing** is concerned with the full build of an application. At this level, the emphasis is less on bug hunting and more on checking that the application and its environment interact with each other correctly. The level of testing that would be conducted at this phase would be more systemwide—features such as correct initialization from the registry, performance, unexpected termination of resources, logon failures, and error recovery.

- **Stress testing** verifies how an application behaves under adverse conditions such as low memory, high network traffic, or insufficient disk space.

- **Regression testing** is the repetition of previous tests after changes have been made to the source code. The purpose of regression testing is to verify that expected bug fixes were successful, that the application still works as expected, and that new bugs have not been introduced by the code revisions.

- **Beta testing** is when a developer distributes a pre-release version of an application to a selected group of users. The users are generally chosen for their familiarity with past versions of a product, their willingness to use the new version under a wide variety of conditions, and a demonstrated ability to communicate what they like and dislike about a product.

- **User acceptance testing** is when a tested version of the specified deliverable is made available to a selected number of users who have already received training in the use of the system. The users chosen to perform the tests are expected to give the system the kind of usage that it will receive in real life.

Developing a Test Plan

A *test plan* is a written version of the entire test suite for an application. A properly created test plan completely describes all of the testing that needs to be done, and identifies what constitutes the success of any particular test. Test plans should be written to provide directions to someone other than the author on how to test an application. The primary criterion for a successful test plan is whether a different tester can pick up the plan halfway through the project and continue testing.

Custom applications can be effectively tested through three methods:

- In-house testing by the developers and the testing/quality assurance (QA) group
- Beta testing by selected users
- User acceptance testing by selected users

Elements of a Test Plan

A test plan provides a formal basis from which to develop repeatable regression tests. As applications evolve, or as new builds are created during the debug cycle, it is essential that the existing stability of the application as a whole has not been damaged. A test plan also provides a basis from which the test strategy can be inspected and discussed by all interested parties.

A good test plan starts with a description of the application and the functionality to be tested, and is followed by a brief discussion of the test objectives. The plan should include the following elements:

- The objectives of the test exercise.

- A description of how the tests should be performed, explaining the various degrees of reliance that should be made on key testing components such as test scripts, manual checklists, and user involvement.

- A description of the environment in which the tests should occur, including the operating system and, if relevant, its version number. For example, the original release of Windows 95 has slightly different characteristics than the same operating system with Service Pack 1 installed. A test plan might need to consider these differences.

- A listing of the test data that must be made available for the tests to be valid.

- A discussion of any restrictions placed on the test team that might affect the reliability of the test results. For example, if you are testing a system designed for hundreds of users accessing a large central database, it can be impossible for a small organization to simulate this volume of usage.

- A declaration of the relative orders of importance placed on different criteria—for example, your concern for robustness compared to that of performance.

- A list of features that should not be tested, with a commentary explaining your reasons.

- An intended test schedule that identifies milestones. This should tie into the overall project plan.

Test Scenarios

After designing a test plan, the next step is to list each test scenario, using the same breakdown of functionality as presented in the design specification. Each scenario should include:

- A reference to the item to be tested.
- The expected results.
- Commentary that describes how the test results confirm that the item being tested is functioning as expected.

Lesson Summary

This lesson defined some of the common terminology pertaining to software testing, and described how to write an effective test plan. A test plan incorporates detailed information about an intended program of testing procedures including:

- Unit testing for small sections of code.
- Integration testing to verify how code sections operate together.
- System testing to verify the overall stability of the entire program.
- Stress testing to determine how the program reacts to conditions of limited system resources.
- Regression testing to ensure that a revision to the code does not introduce further errors.
- Beta testing to gather user input.
- User acceptance testing to reflect real-life usage.

Small development teams of less than four or five people usually have to serve as both programmers and testers. In larger organizations with more personnel, developers and testers often form two distinct teams. Even in this case, programmers can benefit from the information in this lesson, because the entire development process runs more smoothly when both teams understand each other's work.

Lab 13: Debugging the STUpload Application

In this section, you will use the Visual C++ debugger to investigate the STUpload application as it runs. The lab exercises implement the debugger's Variables, Watch, Call Stack, and Disassembly windows, and demonstrate how these windows all contribute to the debugging effort. You will also set breakpoints at various locations and examine the effects of data breakpoints.

Estimated lesson time: 15 minutes

Running STUpload in the Debugger

In this exercise, you will run STUpload in the debugger until the MFC framework calls the application's **CMainFrame::OnCreate()** function. This function executes early in the application's run cycle, before documents and views are created and before the STUpload window appears on the screen. This process provides the opportunity to single-step through **OnCreate()** for an inside view of how an MFC program begins life.

The first step of the exercise is to build a debug version of the program, which is necessary to run the debugger. If you have already created a debug version of STUpload for labs in earlier chapters, skip to the second procedure.

▶ **To build a debug version**

1. Open the STUpload project.

2. In the larger of the two text boxes on the **Build** toolbar, select **Win32 Debug**. Alternatively, you can click the **Set Active Configuration** command on the **Build** menu and select **Win32 Debug**.

3. Click the **Build** button on the **Build** toolbar, or click the **Build** command on the **Build** menu to compile and link the application.

▶ **To stop execution at CMainFrame::OnCreate()**

1. On the **FileView** tab of the Visual C++ Workspace window, expand the list of source files. Double-click **MainFrm.cpp** in the list to open the file.

2. Scroll down to find the beginning of the **OnCreate()** function, which looks like this in the source code:

```
int CMainFrame::OnCreate(LPCREATESTRUCT lpCreateStruct)
```

3. Click the function's opening brace to set the insertion point there. This action identifies the line at which the program should stop.

4. Launch the debugger by choosing **Start Debug** from the **Build** menu and clicking the **Run to Cursor** command.

The debugger begins first, then automatically runs the STUpload program. When **CMainFrame::OnCreate()** gains control, execution halts at the line containing the insertion point. The instruction has not yet executed, but is next in line to do so when the program resumes.

Although no C++ code appears associated with the function's opening brace, code nevertheless exists before the first C++ instruction, as you can see by clicking the **Disassembly** tool in the debugger toolbar. The assembly language instructions that appear in the source window are the function's prologue code, in which a stack frame is created and the class's **this** pointer is stored as a local variable. Click the **Disassembly** tool again to restore the normal Source window.

Stepping Through Code

This exercise demonstrates how to single-step through the **OnCreate()** function using the **Step Into**, **Step Over**, and **Step Out** tools. The exercise also shows how to read information in the debugger's Variables and Call Stack windows while stepping through code.

▶   **To see the Variables and Call Stack windows**

1. If the Variables window does not appear on your screen, click the **Variables** tool on the debugger toolbar to expose the window. In its undocked state, it appears as shown in Figure 13.13.

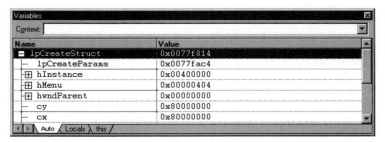

Figure 13.13   The Visual C++ debugger's Variables window

2. Click the plus icon adjacent to the lpCreateStruct name in the Variables window to expand the listing. Because the function's parameter is the only variable on the current function's stack frame, lpCreateStruct is the only variable

listed in the window. It points to a **CREATESTRUCT** structure, the various fields of which appear in the Variables window when the view is expanded. Expanding the view shows that, for example, the structure's **lpszName** field contains a pointer to the application's name.

3. Click the debugger's **Call Stack** tool to expose the Call Stack window (Figure 13.14). This window shows the course taken to reach the **OnCreate()** function, which heads the list. The second function in the call stack list identifies the function that has called **OnCreate()**, and to which control will return when **OnCreate()** finishes. In this case, the caller is **CWnd::OnWndMsg()**, part of the MFC framework.

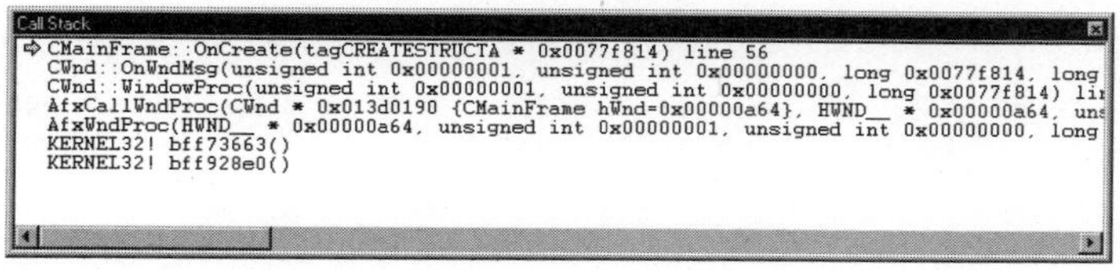

```
Call Stack
⇨ CMainFrame::OnCreate(tagCREATESTRUCTA * 0x0077f814) line 56
   CWnd::OnWndMsg(unsigned int 0x00000001, unsigned int 0x00000000, long 0x0077f814, long
   CWnd::WindowProc(unsigned int 0x00000001, unsigned int 0x00000000, long 0x0077f814) li
   AfxCallWndProc(CWnd * 0x013d0190 {CMainFrame hWnd=0x00000a64}, HWND__ * 0x00000a64, un
   AfxWndProc(HWND__ * 0x00000a64, unsigned int 0x00000001, unsigned int 0x00000000, long
   KERNEL32! bff73663()
   KERNEL32! bff928e0()
```

Figure 13.14   The Visual C++ debugger's Call Stack window

4. Click the **Call Stack** tool again to hide the Call Stack window.

► **To single-step through OnCreate()**

1. Click the **Step Over** tool or press the F10 key to step through the first two or three instructions of **OnCreate()**. Each time you invoke the **Step Over** command, execution halts at the next instruction as indicated by the yellow instruction arrow. Notice how the Variables window shows the application's data changing with each instruction.

2. Continue single-stepping until the instruction arrow points to the line that sets up docking for the application's toolbar:

```
m_wndToolBar.EnableDocking(CBRS_ALIGN_ANY);
```

3. Click the **Step Into** tool to step into the framework's **CControlBar:: EnableDocking()** function. The debugger automatically locates the function's source file Bardock.cpp and opens it. Execution halts at the function's first instruction.

4. Single-step through **CControlBar::EnableDocking()** if you want, then click the debugger's **Step Out** tool to leave. The rest of the function executes, and when control returns to **CMainFrame::OnCreate()**, execution halts at the instruction following the call to **CControlBar::EnableDocking()**:

```
EnableDocking(CBRS_ALIGN_ANY);
```

Setting Breakpoints

This exercise demonstrates how to set breakpoints in another source file. Breakpoints are most commonly set before launching the debugger, but as you will see in this exercise you can set or clear breakpoints at any time, even while the debugger is active.

▶ **To use a breakpoint to interrupt when importing a file**

1. Open the STUploadDoc.cpp source file and scroll down to locate the **CSTUploadDoc::LoadData()** function:

   ```
   BOOL CSTUploadDoc::LoadData(CStdioFile &infile)
   ```

2. In the **LoadData()** function, locate the **while** loop that reads each line of a .dat file, as described in Chapter 4:

   ```
   while(infile.ReadString(strTemp))
       {
           BOOL bValidDate = FALSE;
           CString strFund;
           CString strDate;
           .
           .
           .
   ```

3. Click anywhere on the **while** instruction to set the insertion point there.

4. Press F9 to set a location breakpoint. A small red dot appears in the selection margin to indicate the line has been tagged with a breakpoint.

5. Click the **Go** tool on the debugger's toolbar or press the F5 key. The STUpload application resumes execution, finishing the **CMainFrame::OnCreate()** function that had been interrupted. The STUpload main window now appears. At this point, the STUpload program is active, not the debugger. The debugger does not become active again until the program encounters a breakpoint.

6. On the program's **Data** menu, click **Import** and browse for the Test.dat file in the \Chapter 4\Data folder. When you open the file, control stops at the breakpoint set in the **CSTUploadDoc::LoadData()** function.

7. Right-click the following line and click either **Remove Breakpoint** or **Disable Breakpoint** from the shortcut menu. The first command removes the breakpoint; the second makes the breakpoint unavailable without removing it.

   ```
   while(infile.ReadString(strTemp))
   ```

8. Single-step through a few instructions, noting in the Variables window how variables such as StrDate are correctly initialized.

▶   **To set a data breakpoint**

1. On the **Edit** menu, click **Breakpoints**, or press CTRL+B to invoke the **Breakpoints** dialog box.

2. On the **Data** tab, type **bFirstLine** in the text box labeled **Enter the expression to be evaluated**. This action establishes a data breakpoint that triggers only when the function's bFirstLine variable changes in value.

3. Click **OK** to close the **Breakpoints** dialog box.

4. Click the **Go** command again to resume execution.

You will probably experience a short pause as the **while** loop continues because of the drag on execution speed exacted by data breakpoints. The program soon stops, however, and the debugger displays a message box saying that it has detected a change in the value of bFirstLine. Clicking the message box's **OK** button updates the source window showing the yellow instruction arrow that points to the instruction following the one that has just cleared the bFirstLine flag.

Setting data breakpoints this way is not very helpful for simple variables like bFirstLine that change value only once. However, data breakpoints can be invaluable when tracking down obscure bugs in which a variable is incorrectly altered during execution, and the location in which the variable was incorrectly altered is indeterminable.

▶   **To resume execution and terminate the program**

1. Press CTRL+B again to display the **Breakpoints** dialog box, and click the **Remove All** button at the bottom of the dialog box. This action deletes the data breakpoint attached to bFirstLine, ensuring that the program now runs at normal speed.

2. Click the **Go** command, or press F5 to continue running the STUpload program, and terminate the program normally through its **Exit** command. When the program stops, so does the debugger.

Review

1. What is Structured Exception Handling?

2. What is an HRESULT?

3. Name two ways in which a COM server communicates an error to a client.

4. How does a debug version of a program differ from its release build?

5. Describe MFC's **ASSERT**, **VERIFY**, and **DEBUG_NEW** macros.

6. How does a debugger cause a running program to interrrupt itself?

7. What utility does Visual C++ provide for running and testing ActiveX controls?

8. What is dependency?

9. What information is contained in the four lists that Spy++ can display?

10. What is regression testing?

C H A P T E R   1 4

Deploying Desktop Applications

About This Chapter

After your application is debugged, one task remains: deploying to users. Not as simple a task as you might imagine, deployment requires thought and planning.

In this chapter, you will learn some of the ways a Windows application created with Microsoft Visual C++ can be efficiently deployed. This chapter first presents an overview of deployment methods. You will learn how to use InstallShield, a tool that nearly completely automates the creation of installation programs for Visual C++ projects. You will also learn how installation programs install ActiveX controls and other COM components, and how the Microsoft Zero Administration for Windows (ZAW) initiative will affect program installation in the future.

Before You Begin

Before you start this chapter, you should have read Chapters 2 through 13, and completed the exercises in the text.

Lesson 1: Windows Setup Programs

Deployment consists of two steps. The first step is to transfer all necessary files to the users' hard disks. The second step, which is potentially more complicated, involves configuring the host system so that it recognizes and correctly runs the installed application. To help ensure proper deployment, you should automate the process of getting an application up and running as much as possible. Windows users are accustomed to an installation program that does most of the work for them.

After this lesson, you will be able to:

- Describe how an application is installed on and removed from a user's system.
- List the services provided by a typical installation program.
- Describe various entries that an installation program places in a user's registry.
- Create cabinet and registry files.

Estimated lesson time: 20 minutes

Setup Program Conventions

An installation program should always be named Setup for two reasons:

- To conform to convention.
- To be recognizable to the Add/Remove Programs applet in Control Panel.

Consistent use of the Setup file name has become standard practice for application deployment programs, which helps to minimize confusion among users. The standard Windows user knows how to work with programs named Setup, though the programs can differ in individual style and methods. For purposes of discussion, this lesson refers to installation programs generically as Setup programs.

If your application distribution requires several disks or CD-ROMs, the Setup program should exist on the first disk or CD-ROM of the series to ensure that it is easily located by the Windows Add/Remove Programs applet.

A number of installation services can be provided to users. A typical setup program will:

- Prompt for selected program options.
- Create folders on a user's hard disk as required.
- Copy files from the distribution media to the hard disk.
- Add registry information for shared DLLs.
- Register an application's ActiveX controls and other COM components.

- Add information to the system registry specifying the command needed to remove the application. This allows the Add/Remove Programs applet to identify the application's uninstall program.

- Record the extension used for the application's document files in the system registry to allow users to launch the application from Windows Explorer by double-clicking a document in a file list.

- Add an entry to the Windows **Programs** menu, or a desktop shortcut if stipulated.

- Execute "run-once code" to minimize installation size if the Setup program is not copied to the hard disk.

- Add or make unavailable selected options from the installed application when the Setup program is run again.

The user should need only to select an installation option and insert any additional disks or CD-ROMs as prompted. Microsoft recommends that an installation program include the following four options:

- *Compact* for laptops and systems with limited disk space.

- *Custom* to give users control over what is installed.

- *Typical* to provide a common default suitable for most users.

- *Silent* for unattended installation.

Silent installation is necessary for systems managers who want to install an application across a network. While running in silent mode, the Setup program should not query or display error messages, and must assume intelligent default settings for all cases.

Guidelines for Writing a Setup Program

Keep the following points in mind when you plan a Setup program for your application's deployment. An intelligent Setup program should:

- Store private initialization (.ini) files in the application directory if the application is running locally, or in the directory returned by the **GetWindowsDirectory()** API function if the application is shared.

- Avoid inappropriately copying files to the Windows, WinNT, System, or System32 directories. If your application package includes font files, they should be copied to the system's Fonts folder.

- Check that a file does not already exist on the hard disk before copying it. If the Setup program finds a conflict, it should decide which file is most recent and avoid overwriting a newer file.

- Supply defaults. In particular, the Setup program should provide a common response to every option so users press only the ENTER key at each prompt for a successful default installation.

- Avoid prompting users to insert the same disk more than once.

- Inform users about required disk space.

- Display a progress indicator.

- Store intermediate files in the Temp directory. However, if the Setup program must restart Windows before reading intermediate files, it should confirm that the Temp directory exists on a hard disk and not on a RAM disk. This procedure ensures that the necessary files will still exist after restarting.

- Give users a chance to cancel installations before finishing. The Setup program should keep a log of files that have been copied and settings that have been registered so that it can clean up canceled installations.

A user installs your application either by running the Setup program directly or by running the Add/Remove Programs applet in Control Panel. Add/Remove Programs automatically searches the disk or CD-ROM drive for a program named Setup.exe. If the file is found and the user agrees to finish the installation, Add/Remove Programs starts the Setup program and closes. After Add/Remove Programs closes, the Setup program is responsible for guiding the user through the rest of the installation process.

Uninstall Program Conventions

An installed product should be able to safely, and as completely as possible, remove all traces of itself. This operation, sometimes known as *de-installing* or *uninstalling*, is typically carried out by a separate program with a descriptive name such as Uninstall or Uninst. Alternatively, the Setup program itself can be written to act as the uninstaller. You have much more flexibility when choosing a name for your uninstall program because the location and file name of the uninstall program are identified in the Setup program and written to the system registry during the installation process. This action assures that Add/Remove Programs can locate the correct uninstaller executable regardless of its name.

Uninstalling is an important feature for users, and also is one of the prerequisites for an application to be approved for the Windows compliance logo. Uninstalling includes deleting application files (but not documents) and removing entries added to the system registry.

Because many applications share resources and make modifications throughout the system, deleting an application is rarely a matter of simply deleting files in a single subdirectory. Users must be able to uninstall cleanly and reinstall to correct problems, change configurations, or upgrade applications. The uninstall feature also allows users to free disk space and to abide by licensing agreements when deleting an application from one computer before installing it on others.

Uninstalling a Windows application must be done carefully. A potential problem arises when deleting a program's dependency modules such as DLLs and ActiveX controls. (Dependencies are described in Lesson 5 of Chapter 13.) The uninstall operation must not delete modules upon which other applications depend.

An uninstall program cannot directly determine if a module serves other programs, but can infer whether a module is shared by consulting a usage count stored in a common area of the registry. Usage counts are described in the next section.

Adding and Removing Registry Information

An installation program adds all the necessary information about your application to the registry. User preference data should be written to the registry's **HKEY_CURRENT_USER\SOFTWARE** key. In earlier versions of Windows, this information was written to the Win.ini file. For information specific to the application, add entries to the **HKEY_LOCAL_MACHINE\SOFTWARE** registry key using this format:

```
HKEY_LOCAL_MACHINE\SOFTWARE\CompanyName\ProductName\Version
```

Substitute names for the italicized placeholders that are appropriate for your application.

PATH Environment Variable

Each running application has its own PATH environment setting, containing a list of paths to various folders. The list specifies the paths that the operating system should search when looking for executable modules required by the application. By default, Windows searches certain system folders first in an effort to locate files required for loading an application. Since most applications are installed to unique directories, the path to the application's components must be specified in an application-specific PATH setting.

For example, consider an application in the MyApp folder that uses a DLL in the MyDLL folder. Assuming normal linkage—that is, assuming the application does not call the **LoadLibrary()** API function to load the DLL—the application cannot run unless MyDLL appears in the PATH list. The operating system will search only for DLL files in the default system folders and the folders specified in the PATH variable. If a referenced DLL is not located, the system will refuse to run the application. The application's installation program must therefore specify a PATH setting that includes the MyDLL folder where the required DLL file resides.

To register a PATH, a Setup program should write the desired value in the **HKEY_LOCAL_MACHINE** root under the **\SOFTWARE\Microsoft\ Windows\CurrentVersion\App Paths** key. This is the same string contained in the **REGSTR_PATH_APPPATHS** text macro defined in the Regstr.h file. Notice that the last nested key, **App Paths**, is two words.

The Setup program should create a new registry key having the same name as the application's executable file, and then insert a Path value containing the desired path. Here's an example of how the Path registry value might look for the NewApp program located in the MyApp folder of the preceding code:

```
HKEY_LOCAL_MACHINE\SOFTWARE\Microsoft\Windows\CurrentVersion\
App Paths\NewApp.exe

Default=D:\MyPrograms\MyApp\NewApp.exe

Path=D:\MyPrograms\MyDLL;D:\MyPrograms\MyApp\Utilities
```

The Default value specifies the full path to the executable file. The operating system refers to this value when a user types the application name in the **Run** dialog box without specifying a full path to the executable file. Windows locates the requested executable by searching the **App Paths** key, then reads the full path from the Default value.

The Path value contains NewApp's PATH environment, which includes a reference to the MyDLL folder. When the operating system loads NewApp, it searches the prescribed locations for the DLL that NewApp needs. By including the MyDLL folder in the application's PATH, the Setup program ensures that the system can always locate the required DLL file when running NewApp.

Usage Counts for Shared Modules

For each shared module that it installs, the Setup program should consult the registry and increment the module's usage count. When the application is removed, the uninstall program must decrement the usage count. If the count drops to zero, the uninstaller can delete the module—though usually only after querying the user for permission. If every Setup program were to follow this procedure, dependency modules could be safely removed. Unfortunately, not every developer creating installation programs conforms to this convention; thus, it is customary to query users before removing a file for which the usage count has reached zero.

Usage counts for shared modules are stored in the **HKEY_LOCAL_MACHINE\ SOFTWARE\Microsoft\Windows\CurrentVersion\SharedDLLs** key. Figure 14.1 on the facing page shows an example in the RegEdit utility (described later), in which the usage count for an ActiveX control named msinet.ocx is currently 2.

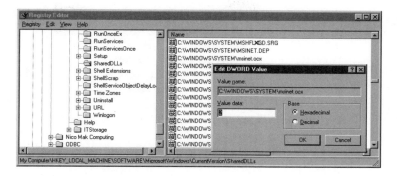

Figure 14.1   Viewing a usage count in the RegEdit utility

Cabinet Files

A *cabinet file* contains files in compressed form, resulting in a single file that serves as a file library. Cabinet files, recognizable by their .cab extension, are often used when deploying large applications because they reduce the number of disks or CD-ROMs required. The application's Setup program reads the .cab files, decompresses their contents into the original files, and writes the files to the user's hard disk.

A .cab file is similar to a .zip file in that it serves as a compressed archive for a group of files. A .cab file can contain any kind of file, and can also have a digital signature that identifies the file's creator and ensures that the file has not been maliciously or accidentally altered. Digital signatures are described in more detail in Lesson 4 of this chapter.

Creating a .cab file requires either the MakeCab or CabArc (Cabinet Archiver) utilities. Both programs are part of the Microsoft Cabinet Software Development Kit (SDK), available as a free download from msdn.microsoft.com/workshop/management/cab/cabdl.asp. MakeCab creates compressed disk images containing a product's files, and is designed to work with Setup programs. CabArc is a console-based program that can read and write .cab files. To run CabArc, type a list of options, the name of the .cab file, and a list of files to compress or decompress. For example, the line

```
cabarc n images.cab \myapp\images\*.jpg \myapp\images\*.gif
```

creates the Images.cab file, and adds, in compressed form, all the .jpg and .gif graphics files in the MyApp\Images folder. The *n* option tells CabArc to create a new file. The Cabinet SDK contains examples and documentation for the CabArc and MakeCab programs.

Registry Files

Setup programs sometimes use registry files to write entries into the system registry. Recognizable by its .reg extension, a registry file serves as a script that lists keys, values, and locations to be added to the registry. Because a registry file is in ASCII format, it can be viewed and edited in a text editor. For example, the registry file for the NewApp program mentioned earlier specifies the program's PATH environment as shown in the following code:

```
REGEDIT4

[HKEY_LOCAL_MACHINE\SOFTWARE\Microsoft\Windows\CurrentVersion\
App Paths\NewApp.exe]

@="D:\\MyPrograms\\MyApp\\NewApp.exe"

"Path"="D:\\MyPrograms\\MyDLL;D:\\MyPrograms\\MyApp\\Utilities"
```

Although long lines in the script have been broken to fit on the printed page, each entry must occupy a single unbroken line in the registry file. No continuation character for registry scripts exists.

The code as shown assumes that the NewApp program is in the MyPrograms\ MyApp subdirectory, and demonstrates a potential problem with registry files. The Setup program must ensure that any paths specified in the script correspond to the location where a user ultimately decides to install the application. Therefore, the Setup program must be prepared to alter a .reg file before using it.

Windows provides the RegEdit utility to read and write registry files. A Setup program can use RegEdit to write (or *import*) the script into the user's system registry, and supply a registry file in the command line like this:

```
regedit newapp.reg
```

This command writes the contents of the NewApp.reg file to the system registry. The following code demonstrates how to create a file named IEpath.reg, which contains a copy of the path information for Internet Explorer:

```
regedit /e IEpath.reg "HKEY_LOCAL_MACHINE\SOFTWARE\Microsoft\Windows\
CurrentVersion\App Paths\IEXPLORE.exe"
```

The */e* switch causes RegEdit to read (or *export*) a section of the registry to a specified file. It is necessary to include the registry key information in double quotation marks only when the key contains a space, as in **App Paths**. Otherwise, quotation marks are not required.

The RegEdit utility provides a simple Windows user interface, so it does not need to be run from the command line. The following exercise demonstrates how to write a .reg file by invoking a command on the program's **Registry** menu.

▶ **To create the IEpath.reg file in RegEdit**

1. On the taskbar, click the **Start** button, and then click **Run**. In the **Open** box, type **regedit**, and then click **OK** to start the RegEdit utility.

2. Beginning with the **HKEY_LOCAL_MACHINE** root, expand the tree view and select the **IEXPLORE.EXE** key as shown in Figure 14.2. The full path to the **IEXPLORE.EXE** key is shown at the bottom of the RegEdit window in the figure.

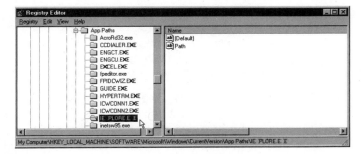

Figure 14.2   Selecting Internet Explorer's PATH entry in the system registry

3. On the **Registry** menu, click **Export Registry File**.

4. Select the desired folder and type **IEpath** in the **File name** box.

5. Click **Save**, and then exit RegEdit.

6. Start a text editor such as Notepad and open the new IEpath.reg file that has been created in your default document directory. The script shows that, like many programs, Internet Explorer includes its own application folder as part of its PATH environment.

A registry file is most useful when a large amount of registry data is being manipulated or when the data is transitory and the Setup program must load and then unload the information again. A Setup program can also use the RegEdit utility to create a backup copy of selected registry information. The uninstall program can then restore the original settings if the user chooses to delete the application.

Lesson Summary

This lesson presented a general overview of the installation process in which a Setup program configures a user's computer to run an application.

A Setup program should ideally provide installation options labeled Compact, Custom, Typical, and Silent. Silent installation allows administrators to run the Setup program unattended when installing the application across a network. Professional-quality Setup programs seek to make the installation process as easy as possible for the user.

If the application requires a custom PATH environment, the Setup program should record the desired variable in the registry. This specifies the PATH setting that Windows makes current when the application runs. The Setup program should also consult the registry when installing shared modules such as DLLs and ActiveX controls, incrementing usage counts for the modules. When the application is removed, the uninstall program decrements the counts and prompts to remove the file when the count reaches zero.

The lesson finished with an introduction to cabinet and registry files. Cabinet files serve as archives that contain other files in compressed form. Microsoft makes available utilities such as MakeCab and CabArc for creating and using cabinet files. Registry files are scripts that can be inserted into the system registry using the RegEdit utility.

Lesson 2: Using InstallShield

As a shortcut for developing setup and uninstall programs, the Professional and Enterprise Editions of Visual C++ include the SDK edition of Stirling Software's InstallShield. (The Learning and Standard Editions don't include this tool, but you can purchase it separately. If you don't have access to this tool, you can still benefit from reading the information in this lesson.)

This lesson introduces the InstallShield toolkit, which enables you to write a script that specifies the steps you want performed during installation. InstallShield then builds a Setup program that installs your product on a user's computer.

With InstallShield, you don't have to write a separate script for uninstallation. InstallShield creates an uninstall program named Uninst that reads a log file created during the setup process. The log file enables Uninst to reverse the steps performed during setup.

InstallShield creates a Setup program for your project that looks and acts much like the Setup program you used to install Visual C++. Microsoft creates Setup programs for many of its products using InstallShield.

An exhaustive description of InstallShield is beyond the scope of this lesson, which is intended only as an introduction to the product. Setup programs today can be surprisingly sophisticated, capable of handling a wide variety of file types, accommodating different operating systems, and handling a bewildering number of potential problems. They must work not only with traditional distribution media such as disks and CD-ROMs, but also across networks and the Internet. InstallShield is not difficult to use, but it offers such a wide array of options designed to address installation issues that gaining familiarity with it can take a while. Furthermore, complete control over the product requires learning its scripting language, InstallScript. As with most programs, practice is the only true teacher.

InstallShield treats your Setup program as a *project*, the same term applied to normal Visual C++ projects. To avoid confusion, this lesson employs the phrases *Setup project* or *installation project* when referring to work done inside InstallShield, and *application project* when referring to the Visual C++ files that the Setup program deploys in their compressed state.

After this lesson, you will be able to:

- Configure InstallShield to run as a Visual C++ tool.
- Step through the InstallShield tutorial.
- Create a simple Setup program using InstallShield.

Estimated lesson time: 15 minutes

Installing InstallShield

If you selected InstallShield when installing Visual C++, the Visual C++ **Tools** menu already contains a command for starting the InstallShield Wizard. However, if the command does not appear in the Visual C++ **Tools** menu and you are not using the Learning or Standard Edition of Visual C++, you should install InstallShield now.

▶ **To install InstallShield**

1. Place the Visual C++ CD-ROM #1 in your CD-ROM drive.

2. In Control Panel, start the Add/Remove Programs applet.

3. Browse to the IShield folder on the CD-ROM and double-click **Setup**.

The Setup program installs InstallShield, places a command on the **Start\ Programs** menu, and adds the **InstallShield Wizard** command to the Visual C++ **Tools** menu.

Running the InstallShield Tutorial

The InstallShield program provides a good tutorial that demonstrates how to develop a sample Setup program for the familiar Notepad utility. The tutorial walks you through various steps, eventually creating a Setup program that places an icon and command on the **Programs** menu. When selected, the command invokes Notepad.

The tutorial shows how InstallShield categorizes your application files into different groups, allowing you to work on different parts of an installation project. Each group contains files with similar characteristics, such as system DLLs, executable files, and Help files.

▶ **To run the InstallShield tutorial**

1. Click **Start**, point to **Programs**, and then click **InstallShield for Microsoft Visual C++ 6**. InstallShield opens.

2. On the **Help** menu, click **Getting Started**.

3. In the **Help Topics** dialog box, expand the list by double-clicking **Welcome to InstallShield**, **Tutorials**, and **Use the Project Wizard**.

4. Double-click the first entry, **Outline: Use the Project Wizard**.

5. Move through the six steps, following the tutorial's instructions.

After running the completed Setup demonstration, be sure to uninstall it by running the Add/Remove Programs applet, as suggested in the tutorial's last step.

The preceding example shows how to start InstallShield from the **Programs** menu, activating the Project Wizard to create a new project or to open an existing project. You can also run InstallShield from inside Visual C++ by clicking the **InstallShield Wizard** command on the **Tools** menu. This alternative is convenient for creating a Setup program for an existing Visual C++ application project, because it fills in information that you would otherwise have to enter manually. When you click the **InstallShield Wizard** command, the wizard appears as shown in Figure 14.3. Select the desired Visual C++ project, click **Next**, and follow the wizard's remaining instructions.

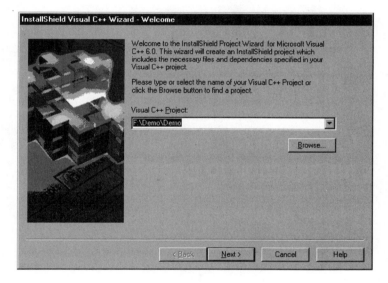

Figure 14.3   The InstallShield Wizard, invoked from the Visual C++ **Tools** menu

Including and Removing Program Files

InstallShield scans the application folder and locates all necessary executable files, adding them to the installation project. Figure 14.4 on the next page shows how the wizard lists the application's dependency files. In this case, the demo.exe application links dynamically to MFC, so InstallShield adds MFC42.DLL to the Setup project. Because MFC42.DLL in turn uses the C run-time library, the MSVCRT.DLL module is also added to the installation project.

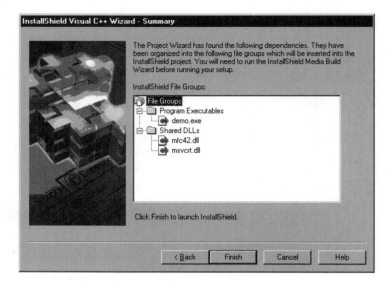

Figure 14.4   Listing an application's dependency files in the InstallShield Wizard

If you intend to distribute your application only to sites where you know the files already exist, you might not want to include dependencies such as MFC42.DLL and MSVCRT.DLL in your Setup program. The InstallShield Wizard does not allow you to alter the list, but you can remove the files from the installation project later. After the wizard finishes, it starts InstallShield automatically.

Creating the Setup.exe Program

After your installation project compiles and runs correctly, the last step is to build the project. This step enables you to create the Setup.exe program and the associated .cab files to distribute to your users. InstallShield provides the Media Build Wizard to walk you through the steps of creating the Setup program. The following list assumes you have created an installation project and are ready to build a Setup program for it.

▶ **To create a Setup program**

1. On the InstallShield **Build** menu, click the **Media Build Wizard** command.

2. In the wizard's first step (titled **Media Name**), type the name of the application project in the **Media Name** box.

3. In the second step, choose the type and size of the media you intend to use for your application's deployment. The wizard offers the choice of various

disk formats, a CD-ROM, a customizable size, and an option named **InstallFromTheWeb** that creates a Setup program that is installable over the Internet.

4. In the third step, choose either **Full Build** or **Quick Build**. The **Full Build** option creates the compressed files required for distribution to users. The **Quick Build** option is intended only for testing purposes, allowing you to quickly build a Setup project and test it without creating actual compressed files. The disk images created by the **Quick Build** option contain links to the application files instead of compressed data. The resultant Setup program will run only on the development computer where the application project is stored.

5. The wizard's third step includes an **Advanced** button. Click this button to expose a dialog box that allows you to enter various settings and to establish a password for the Setup program. You can also specify the folder to which the Setup files will be written. If you do not specify a folder, the wizard writes the disk image files to C:\MyInstallations*project*\Media*project*, where *project* represents the name of the installation project.

6. Click **Next** to skip the wizard's fourth step.

7. In the wizard's fifth step, select the operating systems under which your application can run. InstallShield includes files required for the selected operating systems.

8. The wizard's sixth and final step is titled **Summary**. Click **Finish** to build the Setup program.

9. InstallShield shows the **Building Media** dialog box in which an animated display tracks its progress. When the build process is complete, simply click **Finish** again.

You now have a folder named Disk Images in your chosen installation project folder. The Disk Images folder contains at least one nested folder named Disk1, which holds the disk image for the first disk of the series. If the Setup requires additional disks, their images are contained in folders Disk2, Disk3, and so forth. The contents of each Disk folder must be copied to disks or other media of the type selected in the Media Build Wizard's second step. If the installation creates more than one Disk folder, each receiving medium must be labeled with the disk number to ensure that users can insert disks in the correct order when prompted to do so.

As a final test before shipping your application, run the Setup package on a machine other than your development computer. Test the installed application to ensure that all components have been correctly copied and registered, then uninstall the application to ensure that it is correctly removed.

Lesson Summary

This lesson introduced the InstallShield program, a tool that creates sophisticated installation programs for Visual C++ projects. InstallShield largely automates the entire process of building a Setup program by scanning for dependencies, generating cabinet files, and creating disk images. InstallShield even provides an uninstaller program named Uninst.

Through the Media Build Wizard, InstallShield is accessible from inside the Visual C++ environment where it automatically reads information for the current application project. InstallShield encourages the sorting of project files into distinct categories referred to as file groups, allowing you to specify different characteristics for each group. InstallShield generates a script that governs the installation process, using its own InstallScript language. Complete control over installation is possible by editing the script.

Lesson 3: Registering COM Components on the Client Computer

During installation, a Setup program must register on a user's computer any ActiveX controls or other COM components that the application requires to run. The registry entry for an ActiveX control includes:

- The control's class identifier GUID.
- The location of the control's executable file.
- Characteristics such as the component's threading model.
- Various flags that specify how the component operates—for example, whether the control is visible or invisible, whether it can be activated inside a container's window, and so forth.

ActiveX controls are *self-registering*, meaning they contain their own registry information and can write it to the system registry. By taking on the task of registering themselves, ActiveX controls remove most of the burden from the Setup program. In this lesson, you will also learn how to configure an InstallShield project to correctly install ActiveX controls on a user's system.

After this lesson, you will be able to:

- Describe the self-registration feature possessed by many COM components, including ActiveX controls.
- Describe how exported functions write and remove COM information from the registry.
- Add self-registering components to an InstallShield project.

Estimated lesson time: 15 minutes

Self-Registering Components

To update the user's system registry for installed COM components, a Setup program can use registry files as described in Lesson 1 of this chapter. However, ActiveX controls do not require registry files because they are self-registering.

Chapter 10 explained that an ActiveX control executes as either a stand-alone program or, much more commonly, as a DLL. The latter is known as an *in-process* (or *in-proc*) ActiveX control. An in-process ActiveX control exports a function named **DllRegisterServer()** that, when called, writes to the registry all the information the control requires. The only obstacle is that some other application must load the control and specifically call the **DllRegisterServer()** function.

This task generally falls to either a Web browser (if the ActiveX control is down-loaded from a Web page) or to a Setup program. Because users generally acquire ActiveX controls only over the Internet or by installing an application, registration takes place invisibly—thus, most users never have to worry about registering an ActiveX control.

Control files acquired through other means—e-mail, for example—require manual registration to operate. Windows provides a utility named RegSvr32 that handles this task. RegSvr32 loads a requested ActiveX control or any other self-registering COM component and calls the component's **DllRegisterServer()** function:

```
regsvr32 path\MyControl.ocx
```

where *path* represents where the component is stored. The command:

```
regsvr32 /u path\MyControl.ocx
```

causes the program to call the component's **DllUnregisterServer()** function, which removes from the registry everything that **DllRegisterServer()** wrote. The */u* switch included in the command stands for uninstall.

Adding Self-Registering Components to an InstallShield Project

If your application files include ActiveX controls or other self-registering components, the Setup program you create must call the components' **DllRegisterServer()** function during installation. Likewise, the uninstaller program must call the **DllUnregisterServer()** function for each component if users uninstall your application.

The Setup and Uninst programs created by InstallShield will register and unregister your application's ActiveX components. To configure your installation project to correctly handle self-registering controls, you must create a file group that contains the component files, and then specify the **Self Registered** property for the group.

▶   **To create a group of self-registering components**

1. Open the installation project in InstallShield, as shown in Figure 14.5.

Figure 14.5   Opening an existing project in InstallShield

2. Select the **File Groups** tab in the project workspace and right-click anywhere inside the File Groups workspace.

3. On the shortcut menu, click the **New File Group** command, as shown in Figure 14.6.

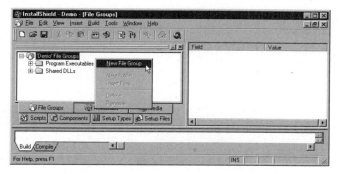

Figure 14.6   Creating a new file group in InstallShield

4. Type **Self-registering Components** for the group's name and press ENTER.

5. With the **Self-registering Components** group selected in the workspace, double-click the **Self-Registered** field in the display area to the right of the workspace.

6. In the **Properties** dialog box, select **Yes, all files in this group are self-registering**, as shown in Figure 14.7. This choice marks the group as containing only self-registering components.

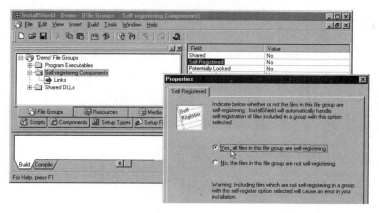

Figure 14.7   Marking a file group for self-registering component files

7. Click **OK**. The value of the **Self-Registered** field changes to **Yes**.

When the Setup program runs on a user's system, it will load each file in the group, call its **DllRegisterServer()** function to register the component, and unload the file. The next step is to add the component files themselves to the new file group.

▶   **To add files to the new Self-registering Components group**

1. In the project workspace pane, click the **Links** sublevel beneath the entry for **Self-registering Components**.

2. Right-click anywhere in the area to the right of the workspace pane. On the shortcut menu shown in Figure 14.8, click the **Insert Files** command.

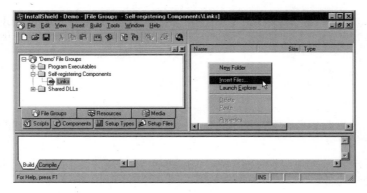

Figure 14.8   Inserting a file into a group

3. In the **Insert file links** dialog box, browse to the first ActiveX control or other self-registering component that you want to add to the installation project and click **Open**.

4. Repeat the steps for all component files you want to add to the group.

Lesson Summary

An ActiveX control contains its own registry information, including:

- The control's class identifier.
- The path to the control's executable file.
- Run-time characteristics and preferences.
- Miscellaneous information for containers.

Each ActiveX control exports a function named **DllRegisterServer()** that, when called, writes the information to the system registry. An ActiveX control also exports a counterpart function named **DllUnregisterServer()** that removes the same information from the registry. These functions make ActiveX controls self-registering and self-unregistering.

Users typically acquire ActiveX controls by viewing Web pages and by installing container applications that use the controls. In either case, registration takes place behind the scenes when the Web browser or Setup program calls the control's **DllRegisterServer**() function. To allow users to manually add or remove an ActiveX control, Windows provides the RegSvr32 utility.

An InstallShield project for a container application requires two extra steps. First, a file group must be added to the project with its Self-Registering flag set to **Yes**. Second, all ActiveX controls and other self-registering components that the application uses must be manually added to the new file group. The second step is necessary because ActiveX controls are not listed in the container's header the way normal DLLs are, so InstallShield will not recognize them as dependencies until specifically instructed to do so. When the resulting Setup program executes, it calls the **DllRegisterServer**() function for each self-registering component in the project.

Lesson 4: Deployment Options

Once the Setup program is created and working properly, you are ready to deploy your application. This lesson discusses how to best get your application into the hands of users, and addresses some issues that you should consider when releasing your application.

Currently, the three most common means of deploying a Windows program are:

- On media such as a disk or CD-ROM.
- Over a network.
- Over the Internet.

After this lesson, you will be able to:

- Describe the advantages and disadvantages of deployment by media, network, and Web site.
- Describe the different setup requirements when deploying an ActiveX control as a product to other developers, as opposed to an ActiveX control serving as an auxiliary file for a container application deployed to users.
- Describe digital signing and explain its purpose.
- Understand how controls are licensed and the effects of licensing on the installation process.
- Design ActiveX controls intended for the World Wide Web.

Estimated lesson time: 20 minutes

Media-Based Deployment

Disks and CD-ROMs provide a cost-effective and convenient means of deployment. In their 3.5-inch form, disks also have the advantage of ubiquity, as nearly all users have access to a disk drive that can read the media.

Disk media are often used for the distribution of application upgrades, which can take the form of simple bug corrections or completely new versions. The upgrade package should include a Setup program that installs only the files that have been revised for the upgrade, making the installation as quick and convenient as possible.

Network-Based Deployment

Deployment via a network is the least expensive method, and is ideal if your application is intended to serve only a set of users within a company or group of companies. Such users are generally linked through a local area or wide area network, or both. Your disk images can be placed on a network share with access granted rights to all intended users, who can then simply run the Setup program over the network.

Deployment of applications with a site license usually involves two steps. First, the organization receives a single set of disks and copies the disk images and Setup program to a server. The users covered by the site license can then install the application over the network.

Web-Based Deployment

Deployment over the World Wide Web has become increasingly common in the last few years. Web-based deployment offers several compelling advantages:

- No packaging costs.
- No distribution costs other than the normal maintenance of a Web site.
- No reseller costs, as the software manufacturer can also fill the role of vendor.
- More efficient distribution to international markets, allowing customers in other countries to access a Web site written in their native languages and download only the application files localized for their languages.
- The opportunity for distribution of evaluation copies.

Time-trial evaluation software is a popular form of deployment over the Web. In this scheme, users download a working version of a program for free, and try it for a predetermined period. At the expiration of the evaluation period, the program politely refuses to run until users purchase a license. When obtained, the license typically arrives via e-mail in the form of a keyword, which the application recognizes as proof of a valid license. Once the keyword is entered into a licensing screen, users continue using the application as before, but now without time constraints.

The Web also serves as an excellent means of distributing application upgrades. The developer can place files in a common area, perhaps protected by a password known only to users. Registered users can be notified by e-mail that an upgrade has been posted, or the application itself can periodically check to determine if an upgrade exists. If an upgrade is available, users should always be informed and given the option of downloading the upgrade.

The potential disadvantages of Web-based deployment must also be considered:

- Inconvenience for users, who might be forced to download many megabytes of data over a low-speed connection.
- Customer base is restricted to users with Internet access.
- Care must be taken to make sure that site passwords are given only to licensed users.

Deploying ActiveX Controls

Lesson 3 of this chapter explained that ActiveX controls must be properly registered on a user's system, but there is a difference between deploying a product that *is* an ActiveX control and deploying a container application that merely *uses* an ActiveX control as an auxiliary component. The difference is particularly important when you have added licensing code to your ActiveX control.

This section discusses issues that you must consider when deploying an ActiveX control as a product, not as a dependency file for a main application. If your product is an ActiveX control (or suite of controls), your customers are most likely not users. Instead, they are likely developers who write applications or Web pages that use the controls, which in turn are distributed to users.

Control Dependencies

An ActiveX control using MFC must link dynamically to the MFC42.dll library file. The installation project for such a control must therefore include the DLL if you are deploying to sites where the file might not already be present. On the other hand, ATL can create ActiveX controls that are self-sufficient, requiring neither MFC nor the C run-time library. If you prefer your ATL control to be independent, do not include code that uses the C run-time library, and set the Release MinDependency configuration when compiling.

If you are deploying a group of ATL controls designed to work together, it's often more efficient to build them using the MinSize configuration instead of MinDependency. Choosing MinSize significantly reduces the size of the controls but makes them dependent on ATL.dll, a library file that Visual C++ installs in the System or System32 folder. Despite the 54-KB library file, the overall deployment size can be reduced when grouping two or more controls constructed using the Release MinSize configuration.

Digital Signing

Through their security settings, browsers can require downloadable software, such as ActiveX controls, to have a digital signature. A *digital signature* provides a way to verify that:

- The contents of the file are identical to when the file was digitally signed.
- The file comes from a responsible source.

A digital signature ensures that a file's contents have not been altered since the file was first made available for download. The signature verifies the source by identifying the legal entity that created the software. When you include a signature with an ActiveX control, you are the legal entity. The legal entity can be held responsible for any destruction caused by signed software when it is downloaded or run.

You provide a digital signature by purchasing a certificate from a *certifying authority*. A certifying authority is a company that validates your identity and issues you a certificate. The certificate contains your digital signature and is a verification of your credentials. In the event of any problems, the certifying authority becomes a witness to your identity. A private key is used to generate the digital signature, which can be validated using a public key that need not be kept secret.

Licensed ActiveX Controls

When deploying a licensed ActiveX control as a product, your installation program should handle licensing requirements automatically. Your developer-customers require the license to use your product in their own applications or on Web pages.

For example, when Control Wizard creates a project for a licensed ActiveX control, it generates a file named License.txt that must be placed in the same folder as the control itself. If you have written your ActiveX control to store license information in the system registry instead of in a file, your Setup program should register the required information during installation.

Regardless of how the license protection is implemented—whether by file, registry entry, or an alternative means—the license must be present on the developer's system or the control will not allow itself to be embedded. This protection is *design-time license protection,* which is verified when a developer attempts to insert the control onto a Visual Basic form or a dialog box template such as the one provided by the Visual C++ dialog box editor. If the license is not correctly installed, Visual C++ displays a message similar to the one shown in Figure 14.9 on the next page, when a developer attempts to place the control on a dialog box.

Figure 14.9   Visual C++ error message when inserting an ActiveX control without a design-time license

Run-time license protection takes place after your developer-customer finishes the application or Web page that uses your ActiveX control. At run time, the container application passes a keyword to the control, providing proof that the license existed during development. After verifying the keyword, the control allows instantiation and runs normally. For this reason, the license is not required on the user's system when the application executes.

Making ActiveX Controls Internet-Friendly

An ActiveX control works best on the Internet when it appears quickly on a Web page, ready to interact with users. To this end, you should ensure that your ActiveX control:

- Is as small as possible.
- Can load its property data asynchronously.

Reducing the Size of an ActiveX Control

The first time a user views a Web page on which the control appears, the user's browser must download the control's file. The control should therefore be small to minimize download time. When coding an ActiveX control, take particular care to reduce the file size as much as possible.

An ActiveX control should be written to completely avoid using the C run-time library. This procedure helps decrease the control's executable size and also removes the MSVCRT.DLL file as a dependency, ensuring that the file is not downloaded along with the control. Some tips for writing an ActiveX control that does not require the C run-time library are as follows:

- Do not include C library calls in your code—use alternative services provided by the operating system. For example, substitute calls to **strcpy()** and **strcat()** with calls to the equivalent API functions **lstrcpy()** and **lstrcat()**.
- Do not make member functions static, as static member functions require initialization by the run-time library.
- If you use ATL to create your control, make sure the compiler predefines _ATL_MIN_CRT. The ATL COM AppWizard sets the definition automatically; if you have created your project without the wizard, add the definition

yourself. In the **Project Settings** dialog box, display the **C++** tab and add _ATL_MIN_CRT to the **Preprocessor Definitions** text box.

Loading Data Asynchronously

By loading its data asynchronously, a control can become active even while the browser continues receiving downloaded properties in the background. This allows the control to become responsive as quickly as possible, even before all of its data arrives. If your ActiveX control requires large blocks of data, you should write the control so that it appears on a Web page ready to interact with a user using only a partial data set.

For example, a control that displays a video clip should not wait until the entire clip is downloaded. Instead, it should display the data already at hand while using a worker thread to continue buffering the rest of the file in the background as the browser receives it.

Deployment Checklist

This section provides a short checklist of miscellaneous items you should consider when deploying a Windows application:

- Make sure the application you are deploying has been built under its release configuration, not its debug configuration. Although Visual C++ by default optimizes the release version for speed, most programmers prefer to optimize for size. Often, this is especially the case when deploying ActiveX controls.

- Before including dependencies with your application, make sure they are legally distributable. Microsoft allows you to distribute both the MFC and the C run-time library modules (MFC42.dll and MSVCRT.dll) along with your Visual C++ application, but other vendors might impose restrictions on their products.

- Because users do not require licenses for ActiveX controls, do not include control license information in the installation package for container applications.

- Make sure your application's Help files are included in the installation package. It is not necessary to distribute the Windows Help Viewer WinHlp32.exe with the Help files, since every Windows system already has the Help Viewer installed. However, if your application uses HTML Help, you should include the HTMLHELP.dll file in your installation package.

- Test your Setup program thoroughly under different scenarios and on different operating systems. Ensure that it reacts correctly when encountering duplicate folder or file names, and under conditions of insufficient disk space and low memory.

- Apply the same tests to your uninstaller program, and ensure it correctly deletes files and cleans the registry.

Lesson Summary

Windows applications are distributed to users through one of three methods:

- On disks or CD-ROMs.
- As a Setup program running on a network.
- As a downloadable file over the Internet.

This lesson described these three methods and discussed some of their advantages and disadvantages. Deployment from a Web site offers the advantages of low cost and is an ideal medium for distributing evaluation copies to interested users.

It's important to understand the difference between deploying an ActiveX control as a product to other developers and as a dependency file to users. The difference is particularly important for licensed ActiveX controls. Licensed controls must include licensing information when distributed to developers so that they can embed the control in their own applications and Web pages. Users do not require licensing information, nor should it be made available to them.

An ActiveX control intended for Web distribution should be designed with the limitations of the Internet in mind. The control should be as small as possible to minimize download time, and should load large blocks of property data in the background while remaining responsive to users. Simultaneous loading of property data in the background is known as asynchronous loading.

As a final checklist for deployment, you should verify that:

- Your application has been built under its release configuration.
- Dependency files are legally distributable to users.
- All auxiliary files such as ActiveX controls, Help files, and font files are included.
- Your Setup and uninstaller programs have been tested and work as expected.

Lesson 5: Zero Administration for Windows

Zero Administration for Windows (ZAW) is a Microsoft initiative designed to reduce costs associated with using networked personal computers in a corporate environment. The initiative's core set of technologies greatly facilitate the management of users, software, and hardware within an organization, and are intended to eliminate the need for an administrator to touch individual desktops on a network.

This lesson first presents a broad overview of ZAW. It then narrows its focus to concentrate on ZAW's Windows Installer and Systems Management Server (SMS), two key technologies that pertain directly to application deployment.

After this lesson, you will be able to:
- List the key features of the ZAW initiative.
- Understand the basics of Windows Installer technology.
- Understand SMS.

Estimated lesson time: 15 minutes

Features of ZAW

The ZAW initiative is part of the Microsoft Windows Client Strategy. ZAW exists in some measure today within Windows NT Server 4, and is slated to become a major part of Windows 2000. Some of the capabilities of ZAW are:

- Automatic system update and application installation.
- Persistent caching of data and configuration information.
- Central administration and system lock-down.

Automatic System Update and Application Installation

Software installation and maintenance is typically a labor-intensive and error-prone process. Under ZAW, this process becomes much simpler through automation. When a system component, device driver, or a new version of the operating system is available, Windows can automatically update itself with the new components. The system can be configured to boot into a minimal network configuration and check for any updates on the Internet. If an update is found, the system can update itself without user intervention.

Persistent Caching of Data and Configuration Information

Previous lessons in this chapter showed how installation programs must store state and configuration information in the host registry. This method of storage can be problematic in a networked and mobile environment, in which users who are primarily away from their desks cannot access their applications or tools from different locations.

Under ZAW, the local host's data can be automatically reflected to servers, allowing users to log on to different computers on the network and work within the context of their host computers elsewhere. This concept of data and configuration information following a user to another computer is known as *persistent caching*.

Central Administration and System Lock-Down

To prevent users from installing hardware and software on their computers as they please, ZAW allows the network administrator to hide devices such as disk drives, presenting the user with a single drive letter that represents their home directory.

The Windows Installer

Perhaps the most important part of ZAW for application deployment is the Windows Installer, which automates application installation across a network. The Windows Installer offers many benefits over the conventional installation procedures described in previous lessons, including the following:

- The ability to automatically repair an installed application. For example, if an application's component file is accidentally deleted, the Windows Installer ensures that it is replaced when the application starts without user intervention.
- Automatic installation on an enterprise-wide system with up to thousands of users.
- Installation on demand, in which COM components are installed only when they are first accessed by a client application. This process speeds installation and prevents unnecessarily cluttering the disks of users who do not need the components.

The Windows Installer is not a program but rather a set of services. Setup programs will still exist under ZAW and will interact with the user as before. The Windows Installer does not replace installer products like InstallShield. Rather, such products will undoubtedly become even more important under ZAW as installation becomes more intricate and technology more sophisticated. In the future, InstallShield and other installer products will undoubtedly generate Setup programs that incorporate the features and services of the Windows Installer.

Systems Management Server

Systems Management Server (SMS) is a ZAW service that continually inventories computers on a network. The software and hardware detected on each computer is then listed in an SQL database. Through SMS, a network administrator has instant access to an up-to-date inventory of all computers on the network, without the expense and disruption of a manual inventory.

SMS makes software deployment more efficient, because it provides query functions by which an installation package can gain access to the SMS database. This process allows a Setup program to automatically test each computer before deployment, and install only on computers that meet a specified set of criteria. When it detects a computer that does not qualify for installation, the Setup program can suggest to the administrator any required changes, such as hardware upgrades.

Zero Administration Kit

ZAW is slated to be an integral part of Windows 2000, and many of its features are already available for Windows NT 4.0. For installing ZAW on Windows NT 4.0, Microsoft provides the Zero Administration Kit, which you can download from:

http://www.microsoft.com/windows/zak/zakreqs.htm

The entire Zero Administration Kit is a self-extracting file roughly 6 MB in size. If you prefer to receive only the documentation, a separate file in Microsoft Word format (415 KB) is also available for downloading.

Lesson Summary

The ZAW initiative is designed to reduce the labor and costs associated with operating a Windows-based network. ZAW's features include:

- Automatic updating of both the operating system and application files. At regular intervals, the system checks data sources such as Web sites, and as new files become available, downloads them automatically.

- Persistent caching, which allows a computer's data and configuration to follow a user to other locations.

- Central administration and system lock-down, allowing an administrator to protect individual systems by hiding devices from users.

The Windows Installer provides services to installation programs running on a network, making application installation faster and more efficient in its use of disk space. As a system service, the Windows Installer is at work even when no Setup program is running. Because it is always active, the Windows Installer is able to repair applications as needed by automatically replacing files that have been deleted or moved.

SMS maintains an inventory of hardware and software on a network, storing the information in an SQL database. Installation programs can query SMS for a computer's configuration before deployment, and install only on workstations that meet the application's requirements.

Lab 14: Packaging and Deploying the STUpload Application

This lab finishes the STUpload project, bundling it into an installation program named Setup. When executed on the client's system, the Setup program decompresses data stored in a .cab file, copies STUpload's executable files to the hard disk, and registers the application's components. In this lab, you will:

- Create a release version of STUpload.
- Create an InstallShield project for the installation program.
- Add dependencies to the installation project.
- Build and test a Setup program and .cab files.

The exercises assume that the customer, StockWatch Data Services Inc., maintains a large network connecting members of its staff. The deployed package will therefore be copied to the network, allowing users to run the Setup program and install STUpload on their individual computers.

As mentioned in Lesson 2 of this chapter, the Learning and Standard Editions of Visual C++ do not include the InstallShield tool, but you can purchase the tool separately. If you do not have access to InstallShield, you should still follow along with the text, but you will not be able to complete Exercises 2 through 4.

Estimated lesson time: 15 minutes

Building a Release Version of STUpload

Now that STUpload has been debugged and thoroughly tested, you are ready to create a release version of the program. The release version is smaller and faster than the debug version created in the previous chapter, because the compiler does not add symbol information to the object files, and also because the compiler optimizes the code to reduce its size.

▶ **To create a release build optimized for size**

1. Open the STUpload project in Visual C++.
2. On the **Build** toolbar, select the **Win32 Release** build context as shown in Figure 14.10 on the next page.

Figure 14.10   Select Win32 Release on the **Build** toolbar prior to creating a release build

3. On the **Project** menu, click **Settings**.

4. In the **Project Settings** dialog box, click the **C/C++** tab and select **Minimize Size** in the **Optimizations** box.

5. Click **OK** to close the dialog box.

6. On the **Build** toolbar, click **Build** to build a release version of STUpload.

Creating the InstallShield Project

Now that you have built a release executable for STUpload, you will create an InstallShield project for the application. The InstallShield project builds the required Setup program that deploys the STUpload application and its auxiliary executable files.

▶   **To create an InstallShield project for STUpload**

1. With the STUpload project still open in Visual C++, click **InstallShield Wizard** on the **Tools** menu.

2. If the STUpload project is not listed in the wizard's **Visual C++ Project** box, click **Browse** and browse to the STUpload.dsw file in the STUpload project folder. Double-click STUpload.dsw to add it to the wizard's **Visual C++ Project** box.

3. Click **Next** to proceed to the wizard's next step.

4. Check the accuracy of the application information, and then click **Next** to proceed.

   The wizard shows a summary of information gleaned from the STUpload.dsw workspace file. As shown in Figure 14.11 on the facing page, the information includes the names of the two ActiveX controls, msadodc.ocx and msdatgrd.ocx, which were added to the STUpload project in Chapter 7. msadodc is the Microsoft ADO Data Control, and msdatgrd is the Microsoft DataGrid control. The wizard read the controls' class identifiers stored in STUpload.dsw, and then consulted the system registry to find the locations of the .ocx files.

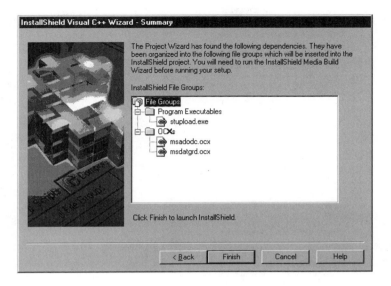

Figure 14.11   Summary page of the InstallShield Wizard

5. Click **Finish** to launch InstallShield, which automatically opens the new STUpload installation project.

Adding Dependencies to the Project

STUpload requires the services of another dependency, the STLoadData.dll component added to the project in Chapter 9. STLoadData is not an ActiveX control, but is nevertheless self-registering because it exports the **DllRegisterServer()** and **DllUnregisterServer()** functions. The component should therefore be added to a file group for which the **Self-Registered** flag is set to **Yes**.

Such a file group already exists in the project, so it's not necessary to create a new group. To contain the project's ActiveX controls, InstallShield has created the OCXs file group and has set the **Self-Registered** flag for the group. This exercise adds the STLoadData component to the OCXs file group.

▶ **To add STLoadData to the OCXs file group**

1. In the InstallShield workspace window, click the **File Groups** tab and expand the list for the OCXs group.

2. Right-click the **Links** entry under OCXs, and then click **Insert Files** on the shortcut menu.

3. Browse to the folder containing STLoadData.dll, select the file, and click **Open**. The list of files in the OCXs group now includes STLoadData.dll.

You will also need to package the data link file used by the StloadData.dll to conncect to the database.

▶ **To add Data Links file group and the data link file**

1. On the **File Groups** tab, right-click the **STUpload File Groups** item. Add a new file group named **Data Links**.

2. Add the **\DataLinks\STLink.udl** file that you created for the lab in Chapter 10 to the Data Links file group.

Note These exercises assume that the Microsoft Data Access Components (MDAC) have been installed on the client machines. For a discussion of the issues surrounding the redistribution of MDAC see the Technical Article "Redistributing Microsoft Data Access Components" in Visual C++ Help.

Building and Testing the Setup Program

This exercise invokes InstallShield's Media Build Wizard to create the Setup program. In addition to the Setup file, the resulting installation package includes various information files and a .cab file containing compressed copies of the four executable files that are installed on the client's network. The executable files are STUpload.exe and its components MSAdodc.ocx, MSDatGrd.ocx, and STLoadData.dll.

▶ **To build the Setup program for STUpload**

1. On InstallShield's **Build** menu, click **Media Build Wizard**.

2. In the Media Build Wizard's first step, type **STUpload** in the **Media Name** box, and then click **Next**.

3. In the list of media types, select the entry for 1.44-MB 3.5-inch disks. This selection determines how you will send the finished installation package to StockWatch Data Services, which will then copy it to a network share visible to all users.

4. Click **Next** four times to move past the Build Type, Tag File, and Platform steps, accepting their default settings.

5. At the wizard's Summary step, click **Finish** to build the project.

6. When the Media Build Wizard finishes, click **Finish** to terminate the wizard.

The Disk Images folder in the C:\MyInstallations\STUpload\Media\STUpload subdirectory now contains a folder named Disk1. Disk1 contains all the files required to install the STUpload application on another computer. You need only copy Disk1 to a single 3.5-inch disk and ship the disk to your client.

To test the installation, place the disk in another computer and run Add/Remove Programs to start the Setup program. If the Setup program asks for a serial number, simply type any text to continue. When you have finished, run the installed STUpload application to make sure all files have been correctly decompressed from the .cab file, and that the three COM components have been correctly registered on the test computer. To remove the program and test the uninstaller, run Add/Remove Programs again and remove STUpload.

Review

1. What are the two stages of deployment?

2. What are cabinet files and registry files?

3. What is the purpose of the InstallShield tool?

4. Must ActiveX controls be registered on a system before they can operate? If so, what examples can you give of a control's registry information?

5. Name three modes of application deployment.

6. What is the main advantage ATL offers over MFC when used to develop ActiveX controls?

7. What are two common ways ActiveX controls are licensed?

8. You have created a licensed ActiveX control and have sold a copy to a development company. Should you provide them with a copy of the control's license as well? Why or why not?

9. Name two characteristics of an ActiveX control designed for use on a Web page.

10. What is Zero Administration for Windows?

APPENDIX

Review Questions and Answers

Chapter 1
Review Questions

1. What is MSF?

   MSF is a collection of models, principles, and practices that helps organizations become more effective in their creation and use of technology to solve business problems.

2. Which models are most directly related to the development of business-oriented software solutions?

   Most directly related to the development of business-oriented software solutions are the Team Model, Process Model, Application Model, and Design Process Model.

3. What is the main focus of the logical design perspective?

   The logical design perspective views the solution from the perspective of the project team.

4. How might a client/server application implement the three tiers of an application?

   A client/server application might implement the three tiers of an application by integrating the business rules into either the data source tier (a thin client/fat server model) or into the client tier (a fat client/thin server model).

5. What are some of the benefits that MFC offers to developers?

   Some such benefits include the ability for developers to quickly and easily generate applications, libraries, and software components. MFC enables rapid development in all aspects of Windows programming including user interface, Internet, component technology, and database

access development—all without sacrificing programming freedom and flexibility. In addition, MFC provides the AppWizard, a step-by-step visual tool that allows developers to quickly and easily generate frameworks to set up a basic application structure, and to generate code to implement fundamental application behaviors.

6. You are writing an MFC application that will allow your network administrator to manage user accounts on an NT network. Which libraries should you install?

   You should install the MFC libraries for Unicode (either shared or static, according to how the application will be distributed). Internal strings used by Windows NT, such as user account names and device names, are Unicode strings, so you will need to install the Unicode libraries if you are planning to write programs that retrieve and manipulate these strings directly.

7. What kind of data can you access through an OLE DB provider?

   OLE DB is capable of dealing with any type of data regardless of its format or storage method. For instance, OLE DB can access data that resides in an Excel spreadsheet, in text files, or even on a mail server such as Exchange.

Page 39

Chapter 2
Review Questions

1. What project configurations are created for you automatically by the MFC AppWizard?

   AppWizard automatically creates the Debug and Release configurations.

2. Where, in the AppWizard, can you configure features of the application windows?

   You can configure features of the application windows on the Window Styles **tab of the** Advanced Options **dialog box in Step 4 of the AppWizard.**

3. What kinds of help are available from the Visual C++ IDE?

   The Visual C++ IDE provides help from the MSDN library, an essential reference for developers, containing more than a gigabyte of technical programming information.

4. What can you set on the C/C++ tab of the **Project Settings** dialog box?

   From the C/C++ page of the Project Settings **dialog box, you can set compiler settings and language features such as calling conventions, processor-dependent settings, optimizations, and preprocessor definitions.**

5. Why might you need to use the **Get Latest Version** feature of Visual SourceSafe?

   You might need to use the Get Latest Version **feature to make sure that you have the latest version of all files in a project. You might also use the** Get Latest Version **command to copy the current versions of the project source files to your working folder, in case you make changes that render your code incompatible with other recently edited modules.**

6. Under what circumstances might you use the Visual SourceSafe **Merge** facility?

   You might use the Merge **facility to merge the changes made to different versions of the same file to recreate a single version of the file.**

Page 73

Chapter 3
Review Questions

1. When developing an MFC application, under what circumstances might you need to call the Win32 API directly?

   When developing an MFC application, you might need to call the Win32 API directly when you need to access system functionality at a fairly low level. For example, if you were developing a utility to modify user accounts on a network, you would be required to use the Win32 networking functions because no MFC classes that provide access to Windows NT network management functions exist.

2. What services are provided by the **CObject** class?

   The CObject class provides serialization (loading and saving data objects to a file), run-time class information, diagnostic and debugging support (validations and dumps), and compatibility with collection classes.

3. Why would you use an MFC extension DLL?

   Because MFC extension DLLs implement reusable classes derived from existing MFC classes, you would use an MFC extension DLL to provide an "extended" version of MFC.

4. Which member function of which MFC class implements the application message loop?

   The Run() **member function of the** CWinApp **MFC class implements the application message loop.**

5. What type of classes can implement message maps?

   Classes derived from the CCmdTarget **class can implement message maps.**

6. Name four categories of Windows messages that can be handled by message maps.

   Four categories of Windows messages that can be handled by message maps are Windows messages, command messages, user interface update command messages, and control notification messages.

7. What is the function of a document template object?

   A document template object associates a document class with a group of resources (such as menus and icons), a frame window, and a view.

8. Which MFC class encapsulates GDI drawing functions?

   The MFC CDC **class encapsulates GDI drawing functions.**

9. How do you ensure that the client area of your application's main window always displays an up-to-date picture of the application data?

   To ensure that the client area of your application's main window always displays an up-to-date picture of the application data, you should call the document's UpdateAllViews() **member function whenever a document's data changes in a way that will affect its visual representation.**

Page 119

Chapter 4
Review Questions

1. Which icons should you supply for an application that meets the Windows 98/Windows NT logo requirements?

   You must supply both standard (32x32 pixels) and small (16x16 pixels) icons for both application and document type to meet the Windows 98/ Windows NT logo requirements.

2. How do you implement ToolTip text for your toolbar buttons?

   To implement ToolTip text for your toolbar buttons, add the \n escape sequence, followed by the ToolTip text, to the end of the Prompt **string in the** Toolbar Button Properties **dialog box.**

3. How can you dynamically change the text of a menu command from within your application code?

   To dynamically change the text of a menu command from within your application code, you would use the SetText **member function of the** CCmdUI **MFC class.**

4. What is the recommended way to update a status bar indicator?

   The recommended method for updating a status bar indicator is to set up an array of status bar indicators associated with string IDs in the application's string table. The recommended way to update text in a status bar pane is to use an ON_UPDATE_COMMAND_UI **entry in a message map to associate a user-interface update handler function with an indicator's string ID.**

5. How would you make an edit control in a dialog box read-only? Why might you want to do this?

   To make an edit control in a dialog box read-only, select the Read Only **check box on the Styles tab of the** Edit Properties **dialog box. A read-only edit control can be used to convey dynamically changing text to a user.**

6. You have created a dialog box template using the dialog editor. How would you display a modal dialog box, based on this template, in your application?

   To display a modal dialog box based on a template created using the dialog editor, you would first use ClassWizard to create a dialog class based on the template. You would then create an instance of the dialog class in your code, and call the base class method CDialog::DoModal() **to display the dialog box.**

Page 161

Chapter 5
Review Questions

1. How is the **DoDataExchange()** function called? How does it determine the direction of the data exchange?

   The DoDataExchange() **function is called by the** CWnd::UpdateData() **function. The** DoDataExchange() **function passes data between the dialog box controls and the application; the** CDataExchange **class member variable m_bSaveAndValidate indicates the direction of the data exchange.**

2. How do you make controls unavailable in a dialog box?

   To make controls unavailable in a dialog box, you would use the CWnd::EnableWindow() **function with the argument** FALSE.

3. Which two functions are used to specify coordinate mapping for an unconstrained mapping mode?

   The two functions used to specify coordinate mapping for an unconstrained mapping mode are the CDC functions SetWindowExt() **and** SetViewportExt().

4. Which function associates a drawing tool object with a device context?

   The CDC::SelectObject() **function associates a drawing tool object with a device context.**

5. What kinds of threads must be created by using a **CWinThread** object?

   You should always use the CWinThread **class to create threads that use MFC functionality, because the** CWinThread **class uses thread-local storage to manage information specific to the thread context in the MFC environment.**

6. What is the difference between a **CCriticalSection** object and a **CMutex** object?

   Though both objects are synchronization classes, CCriticalSection **allows only one thread from within the current process to access an object, while** CMutex **allows only one thread from any process to access an object.**

7. How are Help context IDs specified in a Help project file?

   Help context IDs are stored in files with the .hm extension as part of the Help project.

8. How do you create a hyperlink in a Help project .rtf file?

   To create a hyperlink in a Help project .rtf file, you would format the links as double-underlined text and follow the links immediately by the link destinations formatted as hidden text. A pound (#) footnote mark signifies the link destinations. The footnote text contains the context name, which can either be a name internal to the Help file, or one of the Help context IDs specified in the Help project's .hm file.

Page 245

Chapter 6
Review Questions

1. How do you open a file in text mode?

   To open a file in text mode, create a CStdioFile object and associate it with the text file, and then supply the CFile::typeText **flag to the** Open() **function.**

2. What kind of exception is thrown by the **CFile::Open()** function?

   The CFile::Open() **function throws a** CFileException.

3. What steps are necessary to make a class serializable?

   - **Derive the class from** CObject **or a class that was derived from** CObject.
   - **Provide a default constructor for your class.**
   - **Add the MFC macro** DECLARE_SERIAL **to the class definition.**
   - **Add the** IMPLEMENT_SERIAL **macro to your class implementation file.**
   - **Provide an override of the** CObject::Serialize() **function for your class.**

4. What does the default implementation of the **SerializeElements()** function do?

   The default SerializeElements() **implementation performs a bitwise copy of data contained in an MFC collection to or from an archive.**

5. Which registry key should be used to store application settings that are common to all users of the computer on which the application is installed?

   The registry key that should be used to store application settings common to all users of the computer on which an application is installed is HKEY_LOCAL_MACHINE\SOFTWARE.

6. Where do the MFC profile management classes **WriteProfileString()** and **WriteProfileInt()** store profile settings?

   The MFC profile management classes WriteProfileString() **and** WriteProfileInt() **store profile settings to the registry key specified by the** CWinApp::SetRegistryKey() **function.**

Page 291

Chapter 7
Review Questions

1. How can you connect an ADO application to an ODBC data source?

   You can connect an ADO application to an ODBC data source by using the OLE DB provider for ODBC.

2. What is wrong with the following SQL statement?

   ```
   SELECT * FROM authors WHERE au_lname LIKE M%
   ```

   In the code provided, single apostrophes (') need to enclose M% so that the code reads 'M%'. Note that apostrophes are always used when the value in the WHERE clause is a string value, but not used when the WHERE clause value is a numeral.

3. You need to open a **CRecordset** object so that you can list all the records in a database table to the printer. What value should you supply to the first parameter of the **Open()** function?

   Because you need to make only a single pass through the recordset to list the records to the printer, you should supply CRecordset::forwardonly as the first argument to the Open() function. You should always use the fastest and least memory-consumptive cursor for a given task.

4. What does the **CRecordset::GetDefaultConnect()** function specify?

   This function specifies the data source to be used by the recordset.

5. With which ADO object is the **Errors** collection associated? What does it contain?

   The Errors collection is associated with the Connection object, and contains specific information on provider errors.

6. Which property of the ADO Data control is used to specify an SQL command to retrieve records from the data source?

   The RecordSource property specifies an SQL command to retrieve records from the data source.

Page 341

Chapter 8
Review Questions

1. What is a COM interface?

   A COM interface is a logical grouping of related methods identified by a GUID, known as an Interface Identifier (IID).

2. What is a GUID, and what role does it play in COM?

   A GUID, or globally unique identifier, is a 128-bit numeric identifier that is guaranteed to be universally unique, and to remain unique until approximately 3400 A.D.

3. What are the differences among in-process, local, and remote server COM objects?

   In-process servers, implemented as DLLs, execute within the same process as the object's client application. Local (or out-of-process) servers, implemented as .exe files, reside on the same computer as the client application, but execute in a different process. Remote servers execute on a computer remote from the clients that they are serving.

4. How do you implement standard marshaling?

   You implement standard marshaling by specifying your interfaces using IDL and allowing the MIDL compiler to create marshaling code for you.

5. What is a type library, and how is it used?

   A type library is a binary description that includes interface properties and methods, and method arguments. Type libraries are used in situations when high-performance development languages, such as Visual Basic 6.0, need to be able to access interface methods directly, through the vtable. To make this possible, type libraries provide the Visual Basic client with information on which data types are required by the interface methods.

6. What are the implications of declaring your COM object to be free-threaded?

   COM objects that are created to support the free-threading model must be thread safe, and must provide their own synchronization code. By removing the bottleneck that is created by marshaling, free-threaded objects provide the highest performance and throughput on the server side.

7. What issues must you consider when implementing an ActiveX control?

   When implementing an ActiveX control, you must take into consideration that, although the definition of ActiveX controls requires only that the control support the IUnknown interface, different containers have different requirements. Some containers require certain interfaces for a control to work, while others do not. If you want your control to work with a particular container, your control must implement the interfaces required by the container.

Page 377

Chapter 9
Review Questions

1. Describe the features provided by the templated base class **CComObjectRootEx**.

   The templated base class CComObjectRootEx **provides a default implementation for the IUnknown interface methods** QueryInterface(), AddRef(), **and** Release(). **When you derive from this class, your client can use** QueryInterface() **to acquire an interface pointer to any interface that your COM object supports.** CComObjectRootEx **also provides implementations of the IUnknown methods** AddRef() **and** Release() **to perform reference counting for your object.**

2. Describe the features provided by the templated base class **CComCoClass**.

   The templated base class CComCoClass **provides a default implementation of a class factory, which creates an instance of your server class.**

3. What is a COM map and how is it used?

   A COM map is an element of your class declaration that contains a list of the interfaces that your COM object supports. Add an entry to the COM map by using the COM_INTERFACE_ENTRY **macro. Whenever a client application executes** QueryInterface(), **the object searches this map for a matching interface GUID. If a match is found, the corresponding interface pointer is returned to the client.**

4. What is an object map and how is it used?

   An object map is a table that maintains information used by the framework to instantiate objects through a class factory, establish communication between a client and the root object in the component, perform lifetime management of class objects, and enter and remove object descriptions in the system registry. You can add an entry to the object map by using the OBJECT_ENTRY **macro.**

5. How are the keywords **interface, coclass,** and **library** used in IDL, and how do they relate to each other?

   In an IDL file each COM object definition is identified by a separate coclass **section, and each interface definition by a separate** interface **section. The server's type library is defined within the** library **section. The coclass definitions that are to be exposed through the type library are nested within the** library **definition.**

Page 403

Chapter 10
Review Questions

1. What kind of class represents a COM interface in C++?

   COM interfaces are represented in C++ code by abstract classes.

2. How does a **_com_ptr_t** object help you control the lifetime of a COM server?

   A _com_ptr_t object helps manage the lifetime of your COM server object by calling the IUnknown::AddRef() **and** IUnknown::Release() **methods of the encapsulated interface on your behalf.** AddRef() **is called automatically when a _com_ptr_t object is created as a copy from an existing interface pointer, and** Release() **is called automatically when a _com_ptr_t object goes out of scope.**

3. What are the advantages and disadvantages of COM containment?

   An advantage of COM containment is that the interface on the containing (outer) object can control access to the contained (inner) object, and can control the way in which the inner object's services are used. A disadvantage of containment is that some overhead is incurred by the forwarding of method calls.

4. What is the purpose of the second argument to **CoCreateInstance()**?

   When an outer object creates an aggregated inner object, it uses the second argument of the CoCreateInstance() **function to pass the address of its** IUnknown **pointer (the controlling unknown) to the inner object's class factory. If this address is not NULL, the inner object knows that it is being aggregated, and delegates IUnknown method calls from external clients to the controlling unknown.**

Page 433

Chapter 11
Review Questions

1. How do you implement property persistence for an MFC ActiveX control?

   To implement property persistence for an MFC ActiveX control, you use the property exchange functions provided by MFC, which allow you to serialize properties of different types. The names of these functions begin with the prefix PX_. PX_ functions are placed within the control class's DoPropExchange() function.

2. What is the purpose of the DDP functions, and where are they used?

   The purpose of the DDP functions is to transfer data between property pages and control properties. These functions are used within the DoDataExchange() function of the property page class.

3. What is a connection point?

   A connection point is an interface that helps to manage the connection of source interfaces to a corresponding client object, or sink. Through the connection point mechanism, a pointer to the sink interface is passed to the source object. This pointer provides the source with access to the sink's implementation of its interface methods.

4. How does an object derived from **CComControl** handle Windows messages?

   A CComControl-class object handles Windows messages by implementing a message map.

5. What situations are best suited to using MFC to implement your ActiveX control?

   MFC greatly simplifies the process of creating an ActiveX control. Using the MFC ActiveX ControlWizard, you can quickly and easily create a fully featured ActiveX control. ActiveX controls written in ATL are smaller than their MFC counterparts, and if written properly will perform better. Use MFC where ease and speed of development are more important to you than the size and performance of the control.

Page 465

Chapter 12
Review Questions

1. What is the preferred method of creating a Web browser–style application?

   The preferred method of creating a Web browser–style application is using the MFC AppWizard, and specifying CHtmlView **as the view class.**

2. In an ATL HTML control, how do you define methods to be accessible to the HTML source code of the document displayed by the control?

   In an ATL HTML control, you define methods to be accessible to the HTML source code of the document displayed by the control by adding the methods to the UI dispatch interface that is created for your ATL HTML control project. This UI dispatch interface is used to communicate between the C++ code and the HTML UI. Script in the HTML page displayed by your control can access properties and methods defined for this interface via the DHTML window.external **object.**

3. How does the Microsoft Scriptlet Component handle scriptlet custom events?

   The Scriptlet Component routes all custom scriptlet events through a single event named onscriptletevent. **This event is fired with two parameters. The first parameter specifies the name of the event; the second parameter can be used to pass data associated with the event.**

4. How can you save changes to ActiveX documents deployed on a Web server?

   You can save changes you make to an ActiveX document by using the Save As **option from the** File **menu to create a new version on your own hard disk. An ActiveX document server won't let you save any changes you make to the document back to the Internet host.**

5. How do you specify which menu commands of the ActiveX server application are displayed by an ActiveX document container when it loads an ActiveX document?

   When an ActiveX document container loads an ActiveX document, it displays the menu commands defined on the IDR_SRVR_INPLACE **menu of the ActiveX document server. Edit the** IDR_SRVR_INPLACE **menu (and toolbar) to make the appropriate items appear.**

6. How do you specify the default function for an ISAPI server extension?

   Specify the default function for an ISAPI server extension by using the DEFAULT_PARSE COMMAND **macro in the** PARSE MAP **of your ISAPI extension class.**

7. How do ISAPI server extensions and ISAPI filters differ in the way they are loaded?

   Though both ISAPI server extensions and filters are implemented as DLLs, ISAPI server extension DLLs are loaded into the IIS process when a client first requests them, and stay loaded until the WWW service is stopped. ISAPI filters are loaded when the WWW service is started.

Page 527

Chapter 13
Review Questions

1. What is Structured Exception Handling?

   Structured Exception Handling is a service of the Windows operating system responsible for locating and calling handler code in an application when an error occurs. The application encloses code within a __try block and identifies its error handler code by placing it within an __except block.

2. What is an HRESULT?

   In COM programming, an HRESULT is a defined type for a 32-bit-long integer containing an error code. COM components such as ActiveX controls export functions (or methods) that return HRESULT codes. An HRESULT integer contains bit fields that specify severity, facility, and a code descriptor. HRESULTs are signed integers; zero or a positive value indicates success, whereas a negative HRESULT indicates failure and usually causes an exception to occur.

3. Name two ways in which a COM server communicates an error to a client.

   A COM server can indicate an error has occurred by returning an HRESULT code or by firing the Error **event.**

4. How does a debug version of a program differ from its release build?

   Debug and release builds differ in two main characteristics. First, a program's debug build contains symbol information placed in the object code by the compiler, whereas the release code does not. Second, code in a debug build is not optimized, ensuring that the generated object code closely matches the original source code. Release code is almost always optimized.

5. Describe MFC's **ASSERT**, **VERIFY**, and **DEBUG_NEW** macros.

   ASSERT **and** VERIFY **are very similar, differing in only one respect. Both macros take an expression as a parameter and cause an exception if the expression evaluates to FALSE. The only difference is that** ASSERT **does nothing in release builds, whereas** VERIFY **works in both debug and release code.**

   DEBUG_NEW **replaces calls to the** new **operator, performing the same service but also recording the file name and line number where each** new **statement occurs. This can help locate the cause of memory leaks resulting from a failure to match a new statement with a** delete **statement.**

6. How does a debugger cause a running program to interrupt itself?

   You can place debug breakpoints at designated locations in the program. When the program you are debugging encounters a breakpoint, execution freezes and the debugger gains control. Two types of breakpoints

exist: location and data. Visual C++ also provides conditional and message breakpoints, but these are simply special cases of location breakpoints.

7. What utility does Visual C++ provide for running and testing ActiveX controls?

Visual C++ provides the ActiveX Control Test Container, a general-purpose container program that can embed any ActiveX control. The Test Container can call methods, set and read properties, activate the control's property sheet, and monitor events.

8. What is a dependency?

A dependency is an executable module, usually a DLL or an ActiveX control, that an application requires to execute. Dependencies can themselves have dependencies, forming a hierarchy of modules. For example, an MFC application might make no direct use of the C run-time library; nevertheless, the application is dependent on the library because MFC itself requires the C run-time library.

9. What information is contained in the four lists that Spy++ can display?

Spy++ can display views of current windows, processes, and threads. It can also display a log of messages that a window sends or receives.

10. What is regression testing?

In regression testing, an application is re-submitted to the same battery of tests it has already gone through. Regression testing is applied after changes are made to an application, and ensures that the changes do not introduce new bugs or unexpected behavior.

Chapter 14
Review Questions

1. What are the two stages of deployment?

   The first stage of deployment is the transfer of all necessary files to the user's hard disk. The second stage involves configuring the host system so that it recognizes and correctly runs the installed application.

2. What are cabinet files and registry files?

   Recognizable by their .cab extensions, cabinet files contain collections of files in compressed form. Registry or .reg files hold scripts that can be merged into system registries using the RegSvr32 utility.

3. What is the purpose of the InstallShield tool?

   Given a Visual C++ project, InstallShield creates an installation package consisting of a Setup program, cabinet files, and miscellaneous information files. When run on another computer, the installation package installs the application and automatically configures the computer to run it.

4. Must ActiveX controls be registered on a system before they can operate? If so, what examples can you give of a control's registry information?

   ActiveX controls must be registered on a system before they can be used. Usually, this process is hidden from the user because it is performed automatically by a Web browser or by installation programs. The registry information must include the control's class identifier and its location on the system's hard disk.

5. Name three modes of application deployment.

   Applications can be deployed on media such as disks and CD-ROMs, and over a network or the Internet.

6. What is the main advantage ATL offers over MFC when used to develop ActiveX controls?

   The main advantage ATL offers ActiveX development is that ATL can create controls that have no dependencies. Properly written, an ActiveX control created from ATL requires neither MFC nor the C run-time library, ensuring that only the control's executable file needs to be downloaded from a Web page. ActiveX controls created using MFC can execute only when MFC42.dll and MSVCRT.dll are present on a system.

7. What are two common ways ActiveX controls are licensed?

   Licensing schemes can take many innovative forms, but generally rely on the presence of either a specific file or a particular entry in the system registry.

8. You have created a licensed ActiveX control and have sold a copy to a development company. Should you provide them with a copy of the control's license as well? Why or why not?

Yes, you should provide a copy of the license along with the product itself. ActiveX controls are sold to other developers, who in turn use them to create applications or Web pages designed for users. Licensing code prevents a developer from using an ActiveX control except in the presence of a valid license. When a developer adds an ActiveX control to an application project, the control confirms the existence of the license; only upon confirmation that the license exists can the control then be used.

9. Name two characteristics of an ActiveX control designed for use on a Web page.

An ActiveX control should be small in size, and if it requires large blocks of data, be able to load the data asynchronously. Asynchronous loading allows the control to interact with the user as quickly as possible while buffering downloaded data in the background.

10. What is Zero Administration for Windows?

Zero Administration for Windows (ZAW) is a Microsoft initiative designed to reduce the cost and labor associated with administering a Windows-based network.

Glossary

A

ActiveX All component technologies built on Microsoft's COM, other than OLE technology.

ActiveX control An embeddable, reusable COM object that supports, at a minimum, the **IOleControl** interface. ActiveX controls are typically created for the user interface, but they also support communication with a control container. Multiple clients can reuse these controls, depending upon licensing restrictions.

ActiveX control container An application that supports the embedding of controls by implementing the **IOleControlSite** interface. *See also* control.

ActiveX Template Library (ATL) A set of compact, template-based C++ classes that simplify the programming of COM objects. ATL provides the mechanism to use and create COM objects.

aggregation A composition technique for implementing COM objects. With aggregation, a new object can reuse one or more existing objects. This reuse is achieved by exposing one or more of the interfaces in the original object.

ambient property A run-time property that is managed and exposed by the container. Typically, an ambient property represents a characteristic of a form, such as background color, that is communicated to a control so the control can assume the look and feel of its surrounding environment.

apartment-model threading A threading model that can be used only on the thread that created it. *See also* free threading model, single threading model.

application class Derived from the MFC class **CWinApp**, the class that encapsulates the initialization, running, and termination of a Windows-based application. An application must have exactly one object of an application class.

application framework Or framework. A group of C++ classes in the MFC Library that provides the essential components of a Windows application. The application framework defines the basic operational structure of an application, and supplies standard user-interface implementations that can be incorporated into the application.

assertion A Boolean statement in a program's debug version that tests a condition that should evaluate as true, provided the program is operating correctly. If the condition is false, an error has occurred; thus, the program will typically issue an error message that gives a user the option to abort the program, activate the debugger, or ignore the error.

asynchronous operation In programming for Windows, a task that proceeds in the background, allowing the thread that requested the task to continue to perform other tasks.

ATL *See* ActiveX Template Library.

Automation A technology based on COM, which enables interoperability among ActiveX components, including OLE components. Formerly referred to as OLE Automation.

B

backward compatibility 1. Ensuring that existing applications will continue to work in a new environment. 2. Ensuring that the new release of an application will be able to handle files created by a previous version of a product.

bitmap Also referred to as a pixel image or pixel map. An array of bits that contains data describing the colors found in a rectangular region on the screen (or the rectangular region found on a page of printed paper).

browser A program used to view formatted Web documents.

C

call stack An ordered list of functions that have been called, but have not returned, with the currently executing function listed first. Each call is optionally shown with the arguments and types passed to it. During a debug session, you can view the functions that have been called, but have not returned.

CGI *See* Common Gateway Interface.

child window A window that has the WS_CHILD or WS_CHILDWINDOW style, and is confined to the client area of its parent window, which initiates and defines the child window. Typically, an application uses child windows to divide the client area of a parent window into functional areas.

class factory An object that creates one or more instances of an object identified by a given CLSID. A class factory object implements the **IClassFactory** interface. A class factory is one of the most frequently used types of class objects in COM.

client An application or process that requests a service from an in-process server or another process.

client area Or client rectangle. The portion of a window where an application displays output, such as text or graphics.

clipboard An area of storage, or buffer, where data objects or their references are placed when a user carries out a cut or copy operation.

CLSID A universally unique identifier (UUID) that identifies a type of COM object. Each type of COM object has its CLSID in the registry so that other applications can load and program the CLSID. For example, a spreadsheet might create worksheet items, chart items, and macrosheet items. Each of these item types has its own CLSID that uniquely identifies the item type to the system.

collection class In object-oriented programming, a class that can hold and process groups of class objects or groups of standard types. A collection class is characterized by its *shape* (the way the objects are organized and stored) and by the types of its elements. MFC provides three basic collection shapes: lists, arrays, and maps (also known as *dictionaries*).

COM *See* Component Object Model.

command message In Windows, a notification message from a user-interface object, such as a menu, toolbar button, or accelerator key.

Common Gateway Interface (CGI) A mechanism that allows a Web server to run a program or script on the server and send the output to a Web browser. *See also* ISAPI.

Component Object Model (COM) An open architecture for cross-platform development of client/ server applications based on object-oriented technology as agreed upon by Digital Equipment Corporation and Microsoft Corporation. COM defines an interface similar to an abstract base class, **IUnknown**, from which all COM-compatible classes are derived.

compound document Or container document. A document within a container application that contains data of different formats, such as sound clips, spreadsheets, text, and bitmaps.

connection point In OLE, a mechanism consisting of the object calling the interface, referred to as the *source,* and the object implementing the interface, referred to as the *sink.* The connection point implements an outgoing interface that can initiate actions, such as firing events and change notifications, on other objects. By exposing a connection point, a source allows sinks to establish connections to the source.

containment A composition technique for accessing one or more COM objects via a single interface. Containment allows one object to reuse some or all of the interface implementations of one or more other objects. The outer object manages requests to other objects, delegating implementation when it uses the services of one of the contained objects. *See also* aggregation.

control A discrete element of a user interface that allows a user to interact with application data.

critical section A segment of code that is not re-entrant; that is, the code segment does not support concurrent access by multiple threads. Often, a critical section is used to protect shared resources.

D

data source name (DSN) The name of a data source that applications use to request a connection to the data source. For example, a data source name can be registered with ODBC through the ODBC Administrator program.

Database management system (DBMS) A layer of software between the physical database and the user. The DBMS manages all requests for database action (for example, queries or updates) from the user.

DBMS *See* Database management system.

DDV *See* Dialog data validation.

DDX *See* Dialog data exchange.

deadlock A state in which every process in a set of processes waits for an event or resource that only another process in the set can provide. For example, in data communications, a deadlock can occur when both the sending and receiving sockets are waiting on each other, or for a common resource.

debug version A version of a program built with symbolic debugging information.

debugger A program designed to help find errors in another program by allowing the programmer to step through the program, examine data, and check conditions.

default window procedure A system-defined function that defines certain fundamental behavior shared by all windows.

device context A data structure defining the graphic objects, their associated attributes, and the graphic modes affecting output on a device.

device driver A low-level software component that permits device-independent software applications to communicate with a device such as a mouse, keyboard, monitor, or printer.

dialog data exchange (DDX) In MFC, a method for transferring data between the controls of a dialog box and their associated variables. DDX is an easy way to initialize dialog box controls and gather user data input. *See also* DDV.

dialog data validation (DDV) In MFC, a method for checking data as it is transferred from the controls in a dialog box. DDV is an easy way to validate data entry in a dialog box. *See also* DDX.

dialog editor A resource editor that allows you to place and arrange controls in a dialog box template and to test the dialog box. The editor displays the dialog box exactly as the user will see it. While using the dialog editor, you can define message handlers and manage data gathering and validation with ClassWizard. *See also* dialog template.

dialog template A template used by Windows to create a dialog box window and display it. The template specifies the characteristics of the dialog box, including its overall size, initial location, style, and types and positions of its controls. A dialog template is usually stored as a resource, but templates can also be stored directly in memory. *See also* dialog editor.

dispatch identifier (dispatch ID) A 32-bit attribute value for identifying methods and properties in Automation. All accessor functions for a single property have the same dispatch ID.

dispatch interface In Automation, the external programming interface of a grouping of functionality exposed by the Automation server. For example, a dispatch interface might expose an application's mouse-clicking and text data entry functions. *See also* type library.

dispatch map In MFC, a set of macros that expands into the declarations and calls needed to expose methods and properties for Automation. The dispatch map designates internal and external names of object functions and properties, as well as data types of function arguments and properties.

document object An object that defines, stores, and manages an application's data. When the user opens an existing or new document, the application framework creates a document object to manage the data stored in the document.

document template In MFC, a template used for the creation of documents, views, and frame windows. A single application object manages one or more document templates, each of which is used to create and manage one or more documents (depending on whether the application is SDI or MDI). *See also* MDI, SDI.

document/view architecture A design methodology that focuses on what the user sees and needs, rather than on the application or what the application requires. This design is implemented by a set of classes that manage, store, and present application-specific data.

DSN *See* Data source name.

dual interface An interface that derives from **IDispatch** and supports both late-binding via **IDispatch** and early-binding (vtable binding) via direct COM methods for each of its Automation methods.

dynaset A recordset (or set of records) with dynamic properties that is the result of a query on a database document. A dynaset can be used to add, change, and delete records from the underlying database table or tables. *See also* snapshot.

E

edit control Or edit box, text box. A rectangular control window that a user can use to type and edit text.

entry point A starting address for a function, executable file, or DLL.

environment variable A symbolic variable that represents an element of a user's operating system environment, such as a path, directory name, or configuration string. For example, the environment variable PATH represents the directories to search for executable files.

event 1. In ActiveX, a notification message sent from one object to another (for example, from a control to its container) in response to a state change or a user action. 2. More generally, any action or occurrence, often user-generated, to which a program can respond. Typical events include keystrokes, mouse movements, and button clicks.

event object A synchronization object that allows one thread to notify another that an event has occurred. Event objects are useful when a thread needs to know when to perform its task. For example, a thread that copies data to a data archive would need to be notified when new data is available. By using an event object to notify the copy thread when new data is available, the thread can perform its task as soon as possible.

external name In Automation, an identifier that a class exposes to other applications. Automation clients use the external name to request an object of this class from an Automation server.

F

file input/output (file I/O) The mechanism for making data persistent among program work sessions by creating files, reading from files, and writing to files.

File Transfer Protocol (FTP) A method of retrieving files to a home directory or directly to a computer using TCP/IP.

frame window In MFC, the window that coordinates application interactions with a document and its view. The frame window provides a visible frame around a view, with an optional status bar and standard window controls such as control menus, buttons to minimize and maximize the window, and controls for resizing the window.

free threading model A model in which an object can be used on any thread at any time. *See also* apartment-model threading, single threading model.

FTP *See* File Transfer Protocol.

G

GDI *See* Graphics Device Interface.

GIF *See* Graphics Interchange Format.

Graphics Device Interface (GDI) An executable program that processes graphical function calls from a Windows-based application, and passes those calls to the appropriate device driver, which performs the hardware-specific functions that generate output.

Graphics Interchange Format (GIF) A form of graphics compression.

H

Help context A string and a number (Help context ID) that an application passes during a call to Windows Help to locate and display a Help topic. *See also* Help project file.

Help project file A project file that controls how the Windows Help Compiler creates a Help (.hlp) file from topic files. The Microsoft Help Workshop is used to create a Help project file. The file name extension of a Help project file is .hpj.

Help topic The primary unit of information in a Help (.hlp) file. A topic is a self-contained body of text and graphics, similar to a page in a book. Unlike a page, however, a topic can hold as much information as required. If more information exists in a topic than the Help window can display, scroll bars appear to let the user scroll through the information.

HTML *See* Hypertext Markup Language.

HTTP *See* Hypertext Transfer Protocol.

hyperlink A link used to jump to another Web page. A hyperlink consists of both the display text and the URL of the reference.

Hypertext Markup Language (HTML) Derived from SGML, a markup language that is used to create a text document with formatting specifications that inform a browser how to display the page or pages included in the document.

Hypertext Transfer Protocal (HTTP) The Internet protocol used by WWW browsers and servers to exchange information. The protocol makes it possible to use a client program to enter a URL (or click a hyperlink) and retrieve text, graphics, sound, and other digital information from a Web server. HTTP defines a set of commands and uses ASCII text strings for a command language. An HTTP transaction consists of a connection, request, response, and close.

I

IDL *See* Interface Definition Language.

IID *See* Interface Identifier.

in-process server A COM server implemented as a DLL that runs in the process space of an object's client. *See also* local server, remote server.

interface In COM, a set of related functions; a description of an abstract type.

Interface Definition Language (IDL) The OSF-DCE standard language for specifying the interface for remote procedure calls. *See also* MIDL.

Interface Identifier (IID) A globally unique identifier associated with an interface. Some functions take IIDs as parameters to allow the caller to specify which interface pointer should be returned. *See also* UUID.

Internet A global, distributed network of computers.

Internet Server Application Programming Interface (ISAPI) A set of functions for Internet servers, such as a Windows NT Server running Microsoft Internet Information Server (IIS).

intranet A network within an organization, usually connected to the Internet via a firewall, that uses protocols such as HTTP or FTP to enhance productivity and share information.

ISAPI *See* Internet Server Application Programming Interface.

ISAPI extension A DLL that can be loaded and called by some HTTP servers. Used to enhance the capabilities of applications that extend a Web server.

ISAPI filter An Internet server filter packaged as a DLL that runs on ISAPI-enabled servers.

L

licensing A COM feature that provides control over object creation. Licensed objects can be created only by clients that are authorized to use them. Licensing might afford different levels of functionality, depending on the type of license.

list-box control In Windows, a child window that contains a list of items that can be selected by the user. List boxes can permit the selection of one item or multiple items.

local server A COM server implemented as an executable file that runs on the same computer as the client application. Because the server application is an executable file, the local server runs in its own process. *See also* in-process server, remote server.

locking mode A strategy for locking records in a recordset during update. A record is locked when it is read-only to all users except the one currently entering data into it. *See also* optimistic locking, pessimistic locking.

M

marshaling In COM, the process of packaging and sending interface parameters across process boundaries.

MDI *See* Multiple document interface.

message A structure or set of parameters used for communicating information or a request. Messages can be passed between the operating system and an application, different applications, threads within an application, or windows within an application.

message box A window that displays information to the user. For example, a message box can inform the user of a problem that the application has encountered while carrying out a task.

MFC *See* Microsoft Foundation Classes.

Microsoft Foundation Classes (MFC) A set of C++ classes that encapsulate much of the functionality of applications written for Windows operating systems.

Microsoft Interface Definition Language (MIDL) Microsoft's implementation and extension of IDL. Processed by the MIDL compiler.

MIDL *See* Microsoft Interface Definition Language.

modal A restrictive or limiting interaction created by a given condition of operation. Modal often describes a secondary window that restricts a user's interaction with other windows. A secondary window can be modal with respect to its primary window or to the entire system. The user must close a modal dialog box before the application can continue operations. *See also* modeless.

modeless Not restrictive or limiting interaction. A modeless secondary window does not restrict a user's interaction with other windows. A modeless dialog box remains on a user's screen, available for use at any time, but also permits other user activities. *See also* modal.

Multiple document interface (MDI) The standard user interface architecture for Windows-based applications. An MDI application enables a user to work with more than one document at the same time. Each document is displayed within the client area of the application's main window. *See also* child window, client area, SDI.

mutex object In interprocess communication, a synchronization object in which state is signaled when it is not owned by a thread, and nonsignaled when it is owned. Only one thread at a time can own a mutex.

O

optimistic locking A recordset locking strategy in which records are left unlocked until explicitly updated. The page containing a record is locked only while the program updates the record, not while a user is editing the record. *See also* pessimistic locking.

P

persistent Lasting between program sessions, or renewed when a new program session is begun.

pessimistic locking A recordset locking strategy in which a page is locked once a user begins editing a record on that page. While the page is locked, no other user can change a record on that page. The page remains locked until records are updated or the editing is canceled. *See also* optimistic locking.

pixel The smallest addressable picture element (that is, a single dot) on a display screen or printed page.

platform The hardware and operating system that support an application. A platform sometimes is considered as the hardware alone, as in the Intel x86 platform.

primary key In a database program, a field or group of fields that uniquely identifies a record in a table. No two records in a table can have the same primary key value.

property The data associated with an object.

property page A grouping of properties presented as a tabbed page of a property sheet.

property sheet A type of dialog box that is generally used to modify the attributes of an external object, such as the current selection in a view. A property sheet has three main elements: the containing dialog box, one or more property pages shown one at a time, and a tab at the top of each page that the user clicks to select that page. An example of a property sheet is the **Project Settings** dialog box in Visual C++.

proxy An interface-specific object that packages parameters for methods in preparation for a remote method call. A proxy runs in the address space of the sender and communicates with a corresponding stub in the receiver's address space. *See also* stub, marshaling, unmarshaling.

Q

query A request for records from a data source. For example, a query can be written that requests "all invoices for Joe Smith," where all records in an invoice table with the customer name "Joe Smith" would be selected. *See also* recordset.

R

radio button In graphical user interfaces, a round button operated by the user to toggle an option or choose from a set of related but mutually exclusive options.

raw data Unprocessed, typically unformatted data. Raw data is a stream of bits that has not been filtered for commands or special characters. More generally, it is information that has been collected but not evaluated.

read-only Describes information stored in such a way that it can be played back (read) but cannot be changed (written).

record A collection of data about a single entity, such as an account or customer, stored in a table row. A record consists of a group of contiguous columns (sometimes called *fields*) that contain data of various types. *See also* recordset.

Record Field Exchange (RFX) The mechanism by which MFC ODBC classes transfer data between the field data members of a recordset object and the corresponding columns of an external data source. *See also* DDX.

record view In form-based data-access applications, a form view object in which controls are mapped directly to the field data members of a recordset object, and indirectly to the corresponding columns in a query result or table on the data source.

recordset A set of records selected from a data source. The records can be from a table, query, or stored procedure that accesses one or more tables. A recordset can join two or more tables from the same data source, but not from different data sources. *See also* record.

Red-green-blue (RGB) A mixing model, or method of describing colors, in light-based media such as color monitors. RGB mixes percentages of light-based colors (red, green, and blue) to create other colors. Windows defines these percentages as three 8-bit values called RGB values. Zero percentage of all three colors, or an RGB value of (0,0,0), produces black and 100 percent of all three colors, or an RGB value of (255,255,255), produces white.

reference count A count of the number of pointers that access, or make reference to, an object, allowing for multiple references to a single object. This number is decremented when a reference is removed; when the count reaches zero, the object's space in memory is freed.

referential integrity In database management, a set of rules that preserves the defined relationships between tables when records are entered or deleted. For example, enforcing referential integrity would prevent a record from being added to a related table when no associated record in the primary table exists.

registry In 32-bit Windows, the database in which configuration information is registered. This database takes the place of most configuration and initialization files for Windows and new Windows-based applications.

registry key A unique identifier assigned to each piece of information in the system registration database.

relational database A type of database or database management system that stores information in tables and conducts searches by using data in specified columns of one table to find additional data in another table.

remote server A COM server application, implemented as an executable file, that runs on a different computer from the client application using it. *See also* in-process server, local server.

RFX *See* Record Field Exchange.

RGB *See* Red-green-blue.

rich edit control In MFC, a window in which the user can enter and edit text. The text can be assigned character and paragraph formatting and can include embedded ActiveX objects.

root In a hierarchy of items, the single item from which all other items are descended. The root item has nothing dominating it in the hierarchy.

S

scrolling The process of moving a document in a window to permit viewing of any desired portion.

SEH *See* Structured Exception Handling.

semaphore A synchronization object that maintains a count between zero and a specified maximum value. A semaphore's state is signaled when its count is greater than zero and nonsignaled when its count is zero. The semaphore object is useful in controlling a shared resource that can support a limited number of users. This object acts like a gate that counts the threads as they enter and exit a controlled area, and that limits the number of threads sharing the resource to a specified maximum number.

serialization Also referred to as object persistence. In MFC, the process of writing or reading an object to or from a persistent storage medium, such as a disk file. The basic idea of serialization is that an object should be able to write its current state, usually indicated by the value of its member variables, to persistent storage. Later, the object can be recreated by reading, or deserializing, the object's state from storage.

server 1. In a network, a centrally administered computer that allows network access to all users. 2. An application or a process that responds to a client request.

server object An object that responds to a request for a service. A given object can be a client for some requests, and a server for other requests.

shell A piece of software, usually a separate program, that provides communication between the user and the operating system. For example, the Windows Program Manager is a shell program that interacts with MS-DOS.

Single document interface (SDI) A user interface architecture that allows a user to work with just one document at a time. Windows Notepad is an example of an SDI application. *See also* MDI.

single threading model A model in which all objects are executed on a single thread. Contrasts with multithreaded applications. *See also* apartment-model threading, free threading model.

smart pointer In C++, an object that implements the functionality of a pointer and additionally performs some action whenever an object is accessed through it. Smart pointers are implemented by overloading the pointer-dereference (->) operator.

snapshot In MFC, a recordset that reflects a static view of the data as it existed at the time the snapshot was created. *See also* dynaset, recordset.

SQL *See* Structured Query Language.

status bar A control bar at the bottom of a window, with a row of text output panes. The status bar is usually implemented as a message line (for example, the standard menu help message line) or as a status indicator (for example, the CAP, NUM, and SCRL indicators).

Structured Exception Handling (SEH) A mechanism for handling hardware- and software-generated exceptions that gives developers complete control over the handling of exceptions, provides support for debuggers, and is usable across all programming languages and computers.

Structured Query Language (SQL) A database sublanguage used to query, update, and manage relational databases.

stub 1. An interface-specific object that unpackages the parameters for that interface after they are marshaled across the process boundary, and makes the requested method call. The stub runs in the address space of the receiver, and communicates with a corresponding proxy in the sender's address space. 2. A function with an empty body; used as a placeholder.

synchronization object An object in which the handle can be specified in one of the wait functions to coordinate the execution of multiple threads. The state of a synchronization object is either signaled, which can allow the wait function to return, or nonsignaled, which can prevent the function from returning. More than one process can have a handle of the same synchronization object, making interprocess synchronization possible. *See also* mutex object, semaphore.

T

tab control A common control used to present multiple pages of information or controls to a user; only one page at a time can be displayed.

tab order The order in which the TAB key moves the input focus from one control to the next within a dialog box. Usually, the tab order proceeds from left to right in a dialog box, and from top to bottom in a radio group.

thread The basic entity to which the operating system allocates CPU time. A thread can execute any part of the application's code, including a part currently being executed by another thread. All threads of a process share the virtual address space, global variables, and operating system resources of the process.

toolbar A control bar based on a bitmap that contains a row of button images. These buttons can act like pushbuttons, check boxes, or radio buttons. *See also* status bar.

ToolTip A tiny pop-up window that presents a short description of a toolbar button's action. ToolTips are displayed when the user positions the mouse over a button for a period of time.

type library A file or component within another file that contains type information about exposed objects. Type libraries are created using either the MkTypLib utility or the MIDL compiler, and can be accessed through the **ITypeLib** interface.

U

UDA *See* Universal Data Access.

UNC *See* Universal naming convention.

Uniform Resource Locator (URL) The address of a resource on the Internet. URL syntax is in the form protocol://host/localinfo, where protocol specifies the means of fetching the object (such as HTTP or FTP), host specifies the remote location where the object resides, and localinfo is a string (often a file name) passed to the protocol handler at the remote location.

Universal Data Access (UDA) The Microsoft strategy for providing access to all types of information across the enterprise. UDA provides high-performance access to a variety of information sources.

Universal naming convention (UNC) The standard format for paths that include a local area network file server, as in \\server\share\path\filename.

Universally unique identifier (UUID) A GUID that identifies a COM interface. *See also* IID.

unmarshaling In COM, the process of unpacking parameters that have been sent across process boundaries.

URL *See* Uniform Resource Locater.

user-interface thread In Windows, a thread that handles user input and responds to user events independently of threads executing other portions of the application. User-interface threads have a message pump and process messages received from the system. *See also* worker thread.

UUID *See* Universally unique identifier.

V

variant In Automation, an instance of the VARIANT datatype, which can represent values of many different types, such as integers, floats, Booleans, strings, pointers, and so on.

view A window object through which a user interacts with a document.

vtable A table of function pointers, such as an implementation of a class in C++. The pointers in the vtable point to the members of the interfaces that an object supports. *See also* dual interface.

W

Win32 platform A platform that supports the Win32 API. These platforms include Intel Win32s, Windows NT, Windows 95, Windows 98, MIPS Windows NT, DEC Alpha Windows NT, and Power PC Windows NT.

window class A set of attributes that Windows uses as a template to create a window in an application. Windows requires that an application supply a class name, the window-procedure address, and an instance handle. Other elements can be used to define default attributes for windows of the class, such as the shape of the cursor and the content of the menu for the window.

window handle In the Win32 API, a 32-bit value (assigned by Windows) that uniquely identifies a window. An application uses this handle to direct the actions of functions to the window. A window handle has the **HWND** data type; an application must use this type when declaring a variable that holds a window handle.

window procedure A function, called by the operating system, that controls the appearance and behavior of its associated windows. The procedure receives and processes all messages to these windows.

wizard A special form of user assistance that guides a user through a difficult or complex task within an application. For example, a database program can use wizards to generate reports and forms. In Visual C++, the AppWizard generates a skeleton program for a new C++ application.

worker thread A thread that handles background tasks while a user continues to use an application. Tasks such as recalculation and background printing are examples of worker threads. *See also* user-interface thread.

World Wide Web (WWW) The portion of the global Internet that uses hypertext links to connect pages and resources in a way that lets a user reach any page from any other page.

WWW *See* World Wide Web.

Index

free-threading models. *See* MTAs
full screen, displaying, 50
Full Screen icon, 51
Functional Specifications
  and MSF Design Process, 17
functions. *See also* individual function names
  adding to classes, 129
  control notification message, 172
  DDX/DDV, 163, 167
  modifying, 183
  overriding, 193

G

GDI, 75, 80, 106
Get function, 411
GetBackColor() function, 437
GetChart() function, 512
GetColor() function, 516
getcolor() function, 490
GetDeviceCaps() function, 187
GetDocument() member function, 105
GetFilterVersion() function, 520
GetHtmlDocument() function, 476
GetKey() function, 411
GetProfileInt() function, 272
GetProfileString() function, 272
GetVersionEx() command, 76
.gif files, 121, 221
global entry point functions, 391
glossary of testing terms, 565
goals
  corresponding team roles, 5
  of MSF Design Process, 16
  project, 4
graphic drawing tool, 192
Graphics Device Interface. *See* GDI

graphics editor, 121
  accessing features, 126
  editing toolbars, 126
GUIDs, 346, 351
  ATL wizards and, 397
  ClassIDs as, 343
  CLSID_SimpleCOMServer, 390
  COM objects and, 346
  components and interfaces, 344
  definition files, 395
  formats of, 347
  illustrated, 346
  making definitions available, 422
  numeric representations of, 347
  registries, 348
  string names, 348
  subkeys for COM objects, 362
  type library subkeys, 362

H

handler functions
  implementing manually, 136
  for threads, 202
handlers
  adding, 93–94, 128
  OnLButtonDown, 96
  update, 131
HDC, 458
header files
  COM server, 404
  generating, 407
header information, 409
Help, 53
  adding topics, 217
  application processing, 209
  context-sensitive, 209

O

Object Description Language (ODL) code
  relationship to IDL, 436
Object Linking and Embedding. *See* OLE
object map, 393
object models
  ADO, 324
  DHTML, 469
object synchronization, 365
objects
  ADO, storage of, 325
  associating with controls, 170
  CHttpFilterContext, 521
  CHttpServer, 516
  CHttpServerContext, 516, 521
  COM, creating with ATL, 42
  CStockDataList, 278
  declaring, within a class scope, 414
  Encoder, 344
  public_description, 490, 495
.ocx extension, 436
ODBC, 28, 80, 304
  access through MFC, 306
  API and, 295
  C++ development and, 295
  classes, examples of, 311
  compared with OLE DB, 295
  comparisons and contrasts with DAO, 306
  conformance levels of, 294
  connecting to an RDBMS, 293
  connections, 321
  converting to ADO, 293
  core classes table, 306
  cursor library of, 295
  Data Sources applet in, 294

ODBC *(continued)*
  data sources, SQL Server, 307
  development options, 43
  Driver Manager, 295
  DSNs and, 294
  functions for connections, 307
  functions of, 293
  historical role of, 292
  RDBMS and, 293
  RDO and, 295
  recordsets, 308
  SQL and, 294
OK button, 180
OLE, 45
  ActiveX, 398
  COM and, 398
OLE controls
  relationship to ActiveX controls, 436
OLE DB, 28, 295, 303
  ADO and, 292, 296
  ADO interface to, 323
  ADO object model and, 324
  compared with ODBC, 295
  complexity of, 323
  components of, 296, 304
  templates, Visual C++ and, 293
OLE/COM object viewer, 30
  lab, 373
  opening, 373
OnAppAbout() function, 146
OnClick() function, 485
OnContextHelp() function, 217
OnDataConnect() function, 129, 130,
    133, 273
OnDataEdit() function, 176
OnDataUpload() function, 130

The manuscript for this book was prepared and submitted to Microsoft Press in electronic form. Text files were prepared using Microsoft Word. Pages were composed by Online Training Solutions, Inc. (OTSI) using Adobe PageMaker 6.5, with text in Times and display type in Helvetica Narrow.

Editing, production, and graphic services for this book were provided by OTSI. The hard-working project team included:

Project Editors:	Joyce Cox
	Joan Lambert
	Gabrielle Nonast
Editorial Team:	Leslie Eliel
	Michelle Kenoyer
	Ken Miller
	Rachel Moorhead
	Gale Nelson
Graphics:	Mary Rasmussen
Production Team:	R.J. Cadranell
	Karen Lee

Contact OTSI at:

- E-mail: joanl@otsiweb.com
- Web site: www.otsiweb.com

Learn how
COM+
can simplify your
development tasks

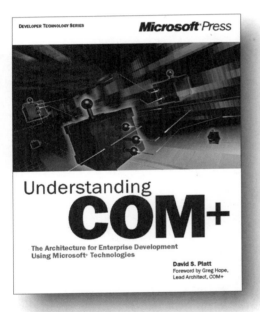

Wouldn't it be great to have an enterprise application's infrastructure so that you could inherit what you need and spend your time writing your own business logic? COM+ is what you've been waiting for—an advanced development environment that provides prefabricated solutions to common enterprise application problems. UNDERSTANDING COM+ is a succinct, entertaining book that offers an overview of COM+ and key COM+ features, explains the role of COM+ in enterprise development, and describes the services it can provide for your components and clients. You'll learn how COM+ can streamline application development to help you get enterprise applications up and running and out the door.

Petzold for the
MFC programmer!

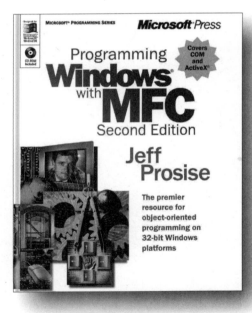

MICROSOFT® PROGRAMMING SERIES
Microsoft Press

Covers COM and ActiveX®

Programming
Windows®
with **MFC**
Second Edition

**Jeff
Prosise**

The premier
resource for
object-oriented
programming on
32-bit Windows
platforms

CD-ROM included

U.S.A.	**$59.99**
U.K.	£56.99 [V.A.T. included]
Canada	$89.99

ISBN 1-57231-695-0

Expanding what's widely considered the definitive exposition of Microsoft's powerful C++ class library for the Windows API, PROGRAMMING WINDOWS® WITH MFC, Second Edition, fully updates the classic original with all-new coverage of COM, OLE, and ActiveX.® Author Jeff Prosise deftly builds your comprehension of underlying concepts and essential techniques for MFC programming with unparalleled expertise—once again delivering the consummate resource for rapid, object-oriented development on 32-bit Windows platforms.

***Microsoft*®**

mspress.microsoft.com

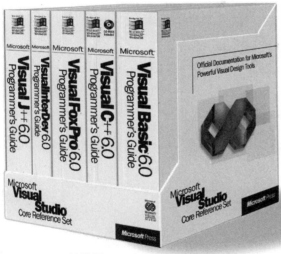

The *Comprehensive* *Official* Resource *for* Microsoft **Visual C++**

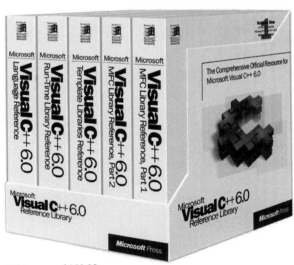

These five volumes deliver the authoritative technical detail you need to maximize your productivity with version 6.0 of the Microsoft Visual C++ development system. This reference set provides official, from-the-source documentation for the MFC library, template libraries, run-time libraries, and language elements in Visual C++ 6.0—all in easy-to-use book form, so the answers you need can always be close at hand!

U.S.A.	**$149.99**
U.K.	£140.99
Canada	$217.99
ISBN 1-57231-865-1	

Microsoft®

mspress.microsoft.com

The industry bible
for
Visual C++
development

PROGRAMMING MICROSOFT® VISUAL C++, Fifth Edition, is the newest edition of the book that has become the industry's most trusted text (previously published as *Inside Visual C++*). Newly expanded and updated for Microsoft Visual C++ 6.0, it offers even more of the detailed, comprehensive coverage that's consistently made this title the best overall explanation of the capabilities of this powerful and complex development tool. You'll find a full discussion of control development with ATL, the latest database programming enhancements, recent COM improvements, C++ programming for the Internet, and loads more.

U.S.A.   **$49.99**
U.K.   £46.99 [V.A.T. included]
Canada $71.99
ISBN 1-57231-857-0

Microsoft®
mspress.microsoft.com

MICROSOFT LICENSE AGREEMENT

Book Companion CD

IMPORTANT—READ CAREFULLY: This Microsoft End-User License Agreement ("EULA") is a legal agreement between you (either an individual or an entity) and Microsoft Corporation for the Microsoft product identified above, which includes computer software and may include associated media, printed materials, and "online" or electronic documentation ("SOFTWARE PROD-UCT"). Any component included within the SOFTWARE PRODUCT that is accompanied by a separate End-User License Agreement shall be governed by such agreement and not the terms set forth below. By installing, copying, or otherwise using the SOFTWARE PRODUCT, you agree to be bound by the terms of this EULA. If you do not agree to the terms of this EULA, you are not authorized to install, copy, or otherwise use the SOFTWARE PRODUCT; you may, however, return the SOFTWARE PROD-UCT, along with all printed materials and other items that form a part of the Microsoft product that includes the SOFTWARE PRODUCT, to the place you obtained them for a full refund.

SOFTWARE PRODUCT LICENSE

The SOFTWARE PRODUCT is protected by United States copyright laws and international copyright treaties, as well as other intellectual property laws and treaties. The SOFTWARE PRODUCT is licensed, not sold.

1. **GRANT OF LICENSE.** This EULA grants you the following rights:

   a. **Software Product.** You may install and use one copy of the SOFTWARE PRODUCT on a single computer. The primary user of the computer on which the SOFTWARE PRODUCT is installed may make a second copy for his or her exclusive use on a portable computer.

   b. **Storage/Network Use.** You may also store or install a copy of the SOFTWARE PRODUCT on a storage device, such as a network server, used only to install or run the SOFTWARE PRODUCT on your other computers over an internal network; however, you must acquire and dedicate a license for each separate computer on which the SOFTWARE PRODUCT is installed or run from the storage device. A license for the SOFTWARE PRODUCT may not be shared or used concurrently on different computers.

   c. **License Pak.** If you have acquired this EULA in a Microsoft License Pak, you may make the number of additional copies of the computer software portion of the SOFTWARE PRODUCT authorized on the printed copy of this EULA, and you may use each copy in the manner specified above. You are also entitled to make a corresponding number of secondary copies for portable computer use as specified above.

   d. **Sample Code.** Solely with respect to portions, if any, of the SOFTWARE PRODUCT that are identified within the SOFT-WARE PRODUCT as sample code (the "SAMPLE CODE"):

      i. **Use and Modification.** Microsoft grants you the right to use and modify the source code version of the SAMPLE CODE, *provided* you comply with subsection (d)(iii) below. You may not distribute the SAMPLE CODE, or any modified version of the SAMPLE CODE, in source code form.

      ii. **Redistributable Files.** Provided you comply with subsection (d)(iii) below, Microsoft grants you a nonexclusive, royalty-free right to reproduce and distribute the object code version of the SAMPLE CODE and of any modified SAMPLE CODE, other than SAMPLE CODE, or any modified version thereof, designated as not redistributable in the Readme file that forms a part of the SOFTWARE PRODUCT (the "Non-Redistributable Sample Code"). All SAMPLE CODE other than the Non-Redistributable Sample Code is collectively referred to as the "REDISTRIBUTABLES."

      iii. **Redistribution Requirements.** If you redistribute the REDISTRIBUTABLES, you agree to: (i) distribute the REDISTRIBUTABLES in object code form only in conjunction with and as a part of your software application product; (ii) not use Microsoft's name, logo, or trademarks to market your software application product; (iii) include a valid copyright notice on your software application product; (iv) indemnify, hold harmless, and defend Microsoft from and against any claims or lawsuits, including attorney's fees, that arise or result from the use or distribution of your software application product; and (v) not permit further distribution of the REDISTRIBUTABLES by your end user. Contact Microsoft for the applicable royalties due and other licensing terms for all other uses and/or distribution of the REDISTRIBUTABLES.

2. **DESCRIPTION OF OTHER RIGHTS AND LIMITATIONS.**

   - **Limitations on Reverse Engineering, Decompilation, and Disassembly.** You may not reverse engineer, decompile, or disassemble the SOFTWARE PRODUCT, except and only to the extent that such activity is expressly permitted by applicable law notwithstanding this limitation.

   - **Separation of Components.** The SOFTWARE PRODUCT is licensed as a single product. Its component parts may not be separated for use on more than one computer.

   - **Rental.** You may not rent, lease, or lend the SOFTWARE PRODUCT.

   - **Support Services.** Microsoft may, but is not obligated to, provide you with support services related to the SOFTWARE PRODUCT ("Support Services"). Use of Support Services is governed by the Microsoft policies and programs described in the user manual, in "online" documentation, and/or in other Microsoft-provided materials. Any supplemental software code provided to you as part of the Support Services shall be considered part of the SOFTWARE PRODUCT and subject to the terms and conditions of this EULA. With respect to technical information you provide to Microsoft as part of the Support Services, Microsoft may use such information for its business purposes, including for product support and development. Microsoft will not utilize such technical information in a form that personally identifies you.

- **Software Transfer.** You may permanently transfer all of your rights under this EULA, provided you retain no copies, you transfer all of the SOFTWARE PRODUCT (including all component parts, the media and printed materials, any upgrades, this EULA, and, if applicable, the Certificate of Authenticity), **and** the recipient agrees to the terms of this EULA.

- **Termination.** Without prejudice to any other rights, Microsoft may terminate this EULA if you fail to comply with the terms and conditions of this EULA. In such event, you must destroy all copies of the SOFTWARE PRODUCT and all of its component parts.

3. **COPYRIGHT.** All title and copyrights in and to the SOFTWARE PRODUCT (including but not limited to any images, photographs, animations, video, audio, music, text, SAMPLE CODE, REDISTRIBUTABLES, and "applets" incorporated into the SOFTWARE PRODUCT) and any copies of the SOFTWARE PRODUCT are owned by Microsoft or its suppliers. The SOFTWARE PRODUCT is protected by copyright laws and international treaty provisions. Therefore, you must treat the SOFTWARE PRODUCT like any other copyrighted material **except** that you may install the SOFTWARE PRODUCT on a single computer provided you keep the original solely for backup or archival purposes. You may not copy the printed materials accompanying the SOFTWARE PRODUCT.

4. **U.S. GOVERNMENT RESTRICTED RIGHTS.** The SOFTWARE PRODUCT and documentation are provided with RESTRICTED RIGHTS. Use, duplication, or disclosure by the Government is subject to restrictions as set forth in subparagraph (c)(1)(ii) of the Rights in Technical Data and Computer Software clause at DFARS 252.227-7013 or subparagraphs (c)(1) and (2) of the Commercial Computer Software—Restricted Rights at 48 CFR 52.227-19, as applicable. Manufacturer is Microsoft Corporation/One Microsoft Way/Redmond, WA 98052-6399.

5. **EXPORT RESTRICTIONS.** You agree that you will not export or re-export the SOFTWARE PRODUCT, any part thereof, or any process or service that is the direct product of the SOFTWARE PRODUCT (the foregoing collectively referred to as the "Restricted Components"), to any country, person, entity, or end user subject to U.S. export restrictions. You specifically agree not to export or re-export any of the Restricted Components (i) to any country to which the U.S. has embargoed or restricted the export of goods or services, which currently include, but are not necessarily limited to, Cuba, Iran, Iraq, Libya, North Korea, Sudan, and Syria, or to any national of any such country, wherever located, who intends to transmit or transport the Restricted Components back to such country; (ii) to any end user who you know or have reason to know will utilize the Restricted Components in the design, development, or production of nuclear, chemical, or biological weapons; or (iii) to any end user who has been prohibited from participating in U.S. export transactions by any federal agency of the U.S. government. You warrant and represent that neither the BXA nor any other U.S. federal agency has suspended, revoked, or denied your export privileges.

DISCLAIMER OF WARRANTY

NO WARRANTIES OR CONDITIONS. MICROSOFT EXPRESSLY DISCLAIMS ANY WARRANTY OR CONDITION FOR THE SOFTWARE PRODUCT. THE SOFTWARE PRODUCT AND ANY RELATED DOCUMENTATION ARE PROVIDED "AS IS" WITHOUT WARRANTY OR CONDITION OF ANY KIND, EITHER EXPRESS OR IMPLIED, INCLUDING, WITHOUT LIMITATION, THE IMPLIED WARRANTIES OF MERCHANTABILITY, FITNESS FOR A PARTICULAR PURPOSE, OR NONINFRINGEMENT. THE ENTIRE RISK ARISING OUT OF USE OR PERFORMANCE OF THE SOFTWARE PRODUCT REMAINS WITH YOU.

LIMITATION OF LIABILITY. TO THE MAXIMUM EXTENT PERMITTED BY APPLICABLE LAW, IN NO EVENT SHALL MICROSOFT OR ITS SUPPLIERS BE LIABLE FOR ANY SPECIAL, INCIDENTAL, INDIRECT, OR CONSEQUENTIAL DAMAGES WHATSOEVER (INCLUDING, WITHOUT LIMITATION, DAMAGES FOR LOSS OF BUSINESS PROFITS, BUSINESS INTERRUPTION, LOSS OF BUSINESS INFORMATION, OR ANY OTHER PECUNIARY LOSS) ARISING OUT OF THE USE OF OR INABILITY TO USE THE SOFTWARE PRODUCT OR THE PROVISION OF OR FAILURE TO PROVIDE SUPPORT SERVICES, EVEN IF MICROSOFT HAS BEEN ADVISED OF THE POSSIBILITY OF SUCH DAMAGES. IN ANY CASE, MICROSOFT'S ENTIRE LIABILITY UNDER ANY PROVISION OF THIS EULA SHALL BE LIMITED TO THE GREATER OF THE AMOUNT ACTUALLY PAID BY YOU FOR THE SOFTWARE PRODUCT OR US$5.00; PROVIDED, HOWEVER, IF YOU HAVE ENTERED INTO A MICROSOFT SUPPORT SERVICES AGREEMENT, MICROSOFT'S ENTIRE LIABILITY REGARDING SUPPORT SERVICES SHALL BE GOVERNED BY THE TERMS OF THAT AGREEMENT. BECAUSE SOME STATES AND JURISDICTIONS DO NOT ALLOW THE EXCLUSION OR LIMITATION OF LIABILITY, THE ABOVE LIMITATION MAY NOT APPLY TO YOU.

MISCELLANEOUS

This EULA is governed by the laws of the State of Washington USA, except and only to the extent that applicable law mandates governing law of a different jurisdiction.

Should you have any questions concerning this EULA, or if you desire to contact Microsoft for any reason, please contact the Microsoft subsidiary serving your country, or write: Microsoft Sales Information Center/One Microsoft Way/Redmond, WA 98052-6399.

Desktop Applications with Microsoft® Visual C++® 6.0 MCSD Training Kit

WHERE DID YOU PURCHASE THIS PRODUCT?

CUSTOMER NAME

Microsoft *Press*

mspress.microsoft.com

Microsoft Press, PO Box 97017, Redmond, WA 98073-9830

OWNER REGISTRATION CARD

Register Today!

0-7356-0795-8

Return the bottom portion of this card to register today.

Desktop Applications with Microsoft® Visual C++® 6.0 MCSD Training Kit

FIRST NAME   MIDDLE INITIAL   LAST NAME

INSTITUTION OR COMPANY NAME

ADDRESS

CITY   STATE   ZIP

(   )

E-MAIL ADDRESS   PHONE NUMBER

For information about Microsoft Press®
products, visit our Web site at
mspress.microsoft.com

Microsoft Press